THE GREENWOOD ENCYCLOPEDIA OF
Women's Issues
WORLDWIDE

Editor-in-Chief

Lynn Walter
University of Wisconsin, Green Bay

Volume Editor

Aili Mari Tripp
University of Wisconsin, Madison

Contributors

Nwando Achebe
The College of William and Mary, Williamsburg, Virginia

Melinda Adams
University of Wisconsin, Madison

Ladan Affi
University of Wisconsin, Madison

Ousseina Alidou
Rutgers University, New Brunswick, New Jersey

Erin Augis
Ramapo College, Mahwah, New Jersey

Gretchen Bauer
University of Delaware, Newark

Tsehai Berhane-Selassie
Ethiopian National Congress

Victoria Bernal
University of California, Irvine

Hannah Britton
Mississippi State University, Mississippi State, Mississippi

Kathleen Maria Fallon
Indiana University, Bloomington

Rebecca Furth
University of Wisconsin, Madison

Asma Mohamed Abdel Halim
Religion and Human Rights Project, Emory University Law School, Atlanta, Georgia

Rebecca Kemble
University of Wisconsin, Madison

Ruth Meena
University of Dar es Salaam, Tanzania

Rebecca Mukyala
Makerere Institute for Social Research, Makerere University, Kampala, Uganda

Mary J. Osirim
Bryn Mawr College, Bryn Mawr, Pennsylvania

Jennifer Seely
Brandeis University, Waltham, Massachusetts

Kathleen Sheldon
University of California, Los Angeles

Judith Van Allen
Institute for African Development, Cornell University, Ithaca, New York

Michele Wagner
University of Minnesota, Minneapolis

Susanna D. Wing
Haverford College, Haverford, Pennsylvania

THE GREENWOOD ENCYCLOPEDIA OF
Women's Issues
WORLDWIDE

SUB-SAHARAN AFRICA

Editor-in-Chief
Lynn Walter

Volume Editor
Aili Mari Tripp

GREENWOOD PRESS
Westport, Connecticut • London

Library of Congress Cataloging-in-Publication Data

The Greenwood encyclopedia of women's issues worldwide : Sub-Saharan Africa /
  Lynn Walter, editor-in-chief; Aili Mari Tripp, volume editor.
    p.   cm.
    Includes bibliographical references and index.
    ISBN 0–313–32787–4 (set : alk. paper)—ISBN 0–313–32145–0 (alk. paper)
    1. Women—Africa, Sub-Saharan—Social conditions.   2. Women's rights—Africa,
Sub-Saharan.   I. Title: Encyclopedia of women's issues worldwide.   II. Walter,
Lynn, 1945–   III. Tripp, Aili Mari.
    HQ1788.G74   2003
    305.42'09767—dc21   2003045526

British Library Cataloguing in Publication Data is available.

Library of Congress Catalog Card Number: 2003045526
ISBN: 0–313–32787–4   (set code)
        0–313–32087–X   (Asia and Oceania)
        0–313–32129–9   (Central and South America)
        0–313–31855–7   (Europe)
        0–313–31888–3   (The Middle East and North Africa)
        0–313–31852–2   (North America and the Caribbean)
        0–313–32145–0   (Sub-Saharan Africa)

First published in 2003

Greenwood Press, 88 Post Road West, Westport, CT 06881
An imprint of Greenwood Publishing Group, Inc.
www.greenwood.com

Printed in the United States of America

♾

The paper used in this book complies with the
Permanent Paper Standard issued by the National
Information Standards Organization (Z39.48–1984).

10 9 8 7 6 5 4 3 2 1

Volume map cartography by Mapcraft.com. Country map cartography by Bookcomp, Inc.

CONTENTS

CONTENTS

SET FOREWORD

The Greenwood Encyclopedia of Women's Issues Worldwide is a six-volume set presenting authoritative, comprehensive, and current data on a broad range of contemporary women's issues in more than 130 countries around the world. Each volume covers a major populated world region: Asia and Oceania, Central and South America, Europe, the Middle East and North Africa, North America and the Caribbean, and Sub-Saharan Africa. Volumes are organized by chapters, with each focusing on a specific country or group of countries or islands, following a broad outline of topics—education, employment and the economy, family and sexuality, health, politics and law, religion and spirituality, and violence. Under these topics, contributors were asked to consider a range of contemporary issues from illiteracy and wage discrepancies to unequal familial roles and political participation and to highlight issues of special concern to women in the country. In this way, the set provides a global perspective on women's issues, ensures breadth and depth of issue coverage, and facilitates cross-national comparison.

Along with locating women's agenda in specific national and historical contexts, each chapter looks at the cultural differences among women as well as the significance of class, religion, sexuality, and race on their lives. And, as women's movements and their non-governmental organizations (NGOs) are among the most worldwide forms of civic participation, their effectiveness in addressing women's issues is also examined. In addition to focusing on national and local organizations, many authors also highlight the major role the United Nations has played in addressing women's issues nationally and in supporting women's networks globally and point to the importance of its 1979 Convention on the Elimination of All Forms of Discrimination Against Women (CEDAW), which is still the most comprehensive international agreement on the rights of women.

Contributors were chosen for their expertise on women's issues in the country or area about which they write. Each contributor provides an authoritative resource guide with suggested reading, web sites, films/videos, and organizations as well as a selected bibliography and extensive references. The chapters and resource guides are designed for students, scholars, and engaged citizens to study contemporary women's issues in depth in specific countries and from a global perspective.

This ambitious project has been made possible by the work of many scholars who contributed their knowledge and commitment. I want to thank all of them and especially the other volume editors, Manisha Desai, Cheryl Toronto Kalny, Amy Lind, Bahira Sherif-Trask, and Aili Mari Tripp. Thanks also to Christine Marra of Marrathon Productions and Wendi Schnaufer of Greenwood Publishing Group for their editorial assistance.

As I read the many chapters of this series what struck me most was the sheer force and determination of the many women and men who are seeking solutions to the problems of inequality and poverty, discrimination, and injustice that lie at the root of women's experiences worldwide. I hope this series will further their vision.

Lynn Walter, Editor-in-Chief

USER'S GUIDE

The *Greenwood Encyclopedia of Women's Issues Worldwide* is a six-volume set covering the world's most populated regions:

Asia and Oceania

Central and South America

Europe

The Middle East and North Africa

North America and the Caribbean

Sub-Saharan Africa

All volumes contain an introduction from the editor-in-chief that overviews women's issues today around the world and introduces the set. Each volume editor broadly characterizes contemporary women's issues in the particular region(s). The volumes are divided into chapters, ordered alphabetically by country name. A few chapters treat several countries (e.g., Tajikistan, Kazakhstan, Turkmenistan, and Kyrgyzstan, which are grouped together as Central Asia) or a group of islands (e.g., the Netherland Antilles).

The comprehensive coverage facilitates comparisons between nations and among regions. The following is an outline showing the sections of each chapter. In rare instances where information was not available or applicable for a particular country, sections were omitted. Variations in a few subheads may have been appropriate in some volumes.

Profile of [the Nation]

A paragraph on the land, people(s), form of government, economy, and demographic statistics on female/male population, infant mortality, maternal mortality, total fertility, and life expectancy.

Overview of Women's Issues

A brief introduction to the major issues to be covered, giving the reader a sense of the state of women's lives in the country.

Education

Opportunities

Literacy

Employment and Economics

Farming [and Herding]

Paid Employment

Informal Economic Activities

Entrepreneurship

Pay

Working Conditions

    Sexual Harassment

Support for Mothers/Caretakers

    Maternal Leave

    Child Care

    Family and Medical Leave

Inheritance, Property, and Land Rights

Social/Government Programs

    Structural Adjustment

    Gender Budgets

Family and Sexuality

Gender Roles and Division of Labor

Marriage

Reproduction

    Sex Education

    Contraception and Abortion

    Teen Pregnancy

Health

Health Care Access

Diseases and Disorders

    [Sexually Transmitted Diseases and] AIDS

    Female Genital Cutting[, Other Traditional Practices, and New Stressors]

    Fistula

Politics and Law
Leadership and Decision-making
    Quota Laws
Suffrage
Political Participation
Women's Rights [and/or Women's Groups]
    Women's Movements
    Lesbian Rights
Military [and Police Force] Service
Religion and Spirituality
Women's Roles
Rituals and Religious Practices
Religious Law
Violence
Domestic Violence
Rape/Sexual Assault
Trafficking in Women and Children
War and Military Repression
Outlook for the Twenty-first Century
Notes
Resource Guide
Suggested Reading
Videos/Films
Web Sites
Organizations
Selected Bibliography

A regional map is in the inside cover of each volume. Additionally, each chapter has an accompanying country or mini-region map. Each volume has an index consisting of subject and person entries; a comprehensive set index is included at the end of this volume.

GLOSSARY

Ajami. Arabic script used for writing local African languages.

Akazu. A small group of close associates of President Juvenal Habyarimana who masterminded the 1994 genocide in Rwanda.

Animism. Attribution of a living soul to inanimate objects, plants, and natural phenomena.

Apartheid. Policy or system of segregation and discrimination based on race (South Africa and Namibia).

Askari. Swahili term for African soldier used in German East Africa (Burundi, Rwanda, and Tanganyika).

Baitos. Village councils (Eritrea).

Basadi. Women (Botswana).

Birr. Ethiopian currency.

Bogadi. Bridewealth (Botswana).

Cedi. The national currency of Ghana.

CFA (Communauté Financière d'Afrique; African Financial Community). Banknote used by fourteen francophone African countries; pegged to the French franc since 1948 and to the euro after 1999.

Ensete. The staple banana-like crop (Ethiopia).

Esusu (also **isusu**). Cooperatives (Nigeria).

Evolué. French term for educated elites (term used in former French and Belgian colonies).

Geer. Prestigious noncasted and casted artisans, such as iron workers, weavers, and carpenters (Senegal).

Griot. Laudatory singer, musician, or oral historian of Western Africa.

IDP. Internally displaced persons.

Ijtihad. Attempting to uncover Allah's rulings on issues from their Islamic sources (Qur'an, Sunnah, Ijma', and other sources).

Infibulation. The full removal of the clitoris, labia minora, and labia majora, and the suturing of the vagina, leaving a small opening to allow for the flow of menstrual blood and urine.

Inyomdi. Wives of the lineage and supreme bodies of arbitration (Igbo, Nigeria).

Inzu. Nuclear family (Rwanda, Burundi).

Iyalode. Yoruba woman chief who headed the women's council that governed women's cultural, social, political, and economic affairs; second in status after the Oba or king (Nigeria).

Iye oba (Yoruba) **or Iyoba** (Benin). Queen mother (Nigeria).

Jeli. Bamanakan (Mali) term for *griot* (see *Griot*).

Kgosi (pl. **dikgosi**). Chief (Botswana).

Kgotla. Traditional village meeting and dispute resolution forum (Botswana).

Khat. Leafy narcotic (Somalia).

Killil. Administrative units in Ethiopia, supposedly inhabited by monolingual tribal groups classified as "nationalities."

Kinyarwanda. The Rwandan language.

Lobola. Bride price (Zimbabwe, South Africa, Mozambique).

Mapoto. Unregistered customary marriages (Zimbabwe).

Marabout. Religious cleric and spiritual leader associated with brotherhoods (Senegal).

Mehr. Bride price given to bride herself (Somalia).

Meticais. Currency of Mozambique.

Mfecane. Zulu and other Nguni wars along with forced migrations in the early nineteenth century that transformed the social, political, and demographic landscape of southern and central Africa (Botswana).

Morafe. Geographically based political units in Setswana language (Botswana).

Motswana (pl. **Batswana**). Citizen.

Muryango. The extended family (Rwanda, Burundi).

Muti. Medicine (Botswana).

Muvyeyi. Mother (Rwanda, Burundi).

Mwami (pl. **bami**).   King (Rwanda, Burundi).

Nakfa.   Currency in Eritrea introduced in 1997.

Njangi.   Rotating credit and savings groups (Cameroon). See also *Tontine*.

Oba.   Yoruba king (Nigeria).

Olori.   Yoruba head wife of the king (Nigeria).

Patrilineal.   Descending lineage and inheritance through the father.

Pharaonic circumcision.   See *Infibulation*.

Polygamy.   Having more than one spouse.

Prefet.   Governor (Rwanda).

Pula.   A cheer for heroes and victories in Setswana language (Botswana).

Qene schools.   Schools run by the Ethiopian Orthodox Church that promote the study and preservation of highly specialized ancient poetry.

Quartiers populaires.   Older neighborhoods (Burundi).

Qur'an.   Holy book of Islam.

Rugo (pl. **ingo**).   Residence (Rwanda, Burundi).

Sangoma.   A diviner, often a woman (Botswana).

Shari'a.   Islamic law, Islamic jurisprudence, and comprehensive codes governing all walks of life.

Sufism.   Mystical and ascetic branch of Islam.

Sunna.   Islamic reference to the traditions of the Prophet Muhammad.

Sunni.   The main orientation of 90 percent of Muslims worldwide that has dominated Islamic religion since 661, when Shi'as left the fold. Sunni Islam is defined through the revelations given to the Prophet Muhammad.

Suntuure.   Pulaar term for a parcel of land on which to cultivate a home garden. (Pulaar is spoken in Guinea, Senegal, Gambia, Guinea, Guinea-Bissau, Mali, Mauritania.)

Talaq (also *Talaqa* in Nigeria).   Divorce according to Islamic law, in which the man utters "I divorce you" three times.

Tontine.   Term for rotating credit and savings group used in francophone West Africa.

Ulama/ulema.   Islamic community of learned men with religious education, religious leaders.

Umuada.   Daughters of the lineage (Igbo, Nigeria).

Umuryango.   Extended family (Rwanda, Burundi).

Urugo. Household (Rwanda, Burundi).

Wali. Governors (Sudan).

Zar. The spirits associated with Sufi brotherhoods and Sufi sects.

Zina. The crime, according to *Shari'a* laws, of sexual relations between people who are not married to each other.

INTRODUCTION

Africa has seen enormous change for women since the demise of coloni-alism in the late 1950s and early 1960s. This volume not only looks at the various countries' historical legacies and continuities, but also documents the major transformations the continent has undergone with respect to the status of women in twenty-two of Africa's fifty-seven countries. Since the 1985 United Nations conference on women was held in Nairobi, a new generation of women's organizations and movements has emerged, ex panding significantly both in numbers and in impact. They differ from earlier associations in their goals, forms of mobilization, and autonomy from the state.

Today, women are taking their claims to land and inheritance to court on a scale not seen in the past. Women are challenging laws and consti-tutions that do not uphold gender equality. In addition, they are moving into government, legislative, party, and other leadership positions that had been the almost exclusive domain of men. In countries like South Africa, Namibia, Uganda, and Mozambique, women have won provisions that guarantee them a greater number of seats in parliament. They are also fighting for female leadership in areas where women were previously mar-ginalized in business, as well as in religious and cultural institutions. They are seeking expanded educational opportunities for girls and improved women's prenatal and health care. In many countries women leaders have led the way in getting governments to be proactive in preventing and treat-ing HIV/AIDS.

Women have taken advantage of the new democratic openings that occurred in the 1990s, even if the openings have been measured and pre-carious. The expansion of independent women's organizations and asso-ciational life more generally accompanied the move away from the older single party systems prior to the 1990s in sub-Saharan Africa. The 1990s saw a shift toward multiparty politics and the demise of military regimes in favor of civilian rule. Women media workers bravely took advantage of new, if limited, expansions in the freedom of speech. The international women's movement as well as an influx of donor funds for women's issues gave added impetus to women's efforts in the areas of income generation and political participation. The expansion of the use of the cell phone, email, and the Internet in the late 1990s, although primarily among urbanites, enhanced networking among women's organizations not only throughout Africa but also locally. These new conditions, coupled with a significant increase in secondary- and university-educated women, opened up new possibilities for women's advancement. At the same time, the tenuousness of political liberalization, continued civil conflict, the revival of conservative interpretations of Islamic law in places like Nigeria and Niger, and the politicization of ethnicity and religion in ways that divide women, have all been factors that have created obstacles for those seeking to change women's status.

This volume provides country-by-country documentation of many of these exciting transformations across the continent, while also emphasizing the continuing constraints that keep women from achieving their full potential. A wide range of countries are covered, from predominantly Muslim (Mali, Niger, Sudan, Somalia) to predominantly Christian (Uganda, Namibia). It looks at wealthier countries (e.g., Botswana, South Africa) as well as some of the poorest in Africa (Mozambique, Ethiopia). It examines countries that have active independent women's movements (Uganda, South Africa, Tanzania) as well as countries that do not (Eritrea, Niger, Cameroon). The volume covers a wide range of countries in terms of colonial legacy: including former British colonies (Uganda, Tanzania, Kenya, Ghana, Nigeria), French colonies (Senegal, Niger, Guinea, Togo), Portuguese colonies (Mozambique), Belgian colonies (Rwanda and Burundi), and from the late 1800s to World War I, German colonies (Tanzania, Burundi, Rwanda, Cameroon, Togo, Namibia).

A word of caution is in order regarding the statistics used in this volume. They should be taken as rough indicators of trends rather than as precise measures. Data collection is poor in Africa generally and is virtually nonexistent in many of countries undergoing civil conflict. Many of the generic statistical categories were not developed with African women in mind. The labor statistics, in particular, do not capture the kinds of work carried out by women in Africa, nor do they adequately reflect the vast amounts of income generated through the informal economy, which is by definition unregulated, unregistered, and unaccounted for. What follows is a summary of some very general trends highlighted in the book in a number of key areas.

A glossary of commonly occurring foreign terms is included at the beginning of the volume. Spelling of these terms is standardized.

EDUCATION

It has been well established that the education of girls has a significant impact on their quality of life and that of their households. Africa has some of the highest rates of illiteracy in the world along with the Middle East and South Asia. Although illiteracy for both men and women over fifteen years old decreased from 72 percent in 1970 to 40 percent in 2000, the gender gap has not decreased. In 1970, 58 percent of the illiterate population were women, while thirty years later, 61 percent of the illiterate population were still women.

Nevertheless, the gender gap has closed in school enrollments. In 1970, for example, the female-male ratio of primary school enrollment stood at 72 percent in sub-Saharan Africa. By 1990 it was up to 85 percent and the gap has continued to close as a result of policy changes. With the tightening economic conditions in many countries, women and girls also became more reliable sources of financial support for parents in societies where adult children were obligated to care for their elderly parents. Women responded to economic crisis in many societies by taking on more income-generating activities, which they drew on to support their households and extended families. Their reliable sustenance to the household meant that girls came to be seen as a future asset, where in the past they might have been more likely to be overlooked for educational opportunities.

At the international level, concern over female education has grown since the United Nations Nairobi Conference on Women in 1985. At the subsequent 1990 World Conference on Education for All, held in Jomtien, Thailand, governments pledged to achieve universal primary education by the year 2000. The 2000 World Education Forum, held in Dakar, Senegal, reaffirmed these goals and took stock of the levels of basic education internationally. The schooling of girls featured prominently in all these events.[1]

In spite of changing international norms regarding girls' education and a closing gender gap in school enrollments, still throughout the continent the average number of girls enrolled at the primary and secondary level stands at 56 percent while the number of boys is 66 percent. While girls make up roughly 41 percent of the total enrolled at the secondary level, at the tertiary level they make up on the average 32 percent of the student body in Africa.

The lowest rates of female enrollment at the primary and secondary level (where below 20 percent of girls are enrolled) are found in the Horn of Africa (Eritrea, Ethiopia, Djibouti, Somalia) and in the predominantly Muslim countries of West Africa (Niger, Mali, Chad).[2] The need for girls to help in household and farm labor, teenage pregnancy, and lingering cultural rationales that privilege boys, keep girls from accessing educational opportunities at rates equal to those of boys. The highest rates of female enrollment are found in southern Africa in Namibia, South Africa, and Botswana, where a larger percentage of girls are enrolled than boys. Women are similarly represented in higher numbers in southern African tertiary institutions, making up 61 percent of the student population in institutions of higher learning in Namibia, 54 percent in Lesotho, and almost half in South Africa, Botswana, and Swaziland.

EMPLOYMENT AND ECONOMICS

In most African countries women do by far most of the agricultural labor. They produce mainly food crops but also cash crops. However, because women do not always market the crops, they are not always able to decide, as the men do, how to spend the income acquired from crop sales. Women's labor is undervalued and not sufficiently recognized in policy measures that tend to privilege male household members in access to land, credit, inputs, and training. Yet at the same time women generally contribute disproportionately to the household in terms of food, shelter, health, and education.

In many countries, women comprise the majority of entrepreneurs in the informal micro and small-enterprise economy, which is the fastest job-creation sector in Africa, contributing to approximately 40 percent of gross domestic product (GDP) in Africa and providing seven of every ten new jobs on the continent.[3]

Women make up 34 percent of the work force in Africa according to official statistics,[4] and have registered declines in work force participation over the past decades. These figures are more indicative of the poor quality of statistical collection in Africa and the problems in classification than they are of actual levels of work force participation. As the state and formal economy eroded after the 1980s in Africa, the informal sector (unregistered, unlicensed, and hence unrecorded economic activity) expanded. Women in Africa produce over 80 percent of food crops and are also involved in the production of traditional farm exports as well as nontraditional exports. They make up the overwhelming majority of the informal economy in many countries. It is difficult to comprehend how the 34 percent rate corresponds to the actual work carried out by the majority women in Africa. Such official data need to be regarded with healthy skepticism.

Women's increased involvement in entrepreneurship, both large-scale and especially small-scale in many countries, is evident from the large numbers of women's business associations at the national level across Africa. It is also evident from the levels of women's savings and credit associations that cater to self-employed women. The average male-female ratio of administrative and managerial workers across Africa is roughly 100:12, and 100:31 for professional and technical positions.[5]

Even though women are not found in large numbers in industry or in the formal sector more generally, employed women nevertheless have attained key benefits for women comparable to other parts of the world. Both the average and median maternity leave in Africa is twelve weeks, and in the majority of cases there is full coverage (100 percent) of wages for that time period. In twenty-one countries, the employer is responsible for the coverage, in six countries the costs are shared (equally) by the employer and government, and in seventeen countries the government is responsible for the costs through a social security scheme.

Inheritance, Property, and Land Rights

Land and land inheritance is a central concern of women in Africa. Since the mid-1990s, women have been active in a variety of land alliances and coalitions in eastern and southern Africa — from Tanzania, Zambia, South Africa, Mozambique, Zimbabwe, Kenya, Uganda, to Namibia — to ensure that any changes in land law incorporate women's concerns. Women's organizations made gains in some countries like Tanzania, where through the 1999 Land Act and Village Land Act they won the right to acquire, hold, use, and deal with land. Their rights of co-occupancy were similarly protected. In other countries women have faced enormous setbacks. In Zimbabwe, for example, a 1999 Supreme Court case gave precedence to customary law in a land inheritance dispute between a brother and sister when it ruled that women as minors could not be considered equal to men before the law because of African cultural norms and "the nature of African society." In this case, the half brother of Venia Magaya, a fifty-eight-year-old seamstress, evicted her from her home after the death of her father. She then sued her half brother for ownership of the land, which under the Zimbabwean constitution and international human rights treaties, she should have had the right to inherit.

Land is the most important resource in much of Africa because people depend on it for cultivation, hence their livelihood. Unequal access to land is one of the most important forms of economic inequality between men and women and has consequences for women as social and political actors. Women provide most of the agricultural labor, yet they generally own only a fraction of the land. Women are commonly responsible for providing for the household; therefore their access to land is critical. But in societies where inheritance is patrilineal (passed through male lineage), women are dependent on their fathers, husbands, and sons to access that land. In patrilineal societies, women generally do not inherit land from either their fathers or their husbands, who frequently want to ensure that all land remains within the clan. Fathers and husbands often do not bequeath land to their daughters and wives because daughters marry outside the clan, and will therefore take the land with them to another clan. In some societies, if the husband dies, the husband's brother inherits the wife and children so that he may provide for them. This practice is dying out, raising fears that if a widow remarries outside the clan, the clan land she has acquired is lost.

Food productivity is determined in part by women's ability to access land and have control over their produce. In a patrilineal society where customary law holds sway, a woman may have jointly acquired land with her husband and may have spent her entire adult life cultivating the land, but she cannot claim ownership of the property because the land titles are registered in her husband's name. If he dies, the land generally goes to the sons, but even if he leaves it to both sons and daughters, he may leave the wife with no land and therefore no source of subsistence. A man may even sell off part of his land to settle a debt without consulting the wife let alone informing her. In both cases, the woman has no basis for contesting those claims. Moreover, women who are childless, widowed, single, separated/divorced, or who have only girl children often have little or no recourse because they cannot rely on men for access to land.

Social/Government Programs

Structural Adjustment

Structural adjustment programs were among the most significant policy interventions affecting women in Africa in the past two decades. The majority of African governments, under pressure from the World Bank and International Monetary Fund, implemented the programs to one degree or another. Bilateral foreign donors also made their continued support contingent on embarking on such an economic reform program. Structural adjustment was an attempt to respond to the severe economic imbalances and crises that had become acute by the 1980s. The crisis was in part due to falling prices of exports and oil price increases, but also to distortions in prices paid to peasants for their crops, urban bias in policies adopted favoring industry and urbanites over rural agricultural producers, over-reliance on subsistence agriculture, overvalued currencies and other such phenomenon that had driven economies into the ground. The adjustment programs addressed these issues by freeing up internal and export trade, allowing rural producers to receive prices for the produce that were more in line with world prices, devaluing overvalued currencies (hence eliminating the black market in foreign currencies), privatizing government monopolies, lifting subsidies on food that had kept prices for urban dwellers artificially low, and reducing the public-sector work force. Because of pre-existing discrimination in women's access to credit, inputs, and land, market liberalization was not always as beneficial to women as it was to men. Since women were still primarily involved in food production, currency devaluation, pricing incentives, and cheaper inputs directed at the export sector did not always assist women in their subsistence agricultural production. Moreover, even though the emphasis on export cash crops pushed more women into this sector, especially into the field of nontraditional exports like flowers, birds, seaweed production, and other such produce, existing gender imbalances and male control of marketing meant that the income obtained from these crops did not always benefit women. Those who produced export crops often found that their husbands did the marketing and thus controlled the income from these crops. Cutbacks in the public sector hit women more severely as they often had less seniority. The introduction of user fees in health care facilities (shifting the burden of health care costs from the government to the patients) put new burdens on women to meet the health expenses of the household.

Government initiatives regarding women have undergone enormous transformations since the 1970s, when national machineries for women were formed to address "women's concerns." Some national machineries were formed after 1975 in response to a UN resolution calling on member states to establish such machineries to promote the integration of women into development and eliminate gender discrimination. Some countries set up women's ministries (Côte d'Ivoire), others established women's bureaus, departments, or divisions within another ministry (Kenya, Ethiopia, Zambia). Still others established commissions, committees, or councils that were to represent and bring all women together nationwide (Ghana, Uganda). The success of these machineries was limited by the extent to which their respective governments gave them funding and other encouragements. Some made modest gains, for example, in the areas of maternity benefits, but rarely did they adopt controversial positions that would have put them at odds with government policy. Thus, for example, in Zimbabwe, the Ministry of Women's Affairs did nothing when the government launched a nationwide roundup of women walking on streets at night in 1983, during Operation Chinyavada, on the pretext that they were prostitutes. In Zambia, the Women's League launched a campaign focusing on women's morality. Government and party authorities frequently used patronage to keep the leaders of the machineries from fundamentally challenging the status quo regarding women's rights.

With political liberalization in the 1990s and the rise of independent women's organizations and agendas, women activists (and some foreign donors) introduced new efforts to influence the national machineries, but also to see that other government ministries and agencies adopted gender-mainstreaming policies. Gender-mainstreaming is defined as a process by which *all* policy (not just that conventionally understood as "women's policy") should be examined for its possible gender-differentiated effects or implications. The outcomes of such initiatives were uneven, and the difficulties encountered have included weak leadership commitments to mainstreaming and a lack of accountability in monitoring and evaluating its effects. Gender units are often accorded low status within organizations and are staffed with junior people, making it difficult for them to carry sufficient weight.

Women activists have especially targeted ministries of finance and economic planning in several countries for gender-mainstreaming with the aim of incorporating women's concerns into the process of developing the national budgets. After the 1995 Beijing conference, several African countries adopted women's budgets patterned along the lines of South Africa's 1994 budget exercise. These initiatives, typically coordinated by finance departments, have involved collaboration among nongovernmental organizations and parliaments. They have involved analysis of existing budgets to determine the differential gender impact on women, men, girls, and boys, with the intention of making recommendations for future budgets to improve the way in which funds are allocated. Such budget initiatives have thus far been adopted with varying degrees of success in countries like Uganda, Mozambique, Botswana, Zimbabwe, Malawi Namibia, and Tanzania.

HEALTH

The female-male ratio in Africa is 101:100, which is similar to the rates in North and South America but higher than the 98:100 ratio in Asia (where in some countries the preference for boys has meant that women and girls suffer disproportionately from poor health and nutrition and in some cases infanticide and abortion if the fetus is determined to be a girl). The female-male ratio in Africa is lower than the 105:100 ratio in Europe. Life expectancy at birth (2000–2005 figures) is fifty-three years for women and fifty years for men in Africa.

Health concerns are paramount in explaining the discrepancy in life expectancy in Africa when compared with Europe. For example, 1 in 16 women in Africa die from maternal causes, while only 1 in 1,400 do so in Europe. Infections, blood loss, and unsafe abortions account for the majority of maternal deaths, most of which are preventable by proper prenatal care and skilled health personnel attending births. The maternal mortality rate is, in fact, going up: according to the UNDP and WHO between 1980 and 1992 there were 606 maternal deaths per 100,000 live births, 870 in 1990, and 940 in 2000.[6] This is despite increases in access to prenatal care and trained midwives for delivery in some parts of Africa, suggesting uneven access to such care. On average, 68 percent of women received prenatal care in Africa by 2000, while half of all deliveries were attended by a skilled professional.

An overwhelming 70 percent of all HIV/AIDS cases can be found in Africa. Women are generally infected at higher rates than men in Africa, where HIV is transmitted primarily through heterosexual relations. They are more likely than men to become infected, in part for physiological reasons. Social and cultural factors also increase their vulnerability to HIV, making it difficult for women to insist on safe sex practices. Women also may have less access to public health care facilities.

Fertility rates are decreasing overall worldwide, contributing to slower population growth rates, and these trends are evident in Africa as well. The average number of children per woman between 1990–1995 and 2000–2005 has gone down from 5.7 to 5.1, although some countries still have high rates, such as Uganda, Somalia, Ethiopia, Angola, the Democratic Republic of Congo, and Liberia. These are all countries that have seen extensive civil conflict and bloodshed throughout these years. Africa also leads the world in births to teenagers, with the highest rates in the aforementioned conflicted countries. On average Africa has 116 births per 1,000 women aged fifteen to nineteen.[7] On average, one-quarter of women in Africa use some form of birth control. Infant mortality stands at about 82.5 births per 1,000 live births.[8]

One growing health concern in Africa has been the practice of female genital cutting. There are two types of cutting that are practiced in Africa. The first is called infibulation (also known as pharaonic circumcision), which may include the excision of the clitoris. The practice includes the removal of the woman's entire external genital area and sewing the wound together leaving a small opening to allow for the flow of menstrual blood and urine. Infibulation is practiced on young girls, even infants, to make girls into desirable brides who are virgins until marriage. Many also believe that infibulation enhances health, aesthetic beauty, and fertility. The resulting scar tissue and smallness of the opening may require defibulation with a knife at the time of marriage and childbirth. The psychological effects of cutting small girls without anesthesia can be traumatic and can undermine trust in their closest female relatives who carry out the procedure. The unsanitary conditions under which the infibulation is performed may also lead to serious complications. Infibulation is practiced primarily in the Horn of Africa, in Ethiopia, Sudan, Egypt, Eritrea and Somalia.[9]

The other form of cutting, clitoridectomy, or the excision of the clitoris, varies widely. There is also a form of female circumcision that involves pricking or nicking the clitoris or removing the prepuce of the clitoris. This is practiced in northern Tanzania, throughout Kenya (except along the predominantly Islamic coast) and a small eastern portion of Uganda, much of Ethiopia, from Egypt down to northern Democratic Republic of Congo, and then across West Africa south of the Sahara. In many societies, clitoridectomy is performed as part of puberty rituals for girls at the time of their first menses and is often seen as analogous to male circumcision. The practice is seen as necessary in establishing a gender identity and in bringing youth into adulthood. Cutting in the context of initiation rituals are often seen as integral to the continuity of the society and culture.[10]

Throughout Africa, local, national, and regional initiatives have been launched by African women's organizations to eradicate the practice by educating women of the health and reproductive health risks involved. Initiation rites have been revised in some cases to drop the actual cutting while maintaining the spirit and essence of the ritual. Women have pursued political strategies to elect leaders who resist the practice. They have provided alternative economic incentives to those women who profit from carrying out the cutting, provided elders with recognition for discouraging the practice, and educated girls themselves about the hazards of the practice. Efforts aimed at changing legislation regarding the practice have been less successful without the necessary groundwork through education and persuasion.

POLITICS AND LAW

Throughout Africa, women had historically been queens, chiefs, sultans, and heads of state. In the preindependence period women were active in the formation of parties in Tanzania, Cameroon, Nigeria, Uganda, and other countries. They played major roles in liberation movements and guerrilla wars in Zimbabwe, Mozambique, Uganda, Eritrea, and South Africa. Women never wielded as much power as men in precolonial Africa. With colonial rule, and even more so in the postindependence periods, opportunities for female leadership diminished considerably. But it was not until the 1990s that women began to seek national leadership in greater numbers. Women sought to be placed on the ballot as presidential candidates in countries like Nigeria, Tanzania, Angola, the Central African Republic, and Guinea Bissau, and ran for the presidency in Liberia and Kenya. Uganda's Wandera Specioza Kazibwe became the first female vice president in Africa. In the mid-1990s Rwanda and Burundi had woman prime ministers and Senegal gained its first woman prime minister in 2000.

Women sought parliamentary seats in greater numbers. By 2003, women held on the average 13.6 percent of the seats in parliaments throughout Africa, compared with 6 percent a decade earlier. In fact, Africa, which had the lowest rates of female participation in politics in the 1960s, has subsequently experienced the fastest rates of growth in female representation of any world region. Some countries, like South Africa and Mozambique, had 30 percent female representation, Rwanda and Namibia had 26 percent, Uganda had 25 percent, and Tanzania had 22 percent in 2003.

By the end of the 1990s the Ethiopian, Lesothoan, and South African legislative bodies even had women speakers of the house. In the 1990s women formed new political parties in countries like Zambia, Zimbabwe, and Lesotho and headed political parties in Kenya, the Central African Republic, and Angola. These are just a few examples of the rapid changes that were evident by the beginning of the new millennium.

What accounts for these changes that began in the 1990s? No single factor can explain the transformations. Rather one must look at a convergence of circumstances. The move toward multipartyism in most African countries opened up spaces for new forms of women's mobilization. It diminished the importance of mass women's organizations linked and directed by the single ruling party, opening up possibilities for the rise of independent women's organizations. These organizations had new leadership that began to push for a broader agenda, which included women's expanded political participation. Women's movements that had once been dominated by organizations engaged in "developmental" activities, focusing on income generation, welfare concerns, and homemaking skills, were now witnessing the emergence of organizations that lobbied for women's political leadership, pressed for legislative and constitutional changes, and conducted civic education.

Although rarely mentioned in studies of democratization in Africa, women's movements actively sought to participate in the political reform movements of the 1990s. They openly resisted corruption and repressive regimes through public demonstrations and other militant action in countries like Kenya, Mali, and Niger. Changing international donor strategies helped spur the growth of national level organizations that supported women's political activities on a nonpartisan basis. Donors supported efforts of women to participate in civic education, constitutional reform, legislative reform, leadership training, and programs for women parliamentarians.

Governmental commitment to women's increased representation on the part of the leadership of the country was another critical factor in advancing women's political representation. One-fifth of countries in Africa adopted some kind of quota system. Thus some of these gains can be attributed to legislative affirmative action measures. In Senegal and Namibia an electoral quota was mandated for all parties by the legislature; in Mozambique, South Africa, and Tunisia, the largest party had set quotas, while Burkina Faso, Eritrea, Tanzania, and Uganda had reserved seats for women. These affirmative action strategies are as controversial in Africa as elsewhere, but what is indisputable is the fact that where they have been implemented, the popular political culture has gradually become more accepting of female politicians.

The international women's movement has also played a significant role in encouraging women to seek political office and influence policymaking, especially after the UN Beijing Conference on Women in 1995. Finally, much of formal politics in Africa is underwritten and controlled by informal patronage politics. Most women tend to operate on the margins of clientelistic networks. This means that women have often found opportunities to advance themselves where state linked clientelistic networks were weakened by economic crisis, as has been the case in recent years in Senegal. Economic crisis has forced many women into formal and informal economic associations and into heightened entrepreneurial activity. Some women with independent sources of income have been able to use these resources to enter politics.

Cultural and social norms have not generally encouraged women's political participation in Africa. Nevertheless, in the 1990s many African countries saw the growth of an unprecedented degree of mobilization to support women electoral candidates, train women leaders, carry out civic education, press for legal changes in the status of women and in the constitution-making process, lobby parties to endorse more women candidates, and develop strategies to get more women into leadership. Women's movements also slowly began to seek legislative change, especially in the areas of land ownership, marriage and inheritance rights, female genital cutting, rape, domestic violence, citizenship rights, and many other such issues.

RELIGION AND SPIRITUALITY

Approximately 50 percent of Africans follow indigenous religious practices, 25 percent are Muslims, and 25 percent are Christian, including Catholics, Protestants, and members of independent churches.[11] There is considerable overlap between these categories and a wide range and interpretation of religious systems.

Women's role as spiritual and moral leaders has been central throughout African history. Women have been priestesses, prophetesses, and spirit mediums. They have claimed key positions of authority as healers, diviners, instructors in initiation rites, circumcisers, keepers of ancestor shrines, and members of secret societies. At times they have been feared for their bewitching powers. Some of their authority diminished with the introduction of Islam and later the onset of colonialism. However, today women are beginning to voice their concerns about a lack of female leadership in established Christian churches, where the majority of the laity and most active parishioners are women, yet they are poorly represented further up the church hierarchy. The problem is less pronounced in the independent churches, where there has been more room for women's leadership. African feminists have been critical of the fact that the churches, especially Catholic churches, have adopted patriarchal hierarchies that accept women's material services but do not listen to their voices, seek their leadership, or welcome their initiatives.

While some women's organizations within predominantly Islamic countries like Sudan have pursued greater secularism as a way of advancing women's rights, other groups like the Federation of Muslim Women's Associations of Nigeria (FOMWAN) have tried to open up the gender discourse within Islam. They have pressed for a redefinition of women's rights, including inheritance and custody rights, equality in education, and the full participation of women within the context of an Islamic state and within the bounds of the Islamic *shari'a* law. Other groups like Baobab in Nigeria seek to advance the rights of women who live under Islamic law through whatever means women locally deem appropriate, whether it means taking a secular stance or using arguments based on Islamic law. There are also regional organizations, like Women Living Under Muslim Laws, which are involved in information sharing, database building, networking, solidarity action, and organizing campaigns throughout Africa and the Middle East. Nigeria has become a focus of international attention with the expansion of institutionalized Islamic law since 2000 in the northern part of the country. The north saw the imposition of harsh punishments on women charged with violating the law, including imposing the death penalty by stoning on individual women singled out and accused of adultery. Women lawyers and activists in northern Nigeria have been actively fighting such cases.

VIOLENCE

Domestic Violence

Norms around domestic violence vary considerably throughout Africa. Researchers have found that in some countries, like Côte d'Ivoire, Malawi, Madagascar, Gabon, Swaziland, Somalia, and Togo, wife-beating is less common than in other parts of Africa. In countries where surveys have been conducted, women have reported physical abuse by a male partner (1986–1993) in rates that are comparable with those in other parts of the world: 60 percent in Tanzania, 46 percent in Uganda, 42 percent in Kenya, 40 percent in Zambia.[12]

Violence in Civil War

Africa has sustained a higher number of civil conflicts than anywhere else in the world. Even though the number of conflicts has been halved since 1994, in the 1990s twenty-four of its fifty-three states have had some form of internal strife. The cost of conflict has been staggering in terms of the numbers who have lost their lives. Women in particular have suffered, not only as victims of killings, but also because together with children they make up the vast majority of refugees who have either had to flee borders or are internally displaced. Women also suffer disproportionately from rape and other forms of sexual violence within the context of conflicts. It is estimated that a quarter of a million women were raped during the 1994 genocide and war in Rwanda. Similar reports of mass rape have been documented in the conflicts in Somalia, Burundi, Liberia, and Uganda. Conflict in southern Sudan, for example, has left over one-third of all households headed by women, and women generally are the only food producers and are primarily responsible for feeding and caring for the children. They desperately need to be able to farm and keep their animals out of harm's way to be able to sustain their households.

Women have often been prime initiators of peacebuilding efforts at the local level, whether it be over access to water and fuel wood in southern Sudan, or collaborating to rescue kidnapped members of feuding clans in Somalia, or talking about common experiences in conflict situations in Uganda. Various organizations have sought to draw women into peace-keeping efforts, like the African Women in Crisis Umbrella Programme, the Federation of African Women's Peace Networks, ABANTU for Development, Center for the Strategic Initiatives of Women (based in the Horn of Africa), and other such regional and Africawide groups.

Even though women suffer enormously from the consequences of war and have sought informally to build peace, they are often left out of official peacekeeping efforts at the national and regional level. For example, a delegation of Burundian women leaders from across the ethnic and political spectrum formed a coalition and came to participate in the Arusha peace talks in 1998, aimed at bringing an end to civil conflict in Burundi. When they arrived, they were first not permitted to participate and then later told not to join together but to be loyal to their own parties. They were eventually permitted two years later to participate in the talks to endorse the peace accord. An All-Party Burundi Women's Conference was convened in Arusha during July 2000, where they insisted that women's concerns be taken up in the peace process, given the particular effects of the conflict on women. They also demanded a 30 percent quota for women in the legislature, the judiciary, and the executive branches of government, as well as in all bodies created by the peace accord. But their initial expulsion from the talks and the delegates' attempts to destroy their hardwon unity illustrates just how many obstacles lay in the way of women's full participation in peace initiatives.

Trafficking in Women and Children

Although African countries have not been as affected by the expansion of sex trafficking as other parts of the world, there are reports of child abductions and trafficking for the purposes of the sex industry in Senegal, Kenya, Ethiopia, and Uganda, with the worst cases appearing in South Africa, where sex trafficking has increased since the country became democratic in 1994. There are estimates of about 38,000 child prostitutes, the youngest about age four, being sold to South Africans and foreigners. The rise in child prostitution and trafficking has increased with the rise of poverty and joblessness. The myth that AIDS can be prevented by having sex with a virgin or that children are not infected by the HIV virus has also contributed to the expansion of the sex industry.

Over 12 million children in sub-Saharan Africa have lost a parent or both parents to HIV/AIDS and the figure is expected to more than double between 2000 and 2010. Without adequate alternatives, many of these orphans are being drawn into the sex trade. Many become street children as well, which places them at higher risk of becoming sex workers.

OUTLOOK FOR THE TWENTY-FIRST CENTURY

Since the early 1990s, new, autonomous women's organizations have increased numerically throughout Africa. They have taken up a wide variety of new concerns and set bold new agendas. Women are organizing at all levels: local, national, and across Africa. They have used the media and Internet in ways not possible in the early 1980s. In some countries they are taking their claims to land, inheritance, and associational autonomy to court. Women are seeking legislative and constitutional reforms to advance the cause of equality. They are also seeking leadership positions in government, legislative, party, nongovernmental, and other organizations that had previously been held exclusively by men. The twenty-first century is certain to be a century of new beginnings for African women.

NOTES

1. UNESCO, http://portal.unesco.org, accessed 2002.

2. Human Development Report (UNDP), *Deepening Democracy in a Fragmented World, 2002* (New York: Human Development Report Office, United Nations Development Programme, 2002), http://hdr.undp.org/reports/global/2002.

3. Margaret Snyder, *Women in African Economies: From Burning Sun to Boardroom—Business Ventures and Investment Patterns of 74 African Women* (Kampala: Fountain Publishers, 2000), 5.

4. Naomi Neft and Ann D. Levine, *Where Women Stand: An International Report on the Status of Women in 140 Countries, 1997–1998* (New York: Random House, 1997), 50.

5. Neft and Levine, 1997, *Where Women Stand*, 64, 8.

6. UNDP, *Human Development Report 1995* (New York: Oxford University Press 1995).

7. UNDP, 2000–2005 figures, http://hdr.undp.org.

8. Ibid.

9. Stanlie M. James and Claire Robertson, eds., *Genital Cutting and Transnational Sisterhood: Disputing U.S. Polemics* (Urbana-Champaign: University of Illinois Press, 2002), 8.

10. Ibid., 10–11.

11. Margaret Strobel, "Women in Religious and Secular Ideology," in 2nd ed. of *Women in Subsaharan Africa*, eds. Margaret Jean Hay and Sharon Stichter (New York: Longman, 1995), 89.

12. Neft and Levine, *Where Women Stand*, 154.

RESOURCE GUIDE

Suggested Reading

Allman, Jean Marie, Susan Geiger, and Nakanyike Musisi, eds. *Women in African Colonial Histories*. Bloomington: University of Indiana Press, 2002.

Amadiume, Ifi. *Re-Inventing Africa: Matriarchy, Religion, and Culture*. London: Zed Books, 1997.

Courtney-Clarke, Margaret (photographer). *African Canvas: The Art of West African Women*. New York: Rizzoli, 1990.

Gladwin, Christina H., ed. *Structural Adjustment and African Women Farmers*. Gainesville: University of Florida Press, 1991.

Hay, Margaret Jean, ed., and Sharon Stichter, contrib. *African Women South of the Sahara*. New York: Longman, 1995.

James, Stanlie M., and Claire Robertson, eds. *Genital Cutting and Transnational Sisterhood: Disputing U.S. Polemics*. Urbana-Champaign: University of Illinois Press, 2002.

Mikell, Gwendolyn, ed. *African Feminism*. Philadelphia: University of Pennnsylvania Press, 1997.

Nnaemeka, Obioma, ed. *The Politics of (M)Othering: Womanhood, Identity, and Resistance in African Literature (Opening Out)*. London: Routledge, 1997.

Ogundipe-Leslie, Molara. *Re-Creating Ourselves: African Women and Critical Transformations*. Trenton, NJ: Africa World Press, 1994.

Oyewumi, Oyeronke. *The Invention of Women: Making an African Sense of Western Gender Discourses*. Minneapolis: University of Minnesota Press, 1997.

Sheldon, Kathleen, ed. *Courtyards, Markets, City Streets: Urban Women in Africa*. Boulder: Westview Press, 1996.

Tripp, Aili Mari. "The New Political Activism in Africa." *Journal of Democracy* 12, no. 3 (2001): 141–55.

Turshen, Meredeth, and Clotilde Twagiramariya, eds. *What Women Do in Wartime: Gender and Conflict in Africa*. London: Zed Books, 1998.

Videos/Films

The following are good sources for films and videos on women in Africa.

California Newsreel: Library of African Cinema, www.newsreel.org/topics/acine.htm.

Icarus First Run Films, www.frif.com.

Women Make Movies, www.wmm.com/index.htm.

Web Sites

Africa Action Strategic Action Issue Area: African Woman's Rights, www.africaaction.org/action/women.htm.
This has documents as well as links to web sites on African women, as well as some international links.

AfricaBib, www.africabib.org/.
The site consists of two bibliographic databases covering Africana periodical literature (Bibliography of Africana Periodical Literature Database) and African Women's literature (African Women's Database). You will also find a comprehensive bibliography on women travelers and explorers to Africa (Women Travelers, Explorers, and Missionaries to Africa: 1763–2000—A Comprehensive English Language Bibliography).

Africa South of the Sahara, Topics: African Women, www-sul.stanford.edu/depts/ssrg/africa/women.html.
Links to information on women in Africa.

Africa Women's News, www.africawoman.net/.

Afrol.com, www.afrol.com/categories/women/msindex.htm.
Articles on African women from various sources (UNICEF, World Bank, IPS, etc.).
Based in Oslo, Norway.

allAfrica.com, http://allafrica.com/women/.
Very current news from a variety of African news sources. From the long established
Africa News Service, founded by Reed Kramer.

Feminist Africa, www.feministafrica.org.
The African Gender Institute's Gender and Women's Studies Project at the University
of Cape Town sponsors the first Africawide feminist electronic journal, *Feminist Africa*.

Flame: African Sisters Online, http://flamme.org/.
Flame is a network of African sisters online committed to strengthening the capacity
of women through the use of ICTs to lobby, advocate, and participate in the Beijing
+5 process regionally and globally.

JENDA: A Journal of Culture and African Women Studies, www.jendajournal.com.
Full-text articles from the e-journal, from vol. 1, no. 1 (2001). Published by Africa
Resource Center, Endicott, NY. Edited by Nkiru Nzegwu.

Organizations

ABANTU for Development
Directorate (London)
1 Winchester House
11 Cranmer Road
London SW9 6EJ United Kingdom
Phone: 44-207-8200066
Fax: 44-207-8200088
Email: directorate@abantu.org
Web site: www.abantu.org

Directorate (Nairobi)
Mbaazi Avenue
P.O. Box 2389
00200 City Square, Nairobi, Kenya
Phone: 254-2-570343/574876
Fax: 254-2-570668
Email: esadirect@abantu.org
Web site: www.abantu.org

ABANTU for Development is an organization with nineteen affiliates that work toward sustainable development in Africa through training, sharing information, and
mobilizing resources.

African Women's Development and Communications Network (FEMNET)
P.O. Box 54562
Nairobi, Kenya

Phone: 254-2-741301/20
Fax: 254-2-742927
Email: femnet@africaonline.co.ke
Web site: www.africaonline.co.ke/femnet

FEMNET works to build linkages and networks of African women's organizations around issues of development with the aim of sharing ideas, knowledge, and experiences.

Forum for African Women Educationalists (FAWE)
P.O. Box 21394
Nairobi, Kenya
Phone: 254-02-573131 (Pilot line)/573351/573359
Fax: 254-02-574150
Email: fawe@fawe.org
Web site: www.fawe.org

FAWE is a network of thirty-three Africa-wide chapters that focuses on improving girls' education through policy change.

Isis-Women's International Cross-Cultural Exchange (Isis-WICCE)
P.O. Box 4934
Kampala, Uganda
Phone: 256-41-543953
Fax: 256-41-543954
Email: isis@starcom.co.ug
Web site: www.isis.or.ug

Isis-WICCE is a global women's organization that is based in Africa. It focuses on sharing strategies, skills, experiences, and information to promote women's empowerment.

SELECTED BIBLIOGRAPHY

Human Development Report (UNDP). *Deepening Democracy in a Fragmented World 2002*. New York: Human Development Report Office, United Nations Development Programme. http://hdr.undp.org.

Neft, Naomi, and Ann D. Levine. *Where Women Stand: An International Report on the Status of Women in 140 Countries, 1997–1998*. New York: Random House, 1997.

Snyder, Margaret. *Women in African Economies: From Burning Sun to Boardroom—Business Ventures and Investment Patterns of Seventy-four African Women*. Kampala: Fountain, 2000.

Strobel, Margaret. "Women in Religious and Secular Ideology." In *Women in Subsaharan Africa*, edited by Margaret Jean Hay and Sharon Stichter, 101–18. 2nd ed. New York: Longman, 1995.

I

BOTSWANA

Judith Van Allen

PROFILE OF BOTSWANA

Botswana has a small population, about 1.6 million, but a large territory of 600,370 square kilometers.[1] Botswana is landlocked, and 80 percent of it is covered by the thornbush and sands of the Kalahari Desert. It is bounded by the Limpopo River on the south and the Zambezi River on the north, surrounded by South Africa, Namibia, Zambia, and Zimbabwe. Arable areas and most of the population lie along the southern and eastern borders with South Africa and Zimbabwe and in the northwest around the large inland Okavango Delta, almost the only permanent source of water in the country. Summers are hot and wet, but the rest of the year is dry, and there are frequent periods of drought. There is no permanent cropland, only seasonal cultivation in the 0.6 percent of the land that is arable. Rain's central importance for human survival in the history of the Tswana people, who predominate in Botswana, is reflected in the use of *pula*, the word for rain in the Setswana language, as a cheer for heroes and victories ("*Pula! Pula!*") and the historical power of those who controlled the chants to bring rain. The symbolism is carried into the modern economy in

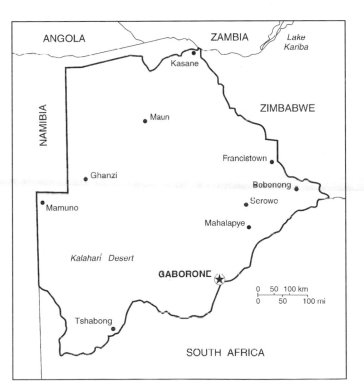

the name of the Botswana monetary unit, the *pula*. In present-day Botswana, as it has been since the Tswana moved into the Kalahari, *pula* is crucial for survival.

The inhabitants of this challenging region have historically relied on year-round herding of cattle combined with short-season cultivation, keeping of small livestock (chicken, goats, some sheep), gathering of wild crops, and hunting of wild game. These patterns have been radically transformed by economic development, so that today more than 50 percent of the population is urbanized or "semi-urbanized," rural residents have many urban connections, and more than two-thirds of the labor force is employed in wage labor, patterns that hold for women as much as for men. The availability of wage work has seriously weakened the patterns of authority within kinship relations as it transformed the kinship context in which people labored to survive. This social transformation lies behind the emergence of a women's movement among women earning their own livings from wages and salaries.

Botswana is relatively homogeneous ethnically, compared with most other African countries. By the mid–nineteenth century the Tswana were organized into hierarchical, kinship, and geographically based political units, *morafe* in Setswana. These polities were forged through a combination of conquest and the acceptance of refugees from the wars raging in southern Africa in the early and middle nineteenth century: the *mfecane*, resulting from expansionary Zulu wars. Some groups, like the Kalanga, perceived as "more like" the Tswana, were incorporated on a fairly equal basis; others, like the Wayeyi and other residents of the Okavango Delta region, and the San throughout the Kalahari, were pressed into servitude or slavery.

Botswana government figures for citizen residents put the current Tswana population at 79 percent, Kalanga 11 percent, other "minority tribes" 6 percent, San 3 percent, and whites 1 percent, although some non-Tswana groups dispute these figures.[2] All except the San and the whites have been largely incorporated, willingly or not, into Setswana culture through the use of Setswana as the national language and as the teaching language in primary schools (with English as the language of government, business, and higher educational levels), and the promotion of Setswana cultural symbols. National unity is expressed in the language of citizenship itself. Just as *Botswana* literally means "land of the Tswana people," the citizenry is designated the *Batswana*, and an individual citizen is a *motswana*. The fictive unity that "We are all Batswana" is perfectly captured on tee-shirts produced by a women's craft collective in Mochudi, north of Gaborone, which show only the eight constitutionally designated "major tribes," represented by their totem animals, pulling the nation, a wagon shaped like a map of Botswana, with the slogan *"Phuthaditshaba"* (We all pull together).

Recently the Wayeyi have sought equality through the courts with the eight "major tribes" and are now pressing their case at the international level with the United Nations.[3] The San people generally remain outsiders, originally enslaved by the Tswana, still subject to discrimination, and currently the center of a controversy over their removal from wildlife areas against their will. It is noteworthy that even though these ethnic conflicts are now surfacing, they are being negotiated through peaceful processes, jural and political. The peaceful resolution of conflicts is often publicly cited in Botswana as an important part of national values and culture that distinguishes the country from its neighbors.

Botswana is a genuine multiparty democracy, and has held regular elections every five years since independence in 1966, with active campaigns and without political violence or fraud. Lively criticism of the government occurs in the independent press, on independent radio, and in the "Freedom Squares" in urban areas in which rallies and speeches take place during election campaigns. Botswana has a parliamentary system, with the president elected by a majority of members of parliament, and it has an independent judiciary that can declare laws unconstitutional. A fifteen-member house of chiefs advises government on matters of customary law but has no legislative authority. Government is known for its extensive bureaucracy, but also for its efficiency, effectiveness, and honesty.

Economically, the country pursues a capitalist market economy and has done so since independence. There are wide disparities in income, with a wealthy class based in commercial meat export to Europe and business, including mining, that dominates politics. According to government figures, poverty has been decreasing, from 59 percent of the population living below the poverty datum line (PDL) in 1985–1986 to 36.7 percent in 2001.[4] Large government expenditures on social services are a strong equalizing factor for people's quality of life, and a serious factor in maintaining the stability of the political system and the reelection of the dominant party, the Botswana Democratic Party. Government provides health services throughout the country that are almost free, ten years of free education, stipends at university level, subsidized house-building programs, food and basic needs targeted for those below the PDL, and widespread drought relief.

At independence in 1966 Botswana was called a "basket case" by international agencies. In thirty years it reached the status of an upper-middle-income country through the good fortune of discovering gem-quality diamonds, the extremely good sense and honesty of its government, and its willingness to use expatriate experts when needed and to be tough in negotiations. Despite its relative weakness, Botswana negotiated favorable arrangements with the giant diamond corporation De Beers for development of its diamonds and with South Africa over the terms of the Southern African Customs Union soon after independence.

In 2002 the gross domestic product (GDP) per capita was equivalent to about U.S.$7,184. Its average growth rate of 7.3 percent between 1970 and

1995 was the highest in the developing world, and it has leveled off at a respectable 3.5 percent. Diamonds account for about 30 percent of GDP and about two-thirds of exports and central-government revenues. On this base, the economy is being slowly diversified and wage employment for women as well as men is increasing, although unemployment remains around 20 percent overall, and slightly higher for women. Botswana's export wealth provides large foreign reserves and low debts, leaving Botswana free of forced structural adjustment programs.[5] Botswana has used its diamond wealth and the foreign aid directed to it to build a significant infrastructure, including roads that link more than 90 percent of the population and a digital telephone network throughout the country. Numerous NGOs work with government departments to increase sustainable agriculture suitable to the region, to develop appropriate technology, and to protect wildlife preserves while promoting the cattle industry—two goals that are not always compatible. Botswana has achieved food security, not by becoming food self-sufficient through its own agricultural production, but by enabling people to purchase food, or if needed, purchasing it for them. As a Botswana delegate to the United Nations said in a debate over African food aid a few years ago, "In Botswana, we have drought, but we do not have famine." In 2002 drought has created severe food shortages in southern Africa, with all countries declaring crises and asking for food aid *except* Botswana and the much richer, much more agriculturally productive South Africa. Government programs provide favorable conditions for foreign investment, and the country is rated as a stable investment site by international agencies. Botswana's main problem today in attracting investment lies outside its borders: the continuing instability of neighboring countries, particularly the Congo and Zimbabwe.

OVERVIEW OF WOMEN'S ISSUES

Botswana has a total population of about 1.6 million people, of which 52 percent are women. Infant mortality was 74 per 1,000 live births in 1999, and maternal mortality was 330 per 100,000 live births. The total fertility rate was 3.3 births per woman by 2002. Life expectancy had dropped to 40 years in 2002. These and other measures of health, especially life expectancy, have been seriously worsened by the HIV/AIDS epidemic.

Women in Botswana, despite class differences, have remarkable opportunities in education, employment, and politics, and have seen notable advances in women's rights in the last twenty years. Since its beginning in the early 1980s, the women's rights campaign in Botswana has clearly spoken out for "rights" over "tradition." As Athaliah Molokomme, a law professor and leader in the women's rights movement put it at the 1988 Democracy Conference in Botswana, "We have to open up those cellars marked 'tradition' and clean them out!" The women's movement has succeeded in building on women's economic position to form an effective political force. The historical context for women's political effectiveness and economic opportunities today can be summed up as "drought, diamonds, and democracy," with a little influence from Christian missionaries.[6]

Women's status in Botswana today is remarkably progressive in African terms, an example of what can happen in a country with rich resources and honest democratic government. Women make up about 52 percent of the population (some men continue to migrate to South Africa as mine labor; more men than women are students abroad).[7] The most serious threat to the quality of women's lives (and men's lives) in Botswana today is HIV/AIDS, and many of the gains for women are at risk unless the epidemic is brought under control. Although there remains a significant differential in quality of life between those women who have benefited most from the opportunities and changes of modernity and those who remain in poverty, both rural and urban, some benefits apply to virtually all women because of government provision of schools, clinics and housing subsidies, the continuing expansion of wage labor available to women, the extension into rural as well as urban areas of women's centers, and women's increasing participation in government. History, sometimes in ironic ways, has put women in Botswana in a position to use the openness of their political system to pursue their interests as they continue to define them. The historical interaction of drought, diamonds, and democracy is complex and paradoxical, but it creates real possibilities for women to organize to overcome the tragedy of HIV/AIDS and to use the tremendous advantages that diamond wealth and honest democratic government provide to promote and secure an improving quality of life for all women in Botswana.

EDUCATION

Opportunities

The Tswana agro-herding survival strategy for living in their dry and drought-stricken land paradoxically resulted in educational advantages for girls and women. The combination of a short farming season that used girls' labor and a year-round need for boys' labor herding cattle meant that when Christian missions established schools, many girls were sent to schools and many boys were not, the opposite of the pattern in almost all the rest of Africa.

The London Missionary Society arrived in 1817 and was particularly devoted to spreading literacy through its schools. Some of the Tswana chiefs also set up their own secular schools. Missionaries and colonial officers complained about the disproportionate number of girls in mission schools. In 1937 the colonial Education Department reported that some 1,400 children were in primary school, and of these 1,170 (83 percent) were girls. Despite attempts by the missions to get the boys into school, the Tswana held on to their boys' labor at the cattle posts, and girls became significantly advantaged in access to schooling.

At independence Botswana launched an ambitious program of expanding education, first making seven years of primary schooling universally available and free and now providing ten years of free schooling to all children who qualify through examinations starting at the end of primary school. Botswana is almost unique in Africa in providing free state schooling. Tanzania, for example, has had policies of free education based on socialist politics, but had to institute school fees as a condition of structural adjustment. Places in the University of Botswana, tuition-free and with room and board provided, are available to all citizens who pass the required examinations.

As the state education system has expanded and as cattle herding has been privatized and transformed into a commercial meat industry, the need for boys' labor has decreased and more boys are able to attend school, but girls continue to outnumber boys at all levels up to the third year of secondary school. By the last year, girls make up 44 percent of students. University enrollment of women was 43 percent of the total in 1989.[8] Girls' dropout patterns in secondary school are largely the result of rules requiring that they leave if they become pregnant. Formerly, they had to attend a different secondary school if they wished to return to school, which made it virtually impossible for most girls. Under pressure from women's groups, the rules were changed in the 1990s so that girls can return to the same school and, if in their senior year, may sit for their examinations. This has enabled some girls to finish secondary school, but the pressure on girls with children to stay at home, whether married or not, is very great, and the cultural values that make them extremely vulnerable to pregnancy remain strong. Girls also are at a disadvantage in junior and senior secondary schools, in terms of curriculum, negative attitudes of male staff about the capabilities of female students, and sexual harassment. Further, girls are expected to do domestic labor after school, whereas boys are free to do their homework, which affects girls' test scores and therefore their access to higher education.

Literacy

The availability of education and the opportunities provided by the short farming season, combined with patterns of male labor migrancy, has resulted in Botswana having remarkable levels of female literacy, particularly as compared to other parts of Africa: almost 90 percent for urban women (who make up more than 50 percent of all women), and 79 percent for all women in the country aged fifteen and above. The lower rural literacy rate reflects the greater rural residency of older women, those past school age when the government expanded education. Male literacy lags 5 percent behind the female rate.[9]

EMPLOYMENT AND ECONOMICS

Farming

Approximately 50 percent of women live in rural areas and engage in farming, although few rural households live completely from the combination of farming, herding, gathering, and hunting that sustained their grandparents and earlier generations. Young women are increasingly seeking other employment. In the precolonial economy, corn (maize or "mealies") was the basic crop, supplemented by onions, squash, and other vegetables, and wild fruits and roots. Cows provided milk and were used for bridewealth, but were slaughtered for meat only on special occasions, like weddings and funerals.

In South Africa diamonds were discovered in 1867 and gold in 1886, and mine recruiters began the process of converting Botswana, along with other areas of southern Africa, into a migrant labor reserve for the mining industry. By the 1930s young men were going as migrant mine workers from almost all parts of what was then the British Protectorate of Bechuanaland, and by 1943 an estimated one-third to one-half of all males fifteen to forty-five years of age were away at the mines at any given time. Although South Africa began to reduce the use of migrants in the 1980s, significant numbers of young men continued to engage in migrant mine labor through the decade.

This migration of men removed their labor from agriculture for significant periods of time and left the burden on women, children, and older men. As boys and young men continued to herd cattle and then migrate as mine workers, girls and young women continued to farm and attend school.[10] But girls' educational advantage diminished as cattle ownership became concentrated, and they also suffered increasing poverty in rural households. The absence of male labor, combined with the gradual concentration of cattle ownership, led to a continuing impoverishment of rural life, which the government has been trying to address since independence. Except for a wealthy few percent of (male) commercial farmers in the most fertile areas of the country, farming is insufficient to meet subsistence needs, and is supplemented by paid agricultural labor, money sent by family members employed elsewhere, and government aid. Rural households have the greatest incidence of poverty, and female-headed households, today upwards of 50 percent of all rural households, have the highest poverty levels of all. Women farmers are disadvantaged relative to men from male-headed households because they generally have less access to cattle for plowing, extension services, development programs, technical training, loans for agricultural development, and male or female labor. In addition, women farmers' own labor is restricted by domestic responsibilities. All these factors lead to lower productivity and therefore greater poverty.[11]

Paid Employment

Diversification of the economy and greatly expanded opportunities for women in wage employment have been made possible by diamond mining: in Botswana, diamonds are indeed "a girl's best friend." In 1967, a year after independence, diamonds were discovered in Botswana, and more diamond mines have been developed since then. Under terms set by the government, new towns have been built at mine locations, with full family amenities and services, so that most Botswana diamond miners are not migrants but permanent resident workers. The diamond-based economic growth and diversification and government expansion that began in the 1980s has led to tremendous increases in urbanization and the expansion of public- and private-sector wage labor in residential and commercial construction, in transportation, communication, and electrification, in manufacturing, meat-packing, and brewing, in finance and banking, and in the service industries, as demand has increased both from wage- and salary-earning Batswana and from the expansion of upscale tourism.

Botswana has tried to encourage decentralization by locating government regional offices as well as the rapidly growing number of schools, clinics, and government-supported housing construction programs throughout the country, and by encouraging (less successfully) the locating of private-sector job-creating enterprises in these areas. This process has promoted a form of decentralized urbanization, with more than 50 percent of the population—and slightly more women than men—now living in cities or "semi-urban areas" in which people meet more than 75 percent of their needs from nonagricultural activities. By 1991 the proportion of the labor force in paid employment had reached 63 percent and was continuing to grow. Women made up almost 40 percent of that labor force. By 1999 women had reached 45 percent of the total labor force in paid employment.

As wage jobs have opened up as a result of diamond-based development, young women have been ready to move into them. Schooling gives young women both skills and aspirations, and the rural sector has become increasingly less attractive. Droughts plagued agriculture in the 1980s, and both cattle ownership and landownership have become increasingly privatized and concentrated (in the hands of wealthy men) through market-oriented, government-sponsored "development" programs. Young women in Botswana, as elsewhere in Africa, expect to engage in productive labor to support themselves and their families. Because of their education and the relative absence of similarly educated young men until very recently, female urban migrants have been able to move into jobs usually monopolized by men throughout sub-Saharan Africa. Even though men continue to dominate the higher-level jobs, in Botswana the face of business, and increasingly of government and the university, is often a female face: shop clerks, grocery checkers, managers, office workers, bank tellers, foreign exchange specialists, administrators, school teachers, university staff, technicians, security guards, cooks, postal workers, government researchers, office cleaners or domestic workers, depending on their level of education, as well as the nursing and other health care jobs generally held by women throughout sub-Saharan Africa. To Westerners, this may seem a familiar pattern. But for Africa it is a striking exception.

Women have been more poorly represented—but often better paid than comparably educated service workers—in the industrial sector. The mining, meat, and brewing industries primarily hire men, although women are employed as diamond sorters and on assembly lines in meat-packing and bottling. Industrial diversification has been somewhat problematic: a new

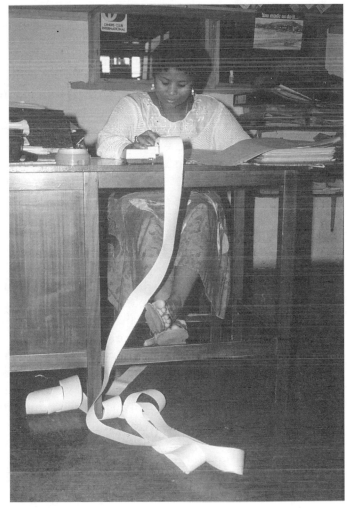

Accountant, Botswana. Photo © TRIP/E. Terry.

Hyundai auto assembly plant opened in 1994 and hired many men, but was shut down in 2000; garment manufacturing shows promise for women's employment, but many garment plants have opened, taken advantage of initial government benefits, and then closed owing wages to workers.

Although the decentralization of education, health care, and some government services keeps at least some paid jobs in rural villages, more of these jobs are in cities and urban areas attracting women migrants. At the top of the women workers pyramid is a small privileged segment, approximately 5 percent (about 6,000 women), of professionals, university faculty and administrators, managers, government officials, and businesswomen. According to a study of the Southern African Development Community (SADC), 36 percent of the combined category of managerial and administrative employees and legislators in Botswana in 1992 were women and 64 percent were men. This is the highest rate for women in such positions in the southern Africa (male) migrant labor recruitment area, and much higher than in other regions of Africa. The figures for such workers in Lesotho were only slightly lower, but for the other SADC countries minus South Africa, the ratios were sharply increased, with 9 percent women to 91 percent men in these positions.[12]

The next 35 percent of women workers—from clerks to teachers to health care workers to secretaries—are fairly well educated, with at least some secondary school, many with some postsecondary technical training, and usually proficient in English as well as Setswana. Women's representation in Botswana increases significantly in the categories of professional and technical workers, with 61 percent women compared to 39 percent men. Lesotho is close behind in female professional and technical workers, but for the rest of the SADC group, the proportions are sharply reversed, with 36 percent women compared to 64 percent men. For all these categories of salaried and waged employment, Botswana is a leader not only in Africa in employing women. These ratios, carried through 1999, put Botswana among the highest hirers of women in managerial, professional, and technical categories in the world.[13]

The remaining 60 percent of women in the labor force are likely to have at least a Standard Four level education and therefore to be literate in Setswana, and to speak at least some English. They work as office cleaners, hotel maids and kitchen workers, industrial workers, laborers, and domestic workers. These women are very likely to have strong connections with their natal villages, although all Batswana women, of whatever class, maintain ties with their "home" villages and visit on holidays or for significant family occasions, like weddings and funerals.

Informal Economic Activities

Since virtually all adult women are expected to engage in some kind of economic activity, women urban migrants who cannot find employment, along with many rural women, are engaged in self-employment. Women tend to be engaged in activities with the lowest returns and limited access to credit, skills training, markets, and materials. Women's activities account for three-quarters of informal-sector enterprises, including artisans (weavers, basket-makers, potters, textile printers), beer-brewers, dress-makers, hawkers of cooked foods, vendors of dried and fresh produce, and other petty traders. A small percentage of women artisans are either employed full-time in producer cooperatives, notably the women who design and weave wool hangings in Oodi and create pottery in Lobatse, or can devote significant time to the production of goods in high demand for the tourist trade and for export, as has sometimes been the case for women who produce silk-screened products in Mochudi or the makers of "Botswana baskets" around Maun. But most artisans must combine these income-generating activities with full-time domestic responsibilities, which in rural areas includes water and fuel hauling and family agricultural labor.

The economic vulnerability of artisan production, even of very popular crafts such as the internationally sold Botswana baskets, provides an uncertain living. Even though the baskets are famous for their fine craftsmanship and the creativity of their design, and are used as a symbol of Botswana culture by both government and private companies, the government has not moved sufficiently to support their production and increase basket makers' incomes. Many talented basket makers are reported to be seeking work as day laborers because the palms and dye plants that have been used since this craft industry started twenty-five years ago have been increasingly hard to find for the last few years, and because the basket makers' location in northwest Botswana makes them dependent on buyers who pay the women low prices and then may sell the baskets for ten times as much in the cities.

Entrepreneurship

Women in Botswana do not have the history of active involvement in market trading found in some other parts of Africa. Opportunities for entrepreneurship therefore are focused in the informal sector. A small number of women own small businesses, but it is difficult for women to establish medium- to large-scale enterprises because of constraints on credit availability, capacity to provide collateral (land is often used as collateral and few women own sufficient land), marital restrictions on property ownership, insufficient training in business skills, and lack of gender sensitivity in government programs designed to promote new businesses, such as the Financial Assistance Program. All these areas are currently under review by a government commission, after pressure from women's groups.

Pay

Women's average wages are lower than men's generally, partly through differential pay for the same jobs, but mostly because men are more heavily represented in the higher-paid job categories, those at the top in almost every area and those in heavy industry. Women's average pay in 2002 was 60 percent of that of men, $5,418 as compared to $9,025.[14] Many recommendations for equalizing job opportunities and pay are included in the National Gender Programme and Plan of Action, but have not yet been implemented.

Working Conditions

Sexual Harassment

Sexual harassment is an ubiquitous problem, in schools, in workplaces, and in public service provision. It is considered an expected, undesirable part of life by most women, and is not generally accepted as a "problem" by most men. Girls in school are subject to sexual harassment by male teachers, women workers by male supervisors, and women seeking public services by the service providers. Sexual harassment by teachers is just emerging as an issue; a recent study indicated that 67 percent of schoolgirls in the northwest had been subjected to some form of harassment or abuse, and government has expressed willingness to explore ways to deal with it. Until changes are made, nothing in the country's code of conduct for teachers, written in 1974, mentions sexual harassment or "consensual" sexual relations, nor does it make any provision for lodging complaints except at regional education offices, which could be hundreds of kilometers distant.

Sexual harassment in the workplace is particularly a problem for the most vulnerable workers, such as domestic workers, cleaners, and farm laborers, but it is a problem for all employed women with male supervisors. In Francistown in 1994, women garment workers took part in protests demanding pay increases, but also demanding an end to sexual harassment.

Support for Mothers/Caretakers

Maternal Leave

For women in full-time formal-sector jobs, maternity leave is provided by law for up to six weeks before and six weeks after childbirth, with pay of at least 25 percent of the regular wage. Working women are expected to bear children. But mothers in paid employment still constitute only a minority of women—perhaps 40 percent of women in paid employment, which means about 20 percent of women in the overall labor force. For the others pregnancy must be combined with work, and if time is taken off from paid work after childbirth, it is likely be unpaid.

Child Care

Women in the most privileged category and women in the next 35 percent who have full-time skilled jobs or live in two-income families can afford to hire other women, either strangers or kinswomen from their village, to do household work and provide child care. But lower-income women cannot. They are likely to have their children living with grandmothers in rural villages. As daughters, they have left their rural villages, either on their own initiative to seek a better life "far and beyond" or because the rural household needs additional cash income. They take jobs in town, often become pregnant but just as often do not marry, sometimes by choice, sometimes because the man is not willing either to marry or to support his child. Young women therefore take their babies "home" to be cared for by the grandmothers. The mothers send money for the children's care, visit when they can, build houses for their parents and/or themselves in the villages, and say that they plan to "retire" to the village when their children are old enough to support themselves. This allows more rural households to access urban wages, but creates a situation ripe for inter-generational conflict as well as cooperation. If the babies are infected with HIV, it creates an added burden for the grandmothers, who must care for sick babies who will never grow up to help with household chores.

This pattern of care by female kin or hired maids constitutes the "daycare system" in Botswana, but there may be attempts to change it: newly elected and appointed women have been discussing the need for on-site daycare for women government employees.

Inheritance, Property, and Land Rights

At independence in 1966 a constitution was adopted that somewhat am-biguously provided for all citizens to be treated equally, and several laws were changed to benefit women. Among the significant changes was a land law guaranteeing women rights of inheritance and ownership (women could already own cattle). However, married daughters do not inherit equally, and customary law does not recognize rights of inheritance by widows and their female children, although the principal heir, the eldest son, is supposed to provide for them. Women's groups advocate for equal inheritance by all sons and daughters, and for widows to be the principal heir and administrator of estates.

Social/Government Programs

Under pressure from women's groups, a National Policy on Women in Development, a National Gender Programme, and a Gender Plan of Ac-tion have been adopted. The Women's Affairs Unit has been elevated to a department. These policies and plans include both goals of gender equality and practical methods of implementation. The National Gender Pro-gramme includes provisions for creating a national machinery for moni-toring and evaluating gender equity programs, procedures, and policies. Botswana has ratified the Convention on the Elimination of All Forms of Discrimination Against Women (CEDAW) and has set up a commission to evaluate all Botswana laws in terms of their impact on women, and their compliance with CEDAW and other international conventions on human rights. This has resulted in repeal or amendment of several laws and the process is continuing.

FAMILY AND SEXUALITY

Gender Roles and Division of Labor

In the past, the division of labor followed common African patterns. Women and girls were responsible for all domestic tasks, including fetching water and fuel. They were also primarily responsible for cultivation, including planting, weeding, scaring birds away from the growing crops, harvesting, and threshing, for care of small livestock, and for gathering of wild crops during the "hungry season" before the new crops could be harvested. Men and boys were responsible for herding and hunting, both of which took place at cattle posts at a distance from villages and fields, and for certain specific agricultural tasks, particularly clearing fields and plowing.

By 1999 female-headed households made up 52 percent of all households, whether headed by women never married, divorced, abandoned, or widowed.[15] Women's continuing single status results both from their own choices and from men's unwillingness to marry and/or support children: urban newspaper letters and advice columns are full of letters from women complaining about "men who only want sex" and from men about "women who only want money." Despite much agitation for reform by women's groups, child maintenance laws are still inadequate and are not effectively enforced. The reluctance of male legislators to act in this area was one motivation for women's groups to take up a strategy of electing women to office.

Women's groups continue to advocate for equalizing the status of wives and husbands in marriage, and have been running educational campaigns on marriage law since the mid-1980s. These educational and advocacy campaigns take place within a context of severely decreasing rates of marriage of any kind. The long absences of men in migrant labor in South Africa over generations seriously disrupted the patterns of marriage and family relations that the Tswana and other groups maintained for centuries. Women's access to education and wage jobs enables them to support themselves outside both rural kinship-based relations of production and urban marriage, and so reduces women's need and motivation to marry. They may very well seek child support from the fathers of their children, however.

Marriage

The contemporary situation has been summed up by Botswanan law professor and activist Athaliah Molokomme as "marriage—what every woman wants, or 'civil death'?"[16] The marriage law is a complicated mix of customary law and Dutch-Roman law (the common law of Botswana), now expressed in statutory provisions for different forms of marriage. These provide for different degrees of control over the wife's property by the husband, but despite reforms, all include the "marital power," which means that the wife cannot sue or be sued except through her husband, and cannot engage in financial transactions without his consent. By choosing marriage "out of community property" and obtaining the husband's consent to a prenuptial agreement excluding the marital power, a married woman has almost the same legal status as a single one. However, her legal domicile is still determined by her husband, he legally has the final say in family decisions, and he is the legal guardian of minor children. These multiple forms of marriage are confusing, and most women are not in a position to obtain exclusion of the marital power.

Customary marriage involved bridewealth *(bogadi)*, which is the provision of a ceremonial gift, traditionally cattle, by the groom's family to the bride's family, and marriage was a long process with many stages, not an event. Today, in village life more than in urban life and in cash more often than in cows, *bogadi* is retained and combined with a church or civil wedding. Even the highly educated may pay *bogadi*. Unlike many other African countries, however, Botswana has not seen an inflation of bridewealth, since by tradition the groom's family sets the amount. *Bogadi* by custom transfers the affiliation of children from their mother's lineage to their father's lineage, thereby reinforcing parental inequality in marriage.

Reproduction

A very high social value is placed on motherhood in Botswana. All women expect and are expected to bear children, and almost all women do, married or not. Social disapproval of women bearing children outside the traditional institutions of betrothal and bridewealth has seriously diminished as the rate of marriage has decreased, although it has not disappeared, particularly in villages and for young women still in school. For those women who are not married, motherhood has replaced marriage as the marker of social adulthood.

Sex Education

Sex education has not been provided in schools, but the HIV/AIDS crisis has led the government to institute a curriculum on HIV/AIDS from the primary level on, which necessarily involves sex education.

Contraception and Abortion

Except for condoms, contraception is not easily available except to those with higher incomes, who can obtain medical services and contraceptives in South Africa. Customary law and Roman-Dutch common law inhibit the independent access of married women and women under twenty-one to family planning services.

Teen Pregnancy

The lack of family planning services leads to particularly serious problems for teenage girls, who are commonly subjected to sexual harassment and intimidated into sex by older men, including teachers and relatives. The customary deference that girls are taught to practice towards elders, particularly male elders, contributes to their vulnerability, as does the poverty in which so many girls live, especially in rural areas. A male teacher, or any other formally employed male in a rural community, has age, status, power, and money on his side. Predatory behavior toward schoolgirls is considered acceptable by many men, and sexual relations resulting from harassment, intimidation, seduction, or bribery are all considered "consensual." *The Botswana Human Development Report 2000* indicated that 20 percent of girls said they had been "asked" by teachers to have sex with them, and that about half accepted, for fear of getting lower grades if they refused. By Form One, the first year of secondary school, 17 percent of girls said that they were ready to leave school because of pressure for sex by teachers and their fears of pregnancy and HIV transmission.

The code of conduct for teachers is as silent on "consensual" sexual relations as it is on sexual harassment, although with the appointment of a new minister following the 1999 elections, the ministry of education's secondary schools department started a process of consultation with women's and human rights nongovernment organizations (NGOs) on a policy covering sexual harassment and pressure for sex. Paradoxically, AIDS itself provides a pressure to retain even abusive male teachers: it is estimated that Botswana will lose 2 to 5 percent of its teaching force per year due to AIDS.

Abortion is legal under extremely restrictive circumstances and is not readily available. Complications from attempted abortions, by a healer (*sangoma*) using traditional medicines or by the woman herself, are commonly said to be the greatest cause of female death in Botswana hospitals, but no official statistics are available. Abortion, at least among girls before marriage, is reported to have been tolerated by the Tswana before Christian influence became dominant, but today it is such a controversial subject that no mention is made of it in women's groups demands. Recent reforms that allow abortion in restricted circumstances were pushed by health care practicioners, not by women's groups, and were intensely opposed by the Catholic and other Christian churches. The intensity of the attempt at social control of abortion is indicated in the criminalization of "concealment of birth," which means that a woman is legally found to have concealed a birth and the baby has not survived. This is a crime in itself, whether or not there is any indication of infanticide, and can bring a prison sentence.

HEALTH

Health Care Access

Botswana has used significant resources to create a nationwide system of health care. Vaccination and other forms of prevention had succeeded in eliminating or controlling disease and significantly increasing life expectancy and general health until the AIDS epidemic struck.

Diseases and Disorders

Because of AIDS, life expectancy has declined drastically, from sixty-seven in 1996 to forty in 2002. Tuberculosis has rebounded. Health experts see HIV/AIDS as implicated in the infant mortality rate of seventy-four per 1,000 births and the maternal mortality rate of 330 maternal deaths per 100,000 live births, despite studies indicating that 99.5 percent of births are attended by skilled health personnel and that prenatal care is available to virtually all women. HIV/AIDS, increased contraceptive use (estimated at 47.6 percent in 1996), and abortion (illegal outside hospitals but widespread) all contribute to a decline in the number of children born to each woman from 4.2 in 1991 to 3.3 in 2002.[17]

AIDS

Botswana has one of the highest HIV/AIDS infection rates in the world.[18] By 2002, more than 38 percent of the population, almost evenly divided between women and men, was infected with HIV, a figure based on anonymous testing of pregnant women in the country's ubiquitous prenatal clinics, which reaches virtually all young women, and of some men in clinics for sexually-transmitted diseases and tuberculosis. This tragic high rate is a result of Botswana's historic position on "the road to the north" (now the line of rail and paved road that connects South Africa commercially with Zimbabwe and East Africa), of decades of the yearly movement of the majority of the adult male population to the South African mines, where they were at high risk of infection and then back to their wives. The high HIV infection rates can thus be attributed to the very success of economic development in tying the whole country together and producing cycles of urban-rural migration and commerce that make even the remotest residents vulnerable to infection. In Botswana, the rate for large cities averages 47 percent, and for the rest of the country, 36 percent. One factor that contributes to women's vulnerability to infection in some parts of

Africa is absent in Botswana: female genital cutting is unknown, and has never been reported in historical accounts.

The government is now putting its considerable resources into the fight against HIV/AIDS. Botswana is attempting to be a leader in the war against the disease, with programs for prevention, treatment, and care. But the virus is so widespread that a generation of young adults, the most highly educated in the country's history, is at high risk of early death. There are more and more deaths every day, although "no one dies of AIDS," but of other infections, particularly tuberculosis.

Arguably the greatest problem facing health workers in wealthy Botswana is neither lack of resources nor of government commitment, but the stigma, prejudices, and myths surrounding the disease that leads to denial of infection. Denial is reinforced by the continued strength of indigenous beliefs that blame the symptoms of AIDS on the animosities and curses of supposed enemies, and the promises of diviners that they can provide "cures."

The greatest problem for girls and women is their lack of equal power in sexual negotiations and therefore their inability to demand safe sex or to refuse sex at all. Girls are taught to be deferential to older men, and both custom and law legitimate husbands' demands for (unsafe) sex from wives, and justify beating of wives who refuse.

The government has launched an aggressive campaign for safe sex, including distribution of condoms, although sex education in schools lags behind advisory reports urging its implementation. If the 1996 figure for condom use of 47.6 percent is accurate, then the long-standing male bias against condoms and the belief that "only prostitutes use condoms" may be breaking down, but slowly. The need to address gender power inequality is acknowledged in the 1995 National Plan of Action, but again implementation lags. Drugs to prevent transmission from mothers to infants and anti-retrovirals are now available in some clinics. The government is planning to extend the distribution of the anti-HIV drug AZT (Azidothymidine) and is discussing a program to provide treatment drugs to all infected citizens. Both De Beers and Anglo-American mining companies already provide HIV/AIDS education, condoms, and treatment for mine workers and their families. The government is also discussing setting up hospices for terminally ill AIDS patients, in recognition of the fact that both hospitals and families—especially women in families—are becoming overwhelmed by the burden of care. The Botswana Network of AIDS Service Organizations (BONASO) attempts to coordinate all the activities of the many private groups working on HIV/AIDS.

But stigma, denial, and gender inequality continue to weaken anti-AIDS efforts. Only an increasingly aggressive government program that directly addresses both the stigma of HIV/AIDS and the inequality of power between women and men—and the engagement of women's rights groups themselves in this effort—has any hope of combating the epidemic.

POLITICS AND LAW

Leadership and Decision-making

Quota Laws

In 1993, Emang Basadi, the women's rights organization, decided to launch a new strategy of targeting political candidates and parties and urging women to vote for those who supported women's rights. They issued *The Women's Manifesto*, setting out problems and goals. In the run-up to the 1994 election, the Botswana National Front (BNF), responding to a number of factors including dissatisfaction from young women in the youth wing and the women's wing, put forth a strong women's plank in their platform, including a provision that 30 percent of all positions in party structures be reserved for women. The Botswana Democratic Party (BPD), with no women's plank or quotas, put up and elected two women candidates and put women into two of the four "specially elected" seats (nominated by the president and "specially elected" by the parliamentary majority). The BNF failed to elect any women, but did move from holding three to seventeen seats in the expanded legislature after the 1994 elections.

Botswana has a long history of relatively peaceful indigenous political life. As the British Protectorate of Bechuanaland from 1885 until independence in 1966, the country was largely left in the hands of the local African authorities, the *dikgosi* or "chiefs" of the eight groups of the Tswana. From the mid–nineteenth century until independence, the Tswana polities managed to fend off repeated attempts at incorporation by South Africa. At independence, Botswana began political life with an elected president and parliament, multiple parties, free speech and vigorous political debate, peaceful political processes, but no army—even though it was a Frontline State surrounded by white minority–ruled regimes. Botswana is unique in Africa for having maintained peaceful multiparty and nonracial democracy since its independence. For almost twenty-five years democratic Botswana kept an open border to refugees, denounced apartheid, and resisted economic pressures, threats, and commando raids from its much more powerful white minority–ruled neighbors. Even though one party, the Botswana Democratic Party, has succeeded in keeping its majority in each five-year election, minority parties and their issues have had significant influence on policy, and the existence of opposition parties has created more political space for "outsiders" like women's groups to maneuver for policy changes and greater representation in government.

Suffrage

Women and men over twenty-one were given the right to vote during the pre-independence elections in 1965, and in the 1990s the voting age was lowered to eighteen.

Political Participation

At independence, women could stand for office, and were given a voice in the "traditional" village meeting and dispute resolution forum, the *kgotla*, presided over by the *kgosi* or "chief," which continues to form the basic level of local government, with severely diminished powers. Registration is relatively easy and women have been active voters in every election. Elections are held every five years, and in the last national election in 1999, overall turnout was 77 percent, and women were a majority of voters, as they are of the population.

Emang Basadi broadened its efforts in the 1990s, reaching out to women activists in the political parties and to the many "nonpolitical" women's civic and church groups, including the YWCA, Red Cross, and Botswana Christian Council (all dominated by women). In 1995, during the run-up to the Beijing Conference on Women, well-attended workshops were held around the country by the NGO Network for Women's Rights and the NGO Coalition. Women in both urban and rural areas had heard Emang Basadi's political education program on the radio, wanted to know more about the women's movement, and urged the NGOs to continue workshops on leadership skills and assertiveness training after Beijing.

Emang Basadi launched annual national conferences for women, starting in 1996, focused on different aspects of gender, development, equal rights, and electoral strategy. The 1997 subtheme was "Issues Women Will Vote for in 1999," six critical areas based on the Beijing Report: poverty alleviation and economic empowerment; education and training; health and population; decision-making and power sharing; violence against women and women's human rights; and the girl child. Participants wore tee-shirts proclaiming, "Democracy without a woman in power belongs to the past," and warning, "Dear President, Members of Parliament, Councillors and All Candidates: In 1999 we will vote for those who advocate for women's rights. Are you one of them?"

Emang Basadi continued its nonpartisan strategy of trying to elect women in 1999. Rallies, workshops, and conferences for the "women's campaign" were organized, and placards at one demonstration proclaimed, "Vote a Woman! Suckle the Nation!" No party had quotas for candidates. The BNF kept its commitment to women's issues, but then split and lost its effectiveness. The BDP put a strong section on gender rights in its platform and fielded the greatest number of women candidates (six). All were elected. After the elections, 1999 was declared "The Year of the Woman" by the *Botswana Gazette*. Reelected BDP president Festus Mogae nominated two women for specially appointed parliamentary seats and appointed women to ten top positions in government and the public service. This increased the number of women members of Parliament to 18 percent of the total, an increase of 100 percent, and women are now 20 percent of the cabinet.[19] Women's groups are working toward the 2004 elections, with the goal that women will again double their representation and this time pass the 30 percent SADC goal.

Women's Rights

A Women's Desk was established in the Department of Home Affairs in 1980, but a broader women's movement started to form with the passage in 1982, with amendments in 1984, of a new and discriminatory citizenship law. The previous law, in effect since independence, had based citizenship on birth in the territory. The new law responded to concerns about refugees becoming temporary "paper" citizens and exploiting Botswana's resources. It based citizenship on descent, but only from the father in the case of married women, a rule based on preindependence Tswana patrilineal customary law. A woman citizen married to a noncitizen could not pass her citizenship to their child, but a male citizen married to a noncitizen could pass on his citizenship. Unmarried women citizens could pass their citizenship on to their children (just as they could pass on their lineage membership under customary law). The new law also made special provision for noncitizen wives to become citizens easily and quickly, but not noncitizen husbands.

This law was enacted into a rapidly urbanizing society, at exactly the time that greatly increasing numbers of women were taking wage jobs and becoming aware of the need for legal rights as they moved both geographically and culturally away from the obligations and protections of kinship-based village life. As urbanization and the pool of salaried and waged women increased, so did opposition to government and customary discrimination against women and support for women's equal rights.

Women's Movements

Growing opposition to the citizenship law led to the formation in 1986 of the women's rights organization Emang Basadi—Stand Up, Women!—a name adapted with a pointed change from the national anthem, which urges men to "stand up and defend the nation," while women are to "stand up beside your men." The original leadership of the organization and wider movement came from the privileged class of highly educated women, but they immediately reached out to the much wider pool of salaried and waged women workers. It is this 40 percent of women, those who have benefited most from economic development and cultural modernity, who find arguments about women's rights and equality most relevant to their daily lives, and who can be potentially mobilized in support of movement goals. Women with lower educational and skill levels, especially domestic workers, are more isolated, less politicized, and more likely to be "targets" of projects by women's organizations than participants in those organizations.

Emang Basadi set out to educate women about their current legal rights and to agitate for increased equal rights, starting with the new citizenship law. It chose not to affiliate with any political party, and in 1986 no political party had even a plank on women's rights or needs. Both the dominant party, the Botswana Democratic Party, and the leading opposition party, the Botswana National Front, had women's wings by 1987, but as elsewhere they were intended to mobilize women to support the party, not to mobilize the party to support women.

Efforts by Emang Basadi to influence government to change the citizenship law failed, and in 1990 women from the organization joined with women from the Women and Law Project of Southern Africa to support a suit filed by Unity Dow, a lawyer and founding director of the Methaetsile Women's Information Center in Mochudi, about fifty kilometers north of Gaborone. Unity Dow was married to a U.S. citizen, and their daughter had been denied a passport. She argued that the citizenship law violated the Botswana constitution. The government appealed to customary law, arguing that the constitution was premised on Tswana patrilineal tradition, and that customary law should take precedence in areas of family law. In 1991 the High Court judge, in a decision upheld on appeal, ruled for Dow, explicitly arguing that women "can no longer be viewed as being chattels of their husbands," but must be viewed as equal citizens in all areas of law.[20] The law was referred back to parliament for revision in 1992, but the government continued to stonewall. After the placement of women in the legislature from the 1994 elections, the new parliament finally took action on the citizenship law and a new nondiscriminatory law, still based on descent, went into effect in January 1996.

Keboitse Machangana, chairperson of Emang Basadi, said of the Citizenship Act victory and its repudiation of custom in favor of equal rights, "Since then, there has been no looking back!"[21] The weekly Gaborone newspaper *Mmegi* (*The Reporter*) editorialized in January 1996: "Women are evolving into a powerful constituency in Botswana. They have always been a potentially strong block as they constitute the majority of voters, especially in the countryside. However, in the past women did not vote as a block rallying around common issues. With the momentum that women's civic associations like Emang Basadi have set in motion in conscientising women about their rights, any political party which does not court women in the future will be doing that at its own peril."[22]

The Botswana Democratic Party apparently learned this lesson. Other discriminatory legislation in significant areas of employment and property law has been changed without additional court cases. The Law Reform Committee has been charged with evaluating all legislation for gender bias, although it is still an all-male committee. Emang Basadi has opened an office with full-time staff and volunteers, and a resource center and library. Many other actions urged in the first *Women's Manifesto* have been taken up by government in addition to these changes in laws, including adoption of the National Policy on Women in Development, the National Gender Program, and the Gender Plan of Action, the elevation of the Women's Affairs Unit to a Department, and the ratification of CEDAW. The Southern African Development Community has established a Gender Unit, located in Botswana and led by a former chair of Emang Basadi. SADC has adopted a target of 30 percent women in each member parliament by 2005. In 1997 the United Nations Development Programme announced a $1.8 million Gender Program for Botswana, which emphasizes training and support for advocacy.

When Miss Botswana, Mpule Kwelagobe (who plans to be a pediatric neurosurgeon), won the Miss Universe contest in 1999, Emang Basadi ran a political advertisement: "To all young Botswana women we say: the sky is the limit, Mpule has set the pace. Mpule has proved that women can take Botswana to greater heights, *Cast your vote for a woman in the coming general elections!*"[23]

Emang Basadi now has its own office and information, resource, and referral center, with a large banner urging, "*Tlhagafalang!*"—Let's Go! Projects include political education, which has both women decisionmakers and voter education components, and organizational development. It has opened a second branch in Mahalaphye, which offers counseling services and training, awareness-building, and economic empowerment programs.

Lesbian Rights

Male homosexual acts are criminalized by a law providing that anyone who permits a male person to have carnal knowledge of him or her "against the order of nature" or who engages in such an act can be jailed for seven years (there is no indication it is applied to heterosexual relations). Lesbian relations are not illegal, but lesbians are very much in the closet. Discussion of homosexuality is beginning, prompted by the South African constitutional protection of sexual preference and organizing for gay rights there, as well as by the condemnations of homosexuality as "un-African" by the government heads in neighboring Zimbabwe and Namibia, and controversies surrounding displays of books on homosexual rights at annual bookfairs in Zimbabwe. Such discussion has been particularly lively on the Internet list serves used by Botswana students overseas. There is no reference to lesbian rights in *The Women's Manifesto*. Lesbianism (at least among girls before marriage) is reported to have been tolerated by the Tswana before European Christian influence became dominant and redefined all homosexuality as "un-African."[24]

Military Service

A small army, all male and volunteer, was created in the mid-1970s to defend the country against incursions by the then-Rhodesian white minority government in its war against the Zimbabwean national liberation movement. The army was expanded in the 1980s as protection against commando raids by the South African Defense Forces. The army has now grown significantly, primarily in response to unrest among some of its neighbors and the desire of government to protect its diamonds and infrastructure as well as its people. But the expanded army has not been politicized and clearly respects civilian political authority. One of the issues raised by Emang Basadi is that the military is completely closed to women.

RELIGION AND SPIRITUALITY

Botswana is sometimes described as 30–50 percent Christian, with the rest practicing indigenous beliefs. But it is more accurately seen as a blending of religions. People in rural villages and in urban areas combine traditional religious beliefs and rituals with Christian ones. From the arrival of Christian missionaries in 1817, Christianity has spread extensively, but has not replaced indigenous animist beliefs.

Women's Roles and Rituals and Religious Practices

Women are particularly active participants in the Christian churches and were the first converts when Protestant missionaries came to Bechuanaland, when women from "royal" or "chiefly" families led services for largely female congregations. Women are also active as practitioners of traditional medicine. Although virtually every village has its Christian church, there is widespread use of *muti* (medicine) and recourse to a *sangoma* (a "diviner," often a woman) for both health concerns and help with personal relations. Small bottles of *muti* are widely sold in supermarkets and pharmacies as well as by practitioners. Periodically, the press reports allege "*muti* murders" of children, usually girls, attributed to a *sangoma* seeking "private body parts" for *muti*, and it is generally believed that these accounts are accurate.

VIOLENCE

Domestic Violence

Domestic violence is endemic, exacerbated by men's high consumption of alcohol, usually beer. There appears to be high social acceptance of domestic violence, even though the contemporary level and severity of such violence exceeds "traditional" cultural norms. Women's rights activists are trying to change attitudes, change the practices of the police and courts, and to offer shelter and legal aid to battered women. They have opened women's centers and human rights centers that focus on issues of violence toward women. In 1994 a Human Rights Center, Ditshwanelo, was opened in Gaborone, with concerns about rape, woman battering by part-ners, and abuse of domestic workers by employers. In mid-1995 they did a study on abuse of domestic workers and then launched a project to or-ganize them. A police task force to investigate domestic violence has now been created in Gaborone.

Rape/Sexual Assault

Rape has become much more prevalent as girls and women are more vulnerable: walking alone to school or work, being alone at home, or being at school or work and victims of teachers and supervisors. Although there are laws to protect underage girls from statutory rape or "defilement," the deference they are taught to practice toward male elders leaves them un-protected in practice, and the laws are not enforced. The first rape crisis group, Women Against Rape (WAR), was formed in 1993, and by 1995 rape cases were beginning to be taken more seriously, at least in public discourse. A law was passed requiring rape cases to be heard *in camera*, and a special police task force on rape was created. However, the incidence of rape as well as the rate at which women report it is believed by activists to be increasing, as Emang Basadi reported in its own study, and only a tiny percentage of reported rapes are prosecuted.[25] Anti-rape activists won a major victory in 1998 with the passage of the Penal Code Amendment Act of 1998, which provides for longer and mandatory sentences for rape.

War and Military Repression

Women in Botswana have been spared the horrors of civil war or mil-itary repression by their own government. But they did live with the fear of attacks from South African Defense Forces commando units during the 1980s. Botswana citizens, mostly women, were killed in such raids. From 1990 on, the raids have ceased, and so far no new warfare has spilled over into peaceful Botswana from its neighbors.

OUTLOOK FOR THE TWENTY-FIRST CENTURY

Women's continued progress in Botswana depends heavily on their own efforts, including their efforts to empower women to be able to protect themselves from HIV/AIDS. Progress also depends on the success of ef-forts to diversify the economy: contrary to slogans, diamonds are *not* for-ever. Women's rights advocates of course continue to face significant opposition at all levels of society and government, despite official decla-rations in support of gender equity. The name-calling days are not over even though these attitudes are slowly changing. A wicked Botswana sense of humor has even dubbed high heels "*emang basadi*," but it has not stopped women from "standing up" for their rights, even in their *emang basadi*. It is easier to face name-calling when it seems that history is on your side, even though the struggle is hard. Some victories are particularly sweet: Unity Dow, the lawyer whose challenge to the citizenship law catalyzed so much, now sits as the first woman High Court judge. *Pula! Pula!*

NOTES

1. One kilometer equals 0.6 miles.

2. Newafrica, 2002, "Botswana Culture and Society" page, www.newafrica.com/ profiles.

3. The Wayeyi object to being called a "minor tribe," on the grounds that there are more Wayeyi than Tawana in the "Tawana" district in which they live. They argue that many people from groups dominated politically by the Tswana identify themselves by the name of the dominant Tswana group of their district for the census, thus creating false "majority tribes." The founder and main spokesperson for the Wayeyi, Dr. Lydia Nyati-Ramahobo, has also been a supporter of women's rights, and the Wayeyi legal strategy was influenced by the Dow case against the citizenship act. The Wayeyi have so far been less successful, however, in the Botswana courts.

4. Republic of Botswana, "Constituent Determinants of Poverty Datum Line explained," *Daily News Online*, July 30, 2002, www.gov.bw.

5. GDP per capita from World Bank, *Gender Statistics* (2002); other economic figures from newafrica, "Botswana Economic Development and Indicators," April 10, 1998, www.newafrica.com/economy/botswana.asp, 1. Unemployment figure from Republic of Botswana, *Women and Men in Botswana*.

6. I am indebted here, as in all my work on Botswana, to the women of Emang Basadi, and the other women activists who are changing their own society. I particularly want to thank Athaliah Molokomme, Leloba Molema, Lydia Nyati-Ramahobo, and the current head of Emang Basadi, Keboitse Machangana.

7. Republic of Botswana, Central Statistics Office, *Women and Men in Botswana: Facts and Figures* (Gaborone: Government Printer, 1998), 4, tab. 1.2.

8. Calculated by the author from charts in Lydia Nyati-Ramahobo, *The Girl-Child in Botswana: Educational Constraints and Prospects* (Gaborone: UNICEF, 1992), 31–34.

9. World Bank, *Gender Statistics Summary Gender Profile* (2002), 1, http:// genderstats.worldbank.org/menu.asp; Botswana Society, *Poverty and Plenty: The Botswana Experience* (Gaborone: Botswana Society, 1997), 217.

10. Isaac Schapera, *Migrant Labour and Tribal Life: A Study of Conditions in the Bechuanaland Protectorate* (London: Oxford University Press, 1947), 25–72.

11. See Pauline Peters, *Dividing the Commons: Politics, Policy, and Culture in Botswana* (Charlottsville: University of Virginia Press, 1994); and Ornulf Gulbrandsen, *Poverty in the Midst of Plenty* (Bergen: Norse, 1996).

12. Botswana figures for women workers here and below calculated by the author from Republic of Botswana, Central Statistics Office, *Administrative/Technical Report and National Statistical Tables, 1991 Population and Housing Census* (Gaborone: Government Printer, 1991), 314, 316, tab. E3, 384–87; tab. E19, E19-1. Lesotho and Botswana comparative figures for 1992 are from Athaliah Molokomme, "Why Gender Is a Key Development Issue for Southern African Development Community," *Southern African Feminist Review* 2, no. 2 (1997): 1–13. Lesotho has similar ratios of female to male employment because of even greater male migrant labor to South African mines, but Lesotho's economy is much poorer than Botswana's and overall urbanization and wage employment rates are much lower. South Africa is excepted because it is much more

highly industrialized than the other countries and because the legacy of apartheid, with its privileging of white women over black men, produces misleading comparisons.

13. World Bank, *Gender Statistics* (2002).

14. *UNDP Human Development Indicators 2002*, http://hdr.undp.org/.

15. Republic of Botswana, *Administrative/Technical Report*, summarized in Republic of Botswana, *Women and Men in Botswana* 10, tab. 1.11; Emang Basadi, *The Women's Manifesto: A Summary of Botswana Women's Issues and Demands*, 2nd ed. (Gaborone: Lentswe La Lesedi, 1999), 20.

16. Athaliah Molokomme, "Marriage—What Every Woman Wants, or 'Civil Death'? The Status of Married Women in Botswana," in *Women and Law in Southern Africa*, ed. Alice Armstrong (Harare: Zimbabwe Publishing House, 1987), 181–92.

17. UNAIDS Epidemiological Fact Sheet on HIV/AIDS and Sexually Transmitted Infections, Botswana, 2002, www.unaids.org; Republic of Botswana, *Daily News Online*, July 30, 2002, August 8, 2002, www.gov.bw.

18. It is sometimes said to have the highest rate, but this claim should be considered in the context of two factors. One is that Botswana's figures are fairly reliable, which is not the case for most of Africa. The Botswana government has a very competent statistic-gathering system, including door-to-door census takers. Pregnant women have access to local health clinics, and those clinics test them for HIV during prenatal visits, as they do men with other sexually transmitted diseases and with tuberculosis. Second, Botswana's small population is fairly concentrated and development itself has made movement between areas easy and common, resulting in relatively small rural/urban differences in the infection rate. In other countries comparably small and interactive populations, such as city populations, have comparably high infection rates, but due to poor transport and poverty, rural areas may have lower rates.

19. Appointments included ministers of local government and of health, and assistant ministers of local government and of the office of the president. One woman has served as minister of foreign affairs, and later as minister of education; one as deputy secretary of foreign affairs and later as assistant minister of local government, lands, and housing.

20. Unity Dow, ed. *The Citizenship Case: The Attorney General of The Republic of Botswana vs. Unity Dow: Court Documents, Judgements, Cases and Materials* (Gaborone: Lentswe La Lesedi, 1995), 39.

21. Keboitse Machangana in public speech in Mmegi (June 5, 1997).

22. *Mmegi/The Reporter* (Gaborone, Botswana), January 12–18, 1996, 15.

23. Caitlin Davies, "Misgivings over Botswana's Miss Universe," *Daily Mail and Guardian Online* (Johannesburg, South Africa), July 8, 1999, 1.

24. For information and discussion of homosexuality in Africa, historical and contemporary, see *Boy-Wives and Female Husbands: Studies of African Homosexualities*, ed. Stephen Murray and Will Roscoe (New York: St. Martin's Press, 1998).

25. Emang Basadi, *Rape in Botswana: Statistics, Profiles, Laws, and Consequences* (Gaborone: Lentswe La Lesedi, 1998).

RESOURCE GUIDE

Suggested Reading

Bozzoli, Belinda. "Marxism, Feminism, and South African Studies." *Journal of Southern African Studies* 9, no. 2 (1983): 139–71. Good summary and feminist critique of analyses of male migrant labor in Southern Africa.

Dow, Unity. *Far and Beyond*. North Melbourne, Australia: Spinifex Press, 2000. A novel that brings to life the current women's issues and conflicts of social change, through the experiences of a sixteen-year-old girl struggling to go "beyond" village life. Notable in that it is written by Dow, the lawyer who won the landmark citizenship case and has become the first female High Court judge.

Holm, John, and Patrick Molutsi, eds. *Democracy in Botswana*. Athens: University of Ohio Press, 1989. Proceedings of a symposium in Gaborone, August 1988. Historical and contemporary perspectives, including papers on women's issues.

Izzard, Wendy. "Migrants and Mothers: Case Studies from Botswana." *Journal of Southern African Studies* 11, no. 2 (1985): 258–80. Studies of female-headed households for the Botswana government.

O'Laughlin, Bridget. "Missing Men? The Debate over Rural Poverty and Women-Headed Households in Southern Africa." *Journal of Peasant Studies* 25, no. 2 (1998): 1–48. Puts the Botswana case in the context of the migrant labor system and its imminent end.

Parsons, Neil. "Seretse Khama and the Bangwato Succession Crisis, 1948–1953." In *Succession to High Office in Botswana*, edited by Jack Parson, 73–95. Athens: Ohio University Center for International Studies. Lively account of Britain's attempt to prevent accession of a popular heir to chieftainship because of his marriage to a white Englishwoman, including accounts of women's demonstrations in his support.

Peters, Pauline. "Gender, Development Cycles, and Historical Processes: A Critique of Recent Research on Women in Botswana." *Journal of Southern African Studies* 10, no. 1 (1963): 100–22.

Smith, Alexander McCall. *The No. 1 Ladies' Detective Agency*. Edinburgh: Polygon, 1998. Superbly written novel, with great wit and a verisimilitude that belies the author's difference in gender and culture from the heroine. It provides rich insights into Botswana culture, current political issues, and women's daily lives.

Van Allen, Judith. " 'Bad Future Things' and Liberatory Moments: Capitalism, Gender, and the State in Botswana." *Radical History Review* 76 (2000): 136–68. Analysis of the historical and contemporary political and economic conditions that made the women's rights movement and its successes possible.

———. "Women's Rights Movements as a Measure of African Democracy." *Journal of Asian and African Studies* 36, no. 1 (2001): 39–63. Uses Botswana as a case study to argue that the presence of an active and successful women's rights movements demonstrates the existence of substantive as well as formal "democracy."

Web Sites

Botswana—Guide to Internet Resources, www-sul.stanford.edu/depts/ssrg/africa/bots.html.
Provides more than seventy URLs related to Botswana, including government, NGO, and university sites, Botswana statistics, discussion groups, and a link to list of news sites.

Botswana Council of Nongovernmental Organizations (BOCONGO), www.bocongo.bw.
Provides a list of all members, with addresses, contact persons, and a description of each organization, plus other pages on programs, reports, and news.

Botswana Government, www.gov.bw/home.html.
Official site, links to ministries, daily news, business/investment, economic, history,

and tourism information. Includes Women's Affairs Department under Ministry of Labour and Home Affairs.

Mmegi/The Reporter, www.mmegi.bw.
Independent NGO-operated weekly Gaborone newspaper, offers good coverage of women's issues from a sympathetic viewpoint.

newafrica, www.newafrica.com/profiles.
Provides country profiles of statistics and basic information on a range of topics including agriculture, culture and society, economy, education, government, health and population, and environment. No specific "gender" page but gender statistics are included in several places.

Southern Africa Human Rights NGO Network (SAHRINGON), www.oneworld. org/aftonet/sahringon.
SAHRINGON links human rights organizations in eleven countries. Site provides a member list, with addresses and contacts, plus information on reports, publications, and campaigns.

UN AIDS, www.unaids.org.
Provides epidemiological fact sheet on HIV/AIDS and sexually transmitted infections, with 2002 updates for Africa by countries.

World Bank Gender Statistics, http://genderstats.worldbank.org/menu.asp.
Provides country statistics, including summaries, demography, population dynamics, labor force structure, education, health, and maternal mortality.

Organizations

Botswana Government Department of Women's Affairs.
Contact: Mrs. M. I. Legwaila, Director
Phone: 267-309-222
Fax: 267-311-944
Email: mlegwaila@gov.bw
Web site: www.gov.bw/government/ministry_of_labour_and_home_affairs.html

Promotes the enhancement and status of women in society and in government.

Botswana Network of AIDS Service Organizations (BONASO)
Contact: Mr. Martin Mosima, Coordinator
P.O. Box 3219
Gaborone, Botswana
Phone/Fax: 570-582
Email: bonaso@botsnet.bw

Coordinates the activities of various organizations working on HIV/AIDS both nationally and in southern Africa.

Ditshwanelo—Botswana Centre for Human Rights
Contact: Ms. Alice Mogwe, Director
Private Bag 00416

Gaborone, Botswana
Phone: 306-998
Fax: 307-778
Email: admin.ditshwanelo@info.bw

Advocates against discrimination based on "gender, ethnicity, religion, sexual orientation, social status or political convictions." Acts as human rights watchdog for Botswana. Part of SAHRINGON.

Emang Basadi (Stand Up, Women!)
Contact: Ms. Keboitse Machangana
Private Bag 0047
Gaborone, Botswana
Phone/Fax: 309-335
Email: ebasadi@global.bw

Women's rights organization, publishes materials, runs educational campaigns, currently focused on recruitment, training, and election of women to local and national government, has resource center and library.

Kagisano Society: Women's Shelter Project
Contact: Ms. Ida Mokereitane, Executive Officer
Private Bag XO46
Gaborone, Botswana
Phone/Fax: 308-691

Provides temporary shelter to women and children survivors of domestic violence, counseling for residents and nonresidents, education about domestic violence to raise public awareness.

Metlhaetsile Women's Information Centre (MWIC)
Contact: Ms. Tholona Phoko, Acting Director
Private Bag 0042
Mochudi, Botswana
Phone: 377-618
Fax: 377-195
Email: mwic@bc.bw

Provides legal aid, counseling, and education for women on rights, AIDS prevention, family planning, violence against women. Founded by Unity Dow in Mochudi, fifty kilometers north of Gaborone. *Metlhaetsile* means "the times have come."

Women Against Rape (WAR)
Contact: Ms. Stefania Rosetti, Coordinator
P.O. Box 319
Maun, Botswana
Phone/Fax: 660-865
Email: war@info.bw

Provides support, assistance, and counseling to survivors of sexual violence, campaigns for greater public awareness and changes in law. Located in northern Botswana.

Women and Law in Southern Africa (WLSA)
Botswana Unit
Contact: Ms. Puseletso E. Kidd, National Coordinator
UB Private Bag 00708
Gaborone, Botswana
Email: wlsa@info.bw

Research Directorate investigates laws, attitudes and practices that impact negatively on women's lives, with the objective of promoting the recognition of women's human rights. Action Unit, established in 1992, uses the research findings to educate, lobby, and advocate for law reform. Other units operate in Lesotho, Mozambique, Swaziland, Zambia, and Zimbabwe.

SELECTED BIBLIOGRAPHY

Botswana National Front. *Manifesto for the General Elections, 1994*. Gaborone: BNF Secretariat, 1994.

Botswana Society. *Botswana in the Twenty-first Century*. Proceedings of a symposium in Gaborone, October 18–21, 1993. Gaborone: Botswana Society, 1994.

———. *Changing Roles of Women in Botswana*. Proceedings of a conference in Francistown, October 31, 1992. Gaborone: Botswana Society, 1993.

———. *Poverty and Plenty: The Botswana Experience*. Proceedings of a symposium in Gaborone, October 15–18, 1996. Gaborone: Botswana Society, 1997.

Bozzoli, Belinda. "Marxism, Feminism, and South African Studies." *Journal of Southern African Studies* 9, no. 2 (1983): 139–71.

Davies, Caitlin. "Misgivings over Botswana's Miss Universe." *Daily Mail and Guardian Online* (Johannesburg, South Africa). July 8, 1999, 1. www.mg.co.za.

Dow, Unity, ed. *The Citizenship Case: The Attorney General of the Republic of Botswana vs. Unity Dow: Court Documents, Judgments, Cases, and Materials*. Gaborone: Lentswe la Lesedi, 1995.

Dutfield, Michael. *A Marriage of Inconvenience: The Persecution of Seretse and Ruth Khama*. London: Unwin Hyman, 1990.

Emang Basadi. *Emang Basadi's Political Education Project: A Strategy That Works*. Gaborone: Lentswe la Lesedi, 1998.

———. *Rape in Botswana: Statistics, Profiles, Laws, and Consequences*. Gaborone: Lentswe la Lesedi, 1998.

———. "A Summary of Botswana Women's Issues and Demands." *Southern Africa Feminist Review* 1, no. 1 (1995): 99–112.

———. *The Women's Manifesto: A Summary of Botswana Women's Issues and Demands*. 2nd ed. Gaborone: Lentswe la Lesedi, 1999.

Gulbrandsen, Ornulf. *Poverty in the Midst of Plenty*. Bergen: Norse, 1996.

———. "To Marry or Not to Marry? Marital Strategies and Sexual Relations in a Tswana Society." *Ethnos* 51 (1986): 7–28.

Izzard, Wendy. "Migrants and Mothers: Case Studies from Botswana." *Journal of Southern African Studies* 11, no. 2 (1985): 258–80.

———. *Rural-Urban Migration of Women in Botswana*. Gaborone: Government Printer, 1979.

Jochelson, Karen. "Women, Migrancy, and Morality: A Problem of Perspective." Review article. *Journal of Southern African Studies* 21, no. 2 (1995): 323–32.

Kerven, Carol. "Academics, Practicioners, and All Kinds of Women in Development." *Journal of Southern African Studies* 10, no. 2 (1984): 259–68.

————. *Urban and Rural Female-Headed Households' Dependence on Agriculture*. Gaborone: Government Printer, 1979.

Landau, Paul. *The Realm of the Word*. Portsmouth: Heinemann, 1995.

Livingston, Julie. "These Children of Today: Older Women's Narratives of Domestic Caring and Conflict in Twentieth Century Botswana." Paper presented at the Berkshire Women's History Conference, Rochester, New York, June 3–5, 1998.

Mmeghi/The Reporter. Gaborone, Botswana, 1987–1996.

Molokomme, Athaliah. *Citizenship: Will My Child Become a Botswana Citizen?* Pamphlet prepared for the Women's Affairs Unit, Ministry of Home Affairs. Gaborone: Government Printer, n.d. [1984].

————. *His, Mine, or Ours? The Property Rights of Women Married Under Botswana Common Law*. Pamphlet prepared for the Women's Affairs Unit, Ministry of Home Affairs. Gaborone: Government Printer, 1986.

————. "Why Gender Is a Key Development Issue for Southern African Development Community (SADC), and Recommendations of the SADC Gender Strategy Workshop to the SADC Council of Ministers Meeting." *Southern African Feminist Review* 2, no. 2 (1997): 1–13, 59–63.

————. *The Woman's Guide to the Law: An Outline of How the Law Affects Every Woman and Her Family in Botswana*. Pamphlet prepared for the Women's Affairs Unit, Ministry of Home Affairs. Gaborone: Government Printer, 1984.

Murray, Stephen, and Will Roscoe, eds. *Boy-Wives and Female Husbands: Studies of African Homosexualities*. New York: St. Martin's Press, 1998.

newafrica. 2002. www.newafrica.com/profiles.

Nyati-Ramahobo, Lydia. *The Girl-Child in Botswana: Educational Constraints and Prospects*. Gaborone: UNICEF, 1992.

O'Laughlin, Bridget. "Missing Men? The Debate over Rural Poverty and Women-Headed Households in Southern Africa." *Journal of Peasant Studies* 25, no. 2 (1998): 1–48.

Peters, Pauline. *Dividing the Commons: Politics, Policy, and Culture in Botswana*. Charlottesville: University of Virginia Press, 1994.

————. "Gender, Development Cycles, and Historical Processes: A Critique of Recent Research on Women in Botswana." *Journal of Southern African Studies* 10, no. 1 (1983): 100–22.

————. "Women in Botswana." *Journal of Southern African Studies* 11, no. 1 (1984): 150–53.

Republic of Botswana. *Constitution of Botswana*. Gaborone: Government Printer, n.d.

————. Botswana Press Agency (BOPA). *Daily News Online*. www.gov.bw/.

————. Central Statistics Office. *Administrative/Technical Report and National Statistical Tables, 1991 Population and Housing Census*. Gaborone: Government Printer, 1991.

————. Central Statistics Office. *Education Statistics Report 1997*. Gaborone: Government Printer, 1997.

————. Central Statistics Office. *Women and Men in Botswana: Facts and Figures*. Gaborone: Government Printer, 1998.

————. Ministry of Finance and Development Planning. Central Statistics Office. *Eighth National Development Plan (NDP8) 1997/98–2002/03*. Gaborone: Government Printer, 1997.

Samatar, Abdi Ismail. *An African Miracle*. Portsmouth, NH: Heinemann Press, 1999.

Schapera, Isaac. *A Handbook of Tswana Law and Custom*. 2nd ed. London: Frank Cass, 1955.

————. *Married Life in an African Tribe*. Evanston, IL: Northwestern University Press, 1966 [1940].

———— . *Migrant Labour and Tribal Life: A Study of Conditions in the Bechuanaland Protectorate*. London: Oxford University Press, 1947.

Solway, Jacqueline. "Drought as a 'Revelatory Crisis': An Exploration of Shifting Entitlements and Hierarchies in the Kalahari, Botswana." *Development and Change* 25, no. 3 (1994).

Southern African Development Community. Gender Unit. *Women in Politics and Decision-Making in SADC: Beyond 30 percent in 2005*. Report of the proceedings of a conference held in Gaborone, Botswana, March 28–April 1, 1999. Gaborone. Government Printer, 1999.

UNAIDS. 2002. "Epidemiological Fact Sheet on HIV/AIDS and Sexually Transmitted Infections — Botswana." www.unaids.org.

World Bank. *Gender Statistics Summary Profile*. 2002. http://genderstats.worldbank.org/menu.asp.

2

BURUNDI

Michele Wagner

PROFILE OF BURUNDI

Burundi is a small country in the Great Lakes region of eastern-central Africa, tucked along the northwestern shores of Lake Tanganyika. Extending along the northeastern shoreline of the lake, its high hills rise from the narrow lake plain and open out to a rolling highland plateau in the center of the country. The western part of the central plateau is relatively high in elevation, about 6,000–6,500 feet, and it is transected by a chain of mountains, running north-south, which divide the watersheds of two of Africa's great rivers, the Congo-Zaire and the Nile. The mountains average 8,000 feet in elevation but the entire chain is no more than ten miles wide. As one descends their eastern slopes and proceeds along the central plateau, the altitude decreases to an average of 5,000–6,000 feet, and the landscape takes on an aspect of grassy rolling hills. Continuing eastward, the altitude continues to decrease until, on its eastern flanks, the central plateau descends to a low, flat, dry savanna. This savanna, averaging 3,400 feet in altitude and characterized by tall grass and acacia trees, contains the riverbed of the Malagarassi River, which serves as the border with neighboring Tanzania. Burundi's breadth of elevation makes for

significant environmental diversity. Nevertheless, it is a small country, only 10,746 square miles (27,834 square kilometers) in area.

Burundi lies slightly below the line of the equator, between 2 and 4.5 degrees south latitude, which is well within the tropical zone. Its climate is modified by its mountainous topography and by the winds of the Indian Ocean, rendering an average annual temperature of 68 degrees Fahrenheit (20 degrees Centigrade). Higher elevations, particularly those of the western central plateau, average slightly cooler temperatures, in the lower sixties, and can drop more than twenty degrees in temperature at night. Lower-altitude regions, such as the western lake plain and the eastern savannas, are generally warmer, average temperatures are in the middle seventies, but midday temperatures can exceed ninety degrees.

Burundi's rainfall averages forty to sixty inches per year. Generally, the highlands received greater precipitation, such as the northern Congo-Nile divide, which averages seventy inches per year. The extreme west and east receive less rainfall: the lake-plain averages thirty to forty inches per year, and the eastern savannas average thirty inches annually. Particularly on the western lake-plain, precipitation can occur as intense, pounding tropical rainstorms. In the central plateau, hailstorms are not uncommon. Precipitation patterns occur as distinct rainy and dry seasons. The primary rainy season occurs in late March to May and a second rainy season occurs in September to early December. A short dry season occurs in January to February, while the period June to August is normally quite dry. Generally, in the central plateau, some precipitation occurs every month.

Burundi's human geography is most strikingly characterized by a very dense population. The estimated total population in 2002 was 6.7 million, with a female-male gender ratio of 104:100, or 3.4 million females and 3.2 million males.[1] The average population density in 2002 was 622 persons per square mile,[2] which is the second densest on mainland Africa. Despite this density, the vast majority of Burundians, more than 90 percent, live in rural areas.[3] Only 65 percent of Burundi's land, however, is used for the predominant rural activities, farming and grazing.

The heaviest concentrations of people live in the central highland plateau, and the central provinces of Gitega, Muramvya, and Ngozi support particularly dense populations. Other particularly dense population clusters used to be located at Makamba in southern Burundi, and in the western lake-plain towns of Kigwena, Rumonge, and Nyanza. However, all of these latter populations have been significantly affected by post-1993 armed conflict. The lowest population densities are found in the eastern savannas, particularly in an ecological zone called Kumosso, which is characterized by erratic rainfall. This dusty, flat region, considered unattractive and unhealthful by most Burundians, whose "ideal" terrain is one of verdant hills, has been a target area for a variety of resettlement schemes in the past and present, including schemes to resettle "unaccompanied" women.

Burundi has several towns, including the administrative seats of each of its provinces. The largest of these is Gitega on central plateau, with a 1997 population of 30,000. On the lake plain, Rumonge had an 1997 population of about 15,000.

About 8 percent of Burundi's population lives in urban settings. Of Burundi's urban population, the large majority lives in the capital city, Bujumbura.[1] Bujumbura, located on the coast near the northern end of Lake Tanganyika, is Burundi's port, center of trade, and seat of government. Its estimated population in 1997 was 310,000.

Roughly based on a nineteenth-century kingdom located on the rolling hills of its central plateau, Burundi endured German colonial conquest and later Belgian colonial administration before gaining its independence in 1962. Postindependence Burundi endured a thirty-year string of authoritarian military regimes characterized by institutionalized oppression and intimidation, internal coups and attempted coups, and bursts of political opposition expressed as acts of ethnically patterned violence that consistently elicited massive, ethnically targeted military reprisal.

A brief period of liberalization in 1993 ushered in the first universal enfranchisement of the adult population, particularly women, and the first democratically elected president. This renaissance came sharply to a halt with the assassination of the president and many of his associates by army paratroopers three months after he took office. The murders plunged Burundi into a period of large-scale massacres that broadened into a civil war in which civilians, including women, became proxy targets for violent conflict between government troops and rebels. In the first five years of this crisis, armed forays into Burundian communities had generated a death toll of well over 200,000 persons, and had displaced well over a million more.

At the center of Burundi's protracted conflict has been a power struggle for control of the state in a context in which Burundians have both conceived of and exercised power as an "all or nothing" contest. From the earliest days of the nation's independence, political actors have used assassination to thwart their opponents' efforts at coalition building. They have relied on manipulation and intrigue to replace transparency and cooperation. Indeed, political groups have even resorted to the systematic and preemptive extermination of an entire group of potential opponents rather than to engage them in negotiation. In this context, effective exercise of power has been restricted to a very small group; however, the challenge to those in power by their opponents, and the power-group's defense against the challenge, have been expressed much more broadly in ethnic terms.

Burundi's "ethnic problem," which is the association of power and privilege with ethnic identity, is rooted in patterns of colonial rule. One of the most enduring colonial legacies has been an oppositional system of ethnic identity under which diverse precolonial identities were merged into three legally-recognized ethnic categories—Tutsi, Hutu, and Twa. Within this system, Tutsi and Hutu were explicitly contrasted and opposed to each other in the allocation of social benefits such as access to education, employment, and other means of socioeconomic advancement. It became both a colonial truism, and with the establishment of the divisive system of indirect rule, a colonial reality, that "Tutsi," as a category, was associated with intelligence, wealth, and relative privilege while "Hutu" was associated with the peasant or laboring class. Twa, depicted in profoundly negative images as backward and prehistoric, remained largely outside the colonial system of extracting and redistributing resources.

Although ethnic ideology drives the supporters and the opponents of the Burundian elite's monopolization of power and ethnic identity plays a vital role in the state's distribution or withholding of resources, the state's lack of power sharing marginalizes Burundian citizens for reasons other than ethnicity. Women, particularly, regardless of ethnicity, have been subject to discrimination—both structural and informal—as well as more menacing intimidation and violence. Burundian women, like Hutus, have been broadly cast, even within the realm of national policy, in a stereotyped manner that emphasizes the primacy of roles in production (and especially reproduction), rationalizes the denial of their access to resources (such as education), and ensures that they remain subject to physical and psychological violence while those who have violated them remain unpunished and often unaccused.

In the war that exists between government soldiers and Hutu rebels at the opening of the twenty-first century, civilians, including women, have been terrorized and murdered by both sides. These civilians, however, were not simply the war's incidental collateral damage: they have been the targets.[5] Their deaths are meant to "send a message"—to convey meaning to the enemy. In massacres committed by both sides throughout the country—including in the capital city of Bujumbura—over 200,000 people have lost their lives, and many more have lost their homes, schools, health care centers, and their sense of what is normal life. Caught between the violent forays into their communities, civilians, and civilian society itself, are under siege.

The most salient feature of contemporary Burundian society is the human displacement that has occurred on a massive scale, including both internal and external, both voluntary and involuntary. By 2001, some 350,000 Burundians were living as refugees in neighboring Tanzania, more than 432,000 people were living in formal IDP (internally displaced persons) locations, at least 200,000 persons were living in ad hoc arrangements, and some 100,000 more were temporarily displaced and awaiting the chance to return home.[6] Information collected at various points in the crisis has demonstrated that consistently the majority of the displaced have been women and children. In 1994, for example, at a time when more than 10 percent of the entire population was displaced, women and children made up more than 70 percent of the displaced population.[7] In other situations, 80–85 percent of those seeking refuge were women and children.

Further contributing to the deterioration of Burundian civil society has been the massive, often intentional destruction of public infrastructure including health centers, schools, and workplaces. By 2001 the conflict had degraded or destroyed about 30 percent of existing infrastructure.[8] Basic services like water and sewage were no longer broadly available. In 2001 only 52 percent of Burundians had access to safe drinking water, and only 47 percent had access to hygienic latrines.[9] Food was also no longer widely available, and food security no longer reasonably anticipated. The conflict and particularly the displacement had affected subsistence farming, which is the work of more than 90 percent of Burundians. In addition, delayed and erratic rainfall beginning in 1998 intensified the farming crisis, resulting in wide-scale malnutrition, particularly in the country's northern provinces.

Despite the limitations on its GDP that come from reliance on subsistence agriculture, Burundi engages in international trade and runs a consistently high trade deficit; in 1998 foreign trade debt stood at about U.S.$1.1 billion. In that same year, export earnings netted approximately U.S.$49 million while import expenditures were in the range of U.S.$102 million. Despite constraints, certain kinds of spending remain large; for example, Burundi's 1999 defense budget was U.S.$62 million.[10] Burundi is managing these discrepancies with huge international assistance. Despite the temporary imposition of international economic sanctions from 1996 to 1999, foreign aid accounted for more than half of the 1999 national budget.[11]

Already economically frail—it ranked 170 out of 174 countries by the United Nations Development Programme (UNDP) 1998 Human Development Index—Burundi confronted conditions that continued to decline by 2000. Multiple and concurrent emergencies occurred and converged, mutually intensifying each other. Three emergencies—an increase in internally displaced people, diminished farm production, and a malaria epidemic—occurred together in 2000–2001. The depth of the crisis that they produced is only beginning to be understood beyond the borders of Burundi.

Burundi's population is continuing to be affected profoundly by converging political and epidemiological crises, the mutual interaction of which has not yet been fully acknowledged or understood. The impact of these crises is most dramatically reflected in human life expectancy rates, which have declined precipitously in recent years, from 47.2 years in 1995 to 41 years (41 for females, 40 for males) in 2002.[12] Mid-2002 estimates of Burundi's infant mortality rate indicate that over the decade of the civil war, infant mortality more than doubled from 110 to 239 deaths per 1,000 live births.[13] Maternal mortality was also high, 21 deaths per 1,000 deliveries.[14] Overall, Burundi's 2002 population was estimated at 6.7 million persons,[15] based on an estimated average annual growth rate of approximately 2.2 to 2.5 percent.[16] It is a dense population, approximately 250 persons per square kilometer. Females compose 51 to 52 percent of all Burundians.

The population structure of Burundi, like that of many developing countries, is skewed toward youth. The crude birth rate is relatively high, in 2002 about 43 births per 1,000 population, while the crude death rate was 21 per 1,000 population.[17] In 2002 the percentage of the total population, both genders, under the age of fifteen (which is generally used as the demographic definition of childhood) was 47 to 48 percent.[18] Adults between the ages of fifteen and forty-nine constituted about 46 percent of the total population.[19] The relative percentage of elders, sixty and older, in the population was low, 3 percent in 2002, and appeared to be on the decline.[20] The gender composition of the population of elders was sixty-one males per one hundred females.[21]

OVERVIEW OF WOMEN'S ISSUES

By 2000, the armed struggle for power, particularly the intentional killing of civilians, and diminished living conditions had created hardship and tragedy for all Burundians, regardless of ethnicity. In this profoundly dehumanized setting, Burundian women found themselves divided by ethnicity and also divided about how to understand and to best respond to the crisis their nation was facing.

Although a failure to share power had created the conflict, most Burundians identified the source of their own insecurity, not as the abstract notion of the failure to share power, but as the clear and concrete threat posed by one or the other set of belligerents. As civilians facing belligerents, women experienced the violence of war, but had no direct means to stop or combat it. This is what all women shared, but what they did not share was a sense of what they could do as civilians to address their situation—in war or in peace. Therefore, while ordinary women struggled to address their specific situation in a myriad of practical ways, a group of educated urban women organized to effect changes for themselves. In organizing, urban women adopted two distinct but overlapping tasks: one focusing on legislating legal and economic parity, the other focusing on peace negotiations and particularly on the building of a postceasefire government to lobby for the place of women in Burundi's political future.

Throughout the course of the war, while their less privileged kinswomen found themselves living directly in combat's way, many of Bujumbura's educated elite women, who due to military protection of particular Bujumbura neighborhoods were less likely to become IDPs, questioned what their lives would be like after the ceasefire. These women had lived through several of their nation's periodic massacres and understood that as civilians, they had little input into the outcome of the war. Their experience of political liberalization in 1993 had also shown them that as citizens they could play a role in the outcome of the peace in postceasefire Burundi. Therefore, despite the war, they continued to press for a prewar agenda of gender mainstreaming and the legislation of women's rights. They sought to build on gains that had been made prior to the war when a small window of opportunity had opened up enabling women to effect the passage of significant gender equity legislation.

EDUCATION

Opportunities

Education is one of the basic infrastructures of Burundian civil society that has deteriorated in the current crisis. By 2002, less than half of Burundi's children, even those aged seven to ten, saw the inside of a classroom.

In the 1980s, education became a site of conflict, between the government and nongovernmental institutions (NGOs), particularly those sponsored by the Catholic Church. The government seized Catholic schools and deported clergy and lay workers. Despite these conflicts, education remained an aspiration for many, and in 1992–1993, in a period of eased political tensions, about 70 percent of Burundian children attended school. Since then, with the deterioration of civil society, school attendance fell. In 1999–2000, 48 percent of Burundian children attended school.[22] Post-2000 patterns of school attendance show that disparities have a strong regional character. In 2002, of Burundi's seventeen provinces, five had primary school attendance rates over 82 percent and above and four had rates of below 50 percent.[23] Gender disparities in school enrolment also had a regional character, with provinces in the center of the country (Gitega, Muramvya) demonstrating significantly less gender disparity than peripheral and war-affected provinces (such as Cibitoke, Kirundo, Bubanza). In terms of national averages, the gender ratio for school attendance was 79.4 girls per 100 boys.[24]

The continuing political nature of the issue of education is suggested by the state of Burundian schools since the beginning of the civil war when many had functioned as IDP shelters. By 2001, at least 500 primary schools were not functional, and at least 28 percent of primary schools had closed. Those continuing to function did so with serious structural and staffing problems. At least 57 percent of schools received no physical maintenance and at least 25 percent did not have functioning latrines. Staffing problems led to overcrowded classrooms, an average of seventy-two primary students per classroom. Of some 14,000 teachers in place, 3,000 had no formal teaching qualification and only a limited education.[25]

Literacy

Although women constitute 52 percent of the national population, only 27 percent of women are literate compared to 48 percent of men, a ratio of 56 women to 100 men.[26] Historically, few Burundians had had access to education, particularly females and rural dwellers. Literacy rates collected fours years after independence in 1966 indicated that the literacy among town dwellers was 32 percent while among rural dwellers it was only 4 percent.[27] At that time only 5 percent of Burundians studied in any educational institution.

Work was carried out to expand literacy in the first decades of independence, and it is reflected in subsequent literacy studies that find that in 1990 among adults born in 1965 or earlier, 43 percent of males and 18 percent of females were literate. In the cohort of Burundians born in the first decades of independence, between 1966–1975, literacy rose to 60 percent of males and 38 percent of females. These gains were countered, however, by events in 1972, in which army death squads specifically targeted educated Hutus. The impact of this was to discourage Hutu parents from sending their children to school.

EMPLOYMENT AND ECONOMICS

The structure of Burundi's work force is largely weighted toward agriculture, which normally accounts for about 93 percent of the national labor force. The government/military is the second largest employer, accounting for 4 percent of labor, followed by industry/commerce and services, each accounting for 1.5 percent of national labor.[28] Market-oriented agriculture accounted for about 50 percent of gross national product (GNP) in the mid-1990s and was based mainly on coffee (75 percent of total exports), tea (5 percent of total exports), cotton, and tobacco.

Burundi's industrial sector is largely oriented toward production of goods for local consumption, and agricultural processing dominates the sector, including industries such as beer brewing, soft drinks, and sugar. Among the other dominant industrial enterprises are

Women work at a reforestation nursery in Rumonge, Burundi. Photo © Sean Sprague/Painet.

cotton textiles (5 percent of total exports), cigarettes, match production, and food processing. Altogether this sector amounts to slightly over 20 percent of gross domestic product (GDP).[29] Most factories are located in the capital city, whose supply system had been interrupted by conflict. One component of Burundi's industrial sector that remains in a nascent state is mining. Burundi has large deposits of nickel, copper, cobalt, phosphates, and platinum-group metals, and it currently produces tin and gold. Another promising sector is hydropower, the main source of electricity, which is likely to find markets in neighboring countries.

Within Burundi, fewer than 5 percent of households have access to electricity.[30] The prevalence of subsistence farming in Burundi is reflected in its generally low per capita GNP. With disruption caused by the war, the per capita GNP declined in the late 1990s, and plunged in 2000–2001 to U.S.$103.[31] The economic growth rate for the last decade of the twentieth century was −3.7 percent.

Farming

More than 90 percent of Burundi's citizens are engaged in the agricultural sector. Among women, 95 percent are farmers,[32] and most are engaged in subsistence farming, which in Burundi centers on mixed farming and livestock raising.

Burundi's temperate climate supports a range of crops, including bananas, beans, peas, cassava, squashes, and corn, which are among the most important staple foods grown and consumed by rural households. Other staples include highland grain crops, such as wheat, sorghum, barley, and highland peas. Lowland crops include yams, potatoes, sweet potatoes, peanuts, and peppers. Cash crops include coffee, which is produced both by small farmers and commercially; tea, which is generally produced on highland plantations; and cotton and palm oil, both of which can be produced by small farmers but have been most successful when grown on commercial plantations. Most families keep some livestock, particularly goats, sheep, and cattle. Large herds are rare due to land shortage.

With more than 90 percent of the national population living in rural areas, the vast majority of Burundians are engaged in agricultural activities, most at a subsistence level. Most farms are smaller than one hectare in size, and worked by the members of a family-based household. The work of family farming is shared among family members, and labor patterns vary by socioeconomic class and family. Nevertheless the primary responsibility for household crops is regarded by Burundian society as belonging to the senior adult female. By contrast, responsibility for the farming of crops regarded explicitly as commodities (such as contemporary cash crops like coffee or more traditional exchange crops like tobacco) and the raising of livestock, which function both as commodities and as items of social exchange, generally belongs to the household's senior adult male. Rural families value children and rely heavily on their labor.

In central Burundi, where the landscape is characterized by hills and valleys, it is generally the case that residential compounds are located on hillsides, not in the valleys. Burundians have traditionally regarded valleys as uninhabitable due to seasonal flooding and the persistent level of humidity that promotes the breeding of insects. This choice, however, has necessitated an enormous expenditure in the carrying of water, a task often assigned to children, especially girls.

Paid Employment

For women working in the urban, salaried sector, occupations range widely from domestic servant to senior executive. Because of historical patterns tending to coalesce socioeconomic status and ethnicity, many occupations are associated with, and sometimes informally restricted to, ethnicity. Gendered patterns, similarly, can be detected in the occupations and hiring practices of Burundi's salaried sector. A 1998 study of the senior service, for example, revealed that only 2.5 percent of employees in this sector were female.

Entrepreneurship

The presence of African women in colonial-era cities was cause for alarm among European commentators and policymakers, including Belgians, who judged such women to be disoriented, separated from custom and hence customary morals, and vulnerable to moral corruption.[33] Particularly unmarried or otherwise "unaccompanied" women were identified as particularly susceptible to moral decline. The impact of this evaluation was that colonial policy actively thwarted women's cash-generating activities and impeded other activities which might be construed as fostering female autonomy. Thus it was despite the weight of colonial policy that African women, particularly those who were not the wives of educated and/or salaried workers of Europeans, resided and even managed to develop small businesses in the city.

Pay

A 1999 study of the salaried sector reported that women earned only 75 percent of what their male colleagues earned.

Support for Mothers/Caretakers

There are no reliable data on the subject of care for children during a woman's working hours. As a result of the armed conflict, many women and children are not only displaced from their homes but also separated from their families.

Inheritance, Property, and Land Rights

Associated with the residence (*rugo*) are the plots of land from which its resources are drawn. Typically, the plots immediately adjacent to the homestead are used to grow plants of immediate recourse, such as medicines and herbs, and the heaviest crops, especially bananas destined for making beer. Most households control one or more nonresidential plots, some inherited (generally by men, but occasionally by women), some purchased (normally by men, but also by wealthier women), where family members or hired laborers grow other crops. One objective in pursuing additional plots is to acquire fields in various microenvironmental zones for crop diversification.

Burundian women can and do purchase additional plots, and hire nonfamily laborers, female or male, to farm them, usually negotiating a crop-splitting arrangement. The present state of insecurity has led to an increase in the number of landless and displaced people, particularly women and children, willing to hire out their labor for the duration of a growing season.

While Burundian urban space and ownership is generally developed from the policies of its two former colonizers, Germany and Belgium, Bujumbura grew out of a center of mid-nineteenth-century slave trade. When Germans arrived to lay claim to the region in the mid-1890s, they established a military post in the slave market's environs. With some slight modifications to optimize healthfulness and harbor capacity, the trade and administrative center of Usumbura (renamed Bujumbura at independence) developed. Regarded by colonizers as separate and distinct from the surrounding milieu characterized by the *rugo* (plural, *ingo*) under the control by chiefs, Usumbura was directly controlled by European colonial authorities. African residence there was regulated and monitored. Only after 1935 did the colonial government begin to lay out housing quarters for Africans, and even then, the permanent residence of Africans in Usumbura was discouraged by allowing African occupation rights but not ownership rights to urban real estate.[34] Although urban growth led to an informal erosion of some of these restrictions, they remained legally intact until 1960, and they ended altogether with independence in 1962. With independence, the racial boundaries that had defined and separated neighborhoods were informally replaced with socioeconomic and ethnic ones. Successive bouts of ethnic tension in the 1960s–1980s made incremental but perceptible impacts on the ethnic character of certain among Bujumbura's neighborhoods, culminating in urban paralysis, violence, and ethnic cleansing in the 1990s.

Burundian women's experience of urban life in Bujumbura has been very much filtered through the history of the settlement itself. As residents of the precolonial slave-trade depot of Uzige, their experiences would have been strongly shaped by their links to male protectors, as wives or servants, or their lack of protective links, which would have rendered them as slaves. In colonial Usumbura, which was designated as a residential space for Africans only insomuch as they provided labor, women's experiences would have been strongly influenced by the colonial assumption that wage laborers should be male. Women's struggles for economic and social latitude, and even autonomy, did take place and by the mid-1980s, women composed about 48 percent of Bujumbura's population, and possibly one quarter of the homeowners, at least in the city's less affluent and older neighborhoods (called *quartiers populaires*).

These gains were not clearly being transformed into future advantages, for in terms of land sales, women constituted only 12.6 percent of buyers, and were particularly underrepresented in purchases of land tracts located in newly opening neighborhoods.[35] The impact of Bujumbura's urban history for women, therefore, has been mixed. On the one hand, women as a group have been subjects of an implication that they are not, or should not be, full-fledged residents of the city by those who have associated urbanization with male-dominated wage labor. On the other hand, Burundian women have not experienced urban life as a group, because their experiences have been bounded or shaped by the parameters of ethnicity.

FAMILY AND SEXUALITY

The backbone of society and the essential unit of a subsistence economy, family is central to how Burundians experience their daily lives. In rural areas, family is often associated with household, for in the Kirundi language, words associated with family, *umuryango* (literally, door), the larger or extended family, *urugo* (homestead, fence), the household, and *inzu* (small house, hut), the narrower or nuclear family, are strongly related to one another, and in relaxed, informal speech are sometimes used interchangeably. Since Burundians lived in dispersed homesteads rather than in villages or towns prior to the colonial period, and in many cases still do, family and household constitute a person's primary collective identity, with one's hill of residence constituting one's broader collective identity. Prior to the colonial period, most Burundians did not conceive of themselves as members of large "ethnic" groups, but rather as members of discrete families or clans.[36]

Gender Roles and Division of Labor

Rural families live on dispersed, self-contained homesteads—that is, a fenced multistructure residential compound sitting on one plot of land and having adjunct plots of land in various locations. The residence itself, called a *rugo*, is normally cluster of houses, storage sheds, granaries, livestock pens, and service sheds arranged around an outdoor courtyard, all of which is surrounded by a secure, woven fence of live ficus trees. Burundians typically regard the *rugo* as domestic space, managed by the primary adult woman whose supervising authority derives from her relationship to the head of household, who is usually her husband. Ideally, the woman manages the household—and either performs or supervises most of the domestic labor, depending on the family's socioeconomic level and resources—while the male head of household superintends its internal workings with a certain degree of "domestic detachment." His role is to represent the household to the larger community beyond its protective fence.

The persistence of this "ideal" vision of household organization and authority in the current context of armed conflict and epidemiological disaster has placed many Burundians in a state of profound dissonance and stress. Vital as family is to Burundian life, many families have deteriorated during the stress of the last decade, particularly as a result of displacement and AIDS.[37] The present reality is that many households are headed by women, and even by children, who according to the "ideal" model are neither equipped individually nor empowered socially to supervise a household and represent it in the public sphere.

Marriage

Marriage has traditionally functioned in Burundi as a means to create bonds of solidarity between two families. Marriages were negotiated by the senior men, who gave much attention to lauding the opportunity to create new bonds produced by the transfer of a young woman from one family to another. At a family-to-family level, marriage was a reciprocal, formally transacted relationship that involved an initial transfer of goods to be finalized by the transfer of a person (the bride). The goods, transferred from the groom's to the bride's family, were socially explained as compensation to the bride's family for her loss and acknowledgment of the care that the bride's family had invested in raising her. Very importantly, the payment also ensured that offspring born of the union would belong to the groom's lineage. Traditionally, marriages were constructed over the course of a series of events, including bridewealth negotiations, ceremonies to prepare, introduce, and join the couple, a cloistering of the bride as she entered her new family, and the formal reintroduction of the newly married couple, and particularly the bride, back into society. Regional variations in marriage practices existed, especially pertaining to the form and amount of bridewealth, and elements of the various ceremonies.

Today, there has occurred a certain "standardization" of wedding customs, particularly among the elite classes, and there are significant differences in customs between elite and ordinary families. Among the socially ascendant, customs identified as "Western" (such as a separate, white-dress church ceremony centering on exchange of vows and rings followed by a public reception and evening dance party) have been combined with customs derived from cattle-keeping families of the central plateau (such as the expression of the bridewealth in terms of cattle, the use of cattle imagery in speeches and dances, and the draped dress adopted by women participants). Among less wealthy families, weddings often include fewer Western customs, and many involve bridewealth payments expressed or "valued" in traditional forms other than livestock, such as hoes, pots of beer, and packets of salt.

Burundi has officially outlawed polygamy, and this has had numerous social consequences. One consequence is that concubinage became widespread, particularly among the well-off government workers in Bujumbura. This practice is believed to have facilitated the spread of HIV/AIDS within wealthy urban families.

Reproduction

Another consequence of monogamy is that the child-bearing capacity of a bride-to-be is of considerable interest, since she cannot be "supplemented" with a second wife should she have fertility problems. Despite a traditional Burundi and a Christian ban on premarital sex, many brides preside over their wedding ceremonies in an evidently pregnant state, with much exclamation made of happy certainty of the young woman's fertility. Adultery is much frowned on for Burundian women, and has been tacitly tolerated for men. New legislation passed in 1993 placed new emphasis on culpability regardless of gender.

Consistent with a reliance on family labor is a pattern of large family size and high birth rates. In 2002, Burundian women averaged 6.3 live births per woman. Another study estimated that 43 births occurred per 1,000 population. This emphasis on large families came at a cost for women: maternal mortality rates in 2002 ranged from 800 to 1,300 deaths per 100,000 live births, depending on region.

Children are highly valued in Burundi, and from a larger family perspective, they are regarded as social capital that a woman uses to consolidate her position in her husband's family. A bride is a "stranger" with little protection inside her new family of marriage, but a mother of numerous children has a foundation of "insiders" who protect her interests with relatives among whom she lives but was not born. Burundi's fertility rate of 6.8 percent is high.[38]

Contraception and Abortion

Despite the growing prevalence of HIV/AIDS, contraception is not widely practiced in Burundi. A 1987 study found that contraceptive prevalence among married women of childbearing age was 9 percent using any method, and 1 percent using a modern method.[39] Professional health intervention is also relatively uncommon in pregnancy and delivery. More than 90 percent of Burundian women give birth at home without the assistance of trained medical professionals.[40]

Burundian law prohibits abortion, except in situations in which the mother's life is clearly at risk. Even then, the approval of two doctors is needed before an abortion may be performed.[41] In many rural areas, this is rarely possible. Instead, women seek assistance from untrained neighbors and others. A 2001 report conducted by a monitoring body for the Convention on the Elimination of All Forms of Discrimination Against Women (CEDAW) affirmed that many women had died from secret abortions, and that 45 percent of those admitted to the hospital as a result of badly performed abortions were girls.[42]

HEALTH

Health Care Access

Access to health care is a vital issue among women, who in Burundian culture bear primary responsibility for the physical well-being of young family members. The destruction of the medical infrastructure has had serious consequences for Burundi's women and families, not the least of which has been unprecedented levels of common diseases, including the outbreak of a malaria epidemic.

Between 1993 and 1998, one in ten health centers closed or was destroyed.[43] By 2000, the system of basic health care was functioning at 80 percent capacity.[44] Many of the centers that remained open offered only the most rudimentary of services due to a shortage of essential drugs and physicians.

Diseases and Disorders

Among the most commonly untreated ailments are malnutrition and malaria.[45] Left untreated, both grew into serious health crises. Malaria rose to new thresholds in late 2001. In November 2001, more than 1 million cases were reported.[46] Particularly alarming was that the disease moved from lower-altitude regions, where it is endemic, to high-altitude zones, where it is rare and where natural resistance is low. Its spread may have been associated with the movement of displaced persons, among whom its incidence was particularly acute.

Malnutrition climbed from moderate to severe in 1998–2000, particularly in insecure and drought-prone provinces and among displaced populations.[47] Its prevalence was particularly high among children: 37 percent of children under five years of age suffered from moderate to severe malnutrition.[48] But in the conflict-ridden western provinces, malnutrition was so prevalent in 1998 that more than 50 percent of the beneficiaries of therapeutic feeding centers were adults.[49] The deteriorated health care structure aggravated the prevalence and severity of other common ailments, particularly diarrhea and acute respiratory infections.[50] Childhood immunization rates dropped at least 20 percent over the course of the 1990s.

AIDS

HIV/AIDS grew through the course of the conflict, and new levels of infection spread to previously low-risk groups, particularly young women and girls. By 2002, approximately 24 percent of adult women, and 3 percent of children under five were believed to be infected with HIV/AIDS.[51] Among young adults ages twenty to twenty-four, the rate of HIV seropositivity has been found to be three times higher than that of men in the same age group. The phenomenon has been linked to an escalation in sexual exploitation and violence, and the breakdown in vital health and education services, leaving these women without access to HIV prevention and treatment services.

AIDS has been a forceful cause of the deterioration of the Burundian family. UNICEF research in 2002 identified 230,000 of Burundi's children to be AIDS orphans.

POLITICS AND LAW

The contemporary nation-state of Burundi is based on (but by no means synonymous with) a precolonial kingdom that extended its rule over portions of the central highland plateau. Political power centered on the Baganwa, a small aristocratic dynasty, from which the *mwami*, or king, was chosen. The Baganwa regarded themselves as separate and distinct from those over whom they ruled. To express this, they called themselves, the "children of the womb of the drum," the drum being the symbol of royal power. Although the Baganwa princes empowered and enriched themselves with shrewd politics, the authority of the *mwami* depended very much on an ideological and mystical dimension. It was a group of royal ritualists and divination specialists who chose the *mwami*, who enthroned him, who protected his sacred insignia and who reinforced his power annually with a ritual of fertility. These ritualists included both men and women. Some of the most important figures, including the keepers of the most scared symbol of power, a particular royal drum, were ritually required to be women.

Leadership and Decision-making

Although women played key roles in the power structure of precolonial Burundi, German conquest and subsequent Belgian administration transformed the structure and exercise of power. Armed Germans and their African soldiers (*askaris*) militarized the notion of power. The Germans sent violent "punitive expeditions" to convince autonomous regions to submit to the *mwami* of Burundi, thereby demonstrating that force could overcome a lack of legitimacy.

Belgium, which administered Burundi (then port of Ruanda-Urundi) on behalf of the League of Nations (and later the United Nations) after Germany's defeat in World War I, demonstrated that not only do leaders not need to be legitimate, but they also need not be responsive to the ruled. The Belgian colonial government established a new administrative system across the country which relied on centrally appointed "chiefs" and "subchiefs." In service of this system, local leaders, including women and Hutus, were systematically removed and replaced by exclusively male "chiefs" who came from royal or wealthy cattle-keeping families.

Belgian administrators ousted royal ritualists, including women, and claimed for themselves the power to appoint leaders. Moreover, under Belgian influence, royal power became secularized, and the *mwami* converted to Catholicism. Other ritualists and diviners, women included, were dispossessed and even threatened or persecuted for witchcraft. Officially, they faded into the general "peasant" population, although at the local level they remained highly regarded.

Under Belgian rule, the colonial chiefs and subchiefs became the linchpin of the system, and their children were targeted for careers in the colonial bureaucracy. Accordingly, chiefs' sons were designated for a western education, and their daughters were educated to become appropriately demure and domesticated wives. Royal women, and women of the royal entourage, who served as envoys, spies, powerbrokers, and dealmakers, found their *evolue* ("evolved," "civilized") daughters crocheting tablecloths. Ritualist women, who had served as prophetesses and kingmakers, found their daughters toiling in the fields.

Political Participation

At independence, women remained in the background while men, like Prince Louis Rwagasore, stepped forward to build political movements. Rwagasore's efforts were soon cut short by his assassination, and political power became associated with the capacity and willingness to commit violence. A rapid succession of coups, first by a young prince who declared himself king, and then by an obscure young soldier who named himself president, demonstrated power's tumultuous and deceitful nature in the newly independent Burundi. The 1966 ascendancy of Michel Micombero to the presidency had initiated a new kind of power: one monopolized by a small, previously insignificant regional faction rooted in the army. Micombero's two successors, Jean-Baptiste Bagaza, who overthrew him in 1976, and Pierre Buyoya, who overthrew Bagaza in 1987, had all been members of that same faction. The militarization of presidential power tended to exclude women, since women could not enter into the army. At best, educated women from well-connected families received political appointments, and women were assured a certain permanency of control over certain gender-specific posts such as those in the Ministry of Women.

By the early 1990s, considerable international donor pressure convinced President Buyoya to loosen his control over Burundian society and liberalize many of his policies, including the formal and informal policies that prevented women from acting as full citizens. In this context, women lobbied for legal parity and newly formed political parties lobbied for elections. In this exciting atmosphere, Melchior Ndadaye, a Hutu of the newly formed Front for Democracy in Burundi (FRODEBU) political party, stood for election, challenging Buyoya. In Burundi's first free elections, the first elections in which the majority of Burundians, including women, were allowed to vote, Ndadaye won.

But elements within the Tutsi-dominated army were unable to accept a Hutu president, and particularly the notion that he might "balance" the ethnic composition of the army. They assassinated him and other top Hutu leaders in October 1993 after only three months in power. The assassination provoked a response throughout Burundi, which rapidly took a bloody and ethnic character. Two large-scale ethnic massacres, one conducted by Hutu civilians against their Tutsi counterparts (which Tutsis refer to as "the genocide"), followed by another conducted by the army against Hutu civilians (which is frequently subsumed under "the war").

Several subsequent presidents and interim presidents—including an interim presidency by a woman, Sylvie Kanigi, a Tutsi who served as acting president as well as prime minister at the height of the bloodshed from October 1993 to February 1994—failed to consolidate power. What became clear in those months of tragedy was that the civilian government and the military were two separate and opposed branches of the government—and the real power lay with the military. Finally, in July 1996, former president and military officer Pierre Buyoya put an end to this contradiction by seizing, and thus consolidating, power. This provoked angry civilians to radicalize and organize an armed resistance. The response followed the "logic" of Burundian politics, but it failed to draw participation and support from women.

Buyoya's 1996 coup, and the army's heavy-handed reaction to the resistance that it had elicited, led to the imposition of sanctions against Burundi by neighboring countries. These sanctions were intended to pressure Buyoya and his opponents into negotiations, as both sides had stepped up their armed attacks. By 1997–1998, the struggle had developed patterns of aggressions. Rebels attacked civilians. The army attacked other civilians. Both sides used civilians as proxy targets in a war against each other.[52] This pattern of killing civilians continued even as peace talks began, first brokered by former Tanzanian president Julius Nyerere, then subsequently mediated by former South African president Nelson Mandela. In August 2000 an agreement was reached. The agreement was hailed as a breakthrough even though parties initially refused to sign it, and at least two coup attempts had taken place over the course of the peace negotiations. Negotiations over its implementation began, and it was at this point that Burundian women increased their involvement in the peace process.

It was during the course of these negotiations that Burundian women organized to lobby for greater institutional participation, and their effort led to the inclusion of women on official delegations. Following this with great interest, refugee women also organized and sent their own female delegates in October 2001. Both sides were keenly interested in the gender and ethnic composition of a new transitional government. The struggle that women of both sides faced and the nature of the milieu in which they struggled can be gleaned by a remark made by Nelson Mandela in talks in mid-2001 that if men began to fight again, women should weigh in against it by withholding their "conjugal rights" (like cooking, he added).

While women delegates to the peace talks pushed for their inclusion in the transitional government, women activists worked to broaden their campaign by holding regional workshops and roundtables. In the refugee camps as well, women made use of existing social structures (such as women's counseling centers) to exchange ideas on what the implementation of the peace accord might mean. A critical difference between these two groups is that Burundian nationals could and did translate their activism into parliamentary seats in the new government. Refugee delegates returned to their camps—and many remained refugees.

In Burundi, new tactics, such as organizing women to empower themselves and encouraging women to denounce rebel violence "as mothers" helped to broaden the movement in late 2001. Other Burundian women reacted to these efforts with skepticism, such as a group of Tutsi women who complained to Mandela mid-2002 that the peace and rebuilding efforts had drawn attention away from their plight as genocide survivors. Drawing women, even women of the same ethnic group, into a shared political discourse was not easy, and working against it was an environment of fear that continued with new armed attacks. In January and February 2002, precisely when the National Assembly was being constituted, new offensives were launched in Bujumbura. At one point, 14,000 people were displaced in two weeks. Approximately 85 percent of those displaced were women and children. At another point, in February, 3,000 persons were displaced and others killed in Ruyigi Province, while health centers were attacked and a school was burnt to the ground. Women continued to struggle, believing that a civilian future would be possible.

Women's Rights

In 1991 Burundi ratified the Convention on the Elimination of All Forms of Discrimination Against Women as an expression of the principle of gender parity. Elaborating on that principle, in 1993 a string of new legislation protected women's rights in much more specific ways: eliminating polygamy, establishing a minimum age of marriage (eighteen for women, twenty-one for men), protecting women's inheritance rights, and allowing women to administer family property. Laws addressing the custody of children, parental authority, and adoption were amended to protect women's interests. Even labor laws were revised to address in a preliminary way the problem of gender discrimination in the workplace.

Although much of the language that had conveyed the case for legal and economic parity had centered on human rights and development, which rapidly appeared to have been sidelined by the war, supporters adapted their discourse to meet the new situation. For example, supporters emphasized that war was a conflict over resources, and therefore it related directly to a poverty-and-development agenda. Another dimension of the prewar gender equity strategy had focused on opening up positions for women in public and private institutions, and promoting women in government employment. This, too, seemed to have been made less urgent by the war. Nevertheless, supporters continued to push for institutional inclusion, and in the process they worked to strengthen their own institutions. Concretizing the principle of institutional participation, women formed and worked through their own gender-based professional associations.

One of the largest and most successful of Burundian women's associations was Collective/Umbrella of Women's Associations and Non-Governmental Organizations of Burundi (CAFOB). Composed of many Burundian member organizations, CAFOB was also linked to a larger regional coalition, the Great Lakes Platform of Umbrella Women's Organizations. Its stated goals were to create opportunities for increased women's involvement in political processes, economic development, and peacebuilding. In pursuit of this goal, CAFOB launched a campaign to influence the gender composition of the government in 1998, observing that the representation of women was minimal. Although it could not change the composition of the ministerial cabinet, CAFOB succeeded in influencing the nomination of a woman as president of the Constitutional Court. In pursuit of its peacebuilding goal, in the late 1990s CAFOB pushed for women's participation in Burundi's peace negotiations. It noted that numerous government delegations to the peace talks had included a total of one woman. Lobbying hard for women's involvement in the talks, by mid-2000 CAFOB had succeeded in influencing the inclusion of women in most of the dozen or so delegations to the negotiations, a remarkable and rapid improvement over the past.

At the peace talks, the negotiations hinging on the formation of a transitional postceasefire government gave CAFOB and other women's advocates another opportunity to expand women's political participation. Organized to a degree that they had never before achieved, women presented their candidatures for positions in the new government. They argued that peace, an assertion of human rights, must be tied to women's rights. Any discussion about rebuilding society must include women as actors and decisionmakers. The success of their lobbying efforts was reflected in the inclusion of an unprecedented four women ministers on the president's transitional cabinet when it was named in late 1999, and a record number of women legislators elected to the National Assembly (18 percent) and to the Senate (19 percent) in January and February 2000.

While elite women worked to mainstream women's rights as human rights, ordinary women experienced the dehumanizing reality of war: even the most elementary human rights, particularly the right to life, were flagrantly violated on a regular basis. Moreover, as elite women sought to open up and transform institutions to include their agenda, rural women watched the institutions most visible in their lives—dispensaries and schools—deteriorate. Ordinary women faced displacement, destruction of their families, and physical and sexual violence. Becoming household heads for the first time in their lives, often under stressful and tragic conditions, women living in combat areas faced dilemmas of how best to protect their children and themselves from violence and hunger. Many women and girls grappled with the question of bartering sex, and risking AIDS, for immediate basic sustenance.

RELIGION AND SPIRITUALITY

Two out of every three Burundians profess membership in an organized religious community. Roman Catholicism is the dominant Christian religion in Burundi, and at least 62 percent of Burundian citizens are Catholic. Five percent of the population practices other Christian faiths, and about 1 percent practice Islam.[53] Women play active roles in Christian communities to the extent that their religions allow. In Burundi's Catholic community, women serving as nuns far outnumber men serving as priests and brothers.

Rituals and Religious Practices

Approximately one out of three Burundians do not belong to an organized religion, and are believed to observe certain pre-Christian spiritual practices, such as consultation with ancestors. Of the cluster of religious practices that existed in Burundi prior to the arrival of Christian missionaries, many are no longer widely practiced, if they are practiced at all. Notable among these is the Kubandwa spirit possession cult that had many adherents, including many women, before it was phased out by the Belgian colonial administration, under missionary pressure. Other practices continue to exist, particularly those related to healing, and women play important roles as diagnosticians, herbalists, and healers.

VIOLENCE

Domestic Violence and Rape/Sexual Assault

Elevated rates of HIV/AIDS infection have been reported in both IDP and refugee camps, and have been related to sexual violence by men against women in a context of the breakdown of family structure. High incidences of sexual violence against women have been documented in the Burundian refugee camps in Tanzania.[54] Refugee agencies have also noted a correlation between food distribution and reported incidents of sexual exploitation and domestic violence.

War and Military Repression

The contexts of sexual exploitation in which young women become infected center on the crisis elements of displacement and poverty. In the process of fleeing from armed conflict, young women and girls become particularly vulnerable to capture, sexual assault, and exploitation during ambushes along the road by soldiers and rebels. Anecdotal evidence to this effect has been substantiated by medical evidence from health centers at IDP sites. These centers have also found that the majority of displaced young women and girls suffer from health problems caused by different forms of physical and sexual violence. An estimated 80 percent have been victims of physical violence and 10 percent victims of rape.[55] In addition, young women who are not displaced, or who have ostensibly found safety in camps, have reported confronting the dilemma of bartering sexual services for food, money, or medicine. This dilemma has been particularly associated with child and female heads of households. IDP statistics indicate that women form the demographic majority, and that an estimated 70 percent of IDP households are headed by women.[56]

UNICEF studies on the state of Burundi's children, which have indicated that there exists a large and growing population of children who have been orphaned or estranged from their families. In 2002, UNICEF identified 230,000 AIDS orphans and 25,000 war orphans. It identified over 5,000 child-headed households. In addition, it noted the existence of 14,000 child soldiers, more than 5,000 street children, and 120 minors in prison sharing cells with adults. Children account for 60 percent of displaced Burundians, and among the displaced are many children who have been separated from their families. In 1998, 4,500 children had been registered as unaccompanied minors.

OUTLOOK FOR THE TWENTY-FIRST CENTURY

In Burundi's quest to rebuild itself as a nation, Burundi's women promise to play a central role in the reclamation of their nation by civil society. It is not clear how much elite women will identify with their ordinary countrywomen. Their discourse "advises," "sensitizes," and "warns" ordinary women, but it does not yet empathize and listen. Without dialogue on a more equal footing the women's movement risks becoming an appendage of the current power group. Women have the potential to become a vital force for reconciliation and change with greater mutual identification.

NOTES

I would like to acknowledge the work of Colman Titus Msoka of the University of Minnesota Department of Sociology, who provided much appreciated assistance for the research for this chapter.

1. Population Reference Bureau (PRB), 2002 *World Population Data Sheet*; UNFPA, *State of the World Population* (1999), 6.6 million.

2. Ibid.

3. United Nations Population Division (UNDP), 1999.

4. Quest Economic Database (August 2001), 8 percent; UN Statistics Bureau, 9 percent. It is difficult to get accurate data statistics for the population of Bujumbura due to population displacement and large-scale migration to and from Bujumbura for security reasons.

5. Human Rights Watch, *Proxy Targets: Civilians in the War in Burundi*, March 1998.

6. UNICEF, *A Humanitarian Appeal for Children and Women, January–December 2002: Burundi*, 2002.

7. Convention on the Elimination of All Forms of Discrimination Against Women (CEDAW), *Initial Reports of State Parties: Burundi* (CEDAW/C/BDI/1).

8. Ibid.

9. UNICEF, 2002.

10. *The Military Balance*, 2000/2001.

11. CEDAW, *Initial Reports of State Parties: Burundi* (CEDAW/C/BDI/1); Minority Rights Group (Filip Reyntjens), 2000.

12. PRB, 2002, 41.

13. There is considerable variation in this statistic. Statistic used is from 2002. PRB, 2002, 116/1,000; UNICEF, 2001, 106/1,000.

14. PRB, 2002; UNICEF, 2002, gives ranges of 8 to 13 per 1,000 births.

15. 6.7 is in PRB, 2002. Although estimates vary, the 1999 United Nations Population Division estimate of 6.56 million, and the estimate of 6.6 published by the

UNFPA, *State of the World*, 1999, have been broadly accepted, as has the UNFPA's 1997 estimate of 6.4 million.

16. The estimated rate of growth varies broadly from 2.85 percent used by the U.S. Department of State in *Background Note: Burundi* (August 2002) to 1.7 percent used by the United Nations Statistical Bureau in the publication *The World's Women 2000: Trends and Statistics* (New York: United Nations, 2000). The UNFPA (1997) used 2.8 percent. U.S. government sources, circa mid-1990s used 2.5 percent. PRB, 2002, uses 2.2 precent.

17. PRB, 2002.

18. UN Statistics Bureau, 2001, 47 percent; PRB, 2002, 48 percent.

19. UNAIDS and Government of Burundi statistics, supported by the UN Population Division 1999 figures.

20. PRB, 2002, 3 percent. Elders had declined from 8 percent in 1965, to 4.4 percent in 1995, to 3 percent in 2002.

21. UN Statistics Bureau, 2001.

22. School attendance data from UNICEF, 2001 and 2002.

23. UNICEF, 2001. In addition, three were 50–57 percent, four were 57–82 percent.

24. Ibid.

25. Ibid.

26. UNICEF, 2002. The UNDP literacy statistics for 2000–2001 were 38 percent female and 55 percent male.

27. U.S. Department of State, *Handbook* (1966).

28. U.S. Government, *Burundi: A Geographic Profile of a Potential Crisis Area*, April 1995.

29. Ibid.; Minority Rights Group (Filip Reyntjens), *Burundi: Prospects for Peace*, November 2000.

30. Ibid.

31. U.S. Embassy, Stockholm, *Country Reports on Human Rights Practices*, 2001; UN Statistics Bureau, 2000; Burundi's 1999 per capital GDP was $128; World Bank, 1998: per capita GNP was $140.

32. Ministry of Social Action and Women's Affairs, May 2001 workshop.

33. Nancy Rose Hunt, "Domesticity and Colonialism in Belgian Africa: Usumbura's *Foyer Social*, 1946–1960," *Signs* 15, no. 3 (1990): 447–74.

34. Ibid.

35. Carol Dickerman, "Urban Housing and Land Markets: Bujumbura, Burundi," University of Wisconsin–Madison Land Tenure Center Research Paper no. 97, September 1988.

36. Members of the aristocratic group, Baganwa, did have a broader, collective identity. Research would need to be conducted to examine Batwa identity, which may have had a stronger collective dimension. The same may have also been the case for Hima pastoralists.

37. UN IRIN (United Nations Investor's Relations Information Network), "IDP Camps 'Blamed' for High HIV Infection Rates," June 23, 2002.

38. PRB, 2002.

39. UN Statistics Division.

40. UNICEF, 2001, 2002.

41. PRB, 2002.

42. CEDAW/C/BDI/1.

43. UNICEF.

44. UNDP, *Human Development Report*, 2000–2001.

45. ITEKA (La Ligue Burundaise des Droits de l'Homme Iteka), *Human Rights Report*, 2001 (2002), www.ligue-iteka.bi.

46. UNICEF, 2002.

47. Ibid.

48. UNICEF, 2001.

49. UNICEF, 1998.

50. UNICEF, 2001, 2002.

51. UNICEF, 2002.

52. Human Rights Watch.

53. Central Intelligence Agency, *The World Factbook 2002*, www.cia.gov/cia/publications/factbook/geos/by.html.

54. Human Rights Watch.

55. UNICEF, 2002.

56. UN IRIN, "IDP Camps 'Blamed.'"

RESOURCE GUIDE

Suggested Reading

Albert, Ethel. "Women of Burundi: A Study of Social Values." In *Women of Tropical Africa*, edited by Denise Paulme. Berkeley: University of California Press, 1971.

Burke, Enid de Silva, Jennifer Klot, and Ikaweba Bunting. *Engendering Peace: Reflections on the Burundi Peace Process*. Nairobi, Kenya: UNIFEM, 2001.

Dickerman, Carol. "City Women and the Colonial Regime: Usumbura, 1939–1962." *African Urban Studies* no. 18 (Spring 1984): 33–48.

Hunt, Nancy Rose. "Domesticity and Colonialism in Belgian Africa: Usumbura's *Foyer Social*, 1946–1960." *Signs* 15 (Spring 1990): 447–74.

Nduna, Sydia, and Lorelei Goodyear. *Pain Too Deep for Tears: Assessing the Prevalence of Sexual and Gender Violence Among Burundian Refugees in Tanzania*. International Rescue Committee, 1997.

Web Sites

Burundian Women's Associations and Grassroots Peacebuilding, www.africa.upenn.edu/burundiwomen/index.htm.

CIA World Factbook, Burundi, www.odci.gov/cia/publications/factbook/geos/by.html.

ITEKA (La Ligue Burundaise des Droits de l'Homme Iteka), www.ligue-iteka.bi. Monitors and defends persons from human rights violations in Burundi by partnering with NGOs and public organizations.

United Nations Development Programme, http://hdr.undp.org.

University of Pennsylvannia, "Burundi" page, www.sas.upenn.edu/african_studies/country_specific/burundi.html.

Organizations

Association des Femmes Burundaises pour la Paix Deputé à l'Assemblé Nationale
P.O. 5721
Bujumbura, Burundi
Phone: 257-223-619
Fax: 257-223-775

Association Pour la Promotion Economique de la Femme (APEF)
B.P. 5314
Bujumbura, Burundi
Phone: 257-213-375
Fax: 257-213-855

Women, small enterprises, credit, savings.

Centre de Promotion Feminine (SOCCODEFI)
B.P. 3450
Bujumbura, Burundi

Collectif d'Actions pour le Development Communautaire et Industriel (CADIC)
P.O. Box 386
Bujumbura, Burundi

Collectif des Associations et ONGs Feminines du Burundi (CAFOB)
B.P. 561
Bujumbura, Burundi
Phone: 257-21-77-58
Fax: 257-21-84-09
Email: cafob@coinf.com, ruvakubusa@yahoo.fre

Igaa Ishiraha Muse Rud Guteza Imbere Abakenuez
Bujumbura, Burundi
Phone: 257-224-167
Fax: 257-213-709

Pain Pour Les Desherites
B.P. 6607
Bujumbura, Burundi
Phone: 1-407-726-5034
Fax: 1-407-726-5034

Swaa Burundi
B.P. 6301
Bujumbura, Burundi
Phone: 257-211-432
Fax: 257-241-533
Email: swaabdi@cbinf.com

Union des Femmes Burundaises
B.P. 2910

Bujumbura, Burundi
Phone: 257-22-66-70

Women for Peace—Burundi
INSS Quarter, Burundi
Phone: 257-223-331

SELECTED BIBLIOGRAPHY

Bukuru, Marguerite, and Marie-Rose Hatungimana. "Strategies and Programmes for the Promotion of Women in the Agricultural Sector of Burundi." In *International Conference, Women in the Development Process*. Berlin: German Foundation for International Development, 1991.

Dickerman, Carol. "Urban Housing and Land Markets: Bujumbura, Burundi." University of Wisconsin–Madison Land Tenure Center Research Paper no. 97. September 1988.

Human Rights Watch. *Proxy Targets: Civilians in the War in Burundi*. New York: Human Rights Watch, March 1998.

———. *Seeking Protection: Addressing Sexual and Domestic Violence in Tanzania's Refugee Camps*. New York: Human Rights Watch, 2000.

ITEKA (La Ligue Burundaise des Droits de l'Homme Iteka). *Human Rights Report*, 2001 (2002). www.ligue-iteka.bi.

Minority Rights Group (Filip Reyntjens). *Burundi: Prospects for Peace*. November 2000.

Population Reference Bureau (PRB). *2002 World Population Data Sheet*.

UN IRIN (United Nations Investor's Relations Information Network). "IDP Camps 'Blamed' for High HIV Infection Rates." June 23, 2002.

UN Statistical Burea. *The World's Women 2000: Trends and Statistics*. New York: United Nations, 2000.

UNFPA (United Nations Population Fund). *State of the World*, 1999.

UNICEF. *A Humanitarian Appeal for Children and Women, January–December 2002: Burundi*. 2002.

U.S. Department of State. *Background Note: Burundi*, August 2002.

U.S. Embassy, Stockholm. *Country Reports on Human Rights Practices*, 2001.

3

CAMEROON

Melinda Adams

PROFILE OF CAMEROON

Cameroon is a geographically, culturally, and linguistically diverse country located in west-central Africa. It covers 184,000 square miles and is approximately the size of California. Cameroon's climate and geography vary from region to region, stretching from the densely forested and tropical climate of the south, to the more sparsely vegetated and drier climate of the central grassfields, to the semiarid Sahel of the north. Cameroon's geographical diversity is matched by its ethnic diversity. Members of more than 200 ethnic groups live in Cameroon. These include the Bamiléké and Bamoun of the central grassfields, the Bassa and Duala of the southern coastal regions, the Beti, Bulu, Fang, and Bakas of the southern forests, and the Fulbe and Kirdi of the north.

The presence of so many ethnic groups contributes to Cameroon's linguistic diversity. English and French are Cameroon's two official languages, but over 250 languages and dialects are spoken in Cameroon. Pidgin serves as a lingua franca in the West, and Fulfulde plays a similar role in the North.

Cameroon has a mixed colonial legacy. Germany, France, and Britain have all controlled parts of

Cameroon's territory. Cameroon was a German colony from 1884 to 1916. The Allies took control of Cameroon from Germany in 1916, and in 1922 Cameroon was officially placed under British and French mandates. France ruled the bulk of the territory as part of French Central Africa. Britain controlled a significantly smaller portion of Cameroon (approximately one-fifth of the total area), administering it as part of Nigeria. The French-controlled territory gained independence on January 1, 1960. On October 1, 1961 the southern portion of the British trust territory joined the already independent French-speaking Cameroon to form the Federal Republic of Cameroon (the northern portion voted to join Nigeria). In 1972, Cameroon's official name was changed to the United Republic of Cameroon. In 1984, Cameroon once again changed its official name to the Republic of Cameroon. Cameroon is divided into ten administrative provinces (Adamaoua, Center, East, Far North, Littoral, North, Northwest, West, South, and Southwest).

Cameroon is dominated by a strong presidency. The legislature and the judiciary are subordinate to the president and the party. A single party, formerly called the Cameroon National Union and now known as the Cameroon People's Democratic Movement, has been in power since independence. Even though opposition parties were legalized in 1990, presidential and legislative elections have been marred by fraud, by the blatant intimidation of the opposition, and by manipulation. Since independence, there have been two presidents of Cameroon; no president has come to power as a result of an election. The first president, Ahmadou Ahidjo, led Cameroon from independence until 1982. Paul Biya came to power in 1982 through a constitutional transfer of power. According to a 1996 constitutional amendment, which has yet to be fully implemented, the president is elected for a seven-year term, which is renewable once.

In the 1960s and 1970s, Cameroon was one of the more prosperous states in Africa. Its oil resources and favorable agricultural conditions contributed to its economic success. Cameroon's principal exports include oil, cocoa, coffee, and cotton. The steep drop in commodity prices in the mid-1980s and the 50 percent devaluation of the CFA franc in January 1994 impacted the Cameroonian economy negatively. Since the late 1980s, the Cameroonian government has engaged in a number of International Monetary Fund (IMF) and World Bank structural adjustment programs, which have required painful austerity measures. Cameroon is a member of the World Bank and IMF Heavily Indebted Poor Countries initiative, which grants debt relief to the poorest countries. The initiative reduces debt service obligations and frees money for spending on health care, HIV/AIDS, education, and other social services. Currently the per capita gross national product in Cameroon is approximately $607.[1]

Cameroon has an estimated population of around 15 million people.[2] The overall male to female ratio is 1.01:1.00.[3] The male to female ratio is slightly higher at birth (1.03:1.00), but lower among the population sixty-five years and older (0.86:1.00). The infant mortality rate is 70.87 deaths per 1,000 live births,[4] and the maternal mortality rate is 550 per 100,000 births.[5] The average birth rate is 4.88 children born to each woman.[6] Overall life expectancy at birth is 54.82 years. Males have a life expectancy of 54.01 years, while that of females is 55.64.[7]

OVERVIEW OF WOMEN'S ISSUES

Given Cameroon's incredible diversity it is difficult to generalize about the position of women in Cameroonian society. Women's roles and conditions vary along religious, cultural, and class lines. Nevertheless, one can point to a gap between legal rights and actual practice that cuts across these various divisions. Generally, Cameroonian law grants women the same legal rights as men; yet in reality, discrimination against women is prevalent in economic, political, and social spheres.

Both domestic and international law affirm equality of the sexes. The preamble to Cameroon's constitution claims: "We, the people of Cameroon, *declare* that the human person without distinction as to race, religion, sex or belief, possesses inalienable and sacred rights."[8] Cameroon signed the Convention for the Elimination of Discrimination against Women without reservations on June 6, 1983, and acceded to it in August 23, 1994. In reality, however, certain customary practices impede Cameroonian women's ability to enjoy the rights guaranteed in these laws. These practices constrain women's ability to freely marry and divorce, to work without their husband's consent, and to inherit property. Moreover, Cameroonian women are less likely to go to school and generally earn less money than their male counterparts.

EDUCATION

Opportunities

Women in Cameroon tend to be less educated than men. Increasing girls' and women's access to education is a crucial component of any program designed to effect long-term change in gender roles and status. According to Cameroonian law, education is compulsory for all children between the ages of six and fourteen. In reality, however, girls have unequal access to education in Cameroon, particularly in the north. The gap in school attendance rates between boys and girls widens as the level of education increases. Sixty-nine percent of school-aged boys are enrolled in primary school, while only 66 percent of girls are enrolled. Thirty-two percent of boys and only 23 percent of girls are enrolled in secondary school.[9] School attendance rates for females drop even more steeply at the postsecondary level. A 1992 study by the Ministry of Women's Affairs found that women composed only 23 percent of postsecondary students.[10]

Recently more women are beginning to enter higher education. For example, of the 2,317 students offered admission for the 2001–2002 school year at the University of Buea, one of six state-run universities in Cameroon, 1,175 were female (50.7 percent) and 1,142 were male (49.3 percent).[11]

Both cultural and economic factors affect girls' access to education. The highest disparities between boys' and girls' education levels occur in the north, which is predominantly Muslim. During periods of economic downturn, school attendance rates for girls decline more rapidly than boys' attendance rates, indicating a preference for the education of boys.[12] Parents must pay uniform and book fees for primary school. Secondary school, due to tuition, is even more costly. These fees make education unaffordable for many children. Parents often must choose which children to send to school and which to keep at home.

Literacy

Girls' lower school attendance rates lead to lower literacy rates among women. The overall literacy rate, defined as the age of citizens fifteen years or older who can read and write, is 63 percent in Cameroon. Literacy rates vary substantially by gender: 75 percent of males are literate, while only 52 percent of women can read and write.[13]

EMPLOYMENT AND ECONOMICS

There are few legal provisions that explicitly constrain women's ability to fully participate in the Cameroonian economy. Still, women make up only about 32 percent of those participating in the formal economy, compared with men, who make up 68 percent of the labor force.[14] Women traders and providers of services like hairdressing and tailoring compose a significant portion of the informal sector. Women also contribute significantly to agricultural production.

Farming

Women produce an estimated 90 percent of food crops in Cameroon.[15] Women's contributions to agricultural production vary according to region. In general, women tend to cultivate subsistence crops while men primarily grow cash crops like coffee and cocoa. Some women grow cash crops as well. One consequence of women's concentration in food rather than cash crop production is that they generally earn less than their male counterparts. Women's lack of landownership limits their production of cash crops, forcing them to cultivate short-term crops rather than invest in cash crops that take several growing seasons to produce a profit. This gendered division of labor is especially strong in the western grassfields and the southern and eastern forest regions.

In the north, women contribute to the production of communal millet and sorghum fields and grow staple food crops in private plots. Depending on the region, women's agricultural responsibilities may also include the processing and marketing of fish, the raising of poultry or other livestock, and the processing of milk products. On average, women in rural areas put in 1.5 to 3 times more hours in a workday than men.[16]

In the past, women responded to this heavy workload by forming small, cooperative farming groups. Beginning in the 1920s, groups of approximately ten or twelve women began farming individual members' plots each day until every member's field had been covered.[17] As wage employment grew, participation in work groups declined. Yet women continue to participate actively in other forms of cooperative organizations.

Small-scale women's projects and corn mill societies enjoyed a relatively strong presence in the 1950s and 1960s. In 1959, the Department of Education bought fifteen corn mills and made them available on loan to several communities. Each society numbered around 75 to 100 women. All society members shared in the purchase and operation of a corn mill. Members paid a monthly fee for the use of the mill. By the end of the first year, thirty villages had repaid their loans, and the government had purchased other mills to distribute to different communities. In the early 1960s, the mill societies spread rapidly. At their height, over 200 societies existed, encompassing some 15,000 members.[18] Often these societies took on additional activities like soap making, poultry raising, or farming of society-owned fields.

In the 1970s, the women's wing of the Cameroon National Union organized women into palm-oil cooperatives in the Southwest and Northwest Provinces, the latter of which were generally more successful and enduring than the former.[19]

The Cameroon Development Corporation (CDC) is the second largest employer in Cameroon, overshadowed only by the government. The CDC produces tea, bananas, palms, and rubber. In an attempt to strengthen the Cameroonian economy, the CDC cultivates tropical plants, processes them, and produces finished products for sale in domestic and international markets. Many women work on the various CDC estates as laborers and, increasingly, in management positions.

Paid Employment

The constitution states that "every person shall have the right and the obligation to work."[20] Similarly, the labor code recognizes every citizen's right to work and considers work a national duty. Labor legislation also guarantees the right to a healthy and secure working environment. To this end, women are prohibited from working night shifts in industrial jobs. All workers are also, at least theoretically, entitled to paid vacations and retirement, health, and disability benefits. The reach of these benefits is limited, however, to those workers employed in the formal sector, a small percentage of the total working population.

Legally, women have the right to equal pay for the same work, equal opportunities for employment, and free choice of a profession or employment. Yet in practice, discrimination against women is prevalent. Women, on average, are paid significantly less than men. The pay disparity may be partially attributable to the fact that men tend to have more seniority than women do. Women continue to be underrepresented in both the private and public sectors. Discrimination is especially strong in the hiring process in the private sector. A 1981 law permits a husband to oppose his wife's employment on the grounds that it adversely affects the home and family. This law directly contradicts both the constitution and the labor code. Still, due to the existence of this provision, employers may seek the husband's permission before hiring a married woman.

Informal Economic Activities

Women are active in the informal sector and comprise the vast majority of petty traders. The economic crisis in the 1980s and 1990s pushed many women to engage in informal-sector activities as a means of coping with growing unemployment and as a way to supplement declining incomes. Even women employed in the formal sector began to supplement their incomes with informal business activities.

Entrepreneurship

Women entrepreneurs are well represented in the catering, tailoring, food processing, and retail trade sectors. The majority of these businesses are quite small and most female entrepreneurs are working at the subsistence level. They generally work alone or rely on help from family members. Lack of access to credit, high competition, lack of business training, and heavy domestic responsibilities limit the growth of women's businesses.

Support for Mothers/Caretakers

Maternal Leave

Cameroon's labor legislation specifically protects pregnant women's right to work and provides for paid maternity leave. Legal provisions enable pregnant women to break employment contracts unilaterally without penalty if their health status no longer allows them to perform their work. Cameroonian law also prohibits dismissals linked to pregnancy or marital status. Pregnant women have fourteen weeks of paid maternity leave that can be extended for six additional weeks in case of illness. Women on leave are compensated at a rate equal to their salary before their work was interrupted. Women are also entitled to nursing breaks for fifteen months after the child's birth.

While Cameroonian labor law provides for maternal leave, women sometimes find it difficult to fully benefit from this guarantee. Cameroonian women, particularly those in professional positions, have noted that women often face pressure to give up all or part of their maternity leave to keep their jobs.[21] Moreover, only a small percentage of female workers, those employed in the formal sector, are entitled to these maternity benefits.

Inheritance, Property, and Land Rights

As in other spheres, women's legal rights and actual experience diverge sharply in the areas of landownership and inheritance rights. The constitution states that the right to "ownership shall mean the right guaranteed to every person by law to use, enjoy and dispose of property."[22] Theoretically, legal provisions governing property rights and landownership do not discriminate against women. In practice, however, laws are interpreted in such ways that disadvantage women. Women's inheritance rights are equal to those of men. Still, customary practices often prohibit women from inheriting land and property because women are expected to marry and join a different family.

Since women often lack a regular income and substantial collateral, such as land, which are required by banks to obtain loans, they turn to alternative sources for credit. Indigenous credit associations, a type of cooperative organization, are prevalent in contemporary Cameroon. The majority of Cameroonian women are members of at least one rotating savings and credit association. The laws governing financial institutions do not explicitly discriminate against women. Again, however, the vast majority of women in Cameroon have a difficult time obtaining credit through banks and credit unions because they fail to meet the financial criteria required by these institutions. Indigenous forms of credit offer women without access to bank loans a way to obtain larger sums of money.

There are at least two types of common local credit associations: (1) the "meeting" and (2) the *njangi* groups, called *tontine* in French and also commonly referred to as rotating savings and credit associations (ROSCAs).[23] Not all credit associations in Cameroon are gender-based; some operate according to ethnic affiliation. Women's credit associations, however, are among the most common and successful because women are more likely to return their loans. Women's meetings, unlike ethnic-based meetings, require savings and grant loans to members at low interest rates. Meetings also serve important social functions. *Njangi* groups may have evolved from cooperative farm work groups. In both, women work together and take turns reaping the benefits of their cooperation. In general,

Business leader at gathering of businesswomen, Cameroon. Photo © TRIP/ASK.

njangi members meet at a regular time and place and pool money or other resources. The money or in-kind contributions are distributed to members on a rotating basis. *Njangi* groups may be personal or impersonal. Personal groups meet regularly and have important social as well as economic functions. Women come together to pool resources, share experiences, and learn new skills, which members can put to use to start individual or group businesses. Many women's groups have one or more *njangi* group to help members raise funds for a variety of purposes, including paying children's school fees, buying kitchen equipment, and raising capital to start small businesses. In addition, personal *njangi* groups support members in times of joy and sorrow, coming together to celebrate births and marriages and mourn deaths. Impersonal ones do not have regular meetings; their primary purpose is to exchange resources.

In addition to indigenous credit associations, a number of national and international nongovernmental organizations (NGOs) give credit to women in Cameroon. Often these NGOs work with established women's groups. In general, the NGO disburses funds to a women's group, which then grants loans to individual members. Although loans are generally given to an individual, the entire group is held accountable for the repayment of the loan. By working with women's groups rather than individual women, NGOs usually achieve a higher repayment rate.

Social/Government Programs

Structural Adjustment

The structural adjustment programs supported by the IMF and the World Bank call for severe cuts in state expenditures and the privatization of services including health care and education. These programs have made it difficult for the government to address these problems. Even if the state were not constrained by budgetary considerations, it lacks the political will to make the status of women a priority. Nevertheless, the rise of women's organizations in the past decade has increased the visibility of women's issues within Cameroon. Nongovernmental organizations and other women's groups play important social, development, political, and advocacy roles.

FAMILY AND SEXUALITY

Gender Roles and Division of Labor

Family relations are currently governed by the civil code, since no comprehensive family code exists. In 1990, a proposal was made to develop a family code, an initiative supported by a number of non-governmental organizations, but it has yet to be adopted. Despite the commitment of numerous organizations to issues related to the family and sexuality in Cameroon, the gap between the letter of the law and de facto realities remains as marked in these areas as elsewhere.

Marriage

There are multiple sources of marriage law in Cameroon.[24] The civil code and a 1981 law on civil status explicitly govern marriage. The 1857 Matrimonial Clauses Act, covering marriage in the former West Cameroon, the 1870 Married Women's Property Act, recognizing women's right to own property, and several East Cameroon statutes are also relevant. Additionally, various customary practices affect both marriage and divorce.

Multiple marriage regimes exist in Cameroon. The bride and groom can choose to have a monogamous or polygamous marriage, although polyandry (multiple husbands) is not permitted. They also decide whether they want joint or separate property. In 1991, approximately 39 percent of Cameroonian women were in polygamous marriages.[25] The couple selects the marriage regime at a ceremony before a registered official, and the selected regime is noted on the marriage certificate. In addition to determining the nature of the marriage, the selected marriage regime affects where spouses settle grievances. In general, couples married polygamously settle disputes in customary courts while those married monogamously settle grievances in civil courts. Women tend to fare better in civil courts.

The minimum age for marriage is fifteen for females and eighteen for males. In reality, however, early marriage continues to take place in some areas of the country. In the Far North, Adamaoua, and Northwest provinces, marriage sometimes occurs as early as eight or nine, although in general it is not until the girl reaches puberty that she leaves her parents to live with her husband. The average age of first marriage varies according to place of residence. Residents of Yaoundé and Douala, Cameroon's two largest cities, tend to marry at a later age than residents of smaller cities and rural areas. Overall the average age of first marriage appears to be slightly increasing. On average, women between the ages of 25 and 49 first married at 16.5, while the average age of first marriage for women of ages 20 to 24 is 17.3.[26]

Customs governing both courtship and marriage vary by ethnic group, and there is significant variation in marriage practices across regions. Cameroonian law requires that both spouses consent to the marriage for it to be considered legitimate. In reality, however, parents often select the spouse, especially for first marriages.

The concept of bridewealth is generally accepted throughout Cameroon, although the actual practice varies by region, ethnic group, and even family. Bridewealth can be defined as the "totality of goods, services, and money, which is given by the family of the groom at the request of the family of the bride in traditional marriage."[27] Under customary law, the payment of bridewealth is the foundation of a marriage. From this perspective, if there is no payment of bridewealth, there is no marriage. Additionally customary law maintains that once the bridewealth is paid the marriage continues to exist until the bridewealth is refunded. Thus despite the fact that the 1981 civil status ordinance explicitly states that the payment or nonpayment of bridewealth has no effect on the validity of the marriage, the payment of bridewealth is generally believed to be a necessary component of a legitimate marriage.

Like marriage, divorce is formally regulated by the civil code. Cameroonian law does not recognize no-fault divorce; only divorce with penalty exists. Offenses considered legitimate grounds for divorce include adultery and serious and ongoing domestic abuse.

Divorce in Cameroon is an arduous process that often leaves women impoverished. Traditional laws and courts frequently do not grant women the property that they are entitled to under civil law. To gain a portion of the property, women must present documentation that shows that they contributed to the accumulation of the estate. In general, judges grant women custody of small children, and men custody of older children. In most cases, women should be able to divorce without refunding their brideprice. The 1981 civil status ordinance, however, states that the court may demand partial or full repayment of the bridewealth "if the court feels that such a person is totally or partially responsible for the divorce."[28] Many women lack the financial means to refund the bridewealth, and it causes an additional hardship for women seeking divorce. The difficulties associated with formal divorce procedures lead many women to abandon the legal process.

Reproduction

Sex Education

In the past sex education was largely a taboo subject in Cameroon. This, however, is changing as the HIV/AIDS epidemic forces the government and NGOs to take proactive steps to stop the spread of sexually transmitted diseases. The government has recently recognized the importance of sex education in reducing the spread of AIDS and other sexually transmitted diseases and in controlling population growth. The 1992 population policy recommended expanding sex education for girls to cover such topics as contraceptive methods, sexually transmitted diseases, and AIDS. The current lack of adequate sex education leads to a range of problems including sexual promiscuity, the spread of HIV/AIDS, high school dropout rates, clandestine abortions, and prostitution.

Despite growing recognition of the importance of sex education, serious barriers to effective sex education remain. Resources devoted to sex education and family planning are inadequate. There are an insufficient number of family planning centers and women's houses, places where girls are exposed to basic sex education and small-business training, in Cameroon. Women in rural areas often do not have access to the resources provided by these facilities. Public service announcements aired on television, before film showings, and printed in the government newspaper, *The Cameroon Tribune*, generally reach only urban and suburban women. In addition, despite the government's shift from a pronatalist to a family planning policy, pronatalist attitudes remain prevalent throughout society, placing pressure on women to have children.

Nongovernmental organizations have initiated educational campaigns that seek to inform parents, teachers, and youth about family planning issues. The Cameroon National Association for Family Welfare (CAMNAFAW), for example, is one association that organizes seminars on reproductive and sexual health and family planning. CAMNAFAW, which is affiliated with the International Planned Parenthood Foundation, seeks to provide a space where people can talk freely about sexual and other health issues. At educational seminars, CAMNAFAW encourages participants to use available family planning resources and distributes condoms and other nonprescription contraceptives to women and youth.[29]

Contraception and Abortion

A 1980 law permits the sale of contraceptives in Cameroon; however, women's access to adequate family planning services is constrained by a 1990 law that prohibits birth control propaganda. A 1991 Demographic and Health Survey found that the use of modern contraceptive methods among women of childbearing age is low. Only 4.2 percent of respondents used "modern methods," and only 19.7 percent employed any type of contraceptive method at all.[30] In 1997 the government drafted a law that would permit sterilization if certain conditions were met. The proposed law only applies to women who are at least thirty-five years old and have had a minimum of five children.

Cameroonian law permits abortion in a limited number of cases. Abortion is authorized if it is necessary to save the life or protect the health of the pregnant woman and in cases where the pregnancy is the result of rape. Both the woman who has or consents to an abortion and the person who performs the procedure face fines and imprisonment if the procedure is performed outside the bounds of these criteria. Despite these penalties, abortion is known to be quite common throughout Cameroon, although exact data are unavailable. Clandestine abortions pose serious health threats to women. A 1991 study found that 40 percent of gynecological and obstetric emergency admissions were the result of clandestine abortions.[31] Few abortion cases go to court since the woman involved is unlikely to report herself. When a woman dies as a result of an abortion, however, abortion providers are severely punished.

Teen Pregnancy

Teen pregnancy is prevalent in Cameroon. Lack of access to sex education and contraceptive devices and early marriage all contribute to high teenage pregnancy rates. Education is the most effective means to combat teen pregnancy. Girls with more education tend to marry and have children later.

HEALTH

While government rhetoric emphasizes that good health is a necessary component of a productive citizenry, the overall health care situation in Cameroon is poor. Key problems include lack of adequate care for mothers and infants, low vaccination rates, especially in rural areas, and the spread of HIV/AIDS.

Health Care Access

Most Cameroonians have access to primary health care, but specialized facilities are extremely limited. In 1995 there were 29,124 hospital beds for a population of nearly 14 million.[32] A 1995 study of Cameroon's health facilities found that there were 206 hospitals, 800 health centers, 62 maternity centers, 312 dispensaries and infirmaries, and 288 pharmacies. The Ministry of Public Health reported in 1997 that there were 729 doctors in Cameroon and 11,844 health personnel.[33] On average, there is one doctor for every 12,500 people in Cameroon.[34] Thus, both facilities and staff are inadequate and are unable to sufficiently serve the entire population.

Structural adjustment programs have led to the privatization of health care. In general, prices are reasonable: the average price of a medical consultation is about a dollar, and the delivery of a child costs around ten dollars.[35] Yet even these relatively low prices place health care out of the reach of some.

Diseases and Disorders

AIDS

HIV/AIDS has had a significant impact on the Cameroonian population. Population estimates specifically take into account the excess mortality linked to AIDS; AIDS leads to lower life expectancy and population growth rates, higher infant mortality and death rates, and changes in the distribution of the population by age and sex.[36] The first AIDS case in Cameroon was reported in 1986. A September 2000 study estimated that some 937,000 people were infected with the HIV virus in Cameroon, which is 11 percent of the sexually active population.

A National Committee for the Prevention of AIDS (CNLS) was created in 1985. In July 1998, the National AIDS Prevention Department was formed to implement the CNLS policies. In September 2000, the government launched a national strategy for the fight against HIV/AIDS. Cameroon received $50 million from the World Bank for this AIDS prevention project in January 2001. The goal of Cameroon–World Bank project was to strengthen the capacity of local communities to fight the spread of AIDS.[37]

Female Genital Cutting

Female genital cutting is primarily practiced in the Far North and Southwest provinces. The prevalence of female genital cutting is estimated at 20 percent nationally.[38] Infibulation is the most common form practiced in Cameroon. Infibulation involves the partial closure of the vulva and the vaginal orifice. Clitoridectomy may be part of the surgery. No Cameroonian law specifically prohibits cutting. Certain laws addressing "grievous harm," however, are potentially applicable to the practice. Article 277 of the penal code states, for example: "Whoever permanently deprives another of the use of the whole or of any part of any member, organ or sense shall be punished with imprisonment for from ten to twenty years."[39] The Ministry of Women's Affairs has criticized female genital cutting and has undertaken a campaign against traditional practices harmful to women. A number of Cameroonian NGOs have also initiated education and awareness campaigns in an effort to eliminate the practice.

POLITICS AND LAW

Leadership and Decision-making

Levels of women's representation and participation in formal political institutions are relatively low. During the single-party era, the ruling political party gradually increased the number of women in decisionmaking positions. With the return to multipartyism in 1990, women face greater competition at both the intra- and interparty levels and women's representation in municipal councils, parliament, and the government has stagnated or declined. Despite relatively low levels of representation in formal political institutions, women wield considerable power that stems from informal sources such as their status as mothers and primary food providers. Older women, who are past childbearing age, are particularly influential and have used their status to challenge the government.

Throughout Cameroonian history, women have been quite dynamic. In the 1950s, for example, women were active participants in the struggle for independence and even launched a women's political party. Women also participated in the lengthy strikes and prodemocracy rallies of the early 1990s. Today, women are active in a vast array of grassroots and nongovernmental organizations in addition to participating in political parties.

Women hold few elected or appointed political positions in Cameroon. Cameroon is divided into ten provinces, which are partitioned into fifty-six divisions. Each province is headed by an appointed provincial governor, and each division is headed by a Senior Divisional Officer, who is also appointed. No woman has ever held either position. A 1996 study conducted by the United Nations found that women comprised only 2.6 percent of ministerial positions in Cameroon and 5.3 percent of sub-ministerial positions.[40] In 2003 there were two women ministers in Cameroon: Madeleine Fouda was the minister of social affairs and Catherine Bakang Mbock was the minister of women's affairs. Several other women have held high political offices since independence, including Yaou Assiatou, the former minister of women's affairs, and Dorothy Njeuma, the current vice chancellor of the University of Buea. Women in the government tend to be confined to leadership positions within social ministries, particularly the Ministry of Education, the Ministry of Social Affairs, and the Ministry of Women's Affairs.

Just as women hold few high-level appointed positions, their representation in elected offices is relatively low. While women's representation in the legislature gradually increased from one in 1960 to twenty-seven in 1990, it has declined in the last decade. Twenty-four women members of parliament were elected in the first multiparty election in 1992 and only ten were elected in 1997. The representation of women fell from a high of 15 percent in the 1988–1992 legislature[41] to 5.6 percent in the 1997–2002 legislature and then went up to 9 percent in 2002.[42] This dramatic drop in women's representation in the legislature is primarily the result of political parties' unwillingness to support female candidates. With the return of multiparty competition, political parties view female candidates as an electoral liability, choosing instead to nominate "safer" male candidates. In addition, in comparison with men, women tend to have less money, political experience, and time to devote to campaigns, which are important resources in a more competitive political environment.

Women also comprise only a fraction of the municipal councilors. The national mean for women's representation at the municipal level was 9.19 percent in 1987 and 13.69 percent in 1996, thus indicating a slight increase in women's representation.[43] The national figures, however, hide vast regional disparities. In the 1996 municipal elections, for example, women's representation ranged from a low of 4.55 percent in the Far North province to a high of 15.64 in the South province.[44]

Analysts offer a number of explanations for women's low levels of representation in elected positions. Many cite the lack of political will on the part of parties, which marginalize women in investiture operations. Political parties tend to place few women on electoral lists as substantive candidates. When women are invested as candidates, they are often placed low on lists or are on lists outside the party's electoral stronghold.[45] Women's overall lower level of education, their lower socioeconomic status, and their heavier workload also constrain their ability to run for public office. Likewise, social norms may discourage females from running for political office. Quite often women simply lack the finances necessary to run an expensive campaign. Finally, many women lack training in how to campaign effectively and hold a public office.

While women are among the most active political militants in Cameroon, coming out in greater numbers than men for political rallies and events, they are often confined to nonpolitical, nondecisionmaking roles. Within Cameroonian political parties, women are typically ghettoized in women's wings, which privilege social and development issues over explicitly political aims. Women's wings relegate women to positions outside the realm of high politics. Their primary roles tend to be to cook, sing, and dance. An historical precedent to contemporary women's wings, the Women's Cameroon National Union (WCNU), had no political purposes. Its role was to extend the "social aspects of the party's programme."[46] The Women's Cameroon People's Democratic Movement (WCPDM), a wing of the contemporary Cameroon People's Democratic Movement, has more formal responsibilities. Unlike its WCNU predecessor, the WCPDM can hold economic, social, cultural, and *political* meetings. This is largely due to women's demands for more active participation in party decisionmaking.[47] In addition, some women are opting to join the main organ of the CPDM rather than the women's wing to gain more influence within the party.

Out of the 168 parties currently registered in Cameroon, only two do not have a separate women's wing.[48] The Social Democratic Front is one party that seeks to integrate women into the mainstream party apparatus. The SDF, which was the first opposition party to be formed in May 1990, is one of the most vocal and strongest opponents of the ruling CPDM.

Quota Laws

No national gender quota laws exist in Cameroon. Both the ruling Cameroon People's Democratic Movement (CPDM) and the major opposition party, the Social Democratic Front (SDF), have, however, set intraparty gender quotas. In 1996 the CPDM announced a 30 percent quota for female candidates in future elections. Similarly, the SDF adopted a 25 percent quota on all leadership positions within the party. Neither party has fully implemented the quotas. Since the quotas exist at party rather than the state level, they are difficult to enforce. In the June 2002 parliamentary and municipal elections, both the CPDM and the SDF presented lists that failed to meet with their own quotas. Committed implementation of intraparty quota systems is especially necessary in Cameroon, since the electoral system works on the basis of lists assembled by parties. Under this system, women's names generally appear at the bottom of parties' lists. After elections, only those candidates listed at or near the top of parties' lists assume seats.

Women's Rights

In theory, domestic and international laws ensure the equal rights of men and women in Cameroon. In reality, women continue to face discrimination in a number of realms. Cameroon signed the Convention for the Elimination of Discrimination Against Women (CEDAW) on June 6, 1983, and acceded to the treaty on August 23, 1994, without reservations. State parties to CEDAW must harmonize domestic laws with the convention's provisions. In an effort to comply with this requirement, the Cameroonian government has adopted several legal measures that aim to address areas of discrimination and has created new positions and institutions that focus on women's issues. The government established a Ministry of Women's Affairs in 1984. In 1988 this ministry was merged with the Ministry of Social Affairs. In December 1997 the government reestablished a separate Ministry of Women's Affairs. Following the 1995 Beijing Conference, the government initiated a national action plan for the advancement of women. Legal reforms include the elimination of the requirement of the husband's authorization for the wife's travel abroad, the provisioning of housing benefits to women workers on an equal basis with men, and the readmission of girls suspended from school due to pregnancy. Women's organizations worked with the Ministry of Women's Affairs to achieve these legal reforms.

Cameroon's national policy for women's advancement developed by the Ministry of Women's Affairs in coordination with civil society actors as a follow-up to the Beijing Conference outlines seven major policy guidelines: (1) improve women's quality of life, (2) improve women's legal status, (3) enhance female human resources in all areas of development, (4) ensure women's effective participation in decisionmaking, (5) protect and promote the girl child, (6) eliminate violence against women, and (7) improve the institutional framework for mainstreaming women in development.[49]

These policies and measures have improved the status of women in Cameroon, yet there are still significant barriers to women's full equality. The government has yet to approve a comprehensive family code, which would harmonize Cameroon's various legal codes, integrate international treaties into domestic law, and better protect women's interests within the family. The Ministry of Women's Affairs is insufficiently funded; central, provincial, and local offices lack the resources to fulfill their broad mandates. In addition, certain legal and customary measures disadvantage women. The 1981 civil status ordinance, for example, allows a husband to oppose his wife's right to work if the protest is made "in the interest of the family." This law contradicts the preamble to the constitution, which recognizes that "every person shall have the right and the obligation to work."[50] Customary practices continue to impede women's ability to own property, work outside the home, and marry freely.

Women's Movements

Although women's participation and representation in formal political institutions has stagnated or even declined in the 1990s, the same decade has been marked by a rise in women's organizations. The growth of non-state women's groups is a positive development that can supplement and challenge state programs to improve the status of women in Cameroon.

Women have played key roles in Cameroonian history. In the 1940s and 1950s, women made important contributions to Cameroon's nationalist movement. Women sent thousands of petitions to the UN Trusteeship Council exposing abuses carried out by the French regime in Cameroon. In 1958, Kom women in the British West Cameroons launched a three-year uprising, known as the Anlu Rebellion, which protested colonial policies affecting women, including rising taxes and laws regulating farming techniques.

Women's activism has continued and has, in fact, even expanded in postcolonial Cameroon, especially since the 1990s. Women have been active participants in the prodemocracy campaigns that spread across Cameroon in the 1990s, and women's organizations along with other civil society groups have put pressure on the government to implement democratic reforms. The government dissolved one women's organization, the Collectif des Femmes pour le Renouveau, and several other civil society organizations for participating in prodemocracy rallies. Women participated in the "ghost town" or *ville mort* campaigns, nationwide strikes sustained for several months in 1991. Following the announcement of the official results of the highly contested 1992 presidential election, a group of women in the Northwest province protected the defeated SDF candidate, John Fru Ndi, by surrounding his compound and stripping when the military made a move against him. According to the official results, Paul Biya won 39.9 percent of the votes cast in the 1992 presidential election while Fru Ndi won 35.9 percent of the vote. National and international observers cited widespread electoral fraud and questioned the validity of the official outcome. Demonstrations and violent incidents occurred in the Northwest province following the announcement of official results. In response to these demonstrations, the government declared a state of emergency in the area that lasted for several months after the elections. In October 1994, thirty women blocked the road to Bamenda, the capital of the Northwest province, to demand the release of nine opposition members whom the government detained for arranging a prodemocracy rally. In both these instances, women elders used their status within the community to challenge the government. Women have been both leaders and active participants in Cameroonian social movements.

The 1990s were marked by a rise in women's organizations in Cameroon. In fact, women's associations comprise one of the most active segments in contemporary Cameroonian society. Political openings in the early 1990s cleared the way for the rise of a stronger and more autonomous non-state sector. A 1990 law allowing for freedom of association facilitated the creation of new women's organizations. As of April 1999, over 200 women's organizations had registered with the Ministry of Women's Affairs.[51] The objectives and strategies of these organizations vary enormously. Some focus on women's human rights, others concentrate on education, health, and development issues. Strategies employed by these diverse groups include conducting research, organizing educational seminars and workshops, offering counseling and legal aid to women, lobbying the government, and networking with national, regional, and international organizations.

Lesbian Rights

While groups focusing on women's rights in general exist in Cameroon, few organizations specifically focus on gay and lesbian rights. Homosexuality is a crime in Cameroon, although it is generally not prosecuted. The penal code prohibits same-sex sexual relationships, stating: "Whoever has sexual relations with a person of the same sex shall be punished with imprisonment for from six months to five years and a fine from 20,000 to 200,000 francs."[52] There is no evidence, however, that anyone is currently in prison for violating this law. Same-sex marriages are also prohibited in

Cameroonian law. There is some evidence of a small gay community in Douala and Yaoundé, but overall gays and lesbians are not very visible in Cameroon.

RELIGION AND SPIRITUALITY

Cameroon is a religiously diverse state. Approximately 40 percent of the population is Christian and 20 percent is Muslim. The remaining 40 percent practice traditional religions or no religion.[53] The Christian population is more or less evenly divided between Catholics and Protestants. The Anglophone (Northwest and Southwest) provinces are predominantly Protestant, while the Francophone southern and western regions are generally Catholic. The northern provinces are largely Muslim. Certain religious doctrines within both Christianity and Islam adversely affect women.

Women's Roles

Women are generally more active in religious movements than men are; yet most religious groups are still led by men. Some Christian denominations allow women to assume leadership positions and even be ordained as ministers; others restrict women to less influential roles. Christian women's groups are some of the most active women's organizations in Cameroon. The Catholic Women's Association and the Presbyterian Christian Women's Fellowship are among the largest church groups with chapters across the country.

Religious Law

The Cameroonian constitution affirms that the "State shall be secular. The neutrality and independence of the State in respect of all religions shall be guaranteed."[54] In addition to affirming the secular status of the state, the constitution also guarantees freedom of religion and worship. Relations between the state and religious groups are outlined in the Law on Religious Congregations. Religious groups must be approved and registered with the Ministry of Territorial Administration. Currently Christian, Muslim, and Baha'i groups are registered with the state. The state does not register traditional religious organizations on the grounds that the practice of traditional religion is personal and private to a particular ethnic group or locality.[55]

VIOLENCE

Domestic Violence

Although reliable statistics are unavailable, domestic violence is common throughout Cameroon. No gender-specific assault laws exist in Cameroon.

Judges' acceptance of the principle that husbands have "disciplinary rights" over their wives has exacerbated the problem.[56]

Since the early 1990s, a number of NGOs have been working to raise awareness about and end the practice of domestic violence. These include the Association for the Struggle against Violence Towards Women (ALVF), the Cameroon Association of Women Jurists, and SOS Battered Women. The story behind the formation of ALVF highlights the seriousness of domestic abuse in Cameroon. Three women were killed in a two-month period in 1990 and no one was brought to justice for these deaths. Responding to these deaths and the lack of justice, members of the Collectif des Femmes pour le Renouveau founded a new organization, the ALVF, in November 1991 that focuses specifically on domestic violence.

Rape/Sexual Assault

The penal code stipulates that any person who forces a woman to have sexual relations with him will be sentenced to five to ten years in prison. Legal opinion is divided over the issue of marital rape. In general, forced sexual relations within a marriage are not recognized as rape.

Trafficking in Women and Children

Child trafficking does exist in Cameroon. An International Labour Organisation conducted a study in Yaoundé, Douala, and Bamenda and found that trafficking composed 84 percent (530,000 out of an estimated 610,000) of child laborers in Cameroon.[57] In most cases, agents pay parents the equivalent of a few dollars for a child claiming that they will train or educate the child. These agents then transport the children to urban areas where they are sold as child laborers and forced to work for little pay. There has been little study of trafficking of adults in Cameroon, although there is some evidence that trafficking of adults, especially women, also exists.

OUTLOOK FOR THE TWENTY-FIRST CENTURY

The status of women in Cameroon is slowly improving. Domestic and international legal guarantees of equality exist. The government has indicated a commitment to improving the status of women in Cameroon by signing CEDAW. Still, in actual practice, women lack equal rights. A long-term strategy for improving the position of women in Cameroon must focus on increasing girls' access to education, especially at the secondary and university levels. Another area of concern is the low percentage of women in decisionmaking positions. The experience of other African states has shown that national gender quotas are an effective means of quickly increasing women's representation in government. The combination of new state institutions designed to monitor and promote the status of women and an active and growing nonstate women's movement has the capacity to significantly improve the position of women in Cameroonian society.

NOTES

1. Bureau of Democracy, Human Rights and Labor, U.S. Department of State, *Cameroon Country Report on Human Rights Practices for 2000*, www.state.gov/g/drl/rls/hrrpt/2000/af/index.cfm?docid=713.

2. Central Intelligence Agency, *The World Factbook 2000*, "Cameroon," www.cia.gov/cia/publications/factbook/geos/cm.html.

3. Ibid.

4. Ibid.

5. Center for Reproductive Law and Policy (CRLP) and Groupe de Recherche Femmes et Lois au Sénégal, *Women of the World: Laws and Policies Affecting Their Reproductive Lives: Francophone Africa* (New York: CRLP, 1999), 66.

6. CIA, *The World Factbook 2000*, "Cameroon." Another source states that between 1995 and 2000, the average total fertility rate is estimated at 5.3 children per woman. See CRLP, *Women of the World*, 66.

7. CIA, *The World Factbook 2000*.

8. Constitution of the Republic of Cameroon, www.richmond.edu~jpjones/confinder/cameroon.htm.

9. CRLP, *Women of the World*, 66.

10. U.S Department of State, *Cameroon Country Report on Human Rights Practices for 2000*.

11. Joyce B. Mbongo Endeley and Shirley Ardener, "Gender-Inclusive Culture in Higher Education: Process and Challenges—The Case of the University of Buea, Cameroon," paper presented at the Women's Worlds Conference, Kampala, Uganda, July 21–26, 2002.

12. A. Aghenebit Mungwa, "The Mandatory Nature of Affirmative Action for Women's Political Rights in Cameroon," paper presented at African Studies Association, Nashville, TN, November 16–19, 2000.

13. CIA, *The World Factbook 2000*.

14. International Planned Parenthood Federation (IPPF), "Country Profile: Cameroon," http://ippfnet.ippf.org/pub/ippf_countryprofile.asp?isocode=cm.

15. "Cameroon: Country Gender Profile," www.gsid.nagoyau.ac.jp/user/prof . . . er/genderx/preview/html/body_camero.htm.

16. FAO, "Fact Sheet: Cameroon—Women, Agriculture, and Rural Development," www.fao.org/docrep/V9319e/v9319e01/html.

17. Audrey Wipper, "Women's Voluntary Associations," in *African Women South of the Sahara*, ed. Margaret Jean Hay and Sharon Stichter (New York: Longman, 1995), 165.

18. See Judy C. Bryson, *Women and Economic Development in Cameroon* (Washington, DC: Office of Women in Development, Bureau for Program and Policy Coordination, Agency for International Development, 1979); and Audrey Wipper, "Women's Voluntary Associations," 171.

19. Mark W. DeLancey, "Women's Cooperatives in Cameroon: The Cooperative Experiences of the Northwest and Southwest Provinces," *African Studies Review* 30, no. 1 (March 1987): 16.

20. Constitution of the Republic of Cameroon.

21. Center for Reproductive Law and Policy (New York) and Association Camerounaise des Femmes Juristes (ACAFEJ), Douala, Cameroon. *Women's Reproductive Rights in Cameroon: A Shadow Report*, 2000, www.crlp.org/pdf/SRCameroon00en.pdf.

22. Constitution of the Republic of Cameroon.

23. Margaret Niger-Thomas, "Women's Access to Credit in Cameroon," in *Money-Go-Rounds: The Importance of Rotating Savings and Credit Associations for Women*, ed. Shirley Ardener and Sandra Burman (Washington, DC: Berg, 1995), 98–99.

24. CRLP, *Women of the World*; CRLP and ACAFEJ, *Women's Reproductive Rights in Cameroon*, 8–10.

25. CRLP, *Women of the World*, 66.

26. Ibid.

27. Beatrice Nambangi, "Bride Price in the Cameroon Context," in *Women, Children and the Law* (Douala, Cameroon: Tencam Press), 24.

28. United Republic of Cameroon, *Civil Status Registration*, June 1981, 22–23.

29. IPPF, "Country Profiles: Cameroon."

30. CRLP, *Women of the World*, 76.

31. CRLP and ACAFEJ, *Women's Reproductive Rights in Cameroon*, 8.

32. CRLP, *Women of the World*, 72.

33. Ibid.

34. IPPF, "Country Profile: Cameroon."

35. CRLP, *Women of the World*, 72.

36. CIA, *The World Factbook 2000*.

37. World Bank, "Supporting Cameroon's Fight Against HIV/AIDS," World Bank News Release 2001/196/AFR.

38. Anika Rahman and Nahid Toubia, *Female Genital Mutilation: A Guide to Laws and Policies Worldwide* (New York: Zed Books, 2000), 117.

39. Ibid., 118.

40. United Nations, www.un.org/womenwatch/daw/public/percent.htm.

41. Mungwa, "The Mandatory Nature of Affirmative Action," 16–17.

42. Pippa Norris and Ronald Inglehart, "Cultural Obstacles to Equal Representation," *Journal of Democracy* 12, no. 3 (2001): 128.

43. Martha Simo Tumnde, "The Participation of Women in Politics and the Democratisation Process in Cameroon," *Journal of Applied Social Sciences* no. 1 (1998): 49–50.

44. Ibid., 50.

45. Rose Zang Nguele, "La Marginalisation des femmes camerounaises dans les institutions nationales," in *Femme camerounaise: Adulation et marginalisation* (Yaoundé, Cameroon: Editions Saagraph and Friedrich-Ebert-Stiftung, 1997), 32–33.

46. OFUNC, *Visages de la femme camerounaise* (Yaoundé: OFUNC, 1975), 89.

47. Mungwa, "The Mandatory Nature of Affirmative Action," 14.

48. Mungwa, "The Mandatory Nature of Affirmative Action."

49. Ministry of Women's Affairs, Policy of Women's Advancement in Cameroon, March 2000.

50. Constitution of the Republic of Cameroon, 3.

51. *Rapport du Cameroun sur le suivi de la Quatrième Conférence Mondiale sur les Femmes*, 14.

52. Behind the Mask, "Cameroon," www.mask.org.za/sections/africapercountry/cameroon.html.

53. CIA, *The World Factbook 2000*.

54. Constitution of the Republic of Cameroon.

55. U.S. Department of State, *Cameroon Country Report on Human Rights Practices for 2000.*

56. CRLP and ACAFEJ, *Women's Reproductive Rights in Cameroon,* 13.

57. U.S. Department of State, *Cameroon Country Report on Human Rights Practices for 2000.*

RESOURCE GUIDE

Suggested Reading

Ardener, Shirley, and Sandra Burman. *Money-Go-Rounds: The Importance of Rotating Savings and Credit Associations for Women.* Washington, DC: Berg, 1995. Edited volume includes chapters on rotating savings and credit associations in Africa, Asia, and diaspora communities. Two chapters specifically examine indigenous credit associations in Cameroon.

Center for Reproductive Law and Policy (CRLP) and Groupe de Recherche Femmes et Lois au Sénégal. *Women of the World: Laws and Policies Affecting Their Reproductive Lives: Francophone Africa.* New York: CRLP, 1999. Examines laws affecting women's reproductive health in a number of Francophone West African countries as well as women's practical experiences. Includes chapters on Benin, Burkina Faso, Cameroon, Chad, Côte d'Ivoire, Mali, and Senegal.

Feldman-Savelsberg, Pamela. *Plundered Kitchens, Empty Wombs: Threatened Reproduction and Identity in the Cameroon Grassfields.* Ann Arbor: University of Michigan Press, 1999. An anthropological study examining women's fears of infertility in Bangangté, a Bamiléké kingdom in Cameroon's grassfields. Examines "birth" and "fertility" not only as biological processes but also as social phenomena with culturally and historically specific meanings.

Goheen, Miriam. *Men Own the Fields, Women Own the Crops: Gender and Power in the Cameroon Grassfields.* Madison: University of Wisconsin Press, 1996. An anthropological study focusing on gender roles among the Nso' of the Northwest province.

Rahman, Anika, and Nahid Toubia, eds. *Female Genital Mutilation: A Guide to Laws and Policies Worldwide.* New York: Zed Books, 2000. Provides background and history on the practice of female genital cutting, examines international law and NGO strategies, and gives national-level legal measures.

van den Berg, Adri. *Land Right, Marriage Left: Women's Management of Insecurity in North Cameroon.* Leiden: CNWS Publication, 1997. A legal-anthropological study of insecurity among Giziga women in the Far North province. Examines the factors that contribute to women's insecurity and how women cope with rising levels of insecurity.

Web Sites

Africa South of the Sahara, www.sul.stanford.edu/depts/ssrg/africa/camer.html. Provides links to a number of web sites on Cameroon.

Association des Femmes Cameroonaise, www.gcnet.cm/afac/accueil.htm. List of Cameroonian women's associations by province and by issue area.

Center for Reproductive Law and Policy, www.crlp.org.
The Center for Reproductive Law and Policy (CRLP) focuses on women's reproductive rights. Of special interest are the report on women's reproductive rights in Cameroon and the chapter on laws and policies affecting women's reproductive rights.

CIA World Factbook, www.cia.gov/publications/factbook/geos/cm.html.
The *CIA World Factbook 2000* provides general background material on Cameroon.

Constitution Finder, www.oncampus.richmond.edu/~jjones//confinder/cameroon. html.
This site has an English-language version of Cameroon's constitution.

Human Rights Watch, www.hrw.org.
Human Rights Watch has several reports on Cameroon, including one that focuses on Cameroon's National Commission on Human Rights and Freedoms. This report is part of a larger, comparative project on government human rights commissions in Africa.

International Planned Parenthood, http://ippfnet.ippf.org.
The International Planned Parenthood Federation web site has country profiles that focus on women's sexual and reproductive health.

Inter-Parliamentary Union, www.ipu.org/wmn-e/classif.htm.
The Inter-Parliamentary Union has comparative data on women in national parliaments.

U.S. Department of State, www.state.gov/g/drl/rls/hrrpt/2000.
This U.S. Department of State web site has annual country reports on human rights records. Short sections of each report are devoted to the rights of women and children.

Organizations

Association for the Struggle Against Violence Towards Women (ALVF)
B.P. 2350
Yaoundé, Cameroon
Phone: 237-220-5294
Fax: 237-222-1873
Email: alvf@camnet.cm

AVLF seeks to eliminate all forms of violence against women through documentation, educational campaigns, lobbying the government, and collaborating with other organizations.

Cameroon Association of Women Jurists (ACAFEJ)
B.P. 14057
Yaoundé, Cameroon
Phone: 237-221-7951
Fax: 237-221-7951
Email: acafej@camnet.cm

ACAFEJ's goals are to fight against discrimination against women and children, to support the rule of law in Cameroon, to develop laws that help women and children, and to enable women lawyers to exchange information and experiences.

Federation of Women's Associations in Cameroon (FWAC)
B.P. 13729
Yaoundé, Cameroon
Phone: 237-222-4001
Fax: 237-222-4001

FWAC coordinates the activities of women's groups in Cameroon. It organizes leadership seminars, raises funds to enable women to attend international conferences, manages a database of women's groups in Cameroon, and develops educational programs.

Human Rights Clinic and Education Center (HURCLED Center)
B.P. 315
Bamenda, Cameroon
Email: bobgambuton@yahoo.com

The HURCLED Center seeks to establish a democratic and human rights culture in Cameroon. It has free legal clinics, organizes workshops and seminars, and disseminates information.

Inter African Committee on Traditional Practices Affecting the Health of Women and Children—Cameroon (IAC)
B.P. 4532
Yaoundé, Cameroon

IAC aims to eliminate traditional practices harmful to women and promote practices beneficial to women. It runs training programs, develops educational materials, launches public awareness campaigns, and engages in research.

International Federation of Women Lawyers—Cameroon (FIDA-Cameroon)
B.P. 126
Limbe, Cameroon
Phone: 237-333-2385
Fax: 237-333-2327
Email: lumah@camnet.cm, luma@cyberkoki.net

FIDA-Cameroon seeks to raise awareness about women's human rights by organizing seminars, workshops, and legal clinics and distributing its publications.

League for Women and Child Education (LEWCE)
B.P. 14702
Yaoundé, Cameroon
Phone: 237-222-4001
Fax: 237-222-4001
Email: pauline_biyong@camnet.cm

LEWCE seeks to promote civic education particularly among women and children. It lobbies government agencies, organizes seminars and workshops, produces a regular journal, *La Cité*, and disseminates various other publications.

National Association of Professional Media Women (NAPMEW)
Phone: 237-220-6842
Fax: 237-221-5691

NAPMEW's objective is to produce programs on television and radio and to carry out seminars and workshops that promote the rights of women.

National Committee of Action for the Rights of Women and Children (CADEF)
B.P. 1984
Yaoundé, Cameroon
Phone: 237-220-6675
Fax: 237-220-6675
Email: cadef@caramail.com

CADEF seeks to promote the rights of women and children by diffusing appropriate United Nations conventions, educating women and children, and investigating the origins and socioeconomic implications of discrimination against women and children.

SELECTED BIBLIOGRAPHY

Ardener, Shirley, and Sandra Burman. *Money-Go-Rounds: The Importance of Rotating Savings and Credit Associations for Women*. Washington, DC: Berg, 1995.

Boyle, Patrick M. "Parents, Private Schools, and the Politics of an Emerging Civil Society in Cameroon." *Journal of Modern African Studies* 34, no. 4 (1996): 609–22.

Bryson, Judy C. *Women and Economic Development in Cameroon*. Washington, DC: Office of Women in Development, Bureau for Program and Policy Coordination, Agency for International Development, 1979.

Center for Reproductive Law and Policy (CRLP) and Association Camerounaise des Femmes Juristes (ACAFEJ). *Laws and Policies Affecting Women's Reproductive Lives: Implementation, Enforcement, and the Reality of Women's Reproductive Lives*. New York: CRLP, 2000.

Center for Reproductive Law and Policy (CRLP) and Groupe de Recherche Femmes et Lois au Sénégal. *Women of the World: Laws and Policies Affecting Their Reproductive Lives: Francophone Africa*. New York: CRLP, 1999.

DeLancey, Mark W. *Cameroon: Dependence and Independence*. Boulder: Westview Press, 1989.

———. "Women's Cooperatives in Cameroon: The Cooperative Experiences of the Northwest and Southwest Provinces." *African Studies Review* 30, no. 1 (1987): 1–18.

Feldman-Savelsberg, Pamela. *Plundered Kitchens, Empty Wombs: Threatened Reproduction and Identity in the Cameroon Grassfields*. Ann Arbor: University of Michigan Press, 1999.

Goheen, Miriam. *Men Own the Fields, Women Own the Crops*. Madison: University of Wisconsin Press, 1996.

Hay, Margaret Jean, and Sharon Stichter, eds. *African Women South of the Sahara*. 2nd ed. New York: Longman, 1995.

Holtedahl, Lisbit. "Magic and Love on the Road to Higher Education in Cameroon." In *Transforming Female Identities: Women's Organizational Forms in West Africa*, edited by Eva Evers Rosander. Uppsala: Nordiska Afrikainstitutet, 1997.

Human Rights Internet. *African Directory: Human Rights Organizations in Sub-Saharan Africa.* Ottawa: Human Rights Internet, 1996, 19–27.

Idole Mekounde, Anastasie. "La Naissance du Groupe Nsaw-Mboum des Femmes de Ngaoundéré." In *Transforming Female Identities: Women's Organizational Forms in West Africa*, edited by Eva Evers Rosander. Uppsala: Nordiska Afrikainstitutet, 1997.

Le Vine, Victor. *The Cameroon Federal Republic.* Ithaca: Cornell University Press, 1963.

Ngassa, Vera. *Gender Approach to Court Action.* Yaoundé, Cameroon: Editions Saagraph and Friedrich-Ebert-Siftung, 1998.

Ngoh, Victor Julius. *History of Cameroon Since 1800.* Limbe, Cameroon: Presbook, 1996.

Niger-Thomas, Margaret. "Women's Access to and the Control of Credit in Cameroon: The Mamfe Case." In *Money-Go-Rounds: The Importance of Rotating Savings and Credit Associations for Women*, edited by Shirley Ardener and Sandra Burman. Washington, DC: Berg, 1995.

Rahman, Anika, and Nahid Toubia, eds. *Female Genital Mutilation: A Guide to Laws and Policies Worldwide.* New York: Zed Books, 2000.

Rowlands, Michael. "Looking at Financial Landscapes: A Contextual Analysis of ROSCAs in Cameroon." In *Money-Go-Rounds: The Importance of Rotating Savings and Credit Associations for Women*, edited by Shirley Ardener and Sandra Burman. Washington, DC: Berg, 1995.

van den Berg, Adri. *Land Right, Marriage Left: Women's Management of Insecurity in North Cameroon.* Leiden: CNWS Publications, 1997.

4

ERITREA

Victoria Bernal

PROFILE OF ERITREA

Eritrea is a small country located on the east coast of Africa in a region known as the Horn of Africa. About the size of Kentucky, Eritrea is bordered on the south by Ethiopia and Djibouti, on the north and west by Sudan, and on the northeast by the Red Sea, where its coastline stretches for 600 miles. Eritrea is a new nation that gained international recognition as an independent state in 1993.

Historically, Eritrea came into being as a political entity when it was carved out of eastern Africa by the Italians, who ruled it as their colony from 1886 until 1941. In 1942 Eritrea passed from the Italians into the hands of the British, who administered it as a trusteeship until 1952. Eritrea was then federated to Ethiopia under an arrangement that left considerable local autonomy. However, in 1962 Ethiopia violated the terms of federation and annexed Eritrea. From 1962 until 1993 Eritrea was officially a province of Ethiopia. Independence from Ethiopia was achieved after three decades of war. Eritrea's first major independence movement, the Eritrean Liberation Front (ELF) began in 1960. The Eritrean People's Liberation Front (EPLF),

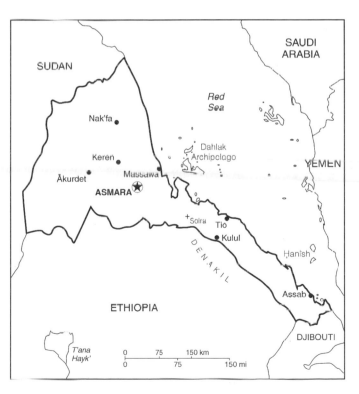

which ultimately succeeded in winning independence for Eritrea, first emerged as a splinter group that broke away from the ELF in 1971. The EPLF was a revolutionary mass movement that sought not only to liberate Eritrea from Ethiopian rule, but to transform Eritrean society from within. The status of women was among the issues taken up by the EPLF and within its own ranks it made considerable strides in altering gender relations towards greater equality.

Three decades of war have had a profound impact on Eritrea. Over the course of the struggle, tens of thousands of Eritreans joined the forces of the EPLF. Many others lived as civilians in "liberated areas" of Eritrea under EPLF control. Other civilians, like those in Asmara, the capital city, remained living directly under Ethiopian rule. The war of independence also gave rise to an Eritrean diaspora. Perhaps as many as 1,000,000, according to UNICEF, fled to other countries where they lived as refugees and exiles.[1]

The armed struggle ended in 1991 and official independence was declared in 1993 after an internationally supervised national referendum in which Eritreans voted overwhelmingly in favor of independence. By 1993, when independence became official, women composed one-third of the roughly 95,000 fighters in the EPLF. Today the EPLF calls itself the People's Front for Democracy and Justice (PFDJ) and is in effect the ruling party of a one-party state. Since gaining independence, Eritrea has faced the great tasks of reconstruction and economic development in the wake of thirty years of war and neglect. Regrettably, this process was further delayed by the outbreak of a border war with Ethiopia that began May 1998 and raged on and off for two years.

Eritrea is one of the least developed countries in the world and was left with its infrastructure largely destroyed and its economy crippled. Its gross domestic product (GDP) per capita is estimated to be about $150, less than half the $350 average for sub-Saharan Africa. Eritrea's predominantly rural population is engaged in agriculture and animal husbandry. Its terrain is roughly divided into highlands occupied by farmers and lowland plains inhabited by agro-pastoralists. Agricultural production has not been sufficient to meet domestic consumption in most recent years. In addition to the disruptions of production caused by war and associated population displacements, Eritrea is prone to droughts. Food aid from international sources and remittances from Eritreans abroad help to sustain the population. The industrial sector is small. In such a nonindustrialized economy land is a key resource.

There are nine major ethnic divisions, most of whose inhabitants speak Semitic or Cushitic languages. The Tigrinya and the Tigre make up four-fifths of the population. The population is fairly evenly divided between Orthodox Christians and Muslims, although Christians have historically dominated Eritrea's political economy and continue to do so. There is no official national language, but Tigrinya, Arabic, and English are used as official languages in practice. In 1997 Eritrea introduced its own currency, the *nakfa*. The country has a population of roughly 4 million.

For Eritreans born in 2000, average life expectancy at birth is estimated at 52 years, with female life expectancy at 53.3 years and male life expectancy at 50.6 years. For Eritreans born between 1995 and 2000, the UNDP estimates that nearly one third (31.7 percent) will die before reaching the age of forty. For women born during this period the probability at birth of surviving to age sixty-five is 47.1 percent, while for men it is 40.7 percent. Even so, the population is predicted to rise to 5.7 million by the year 2015, up from 3.7 million in 2000. Based on 1995–2000 figures, the average number of births per woman is estimated as 5.7. During that same period only 21 percent of births were attended by trained health staff. The infant mortality rate was calculated at 73 per 1,000 live births in the year 2000, while the under-five mortality rate was 114 per 1,000 live births. The most recent figures on maternal mortality indicate that for the period 1985–1999 there were 1,000 maternal deaths per 100,000 live births.[2]

OVERVIEW OF WOMEN'S ISSUES

Women in Eritrea face the challenges of life in a poor country that has experienced foreign domination in various forms and decades of war during the past century. As women they also face the particular challenges of cultures that have conventionally accorded authority positions in the family and the community to men and have socialized women to subordinate roles. Women's circumstances vary considerably depending on whether they live in a village or an urban center, and depending on their ethnic, regional, and religious affiliations. Women who are demobilized fighters, returned refugees, displaced persons, members of female-headed households, disabled individuals, or orphans are particularly vulnerable. At the same time, Eritrean women can draw to various extents on the revolutionary culture of the EPLF, which broke down many gender barriers. Since independence, the major question concerning women's issues has been the extent to which the EPLF, now the PFDJ, would continue to champion gender equality and the extent to which any attempts at reform would be met with opposition on the part of local communities. To date the results are mixed. The former guerrilla movement, now the ruling party of government, remains a progressive force in a conservative society, but has dealt with gender equality largely in terms of equal rights under the law. This approach appears inadequate to bring about the social transformation necessary for gender equality.

The nexus of issues that govern the situations of women in Eritrea today revolve around land tenure, marriage laws and practices, access to education, and opportunities for employment. As a revolutionary mass movement the EPLF made strides in all of these areas: conducting land reform that extended land rights to women; promoting marriage laws that outlawed such practices as child marriage, the repudiation of nonvirgins and dowry; conducting mass literacy campaigns; and within its own ranks training women to be soldiers, doctors, and mechanics, and encouraging them to acquire other nontraditional skills. At independence the leader of the EPLF, Isaias Afewerki, became Eritrea's head of state and the PFDJ became the ruling party. This government has generally asserted a progressive stand on women's right to equality, but official efforts to challenge entrenched patriarchal authority have been weak and the focus of the government on capitalist development has overshadowed concerns about social equity and gender equality.

EDUCATION

Opportunities

Enrollment in primary education is still far from universal: only 52 percent of boys and 41 percent of girls attend school.[3] These figures represent progress made since independence as the average enrollment rate in 1991–1992 was only 36 percent.[4] However, the gap between male and female enrollment has actually increased and girls are twice as likely to repeat classes and drop out of school than are boys. There is, moreover, a much greater gender gap at higher levels. At technical schools and Eritrea's one university—the University of Asmara—women students make up only about 10 percent of total enrollment.[5]

Among the impediments to women's education are the reliance on female labor for domestic chores, early marriage and childbearing, social restrictions on female mobility coupled with long distances from home to school. Eritrean schools are not entirely free, but depend in part on parents to pay for textbooks, administrative fees, and various other costs. Families with limited resources are more likely to spend them on educating sons than daughters. This suggests that strategies aimed specifically at increasing girls' enrollment and retention rates are necessary along with general measures for improving the quality and availability of education. In addition, the more opportunities that can be opened for women to be gainfully employed, the more likely families will come to see girls' education as a worthwhile investment.

Literacy

Literacy remains a major challenge in Eritrea, where 80 percent of the population is illiterate. The government has stated goals of eradicating illiteracy and making education available to all and has taken some concrete measures. Between 1991 and 1998 the number of teaching staff nationwide was increased by about 50 percent and now totals 8,000.[6]

EMPLOYMENT AND ECONOMICS

Farming

The majority of Eritreans are self-employed and 80 percent contribute to their own subsistence by farming or herding. About two-thirds of farmers are agriculturalists and one-third are agro-pastoralists who combine herding and farming. Only about 5 percent of the population practice pastoralism exclusively and livestock products contribute only 5 percent to the GDP. Agriculture is the backbone of the Eritrean economy with the majority of farming families cultivating cereal crops on small rainfed plots. Plowing is commonly done by men using oxen as draft animals: both men and women carry out the other farm work. Women are responsible for storing and processing the products of the farm, for milking dairy animals, and for raising chickens if there are any. Women spend much of their day engaged in unpaid domestic labor in rural and urban areas where food preparation is laborious and running water is unavailable.

Paid Employment

Government data on women's employment in 1993 show that out of a total of 18,913 employed women 7,925 (42 percent) were civil servants, and women accounted for 31 percent of civil service employees. The next largest number of employed women, 7,018 (37 percent), were in manufacturing, where they reportedly accounted for 48 percent of the labor force. Women in manufacturing were concentrated in the textile and tobacco industries. In the civil service women generally held secretarial or custodial positions. According to the International Labour Organisation (ILO) women compose nearly half the total employees in public enterprises, but very few women are employed in professional or managerial positions.

One notable feature of the EPLF was its training of women for non-traditional occupations. This momentum appears to have slackened after independence. Only 23 percent of students in vocational training schools were women in the mid-1990s, and of those receiving technical training only 13 percent were women, while in midwifery and nursing women composed 68 percent and 37 percent of students respectively.[7]

Informal Economic Activities

The formal sector of the economy is very small and therefore many women as well as men must create employment for themselves by engaging in informal-sector activities. Women are particularly active in services and petty trade. An ILO sample survey of 100 informal-sector enterprises in 1993 found that 20 percent were owned by women. It is estimated that about one in three Eritrean households is now female-headed and many women therefore must assume active roles as providers for their families. Some women are migrating to urban areas for other opportunities and become petty traders selling fruits and vegetables, handicrafts, beer, and tea.

Entrepreneurship

There are a small number of woman-owned businesses in the urban service sector such as bars, restaurants, and grocery stores. According to Ministry of Agriculture data 68 percent of grocery store owners are women. This was the only economic area in which women reportedly were more active than men.[8] Small shops are often located in residential areas and it is not unusual for the shop to adjoin the owner's residence. Shop-keeping may be more compatible than other endeavors with women's domestic responsibilities. The predominance of women in shopkeeping may thus be a reflection of the limits placed on women's mobility due to their involvement in unpaid labor within their households, which precludes them from pursuing other occupations. However, much of the available data from government or other sources are contradictory and incomplete.

Pay

Eritrean law provides for equal pay for equal work and prohibits discrimination against women, but these must be regarded as statements of goals rather than descriptions of behavior in practice. An indication of the persistent and perhaps even growing economic disparities between men and women is that of 615 demobilized fighters who obtained loans from the Commercial Bank of Eritrea through the end of 1996. The overwhelming majority (86 percent) were men and they accounted for 91 percent of the funds dispersed.

Support for Mothers/Caretakers

Maternal Leave

The constitution provides for sixty days of paid maternity leave. The number of employed women who actually are able to receive this benefit is not known. It seems likely, though, that women employed in the public sector would have greater access to paid maternal leave than women employed by private businesses.[9]

Inheritance, Property, and Land Rights

Under most customary land tenure systems in Eritrea women did not have the right to own land. Daughters worked on their fathers' land and wives on their husbands' land, while only sons stood to inherit ownership of the land. During the liberation struggle, the EPLF carried out land reform in areas under its control, extending ownership rights to women. In 1994 the government of Eritrea introduced new land tenure regulations that accorded ultimate ownership of land to the state but gave every adult, including women, the right to own and inherit land in practice. This is a significant economic and symbolic act in terms of promoting gender equality. Eritrean women thus have the legal right to be the de facto owners of land, but as with other rights accorded by government decree, women's capacity to exercise this right varies and may be limited in communities where patriarchal authority remains the norm and customary practices prevail. Furthermore, even Eritrean women who own land may lack the means of working it. Plowing is considered a task solely for men and this, along with a lack of draft animals, presents an obstacle to female-headed households. The ownership of livestock similar to that of land is usually vested in the male head of household.

FAMILY AND SEXUALITY

Gender Roles and Division of Labor

In its report on the status of women in Eritrea to the United Nations Fourth World Conference on Women in 1995, the government of Eritrea noted that "women still carry an unacceptable burden of social and family responsibility and are still victimized by outmoded social values and relations."[10]

Marriage

With nine major ethnic groups Eritrea has an array of marriage customs. Some of the common features of marriage practices in past generations are that marriages were arranged by families, brides were betrothed as children, and great importance was placed on the virginity of the bride at marriage and upon her fertility within marriage. Important measures in Eritrea's civil code raise the legal age of marriage from fifteen to eighteen and outlaw bridewealth, legal measures that seek to empower women in marital matters.

Reproduction

Contraception and Abortion

While the government of Eritrea supports family planning, large families and high fertility for women continue to be socially valued by Eritreans, and the resources to promote family planning are limited. According to the International Planned Parenthood Association, unwanted pregnancy and unsafe abortion are emerging as public health problems.[11] The law allows abortions only to preserve the mental or physical health of the mother.

HEALTH

Health Care Access

Eritrea's health infrastructure is inadequate and there is a shortage of trained personnel and medical supplies. Public health measures, such as access to clean water, are lacking in most areas. Life expectancy at birth was estimated to be fifty-three years for men and fifty-seven years for women in 2001. The most pressing health issues for women are those related to childbearing and female genital cutting. The infant mortality rate is 80 per 1,000 births based on 2001 estimate while the fertility rate is 6 children per woman.[12] The maternal mortality rate is 1,400 per 100,000 live births (a rate that is among the ten highest in the world). There is 1 doctor for every 50,000 inhabitants. In the mid-1990s nearly four out of ten children under age three were chronically malnourished.

Diseases and Disorders

AIDS

In comparison to many other countries in sub-Saharan Africa, the prevalence of HIV/AIDS is relatively low in Eritrea, with 3.2 percent of the population infected in 1997.[13] However, data on the HIV/AIDS situation in Eritrea are limited. It is feared that the disease will spread rapidly due to the massive population movements associated with war, including the repatriation of refugees and to the demobilization of 200,000 troops from the recently settled border war.

Female Genital Cutting

Female genital cutting is widely practiced and it is estimated that about 95 percent of women have undergone some form of surgery. A survey of

436 Eritrean women found that 73 percent of them believed that female genital cutting should be abandoned, yet 79 percent stated that they either had or intended to have their daughters cut.[14]

POLITICS AND LAW

Suffrage and Political Participation

Eritrean law grants universal suffrage to its citizens. Women can and do vote and they also run for office. The EPLF promoted considerable gender equality within its ranks, but not, however, at the top echelons of leadership. In 1984 none of the thirty-seven members of the EPLF Central Committee were women and by 1991, when the war for independence ended, only six out of seventy-one members or 8 percent of the Central Committee were women.[15] At lower levels of authority, however, women were better represented within the EPLF. For example, about one-fourth of the delegates to the second National Congress of the EPLF in 1987 were women. The political participation of women within the EPLF must be seen in contrast to local cultures within Eritrea that vested authority in male elders, all-male village councils, and male household heads and that generally excluded women from official leadership positions and from membership in recognized decisionmaking bodies. At independence the population of Eritrea varied greatly in terms of the degree to which they had experienced or participated in EPLF initiatives.

The government has taken proactive measures to ensure women's political participation by reserving legislative seats for women candidates. The constitutional provisions regarding the National Assembly make no mention of reserved seats for women, but by law 20 percent of seats in the National Assembly are reserved for women candidates and 10 percent of seats are reserved for women in village councils (baitos). In 1995 there were twelve women out of seventy-five members of the Central Committee of the PFDJ and ten women out of thirty representatives of the Provincial Council, which represents the population across all the provinces of the country. The Central Committee and the Provincial Council make up the National Assembly, which is the legislative body of the Eritrean government. Women thus made up about 22 percent of the National Assembly in 2003. One third of all government employees are women.[16] Today there are two (13 percent) women ministers (one heading the Ministry of Justice and the other heading the Ministry of Labor and Human Welfare), and women constitute 11 percent of Eritrea's ambassadors, and 16 percent of its judges. There are no women sitting on the Supreme Court, however.

Women's Rights

Several areas important to consider in assessing women's rights in Eritrea including the EPLF's mobilization of women for the nationalist cause, the policies and practices of the PFDJ as the ruling party of government since independence, and the constitution of Eritrea. The existence and activities of women's organizations is also significant.

The government of Eritrea to date has kept political activity and organization circumscribed. There are no political parties besides the PFDJ and very few local nongovernmental organizations. The private press, after flourishing briefly, was closed down in September 2001 and a number of journalists remain in jail. Therefore, rising within the ranks of the EPLF and later the PFDJ has been the main avenue to positions of political power for women.

The preeminent law of any land is presumably the constitution. Eritrea's constitution makes strides toward empowering women in a number of ways. For one thing, women made up twenty-two out of the fifty members of the Constitution Commission, which was charged with drafting a national constitution. The constitution, which was ratified in 1997, has yet to be implemented. The stumbling blocks appear to be the PFDJ-dominated government's unwillingness to usher in a new political era of multiparty politics and to hold elections. Despite the government's failure to fully implement the constitution, the Eritrean constitution nonetheless lays out core values and ideals and many of these are already operating as law in Eritrea's civil code.

The preamble to the constitution articulates the goal of creating "a society in which women and men shall interact on the bases of mutual respect, fraternity, and equality." The body of the constitution includes numerous provisions for the equality of all Eritreans as citizens of the nation and Article 14 prohibits any form of discrimination, including discrimination on the basis of sex. Article 3 of the constitution states that "Any person born of an Eritrean father or mother is an Eritrean by birth," thus making it clear that women can pass on their nationality to their children regardless of paternity. Section 2 of Article 7 states, "Any act that violates the human rights of women or limits or otherwise thwarts their role and participation is prohibited." Similarly, Article 22 of the constitution deals with family relations and asserts that "men and women . . . shall have equal rights and duties as to all family affairs." In spite of these many progressive constitutional provisions, women have a long way to go before their rights are fully realized in practice.

Women's Movements

There were no women's organizations in Eritrea before the EPLF formed the National Union of Eritrean Women (NUEW) as a mass organization for women during the liberation struggle. Shortly after independence, the NUEW declared itself a nongovernmental organization. However, it remains tightly linked to the PFDJ and thus to the government. In fact, the NUEW represented the Eritrean government at the June 2000 Beijing Plus 5 meetings held at United Nations headquarters in New

York. The NUEW is the major organization of women in Eritrea and claims a membership of over 200,000. As a mass organization of the EPLF, the NUEW did not have to start from scratch at independence but on the contrary already had branches all over the country. This was important in overcoming one common problem of African women's organizations, which is that the leadership is urban and has to work hard to connect with rural women and establish organizational bases outside the city. The NUEW already had a national membership base and an organizational presence in rural areas.

The NUEW has focused on a number of activities to improve the condition of women, including literacy programs, microcredit programs, and vocational training. The ability of the NUEW to play a leadership role and to advance the cause of women's empowerment and gender equity is complex to assess. On the one hand, the close links between the NUEW and the government ensure that the NUEW leadership has access and communication with national decisionmakers. As insiders, NUEW leaders may be able to raise gender issues effectively. On the other hand, the NUEW has been criticized historically for failing to take independent positions on issues and serving instead as a means of implementing the EPLF's and the PFDJ's policies.

In 1995 a new organization, Eritrean Women War Veterans Association (BANA), was formed by women ex-fighters to help women who had been demobilized by the EPLF and to bring public attention to women's issues. BANA's members pooled the 10,000 *birr* (Ethiopian currency was still being used in Eritrea at that time) that each woman was paid at demobilization and organized cooperative enterprises such as bakeries and fish marketing as well as training programs to give women marketable skills. In 1996, however, the government closed BANA down, arguing that it duplicated the work of other organizations. In addition to the NUEW, which had close ties to government, there was also a government department of Reintegration of Demobilized Fighters (MITYAS) charged with helping former combatants.

Some Eritreans believe that BANA was closed down largely at the request of NUEW leaders who wanted to assure the primacy of NUEW by eliminating any potential competition. In all fairness to the NUEW, it should be pointed out that nongovernmental organizations in all areas have been limited by the government and the lack of independent women's organizations is not solely a result of competition among women, but more a result of the larger political climate, which remains highly centralized by the government and allows little scope for civil society activities.

Military Service

Women, like male citizens, are required to participate in national service, which includes six months of military training followed by one year of service in various nation-building projects, usually located in rural areas.

Carpentry class for former soldiers of the Eritrean People's Liberation Front, Asmara, Eritrea. The class was sponsored by Bana, which means "ray of light," a group for demobilized women fighters that was eventually banned by the government. AP/Wide World Photos.

The inclusion of women in military training and national service carries forward the EPLF practice of a mixed army. However, unlike EPLF practices, married women and those raising children are exempt from national service, a practice that would seem to reinforce the primacy of women's roles in reproduction and domestic service rather than nation building.

VIOLENCE

Domestic Violence

There are limited data available with which to assess the prevalence of violence against women in Eritrea. Civil codes introduced at independence provide a legal basis for women to fight against domestic violence. However, few cases are brought to the courts.

Rape/Sexual Assault

Rape is regarded as a serious crime, but most often goes unreported by the victim due to shame or is handled outside the legal system by the victim's family. It is worth noting that women are visible in public places in urban areas day and night where they seem to move without fear and without need of male guardianship. Women are not publicly harassed or intimidated as they move about and they do not appear to fear for their own safety.

OUTLOOK FOR THE TWENTY-FIRST CENTURY

Women in Eritrea face an uncertain future. Even as Eritreans remained engaged in tasks of reconstruction and nation building following the three-decade-long war of liberation, they entered a new war with Ethiopia in 1998. This war, which officially ended in 2000, was ostensibly a disagreement over national borders, but may well have deeper causes in rivalries between the Ethiopian and Eritrean regimes and the dissatisfaction of Ethiopians with having lost their access to the Red Sea. The border war exacted a toll on the Eritrean economy by disrupting production and foreign investment and diverting resources from development to the war effort. Currently, drought conditions mean a new threat of famine in Eritrea. It is against this backdrop of poverty and warfare that Eritrean women struggle to survive and make a better future for their children. Progress in the areas of education, health care, and employment for women is limited by bleak economic conditions. Women's political activism is constrained by the centralized, authoritarian practices of the PFDJ-government. Nonetheless the seeds of social transformation were sown by the EPLF and its women revolutionaries. The overall direction of change in Eritrea toward greater gender equality appears set and the constitution and civil code have laid the legal groundwork for greater emancipation of women. Women are participating in national and local politics more than they ever had before. The ground on which patriarchal authority structures were built is not as solid as it once was. But, there can be no doubt that Eritrean women will have to struggle to claim their rights and to find their own political organizations to make their distinct voices heard.

NOTES

1. UNICEF (United Nations Children's Fund), *Children and Women in Eritrea* (Asmara: UNICEF, 1994).

2. Human Development Report (UNDP), http://hdr.undp.org.

3. EIU (Economist Intelligence Unit), "Country Report: Eritrea," 2002.

4. IMF (International Monetary Fund), "The Gender Gap in Education in Eritrea in 1991–98: A Missed Opportunity?" 2001, working paper prepared by Z. Brixiova, A. Bulir, and J. Comenetz.

5. ILO (International Labour Organisation), *Foundations for Sustained Employment in Eritrea*, 1993, report of an ILO Employment Advisory Mission to Eritrea.

6. IMF, "The Gender Gap."

7. Government of Eritrea, *The Status of Women in Eritrea*, 1995, Eritrean National Report to the Fourth World Conference on Women.

8. Ibid.

9. Ibid.

10. Women Watch, the UN Internet Gateway on the Advancement and Empowerment of Women, www.un.org/womenwatch/confer/.

11. IPPF (International Planned Parenthood Federation), *Country Profile: Eritrea*, undated.

12. PRB (Population Reference Bureau), *Eritrea: Demographic Highlights* (Washington, DC, 2001).

13. CIHI (Center for International Health Information), *Health Statistics Report: Eritrea* (Arlington, VA, 1999).

14. Gary Davis et al., "Female Circumcision: The Prevalence and Nature of the Ritual in Eritrea," *Military Medicine* 164, no. 1 (1999): 11–16.

15. Amrit Wilson, *Women and the Eritrean Revolution: The Challenge Road* (Trenton, NJ: Red Sea Press, 1991).

16. Government of Eritrea, *The Status of Women in Eritrea*.

RESOURCE GUIDE

Suggested Reading

Bernal, Victoria. "Equality to Die For? Women Guerilla Fighters and Eritrea's Cultural Revolution." *Political and Legal Anthropology Review* 23, no. 2 (2000): 61–76.

Davis, Gary, Julius Ellis, Milo Hiibbert, Romeo Perez, and Erlene Zimbelman. "Female Circumcision: The Prevalence and Nature of the Ritual in Eritrea." *Military Medicine* 164, no. 1 (1999): 11–16.

Frankland, Erich, and Tammy Noble. "A Case of National Liberation with Feminist Undertones: The Secession of Eritrea." *Small Wars and Insurgencies* 7, no. 3 (1996): 401–24.

Killion, Tom. *Historical Dictionary of Eritrea*. African Historical Dictionaries no. 75. Lanham, MD: Scarecrow Press, 1998.

Silkin, Trish. " 'Women Can Only Be Free When the Power of Kin Groups is Smashed': New Marriage Laws and Social Change in the Liberated Zones of Eritrea." *International Journal of the Sociology of Law* 17 (1989): 147–63.

Stefanos, Asegedet. "Women and Education in Eritrea: A Historical and Contemporary Analysis." *Harvard Educational Review* 67, no. 4 (1997): 658–88.

Tesfagiorgis, Gebre Hiwet. "When the Drafting of a Constitution Is Not Confined to Men of Stature or Legal Experts: The Eritrean Experience." *Eritrean Studies Review* 2, no. 2 (1998): 143–61.

Wilson, Amrit. *Women and the Eritrean Revolution: The Challenge Road*. Trenton, NJ: Red Sea Press, 1991.

Woldemikael, Tekle. "Political Mobilization and Nationalist Movements: The Case of the Eritrean People's Liberation Front." *Africa Today* 38, no. 2 (1991): 31–42.

Zerai, Worku. *Participation of Women in the Eritrean National Liberation Struggle*. M.A. thesis, Institute of Social Studies, the Hague, Netherlands, 1994.

Video/Film

The Dream Becomes a Reality. 1995. Eve Egensteiner, prod. Anthropologist and filmmaker Eve Egensteiner interviewed women combatants of the Eritrean People's Liberation Front, which brought Eritrea to independence in 1991. Women made up one-third of the frontline fighters and held positions of leadership. VHS PAL. 45 minutes.

Web Sites

Asmarino.com, www.asmarino.com.
Eritrean news and discussion.

Dehai: Eritrea Online, www.dehai.org.
Eritrean news and discussion.

People's Front for Democracy and Justice, www.shaebia.org.
Web site of the Eritrean government.

SELECTED BIBLIOGRAPHY

CIHI (Center for International Health Information). "Health Statistics Report: Eritrea." Arlington, VA, 1999.

EIU (Economist Intelligence Unit). "Country Report: Eritrea." 2002.

"Eritrea 1995: Results from the Demographic and Health Survey." *Studies in Family Planning* 28, no. 4 (1997): 336–40.

Government of Eritrea. "The Status of Women in Eritrea." Eritrean National Report to the Fourth World Conference on Women, 1995.

ILO (International Labour Organisation). "Foundations for Sustained Employment in Eritrea." Report of an ILO Employment Advisory Mission to Eritrea, 1993.

IMF (International Monetary Fund). "The Gender Gap in Education in Eritrea in 1991–98: A Missed Opportunity?" Working paper prepared by Z. Brixiova, A. Bulir, and J. Comenetz, 2001.

IPPF (International Planned Parenthood Federation). *Country Profile: Eritrea*. undated.

PRB (Population Reference Bureau). "Eritrea: Demographic Highlights." Washington, DC, 2001.

UNICEF (United Nations Children's Fund). *Children and Women in Eritrea*. Asmara: UNICEF, 1994.

5

ETHIOPIA

Tsehai Berhane-Selassie

PROFILE OF ETHIOPIA

Ethiopia is one of the oldest nation states in the world and one of only three African states that sustained their independence from colonial aggression in the nineteenth and twentieth centuries (save for a brief Italian occupation between 1935 and 1940). Ethiopia's political history has affected the status of women in important ways.

Until 1974, Ethiopia was ruled by monarchs and tributary kingdoms, princedoms, sultanates, and chief-doms. Women participated in politics and the army, albeit in very subordinate roles. When the monarchy developed a centralized system of government between 1890 and 1930, it reduced the role of the tributary rulers, thus removing personalized governance at several centers and concentrating power in the hands of a single monarch, the Emperor Haile Selassie I, who ruled from 1930 to 1974. Selassie, who maintained neutrality in international politics, had nonetheless allowed the influence of Western ideas of femininity among upper-class women.

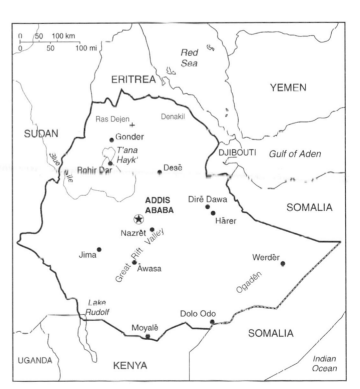

Attempts by various subsequent governments to bring women into formal politics have never been supported by systems for gauging and formulating policies in line with their interests. After Selassie was overthrown in 1974 in a military coup led by Major Mengistu Haile Mariam, the military leaders declared socialism to appease civilian revolutionary forces, thus ushering in the so-called revolutionary period. They established the Revolutionary Ethiopian Women's Association (REWA) in 1976 to carry out sensitization around what they called the "woman question." When Somalia invaded the country in 1978, Mengistu had to acquire weapons and therefore allied the country with the Soviet bloc. Large numbers of women were affected in the 1980s when Mengistu's military government set in motion an ill-advised and politically motivated focus on cultural enrichment. Using the Soviet "nationalities" model, a social engineering program was implemented that involved transplanting whole populations to distant areas where they became resented by local populations in order to purportedly escape famine and starvation caused by impoverished soil in their home regions. Faced with guerrilla rebel groups that were supported by the West, Mengistu drew Ethiopia into the Cold War, which lasted until he was overthrown in 1991.

The Ethiopian Peoples' Revolutionary Democratic Front (EPRDF), which took power in 1991, had ideological leanings similar to those of Mengistu. Following the old Soviet model, therefore, they set up a federal state on the basis of exclusive tribal territories known as *killil*, supposedly inhabited by monolingual groups they classified as "nationalities." To implement the policy, they continued the top-down social engineering approach for the purposes of constructing the *killil*, and gave nine of the "states" the constitutional right to secede if they so wished. To entrench national divisions, they encouraged their supporters to assert their territorial and "cultural" rights, the return to "tribal values," and the reinvention of tribal "traditions." Under such policy, young men began kidnapping and raping women to claim them for marriage in the name of asserting their "tribal" laws, thus causing serious violations of women's rights. The imposition of *killil* and tribal "traditions" also led to ethnic cleansing during rivalries between supposedly homogenous groups that tried to assert their *killil* rights, and large numbers of women and girls were murdered. Among the victims were those who had been transplanted to different regions by the military regime, or whose families had been settled in more remote periods.

Today, women make up roughly half of Ethiopia's estimated total population of 66 million. Levels of life expectancy, which are among the lowest in the world, stand at around 44.6 years at birth for women and 43.2 years for men. Nevertheless, the average annual increase of population from 1995 to 2000 remained at 5.16 percent in urban areas and 1.91 percent in rural ones, higher than a decade earlier.

OVERVIEW OF WOMEN'S ISSUES

Relations of power between men and women have been influenced by the monotheistic religions of Christianity, Islam, and Judaism, and by polytheistic spirit cults. These religions, which have for centuries influenced one another, crisscross over 80 languages and 150 dialects spoken in Ethiopia. The influence of the religious, social, and economic forces on women's lives became especially salient during 1974–1991, when the government used language to classify people into "nationalities." Similarly, in the post-1991 period, the former guerrillas used the same model to divide the nation into "federal" states.

Economic developments that affect women's lives in general remain linked to the subsistence agricultural base, and the country's heavy dependence on foreign aid from the West, including loans from the World Bank and the International Monetary Fund (IMF). The statistics provided for the year 2000 show that only 24 percent of the total population had access to improved drinking water sources.[1] This broke down to 77 percent of the urban and 13 percent of the predominantly rural population that had access to drinking water. The percentage with access to improved sanitation facilities was a mere 15 percent: 58 percent of the urban and 6 percent of the rural population. Access to employment, public health, and other amenities is even lower.

Young women are burdened with marital and motherhood responsibilities as caretakers, service providers, and agricultural workers. Over the last decade, about 49 percent of fifteen- to nineteen-year-old girls (as opposed to 8 percent of boys) have been married and burdened with hard work since their early teens. These early marriages contravene girls' universal rights to education and other rights of the child. Under such political and economic conditions, the chances of women's personal advancement and of improving their health, education, and employment are severely restricted.

Of course, state policies and national economic conditions alone do not account for the limitations or abuses of women's rights in Ethiopia. Gender perceptions, socializing processes, customary practices, and views based on religious and local political ideologies assign different roles to girls and boys. They mostly restrict girls' potential for self-development. Such practices and beliefs as well as the political and cultural manipulation of differences along linguistic lines have increased women's powerlessness and vulnerability. They have made it difficult to create a sustained movement that can advocate for women's universal rights. The Women's Bureau, which succeeded REWA in the current prime minister's office, has been ineffective in asserting the rights of women in the face of a tribe-based "federal" state. Women remain especially vulnerable to abuse, unwanted pregnancies, backstreet abortions, and especially wide-ranging violations of their physical safety and security.

Urban-based Ethiopian women elites introduced "gender-based" forms of analysis around 1989–1991, but their influence on policy formulation has been minimal, if not negligible. The protracted campaigns around women's rights in the late 1980s and early 1990s are now limited to education against traditional practices that affect the health of women and children by a voluntary association. An independent women's group, the Ethiopian Women Lawyers Association (EWLA), has recently taken up advocacy on behalf of physically abused victims of sexual predators and domestic workers who travel to work in the Middle East. Virtually no other agency or organization is involved in effective advocacy for the rights of women and girls in general and even EWLA has faced government suppression.

EDUCATION

Opportunities

The formal education for girls that resumed in earnest after 1941, when the war with Italy ended, affected only girls from a few urban families who accepted the importance of girls' education and equality with boys. The enrollment of girls in the elementary schools to this day remains lower than that of boys, with the numbers diminishing progressively at the secondary and tertiary levels. Prior to the revolution of 1974, only 32 percent of all school-age girls were enrolled in primary schools, and they were mostly from the urban centers around the country. By 1998 only 30 percent of school-age girls were enrolled in primary schools.[2] The ratio of girls to boys in primary schools stood at 73 percent.

The lack of a wide distribution of secondary schools means that rural students have to leave their homes and take up residence in overcrowded accommodations in the urban areas. They commute periodically to collect their supplies from home, and in that context secondary school girls often find themselves exposed to molestation or unwanted attention en route to school as well as in their urban dwellings. By 1998, the female secondary net enrollment ratio stood at 12 percent while the ratio of girls to boys at the secondary level stood at 63 percent. At the tertiary level this ratio was only 24 percent.[3]

Girls' low level of enrollment, poor performance, and frequency of attrition are often blamed on parental attitudes, the tradition of helping mothers at home, emphasis on marrying girls off at young ages, unintended pregnancy, and lack of role models. Parents' preference to pay for their boys' rather than their girls' education curtails girls' capacity to pass through the education system. Other reasons for girls' low enrollments include the lack of finance for presenting themselves in schools properly dressed and equipped with sanitary napkins.

Equally critical have been various governments' neglect of improving the school environment for girls' education. Often studies overlook the brutal pressures of male peers, including deliberate raping and teasing of studious girls. These attitudes and practices compelled girls to abandon schooling, even on university campuses in the 1990s. In what became an unchecked phenomenon of the 1990s, boys in their teens forced very young high school girls to become their "wives" at knifepoint. The educational opportunities of most rural girls are made worse by their restricted mobility for fear of kidnapping and forced marriage.

Although the country's few professional women were graduates of the all-girls' schools of the pre-1974 period, those schools have long been made coeducational. Other all girls' private schools, often run by religious organizations, are coming under similar pressures to become coeducational even though their girls successfully compete in tertiary level institutions. In the early 1990s, some elite women attempted to make special space for girls on campuses and advocated for positive discrimination in women's enrollment in the university. In spite of such advocacy, the government has yet to adopt any useful policy on the education of girls. Aware of such pitfalls in the learning environment, state officials and those of lower rank seem to continue with the tradition of sending their daughters to other African countries while ministers and those in the diplomatic corps strive to find places for their girls in schools in Europe, America, or elsewhere abroad.

None of this has been improved by the so-called education sector review of the post-1991 state. In the new educational policy, the learning of the lingua franca, Amharic, and the second official language, English, are deferred until after the seventh year of schooling, in preference for learning local languages. This effectively excludes "others" from engagement at the national level, though it is theoretically meant to bring local languages into the literary fold. Eroding the teaching of Amharic makes it harder for girls to access the national language, which became current in the thirteenth century. As it still remains the working language of the federal administration and is in use by the Tigray ethnic group that has dominated the political scene since 1991, restricting it practically helps only those from the Tigray area, the home base of the ruling ethnic group. Among the rest, boys are more likely than girls to pick it up while socializing outside of the home.

In the new system, free education stops two years through high school, becoming yet one more restrictive element in girls' chances of acquiring tertiary education. Despite the uphill struggle against social expectations, peer pressure, and restrictive educational policy, the high number of young women in evening classes in Addis Ababa and elsewhere shows that young women themselves work hard to acquire education and are interested in trying to improve their skills for employment and higher salaries.

Literacy

Under the monarchs, literacy was discouraged except among the clergy. Only a few mainly male aristocrats learned to read and write, and the few women who made it to the highest level of competence in traditional literature (*qene* schools, as they were called) were considered mavericks. Women's literacy in Arabic has never existed in Ethiopia, even though it was at times taught informally. Universal literacy has never been compulsory in Ethiopia; nor have formal education policies been discriminatory against girls.

When formal and "modern" education began in Ethiopia at the turn of the twentieth century, a special school was built for girls. The earliest girl pupils took up nursing and teaching. One woman sought and acquired the emperor's permission to learn and pilot the first plane bought by Ethiopia in 1930. Another took up music lessons in Switzerland. Such beginnings were harshly interrupted by the Italian occupation of the country in 1935–1940, a period now recognized as involving the first battles of World War II. In the euphoria of emulating Western civilization in the post-war years, Emperor Haile Selassie I paid special attention to the education of girls. Even the 1987 constitution of the socialist military state strongly supported female education.

However, socializing processes emphasized inequality with men and encouraged a femininity that promoted women solely as wives, mothers, and care providers. Informal literacy contributed very little to bring about change. The figures for the literacy campaigns undertaken sporadically since the 1960s, give a false picture of achievement, as the lack of facilities undermined the use of reading and writing. Shortages of newspapers or writing materials forced those who could read to lapse into illiteracy. In the mid-1980s, an intensive literacy drive yielded a 60 percent rate of literacy, but the figure went down to a very low rate of about 10 percent by the late 1990s. The UN Educational, Scientific, and Cultural Organization (UNESCO) estimated in 2000 an adult illiteracy rate of 56 percent for men and 67 percent for women. Women often report that their attendance of literacy classes was interrupted due to sight problems or overload of work, but most who received certificates for completing the literacy classes never sustained their knowledge for lack of reading material.

EMPLOYMENT AND ECONOMICS

Farming

Largely illiterate, young, and agrarian, 88 percent of the Ethiopian population works the land.[4] Government policies have exacerbated the fragility of the natural environment and contributed to thirty years of recurrent environmental disasters. There is only a slow expansion of private-sector employment and alternative economic systems. This has left the state monopolizing employment and its officials controlling most business investments. This economic environment has had very negative consequences for women.

There is little effort to enhance the variety of inherited knowledge in the areas of work at the base of the Ethiopian economy, namely subsistence farming, seminomadic cattle herding, and artisanship. Government inadequacy in developing water technology and reforestation has not only resulted in the country's image of famine and misery, but has also seriously affected the well-being and health of women and their children. Moreover, the Ethiopian topography and its proximity to the ever-expanding Sahel, the southeastern fringes of the Sahara desert, mean that recurrent droughts afflict parts of the country. Given women's chores of servicing the needs of their households, they literally have to negotiate the rugged landscape for water and fuel. In the case of the seminomadic cattle herders, they mediate in finding grounds for putting up their makeshift homes and in cultivating their supplementary foods.

Following traditional gender roles among subsistence farmers, women's work is considerably harder than that of men. Women contribute significantly in weeding, harvesting, winnowing, and storing grain. Nonetheless, women are prohibited from farming with ox-drawn plows, and men perform most of the harvesting and hauling of the grains. Women who cultivate tubers, legumes, *ensete* (a plant resembling the banana), and the commercial crops, coffee and tea, prepare the soil as well as perform the rest of farm work. Indeed, among *ensete* cultivators, harvesting is one of women's food-processing roles. In the escarpments and associated lowlands, where seminomadic cattle herders make up an estimated one-tenth of the total population, only women cultivate supplementary cereals and other food. However, they are marginal to the pre-

Seminomadic woman with baby, Ethiopia. Photo © TRIP/B. Seed.

dominant occupation of cattle herding. Indeed, mostly perceived as bearers of children, women barely feature in owning or inheriting cattle wealth. Still, their substantial role in supplementing the nutritional needs of their families by cultivating grains is not to be underestimated. In all zones, women prepare butter and look after small livestock, some of which are marketed for income to be used in meeting the families' additional needs.

In many parts of the country, women relieve the drudgery of their daily lives by well-established customs of organizing work groups. Although these arrangements are reciprocal, they provide women with an important social base and a supportive work environment. Women face difficulties in playing their expected role of providing for their families. This is further exacerbated by the limited choices they have in waged employment, especially in the urban areas.

Paid Employment

In 1990–1991 women wage earners composed only 5 percent of the total labor force; men composed 8 percent. By 1996–1997 this rose to 10 percent, but if nonwage work is included, women composed around 40 percent of the overall labor force. Self-employed women composed 28 percent of the total; men composed 59 percent. During 1985–1997 women held only about 8 percent of total administrative and managerial positions.

The cycle of failure, caused by the low regard for girls' education and underlined by textbook images and the absence of role models, has been reflected in the employment sector, which inhibits change in women's status. To take a few areas, the highest number of women scientists and engineers were employed in the National Institute of Health Research (21 out of 110 employees), the Ethiopian Nutrition Institute (16 out of 70), and the Institute of Agricultural Research (14 out of 284). The statistics on women teachers and students at the tertiary levels shows the same pattern in the 1990s, two decades after sensitization about women began by the Revolutionary Ethiopian Women's Association under the military regime, albeit to support the state's revolutionary programs.

Informal Economic Activities

Unlike farmers and cattle herders, women have prominence in communities of pottery makers, wood-carvers, beekeepers, and weavers. These women are petty traders who exchange products from the different parts of the country, while their husbands supplement their meager household economy by farming. Women bring trading items such as secondhand clothing, utensils, oil, and other household necessities, traveling long distances between their own localities and small trading towns. Many women small-scale traders also risk rape (with its added danger of contracting HIV/ AIDS) when traveling between towns, and most others face police harassment in the open markets of the urban areas, especially in the capital. Local authorities often make licenses difficult to obtain, and only a few can afford to rent the shops and stalls in the market halls where they can sell their wares.

Both as married women and single household heads, urban homemakers are mostly economic dependents, surviving either on their husbands' incomes or, especially since 1991, on remittances by children and relatives abroad. Many head their own households, with responsibility for large numbers of underage children, both of their own and of parents who have gone abroad or have died of HIV/AIDS. A substantial number of urban women engage in informal economic activities, making income as retailers, small business owners, domestics, and office workers. Many try to make ends meet as street hawkers, retailers, and commercial sex workers.

Entrepreneurship

A relatively small number of women own small businesses, trading in handicrafts, imported clothing, and other consumer goods. Very few women travel internationally in order to import electrical and other goods, and in that respect Ethiopian market women lag behind the dominance of informal trade by women elsewhere in Africa.

Pay

Women's remuneration and chances for promotion are poor compared with men's. There has been little regulation of equal pay for equal work, promotion, or other aspects of work-related equity. According to the 1999 International Labour Organisation figures, the per capita adult economic activity rate percent of gross domestic product was $90 for men and $72 for women.

Support for Mothers/Caretakers

In the wage-labor environment, there are no salary adjustments or other systems of support to families with large numbers of children.

Maternal Leave and Child Care

Despite their low involvement in the waged labor force and poor access to education, in addition to the weaknesses within the overall economy, some aspects of wage employment have been beneficial to women. There are few government supports for childcare, but in 1989 REWA's advocacy around women's employment benefits yielded a ninety-day maternity leave for working mothers, with full pay coverage by the employer.

Inheritance, Property, and Land Rights

Historically, land belonged in theory to the monarchs, and in practice, to communities that inherited it from their ancestors. Those communities that allowed women's rights to property ownership and inheritance traced their descent through both men and women. Women's rights to land also correlates to traditional technologies. In the areas where ox-plows predominate, inheritance and descent are traced through both men and women, and women are therefore entitled to land. But these entitlements are often affected by their dependence on men for the use of the ox. Even within those areas, women in the northeast are not allowed to inherit or own landed property. Outside the ox-plow areas, where digging sticks are used, the communities are mostly patrilineal and women have no rights to land-ownership as descent and inheritance are passed down through men.

The 1958 constitution, however, entitled all women to inherit, own, and buy land. However, elite women in urban areas fared better in asserting their rights to own land than their rural counterparts, mainly because of the difficulties of asserting such rights in the courts. It proved an uphill struggle for women to bypass "traditions," male control, and bureaucracy to assert their constitutional rights to land. With the same constitution, bringing women under men's tutelage (fathers, husbands, and the like) for purposes of public representation, women's inheritance of property could be asserted only when men challenged their right to inherit the property of their mothers or wives. Nonetheless, in the pre-1974 period, some women could and did win court cases even in localities where they had been traditionally excluded from landownership. However, those were mostly in cases where property matters arose during divorce. In the post-1974 period, land was nationalized and it belonged to the socialist state. In that context, a land reform program redistributed plots to those who lived and worked on them, initially leaving out many women in female-headed and polygamous households. It took a few years before the mistake could be corrected.

Land rights remain unclear under the regime that came to power in 1991. Theoretically, the state still owns all land, but the regime seems to apply different laws in different ethnic regions, sometimes using the 1958 constitution, other times using some arbitrary law. In many administrative units *(killils)*, the government oversees a return to tribal laws, which gives men the right to assume control of property according to "old" communal rights laws that excluded women. In some urban areas in the north, land has been returned to those who owned it before the socialist revolution of 1974, but not in the rest of the country. In all the confusion, women's dependence on men for legal representation continues to obscure their rights even further.

Social/Government Programs

When government development programs were launched in the 1960s, the focus on "economic growth" and increasing farm production was based on false assumptions, especially about the position and role of women. The government created a major gap between the population's subsistence economy on the one hand, and the market-orientation of government elites and development workers on the other. This resulted in a missed opportunity to enhance the benefits of development for women.

For instance, an extension unit, Rural Women's Agricultural Department, set up within the Ministry of Agriculture in 1960. It was responsible for deploying women who were trained in nutrition, vegetable gardening, environmental hygiene, cooking, and other such subjects. Mostly high school graduates with two years' training in those vocations, the women extension workers were deployed as much as possible within their "home" bases, or at least in areas where they spoke the local languages. Their purpose was to educate rural women. However, the unit was underresourced and less privileged than its extension counterpart that worked with male farmers. Unlike the women extension workers, the extension workers in this latter unit were provided with motorcycles and funding with which to develop model farms and houses.

Women potters, who were the backbone of their community's economy, were similarly marginalized. Coming in the context of five-year development plans based on agricultural loans from the World Bank, the International Monetary Fund, and other international donors, one project aimed to expand the cultivation of commercial crops, notably coffee, tea, and soybeans for export. There was no consultation with those leading the Rural Women's Agricultural Department within the Ministry of Agriculture, its women extension workers, or the rural women in the project areas. The project relegated the farmers and the potters to marginal lands, as exemplified by two major showpiece plans, the Chilalo Agricultural Development Unit and the Wolayta Agricultural Development Unit (WADU). In the case of WADU, commercial coffee production exposed local Wolayta farmers to hunger by marginalizing *ensete*, the staple banana-like crop, that has the potential of sustaining communities over several years of drought. With the marginalization of WADU, women who harvested and processed this crop were forced to seek alternative incomes to feed and look after their families. The commercial farms were mechanized and both men and women were displaced. In places like Wolayta the potter communities, of which women were the backbone, were forcibly resettled and obliged to be crop cultivators on poor agricultural land. In one stroke, the potter women lost their centrality to the economy and their society. Despite the development of some public services such as education and health, these and other services did not significantly help to improve the quality of life of the marginalized population. They were not given alternative means of survival, and the scheme began a trend of migration to the urban areas.

FAMILY AND SEXUALITY

Gender Roles and Division of Labor

The economic and social crisis has set in motion a trend of increasing single motherhood and reduced male parental responsibilities. A long-term population trend shows a decrease in women's fertility from 7.0 live births per woman in the mid-1980s to 5.4 in 1995–2000, and to 6.0 children per woman in the shorter period of 1991–1998. There was also an increase in marriages of fifteen to nineteen-year-olds (to 59 percent) during 1991–1998. Young families face poverty, including lack of employment and urban housing. Men are increasingly turning away from marriage and parental responsibility, while young women are burdened with motherhood without sufficient support. Subsequently there has been a sharp a rise in the number of children flooding the streets in urban areas.

Marriage

Early marriage is prevalent in northern Ethiopia, where girls as young as eight to ten years old are married off. The parents arrange marriages involving transfer of plots of land, farming equipment, or similar other property as bridewealth. Until they reach the age of puberty, the girls are brought up by their future mothers-in-law with their husbands-to-be, who are only two or three years older than themselves. They serve their marital family in the name of learning household work and administration. With the bond they develop in growing up together, couples in early marriage often reject each other as sexual partners and divorce immediately after they have their first intercourse. The girls cannot return to their parental homes because of the shame associated with divorce, and their families face the difficulty of returning the goods exchanged at the time of their marriage. The girls therefore run away to urban areas. Until they reach the age of thirty or so, the men then may frequently engage in serial marriages, some marrying up to ten times as they "look for the right woman" among the teenagers who have not been married off as children. Only the marriages of boys singled out to be priests seem to remain intact. That is because they receive special attention from parents in orientating them to be married couples and marry girls who have grown up within their own parental homes.

Reproduction

During 1995–2000, births per 1,000 women were reported to be 152, and the total fertility rate over the same period was 6.3 children per woman.

Maternal mortality per 100,000 was recorded as 560 (out of a threshold of 100) for the period 1980–1992. Infant mortality rates of 109 and 121 respectively per 1,000 births of girls and boys during the same period meant a high number of women losing their infants. Women's fertility rate decreased from 7.0 live births per woman in the mid-1980s to 5.4 in 1995–2000.

Sex Education

There has been some promotion of healthy sex education for women. This includes the campaigns mounted by the United Nations Population Fund, World Health Organization, and the Inter-African Committee on Traditional Practices Affecting the Health of Women and Children (an organization linked to the United Nations and Economic Commission on Africa), to conduct education programs against early marriage, genital cutting, fistula, and the spread of sexually transmitted diseases and HIV/AIDS. Although all of these campaigns address women's economic, social, and political lives, their contribution to women's autonomous development has been minimal.

Contraception and Abortion

In the early 1990s, many women reported that their traditional natural birth control systems included the suckling of babies for a number of years. Men reported abstinence or interruption at the critical moment and counting the days of menses as the main means of controlling pregnancy. On the grounds that the quality of life would improve with child spacing and improved health for women, the Ethiopia Planned Parenthood Association has been campaigning for family planning. Its campaigns for modern contraceptives were initially slowed down by reports of forced uterine closures circulating in the society. Besides, strict religious groups protested that contraception is interference with "God's will."

The situation has been improving in recent years, and people have been more accepting of condoms, especially after they have come to accept the cause for the spread of HIV/AIDS. Despite improvements, most men avoid the use of male condoms, insist on having large families and prohibit women's use of pills or other devices, especially their wives. Generally, women now accept the idea of birth control and prefer oral contraceptives, but only 4 percent of married women used contraceptives over a monitoring period of 1991–1998. The majority of women lack access to any contraception, and some devices such as female condoms are unknown.

Teen Pregnancy

Girls in early marriage are apt to bear children from the time they are thirteen or so. The practice of early marriage represents a total manipulation of children for the circulation of wealth among local people. The practice has not been stopped by the legal prohibitions introduced in the mid-1970s, nor in the 1980s by the educational programs of the Revolutionary Ethiopian Women's Association, set up under the Mengistu regime and continued into the 1990s by the Inter-African Committee on Traditional Practices Affecting the Health of Women and Children in Africa. Mothers often claim that in marrying off their daughters, they enjoy securing the future of their children while they are still alive. The circulation of wealth associated with early marriage rises and wanes according to the level of economic prosperity, with the arrangements becoming frequent during hard times. This makes early marriage one of those problems that can only be solved by improvements in the overall economy. Meanwhile, it exposes an unknown number of girls to all sorts of health hazards, including pregnancy, before their bodies are strong enough to carry babies.

HEALTH

Health Care Access

In general, women have very poor access to health facilities in Ethiopia. By the year 2000, only 1 in 6,000 had access to qualified medical doctors, and there has been little help to ease women's responsibilities to look after family members infected by HIV/AIDS. By 2002, over 3 million (5 percent) were said to be infected with HIV/AIDS in the country. Only about 20 percent of pregnant women have access to prenatal care, and qualified birth attendants assist in only 8 percent of women giving birth. Many communities around the country emphasize rest and food for new mothers, but not all aspects of maternal care are positive. Many women live long distances from health facilities. Other women continue hard work such as carrying water well into their pregnancy, with such consequences as uterine rupture and miscarriage.

Diseases and Disorders

Several health issues feature prominently in Ethiopia today. Maternal mortality is generally the result of the interrelated factors of malnutrition, viral hepatitis, fistula, and the physical complications of very young mothers' pregnancy. Most women, their infants and growing children suffer from poverty-related malnutrition, anemia, mental distress, and some consequences of traditional practices that harm their health.

Sexually Transmitted Diseases and AIDS

The spread of sexually transmitted diseases (STDs) has been well known about in the country, as far back as the sixteenth century. Traditional treatments for syphilis and gonorrhea included something that resembled Turkish baths, abstinence, and strict monogamy. Nonetheless, population mobility due to frequent wars, warfare, and mass migrations over the last two centuries have contributed to the frequency of transmission.

The spread was aggravated by certain beliefs, for example, that only females were the transmitters or that such diseases were environmentally rooted. In the process of running away from early marriage, some girls are also exposed to rape and engage in commercial sex, resulting frequently in STDs. Despite the reluctance of the government to acknowledge the prevalence of HIV/AIDS, the disease and related deaths were widespread by the early 1990s. The perception that women were the only transmitters encouraged men's promiscuous behavior and increased the spread of the diseases to the detriment of their wives and rural women.

The belief in the environmental roots of diseases inhibited women from bathing in certain seasons for fear of catching diseases, for instance, from the moon. Despite the knowledge that some diseases such as syphilis and gonorrhea are sexually transmitted, ecology-focused beliefs about their occurrence have been transposed to other diseases such as HIV/AIDS.

Confusing myths about its "known" antiquity were linked up with perverse romanticism regarding sexual encounters and male prestige. One of the legends circulating was that AIDS was harmless. A cynical jingle, "die with AIDS, drive the DX" (the much admired deluxe car model), also undermined the promotion of condoms. The government's reluctance to officially admit the existence and spread of HIV/AIDS contributed to undermining sensitization programs at the early stages. Nongovernmental organizations in Addis Ababa such as the Sisters of Charity and the Organization for Social Service for AIDS tried to give moral and social support to girls dying of HIV/AIDS-related diseases. Most of these girls had contracted the HIV/AIDS virus while working either as domestics in places far away from home or as bar maids in brothels. By the early 1990s almost all hotels and many commercial sex workers were promoting condoms.

It cannot be emphasized enough that the long-drawn-out wars that began in the 1960s required the deployment of more than half a million soldiers and militia by the mid-1970s. Their sudden demobilization in the early 1990s and the lack of public preparation contributed to the fast increase in HIV/AIDS. The displacement, homelessness, and retrenchment of thousands of others who were seen to be supporting the military regime have increased the mobile population, who are potentially at risk for spreading the diseases. Nonetheless, by and large the population now accepts the facts relating to sexually transmitted diseases and the value of modern medication. However, attempts at having measures of safety and protection are frustrated by poverty and lack of facilities.

Female Genital Cutting

Genital cutting is practiced widely in Ethiopia. The pressure to practice it comes from diehard customs of beauty, social and peer pressure, archaic notions of sexuality, and even the symbolic importance attached to womanhood. Genital cutting ranges from clitoridectomy to incision (removal of the labia majora) and to infibulation (the removal of the labia major and sewing the remainder together, leaving a small opening). The age of cutting depends on the purported purpose for it. Among eastern Ethiopians and along the Red Sea coast, where infibulation, the most precarious operation, is performed on girls of eight years and above, the claimed purpose is "beauty" and protection of the virginal hymen for the use of a future husband. Cutting off of the labia majora is also performed on women among a small number of people in the south, where the death of a husband is considered polluting and the widow has to undergo a cleansing ritual. The widow stays away from her community for two years, subjecting herself to sexual relations with a man from a neighboring tribe. The operation, performed on her return, endows her with the status of an honorary senior male.

In some parts of the south, men have irrational fears about the natural female genitalia, which they believe will consume their penis unless it has been cut. In these regions, women's genitalia are always cut prior to their weddings. Elsewhere in the country, clitoridectomy is performed, purportedly to protect the girl's chastity as a child and to prevent her promiscuity as an adult. One type of clitoridectomy involves slightly bleeding the clitoris, the most sensitive organ of female sexuality, while another form involves completely removing it. Some highlanders, who draw on Christianity to rationalize the practice, perform this operation when the infant is about eight days old, most performing only a symbolic version of the ritual. Some avoid the operation altogether if they feel their girls can avoid scrutiny.

Campaigns against female genital cutting that have been ongoing for a number of years, are often done in association with childbirth practices. The Inter-Africa Committee on Traditional Practices Affecting the Health of Women and Children, with its regional headquarters in the Ethiopian capital, conducts educational programs for traditional birth attendants, who are traditionally the specialists in the cutting. Some urban parents are listening to the advice of medical professionals and stopping the practice altogether, while foreign-educated young men are abandoning their wives who have been genitally cut in favor of women who have not been cut. Given the shame associated with the avoidance of cutting, religious and ritual leaders and other public opinion makers have yet to be involved openly in changing attitudes.

Fistula

Fistula most often occurs when a girl experiences a long and difficult labor with no access to adequate medical attention. The resulting extensive tissue damage to the birth canal, which can also involve the loss of the child, means that women lose control of their bladder and bowels unless treated. It is reported in the oral tradition of the northwest that historically bonesetters used to shape and fix gourds in order to reconstruct the affected area. When bonesetters were not available, some women went to the monasteries of the central highlands, where they received attention and care until they died. In many other areas, they died rejected by husbands and isolated from society. In modern times, Ethiopian women have had access to one of only two fistula hospitals in Africa specializing in the problem. One hospital was established in the capital by an English couple who noticed the huge magnitude of the problem over fifty years ago. It was servicing young mothers from all parts of Ethiopia.

POLITICS AND LAW

Political Participation

Under the monarchy and since it was overthrown in 1974, some women have been appointed to decision-making positions such as ministers, and since the mid-1980s a few have held positions in the judiciary. Women representatives in the National Assembly were in considerably higher numbers than in the old parliament during the monarchy, today constituting 7.7 percent of the legislature. Though the Revolutionary Ethiopian Women's Association and its successor, the Women's Bureau, have promoted women's political involvement, they have not been successful mainly because the effectiveness of these offices has been inhibited by a lack of resources. Moreover, the lack of autonomous women's organizations has meant that Ethiopia has not had the kinds of nonpartisan women's organizations that promote women running for office and leadership training.

In many ways, the marginal status of women in politics is rooted in the country's long political history and oral traditions. Major traditional images portray women as having legitimized the monarchies and other political entities, destroyed the state in wrath, or saved it in times of disastrous wars. Yet women are rarely featured prominently at the center of power. An ancient queen, Makeda (otherwise known as the Queen of Sheba), who lived around the tenth century B.C., is regarded the founder of Ethiopia's monarchy. Queen Yodit (Judith), who assumed power after a rebellion, reigned for forty years in the tenth century. She is remembered for launching the Zagwe dynasty, which ruled between the ninth and thirteenth centuries. More recent women leaders include nine women provincial governors who were appointed by Emperor Zera Yakob (1434–1468) in reaction to the inefficiency of his male appointees. Others stood in for sons who were minors. Among those, Empress Eleni, widow of Emperor Lebna Dingil (1508–1540), acquired fame for saving the country from Muslim rebels from the east.

Though the public continues to delight in such histories, the twentieth century saw a deliberate marginalization of women from the center of power. This began by the ouster of Empress Tayetu, who was famed as a warrior and politician and was also consort of Emperor Menelik II (1889–1913). She is mostly remembered in connection with her role at the famous Battle of Adewa in 1896, when European (Italian) colonialism was defeated for the first time on African soil. Along with 100 high-ranking women, Tayetu was responsible for the supply unit of the Ethiopian army and commanded a contingent of her own on the battlefield. The fighters included women responsible for provincial treasuries and female soldiers responsible for administering military land. A very opinionated woman, Empress Tayetu was one of the first ministers appointed by Menelik II in his effort to create a European model of the "modern" state. On the death of her husband, the court appointed her stepdaughter, Zewditu, to be the Queen of Kings. Though Empress Zewditu (1916–1930) ruled in her own right, a male heir to the throne, Ras Teferi (the future Emperor Haile Selassie I, 1930–1974), was appointed at the same time and granted more power than her.

Probably feeling threatened by politicians like Tayetu and her stepdaughter, Zewditu, Emperor Haile Selassie deliberately left women out of politics and the army when he followed Zewditu on the throne. In the postwar period, the marginalization of women was accompanied by the spread of different versions of history. For instance, Queen Yodit, also nicknamed Gudit ("the awful one"), is now remembered mostly for sacking the trading city-state of Aksum and its historical monuments. Gudit is now the nickname for a current female education minister, Genet Zewde, who is accused of dismantling Ethiopia's educational institutions. Given the interest of Ethiopians in their history, such portrayals significantly work against women's positions in politics. Accompanied by their absence from effective political positions, such stereotypes give the impression that women are incompetent as decision-makers.

In the context of "modernity," which began in Ethiopia at the turn of the twentieth century with the centralization of the state, the government programs of social engineering seriously changed traditional attitudes towards women and marginalized them completely from politics. In the early 1930s, new stereotypes of femininity restricted high-class women to such organizations as the Ethiopian Women's Welfare Association, which sponsored fashion shows, charities, and welfare-oriented activities. The earliest such organization made gas masks to protect soldiers from the gas bomb attacks by the Italians during the invasion in 1935–1936. Coupled with the lack of advocacy for political equality or emancipation, such women's organizations did not leave the country a legacy of change in gender relations.

The government in the post-1974 era of socialism not only imposed its ideology on women, but also established the Revolutionary Ethiopian Women's Association in 1976 to lead women in Ethiopia. One woman appointed at the ministerial rank represented REWA within the ruling party's Politburo, while a former female high court judge headed the organization, which claimed to have 5 million members. REWA created rural showcases of female income-generating projects and tried to fight for women's rights in the National Assembly, successfully passing a bill that allowed women the right to three months' paid leave after giving birth. REWA also tried to campaign against early marriage in the northern highlands, and against lip and tooth incision and facial scarification in some parts of the southwest. They also worked with the state-sponsored rural peasant associations to politicize women.

To some extent they sensitized women about asserting their rights in challenging the household division of labor, in participating in grassroots decisionmaking bodies, in promoting the education of girls, and in carrying out development programs that were mainly meant to generate household income. REWA helped push to get Ethiopia to ratify the United Nations Convention on the Elimination of All Forms of Discrimination Against Women in 1981.

However, REWA's numerical strength was also used to organize military supplies for combating the guerrilla wars and to provide political support to the government's social engineering programs, such as changing the settlement patterns in the rural areas. Because of the women-only approach inspired by the "woman question," the mobilization and advocacy of REWA for the rights of women failed to create legal, social, or state structures that supported women's interests. Its influence on legislation was in terms of women as mothers, rather than in terms of the overall status of women's health, education, or employment opportunities in society and public offices that were controlled by the state. During the land distribution program, REWA was not able to draw attention to polygamy and single women household heads. Indeed, the officers of REWA unwittingly created male resistance, which found more ways of marginalizing women from mainstream decision-making, for instance, in the farms. Because REWA helped to organize women into the socialist structure, its success in attracting women activists was limited. The men effectively concentrated power and decision-making in their hands and marginalized the officers of REWA.

Women's Rights

The military regime also used the war in the north and its defense costs to justify its lack of attention to women's rights. It used the grassroots women's associations linked to REWA to support the peasant associations in their endless mobilization meetings and parades in support of the regime. By the late 1980s, even the control of farm products and crop cultivating and marketing decisions excluded women. The transfer of such power into men's hands led to household food shortages and silent malnutrition in many parts of the country, causing nongovernmental organizations to respond to the shortages and combat the effects of the recurring droughts. By the dawn of the 1990s many rural women had lost confidence in REWA.

The Women's Bureau, set up after Mengistu's overthrow, lost the little influence the state had with women. Headed by a minister, the bureau continues to be underfunded and powerless to stem the political turbulence that has been stirred up in the name of reasserting "tribal laws" that override women's rights. It is unable to advocate on behalf of women who suffer wide abuse of their rights such as those who are unable to choose where they live, their marriage partners, and educational and employment opportunities. The office has no resources to stop the kidnapping, rape, and unwanted marriages that force girls to flee the rural areas, and that contribute to women's internal displacement and even cross-border migration in search of political asylum and domestic employment. Parliamentarian women, political appointees, or those charged with the work of the women's affairs unit seem to lack clout, even those who are urban-based professional women.

Women's Movements

From about the mid-1990s various women's professional associations have been engaged in advocacy on women's behalf. For instance, the Ethiopian Women Lawyers Association (EWLA) has been taking up some issues such as domestic employment in the Middle East as well as cases of rape, kidnapping, and forced marriage. However, EWLA suffered censure and freezing of its funds when it criticized the court system. The Inter-Africa Committee on Traditional Practices Affecting the Health of Women and Children similarly advocates on behalf of women and children but limits its focus mainly to such harmful cultural practices as female genital cutting. As any civic activism is considered defiance of the state, the effectiveness of women's nongovernmental organizations in influencing legislation or raising awareness of women's interests remains limited. As guests of the state, even United Nations agencies are equally circumscribed.

Military Service

During the resistance guerrilla wars against Italian forces in 1935–1941, thousands of ordinary women participated; some of them, like Lekelesh Beyan and Shewareged Gedle, emerged as famed guerrilla leaders. Though at least 3,000 women war veterans were awarded medals, their involvement was never translated into women's employment in the standing army that was set up following the war.

RELIGION AND SPIRITUALITY

Alongside African spirit and ancestor worship, three monotheistic religions have been prevalent in Ethiopia over the centuries. Judaism has been present from time immemorial, Christianity since about A.D. 325, and Islam since its beginnings in the seventh century. The majority of the population belongs to one or the other of these three main religions, with roughly half Muslim and 40 percent Ethiopian Orthodox. The remainder practice other forms of religions, including spirit and ancestor worship. People of all religious affiliations also consult with diviners and astrologers. Their attachment to the formal religions tends to shift with the degree of their prosperity.

Rituals and Religious Practices

Men are predominantly in the leadership of the monotheistic religions, which all segregate men and women and maintain a strict hierarchy in leadership. The Ethiopian Orthodox Church (sometimes incorrectly referred to by foreigners as "the Coptic" [Egyptian] church) allows women to provide supportive services to priests. Prior to 1974, women worked as administrators of its properties. Even though Ethiopian Muslim women in the east wore clothing that distinguished them from the rest of the population, it has been only since the 1990s that many began to cover their faces, coinciding with the expansion of Islamic fundamentalism in Ethiopia.

In broad terms, the popular teachings of the Ethiopian Orthodox Church hold women as the cause for the demise of mankind, having misled the original man, Adam, by giving him the forbidden fruit of the fig tree (not apple). On the other hand, the Virgin Mary is held to be the cause for the transition of mankind from the Era of Damnation to the Era of Mercy because she was the mother of Christ. While Eve is used to put down women, Mary is used to extol them. Indeed, Christians encourage women in labor by a litany to Mary, a patron saint of birth. The perception about the Virgin Mary is transposed into respect for women, but expressly as mothers of men who might turn out to be kings or church patriarchs.

The most common form of nonmonotheistic spirituality revolves around worshipping the fertility goddess, Atete. Often associated with water and fresh grass, the spirit is worshipped mostly around New Year (September 10/11). Celebrating her includes caressing a string of beads, the fetish that worshippers keep to represent her. Without being named, the same goddess is understood to be the object of worship on the first day of Genbot, around May 10 or 11, alongside the feast of the Virgin Mary. Although men join in, women are more fervently devoted to her, because they believe that she will protect the health of the neighborhood and their families.

Spirit possession is another form of spirituality that attracts women. Some of the spirits can be evoked by coffee sessions, which are accompanied by grass, flowers, and incense. Believed to be the hidden children of Adam and Eve, the spirits, known by the collective name *zar*, are believed to behave like human beings. They possess the opposite sex to the one whom "they" claim to wed. Most urban people, strict Christians and those who belong to churches introduced in the twentieth century, downplay their importance. Some consider them as the evil forces of Bible fame. For the majority, especially from the rural areas, however, they are real, providing cause for receiving and giving attention to those who are possessed. Women, in particular, placate the possessed, singing and feasting and socializing around the "problem." With some of the *zar* demanding the ritual sacrifice of a chicken or a sheep, fussing over "the problem" gives weight to celebrations, especially New Year. Only the homes of a few *zar*-possessed women develop into cult centers. Indeed, there have been no other cults of any of the goddesses or spirits since an emperor campaigned to destroy the worshippers of Deseq and Dino in the fourteenth century. Identifying the specific names and characters of the *zar* is left to experts in astrology and herbal medicine. Such savants belong to the clergy of the Orthodox Church or to Islam, and women rarely number among them.

VIOLENCE

Domestic Violence

Domestic violence such as wife-beating, psychological abuse, and rape (including marital rape) appears to be common, even though all of these are theoretically punishable by law. In fact, as far back as the 1890s, rape entailed capital punishment, and it still draws imprisonment or heavy fines. Very often, however, attitudes regarding male superiority prevent criminalization of such abuses. For example, semi-joking stereotypes suggest that women love to be beaten because it proves how much attention they receive from their husbands.

Rape/Sexual Assault

Considering the emphasis on girls' virginity and chastity, rape is precarious for women socially, psychologically, and physically. Ironically, the unstated rule that a rapist is obliged to marry his victim to save her from public shame has encouraged kidnapping and forced marriage. Bringing abusers to the law courts, or to elders in most communities, is possible. Rapists or abusers can face legal punishment or censure, but often victims find it impossible to find support from male relatives. Consequently, social pressure tends to deflect male criminality toward women, sometimes even when cases of domestic abuse reach the courts or the elders.

The practice of kidnapping and raping a woman for marriage has become more frequent since 1991 because of the assertion of ethnic nationalism. Many young men, especially in the rural areas, have felt emboldened by ethnic fervor to kidnap, rape, and thus forcefully claim girls as their "wives." As a result, even though the law protects women from rape or kidnapping, several young rape victims, with very limited capacity to take their cases to court, have reportedly committed suicide or have murdered their rapists. In the first few months of 2001 alone, several such girls were brought to court for fatally attacking their rapists. This added an unexpected dimension to women's measure of self-defense, and generated a new dimension to the incidental criminality of women.

Trafficking in Women and Children

If lack of a viable environment for girls' education until 1991 inhibited women's rights, the return to tribal politics and "traditions" since 1991 has left women open to victimization, not least by predatory sex offenders and traffickers abroad. Employment agencies have proliferated since 1991 in a new urban phenomenon capturing unskilled workers' attention. The agencies specialize in finding jobs for unskilled women abroad, their main clients being school dropouts and unemployed high school graduates who are girls between the ages of fourteen and twenty. They reportedly charge high fees, at times as high as $2,000, and bond the girls and their families against overwhelming debts. Coordinating their operations from bases in neighboring countries, the owners ultimately entrap the girls in the traffic of commercial sex and abusive domestic service in the Middle East. It appears that some of them have been in operation since the early 1980s. It is this recent phenomena that the Ethiopian Women Lawyers Association has been campaigning against, though with few results.

Sadly, any cooperation to stop the traffic is precluded by several factors. These include the lack of communication among the girls, which prevents their stories from reaching the ears of others; growing poverty and hopelessness among the youth; the increasing desire of both parents and girls to escape the worsening economic and political conditions; and the involvement of high officials in the employment racket, which also shelters the abusers. Remittances from abroad were reported to be over $320 million in 2000, and are said to make a major contribution to the national budget.

War and Military Repression

Systematic violations toward women during wars are known, but the extent of systematic wartime rape, for example, is difficult to establish as reliable data have yet to be compiled. The most intensive internal wars of the twentieth century began in 1960 with the secessionist Eritrean movement. From the mid-1970s, the guerrilla groups increased in size, with the original Eritrean People's Liberation Front organizing ethnically based parties such as the Tigray People's Liberation Front and the Oromo Liberation Front, all aiming at breaking away from Ethiopia. At the same time, other nationwide parties such as the Ethiopian People's Revolutionary Party and MEISON (Amharic, for the "All Ethiopian Socialist Movement") locked the military government in an armed struggle. There were women warriors both on the government and the guerrilla sides. Taking advantage of the internal dissent engaging the army in the northern parts of the country, irredentist Somalia invaded in 1978 to liberate the Ogaden in the southeast. The state had to divert all resources to the war front, reportedly appropriating $800 million per day for defense spending in the early 1980s. The wars between the government and guerrilla groups credited with conducting "the longest war in Africa" encouraged the politicization of differences, and thereby heightened hostilities between ethnic/linguistic groups. Women suffered all the usual consequences of conflict. They devoted emotional and material resources on husbands, daughters, and sons, most of whom became liable to forced recruitment by the protagonists.

It is difficult to give any figures regarding these conflicts, because the reports on the atrocities committed by both sides were documented primarily for propaganda purposes. The political alignments of reporters during the cold war also led to strong biases. What can be stated for certain is that internally displaced people from the fighting regions of the north swelled the cities, generating the huge number of street children and adults now found in Ethiopia's cities. Thirty years of war resulted in heavy losses of lives. The government politicized even the war-related famines so that during the droughts and famine of 1984, it transported thousands of families from the affected areas to the western and southwestern regions.

Due to the intensity of the wars, it became possible for the state of Israel to spirit out a whole population, namely the Bete Israel (also known as Falasha or, by foreigners, as the "Black Jews of Ethiopia"), airlifting them to Israel in "Operation Moses" and "Operation Solomon" between the 1980s and the early 1990s. The Tigray People's Liberation Front also marched peasants from Tigray in a show of its control over the region, and eventually appropriated lands that belonged to Amharic speakers in Bagemder in northwest Ethiopia. Women and children were the ones mainly shunted back and forth by all sides. Though they eventually intermarried, those who were transplanted by the military regime, for instance, were resented by most of the local population, including those in Bagemder.

The legacy of all these developments is felt strongly to this day with the new government policy of political restructuring along linguistic lines. It has resulted in the harassment and murder of thousands of minorities who do not speak the dominant language and of populations forcibly moved by the government. The new regime has sought to create exclusively monolingual territories, erupting in conflicts over land, housing, and employment opportunities. Women have suffered the most, both among the newly transplanted populations and among other minorities who always had lived among what now are held to be monolingual populations.

OUTLOOK FOR THE TWENTY-FIRST CENTURY

Ethiopia became signatory to the Convention on the Elimination of All Forms of Discrimination Against Women in 1981, the African Charter on Human Rights in 1983, and the Universal Human Rights Charter in 1991. Being a developing country that relies heavily on foreign aid, Western donors' demands for the respect of human rights have obliged the Ethiopian People's Revolutionary Democratic Front (EPRDF) regime to incorporate the Universal Human Rights Charter into its constitution. So far, no Ethiopian government has implemented effective programs to bring women's interests into mainstream education, employment, or overall improvements in the quality of life. Stereotyped views about women's inferiority prevail, even though most men emphasize the respect they have for them. Stories of atrocities from the past thirty years of civil war continue to serve political purposes in the game of victors and vanquished. They encourage the region's traditions of masculinity, warriorhood, revenge, and hostility. These values overshadow the political process, preventing democracy and autonomy for women's organizations in particular. On top of this, the current government's political manipulation of linguistic, ethnic, and other differences has sown the seeds of women's segregation and isolation from mainstream development.

Gender advocacy comes mainly from the ongoing international and national campaigns against female genital cutting, the Africawide focus on HIV/AIDS, and other similar international processes. Influences by the United Nations Development Programme and other consultative processes might generate better understanding of rural women's inherited knowledge of ecological interdependence and their autonomous spirit. The emergence of nationwide local nongovernmental organizations, such as the Ethiopian Women's Lawyers Association, might eventually prove the antidote to the current state's negative uses of Ethiopian diversity. However, independent organizations continue to face government imposed constraints on their activities. For example, EWLA had already been interrupted when the government froze its assets and banned it in September 2001. The ban was lifted in October 2001, after a popular outcry by women.

NOTES

1. All statistics are from the World Health Organisation (WHO) and United Nations Fund for Children (UNICEF), 2000.

2. According to the United Nations Development Programme's Human Development Indicators 2002.

3. Ibid.

4. Ibid.

RESOURCE GUIDE

Suggested Reading

Berhane-Selassie, Tsehai. "Ethiopian Rural Women and the State." In *African Feminism: The Politics of Survival in Sub-Saharan Africa*, edited by Gwendolyn Mikell. Philadelphia: University of Pennsylvania Press, 1997.

———. "Gender and Occupational Potters in Wolayta: Imposed Femininity and 'Mysterious Survival' in Ethiopia." In *Gender Issues in Ethiopia*. Addis Ababa: Addis Ababa University, 1991.

———. *Gender Issues in Ethiopia*. Addis Ababa: Addis Ababa University, 1991.

———. "Women Guerilla Fighters." *North East African Studies* 1, no. 3 (1980).

Cassiers, Anne. "Ethiopian Pottery." *Africa Arts* no. 3 (Spring 1971): 45–47.

Eshete, Almaz. "Women and Cooperatives: The Ethiopian Experience." In *All Are Not Equal: African Women in Cooperatives*, edited by Linda Mayoux. London: Institute for African Alternatives, 1988.

Esmonde, Peter, W. "Education and Gender in Rural Ethiopia: The Case of Dalocha." Proceedings of the Eleventh International Conference of Ethiopian Studies, Addis Ababa, 1991.

Kebede, Hanna. "Gender Relations in Mobilizing Human Resources." In *Ethiopia: Options for Rural Development*, edited by Siegfried Pausewang, Fantu Cheru, Stefan Brüne, and Eshetu Chole. London: Zed Books, 1990.

Lydall, Jean. " 'Women Are Beaten': Hamar Explanations of Heir Traditions of Beating." Paper presented at the Eleventh International Conference of Ethiopian Studies, Addis Ababa, 1991.

Negussie, Birgit. *Traditional Wisdom and Modern Development: A Case Study of Traditional Peri-Natal Knowledge Among Elderly Women in Southern Shewa, Ethiopia*. Stockholm: Stockholm University Institute of International Education, 1988.

———. *Reproduction and Family Planning in Ethiopian Society: A Survey of Existing Knowledge, Annotated Bibliography*. Stockholm: Institute of International Education, 1987.

Olmstead, Judith. "Farmer's Wife, Weaver's Wife: Women and Work in Two Southern Ethiopian Communities." In *Women in Africa: Studies in Social and Economic Change*, edited by Edna G. Bay and Nancy Hafkin. Stanford, CA: Stanford University Press, 1976.

Pankhurst, Helen. "What Change and for Whom." In *Ethiopia: Options for Rural Development*, edited by Siegfried Pausewang, Fantu Cheru, Stefan Brüne and Eshetu Chole. London: Zed Books, 1990.

Prouty, Chris. "Eight Ethiopian Women of the Zemene Mesafint (c 1769–1855)." *North East African Studies Notes* 1, no. 2 (1979).

———. *Empress Taytu and Menilek II: Ethiopia, 1883–1910*. Trenton, NJ: Red Sea Press, 1986.

Sergew, Hable Selassie. "The Problem of Gudit: A Woman Revenges Male Oppression." *Journal of Ethiopian Studies* 10, no. 1 (1972).

Video/Film

The Women Who Smile. 1990. Joanna Head and Jean Lydall, directors. Zum Hainteich 27 49326, Melle, Germany.

Web Sites

Department of Reproductive Health and Research including UNDP/UNFPA/WHO/ World Bank. Special Programme of Research, Development and Research Training in Human Reproduction, www.who.int/reproductivehealth/publications/rhr_01_11_ annual_report_2000/atr2000.

Integrated Regional Information Networks (IRIN) of the United Nations, www. reliefweb.int/irin/cea.

International Labour Office (ILO), *Key Indicators of the Labour Market* (KILM) database and *Yearbook of Labour Statistics* (Geneva), www.ilo.org/kilm.

Population Division and Statistic Division of the United Nations Secretariat, as based on Women's Indicators and Statistics Database (Wistat), www.un.org/depts/unsd/ gender/wistat.wistat.html.

Organizations

African Federation of Women Entrepreneurs (AFWE)
P.O. Box 3001
Addis Ababa
Ethiopia
Phone: 251-1-517200 ×301
Fax: 251-1-512785

Agency for Cooperation and Research in Development (ACORD)
P.O. Box 24082
Code 1000
Addis Ababa
Ethiopia
Phone: 251-1-534809
Fax: 251-1-516650
Email: abaynesh_biru@hotmail.com

The Centre for Research, Training, and Information on Women in Development
  (CERTWID)
Institute of Development Research
Addis Ababa University
P.O. Box 1176
Addis Ababa
Ethiopia
Phone: 251-1-12338
Fax: 251-1-551333

Ethiopian Media Women's Association (EMWA)
P.O. Box 62094
Addis Ababa
Ethiopia
Phone: 251-1-157244

Ethiopian Women Lawyers Association (EWLA)
P.O. Box 1215
Addis Ababa
Ethiopia
Phone: 251-1-201780
Email: ewla@telecom.net.et

Hope for Women
P.O. Box 1509
Addis Ababa
Ethiopia
Phone: 251-1-518400-352

Inter-African Committee on Traditional Practices Affecting the Health of Women and
    Children in Africa
c/o UNECA
P.O. Box 30001
Addis Ababa
Ethiopia
Phone: 251-1-517200/51
Fax: 251-1-51 4682

National Committee on Traditional Practices
P.O. Box 12629
Addis Ababa
Ethiopia
Phone: 251-1-181163/624502
Fax: 251-1-621243
Email: nctpe@telecom.net.et

Network of Ethiopian Women Association
(seventeen organizations formed in 2003)
Contact through Ethiopian Media Women's Association (EMWA)

SELECTED BIBLIOGRAPHY

Aredo, Dejene. "The Gender Division of Labour in Ethiopian Agriculture: A Study
    of Time Allocation Among People in Private and Co-operative Farms in Two
    Villages." Addis Ababa, 1980.
Beddada, B. "Female Circumcision in Ethiopia." *Traditional Practices Affecting the
    Health of Women and Children*. EMRO Publication no. 2. Alexandria: World
    Health Organization, 1979.
Berhane-Selaisse, Tsehai. "Ethiopian Rural Women and the State." In *African Femi-*

nism: The Politics of Survival in Sub-Saharan Africa, edited by Gwendolyn Mikell. Philadelphia: University of Pennsylvania Press, 1997.

————. *In Search of Ethiopian Women*. London: CHANGE International Reports, Women and Society, 1984.

Berhane-Selassie, Tsehai, ed. *Gender Issues in Ethiopia: Proceedings of the First University Seminar on Gender Issues in Ethiopia, 24–26 December 1989*. Addis Ababa: Institute of Ethiopian Studies, Addis Ababa University, November 1991.

Crummey, Donald. "Women and Landed Property in Gondarine Ethiopia." *International Journal of African Historical Studies* 14, no. 3 (1981), 444–65.

Druce, Nell, and Jenny Hammond, eds. *Sweeter Than Honey: Ethiopian Women and Revolution: Testimonies of Tigrayan Women*. Trenton, NJ: Red Sea Press, 1990.

Haile, Daniel. "Law and the Status of Women in Ethiopia." Addis Ababa: UN/ECA, ATRCW, 1980.

Haile, Fikrte. "Wood Bearers of Ethiopia." *World Health* (April–May 1990).

Olmstead, Judith. *Woman Between Two Worlds: Portrait of an Ethiopian Rural Leader*. Urbana-Champaign: University of Illinois Press, 1997.

Pankhurst, Helen. *Gender, Development and Identity: An Ethiopian Study*. London: Zed Books, 1992.

Pankhurst, Rita. "Senedu Gebru: A Role Model for Ethiopian Women." In *Gender Issues in Ethiopia*, edited by Tsehai Berhane-Selassie. Addis Ababa: Addis Ababa University, 1991.

Poluha, Eva. *Central Planning and Local Reality: The Case of a Producers Cooperative in Ethiopia*. Stockholm: University of Stockholm Studies in Social Anthropology, 1989.

Prouty, Chris. *Empress Taytu and Menilek II: Ethiopia, 1883–1910*. Trenton, NJ: Red Sea Press, 1986.

6

GHANA

Kathleen Maria Fallon

PROFILE OF GHANA

Modern-day Ghana, previously referred to as the Gold Coast by the British, was colonized by the Portuguese, Dutch, and ultimately the British. In 1957, Ghana became independent from Britain, becoming the first sub-Saharan African country to gain independence from a colonial power. Kwame Nkrumah was elected as president in 1960 and maintained leadership until 1966. Since 1966 there have been six coups followed by military regimes and three attempts to establish and maintain a democratic state. The most recent coup took place in 1981, when the Provisional National Defense Council, (PNDC) headed by Flight Lieutenant Jerry Rawlings, came to power and suspended the constitution. In 1992, however, the PNDC allowed for the first multiparty democratic election since the overthrow in 1981. This event marked the fourth attempt at establishing a democratic state. Since 1992, Ghana has had a democracy, and as of 2001 has been ruled by President John Kufour of the New Patriotic Party.

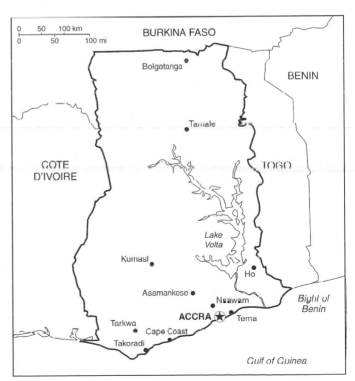

Ghana is one of the most developed countries within sub-Saharan Africa. Major exports include cocoa, gold, and timber. Additional exports include tuna, bauxite, rubber, and some agricultural products, such as pineapples. The gross domestic product is based primarily on agriculture, since at least 50 percent of the nation is employed in the agricultural sector. Beginning in 1983, Ghana has implemented stringent economic reforms with guidance and pressure from the World Bank and International Monetary Fund in order to decrease inflation and government controls, and increase privatization. Despite some of Ghana's successes, it still remains dependent on international funds; in recent years the cedi (the national currency) depreciated leading to public discontent.

Geographically Ghana is slightly smaller than the state of Oregon, lies on the West African coast between Togo and Côte d'Ivoire, and has one of the world's largest artificial lakes — Lake Volta. The climate ranges from humid tropical rain forests in the south to dry Sahelian plains in the north. From January until March, Ghana experiences a dry season when the Harmattan winds (winds from the Saharan desert) blow toward the south. The rainy season occurs from mid-March to July and again in September through October. Of the land in Ghana, approximately 12 percent is arable, 7 percent has permanent crops, 22 percent has permanent pastures, and 35 percent has forests and woodlands.

Although English is the official language, Akan is the predominant language spoken. Of course, numerous languages are spoken throughout Ghana. There are over eighty ethnic groups, and the largest groups include the Akan, Moshi-Dagomba, Ewe, and Ga. The predominant religions practiced include indigenous religions, Islam, and Christianity.

The population of Ghana has increased from 12 million in 1984 to 19.5 million in 2000. The life expectancy is 58 years, and the average woman will give birth to approximately 4.3 children. In 1999, the infant mortality rate was fairly high. About 57 out of 1,000 infants die after birth. In addition, for every 100,000 women giving birth, 210 women die.

OVERVIEW OF WOMEN'S ISSUES

Women in Ghana come from all walks of life. They vary according to ethnic group, religious affiliation, educational attainment, wealth, marital status, urban and rural residence, and many other factors. While we cannot examine the situation for all women of Ghana since their experiences vary widely, we can examine general patterns that have affected them.

There are patterns of education, employment, family and sexuality, health, politics, religion, and violence in relation to women. For example, colonization influenced the means by which both men and women have access to education and employment. Similarly, colonization and indigenous cultural values and expectations have affected family and sexuality practices, as well as religious practices. On the other hand, economic and political instability within Ghana created patterns that affect women's access to health care, their participation in politics, as well as their influence on state laws.

EDUCATION

Under British rule, missionaries were the first to establish formal schools; the British government soon followed suit. The British schools were established mainly for the education of boys in order to assist them in obtaining formal-sector jobs, or jobs formally recognized by the state, in cities. Some schools were established for girls; however, the instruction focused on domestic chores, such as sewing or cooking. The Western domestic value of the housewife role was taught in the schools. Such instruction promoted the belief of Ghanaians that girls would eventually become housewives and hence had no reason to attend more academically oriented schools. On the other hand, under colonial rule, boys were expected to eventually earn money and were encouraged to attend schools since jobs obtained as a result of education earned more than physical labor would. This colonial implementation of education disadvantaged women relative to men. Moreover, it reinforced the domestic roles of women; it formed and reinforced the values that placed women in the domestic sphere and men in the public sphere. In the 1960s these values slowly changed as more girls began to enter secondary schools and emphasis on the domestic sphere dissipated within the school system.

Opportunities

Girls still do not have the same access to educational opportunities as boys today. Statistics compiled by the Ghana Statistical Service and the Ministry of Education demonstrate girls' lack of access to education.[1] Out of the total primary school enrollment in 1990–1991, 55 percent were boys and 45 percent were girls. In 1996–1997, the primary school enrollment in Ghana only increased slightly for girls: 47 percent for girls in comparison to 53 percent for boys. The gender gap further increases when examining secondary schools: in 1990–1991 the total enrollment consisted of 67 percent boys and 33 percent girls. The gender breakdown did improve gradually. In 1996–1997 boys made up 57 percent of the total enrollment and girls made up only 43 percent. The gender gap widens more significantly in institutions of higher education. Although there are no statistics for the 1996–1997 school year, the total enrollment at the University of Ghana in 1990–1991 consisted of 76 percent males and 24 percent females. Although the gender gap is minimal at the primary level, girls' access to secondary and higher levels of education remains lower in comparison to boys' access.

Three main reasons could explain this continued difference between male-female enrollment. First, women are primarily seen as mothers while men are viewed as financial supporters in sub-Saharan Africa. Kinship lineage emphasizes the importance of the family and women feel the resulting pressure to bear children in order to continue their lineage. The social status of women hinges on having children, and it becomes their primary responsibility. If they have several children, they gain respect from relatives since they have assured the continued line of the family. Due to these expectations, many girls feel pressure to have children and do not finish their education because of teenage pregnancies.

Girls are additionally expected to care for younger siblings and are taken out of school for this purpose. With each additional younger sibling, the likelihood of dropping out of school increased among girls.[2] Men, on the other hand, are expected to provide monetary support for the household and their parents. Since there are no social security benefits in Ghana, parents depend on children for financial support. Although norms are changing fast, traditionally women were expected to contribute to their husbands' earnings and care for their children. Men were expected to be financially responsible for their parents. Therefore, families tended to send boys, over girls, to school for the purpose of obtaining a higher paying job. The socially expected role of woman in sub-Saharan Africa was seen by many as that of a caretaker, while the man was socially expected to fulfill the role of the income provider.

Despite the benefits that education offers girls and women, they remain at a disadvantage in gaining access to education compared with boys and men. They tend to be bound to the societal expectations of their gender roles. In addition, women's lack of access to education impacts their participation within the employment sector. As education increases so do employment opportunities. Therefore, men tend to have greater access to a wide variety of employment opportunities, while women are limited in their employment opportunities.

Literacy

Men are more literate than women. The illiteracy rate of men is 20.6 percent, as compared with 38.5 percent among women.

EMPLOYMENT AND ECONOMICS

Farming

Due to women's lack of access to fertile land, many women do not have the opportunity to plant cash crops in order to increase their earnings. Plus, women who are heads of the household have to care for many dependents while also living off the meager earnings gained through farming. Women work fifteen to twenty-five hours longer than men each week because of their housework responsibilities.[3] These hours cut into the time they could be spending on the farm.

Paid Employment

Even within the formal sector, women's activities have been affected by their educational opportunities. Those women who have entered the formal sector tend to enter jobs that are gender segregated, meaning that most women work as teachers, nurses, seamstresses, or caterers. Their domestic chores are simply transferred out of the home. Most important, few women within this sector hold higher status or decisionmaking positions. For example, women who are teachers are predominantly found in primary and junior secondary schools and not in senior secondary schools or in institutions of higher education.

Within organizations, women comprise less than 10 percent of individuals who influence policy and take decisions within organizations.[4] In 1995, within the civil service sector, no women were chief directors, 10 percent were directors, 15 percent were deputy directors, and only approximately 14 percent were assistant directors. Out of all the individuals who worked in the administrative section of the civil service, only 12 percent were women. In addition, of all the women who participate in the formal sector over 60 percent are estimated to hold jobs that do not require any decisionmaking skills.[5] Thus women have little influence on policies or outcomes that would affect their lives.

Although educational experiences generally affect women entering these positions, other factors have prevented women from holding higher positions of authority.[6] First, few women have role models to look up to. Since most women participate in employment guided by expectations, girls and women may simply not aspire to top positions since they do not often see women in them. Second, since women do not have as much education as men, they may not have the same opportunities to be promoted within an organization. Third, a number of women within the formal sector complain that they face discrimination within the workplace. Because many men do not believe women should hold positions of authorities and should rather remain subordinate to men, they may not believe women should be promoted. Some men may fear that their company will lose profits if they promote women since women may take time off for maternity leave.

Informal Economic Activities

Due to the disadvantages women face, and the history of women's limited participation within the educational system, most choose to work within the informal sector. Because nearly 40 percent of women, as compared to 20 percent of men, are illiterate, most women work in the infor-

Women traders at the Kejetia market, Ghana. Photo © TRIP/M. Barlow.

mal sector, or the sector that is not formally recognized by government and business institutions, as either farmers or small-scale traders.

Yet even within the informal sector, women still face many additional disadvantages. They have not been encouraged to farm cash crops; they have little access to fertile land; they must spend more time on household activities than men; and women who are heads of households must care for more dependents. Moreover, they have little access to formal loans to improve their business ventures.

Pay

The 1992 constitution guarantees that individuals will not be discriminated against according to gender, that they will have right to equal pay for equal work. Yet women earn less than men at all levels of education and earn roughly 75 percent of what men earn overall.[7] However, these estimates reflect primarily the returns from wage labor. Many women do not participate in the wage labor force, but rather work in the informal sector, generally as traders or farmers. In the informal sector their earnings may be considerably greater than in the formal sector, where women's wages may be below those of men.

Support for Mothers/Caretakers

Women must spend time on household activities, and women in female-headed households must cater to a number of dependents. Whereas men may concentrate their time and effort on farming, women still have to prepare meals as well as care for the house, children, and other dependents. In addition, there are more dependents living in households headed by women, than in households headed by men. This makes households headed by women among the poorest.[8]

Maternal Leave

According to the constitution, mothers will be given three months' paid leave before and after giving birth. However this law only applies to the formal sector and many companies do not comply knowing that repercussions are relatively rare.

Child Care

The constitution advocates the provision of child care facilities, but does not indicate the manner in which these facilities will be provided. It is still common that girls are taken out of school to look after siblings while their mother works.

Inheritance, Property, and Land Rights

Women do not have equal access to land as men do. Among most ethnic groups within Ghana, women must ask for land from either the chief of the village in which they live or from the head of their family lineage, who also tends to be male. When women do receive land from these individuals, the land is usually smaller and less fertile than the land that men receive. Similarly, when a woman marries, her husband will usually give her a small piece of land to farm, which is not as fertile, and which is not her property. When a woman's husband dies her property often goes to his family. If she gets divorced she will most likely lose all of her land to her husband.

Social/Government Programs

Laws have been implemented to protect women from discrimination. In 1985 the Convention for the Elimination of All Forms of Discrimination Against Women was ratified and should provide for nondiscrimination in employment and pay and the guarantee of job security in the event of marriage or maternity. The 1992 constitution also guarantees that individuals will not be discriminated against according to gender, and that they will have the right to equal pay for equal work and maternity leave. It also advocates for the provision of child care facilities, but does not indicate the manner in which these facilities will be provided. Although these laws are implemented to protect women from discrimination, they only protect women within the formal sector. Moreover, the laws are not always carefully monitored and some companies simply do not comply. Hence, despite the existence of laws to protect women from discrimination within the formal sector, they are not fully enforced and women still find themselves at a disadvantage.

Both women farmers and traders are at a disadvantage in procuring loans in order to start or improve upon their business enterprises. Most formal credit agencies do not view women as potential recipients of loans because of their low educational levels and because they do not own enough collateral, such as homes or land, to put up against their loans. Due to historical and family reasons many women do not have the opportunity to gain an advanced education or access to fertile land. However, when they do have the chance to improve their farming techniques or increase their business output, they are denied this opportunity by formal lenders because of their low educational status and lack of landownership.

Many women must rely on informal means of obtaining loans, which most likely involves family and friends, who lend them money in order to improve their business ventures and to increase their profits. Because women must rely on informal means for loans, their ventures are also limited and they do not have the same advantage as men, who are more educated and own more land.

FAMILY AND SEXUALITY

Gender Roles and Division of Labor

Historical development and cultural expectations influence the division of labor between the sexes.[9] Both boys and girls are expected to help around the house by doing the dishes, laundry, cleaning, and farming. However, as they get older, girls provide more help for the mothers within the home, while the amount of chores that boys do decreases. Boys are more often encouraged to continue their education instead of help with the chores. As adults, women are expected to cook meals, clean the house, do laundry, and care for children, elderly, and other dependents. Men are expected to provide money for some food, clothing, schooling tuition, and other types of amenities, such as furniture, within the home. In many cases, men can no longer afford to provide money for all these services, and must rely on their wives to supplement their income. Women will use some of their income to contribute to food, clothing, and tuition. Interestingly, most women and men keep their income separate, and they will not confide in their partner the amount of money they have. This provides some independence for women, since they may determine how they will spend the money they earn. The reason married individuals tend to keep separate incomes is most likely related to the expectations of customary-law marriages, which emphasize family lineage rather than unified nuclear families.

Marriage

In Ghana there are three types of marriages: marriage under customary law, the marriage ordinance, and the Marriage of the Mohammedens Ordinance. The most common type of marriage—marriage under customary law—includes the possibility of polygamous marriages and the payment of bridewealth to the wife's family, but this varies by ethnic group. There is an oral contract between a woman and a man, which leads to an alliance between their two extended families. Through marriage, the man gains rights over his wife. He may choose to marry additional women, and he may also legally have an affair. The wife, however, may not take on additional husbands, nor may she have an affair. If she does have an affair, her husband has the right to divorce her and demand fines be paid by her lover and herself. If the husband and wife were to decide to divorce, this is generally achieved through negotiations between their extended families.

The marriage ordinance is based on a registration system for monogamous relationships. This ordinance is very similar to marriage practices in the United States. Unlike the customary marriage, the marriage ordinance does not involve the participation of extended family members. It is primarily used for the purposes of forming nuclear families. However, individuals often also participate in a customary marriage to symbolize the union of their families. Divorce through this type of marriage is settled through court.

The Marriage of the Mohammedens Ordinance involves the registration of marriages and divorces under Islamic law. Under such law, the husband is to pay a bridewealth to his wife. He may also take up to four wives and may have additional mistresses. Although those individuals who are married under this law are required to register within a week of their marriage and divorce, few individuals do this. Depending on their ethnic group and their religious beliefs, Ghanaians will choose to marry according to one of these three types of marriages.

Reproduction

The role of reproduction also affects women's social status. When a woman marries, one of her primary goals is to continue the family lineage and there is tremendous pressure for her to reproduce. Simultaneously, children contribute significantly to agriculture: the more children a woman has, the more help she and her husband will have to farm food crops. A woman may also have more children so that some may care for her in her old age when she can no longer work and gain an income. For all of these reasons, women generally gain more status within their community when they have more children. In 1999 women had an average of 4.3 children.[10]

Sex Education

Authorities attempt to target adolescents on topics of human reproduction both in and outside of the educational system through the Ghana Reproductive Health Service Policy.

Contraception and Abortion

One of the primary goals of the Government of Ghana is to control population growth. As part of the Ghana Reproductive Health Service Policy, there are information, communication, and education offices that encourage individuals to make informed decisions regarding their reproductive health.[11] They target school-aged and adolescent children, religious bodies, clients with reproductive health diseases, policymakers, and opinion leaders. These efforts appear to have had minimal impact, since only 20 percent of married women and only 33.5 percent of married men use birth control.[12]

The low use of birth control is due to pressure to have many children. It also has to do with the government ban on the advertisement of contraception in the mass media in 1986 that was imposed in order to maintain moral standards.[13] However, the government does attempt to provide knowledge about birth control and affordable contraceptive services for individuals through health services. The government has also approved advertisements that promote condom usage in order to reduce the prevalence of AIDS. Through these methods, the government hopes to reach individuals regarding contraception while still maintaining a moral standard.

The government has taken a similar stance in relation to abortion. Abortion is only legal if the pregnancy is the result of rape, incest, defilement of a handicapped woman, if the child may develop a serious handicap or disease, or if the pregnancy threatens the life of the woman. In this last case, only a registered nurse or doctor may perform the abortion. Otherwise, abortion is illegal with penalty of up to five years in prison for the individual undergoing the abortion, as well as the individual helping with the abortion.

Teen Pregnancy

More than 60 percent of women have been pregnant by the age of 20.[14] Although the Ghana Reproductive Health Service Policy includes school-aged and adolescent children among its focus, it has not successfully won the battle against societal pressures for women to have many children.[15]

HEALTH

Health Care Access

Similar to reproductive health, access to general medical facilities and medicine also affects women's status. Only about 60 percent of all individuals have access to medical facilities, and within rural areas, only 45 percent have access to medical facilities.[16] In 1995, the health care system was made up of 177 hospitals, 733 health centers, and 869 clinics—that is, 1 clinic for every 10,512 persons. Since medical care is not readily accessible to many Ghanaians, one of the main objectives of Ghana's health policy is to increase access to medical facilities. One means of achieving this is through the promotion of a decentralized Primary Health Care system, which provides cost-effective services. Originally, the government subsidized public health care services; unfortunately, economic policy reforms have led to the withdrawal of subsidies for health care.

Diseases and Disorders

Recently, poverty alleviation programs supported by donor agencies, such as the United Nations Development Programme and the U.S. Agency for International Development, have begun to support health care services. For example, immunization coverage has increased, as has the distribution of vitamin A and support to community-based services.[17]

AIDS

The government is also attempting to target the growing rates of HIV and AIDS infection. From 1986 until 1995 there were 17,564 AIDS cases reported, and women constitute the majority of these cases. In 1994, there were an estimated 172,000 adults with HIV, approximately 2.3 percent of the population. As part of a general policy, the government is attempting to track the prevalence of HIV/AIDS and to provide information about the disease to health care providers. There is also a mass media prevention campaign featuring entertainment, education, promotion of condoms and interpersonal communication, family life education, and advocacy.[18] Although the government banned advertisements of contraceptives via the mass media, it has allowed for advertisements of condoms in order to prevent HIV/AIDS infection.

Female Genital Cutting

The government has similarly targeted the practice of female genital cutting (FGC). In 1994 a criminal code was passed that made FGC a second-degree felony punishable by imprisonment for a minimum of three years. Despite this law, approximately 30 percent of all girls and women have undergone FGC in Ghana. The practice is most prevalent among women from northern ethnic groups, who are predominantly Muslim. Among these women, most claimed that it was necessary for marriage, as well as for religious reasons.[19] The reproductive health service policy seeks to target groups of individuals regarding FGC. These groups include politicians, policymakers, community leaders, religious bodies, women's groups, men's groups, circumcisers, and other groups.[20] They attempt to integrate FGC services into all reproductive health services, and the school health education program to eliminate the practice of FGC.

POLITICS AND LAW

Leadership and Decision-making

Quota Laws

The Representation of the People (Women Members) Act of 1959 (Act no. 72) provided for the election of ten women to parliament.[21] With the implementation of this act, women came to represent 10 percent of the 104-member General Assembly. Even when Nkrumah declared Ghana a one-party state in 1964, women representatives were still voted into the assembly. As far back as 1965 there were already nineteen women representatives.

However, in 1966, Nkrumah was overthrown by General Joseph Ankrah. In the succeeding regimes and republics, women's representation within the government declined.[22] In the Second Republic (1969–1972), only one woman was a member of parliament, and in the Third Republic (1979–1981), only five women were members of parliament. Flight Lieutenant Jerry Rawlings came to power through a coup in 1981, and his regime maintained power until the latest transition to democracy in 1992, when he was elected president. His regime, the Provisional National Defense Council, like those of his predecessors, did not have an equal representation of women. For example, in 1985 there was only one woman out of sixteen cabinet members and one woman out of twenty-nine state ministers. In 1990 there were no women holding the position of cabinet member or state minister.[23]

Political Participation

Although women still do not have equal representation within the government, their representation has recently increased. In the 2000 parliamentary elections, eighteen women gained seats, increasing women's representation to 9 percent. The current president, John Kufour, has also appointed five female state ministers. These numbers indicate an increase in the representation of women, but they still are clearly not in parity with the representation of men. Their power over decision-making within the formal political process is limited. Women who hold ministry positions are generally placed within positions in areas typically associated with women. For example, the Honorable Gladys Asmah is the minister of environment and women's affairs, and the Honorable Christine Churcher is the minister of state at the Ministry of Education, which focuses on primary and secondary education with an emphasis on the girl child.

Before Ghana gained independence from Great Britain in 1957, women participated in the anticolonial struggle when they perceived a threat to their economic and social well-being.[24] They were active participants in boycotts against policies implemented by the colonial government, such as taxation. When Kwame Nkrumah became president in 1960, he attempted to incorporate women into the government system. Since the transition to democracy in 1992, women's organizations have been actively working to improve women's participation and citizenship rights through the formal political process. Prior to the transition, members of women's organizations found it difficult to address women's political issues due to the presence of the 31st December Women's Movement. Rawlings started the 31st December Women's Movement in 1982, and his wife, Nana Konadu Agyeman Rawlings, became president of the organization in 1985. The main purpose of the organization was to encourage women to become involved economically, socially, and politically in the state. It was also used as an apparatus of the state to mobilize women under PNDC rule.[25] Thus it prevented women's organizations from addressing women's political issues, especially if these organizations did not promote the rule of the PNDC. With the transition to democracy, the 31st December Women's Movement became tied to the National Democratic Congress, the political party that evolved from the PNDC. As it did under PNDC rule, the 31st December Women's Movement continued to co-opt women's organizations.[26]

Women's Rights and Women's Groups

Yet with the transition, women's organizations managed to successfully encourage women to participate in the formal political process, as well as to improve women's citizenship rights. First, a number of women's organizations have been encouraging women to vote in the elections. The Young Women's Christian Association and the Women's Section of the Christian Council hold special meetings to inform their members about the importance of voting and expressing their economic and political concerns by participating in the electoral process. Their emphasis is not only on general participation within the formal political process, but also on participation as female members of society. Other organizations, such as the Association for the Social Advancement of Women in Africa and Women in Law and Development in Africa transformed some of their activities specifically to incorporate nonpartisan political issues. They do not limit their activities to their members, but focus on encouraging women in Ghana to become active in politics.

An organization of women lawyers called the Ghana chapter of the International Federation of Women Lawyers—better known as FIDA—in conjunction with other organizations, works to transform laws that affect women. In 1994, FIDA successfully supported an amendment that made the practice of *Trokosi*, which is a form of ritual servitude, illegal. FIDA has also worked to address other women's concerns, such as female genital cutting, and successfully passed a law against it in 1994. Similarly, the organization pushed for and succeeded in increasing punishment for rape and defilement. They have also lobbied the government on marital rape and domestic violence and hope to push bills through parliament in the near future on these issues.

Women's organizations have attempted to redefine women's rights within the public sphere. Since 1997, there have been approximately thirty women who have been murdered in a rash of serial killings. Sisters' Keepers, a network of women's organizations, has coalesced to address women's concerns and has focused on the ongoing murders. Members of Sisters' Keepers, along with other women's organizations, have organized two massive demonstrations protesting the lack of action taken by the police force and the government. They have demanded that more attention be given to the murders and that women's public safety be made a primary concern of the government. Overall, women's organizations have mobilized women in order to address their issues within the formal political process.

In sum, although women continue to face a number of obstacles within the political sphere, women's organizations remain active in attempting to transform laws and improve women's representations and social status.

RELIGION AND SPIRITUALITY

Religion in Ghana helps to shape everyday practices and beliefs for both men and women. Throughout Ghana, 38 percent of the population adheres to indigenous religions, 30 percent to Islam, 24 percent to Christianity, and the remaining 8 percent follow other religious beliefs.[27] Islam is generally practiced in northern Ghana and Christianity is practiced in the southern part of the country. Although there is a geographical divide between these religious followings, there has been little conflict between Muslims and Christians in Ghana. Ghanaian Muslims, for the most part, are Sunni and follow the tenants of daily prayer, giving alms, fasting, and making a pilgrimage to Mecca. Generally, however, they are not conservative or strict in their practices.

Women's Roles

Indigenous religions are practiced throughout Ghana, and their practices vary according to ethnic group and location. In many instances women have opportunities to hold positions of authority. Male and female adherents of indigenous religions may aspire to be shrine priests or priestesses. They may become elevated to the station of priests or priestesses when a known spirit possesses them. For example, in Larteh, the main priestess presides over the Akonedi shrine because the spirit of Akonedi, who died during childbirth, possessed her. By becoming possessed, the priestess has taken on the role of the shrine priestess for Akonedi. Although individuals consult her to help them with their concerns, one of her primary roles is to help women become pregnant. The roles of shrine priests and priestesses differ according to the spirits that possess them, as well as the indigenous beliefs that are practiced. Yet once individuals have become priests or priestesses, they may act as diviners and counselors for the community. Women have had the opportunity to gain high-status positions and power through indigenous religions. However, with the introduction of Christian missionaries in Ghana, women began to lose their status as more Ghanaians converted to Christianity.

Toward the end of the nineteenth century in Ghana, British missionaries strongly believed that if they could teach Ghanaians to read the Bible in English, they would most likely convert to Christianity. Therefore, missionaries concentrated most of their energies on educating Ghanaian children. In order to encourage individuals to participate, they would offer incentives, such as education along with free food and clothing. Through education, the children (mostly boys) could enter service-sector jobs that were opening up in the Gold Coast, which was the name for Ghana under British colonial rule. At the beginning of the twentieth century, this new approach by the missionaries led to a greater number of conversions to Christianity.

In the process of educating West Africans, however, the missionaries found themselves in a precarious position. Newly educated African converts began to question the validity of the European missionaries. Despite the fact that the Bible emphasized equality between individuals, the European missionaries rarely regarded West Africans as equals. Mission organizations let very few West Africans play leadership roles and Africans were not allowed to hold high positions, such as a bishop, within a church. Women were no longer viewed as having the ability to hold a high status position within the Christian religion. This led to West Africans separating from the missionary churches to form their own independent churches. Participation increased in African Churches because they did not exclude individuals who still practiced West African cultural traditions.[28]

The development of African indigenous Christian churches within Ghana is important to the status of women within Christianity. The majority of the members of African indigenous Christian churches are women, and this may be due to the fact women may again attain high status positions within the church. By combining indigenous religions with Christianity, positions have been created that are similar to those found within indigenous religions.[29] For example, within indigenous Christian churches, women have access to healing and diving powers by becoming prophetesses through possession from the Holy Spirit, rather than through some other type of spirit, as found within the indigenous religions. Thus, although the introduction of Christianity stripped women of high status positions, the development of African indigenous Christian churches allowed women to regain the status they originally held within indigenous religious institutions.

VIOLENCE

Domestic Violence

If husbands beat their wives, the wives have no recourse. According to the law, women's consent to be beaten or raped is assumed once they marry. Women may only file charges if the beating continues after they have divorced or if they are legally separated. Currently, there are no shelters to protect women from domestic violence. However, the strength of extended families may give some women the shelter needed to protect them from battering.[30]

Despite the lack of laws to protect women, there has been increased awareness about domestic violence in Ghana. A number of organizations, including the Gender Center and the United Nations Fund for Women, conducted a nationwide survey in 1997 about domestic violence. The goals of this survey were to determine the prevalence of domestic violence and the means by which women handled it, as well as to create a general awareness of the problem. In the wake of the aforementioned serial killings, people have become not only more aware of violence against women in general, but also of the need to address domestic violence against women. Two women's organizations, Leadership and Advocacy for Women in Africa and FIDA, have drafted new legislation that would criminalize domestic violence.

Rape/Sexual Assault

Although the rate of rape is not known, it is understood that its prevalence is fairly high.[31] In 1993 the punishment for rape was amended to a first-degree felony. If found guilty, the perpetrator must spend a minimum of three years in jail and pay a fine. Statutory rape is also illegal, which could lead to imprisonment of twelve months to ten years. Marital rape, however, is not illegal. Since men gain all rights over women once they marry, rape is not considered an offense. In 2000, women's organizations and the Law Reform Commission requested that an amendment criminalizing marital rape be added to the constitution.

Trafficking in Women and Children

In addition to domestic violence and rape, a ritual servitude called *Trokosi* is practiced among some individuals within the Ewe ethnic group. A virgin girl, usually younger than ten years of age, is given to a traditional priest by her family in order to atone for sins committed by a family member or family ancestor.[32] Once the girl is given to the priest, she marries him, has his children, and works for him within his religious shrine. Once he no longer values her presence, he will ask her to leave the shrine, and her family, in most circumstances, must then provide another virgin girl to atone for the sins committed. Currently, the number of girls involved in the *Trokosi* practice is estimated at approximately 4,000. FIDA, in conjunction with other organizations, has worked to abolish *Trokosi*, and it is now illegal according to the constitution. A number of women's organizations are also actively working to create an awareness of the harmful effects this practice has on the young girls given to the priests. Although this awareness has prevented some families from giving one of their children to a priest, the practice still continues.

OUTLOOK FOR THE TWENTY-FIRST CENTURY

Women in Ghana face many challenges. Of course, these challenges vary according to their ethnic group, their religious affiliation, their age, as well as their living situation—if they are in an urban or rural area or if they live with an extended or nuclear family. Certain gendered patterns have emerged. They must cope with limited access to education, employment, land, loans, and health care, increasing exposure to sexual discrimination and AIDS, and limitations to reproductive control, as well as other obstacles. Despite these obstacles, women's status in Ghana continues to change over time.

Although women still do not have equal access to education and employment, their public participation has continually increased. Although laws have not protected women against marital rape or domestic violence, laws have recently been passed to prevent the practice of *Trokosi* and female genital cutting. In addition, laws that address marital rape and domestic violence are expected to come before the parliament in the near future. Women's organizations are actively working to improve women's social status. Therefore, despite the current inequities women face, their social status will most likely continue to improve over time.

NOTES

1. La Verle Berry, *Ghana: A Country Study* (Washington, DC: U.S. Government Printing Office, 1995), www.ghana.edu.gh/educationstats.xls.

2. Cynthia B. Lloyd and Anastasia J. Brandon, "Women's Role in Maintaining Households," *Population Studies* 47 (1993).

3. Ibid.; University of Sussex, "Background Paper on Gender Issues in Ghana," Overseas Development Administration, Sussex, 1996; Shiyan Chao, "Ghana: Gender Analysis and Policymaking for Development" (Washington, DC: World Bank, 1999).

4. Esther Ofei-Aboagye, *Women in Employment and Industry* (Accra: Gold-Type, 1996).

5. E. Ardayfio Schandorf, "Ghanaian Women in the Formal Economy," *Greenhill Journal of Administration* 7 (1990); Ofei-Aboagye, *Women in Employment and Industry*.

6. Ofei-Aboagye, *Women in Employment and Industry*.

7. K. Herz Barbara, Masooma Habib Subbarao, and Laura Rancy, "Letting Girls

Learn" (Washington, DC: World Bank, 1996); Human Development Report, UNDP, 2002.

8. Chao, "Ghana."

9. Yaw Oheneba-Sakyi, *Female Autonomy, Family Decision Making, and Demographic Behavior in Africa* (Lewiston, NY: Edwin Mellen Press, 1999).

10. World Bank, *World Development Indicators* (Washington, DC: World Bank, 2000).

11. Center for Reproductive Law and Policy, "Women of the World: Laws and Policies Affecting Their Reproductive Lives" (New York: Center for Reproductive Law and Policy, 1997).

12. Chao, "Ghana."

13. Center for Reproductive Law and Policy, "Women of the World."

14. Chao, "Ghana."

15. Center for Reproductive Law and Policy, "Women of the World."

16. Ibid.

17. U.S. Agency for International Development, "Ghana: The Development Challenge," 2002, www.usaid.gov/country/afr/gh.

18. Center for Reproductive Law and Policy, "Women of the World."

19. Ibid.

20. Ibid.

21. J. Sandra Pepera, "Political Parties and Social Representation: The Case of Women," in *Political Parties and Democracy in Ghana's Fourth Republic*, eds. Kwame A. Ninsin and F. K. Drah (Accra: Woeli Publishing Service, 1993), 133–45.

22. Ibid.

23. C. K. Brown, N.K.T. Ghartey, and E. K. Ekumah, *Women in Local Government* (Accra: Friedrich Ebert Foundation, 1996).

24. Pepera, "Political Parties and Social Representation."

25. Takyiwaa Manuh, "Women, the State, and Society Under the PNDC," in *Ghana Under PNDC Rule*, ed. E. Gyimah-Boadi, 176–95 (Dakar, Senegal: CODESRIA, 1993); E. Gyimah-Boadi, "Associational Life, Civil Society, and Democratization in Ghana," in *Civil Society and the State in Africa*, eds. John W. Harbeson, Donald Rothchild, and Naomi Chazan, 125–48 (Boulder: Lynne Rienner, 1994).

26. Manuha, "Women, the State, and Society."

27. Central Intelligence Agency, *World Factbook 2000* (Washington, DC: Central Intelligence Agency, 2000), www.odci.gov/cia/publications/factbook/geos/si.html.

28. Brigid Sackey, "Aspects of Continuity in the Religious Roles of Women in 'Spiritual Churches,'" in *Women's Studies with a Focus on Ghana*, ed. Mensah Prah (Koln: Druckhaus Sud, 1995).

29. Ibid.

30. National Council on Women in Development (NCWD), "National Report for the Fourth World Conference on Women," Accra, 1994.

31. Center for Reproductive Law and Policy, "Women of the World."

32. Ibid.

RESOURCE GUIDE

Suggested Reading

Aidoo, Ama Ata. *Changes: A Love Story*. New York: Feminist Press, City University of New York, 1995. This is a well-written novel that discusses a number of issues that Ghanaian women, especially educated Ghanaian women may face during their lifetimes.

Allman, Jean, and Victoria Tashjian. *"I Will Not Eat Stone": A Women's History of Colonial Asante*. Portsmouth, NH: Heinemann, 2000. Allman and Tashjian provide a detailed history of women's activities among the Asante in Ghana by focusing on commodity labor, reproduction, and family labor.

Angelou, Maya. *All God's Children Need Traveling Shoes*. New York: Random House, 1997. Angelou provides amazing and insightful stories that describe her experiences of living as an African American in Ghana during the 1960s.

Clark, Gracia. *Onions Are My Husband: Survival and Accumulation by West African Women*. Chicago: University of Chicago Press, 1994. This academic piece examines how women organize and network within the marketplace within Kumasi.

Horne, Nana Barnyiwa. *Sunkwa: Clingings Onto Life*. Trenton, NJ: Africa World Press, 2000. This is a compilation of poems written by Horne that present nuances of life within Ghana.

Oppong, Christine. *Seven Roles of Women: Impact of Education, Migration, and Employment on Ghanaian Mothers*. Chicago: University of Chicago Press, 1987. Oppong provides a detailed analysis of the varied roles women take on how they attempt to balance the roles.

Robertson, Claire C. *Sharing the Same Bowl: A Socio-Economic History of Women and Class in Accra Ghana*. Ann Arbor: University of Michigan Press, 1984. Robertson explores how women manage during economically tight times. Throughout, she provides short segments of life histories taken directly from in-depth interviews among Ga women.

Salm, Steven J., and Toyin Falola. *Culture and Customs of Ghana*. Westport, CT: Greenwood Press, 2002.

Videos/Films

Africa: A Voyage of Discovery—The Rise of Nationalism. 1984. Presented by Basil Davidson. MBT/RM Arts/Channel 4. This is the seventh segment of eight different topics. In this segment, Ghana is used as one example to demonstrate the independence transition in Africa.

Asante Market Women. 1983. Produced by Grenada Television International. Madison, WI: Videography for the African Continent at University of Wisconsin. This colorful film explores the daily activities of market women in Kumasi.

Laura: The Taxi Driver. 1992. By Michele Badarou, Jeanne Falade, and Noellie Lloupo. Princeton, NJ: Films for the Humanities. This is a short film that captures the attitudes of individuals toward working women in Benin, although it presents general concerns women face within West Africa. Specifically, the film is focused on Laura, a mother and taxi driver.

Pain, Passion, and Profit. 1992. By Gorinder Chandha. International Broadcasting Trust. In this film, Anita Roddick, founder of the Body Shop, travels to Ghana and Kenya to speak with women entrepreneurs about their businesses.

Wonders of the African World: Confronting the Legacy of the African Slave Trade. 1999. Presented by Henry Louis Gates. Produced by Jamila I. White. PBS Video. This is one segment of a six part series in which Gates explores slave castles in Ghana and other areas of West Africa.

Web Sites

Africa Online, www.africaonline.com/site/gh/index.jsp.
Here you can find news headlines and connect to other sites that address sports, music, entertainment, and the like.

Africa South of the Sahara, www.sul.stanford.edu/depts/ssrg/africa/women.html.
This is a site that has been together at Stanford University and it provides a list of resources that address a number of women's issues in sub-Saharan Africa.

allAfrica.com, http://allafrica.com/women/.
This site provides a listing of headlines across sub-Saharan Africa as they pertain to women. The geographical areas are highlighted, so you may easily obtain information in the area you are interested in.

Ghana.com, www.ghana.com.
This site takes you to an Internet service site in Ghana. There is a list of other web sites that you can connect with, as well as different substantive areas you can check out.

Ghana Forum, www.ghanaforum.com/directory.htm.
This is the Ghana web directory. You can browse connections to different websites according to topics, such as education, health and medicine, leisure, and the like.

My joy online.com, www.myjoyonline.com.
Another site with headline news, a chat room, and connections to other information regarding, sports, business, and the like.

The Republic of Ghana, www.ghana.gov.gh.
This is the official web page for the government of Ghana.

WebStar, www.webstar.com.gh.
This link provides a wealth of information on Ghana, including information on travel.

Organizations

A basic list of various indigenous women's organizations and resources may be found at www.euronet.nl/fullmoon/womlist/countries/ghana.html.

FIDA—Ghana
P.O. Box 2345
Accra, Ghana
Web site: www2.h-net.msu.edu/deitutu/fida/contact.html

This organization is headed by women lawyers who are interested in advocating for women's rights in Ghana.

International Association for the Advancement of Women in Africa (ASAWA)
No. 6 Ridge Street, P.O. Box 5737

Accra North, Ghana
Web site: http://web.tiscali.it/win/067.html

This organization actively works to empower women and improve women's social status in Ghana.

Leadership and Advocacy for Women in Africa (LAWA)
H/N 49, 3rd Crescent
Asylum Down
P.O. Box 4889
Accra, Ghana
Web site: www2.h-net.msu.edu/gyimah/aboutus.html

This organization is headed by women lawyers who are interested in advocating for women's rights in Ghana.

Women in Law and Development in Africa (WiLDAF)
Dorcas Coker-Appiah
Gender Centre
P.O. Box 6192
Accra-North, Ghana
Email: wildaf@ghana.com
Web site: http://web.tiscali.it/win/067.html

This organization actively works to empower women and improve women's social status in Ghana.

SELECTED BIBLIOGRAPHY

Agyeman, D. K. "Sociology of Education." In *Introduction to Education in Ghana*, edited by Okechukwu C. Abosi and Joseph Brookman-Amissah. Cape Coast: Sedco, 1992.

Aubrey, L. "Gender, Development, and Democratization in Africa." *Journal of Asian and African Studies* 36, no. 1 (2001): 87–111.

Berry, La Verle. *Ghana: A Country Study*. Washington, DC: U.S. Government Printing Office, 1995.

Brown, C. K., N.K.T. Ghartey, and E. K. Ekumah. *Women in Local Government*. Accra: Friedrich Ebert Foundation, 1996.

Center for Reproductive Law and Policy. "Women of the World: Laws and Policies Affecting Their Reproductive Lives." New York: Center for Reproductive Law and Policy, 1997.

Chao, Shiyan. "Ghana: Gender Analysis and Policymaking for Development." Washington, DC: World Bank, 1999.

Chinnery-Hesse, Mary. "Women and Decision Making." *Labour and Society* 1 (1975) 33–35.

Clark, Gracia. "Mothering, Work, and Gender in Urban Asante Ideology and Practice." *American Anthropologist* 101, no. 4 (December 1999): 717–29.

Clark, Gracia, and Takyiwaa Manuh. "Women Traders in Ghana and the Structural Adjustment Program." In *Structural Adjustment and African Women Farmers*, edited by Christina H. Gladwin. Gainesville: University of Florida Press, 1991.

Dei, George J. Sefa. "The Women of a Ghanaian Village: A Study of Social Change." *African Studies Review* 37, no. 2 (1994): 121–45.

Dolphyne, Florence Abena. *The Emancipation of Women: An African Perspective*. Accra, Ghana: Ghana Universities Press, 1991.

Duncan, Beatrice Akua. *Women in Agriculture in Ghana*. Accra: Gold Type, 1997.

Graham, C. K. *The History of Education in Ghana*. London: Frank Cass, 1971.

Gyimah-Boadi, E. "Associational Life, Civil Society, and Democratization in Ghana." In *Civil Society and the State in Africa*, edited by John W. Harbeson, Donald Rothchild, and Naomi Chazan, 125–48. Boulder: Lynne Rienner, 1994.

Herz, Barbara, K. Subbarao, Masooma Habib, and Laura Raney. "Letting Girls Learn." Washington, DC: World Bank, 1996.

Levin, C. E., M. T. Ruel, S. S. Morris, et al. "Working Women in an Urban Setting: Traders, Vendors and Food Security in Accra." *World Development* 27, no. 11 (November 1999): 1977–91.

Lloyd, Cynthia B., and Anastasia J. Brandon. "Women's Role in Maintaining Households." *Population Studies* 47 (1993).

Manuh, Takyiwaa. "Ghana: Women in the Public and Informal Sectors under the Economic Recovery Programme." In *Mortgaging Women's Lives*, edited by Pamela Sparr, 61–77. London: Zed Books, 1994.

———. "Wives, Children, and Intestate Succession in Ghana." In *African Feminism: The Politics of Survival in Sub-Saharan Africa*, edited by Gwendolyn Mikell, 77–95. Philadelphia: University of Pennsylvania Press, 1993.

———. "Women, the State, and Society under the PNDC." In *Ghana Under PNDC Rule*, edited by E. Gyimah-Boadi, 176–95. Dakar, Senegal: CODESRIA, 1993.

Mikell, Gwendolyn. "Ghanaian Females, Rural Economy, and National Stability." *African Studies Review* 29, no. 3 (September 1986): 67–88.

———. "Pleas for Domestic Relief: Akan Women and Family Courts." In *African Feminism: The Politics of Survival in Sub-Saharan Africa*, edited by Gwendolyn Mikell, 96–123. Philadelphia: University of Pennsylvania Press, 1997.

National Council on Women in Development (NCWD). "National Report for the Fourth World Conference on Women." Accra, 1994.

Odaga, Adhaimbo, and Ward Heneveld. "Girls in Schools in Sub-Saharan Africa: From Analysis to Action." Washington, DC: World Bank, 1995.

Ofei-Aboagye, Esther. *Women in Employment and Industry*. Accra: Gold-Type, 1996.

Oheneba-Sakyi, Yaw. *Female Autonomy, Family Decision Making, and Demographic Behavior in Africa*. Lewiston, NY: Edwin Mellen Press, 1999.

Okonjo, Kamene. "Women and the Evolution of a Ghanaian Political Synthesis." In *Women and Politics Worldwide*, edited by Barbara J. Nelson and Najmka Chowdhury, 285–297. New Haven, CT: Yale University Press, 1994.

Oppong, Christine, and Katherine Abu. *Seven Roles of Women: Impact of Education, Migration, and Employment on Ghanaian Mothers*. Geneva: International Labour Office, 1987.

Pellow, Deborah. *Women in Accra: Options for Autonomy*. Ann Arbor: Reference Publications, 1977.

Pepera, J. Sandra. "Political Parties and Social Representation: The Case of Women." In *Political Parties and Democracy in Ghana's Fourth Republic*, edited by Kwame A. Ninsin and F. K. Drah, 133–45. Accra: Woeli Publishing, 1993.

Robertson, Claire. *Sharing the Same Bowl*. Bloomington: Indiana University Press, 1984.

Sackey, Brigid. "Aspects of Continuity in the Religious Roles of Women in 'Spiritual Churches.' " In *Women's Studies with a Focus on Ghana*, edited by Mensah Prah. Koln: Druckhaus Sud, 1995.

Schandorf, E. Ardayfio. "Ghanaian Women in the Formal Economy." *Greenhill Journal of Administration* 7 (1990).

University of Sussex. "Background Paper on Gender Issues in Ghana." Overseas Development Administration, Sussex, 1996.

U.S. Agency for International Development. "Ghana: The Development Challenge." 2002. www.usaid.gov/country/afr/gh.

World Bank. *World Development Indicators*. Washington, DC: World Bank, 2000.

7

GUINEA

Rebecca Furth

PROFILE OF GUINEA

The Republic of Guinea is situated on the West Coast of Africa. The Atlantic Ocean forms Guinea's western frontier with a shoreline 320 kilometers (515 miles) long. Inland, Guinea shares borders with Senegal, Guinea-Bissau, Mali, Sierra Leone, Liberia, and Côte d'Ivoire. Guinea's population is divided among seven principal ethnic groups. Susu represent 20 percent of the population, Fulbe (Peuls) 40 percent, Malinke 30 percent, and Guerze (Kpelle), Toma, Kissi, Mano, among other groups make up the remaining 10 percent. Malinke, Susu, and Pular are the most commonly spoken languages in Guinea. Malinke and Susu are closely related Mande languages and are spoken in Upper Guinea and Maritime Guinea respectively. Pular, spoken by the Fulbe, is the common language of the Middle Guinea and is spoken in markets across the nation, where Fulbe make up a majority of businessmen. Islam is the most widely practiced religion in Guinea; 85 percent of the Guinean population is Muslim, 8 percent of Guineans are Christian, and 7 percent continue to practice indigenous religions.

A former French colony, Guinea was the first West African

nation to declare independence from France. In 1958 the Guinean populace took a dramatic stand against colonial rule by voting to reject French president Charles de Gaulle's referendum proposing the creation of a "French Community" made up of semiautonomous African nations under French control, in favor of unconditional liberty. Sékou Touré and his political party, Parti Democratique de la Guinée, led the Guinean people to independence and Touré presided as the country's president until his death in 1984. Guinea's official independence date is October 2, 1958.

Sékou Touré's rule began with great optimism but devolved into years of despotic oppression, economic decay, and national isolation. In 1984, after Touré's death in a Cleveland hospital, the army waged a successful military coup and took power. Lansana Conté became the leader of the military government. Guinea functioned under military rule until 1993, when the first democratic elections transformed Lansana Conté from a military leader into the nation's democratic president. Conté's political party, Parti de l'Unité et du Progrès, continues to dominate national politics, often through coercion, but is challenged by several strong opposition parties including the Rassemblement du Peuple de Guinée, Union pour le Progrès et le Renouveau, and the Union des Forces Républicaines (UFR).

Guinea possesses a lush environment and a wealth of natural resources, which are distributed throughout the country's four regions: Maritime Guinea (also called Lower Guinea), Middle Guinea, Upper Guinea, and the Forest Region. In Maritime Guinea, palm oil, pineapple, banana, and rice are the principle agricultural products, which along with fishing form a substantial portion of the region's economy. Guinea has 30 percent of the world's bauxite (aluminum ore).[1] Bauxite deposits exist throughout Guinea but currently the ore is mined and processed only in the coastal region in the towns of Fria, Boké, and Sangaredi. The large port at Kamsar serves as one of the major shipping points for transporting bauxite from Guinea to Europe, Canada, and the United States. Middle Guinea is characterized by the Futa Jallon mountain range. The Futa Jallon is known as the watershed of West Africa as it is the source of almost every major West African river including the Senegal, the Gambia, and the Bafang. The Niger River also starts in Guinea on the southeastern edge of the Futa Jallon near the border with Sierra Leone. The flood plains of the Niger River, which flows through Upper Guinea, provide fertile ground for rice production. Upper Guinea also has a number of gold mines, particularly around the town of Siguiri. The Forest Region produces coffee, cola nuts, and rice. It also has a number of diamond mines as well as iron and uranium deposits. Unfortunately, the once rich forest resources of Guinea's Forest Region have been largely depleted over the last decade as improved roads have facilitated logging and a growing population has strained natural resources. Population pressures have been exacerbated by a huge influx of refugees from the wars in Sierra Leone and Liberia, which have accelerated the clearing of forests for agricultural land.

Guinea's population is estimated at 8.3 million.[2] In addition, approximately 500,000 refugees from Sierra Leone and Liberia are estimated to be living in Guinea.[3] Women constitute 51 percent of the Guinean population, 40 percent of whom live below the poverty level.[4] Gross national product per capita is approximately $530 per year.[5] Guinea has experienced an accelerated rate of urbanization since independence. Population estimates from the 1960s found that only 14 percent of Guineans lived in urban settings,[6] while in 2000 the urban population had reached 30 percent.[7] Infant mortality is estimated at 98 per 1,000 births and maternal mortality at 528 per 100,000 live births.[8] The total fertility rate in Guinea is 5.5 births per woman.[9] The average life expectancy is fifty-four years (1999).[10]

OVERVIEW OF WOMEN'S ISSUES

Women are the backbone of economic and domestic life in Guinea. They are valued as mothers and as wives and their voices are considered vital in many family affairs and some political issues. Women's commercial activities also fuel the informal economy in Guinea and ensure the well-being of their families. Nonetheless, women in Guinea face a number of challenges. Poverty defines women's existence in Guinea and threatens their progress in all respects. The quality of health care is poor and unavailable to some rural women, while illiteracy presents a giant obstacle to women's advancement. In addition, unequal pay and other forms of job discrimination threaten women's ability to become leaders in the work force. Perhaps most significantly, women's political representation remains limited and, although women are central to political mobilization, they tend to be alienated from political decision-making.

EDUCATION

Prior to the colonial era, Islamic schools served as the major forum for education where Guineans learned to read and write Arabic and local languages using the Arabic alphabet. Boys studied with Islamic teachers, often residing with these scholars and exchanging household and farm labor for room, board, and schooling. Girls were also taught in Islamic schools, but their education was limited and few were permitted to study long enough to read or write without assistance. The French introduced European-style schooling and promoted both vocational and academic education. Only a small number of schools were constructed during the colonial era, providing enough education to cultivate a class of Guinean administrators. Very few girls attended French schools.

Opportunities

After independence, Sékou Touré initiated a massive education campaign. He attempted to create a more African educational system by redesigning the national curriculum and creating pedagogical materials in local languages. The new system aimed to teach African values, provide free education for all, expand secondary schools, and establish national universities in Conakry and Kankan. It also sought to bring national ideology, social, and economic issues and political policy into the curriculum. Beginning in 1969, schools were taught in local languages, integrating a limited amount of French only in the third year of school. School j increased dramatically from 45,000 in 1958 to over 285,000 in 1973;[11] however, overcrowding, poor teaching quality, and a weak curriculum compromised the quality of education during the Touré era. Despite the increase in school attendance during Touré's regime, the percentage of girls attending school had only reached 17 percent in 1989.[12]

The current government has made female education a central focus of its development program. In the last decade, the percentage of girls attending school has improved to 37 percent.[13] Girls represented 69 percent of male enrollments at the primary level and 38 percent of male enrollments at the secondary level in 1998.[14] In addition to national schools, private and Franco-Arab schools—educational institutions that teach in both French and Arabic and include Islamic education—are expanding in Guinea, offering greater choice to parents and students.

Literacy

An effort is being made to address illiteracy among women. Only 25 percent of urban women and a mere 6 percent of rural women are literate compared with 60 percent of urban men and 36 percent of rural men.[15] UNICEF has spearheaded a widespread literacy campaign in which a local person is trained to teach women to read and write in their choice of language (French, local language in the phonetic alphabet, or local language in the Arabic alphabet) in adult learning schools called *Centre Nafa.*

Adult literacy class in Niefang, Guinea. Photo © Sean Sprague/Painet.

EMPLOYMENT AND ECONOMICS

Studies of women's labor in Guinea estimate that women work fifteen to seventeen hours per day seven days a week on domestic, agricultural, professional, or commercial activities.[16] Women are responsible for producing a majority of subsistence goods in Guinea; 82 percent of working women are employed in agriculture.[17] Women's economic production is essential for the well-being of their families, particularly in rural areas, where men often migrate seasonally or for several years at a time to urban areas or to neighboring countries in search of wage labor. Under these conditions, women are often left to care for children and elderly relatives, sometimes with very little or intermittent economic support from their spouses.

Farming

In rural areas, women farm grain crops and household gardens. Their labor is burdened by very low cash income, poor access to water, dilapidated roads, and scarcity of health facilities. Almost all women farm both fields and home gardens using very labor-intensive manual methods, such as hoes, hand seeding, and hand harvesting. The poor state of roads in Guinea makes it very difficult for women to get surplus agricultural produce to market, thus further limiting their access to cash. In addition to farming, women tend to domestic animals, care for the sick, and prepare food for their households. Rural areas are at least twice as poor as urban centers, where markets, business, and transportation provide greater opportunities for both women and men. Farmers represent 61 percent of the Guinean population and 80 percent of the populace living below the poverty line.[18]

Entrepreneurship

In addition to farming, approximately 12 percent of working women are engaged in commercial activities.[19] These activities range from the sale of very small amounts of surplus agricultural goods, to international commercial trade of cloth, household utensils, and agricultural produce. Unlike other West African countries such as Ghana, Guinean women's involvement in commerce is relatively recent, stemming primarily from the expansion of markets during the latter part of the colonial era.

The socialist government of Sékou Touré encouraged the development of cooperatives and women's collectives in Guinea in the 1960s and 1970s. The legacy of these collectives remains and a number of women's groups exist in urban and rural areas. These groups enable women to pool financial resources together and engage in a variety of economic activities including cloth dying, gardening, oil selling, or making embroidered items and home decorations. Women's groups have been the focus of many nongovernmental organizations (NGOs) and small credit initiatives, but many still experience problems of very low profit, internal disputes, and challenges in marketing products.

Several different forms of credit are available to women entrepreneurs, but access to substantial amounts of credit is very limited. A number of organizations such as Crédit Rural, Crédit Mutuel, and PRIDE provide small loans to women. However, many women find paying back their loans with interest to be burdensome and choose to participate in traditional credit schemes known as *tontine* in French-speaking Africa. Common throughout Africa, *tontine* groups are composed of a fixed number of women, often relatives or members of the same community, who submit money to an informal rotating bank. Each woman contributes a set sum every month and one woman receives the cumulative sum of all contributions in that month. Women contribute to the *tontine* until each participant has had a turn receiving the aggregate monthly sum. When the cycle is complete, the *tontine* starts a new rotation, disbands, or changes membership. The *tontine* provide women with capital to help them invest in or expand their commercial activities.

Pay

While women are prevalent in agriculture and commerce, they are highly underrepresented in industry, construction, transport, communications, banking and public administration. Women make up a very small percentage of salaried workers in Guinea; 22 percent of salaried government functionaries and 20 percent of contracted government functionaries are women,[20] a majority of whom hold lower-paying service jobs such as secretaries, nurses, and community educators. In the professional levels of the private sector, women represent only 15 percent of salaried workers.[21] Professional women typically work as teachers, agricultural educators, midwives and nurses, secretaries, and assistants. Pay ranges widely between the type of task and the sector in which the woman is employed (public or private).

Support for Mothers/Caretakers

Maternal Leave

Women with salaried jobs in the public and private sectors are entitled to three months of maternity leave, at half pay, through social security benefits. Unfortunately, many private organizations and businesses hire on a contractual basis, which enables workers to avoid paying social security and income tax, but also denies them maternity leave benefits.

Child Care

Guinea possesses few formal settings dedicated to child care, but women and their families employ a number of social networks to ensure the care and safety of their children. Female farmers and merchants take nursing infants to work with them, sometimes enlisting the assistance of a young girl to watch the child while its mother engages in difficult physical tasks or negotiates with clients. Children who have been weaned are frequently left at home under the care of a young girl or another female relative. Caring for children is most often considered a family duty and is not remunerated. Elite families in urban centers may hire a private nanny, frequently a live-in caretaker, to care for their children. In addition, Conakry and other large cities have seen the emergence of a number of *jardins d'enfants* (nursery schools) over the last decade. These schools, which are usually private and expensive, seek to give young children aged three to five a head start on school and a safe place to stay while their parents are at work. UNICEF and other aid agencies have also established children's centers in Kindia and other cities around Guinea to protect and educate children of vulnerable families and refugees while their parents are at work.[22]

Inheritance, Property, and Land Rights

Among most cultural groups in Guinea, grooms are required to provide bridewealth to their brides and their relatives. The portion of the bridewealth given to the bride—usually cattle, money, clothes, and/or gold—and any gifts from a bride's family belong to her alone. In the Futa Jallon, men must also provide wives with a parcel of land on which to cultivate their home garden, called *suntuure* in Pular. Many women own cattle and other livestock, maintaining rights to this property and any monetary benefit obtained from its sale. In addition, according to Article 325 of the Guinean civil code, any income a woman obtains from commercial activities, gifts, or a salaried job belongs entirely to her. Saddled with the burden of providing for their families, many men today prefer women who work because their income helps purchase basic goods for the household and luxury items. Although women's income is supposed to be spent freely, women are often obliged to support their families when their husbands fail to provide the financial resources to fulfill household requirements.

Women generally do not own or inherit land but they do obtain use rights to land from husbands and male relatives where they farm crops and garden. Women can legally purchase land, but this is easier in urban areas, where land sales are more common. Although women do obtain use rights to land, their access is generally restricted. Most of women's agricultural labor is carried out on lands under men's control where women's claim to the harvest is minimal or nonexistent. User rights to and ownership of land in rural areas varies according to culture. In the Forest Region, women can own tree crops such as palm and coffee and they maintain rights to those crops regardless of transfers of the landownership. Susu women on the coast can inherit land from their fathers and sometimes husbands inherit land from their wives, but a majority of land remains in the hands of men. In Upper Guinea land is generally held communally by lineages and women can only gain access to land through male relatives. In addition, access to land may be more or less difficult depending on the social category to which a woman belongs. For example, in the Futa Jallon highlands, descendants of slaves, including men, do not have ownership rights to land according to customary law. Women of slave descent are thus further removed from landowners than "free" women and are therefore more likely to have difficulty obtaining needed land without the support of their male relatives.[23]

Social/Government Programs

Structural Adjustment

In 1985 the Guinean government began initiating structural adjustment programs. A major element of this economic restructuring included privatizing a number of government industries including plastics, bottling, and cigarette factories; the transportation industry; and import and export companies. To facilitate privatization, the government promulgated laws legalizing private ownership, asserted equality between national and international businesses, and created a forum for mediating economic and financial disputes. While private industry has grown in Guinea, the overall effect of liberalization on the Guinean economy has been limited. Although a majority of the populace is engaged in agriculture, very few investments have been made in the agricultural sector and private industries and small businesses have been hampered by corruption, legal obstacles, and poor infrastructure.

FAMILY AND SEXUALITY

Gender Roles and Division of Labor

Most cultures in Guinea are strongly patriarchal, but women have marked authority in particular affairs. Women help arrange marriages, baptisms, and other life-cycle events. While men do the principal negotiating for marriages, women make many of the arrangements, including matchmaking, behind the scenes. In Fulbe marriage ceremonies, the witness of an elderly woman, usually a paternal aunt, is necessary in the negotiations that take place among men at the asking ceremony. Elderly women hold special status in households throughout Guinea. They are usually consulted in domestic disputes and other family problems and their advice is sought and recommended by men and women alike.

The division of labor is highly gendered in most Guinean households. Women are expected to cook, keep house, care for children, and assist with farming and herding activities. They are also expected to be gracious hostesses and defer to their husbands. Men ideally are to carry the responsibility of providing shelter, clothing, and the financial means to support the household. This division of household labor and responsibilities is codified in Articles 324–329 of the Guinean civil code, although in reality, roles and responsibilities are much more complicated. Women often play a dual role, fulfilling their conventional responsibilities as wives and mothers while working in fields, professional jobs, or commerce to provide shelter, clothing, and food for their families.

Marriage

Guinean laws mandate that marriage be carried out in front of state officials and that both the groom and the bride agree to the marriage of their own free will. Nonetheless, few marriages are actually registered with the state. The state wedding ceremony, commonly called *la signature*, has come to represent cosmopolitanism and wealth and is more common in urban areas among the educated elite than it is in rural areas or among the uneducated populace. Many girls agree to marry against their own personal wishes out of respect for their elders or fear of sparking anger from their relatives. Divorced women and widows have more say about who they marry than girls who have never been married. Marriages are often viewed as family affairs that strengthen family relations and couples are expected to put family interests above their own desires. However, so-called love marriages, in which couples court before marriage, are becoming more common in urban areas. In addition, in large cities and mixed communities, different ethnic groups such as the Malinke, Fulbe, Susu, and others intermarry, although homogeneous ethnic marriages are generally preferred. Some communities are barred by social taboos from intermarrying. For example, high-status groups, such as nobles, in the Malinke and Fulbe communities do not commonly intermarry with women from blacksmithing or woodworking families. Women's marriage prospects are shaped to a large extent by their family origins, wealth, beauty, and education.

As in most societies, women in Guinea are central in domestic politics and family life. Polygamy is common in Guinea, with about 50 percent of married men having two or more wives. From the precolonial period into the early part of the twentieth century wealthy men could have as many wives and concubines as they could afford. Today, Islamic law is generally respected in much of Guinea and even wealthy men do not surpass the prescribed Islamic limit of four wives. The Sékou Touré government made polygamy illegal in 1968 and promoted monogamy, but the law, which remains in the civil code, was never enforced or heeded. The current president of Guinea, Lansana Conté, has three wives.

Guineans have mixed feelings about polygamy. For men, having many wives and, even more importantly, many children is a symbol of wealth and status; but supporting many wives is expensive and if wives do not get along, men find themselves constantly mediating disputes. For women, cowives often bring out feelings of jealousy or rivalries over resources, especially in households where husbands do not have the means to support their large families. However, some women appreciate their cowives and derive comfort from their polygamous families. Cowives can help relieve the burden of household tasks, offer company, and provide support. Wives in polygamous families take turns cooking, share childcare, and assist each other in household activities; this collaboration enables women to spend more time on activities of their choosing, such as commerce, socializing, or relaxation.

Reproduction

Sex Education

Historically, elder women and men instructed youth about sexual matters either privately before marriage or during rites of passage. Today, many young Guineans learn about sex through imported magazines and cinema from Europe, the United States, and Asia; from satellite TV; and from a range of pornographic videos that are available in urban centers. A study of sexual activity among youth between the ages of fifteen and twenty-five revealed that the average age of first sexual intercourse was 16.3 years for girls and 15.6 years for boys;[24] the study also found that many youth had misconceptions about sex, pregnancy, and birth control. Twenty-five percent of the young unmarried women surveyed had become pregnant and 22 percent of these pregnancies had ended in abortion.[25] The Guinean educational system does not support a sex education curriculum.

Contraception and Abortion

Reproduction is a defining element of women's status in the household and in society. Choosing not to have children is virtually unheard of in Guinea. Women who are unable to conceive are considered unlucky or even cursed. Although family planning is becoming more widespread, modern methods are used mainly for child spacing and not for limiting the number of children a couple conceives. Recognizing the expense of supporting large families, some couples are choosing to limit the number of children they have. In other families, women who desire to stop having children sometimes encounter pressure from their husbands or from their mother-in-law and other female in-laws who believe that more children will bring good fortune and boost the status of the husband and his extended family.

While few data on abortion are available in Guinea, one study estimates that as much as 20 percent of women's deaths result from abortions or complications from miscarriages.[26] Another study of miscarriages received at one of the main hospitals in Conakry found that 25 percent of abortions were performed in nonhygienic conditions.[27] Abortion in Guinea is illegal and thus safe abortions are not available at health clinics or hospitals. Guinean women have a variety of herbs available to them that are believed to "clean the belly" and cause menses.[28] While some women may use these herbs early in pregnancy to induce an abortion, others use them to stimulate regular menses.

Teen Pregnancy

Teen pregnancy is quite common in Guinea. The legal age for marriage is seventeen, but many girls are married as early as fifteen years; in fact, some studies show that as many as 38 percent of girls between the ages of fifteen and nineteen are married.[29] Some Guineans assert that early marriage has become more necessary in recent years because of the rise in pregnancy among unmarried girls. No data are available on the number of out-of-wedlock pregnancies but they have become relatively common in urban and rural areas. Attitudes about sex before marriage vary in Guinea. Some Susu communities will let a couple live together and have sexual relations if they are formally engaged. The Toma prohibit sexual intercourse for men and women before they are fully initiated into their respective secret societies, which can be as late as eighteen years for women and thirty years for men. The increasing occurrence of pregnancy among girls who have not completed initiation has become a subject of heated cultural debates about modernity, sexuality, and family in Toma society. Fulbe are staunchly against sexual relations before marriage and a woman is expected to be a virgin on her wedding night. The large number of out-of-wedlock pregnancies among the Fulbe has also become a subject of much debate and concern and is contributing to changing views about the social status of illegitimate children.

HEALTH

Health Care Access

While women in urban areas have access to a number of health facilities, women in rural areas frequently reside long distances from health services. In addition, for those who can access health resources, the cost of treatment and medication remains an obstacle to good health for women with little expendable cash. As a result, maternal mortality in Guinea remains high at

528 per 100,000 births.[30] Anemia and iodine deficiency further compromise women's health in pregnancy and childbirth. An estimated 60 percent of pregnant women in Guinea are anemic and over 68 percent of women show signs of iodine deficiency.[31]

Furthermore, many conventional birthing practices promote stoicism and strength on the part of women in pregnancy and childbirth. Among the Fulbe, for example, many women give birth alone, without the assistance of a relative or a trained health professional. When women experience complications, they call for help, but often help comes too late. Illness and discomfort are considered normal in pregnancy and women are sometimes reluctant to consult a health professional for fear that they might appear weak. Together with NGOs the Guinean government has been promoting antenatal and postnatal checkups and is encouraging women to seek the assistance of a trained provider during childbirth. In some cases, traditional birth attendants are being trained to provide better assistance to their clients and to identify danger signs so they can get women to the appropriate health facility in time.

Diseases and Disorders

Poverty poses a serious threat to women's health, particularly with regard to sexually transmitted infections and HIV/AIDS. Many women, some young and unmarried, others married with children, seek boyfriends who will provide them with gifts and sometimes money to help them purchase needed or desired goods. Women and men do not consider such arrangements prostitution, although they do breach a number of social norms. Nonetheless, promiscuity on the part of men and women, combined with polygamy and levirate marriage (wife inheritance)—a practice whereby a man inherits the widow of his deceased brother—threaten to fuel the spread of HIV/AIDS in Guinea.

AIDS

HIV/AIDS prevalence in Guinea is not well documented. In 1998 HIV/AIDS infection in the country was estimated at between 2 percent and 4 percent.[32] A national HIV/AIDS prevalence survey conducted in 2001 found that an average of 4.4 percent of pregnant women tested positive for HIV/AIDS in urban areas, suggesting that the infection rate in the general population is much higher than previously assumed.[33] The government promotes condom use and HIV/AIDS information is disseminated through radio broadcasts in local languages and on national television. The government developed the National Program to Combat AIDS specifically to address issues related to HIV/AIDS in the country and several NGOs including SidAlerte and Coopération d'Aide à l'Enfance, are working to educate the populace and provide services to people living with HIV/AIDS.

Female Genital Cutting

In addition to HIV/AIDS, female genital cutting presents a substantial threat to women's health in Guinea. Article 265 of the penal code, promulgated in 1994, forbids female genital cutting, but the law is not enforced and female genital cutting is widely practiced throughout Guinea. According to one government estimate, 98 percent of women between the ages of fifteen and fifty have been excised. In most Guinean societies, the practice marks an important rite of passage in which a girl is formally acknowledged a woman. A variety of different forms of excision are practiced in Guinea. The most extreme form of excision, infibulation—the full removal of the clitoris, labia minora, and labia majora, and the suturing of the vagina—is least common but not unknown, while clitoridectomy—the removal of the clitoris and sometimes the labia minora—is quite common.

In most parts of Guinea, girls are excised before or around the age of ten. The operation, which is usually carried out on a group of girls at one time, is followed by a month of careful surveillance and recovery at the home of a female relative, often a paternal aunt. After the month of recovery, when the girls have healed, the families celebrate with gifts, song, and ceremony. Many women and girls in Guinea take tremendous pride in their excisions and remain unaware or dismissive of the health risks associated with genital cutting. Women who want to prevent their daughters from undergoing the practice face significant pressure from other female relatives and often have little control over their daughter's excision, which is usually planned and controlled by her paternal aunts and/or grandmother.

A number of NGOs, including Cellule de Coordination sur les Pratiques Traditionnelles Affectant la Santé des Femmes et des Enfants (CPTAFE; Coordination Unit on Traditional Practices That Affect Women's and Children's Health) and large donor organizations as well as United Nations agencies, are waging ardent campaigns to end the practice with minor success. In 1999, 450 traditional excisers agreed to abandon the practice and turned in their cutting instruments.[34] In addition, while the percentage of women who undergo excision remains high, forms of female genital cutting are changing. The UN Children's Fund (UNICEF) found that 51 percent of grown women in Guinea had undergone the most extreme forms of excision while 27 percent of girls are subject to these more dangerous practices today.

POLITICS AND LAW

Leadership and Decision-making

In the last years of colonial rule, Sékou Touré's Parti Democratique de la Guinée (PDG) gained strength and popularity through courting the votes of women. Unfortunately, Touré's rhetoric was stronger than the political practice of the 1960s and 1970s. At the local level, women's committees were relegated to organizing political receptions and conducting semidomestic tasks such as preparing food and tidying meeting rooms. They were also mobilized to sing songs, dress in clothes that promoted Touré's political party, and chant political slogans, but they were given little decision-making responsibility. Women who became powerful or criticized the government faced imprisonment or death. One of the most active women in the Touré government, Loffo Camara, was accused of being an antirevolutionary. Touré had her arrested in 1970 and executed by a firing squad in 1971, without a trial. Few women were appointed to political posts or other jobs where they could be involved in decisionmaking and while the government did hire women as functionaries, most were hired in relatively low paying, low status, jobs as secretaries, midwives, and agricultural educators.

Since Lansana Conté came to power in 1984, the government has continued to talk about the importance of promoting women; however, women remain marginalized in Guinean politics. In the year 2000, only four of twenty-five government ministers were women. After the 2003 elections, 22 (19 percent) of 144 members of the national assembly were women.[35] No women are in leadership of any of the over 300 rural development communities (*communauté rural de dévelopment*), which have replaced the PRL, *Parti revolutionaire locale*, the political organization that oversaw the implementation of national policy at the local level, as democratically elected committees with representation at the district and subprefectoral levels.[36] A woman leads only one of the forty political parties that have sprouted in Guinea over the last ten years.[37] However, some women are overcoming adversity and are gaining prominence in Guinean politics. Madame Kaba Rougi Barry served as a very popular mayor of the commune of Matam, a major section of Conakry, throughout the 1990s. Barry stepped out of her post as mayor in 2000 to run for political office in communal elections in Matam as a representative of the UFR political party. Although the UFR lost its place in the legislative elections, Barry remains a prominent political figure in the nation's capital. Despite the lack of women's representation in the government, NGOs are making significant strides in promoting women's issues and changing government policy. Pressure from CPTAFE, other NGOs, and international organizations led to the government's legislation banning female excision.

Mbalia Camara, a pregnant housewife and avid PDG supporter, was murdered by a Susu political leader for the colonial government 1955 and became a symbol for women's rights and political involvement for the PDG. After independence in 1958, the government of Sékou Touré promoted women's equality and made women and men equal under the law. Since 1958, all citizens of Guinea, male and female, are eligible to vote at age eighteen.

Each PRL had a women's committee, led by an elected woman that promoted women's involvement. A national committee, *comité national des femmes*, advanced women's issues at the national level. The Touré government saw women's labor as an essential factor in the development of the nation. To encourage women's involvement in the workforce, the government set up professional schools for women to gain secretarial, sewing, and embroidery skills. Women were also integrated into the national police force and military.

Women's Rights

Article 8 of the constitution states that all human beings are equal under the law, ascribing the same rights to men and women, and Article 18 states that a person cannot be fired or discriminated against in his/her job because of gender. The national committee for the elimination of discrimination against women (*Comité Pour l'Élimination de la Discrimination à l'Égard des Femmes*, CEDEF) also promotes women's rights. However, legal codes remain ambiguous and often include conditions that protect men's rights over women's and make it difficult for women to find security in the law.

Women's Movements

The most remarkable women's movement in Guinean history, the women's revolt, sent shock waves through the nation and galvanized government reforms. The revolt began in June 1977 in Nzerekoré, a town in the Forest region of Guinea, when the "economic police," officers who enforced the national ban on private commerce, harassed a market woman. Tired of the abuses of these officers, who were known for extracting bribes and forcing women to remove their skirts, the woman called for help and was aided by fellow market women. Outnumbered, the economic police were forced to retreat. Encouraged by their success and fed up with government oppression and restrictions on commerce, the women marched to the homes of the governor and the rural development director, gaining the support of the populace on the way and forcing both political leaders to flee. The movement spread to other towns in the Forest and later to Kankan.

On August 27, 1977, an officer stopped a housewife in a Conakry market to inspect her shopping bag for contraband. Angry at this violation the woman began to protest. Her cries called the attention of the market women in the neighborhood and eventually neighborhood women as a whole. The crowd marched on police stations before turning to the presidential palace. At the presidential palace, the crowd of women demanded an audience with Sékou Touré. In response to the women's complaints, Touré promised to disband the economic police. However, the women were not satisfied and returned to the presidential palace the following day. They rejected Touré's characteristic calls for revolution and anticolonialism and accused him of imperialism, racism, and being an antirevolutionary; moreover, they openly called for him to step down. Such overt challenges to Touré's political leadership were unheard of in Guinea.

On August 29, 1977, the women marched again on the presidential palace. Touré called in the army, which fired on the women as they approached the palace, killing 60 and wounding more than 300. While the army assault put an end to the women's revolt in the capital, the events in Conakry reverberated throughout the country and over the next ten days demonstrations and attacks on the economic police and other government representatives occurred in over thirty towns throughout Guinea. The women's revolt effectively altered Touré's power and authority for the remainder of his rule. In response, Touré loosened restrictions on commerce in the late 1970s and began to reform government policy in the early 1980s.

RELIGION AND SPIRITUALITY

Islam is by far the dominant religion in Guinea. While more conservative forms of Sunni Islam, such as Wahhabiyya, are gaining popularity, most Guineans belong to one of several Sufi (mystic sect of Islam) brotherhoods. Women in Sufi households are given tremendous freedom in dress and movement. Purdah, or wife seclusion, is not practiced by these Sufi orders and is generally looked down upon. Increasingly, women are studying the Koran and gaining prestigious religious titles, including the title of Hajja, the title given to women who have made a pilgrimage to Mecca. However, one study argues that religious teachers offer different teaching methods to women and men. While men are taught to read the Koran and thus gain religious titles by reading prescribed texts, women are merely read too, thus rendering their titles less prestigious than men's and ensuring that men maintain control of religious knowledge.[38]

Christianity has a very small presence in Guinea compared to Islam. Christians make up approximately 8 percent of the population. Catholic and Protestant churches have their main influence in the Forest Region and Maritime Guinea. Outside of Islam and Christianity, indigenous religions continue to be practiced in communities in the Forest and on the coast. Within indigenous religions, some women act as spiritual leaders imparting religious and spiritual knowledge; this is particularly true of the Forest Region, where women preside over women's secret societies.

VIOLENCE

Domestic Violence

Under some conditions, it is culturally acceptable for men to beat their wives. However, beating is expected to be limited and a family member or neighbor usually stops a violent domestic dispute before it escalates. Men who beat their wives often or who injure their wives are considered abusive. Women can use "unprovoked" or excessive abuse as grounds for divorce.

Rape/Sexual Assault

Domestic violence, rape, and sexual assault are common problems in Guinea, the severity of which have been made clear by the abuses of refugee women from Sierra Leone and Liberia. A report by the UN found that refugee women had undergone sexual abuses both during and after their flight to Guinea. A call by the president to the population of Conakry in September 2000 to rid the city of "rebels" led to the beating and rape of numerous women of Sierra Leonian and Liberian origin.[39]

Trafficking in Women and Children

Prostitution, particularly of young women and girls, appears to be on the rise in Guinea.[40] This is particularly true among poor families who may use their daughters as a source of revenue. The Coordination Unit on Traditional Practices That Affect Women's and Children's Health has recently expanded its organizational focus to include combating child prostitution in Conakry.[41] In addition to child prostitution, the UN and local NGOs note an increase in the traffic of children, particularly among the refugee population. Trafficking appears to occur both within Guinea and across national borders, into Guinea from Mali and other countries to the west and out of Guinea to Senegal.

OUTLOOK FOR THE TWENTY-FIRST CENTURY

The steps the government is taking to increase the number of girls in school and their representation in higher education, if successful, will have a great impact on women's social, political, and economic life in Guinea. Pressure from international organizations and local NGOs in these early years of the twenty-first century appears to be moving the government from rhetoric to action with regard to women's issues. Life for women in Guinea is fraught with many obstacles, but Guinean women have shown in the past that they can confront and overcome adversity.

NOTES

1. *CIA World Factbook*, www.cia.gov/publications/factbook/geos/gv.html.
2. UNFPA, *State of World Population 2001*, "Demographic, Social, and Economic Indicators," www.unfpa.org/swp/2001/english/indicators/indicators2.html.

3. UNICEF Conakry, "Situation des enfants et des femmes: Programme de co-operation 2002–2006," November 2000, 79.

4. République de Guinée, www.chez.com/justinmorel/guinch.htm.

5. UNICEF Conakry, "Situation des enfants et des femmes," 13.

6. Claude Rivière, *Guinea: The Mobilization of a People* (Ithaca: Cornell University Press, 1977), 30.

7. UNICEF Conakry, "Situation des enfants et des femmes," 13.

8. Ibid., 13.

9. Ibid., 102.

10. World Bank, "Document intérimaire de stratégie de réduction de la pauvreté," Republic of Guinea, October 2000, 4.

11. Rivière, *Guinea*, 229.

12. Saran Kamara, "L'Alphebetisation une forme de lutte contre la pauvreté des femmes en Guinée," Faculty of Letters and Humanistic Sciences, University of Conakry, 2000.

13. Ibid., 5.

14. Human Development Report, http://hdr.undp.org.

15. World Bank, "Document intérimaire de stratégie de réduction de la pauvreté."

16. UNICEF Conakry, "Situation des enfants et des femmes," 113.

17. Ibid., 119.

18. World Bank, "Document intérimaire de stratégie de réduction de la pauvreté."

19. UNICEF Conakry, "Situation des enfants et des femmes," 11.

20. Ibid., 33.

21. Ibid.

22. UNICEF, www.unicef.org/emerg/Country/Guinea/010930.htm.

23. Julie Fischer, "Report on Natural-Resource Management Practices and Tenure Constraints and Opportunities in the Diaforé Watershed, Fouta Djalon, Guinea," Land Tenure Center, 1995.

24. Regina Gorgen, Mohamed L. Yansané, Michael Marx, and Dominique Milli-mounou, "Sexual Behavior and Attitudes among Unmarried Youths in Guinea," *International Family Planning Perspectives* 24, no. 2 (1998): 65–71.

25. Ibid.

26. UNICEF Conakry, "Situation des enfants et des femmes," 11.

27. Ibid., 103.

28. Elise C. Levin, "Women's Childbearing Decisions in Guinea: Life Course Perspectives and Historical Change," *Africa Today* 47, nos. 3–4 (2001): 63–81.

29. UNICEF Conakry, "Situation des enfants et des femmes," 120.

30. Ibid., 102. Statistics from 1999.

31. Ibid., 104.

32. World Bank, "Document intérimaire de stratégie de réduction de la pauvreté," 2.

33. World Bank Report no. PID11064, June 20, 2002.

34. UNICEF Conakry, "Situation des enfants et des femmes," 116.

35. www.ipu.org.

36. Republic of Guinea, *Programme national des infrastructures rurales: Gender and Transport*, rapport de la mission d'identification, April 1999, 9.

37. Dr. Mariama Beavogui, the daughter of Lansana Beavogui who served as prime minister during the Sékou Touré era, formed the PRN to oppose Conté's military government.

38. Roger Botte, "Pouvoir du livre, pouvoir des hommes: la religion comme critère de distinction," *Journal des Africanistes* 60, no. 2 (1990): 37–53.

39. UNICEF Conakry, "Situation des enfants et des femmes," 135. See also Amnesty International, "Guinea: Maintaining Order with Contempt for the Right to Life," AI Index AFR 292002, May 2002.

40. UNICEF Conakry, "Situation des enfants et des femmes," 79.

41. See Saliou Samb, "Guinée: Une ONG sonne l'alerte pour lutter contre la pédophilie," Inter Press Service, Agence Presse du Tiers Monde (IPS), January 2002, www.famafrique.

RESOURCE GUIDE

Suggested Reading

Adamolekun, 'Ladipo. *Sékou Touré's Guinea: An Experiment in Nation Building*. London: Methuen, 1976.

Derman, William. *Serfs, Peasants and Socialists: A Former Serf Village in the Republic of Guinea*. Berkeley: University of California Press, 1973.

Gessin, Monique. "Conuagui Women (Guinea)." In *Women of Tropical Africa*, edited by Denise Paulme. London: Routledge and Kegan Paul, 1963.

Levin, Elise C. "Women's Childbearing Decisions in Guinea: Life Course Perspectives and Historical Change." *Africa Today* 47, nos. 3–4 (2001): 63–81.

O'Toole, Thomas. *Historical Dictionary of Guinea*. London: Scarecrow Press, 1995.

Rivière, Claude. *Guinea: The Mobilization of a People*. Ithaca: Cornell University Press, 1977.

Salm, Steven J. *Culture and Customs of Ghana*. Westport, CT: Greenwood Press, 2002.

Web Sites

Boubah.com, www.boubah.com.
Guinean Independent News site (in French).

Famafrique, http://famafrique.org.
Sources on women in French-speaking Africa.

MiriNet, www.mirinet.com.
Main web service in Guinean with links to other Guinea-related web sites.

Republic of Guinea, www.guinee.gov.gn.
The official web site of the Guinean government (in French).

Organizations

Association des Femmes Entrepreneurs de Guinée (AFEG)
B.P. 790
Conakry, Guinea
Fax: 224-41-32-06

Association des Femmes pour la Recherche et le Developpement
B.P. 295
DNM Conakry, Guinea
Phone: 224-44-42-48/44-43-21
Fax: 224-41-35-73

Association Feminine d'Information e d'Aide à Creation d'Entreprise (CFIAC)
B.P. 3210
Conakry, Guinea

Association Guinéenne des Femmes Travailleuses de Guinée
Bourse du Travail
B.P. 237
Conakry, Guinea
Phone: 224-41-41-87/41-50-44
Fax: 224-44-36-35

Coordination des ONG Feminines de Guinée
B.P. 2176
Immenble Kebe Ave.
Conakry, Guinea
Phone: 224-44-20-47
Fax: 224-44-27-77

Groupement des Femmes d'Affaires de Guinée
B.P. 3009
Conakry, Guinea
Phone: 224-41-18-92/41-20/65
Fax: 224-31-37-12

SELECTED BIBLIOGRAPHY

Adamolekun, 'Ladipo. *Sékou Touré's Guinea: An Experiment in Nation Building*. London: Methuen, 1976.

Astone, Jennifer. "Gender, Agriculture, and French Colonialism: The Suntuure in the Fuuta Jalon, Guinea 1912–1958." Masters thesis, Binghamton: State University of New York, 1993.

———. "Negotiating Work Burdens: Women's Home Gardens in Fuuta Jalon, Guinea 1930–1995." Ph.D. diss., Binghamton: State University of New York, 1996.

Botte, Roger. "Pouvoir du livre, pouvoir des hommes: la religion comme critère de distinction." *Journal des Africanistes* 60, no. 2 (1990): 37–53.

———. "Stigmate sociaux et descriminations religieuses: L'Ancienne classe servile au Fouta Jalloo." *Cahiers d'Etudes Africaines* 34, nos. 1–3 (1994): 133–55.

Derman, William. *Serfs, Peasants and Socialists: A Former Serf Village in the Republic of Guinea*. Berkeley: University of California Press, 1973.

Devey, Muriel. *La Guinée*. Paris: Karthala, 1997.

Dupire, Marguerite. *Organisation Social des Peul: Étude d'ethnographi comparée*. Paris: Librairie Plon, 1970.

Fischer, Julie. *Report on Natural-Resource Management Practices and Tenure Constraints and Opportunities in the Diaforé Watershed, Fouta Djalon, Guinea*. Land Tenure Center, 1995.

Gessin, Monique. "Coniagui Women (Guinea)." In *Women of Tropical Africa*, edited by Denise Paulme. London: Routledge and Kegan Paul, 1963.

Hoffer, Carol P. "Madam Yoko: Ruler of the Kpa Mende Confederacy." In *Women, Culture, and Society*, edited by Michelle Zimbalist Rosaldo and Louise Lamphere. Stanford: Stanford University Press, 1974.

Kaba, Camara. *Dans la Guinée de Sékou Touré: Cela a bien eu lieu*. Paris: L'Harmattan, 1998.

Kaba, Lansiné. *Le "non" de la Guinée à De Gaulle*. Paris: Éditions Chaka, 1990.

Kamara, Saran. "L'Alphebetisation une forme de lutte contre la pauvreté des femmes en Guinée." Faculty of Letters and Humanistic Sciences, University of Conakry, 2000.

Levin, Elise C. "Women's Childbearing Decisions in Guinea: Life Course Perspectives and Historical Change." *Africa Today* 47, nos. 3–4 (2001): 63–81.

O'Toole, Thomas. *Historical Dictionary of Guinea*. London: Scarecrow Press, 1995.

Republic of Guinea. *Programme National des Infrastructures Rurales: Gender and Transport*. Rapport de la mission d'identification, 1999.

Rivière, Claude. *Guinea: The Mobilization of a People*. Ithaca: Cornell University Press, 1977.

Suret-Canale, Jean. *La République de Guinée*. Paris: Éditions Sociales, 1970.

UNICEF Conakry. "Situation des enfants et des femmes: Programme de cooperation 2002–2006." www.unicef.org/emerg/guinea.htm. UNICEF offers most information in a choice of languages.

World Bank. "Document intérimaire de stratégie de réduction de la pauvreté." Republic of Guinea. October 2000. www.worldbank.org/afr. World Bank offers most information in a choice of languages.

8

KENYA

Rebecca Kemble

PROFILE OF KENYA

Kenya is located on the east coast of Africa and bordered to the north by Somalia, Ethiopia, and Sudan, to the west by Uganda, and to the south by Tanzania. It is bisected east to west by the equator, and north to south by the Great Rift Valley. By area it is 224,961 square miles, about the size of the state of Texas. Kenya has a wide range of geographical and ecological regions ranging from the tropical coastal plains on the Indian Ocean to the glaciers of Mt. Kenya. Over 70 percent of the country is considered arid, receiving fewer than twenty inches of rainfall per year. Only 7 percent of the land is suitable for agricultural production, and that is concentrated in the central and western highlands of the Rift Valley, where most of the population resides.[1]

In 2000 the total population of Kenya was 30.7 million, 43.5 percent of whom were under the age of fifteen, with the majority of the population, 66.6 percent, residing in rural areas. Life expectancy at birth in 2000 was 52.2 years with an infant mortality rate of 77 live births per 1,000. Fertility per woman sharply declined between 1975 and 2000 from 8.1 children per woman to 4.6, for a reduction in the total population growth rate during that same period from 3.3 percent to 1.8 percent.[2]

There are over forty identified ethnic groups in Kenya, with five of these composing 75 percent of the population (Kikuyu 22 percent, Luhya 14 percent, Luo 13 percent, Kalenjin 12 percent, Kamba 12 percent). The national language is Kiswahili, a trade language developed on the East African coast that combines elements of Bantu grammar with Arabic and Portuguese vocabulary. Kiswahili is taught in primary schools and is the common language of business in the more ethnically diverse towns and cities. English is widely spoken in urban areas and is the language of instruction at the secondary and tertiary levels of education.

Kenya was colonized by the British at the turn of the century and gained political independence in 1963 after an armed struggle and a decade-long state of emergency. At independence, full franchise rights were extended to all citizens of the Republic of Kenya regardless of race, sex, or religion. The independent state inherited its administrative structure of seven provinces and forty-eight districts from the colonial state with relatively minor alterations.

Politically, the Republic of Kenya adopted a tripartite system of government with executive, legislative, and judicial branches. In theory, this system was to provide checks and balances so that power would not become concentrated in one branch. However, in practice the executive branch in the person of the president has wielded much more influence over the other two branches than vice versa.[3] Because of this concentration of power, Kenya effectively became a single-party state from 1969 until 1991, when a constitutional amendment reinstated a multiparty system.

OVERVIEW OF WOMEN'S ISSUES

Family matters and property rights are central to Kenyan women's issues today. In order to understand these it is necessary to have an appreciation of the profound transformations most Kenyan communities experienced as the result of colonialism. Kenyan society was affected by colonialism more deeply than most other African countries (with the notable exceptions of South Africa and Zimbabwe) due to the settlement in Kenya by Europeans from the very beginning of the colonial period.

Settlement was officially encouraged by means of various incentives and economic policies. The most far-reaching of these policies, which have had an inestimable impact on all aspects of life in Kenya to this day, involved the alienation of vast tracts of the most fertile land for European settlement and cash-crop production for export markets. The African population was forcibly removed to what the colonial government termed "native reserves" to pave the way for the development of large-scale livestock ranches and agricultural plantations owned by English settlers and to a lesser extent Afrikaners fleeing the Boer War in South Africa.

In addition to land alienation by force and the movement of the African population into reserves, a prohibition on the cultivation of cash crops in the reserves as well as tax and pass laws were instituted to ensure an adequate supply of labor for the European ventures both in agriculture and in the fast-growing city, Nairobi. African families were required to produce a cash income in order to pay taxes. Strictly enforced pass laws similar to those established in South Africa during the apartheid era restricted the movement of people out of the reserves to those in possession of a work permit. Most people issued with work permits were men whose families were not allowed to accompany them to their places of work. This created a social dynamic in which women and children remained in the reserves engaged in subsistence activities, while men migrated out in order to produce a cash income.[4] Many men thus received experience, training, and education in the "modern" European sectors of colonial Kenyan society, while most women relied on traditional languages, technologies, and knowledge for their survival.[5]

Recent estimates show that upward of 40 percent of small farms are managed by women, demonstrating the persistence of this dynamic of de facto single mother–headed households in the rural areas, although the laws and policies that originally created it have long since been abolished.[6] Unfortunately, the compulsion of economic necessity is a well-established fact of existence for most Kenyans and no longer has to be artificially created through government initiatives.[7]

EDUCATION

Opportunities

The Kenyan government has recognized that "females are disadvantaged at all levels of education in terms of access, participation, completion and performance."[8] Whereas the final legal basis to these disadvantages was recently abolished, customs, social attitudes, and financial obstacles limit girls' access to education.[9]

Formal education in Kenya has undergone significant changes over the past seventeen years. In 1985, the 8-4-4 system (8 years of primary, 4 years of secondary, 4 years of university) replaced the old 7-4-2-3 system, which was based on the English model. This new system was intended to meet the increasing demands of the economy for technically and professionally qualified personnel with a more vocationally oriented curriculum. The content of this curriculum is heavily gender biased and reinforces negative stereotypes about women, though there are some government efforts to address this problem.[10] Girls are also channeled into courses of study that are more suitable for traditional female roles, such as home science, nursing, and teaching.

At the primary school level there is now gender parity in enrollment, which represents a great improvement over the past thirty years.[11] Girls' enrollment in secondary school continues to lag slightly behind that of boys, with girls representing 47 percent of the total. However, males still substantially outnumber females in higher education, with women composing only 29 percent of university enrollments.[12]

Although Kenyan law stipulates that education be available to all children through the twelfth grade, cost-sharing initiatives that compel parents to pay substantial amounts of money for educational expenses have had the effect of generally high dropout rates before the end of primary school. In 1996 only 79 percent of primary school age children were enrolled in school.[13] Girls suffer higher dropout rates than boys due to pregnancy, lack of facilities, and the tendency of parents to withdraw girls before withdrawing boys when they can no longer afford school fees.[14]

There is a critical shortage of schools, particularly at the secondary level and particularly for girls. Fewer than half the numbers of primary school leavers are able to enroll in secondary school. Those girls' and coed secondary schools that do exist tend to be more poorly resourced than boys' schools in terms of laboratory equipment, library materials, and teaching staff.[15]

An estimated 8,000 girls drop out of school each year due to pregnancy, though this number is probably low. While the mandatory expulsion of pregnant students is no longer legal, many girls who become pregnant drop out of their own accord never to resume their schooling. Some of these pregnancies occur as the result of rape by schoolteachers, who are rarely charged with any offence. Even when they are charged, the law is lenient toward sexual offenders against children under age fourteen. The offence is not considered rape but "defilement," which carries a maximum penalty of five years imprisonment.[16]

Literacy

Literacy is defined as being able to read as well as write. Seventy-six percent of women over the age of fifteen were considered literate in 2000, as compared to 89 percent of men.[17]

EMPLOYMENT AND ECONOMICS

Farming

Since the beginning of the colonial period the mainstay of the Kenyan economy has been the agricultural sector, which provides more than 70 percent of total employment. Of those employed in agriculture, 80 percent are women.[18] In addition to food for local consumption, tea, coffee, cut flowers, and vegetables are grown for export. While some large-scale farms still remain operational, since the mid-1980s small farmers have undertaken an increasing proportion of the nation's cash-crop production on a contract basis. Part of the larger trend of globalization of the food industry, contract farming transfers most of the risk in production to the farmer, while the marketing agents reap the bulk of the profits.[19]

Farmers with holdings as small as one acre or less sell their produce to export agents based in Nairobi who then transport and market it to buyers in Europe. Some firms have contracts with large supermarket chains in Europe and grade, clean, package, label, and apply price tags to the products before shipping. While these value-added services create jobs for some people in the short run, in the long run all Kenyans, and particularly Kenyan women, lose out as family land that once provided subsistence and security is transformed into a commodity whose yields are largely controlled by men.[20]

Paid Employment and Informal Economic Acitivities

Relatively few women participate in the formal economy; only 12 percent earn a wage or salary and 17 percent are self-employed.[21] Many women who are formally employed also engage in other income-generating activities to supplement relatively low wages.

Entrepreneurship

Devaluation of the currency, transfer of government corporations to the private sector, downsizing of state agencies through surrender of its social welfare responsibilities to the private sector, and promotion of civil society organizations as contractors to the state undermined the progress professional women had made in the first decades of independence through massive layoffs and agency closures. The removal of price controls and subsidies has also worsened the situation for women traders and farmers.[22] Many professional women have taken early retirement and invested their severance packages into starting up small businesses in retail and wholesale trade, transportation, small livestock and poultry production, and the service industry.

Kenyan potter. Photo © TRIP/J. Highet.

Pay

Women have less access to employment opportunities and earn less for equal work as compared to men.[23] Poverty is reflected in high levels of food insecurity and unemployment, low personal incomes and wages, as well as lack of access to basic needs and services such as health, education, water, and sanitation. According to United Nations statistics, nearly half the Kenyan population lives below the absolute poverty line, which is defined as the cost of a 2,250-calorie-per-day diet, plus a modest allowance for nonfood items. Nearly two-thirds of the population survives on less than $2 per day.[24]

Support for Mothers/Caretakers

Urban residents rely on family members in the rural areas to provide additional nonmonetary support in the form of food and child care. Kenyan law allows for a two-month, fully paid maternity leave, though a woman must forfeit her one-month annual leave, which effectively means maternity leave is only one-month. There are no legal provisions for allowing unpaid maternity leave, so if a woman needs more time off than the two months, she risks losing her job.[25]

Inheritance, Property, and Land Rights

Land ownership is the single most politically sensitive and explosive issue in Kenya. Within the past ten years thousands of people have died and hundreds of thousands more have been internally displaced due to politically motivated, violent clashes over land in the Rift Valley, Western, and Nyanza provinces.[26] Landlessness and the unjust nature of colonial land policy were never adequately addressed at independence, and the clashes represent, in part, the culmination of decades of mounting tension as the result of these unmet social needs.

In a country where two-thirds of the population reside in the rural areas and much of the urban population have strong family ties and claims to land, land tenure is a matter of great concern to everyone, but even more so to women whose formal ownership, access to, and control over land are minimal. Traditionally, land has not been seen as a commodity to be bought, sold, and used as collateral. Before the turn of the century and the onslaught of colonialism, land was held in common with no individual having rights to transfer or dispose of it without the consent of the family or community. It was deeply embedded in social relations and had cultural value and meaning above and beyond being a factor of agricultural production.

For many agricultural communities, land is still the source of physical survival, wealth, and social welfare, and it is a major factor in family relations. In few indigenous Kenyan traditions do women have transfer rights over land. They gain access and rights to use land through fathers, husbands, or sons. A woman's access to land, and therefore to survival for herself and her children, thus depends upon maintaining good social relations with her male relatives.

Privatization of land in the native reserves was first introduced as a colonial development project during the state of emergency in the 1950s. By developing a class of indigenous private landowners who had an individual stake in the colonial economy, it was believed that grassroots political pressure for wholesale land redistribution, which had spawned a guerrilla war in the forests around the Aberdare Mountains and Mt. Kenya, would abate. The specific outcomes envisioned for land consolidation and registration included increased individual security of tenure, a reduction in the number of land disputes, greater access to credit, increased investment, and the development of a market in land.[27]

Women's security of land tenure was dramatically reduced by land registration. Once a family's land was surveyed and registered, a title deed was issued in the name of the male head-of-household. Even though women were and remain the primary food producers and users of traditional family land, very few have ever been issued with title deeds. Most of the female-owned property in Kenya is located in urban areas where there are no traditional encumbrances. Even in this category of landownership there is marked gender inequality. Women are legally recognized as owning about 20 percent of urban housing structures, and those structures tend to be of the lowest quality with the least security of tenure.[28] Many of these instances of legally recognized female ownership are cases of a man wanting to disguise his interest in a property by registering it in the name of a female relative.

Thus, with the privatization of family land men's customary rights, which were formerly fluid, negotiable, and subject to family and community consensus, became legally entrenched and absolute. There is no provision for the recognition of women or children's use or inheritance rights on a title deed. The deed-holder not only gains the force of law, but also market value just as the crafters of the privatization policy envisioned. Instead of being a source of communal support that requires the participation of all family members in decisionmaking processes, privately held land can be sold or mortgaged without regard to the well-being of all those who depend upon it for their livelihoods. The deed-holder can thus enrich himself at the expense of his family and render them landless.

In a small step toward gender equity in land tenure, parliament passed the Law of Succession Act, which came into effect in 1981. This act provides for measures protecting the property rights of widows and children in the event that a man dies without making a will. It allows female children a share in their deceased father's property, though in practice courts have ruled against allowing married daughters to inherit. They have argued that a woman's presumed access and rights to the property of her husband preclude the inheritance rights to her father's. Similarly, a widow forfeits the rights to her deceased husband's property upon remarriage.[29]

Social/Government Programs

Structural Adjustment

Kenya's economy showed two decades of impressive growth after independence. Since the mid-1980s, however, Kenya has experienced steady economic decline. This decline is attributable in part to deteriorating terms of trade globally, but internal mismanagement and corruption also play a large role in the weakening of Kenya's economy and infrastructure. A recent Transparency International report places Kenya among the top ten most corrupt countries in the world, rating it 96 out of 102.[30]

In 1997 major international financial institutions and foreign governmental donors suspended financial assistance to Kenya due to political violence during the presidential election that year, the government's failure to address corruption, and its abandonment of economic reform measures implemented under the structural adjustment programs (SAPs) of the early 1990s. Donors were poised to renew funding in 2000, but suspended aid in large part due to the continued cancellation of anticorruption measures, including a 2000 court ruling that the Kenya Anti-Corruption Authority's investigative and prosecutorial powers were unconstitutional.[31]

Women are more vulnerable to poverty than men due to their limited access to economic resources including land, credit, adequate training, and support services. Women are virtually absent from economic decisionmaking at the national level, and have little or no input into the formulation of financial, monetary, commercial and other economic policies, or tax systems and rules governing pay. Women's increased susceptibility to poverty exposes them more to the negative effects of economic liberalization policies. While deemed necessary from a sustainable management perspective, the reforms introduced as part of the SAP in the early 1990s such as cost sharing and cost recovery in the provision of health care, education, sanitation, and water, rendered these services inaccessible to most women who are the majority among the poor.

Even relatively better-off women have been seriously affected by the SAP. The removal of price controls and subsidies has also worsened the situation for women traders and farmers.[32] The devaluation of the currency, the transfer of government corporations and social welfare responsibilities to the private sector, and support of civil society organizations as contractors to the state have all undermined the progress professional women had made in the first decades of independence through massive layoffs and agency closures.

FAMILY AND SEXUALITY

Gender Roles and Division of Labor

The personal law section of the constitution specifies that gender discrimination is not prohibited in marriage, divorce, adoption, burial, or devolution of property. However, in many ways, marriage is the foundation of Kenyan society. For both women and men of all ethnicities and religions, social and property relations revolve around marriage and the extended families of both husband and wife. As economic conditions deteriorate, Kenyans rely more and more on extended family networks for various forms of support for educational, health care and funeral expenses, employment, food, and housing. Kenyans spend a considerable amount of time maintaining these relationships through informal visits and attendance at family functions such as graduations, church weddings, and funerals.

Marriage

There are four legally recognized forms of marriage in Kenya: statutory, Islamic, Hindu, and African customary marriage laws, which themselves have multiple variations based on the various practices of the different ethnic groups. Polygyny (a man marrying more than one woman) is allowed under Islamic and African customary laws, while Hindu and statutory laws require both parties in a marriage to be monogamous. Kenyan law also recognizes the various divorce provisions under each of these marriage systems.

Most Kenyans marry under the customary laws of their ethnic group, and an increasing number supplement this with a Christian church wedding. In addition to being commitments between two individuals, customary marriages also embody formal social contracts and allegiances between families, lineages, and clans. Marriage is more of a process than an event and involves the exchange of wealth and social obligations. The marriage process can span a number of years, in some traditions only being fully recognized upon the birth of the first child.

In most communities, bridewealth is given by the husband's family to a variety of people in the woman's extended family over the course of a series of social events beginning before the marriage is complete and extending in some cases throughout the early years of the new family's development. Traditionally, bridewealth consisted of a combination of livestock, foodstuffs, and traditionally brewed beverages. Although in negotiations bridewealth is still discussed in these terms, the material exchange is increasingly tendered in cash.

Bridewealth exchange does not represent the purchase of a wife, but is rather the substance of family and social bonds. It is a concrete form of social and marital security. As discussed above in the section on land rights, most indigenous Kenyan communities are traditionally patrilineal[33] and patrilocal,[34] which renders women dependent upon their relationships with men for property rights and social status. After bridewealth exchanges are complete, the husband and his extended family have distinct responsibilities to the wife and her children. The members of the wife's natal family have direct, material interests in supporting the woman's rights within the marriage and ensuring that her needs are adequately addressed since they would be required to return all bridewealth payments in the event of divorce. Because marriage is such a complex, multifaceted process involving large numbers of people, instances of divorce are rare.

Reproduction

Contraception and Abortion

In the late-1970s Kenya had the highest fertility rate in the world, an average of 8.1 children per woman, and one of the highest population growth rates, nearly 4 percent.[35] As the social and economic consequences of this population explosion became evident to policymakers, the Kenyan government initiated widespread family planning initiatives in the early 1980s. These programs have taken some time to gain acceptance, but since the 1980s there has been a marked increase in the use of modern methods of contraception from 10 percent of women between the ages of fifteen and forty-nine in 1984 to 32 percent in 1998.[36] Kenyan women have always practiced various traditional forms of birth control, and the reported use of these methods is increasing as well.[37]

Abortion on demand is still outlawed in Kenya, though there is growing support in the government for its legalization. Currently, abortion is legally permitted only in cases where the mother's life is in jeopardy. A government study attributes one-third of the deaths factored into Kenya's high maternal mortality rate (590 maternal deaths per 100,000 births) to complications arising from unsafe abortions.[38] While thus far unable to change the law to legalize abortion, policymakers acknowledge its practice and have mandated that women who get abortions have access to quality post-abortion care, including counseling, education, and family planning services.[39] These services, together with emergency treatment for incomplete abortions, are to be made available at every district hospital in the country.[40]

HEALTH

Health Care Access

Budgetary provisions by the Kenyan government are insufficient to provide a minimum essential health care package for all Kenyans. Kenya ranks last among African countries in government expenditures for health care. Only 28.1 percent of total health care expenditures are provided by the state, while the other 71.9 percent is paid by private sources, mostly out-of-pocket expenditures by the consumer.[41] Since the early 1990s, when the SAP was implemented and a large amount of government support was withdrawn from the health care sector, nearly half of all health care services have been provided by private or religious hospitals and clinics. Government facilities that do still function charge user fees that are more afford-able than the charges at private clinics and hospitals, but these fees are still too expensive for a significant portion of the population.[42] Government health care facilities are also overcrowded, understaffed, and underresour-ced.

Diseases and Disorders

Because of the privatization of the health care sector, women's lack of access to economic resources limits their access to and use of basic health resources, including primary health services for the prevention and treat-ment of childhood diseases, malnutrition, anemia, diarrhea, communicable diseases, malaria, tuberculosis HIV/AIDS, and other tropical diseases.[43]

Over 20 million Kenyans—more than half the population—suffer from malaria, a parasitic infection of the blood carried by mosquitoes. Malaria accounts for 30 percent of all outpatient visits to health care facilities and 19 percent of hospital admittances.[44] Each year 26,000 young children die from malaria. Pregnant women tend to experience malarial infections more severely than other adults. They suffer anemia, tend to have low-birth-weight babies, and run a much greater risk of death from the disease. While most malaria is treatable with drugs, many people can't afford the medi-cine. There have also recently been incidences of drug-resistant strains of malaria in certain parts of the country.[45]

AIDS

Kenya is one of nine African countries hardest hit by the HIV epidemic. Life expectancy in Kenya has declined from fifty-nine years to fifty-two years in the last decade because of AIDS. An alarming 14 percent of the adult Kenyan population—2.2 million people—are infected with the HIV virus. In the year 2000, a quarter of a million Kenyans died of AIDS, and there were an estimated 860,000 orphaned children whose parents died of AIDS.[46] Along with the AIDS epidemic, tuberculosis incidence has in-creased ninefold, with nearly half the population carrying a latent tuber-culosis infection.[47]

Women comprise more than half the HIV/AIDS cases. This number is likely to increase, as young women between the ages of fifteen and twenty-four suffer more than double the infection rate of men in that same age category. This is in large part due to the age differential in sexual partners (i.e., young women having as partners older men who have already been exposed to HIV).[48] Infection rates among pregnant women attending pre-natal clinics in urban areas have remained steady at about 15 percent throughout the 1990s, but the prevalence of infection among women in rural areas is continuing to rise—from about 3 percent in 1990 to 23 percent in 2000.[49] The UNAIDS/WHO epidemiological study also indicates dra-matically higher infection rates in Western and Nyanza provinces in the western part of the country.[50]

HIV/AIDS is having devastating effects on Kenyan families, with women shouldering the bulk of the burden of care of sick family members, as well as the care and maintenance of orphaned children of relatives.

Female Genital Cutting

Young women and men in most indigenous Kenyan communities par-ticipate in coming-of-age rituals, which mark their passage from childhood into adulthood. In some (but not all) of these communities male circum-cision and various forms of female genital cutting occur as part of these rituals. Since the turn of the twentieth century, Europeans have attempted to regulate, control, or ban these practices, calling them barbaric, unhy-gienic, and immoral. The net effect of these campaigns was to strengthen, not weaken, adherence to these practices and to provide a focus for anti-colonial sentiment and action.[51] Kenyan women are thus very sensitive to Western human rights campaigns against female genital cutting.

Missionaries and colonial administrators failed to understand the full cultural context within which these practices took place, and the extent to which girls themselves desired the procedure. The cutting was not an end in itself. It symbolized deeply held cultural values, and an attack on the practice was tantamount to an attack upon the cultural institutions that defined people's identity. Initiation consisted not only of the cutting pro-cedure, but also of months of teachings by older women about sexuality, birth control, childbearing, and other matters concerning family life. Suc-cessful initiation had an impact not only on the social status of the initiate, but on that of her mother as well. In many communities, only women with circumcised children could attain the status, respect, and decision-making powers of an elder.

Current campaigns to eradicate female genital cutting run the risk of fierce opposition if they fail to take into account the deeply held beliefs and identity issues that form the basis of the practice. For the past fifteen years the government has attempted to outlaw female genital cutting, but opposition has been too strong for any such measure to pass.[52] However, in December 2001 parliament passed the Children's Bill, which includes provisions that ban children from forced marriage and forced female genital cutting.[53] In practice, the law may not have much effect, since the people it was designed to protect have little access to accurate information about their legal rights, and few resources with which to pursue those rights in court.

Recently there have been some highly publicized cases of cohorts of girls from different communities being initiated without cutting.[54] However, it remains to be seen whether these few cases represent public relations successes by anticircumcision activists, or whether they in fact mark the beginning of a long-term trend toward a widespread shift in attitudes toward female genital cutting and the eventual abandonment of the practice.[55]

POLITICS AND LAW

Political Participation

Despite the fact that the government has consistently stated its intention to promote gender equality through legislation, it has failed to implement constitutional provisions to domesticate these international and regional human rights treaties that promote and protect women's rights. Kenyan women lag far behind their counterparts in other African countries with respect to political representation. As of 2002 at the national level, women held only 7 percent of the parliamentary seats and three women cabinet ministers were appointed.[56]

While not adequately represented in publicly held positions of leadership, Kenyan women are very active in grassroots women's groups. There are over 24,000 women's groups registered with the Ministry of Culture and Social Services. Most of these are small, village-level groups organized around matters of immediate concern for mutual aid and income generating purposes. However, their membership can easily be mobilized for more political aims. For example, women's groups are increasingly protesting the sale and consumption of *changaa*, a cheap and dangerous high-proof alcohol brewed locally that has been the cause of many disabilities and deaths in recent years.

Maendeleo Ya Wanawake (MYW) or Women in Development is the oldest and largest national-level women's organization. It was founded at the height of the state of emergency in 1952 by the female relatives of colonial officials to educate African women in modern European methods of hygiene, child rearing, and cooking. Ideologically, it served as a counterinsurgency measure used to suppress the increasingly militant opposition to British rule, and it was also used to gather intelligence. Throughout its rather tumultuous history, MYW has been either formally or informally allied with the ruling party, and has had the effect of overshadowing and undercutting attempts by more activist women to forge an alternative, national-level women's alliance.[57]

The Greenbelt Movement began in the late 1970s as an afforestation project of the National Council of Women in Kenya, but has since grown into an environmental activist organization thanks to Dr. Wangari Maathai. She began her tree-planting efforts not only to help curb soil erosion, but also to help the burgeoning population become self-sustaining in its use of fuel wood, as well as to create an income generating activity for women in rural communities. There are now 5,000 grassroots nurseries throughout Kenya and over 20 million trees have been planted.

In the late 1980s Maathai and the membership of the Greenbelt Movement successfully opposed the construction of a skyscraper scheduled to be built in the middle of Uhuru Park, Nairobi's most accessible and important public space. Her vocal opposition to the location of the proposed complex led the government of former President Daniel arap Moi to label both Maathai and the Greenbelt Movement subversive. She was vilified in parliament and forced to vacate her office of ten years with twenty-four hours notice. Nevertheless, thanks to Maathai's opposition, foreign investors withdrew their support for the Uhuru Park complex and the project was canceled.

In addition to the Greenbelt Movement, Kenyan women belong to a wide variety of organizations, ranging from women's activist groups that focus on improving women's access to education, health, and other resources, to nonpartisan women's political organizations that promote women's political leadership, to professional, entrepreneurial, and development associations.

Women's Rights

Although Chapter 5 of the Kenyan constitution guarantees fundamental rights and freedoms to all citizens regardless of race, tribe, place of origin, residence or other local connection, political opinions, color, creed, or sex, women's rights are not fully realized for a number of reasons. The constitution itself specifically suspends the prohibition against gender discrimination in another section pertaining to "personal law." Section 83 states that the prohibition against discrimination on the basis of sex does not apply to marriage, divorce, adoption, burial, or devolution of property, the very areas most relevant to women's ability to determine their own lives.

Additionally, the recognition of different legal regimes (i.e., Islamic, Hindu, and African customary laws) and persistent cultural practices continue to conflict with these constitutionally guaranteed rights. Kenya has signed on to numerous international human rights treaties including the International Covenant on Civil and Political Rights, the International Covenant on Economic, Social, and Cultural Rights, the Convention on the Elimination of All Forms of Discrimination Against Women, the African Charter on Human and Peoples' Rights, and the Convention on the Rights of the Child.[58]

RELIGION AND SPIRITUALITY

The majority of Kenyans are Christians (38 percent Protestant, 28 percent Catholic), while about 25 percent practice indigenous religions and 6 percent are Muslim. Among the Asian community there are Hindus, Sikhs, Parsees, and Bahais.[59]

Christian missionary activity commenced at the beginning of the colonial period at the end of the nineteenth century, particularly in the fertile highland regions where the bulk of land alienation took place. In the 1930s the first indigenous Christian church, the African Independent Pentecostal Church of East Africa, was founded. The AIPCEA was later to play a critical role in the independence movement of the 1950s. Today there are still many mission churches, as well as independent evangelical sects, that have broken ties with other Christian or Protestant denominations. The number of Kenyan clergy has grown since independence, and most of the Roman Catholic and Church Province of Kenya (Anglican) hierarchies are indigenous Kenyan.

Though Christian feminist theologians have decried the sexist underpinnings of church structure and theology, many Kenyan women have used the church as a means of empowerment at both the grassroots and national levels.[60] Thousands of women's self-help groups are organized under the auspices of churches, and through these groups women have access to opportunities for developing leadership, organizational, and financial management skills not readily available to them in the public or business sectors.

Over half of Kenya's Muslim population is of Somali origin. The remainder is largely made up of indigenous coastal people and the Swahili-speaking community on the coast, which has maintained uninterrupted contact with Muslims from the Arabian Peninsula since the fourteenth century.[61] As with the wide variety of Christian practice in Kenya, Kenyan Muslims practice diverse forms of Islam. Similarly, in practice Islam provides both opportunities for women's empowerment, as well as philosophical justifications for their oppression.[62]

VIOLENCE

Domestic Violence

Domestic violence against women is a serious and widespread problem. Wife-beating is prevalent and largely condoned by much of society. African customary traditions permit a man to "chastise" or discipline his wife by physical means. Poverty, lack of alternative housing options, and dependence on male relatives make it difficult for women to leave violent family situations.

In a surprising victory by Kenyan human rights activists, the Domestic Violence (Family Protection) Bill was passed into law in July 2002. The law allows courts to intervene in cases of domestic violence and "to provide for the grant, enforcement and variation of court orders for protection from such violence."[63] Though the law does not recognize marital rape, it does recognize sexual and psychological as well as physical violence. As with most other laws pertaining to women and children, it will only be effective to the extent that public authorities make adequate efforts to enforce the law, and victims understand their rights under the law and have the wherewithal to defend them in court.

Rape/Sexual Assault

According to the government, 1,199 cases of rape were reported to the police in Nairobi during 2001.[64] The available statistics undoubtedly underreport the number of incidents, as cultural norms deter women from going outside their families or ethnic groups to report sexual abuse. Gender-based violence not only exposes women to sexually transmitted diseases, but also to the risk of acquiring HIV/AIDS. The high levels of HIV in the population mean that sexual violence against women and children carries a significant risk of transmission of the virus and of subsequent illness and death.

The law carries penalties of up to life imprisonment for rape, although actual sentences usually are no more than ten years. Sexual assault of a child under the age of fourteen is considered defilement and carries a lighter penalty. The rate of prosecution remains low because of inhibitions against publicly discussing sex, fear of retribution, disinclination of police to intervene in domestic disputes, and unavailability of doctors who otherwise might provide the necessary evidence for conviction.

Trafficking in Women and Children

Trafficking in women for prostitution is not as widespread a problem as it is in other eastern and southern African countries. However, there have been reports that Kenyans were trafficked to Saudi Arabia under the guise of employment opportunities. They report having been misled into accepting jobs, only to work in what they described as "modern slavery."[65] There have also been press reports of trafficking in girls for the domestic labor market in urban areas, though to date there is little research to document the true extent of this practice.

OUTLOOK FOR THE TWENTY-FIRST CENTURY

Deteriorating economic conditions, sporadic but intense violence in various parts of the country, drought, food shortages, and the devastating effects of malaria and HIV/AIDS have marked the past decade in Kenya. Worsening standards of living as measured by health and economic indicators have had a huge impact on Kenyan women in particular. Without economic reform and the political will to eradicate corruption at the highest levels of Kenyan society, it is not realistic to expect much change for the better.

The silver lining of the dark cloud of the collapse of many government-sponsored services, however, is that Kenyans have been compelled to devise local-level responses to their needs. In the long run, the solutions that emerge from local conditions will be more sustainable than the top-down government programs of the past. With their tradition of self-help groups, women are well placed to develop and lead such local initiatives.

NOTES

1. Central Intelligence Agency (CIA), *CIA World Factbook*, www.cia.gov/cia/publications/factbook/geos/ke.html#intro, 2002.

2. United Nations Development Programme (UNDP), *Human Development Report 2002: Deepening Democracy in a Fragmented World* (New York: Oxford University Press, 2002), 164, 176.

3. Sylvie Morel-Seytoux, *Review of Gender Issues in the USAID/Kenya Integrated Strategic Plan 2001–2005: Democracy and Government, Economic Growth, Population and Health, Natural Resource Management* (Nairobi: International Center for Research on Women, 2000), 1.

4. See A. Fiona D. Mackenzie, *Land, Ecology, and Resistance in Kenya, 1880–1952* (Edinburgh: Edinburgh University Press, 1997); Claire C. Robertson, *Trouble Showed the Way: Women, Men, and Trade in the Nairobi Area, 1890–1990* (Bloomington: Indiana University Press, 1997); and Bruce Berman, *Control and Crisis in Colonial Kenya: The Dialectic of Domination* (Athens: Ohio University Press, 1990).

5. There were some notable exceptions, however. For an excellent account of these as well as the highly gendered nature of colonial housing and labor policy, see Luise White, *The Comforts of Home: Prostitution in Colonial Nairobi* (Chicago: University of Chicago Press, 1990).

6. Morel-Seytoux, *Review of Gender Issues*, 3.

7. Bessie House-Midamba, *Class Development and Gender Inequality in Kenya, 1963–1990* (Lewiston, NY: Edwin Mellen Press, 1990).

8. Republic of Kenya, *National Development Plan for the Period 1994 to 1996* (Nairobi: Republic of Kenya, 1994), 255.

9. Until recently the Ministry of Education required that girls who became pregnant as students be expelled from school. See Center for Reproductive Law and Policy, *Women of the World: Laws and Policies Affecting Their Reproductive Lives, 2001* (New York: Center for Reproductive Law and Policy, 2001), 65.

10. Ministry of Health, *National Reproductive Health Strategy, 1997–2012* (Nairobi: Ministry of Health, 1996); Republic of Kenya, *National Gender and Development Policy* (Nairobi: Republic of Kenya, 2000).

11. Republic of Kenya, *National Gender and Development Policy*, 30–31.

12. Ibid., 21.

13. Bureau of Democracy, Human Rights, and Labor, U.S. Department of State,

Kenya Country Report on Human Rights Practices for 2001, www.state.gov/g/drl/rls/hrrpt/2001/af/8386.htm, 2002.

14. Republic of Kenya, *National Report on Progress Made in Implementing the Beijing Platform for Action 1995–2000* (Nairobi: Republic of Kenya, 2000), 28; House-Midamba, *Class Development and Gender Inequality in Kenya*, 63.

15. House-Midamba, *Class Development and Gender Inequality in Kenya*, 66.

16. Bureau of Democracy, Human Rights, and Labor, *Kenya Country Report*, sec. 5.

17. http://hdr.undp.org.

18. Royal Netherlands Embassy, *Kenya Country Gender Profile* (Nairobi: ACTS Press, 1994).

19. Peter D. Little, and Michael J. Watts, eds., *Living Under Contract: Contract Farming and Agrarian Transformation in Sub-Saharan Africa* (Madison: University of Wisconsin Press, 1994).

20. See Catherine S. Dolan, *Tesco Is King: Gender and Labor Dynamics in Horticultural Exporting, Meru District, Kenya* (Ann Arbor, MI: UMI Dissertation Services, 1997); Wanjiku Lois Chiuri, *The Effects of Change in Land Tenure and Resource Management on Gender Relations and the Subsequent Changes in Highland Ecosystems* (Ann Arbor, MI: UMI Dissertation Services, 1996); Stevie Moses Nangendo, *The Web of Poverty: Women and Sugarcane Farming in Bokoli Location, Bungoma District, Kenya* (Addis Ababa: Organization for Social Science Research in Eastern and Southern Africa, 1998); Edwins Laban Moogi Gwako, *The Effects of Women's Land Tenure Security on Agricultural Output Among the Maragoli of Western Kenya* (Ann Arbor, MI: UMI Dissertation Services, 1997).

21. United Nations Statistics Division, www.unstats.un.org/unsd/demographic/ww2000/table5e.htm, 2002.

22. Women's Bureau, Department of Social Services, Ministry of Culture and Social Services, *Platform for Action for Improving the Welfare of Women in Kenya* (Nairobi: Ministry of Culture and Social Services, 1997).

23. UNDP, *Human Development Report 2002*, 224, 238; United Nations Statistics Division, *World's Women 2000: Trends and Statistics*, www.unstats.un.org/unsd/demographic/ww2000/table5g.htm, 2002.

24. UNDP, *Human Development Report 2002*, 158.

25. Center for Reproductive Law and Policy, *Women of the World, 2001*, 62.

26. Kenya Human Rights Commission, *Ours by Right, Theirs by Might: A Study on Land Clashes* (Nairobi: Kenya Human Rights Commission, 1996).

27. R. J. M. Swynnerton, *A Plan to Intensify the Development of African Agriculture in Kenya* (Kenya Colony and Protectorate: Department of Agriculture, 1954).

28. Kenya Human Rights Commission, *Women and Land Rights in Kenya* (Nairobi: Kenya Human Rights Commission, 1998), 6–8.

29. Ibid., 17–18; Center for Reproductive Law and Policy, *Women of the World, 1997*, 67.

30. Transparency International, *Transparency International Corruption Perceptions Index, 2002*, www.transparency.org/pressreleases_archive/2002/2002.08.28.cpi.en.html.

31. *CIA World Factbook*.

32. Women's Bureau, *Platform for Action*.

33. Family lineage traced through men.

34. Marital residence determined by the location of the man's family.

35. National Council for Population and Development et al., and Macro Inter-

national, *Demographic and Health Survey, 1998* (Nairobi: National Council for Population and Development, 1999).

36. Ibid., 86.

37. Ibid.; Beth Maina Ahlberg, *Women, Sexuality, and the Changing Social Order: The Impact of Government Policies on Reproductive Behavior in Kenya* (Philadelphia: Gordon and Breach, 1991).

38. Ministry of Health, *National Reproductive Health Strategy, 1997–2012*, 27.

39. Republic of Kenya, *National Population Policy for Sustainable Development* (Nairobi: Government of Kenya, 2000).

40. Center for Reproductive Law and Policy, *Women of the World*, 2001, 58.

41. World Health Organization, *Selected Health Indicators for Kenya*, www3.who.int/whosis/country/indicators.cfm?country=ken&language=english, 2002.

42. Center for Reproductive Law and Policy, *Women of the World*, 2001, 54.

43. Women's Bureau, *Platform for Action*.

44. Division of Malaria Control, Ministry of Health, *National Malaria Strategy, 2001–2010* (Nairobi: Ministry of Health, 2001), 3–4.

45. Ibid., 4.

46. Centers for Disease Control, *National Center for HIV, STD, and TB Prevention: Kenya Country Profile*, www.cdc.gov/nchstp/od/gap/countries/kenya.htm, 2002.

47. USAID Synergy Project, *HIV/AIDS in Kenya*, www.synergyaids.com/documents/kenya%20brief%20rev%203a.pdf, 2002.

48. UNAIDS/WHO Epidemiological Fact Sheet: 2002 Update, www.unaids.org/hivaidsinfo/statistics/fact_sheets/pdfs/kenya_en.pdf.

49. Ibid., 5.

50. Ibid., 16.

51. Lynn Thomas, " '*Ngaitana* (I Will Circumcise Myself)': Lessons from Colonial Campaigns to Ban Excision in Meru, Kenya," in *Female "Circumcision" in Africa: Culture, Controversy, and Change*, ed. Bettina Shell-Duncan and Ylva Hernlund (Boulder: Lynne Rienner, 2000).

52. Center for Reproductive Law and Policy, *Women of the World*, 2001, 64.

53. Bureau of Democracy, Human Rights, and Labor, *Kenya Country Report*, sec. 5.

54. Ibid.; Family Planning Association of Kenya, *Options for Improving the Status of Women*, www.fpak.org/circ1.html, 2000.

55. Thomas, "*Ngaitana*," 147.

56. Morel Seytoux, *Review of Gender Issues*, UN Statistics Division, 2; *World's Women 2000: Trends and Statistics*, www.unstats.un.org/unsd/demographic/ww.2000/table5g.htm.

57. See Lisa Aubrey, *The Politics of Development Cooperation: NGOs, Gender, and Partnership in Kenya* (New York: Routledge, 1997).

58. *Women of the World*, 2001, 56.

59. George Thomas Kurian, *Encyclopedia of the Third World*, 4th ed., vol. III (New York: Facts on File, 1992), 970–71.

60. Anne Nasimlyu, *Christian Feminism*, www.kenyaconstitution.org/docs/09bd001.htm, 2001.

61. Kurian, *Encyclopedia of the Third World*, 970–71.

62. Namyalo Sauda, *Islam and Women's Rights*, www.kenyaconstitution.org/docs/09bd002.htm, 2001.

63. As quoted in Amnesty International, *Domestic Violence: Torture Behind Closed Doors*, www.web.amnesty.org/web/content.nsf/pages/gbr_kenya.

64. *Women of the World*, 2001, 63.

65. U.S. Department of State, *Kenya Country Report on Human Rights Practices for 2001*, www.state.gov/g/dri/ris/hrrpt/2001/af/8386.htm, 2002.

RESOURCE GUIDE

Suggested Reading

Ahlberg, Beth Maina. *Women, Sexuality, and the Changing Social Order: The Impact of Government Policies on Reproductive Behavior in Kenya*. Philadelphia: Gordon and Breach, 1991.

Center for Reproductive Law and Policy. *Women of the World: Laws and Policies Affecting Their Reproductive Lives, 2001*. New York: Center for Reproductive Law and Policy, 2001.

Fox, Diana, and Naima Hasci. *The Challenges of Women's Activism and Human Rights in Africa*. Lewiston, NY: Edwin Mellen Press, 1999.

House-Midamba, Bessie. *Class Development and Gender Inequality in Kenya, 1963–1990*. Lewiston, NY: Edwin Mellen Press, 1990.

Mackenzie, A. Fiona D. *Land, Ecology, and Resistance in Kenya, 1880–1952*. Edinburgh: Edinburgh University Press, 1997.

Sobania, Neal. *Culture and Customs of Kenya*. Westport, CT: Greenwood Press, 2003.

Thomas-Slayter, Barbara, and Diane Rocheleau. *Gender, Environment, and Development in Kenya: A Grassroots Perspective*. Boulder: Lynne Rienner, 1995.

United Nations Development Programme. *Human Development Report 2002: Deepening Democracy in a Fragmented World*. New York: Oxford University Press, 2002.

Web Sites

Amnesty International, *Domestic Violence: Torture Behind Closed Doors*, www.web.amnesty.org/web/content.nsf/pages/gbr_kenya.

Coalition on Violence Against Women (COVAW[K]), www.nbnet.co.ke/covaw.

Family Planning Association of Kenya (FPAK), www.fpak.org.

Federation of Women Lawyers—Kenya (FIDA KENYA), www.fidakenya.org.

National Center for HIV, STD, and TB Prevention, *Kenya Country Profile*, www.cdc.gov/nchstp/od/gap/countries/kenya.htm.

United Nations Statistics Division, *World's Women 2000: Trends and Statistics*, www.unstats.un.org/unsd/demographic/ww2000/table5g.htm.

USAID Synergy Project, *HIV/AIDS in Kenya, 2002*, www.synergyaids.com/documents/kenya%20brief%20rev%203a.pdf.

U.S. Department of State, *Kenya Country Report on Human Rights Practices for 2001*, www.state.gov/g/drl/rls/hrrpt/2001/af/8386.htm.

Organizations

Coalition on Violence Against Women (COVAW[K])
P.O. Box 10658-00100 GPO
Nairobi, Kenya
Phone: 254-2-574357/8
Hotline: 254-2-574359
Fax: 254-2-574253
Email: covaw@iconnect.co.ke
Web site: www.nbnet.co.ke/covaw

COVAW is an advocacy and counseling nongovernmental organization committed to the eradication of all forms of violence against women.

Family Planning Association of Kenya (FPAK)
P.O. Box 30581
Nairobi, Kenya
Phone: 254-2-604296
Fax: 254-2-603928
Email: info@fpak.org
Web site: www.fpak.org

FPAK is a nationwide, volunteer-based, nonprofit, nongovernmental organization whose major objectives are to improve accessibility and availability of quality reproductive health information and services; to respond to reproductive health needs of the youth; to advocate for gender equity and enhancement of the socioeconomic status of women to enable them to exercise control over their reproductive health; and to enhance male participation in family planning and reproductive health.

Federation of Women Lawyers—Kenya (FIDA KENYA)
P.O. Box 46324
Nairobi, Kenya
Phone: 254-2-717169/711853/718370
Fax: 254-2-716840
Email: fida@Africaonline.co.ke
Web site: www.fidakenya.org

FIDA Kenya is a nongovernmental, nonpartisan, Kenyan women lawyers organization committed to the enhancement of the legal status of Kenyan women through legal aid, monitoring women's rights, advocacy, education, and referral.

Greenbelt Movement
P.O. Box 67545
Nairobi, Kenya
Phone: 254-2-504264

The Greenbelt Movement started out planting trees but has now broadened its scope to incorporate all areas of community environmental action in East Africa.

SELECTED BIBLIOGRAPHY

Ardener, Shirley, and Sandra Burman. *Money-Go-Rounds: The Importance of Rotating Savings and Credit Associations for Women*. Washington, DC: Berg, 1995.

Aubrey, Lisa. *The Politics of Development Cooperation: NGOs, Gender, and Partnership in Kenya*. New York: Routledge, 1997.

Berman, Bruce. *Control and Crisis in Colonial Kenya: The Dialectic of Domination*. Athens: Ohio University Press, 1990.

Chiuri, Wanjiku Lois. *The Effects of Change in Land Tenure and Resource Management on Gender Relations and the Subsequent Changes in Highland Ecosystems*. Ann Arbor, MI: UMI Dissertation Services, 1996.

Division of Malaria Control, Ministry of Health. *National Malaria Strategy, 2001–2010*. Nairobi: Ministry of Health, 2001.

Dolan, Catherine S. *Tesco Is King: Gender and Labor Dynamics in Horticultural Exporting, Meru District, Kenya*. Ann Arbor, MI: UMI Dissertation Services, 1997.

Gibbon, Peter, ed. *Social Change and Economic Reform in Africa*. Uppsala: Nordiska Afrikainstitutet, 1993.

Gwako, Edwins Laban Moogi. *The Effects of Women's Land Tenure Security on Agricultural Output Among the Maragoli of Western Kenya*. Ann Arbor, MI: UMI Dissertation Services, 1997.

Kenya Human Rights Commission. *Ours by Right, Theirs by Might: A Study on Land Clashes*. Nairobi: Kenya Human Rights Commission, 1996.

———. *Women and Land Rights in Kenya*. Nairobi: Kenya Human Rights Commission, 1998.

Kibwana, Kivutha. *Law and the Status of Women in Kenya: The Example of Laikipia District*. Working Paper no. 481. Nairobi: Institute for Development Studies, 1992.

LeVine, Robert A., Suzanne Dixon, Sarah LeVine, Amy Richman, P. Herbert Leiderman, Constance H. Keefer, and T. Berry Brazelton, eds. *Child Care and Culture: Lessons from Africa*. New York: Cambridge University Press, 1994.

Little, Peter D., and Michael J. Watts, eds. *Living Under Contract: Contract Farming and Agrarian Transformation in Sub-Saharan Africa*. Madison: University of Wisconsin Press, 1994.

Ministry of Health. *National Reproductive Health Strategy, 1997–2012*. Nairobi: Ministry of Health, 1996.

Morel-Seytoux, Sylvie. *Review of Gender Issues in the USAID/Kenya Integrated Strategic Plan, 2001–2005: Democracy and Government, Economic Growth, Population and Health, Natural Resource Management*. Nairobi: International Center for Research on Women, 2000.

Mutoro, Basilida Anyona. *Women Working Wonders: Small-Scale Farming and the Role of Women in Vihiga District, Kenya—A Case Study of North Maragoli*. Amsterdam: Thela, 1997.

National Council for Population and Development et al., and Macro International. *Demographic and Health Survey, 1998*. Nairobi: National Council for Population and Development, 1999.

Ongile, Grace Atieno. *Gender and Agricultural Supply Responses to Structural Adjustment Programmes: A Case Study of Smallholder Tea Producers in Kericho, Kenya*. Uppsala: Nordiska Afrikainstitutet, 1999.

Parpart, Jane L., and Kathleen A. Staudt. *Women and the State in Africa*. Boulder: Lynne Rienner, 1989.

Republic of Kenya. *National Development Plan for the Period 1994 to 1996*. Nairobi: Republic of Kenya, 1994.

———. *National Gender and Development Policy*. Nairobi: Republic of Kenya, 2000.

————. *National Population Policy for Sustainable Development*. Nairobi: Government of Kenya, 2000.

————. *National Report on Progress Made in Implementing the Beijing Platform for Action, 1995–2000*. Nairobi, Republic of Kenya, 2000.

Robertson, Claire C. *Trouble Showed the Way: Women, Men, and Trade in the Nairobi Area, 1890–1990*. Bloomington: Indiana University Press, 1997.

Royal Netherlands Embassy. *Kenya Country Gender Profile*. Nairobi: ACTS Press, 1994.

Shell Duncan, Bettina, and Ylva Hernlund, eds. *Female "Circumcision" in Africa: Culture, Controversy, and Change*. Boulder: Lynne Rienner, 2000.

Steeves, H. Leslie. *Gender Violence and the Press: The St. Kizito Story*. Monographs—International Studies, Africa Series no. 67. Athens: Ohio University Center for International Studies, 1997.

Swynnerton, R. J. M. *A Plan to Intensify the Development of African Agriculture in Kenya*. Kenya Colony and Protectorate: Department of Agriculture, 1954.

White, Luise. *The Comforts of Home: Prostitution in Colonial Nairobi*. Chicago: University of Chicago Press, 1990.

Women's Bureau, Department of Social Services, Ministry of Culture and Social Services. *Platform for Action for Improving the Welfare of Women in Kenya*. Nairobi: Ministry of Culture and Social Services, 1997.

Wurster, Gabrielle, and Gundrum Ludwar-Ene. *Gender, Age, and Reciprocity: Case Studies of Professionals in Kenya and Nigeria*. Working Paper no. 255. Bayreuth, Germany: University of Bayreuth, 1996.

9

MALI

Susanna D. Wing

PROFILE OF MALI

The Republic of Mali has an estimated population of 11,008,518. This former French colony gained independence in 1960 and became the largest country in West Africa, covering an area of 471,115 square miles (about twice the size of Texas). The Niger River cuts through Mali, providing an important resource to this landlocked country in the Sahel region that has seven bordering states (Mauritania, Senegal, Guinea, Côte d'Ivoire, Burkina Faso, Niger, and Algeria).

Mali is one of the ten poorest countries in the world with an annual per capita income of $240.[1] Despite increasing migration to cities and towns, over 70 percent of Malians live in rural areas where they work as farmers, pastoralists, herders, and fishermen. Mali currently ranks 153 out of 162 countries on the United Nations Human Development Index (an index that measures the overall quality of life in a country based on educational, health, and economic indicators). However, life expectancy and mortality rates have improved over the years. Today, life expectancy at birth is fifty-one years (in 1970–1974 this was a mere forty-two years), while maternal mortality remains high at 580 per 100,000 births.[2]

In 2001, 121 infants died for every 1,000 births and every woman gave birth to nearly 7 children (the fertility rate is 6.81).[3]

Large families are the cultural norm and are encouraged by the widespread practice of polygyny, in which a man may have more than one wife. Over 90 percent of the population adheres to Islam, 9 percent to indigenous religions, and 1 percent to Christianity. Mali is ethnically diverse, although no single group dominates the country politically or economically. Fifty percent of all Malians belong to the Mande linguistic group, made up, in part, of the Bambara, Malinke, and Soninke peoples. Other ethnic groups include the Peul (Fulani), Bobo, Senoufo, Minianka, Songhai, Dogon, Bozo, Sarakolé, Tuareg (Tamashek), and Moor. Bamanakan, the Bambara language, is the lingua franca of the country and French is the official language of the country.

Many experts regard Mali as a model of democratic transition. Democratic elections in 2002 marked a change in leadership as former president Alpha Oumar Konaré stepped down after concluding his constitutional limit of two five-year terms in office. Current president Amadou Toumani Touré (popularly known as ATT) gained notoriety in 1991 as the leader of the coup d'état that ended the twenty-three-year dictatorship of General Moussa Traoré. President Touré's election in 2002 marks the first democratic change in leadership for the country. The positive changes in the overall political scene during the past decade contributed to the advancement of women throughout Mali.

OVERVIEW OF WOMEN'S ISSUES

Rural and urban environments, as well as cultural differences between ethnic groups, have an important influence on the daily lives of women. However, since the fall of the centralized government of General Traoré, the more open political environment in Mali has allowed more opportunities for all women to organize collectively in credit, professional, and village associations. This opening, in conjunction with the increasing flow of donor support for educational programs, family planning, as well as civic education clinics has brought about positive changes in the lives of Malian women. Nevertheless, many women still face tremendous obstacles as they strive to improve their daily lives.

EDUCATION

Opportunities

Educational opportunities for women and girls have increased dramatically over the last ten years. This has been the result of active associations and educational nongovernmental organizations (NGOs) working in conjunction with the Malian government to strengthen ties between communities and schools. International donors have played an important role in improving the overall educational system in Mali, and more specifically, in helping to ensure equal access to quality education. The National Education Plan, adopted in 1998, focuses on decentralized education and community schools. The widespread construction of community schools has increased the educational opportunities for children and minimized the distance that children travel to school, helping assuage parents' fears for the safety of their children, particularly girls, who once had to walk long distances to attend classes. In addition to community schools that follow a traditional curriculum and provide bilingual education in both French and maternal languages, *medarsas* are a popular educational choice for many families. These Koranic schools, monitored by the Ministry of Education, are expected to teach, largely in Arabic, the same curriculum as public schools

The likelihood of a girl attending primary school was often determined by where she lived. In 1994, primary school enrollment of girls in rural areas was 14 percent, or nearly one-half the attendance levels of girls in urban areas (27 percent). The rural/urban distinction was negligible for boys, where 55 percent of rural boys and 58 percent of urban boys attended primary school. In 1998, 34 percent of all girls were attending primary school, representing seventy percent of male enrollments.[4]

Cultural and economic factors combine to limit girls' access to schools, and these factors are likely to play a more important role in rural settings. When resources are scarce, parents prefer to educate sons rather than daughters. Daughters are frequently perceived as a poor investment because they are often removed from school and married at a young age. Once a girl marries, her responsibilities turn to her new family. A son, on the other hand, is expected to provide for his parents—an investment in his future is an investment in his parents' security. In addition, school fees, as well as the income lost by giving up a girl's domestic labor, can be a strain on a family. The economic status of a family has an immediate impact on the level of education for both males and females in the family. In 1995–1996, the median grade completed by fifteen- to nineteen-year-olds in the richest 20 percent of Malian households was only fourth grade. However, for those in the poorest 20 percent of households this number fell to nearly no schooling at all (well below the first-grade level).[5]

The disparities between education for the rich and poor and the urban and rural are further exacerbated when we consider the gender bias that persists in the classroom. Girls who have had the chance to go to school have faced sexual harassment by their teachers. Increasing access to education does not ensure the quality of a girl's education; therefore, as the enrollment of girls in schools increases, efforts must be made to reduce the existing gender biases. In some cases, girls at school are expected to clean up after other students and when students' hands are raised, girls are routinely passed over by teachers in favor of boys. Until social norms change such that both boys and girls are treated equally in the classroom, girls' education will be hindered.

Literacy

Although literacy for women lags significantly behind that of men, the gap is narrowing. In 1995, male literacy was 39 percent while that of females was a mere 23 percent.[6] By 2000, literacy rates had increased to 49 percent for males and 34 percent for females. The young adult literacy rate is an important sign of change. For those aged fifteen to twenty-five, 72 percent of the males and 60 percent of the females are literate.[7] This dramatic improvement reflects not only an overall increase in the educational levels of Malians, but also a steady narrowing of the educational gap between males and females.

Another important aspect of education for women has been the increase in adult literacy programs. The Progress through Literacy and Numeracy Project (PLAN), a project run by the international nongovernmental organization CARE, provided training to adults in forty-five communities in the Macina area. The courses included training in child nutrition, treating well water, public hygiene, and other issues. Women who were able to take part in the program showed not only increased access to credit, but also an improved tendency to purify drinking water for the household.[8] Several similar programs exist and help to improve the welfare of women and their families.

EMPLOYMENT AND ECONOMICS

Farming

In Mali, 78 percent of active women work in agriculture. As men migrate to cities in search of work, women increase the time they spend in the fields. The household structure is male dominated and during a husband's absence, a member of the extended family is often considered to be in charge of the rural household. A husband's absence often results in a de facto female head of the household. Because women are not recognized as running the household in cases in which their husbands or male relatives are absent, women do not benefit from resources and revenues available for households. For instance, rural extension programs and education are not extended to women, despite their active role in agriculture. The World Bank has recognized this conflict and promoted female access to extension services.[9]

Paid Employment

The labor force in Mali works predominately in the agricultural sector, with 83 percent of the male labor force working in agriculture in 1990, compared to 89 percent of the women laborers. Both sexes had only 2 percent of their labor force in the industrial sector. The service sector of the economy was predominately occupied by men, representing fifteen percent of the male labor force, whereas 9 percent of the female labor force worked in services.[10]

The Malian economy depends on agriculture, which represents 47 percent of the country's gross domestic product (GDP). Other sectors include services (33 percent of the GDP), industry (20 percent), and manufacturing (6 percent).[11]

In 2000, women made up 46 percent of the 5 million people in the formal economy.[12]

Millet grinding, Mali. Photo © TRIP/W. Jacobs.

Informal Economic Activities

Most of the economic activity in the country takes place in the informal sector and is not represented in these figures generated by Mali's *EIU Country Report*.[13] The minister of employment estimates that nearly 50 percent of the economically active population participates in the informal economy. Over 60 percent of the total production of goods and services in the mid-1990s was from the informal sector.[14] This is the very sector in which women are most active. While some women have invested in market stalls in towns or urban areas, others may simply sit along the roadside selling goods to passersby. These transactions are all part of a vibrant informal economy. In some cases women prepare foods at home, enlisting their daughters to sell the goods at the market, a transportation depot, or along the roadside. Women often prepare roasted corn or the popular dish of rice and sauce in the market. In the capital city, Bamako, women sell fish that are freshly caught from the Niger River. These activities are divided by gender. Whereas it is common to see women selling produce, cooked food, and small-scale dry food stuffs, the men predominately sell the meat in the market and control the majority of the stores selling dry goods or cloth.

Women's low level of literacy and numeracy affects their ability to manage their economic activities. Their lack of landownership, or the small size of the land that they manage, makes it difficult to access credit needed to establish or expand their economic endeavors. In response to the lack of credit many women have successfully established their own rotating credit associations. These associations, providing funds to individuals in need, are a form of insurance as well as an opportunity for participants to pursue entrepreneurial projects. Unfortunately, development practitioners, in an effort to alleviate poverty, have encouraged women to produce vegetables to such a degree that supply exceeds demand and many women are left with perishable vegetables that they cannot sell.

Support for Mothers/Caretakers

Maternity leave is provided only to those employed in the formal sector. Women who work full-time in the formal sector receive government assistance in the form of full pay for fourteen to seventeen weeks. In addition, medical benefits provide these women with medical coverage during pregnancy and childbirth.

Inheritance, Property, and Land Rights

In 1985, Mali ratified the Convention on the Elimination of All Forms of Discrimination against Women. According to Mali's constitution, discrimination based on gender is illegal and women are given equal rights to men. However, in practice traditional law plays an important role in determining inheritance and property ownership. As a result, women rarely have control over their own property and when their husbands die they are rarely given control of land. The dissemination of information concerning constitutional law is important so that both women and men become aware of women's rights. The cultural biases against equal inheritance are deeply rooted in the tradition that men are expected to provide entirely for their families. For this reason they receive the greater inheritance so that they can provide for those that depend on them. The practice of "widow inheritance" in which a male relative, usually the husband's brother, marries the widow and takes on responsibility for his late brother's family is commonplace. This system unfortunately often fails to protect single mothers or widows who do not wish to marry their brother-in-law following the death of their husband. If single women are not taken back into their family, they often do not have the resources to support themselves.

Social/Government Programs

Structural Adjustment

The CFA (Communauté Financiere Africaine) franc, the currency used in Mali and other francophone West African states, was devalued by 50 percent in 1994. This policy was part of structural adjustment reforms of the economy and was designed to lower the cost of exports and stimulate export opportunities in the economy. While the export of rice has increased, longer working hours and rising production costs have been reported. Devaluation created new opportunities for women, who diversified their activities, increased incomes, and improved their socioeconomic status. Men's incomes declined with devaluation and as a result, the government has cut back on social expenditures and women have assumed these obligations that often reflect the family's social status.

Another aspect of economic reforms is the fact that in many cases the best quality land, once used for domestic food production, has been committed to the growth of cash crops. As a result, women are left to grow the food for the household in poor-quality soil. Women also have assumed the responsibility for increased costs of education and health care that accompanied structural adjustment. When money is tight and educational costs increase, it is often the young girls who forego their schooling. The Malian government, along with donors, have responded to this problem by increasing access to health care and education through two programs: the Decade of Development in Education and Health and Social Development Program.

FAMILY AND SEXUALITY

Marriage

For the majority of Malian women, their principal responsibility as wives is to produce and care for their husband and children. A young girl's family often selects a husband, although this practice is changing, certainly in urban areas. On average, 50 percent of Malian girls are married (or have been married) between the ages of fifteen and nineteen. In sub-Saharan Africa, only Niger, Mali's neighbor to the East, has a higher rate of marriage at such a young age (64 percent). As in most countries, there is clear gender disparity in the median age for marriage, which is nineteen for Malian girls and twenty-eight for men.[15]

Most marriages are polygynous. However, the rates of polygynous unions vary between rural and urban populations as well as by age. In rural areas, over 61 percent of women ages forty to forty-four are in a polygynous marriage compared to 49 percent of urban women in this age group. In urban areas, 20 percent of young women (ages fifteen to nineteen) are in polygynous marriages, and over 31 percent of their rural counterparts have at least one cowife.[16] Before a civil marriage, the couple must agree to either a polygynous or monogamous marriage. However, it is relatively easy for the husband who has agreed to a monogamous union to choose to marry another wife at a later date, as long as his wife agrees. It is difficult for a wife to oppose her husband's choice to marry another woman given that she is often dependent on her husband's financial support. Her opposition to his choice may simply lead to a divorce.

Women's associations argue that another complication for women's rights with respect to marriage is the practice of a traditional union rather than a civil marriage. While customary and/or religious laws sanction traditional marriages, the government only recognizes the legality of a civil marriage. Therefore, women must have a civil marriage in order to be protected (for instance, from abandonment) by constitutional law. As is the case with civil law, both customary and religious laws require a husband to provide for his wife. If he does not abide by these laws, he is likely to face sanctions from the community. Civil marriage ceremonies are often extravagant affairs in which families spend fortunes. Frequently such marriages are delayed or never occur due to the excessive costs. Women's associations campaign for less costly celebrations in order to prevent families from spending well beyond their means, but also to ensure that a woman has legal protections in the union.

Reproduction

In Mali, wives are expected to have numerous children; therefore, family planning is often perceived as a woman shirking her familial responsibilities. Indeed a woman's primary value is often linked to her ability to produce a large family. Unfortunately childless unions often result in the dissolution of the marriage and accusations of a woman's infertility. It is almost never the case that a man's fertility is questioned when a wife does not bear children.

Contraception and Abortion

Contraceptive use is relatively rare. In 1977 a mere 1 percent of women aged fifteen to forty-nine used contraception. This number had increased to only 7 percent by 1996.[17] A recent study on family planning in Bamako revealed that many women kept their contraceptive use a secret from their husbands for fear of reprisals. Husbands are believed to have the ultimate authority over reproductive decisions made in the marriage. The biggest deterrent among women who had never tried family planning was their fear of their husband's disapproval. There is little support for contraceptive use among Malian men, many of whom believe that clandestine contraceptive use is sufficient grounds for divorce or punishment. Malian women will sometimes rely on their husband's elder sisters or aunts to intervene when their husbands oppose family planning.[18]

Another factor contributing to the low rates of contraceptive use is the fact that access to proper medical facilities is costly and time consuming. Some women who tried birth control methods discontinued their use due to side effects.[19] Without adequate medical observation, women are unlikely to explore unfamiliar methods of family planning.

Mali's laws do not allow abortion, regardless of the circumstances. However, this has been challenged through a liberal interpretation of the country's Population Policy Statement, which says that violence, injury, or homicide may be permissible as a "necessary" or legitimate act of self-defense. This has been interpreted to mean that pregnancies may be terminated if the life of the mother is in danger. UNICEF states that abortion is the cause of one out of twenty maternal deaths in Mali. The National Population Policy Statement has claimed that the increase in clandestine abortions is an urgent social crisis and calls for the promotion of family planning.[20]

Teen Pregnancy

Nearly half (46 percent) of Mali's population is under fifteen years old and 19.3 percent is between fifteen and twenty-four years of age. Teenagers aged fifteen to nineteen contribute approximately fourteen percent to the total fertility rate, with 10 percent of all women in Mali having had a child by the time they were fifteen. At age seventeen, 46 percent of Malian women are pregnant or already have a child, and by nineteen years of age, 69 percent have had children. There is an important difference in adolescent childbearing rates between rural areas, where 49 percent have had children as adolescents, and urban areas, where this falls to 30 percent.[21]

HEALTH

Health Care Access

Statistics reveal the devastating state of health care in Mali. The mortality rate for children under five is the fifth highest in the world — 237 of every 1,000 children under five will die every year.[22] In one out every ten pregnancies, a woman will die from complications.[23] The lack of access to health care has contributed to these high mortality rates. Only 24 percent of Malian women will give birth with a trained health care professional in attendance.[24] Despite these numbers, access to health care is improving with the establishment of village clinics. In particular, the government, in conjunction with the World Bank, United Nations Children's Fund (UNICEF), and others have helped villages establish maternal health clinics to assist women with obstetric needs. Systems have been established to transport victims of medical emergencies to hospitals in a matter of hours, rather than the days it may have taken previously.

Diseases and Disorders

One of the most common health risks in Mali is malaria, which infected 3,688 out of 100,000 people in 1997.[25] The majority of cases were children under five years old. Other diseases include dengue fever, hepatitis, schistosomiasis, dysentery, and meningitis. Guinea worm, a painful disease caused by parasites in water, was virtually eradicated by the year 2000 following a campaign led by Touré in conjunction with the U.S.-based Carter Center, UNICEF, and the World Bank. Unfortunately, as donors and government officials have turned their attention away from what appeared to be a successful eradication of the disease, there has recently been a dramatic increase in the cases of infection. In addition to the pain and suffering caused by the disease, the World Bank estimated, conservatively, that Mali would achieve a 29 percent economic return if the disease were wiped out. These numbers are based on the recovery of time lost by those infected who could not perform their agricultural tasks.[26]

AIDS

Relative to other sub-Saharan countries, Mali has a low rate of HIV infection among the adult population. In 1999, 2 percent of the population (aged fifteen to forty-nine) had HIV/AIDS; however, 55 percent of these cases were women.[27] Urban and rural populations have been affected by HIV/AIDS in varying degrees. In urban areas the HIV rate ranges from 2.5 percent in low-risk groups to 42 percent in high-risk groups. In rural areas the infection rate is 2.2 percent in low-risk groups and 53 percent in high-risk groups.[28] There is a concern that the flow of migrant labor between Mali and Côte d'Ivoire (which has a substantially higher rate of HIV/AIDS infection) will result in the spread of the disease in Mali.

In 1999, 42,000 women between the ages of fifteen and forty-nine years of age were living with HIV.[29] Women's vulnerability to AIDS is increased, in part, due to the socioeconomic disparities between women and men. The lack of access that women have to resources such as land, credit, extension services, and technology has meant that women suffer greater poverty than men. Poverty, in turn, limits access to health and social services. Poverty may even lead some women and young girls into commercial sex work in order to survive.[30] Gender disparities also contribute to a woman's inability to negotiate sexual relations with her partner, putting her at increased risk of infection. The spread of HIV/AIDS has also been linked to the practice of female genital cutting.[31] Surgeries performed without sterilization may contribute to the spread of the virus.

Female Genital Cutting

A study in 1996 revealed that in a sample of approximately 9,700 women (age fifteen to forty-nine), 94 percent reported that they had been subject to female genital cutting.[32] In Bamako the reported rates were 95 percent and in nearby Koulikoro 99 percent of the women interviewed stated that they had undergone the procedure.[33] This practice has both religious and cultural roots in Mali. All ethnic groups in Mali except for the Tamashek

(Tuareg), Songhay, and Dogon practice female genital cutting (although cases have been reported in each of these groups, perhaps as a result of the common interpretation that it is required by Islam).

Education levels are closely linked to an individual's opinion on the procedure. Of women who had obtained a secondary education or higher, only 48 percent advocated the practice. Eighty percent of rural women support cutting, while 65 percent of urban women were in favor its continuation [34]

Although female genital cutting is a topic of much heated debate in Mali, it is not a priority for the majority of women. These women, many of whom lack sufficient resources to buy food and medication for their families, are more concerned with poverty.[35] Nevertheless, women's associations have taken the lead in challenging the practice through educational campaigns.

It should be noted that the majority of Malian women do not necessarily actively support the practice; rather, they are indifferent, or never thought to question the authority of elders who strongly support the practice. A recent study argues that female elders may "resent the intrusion of those men who speak out against excision, one of the few cultural areas in which they have control."[36] Female elders play an important role in the rites of passage for girls entering adulthood. Genital cutting has been one of the few cultural areas that women controlled, yet the shifting of the practice to younger and younger girls has separated it from its former role as a rite of passage. In so doing it has diminished this "traditional" role of female elders.

The politics of the debate on female genital cutting are deeply rooted in social relations. Based on surveys and interviews conducted throughout the country, it is argued:

> For the majority of Malians who live in multi-generational, patriarchal family compounds, to critique or even question a practice which has become reified as "tradition" is not to question an abstract notion, but to challenge the authority and will of an elder (male or female) who is owed respect and obedience and with whom one is in daily contact. This challenge could result in being expelled from the compound and socially isolated—a situation which in Mali, and especially for women, could threaten one's very subsistence.[37]

Those who oppose the practice are often seen as too Westernized and thus alienated from their cultural ways. They are also more likely to have positions of power relative to the majority of Malian women. For this reason, men are more likely to state their opposition to female genital cutting than are women (35.7 percent of men believed it was a "bad thing," while 22.9 percent of women stated this view).[38]

Activists against the practice have pushed for legislation to criminalize female genital cutting; however, this remains a sensitive issue for legislators. In July 2002 the government took an official position on the issue, adopting a decree that supports the end to the practice. Up to this point, the government has taken an educational approach, promoting sensitization on the issue by way of the Ministry for the Advancement of Women, Children, and Family.

Historically, women have not been encouraged to speak in public. This is similar to many other cultures in which the public realm has been perceived as the place for men to be active, whereas women have been kept in the private or domestic sphere. In Mali, topics that were considered taboo were discussed through a singer or *griot* (in Bamanakan they are referred to as *jeli*). The *griots* are men who have inherited the role of oral historian and pass along the history and traditions of their culture through song. Today, family planning as well as female genital cutting falls into this category. Recently, organizations such as women's associations and organizations promoting family planning practices have turned to the *griot* to help educate people about topics that would have been considered improper to be discussed in public. A remarkable example of this transition in topics open for discussion is the example of female genital cutting. Once a subject that would never be publicly discussed, and certainly not in mixed company, it is being debated on television. In 1998 the national television station broadcast interviews with individuals approached randomly in the streets of Bamako. Both men and women spoke about how they viewed the practice. The opening of a public debate on the practice is an important sign of the changes occurring within Malian society.

POLITICS AND LAW

Suffrage

Malian women have always been politically active. Under French rule, Africans living in the French territory of Afrique Occidentale Francophone (AOF) were allowed to vote for deputies to send to the French National Assembly. However, eligible voters were restricted to categories such as merchants, bureaucrats, and literate citizens. These groupings nearly entirely eliminated women from the electorate. Women in France won the right to vote in 1944 and pushed to broaden the electorate in French colonies so that women would be included. In 1951 the French assembly amended voting laws in the colonies to include mothers with two children, "living or dead for France," referring to the African soldiers who fought for the French in World Wars I and II, many of whom lost their lives. This law allowed the mothers of those soldiers to vote, and the electoral laws favored women and resulted in women outnumbering men at the polls.[39] Today, women are encouraged to vote by women's associations, which hope they will use their majority status to promote women's interests.

Political Participation

Women's associations have been influential in promoting female politicians and in 1997, the Coordination des Associations et ONG Féminines au Mali (CAFO) was instrumental in the election of Bintou Sanankoua to the National Assembly.[40] Despite these efforts, Malian men still far outnumbered women in public office in 2000. However, in a five-year period 1992–1997, female representatives in the National Assembly jumped from 2 percent to a remarkable 12 percent. In 1998 the first elections were held in the 682 newly created local communes. While women were elected to city counselor seats, men were elected to these positions in far greater numbers (82 women to 488 men). In the same year, not a single woman was elected mayor.[41]

Overall women have free access to politics and elected office. There are, however, no constitutionally sanctioned quotas for women's political participation. ADEMA-PASJ (Alliance pour la Démocratie au Mali–Parti pour la Solidarité et la Justice), the majority party from 1992 to 2002, adopted a quota system for its own party lists, requiring one-third of all candidates to be women. This is likely to have been the principal reason for the sharp increase in female legislators from 1992 to 1997. The 2002 legislative elections resulted in a slight drop in the percentage of female deputies in the National Assembly, with just 10 percent of the deputies being women. It remains uncertain whether the current ADEMA-PASJ party leadership will continue to support quotas and whether other political parties will choose to adopt them.

Following independence in 1960, the socialist government of Modibo Keita came to power. The ruling party, the Union Soudanaise–Rassemblement Démocratique Africain (US-RDA), created a governmental commission to address women's issues. In 1968, a coup d'état led by General Moussa Traoré brought the CMLN (Comité Militaire pour la Libération Nationale) to power, dissolving the National Assembly and annulling the constitution. During this time, the government regulated women's economic affairs by requiring the endorsement of their husbands for any economic activity. In 1979, Traoré created the Union Démocratique du Peuple Malien (UDPM) and organized single-party elections.

Under the guise of promoting social interest groups, UDPM supported a workers union as well as the creation, in 1979, of the official women's branch of the ruling party, the Union Nationale des Femmes Maliennes (UNFM). This organization, like so many other official women's organizations in sub-Saharan Africa at the time, was run by the first lady, in this case Mariam Traoré. It was not until the violent overthrow of the Traoré regime in March of 1991 that women's associations were free to flourish. The end of the UDPM regime took place at a time when repressive leaders across the continent were falling from power at an astonishing rate. Women participated actively in these political transitions and in Mali they were at the frontlines during the protests that led to Traoré's demise. The creation of the Third Republic in Mali allowed independent women's groups to exist, free from government control. The rapid increase in the numbers of these organizations is evident in CAFO, the umbrella organization for women's NGOs. This organization had fifty members in 1994; by 1998 that number had more than tripled to 191.

Women's Rights

The Malian government created the Commisariat de la Promotion des Femmes (Commissariat for the Advancement of Women, CPF) in 1993. The CPF was established to advise the government on gender issues. In 1997, the Ministère pour la Promotion de la Femme, de l'Enfant et de la Famille (Ministry for the Advancement of Women, Children, and Family) was created. The Ministry serves as the principal arm of the government that handles women's issues. These include the recent program for gender equity, Programme d'Appui au Renforcement de l'Équité Hommes/Femmes (Support Program for the Strengthening of Equality for Men and Women) supported by the United Nations Development Programme (UNDP). This program promotes women's participation in the public sector and in development, the advancement of women's rights, and maintains a database on the status of Malian women. The goal is to "rehabilitate" the image of a woman's position in society and her productive role in the national economy.

The sensitization of both men and women concerning women's rights is one of the principal challenges for the government and for women's associations. Women's associations have focused on the need to inform Malian citizens, both men and women, about the protections of women's rights in the constitution. This may include discussions on marriage and divorce, voting rights, inheritance, and other important topics. These organizations have been successful to a degree, but predominately in urban areas and towns. The rural areas are much slower to change.

Military Service

Nearly 2,500 women and 8,000 men serve in the armed forces.[42]

RELIGION AND SPIRITUALITY

The constitution prohibits religious-based political parties. Islamic leaders in this predominantly Muslim country recently accused President Konaré of pursuing not simply a secular course for politics, but rather an "anti-religious" one.[43] In May 2001, Muslim groups joined together to protest the reforms of family law that the government has continued to pursue. The head of an Islamic Woman's Association argued that " 'foreign values' were being imposed with these laws that would give women equal inheritance rights and eliminate men's legal status as 'heads of the family.' "[44] In July 2002 the National Assembly passed the revised family law. The Malian League of Imams and Learned Persons for Islamic Solidarity (LIMAMA; Ligue Malienne des Imams et Érudits pour la Solidarité Islamique) has protested the passing of the law, which they argue does not reflect the position of the Islamic Community. Although the leaders of LIMAMA are men, women are active participants in the organization.

Religious Law

Religious law, particularly law dealing with inheritance, is a very contentious issue for Malian women. Many women fear that the imposition of equal inheritance rights for women will not only take away the role of the male head of the household, but in so doing, take away his financial responsibility to his family. Even with the passage of a reformed family code in Mali, it will be very difficult to enforce given the low levels of literacy, the lack of awareness of women's rights, and the fear of challenging the cultural norms and of being ostracized by the community.

VIOLENCE

Domestic Violence

Although there are no official statistics on domestic violence against women, it is believed to be widespread. Spousal assault is a crime; however, there is very little enforcement of this law. Economic difficulties often top women's daily concerns, followed by marital difficulties, including "unwanted marriages and divorces, conflicts relating to polygyny, husbands not contributing their share of the household budget, or domestic violence."[45] Women's associations are increasingly involved in the campaign to educate women about their rights and to help protect them from such abuse.

Rape/Sexual Assault

Rape is punishable by five to twenty years of forced labor and a one to five year residence ban. There is no law that includes a provision for marital rape.[46]

Trafficking in Women and Children

Several organizations have started campaigns against trafficking in children from Mali. In June 2001 the National Assembly passed a law to prohibit child trafficking and to make it punishable by five to twenty years in prison. It is estimated that "15,000 Malian children between the ages of 9 and 12 have been sold into forced labor on cotton, coffee and cocoa farms in northern Côte d'Ivoire over the past few years; an even greater number have been pressed into domestic service."[47] Frequently these children, predominately boys, work for Malians that own the farms. The Ministry for the Advancement of Women, Children, and the Family and the Ministry of Employment, Public Services, and Labor are working in coordination with the Ministry of Foreign Affairs as well as the Ministry of Territorial Administration to develop programs to find and rehabilitate victims of trafficking.

Whereas boys may fall victim to trafficking for agricultural work, a large number of girls are employed in urban households as domestic servants. These girls are subject to violence within the households in which they work and have little job security or access to government-sanctioned protections for workers. Domestic servants often work long and exhausting days. Trafficking of domestic servants takes place in the form of "placement agencies" that act as liaisons between families with young girls that they would like to have employed and those seeking domestic servants. Although this is an illegal practice, those who support it believe that it should be legalized because they argue that they are an employment placement service. Mistreatment of servants is of concern to NGOs and other organizations.

OUTLOOK FOR THE TWENTY-FIRST CENTURY

Mali has gained international recognition for its achievements in political and economic liberalization. The country has become the darling of the donor community. This has led to the reduction in debt and the steady flow of development assistance. Along with this attention, women's associations have flourished and benefited immensely from a donor community interested in supporting gender equity. While women are certainly more visible in the public realm and women's rights are increasingly discussed, the divide between urban and rural women remains. The continued reliance of the Malian economy on agriculture and cash crops makes its economic growth unstable and dependent on a volatile world market. Economic downturns overwhelmingly strike the lives and health of women. Until Mali is able to achieve substantial economic growth, the lives of the majority of Malian women will remain precarious.

NOTES

1. 2000 figures from the World Bank, www.worldbank.org/data.
2. UNDP, *Human Development Report 2001*, www.undp.org/hdr2001/indicator/cty_f_mli.html.

3. *The World Factbook: Mali*, www.cia.gov/cia/publications/factbook/geos/ml.html.

4. Human Development Report.

5. World Bank, www.worldbank.org/research/projects/edattain/wgaps_s.Jpg.

6. Ibid.

7. The World Bank, *Mali Summary Gender Profile*, www.worldbank.org/afr/gender/mali.pdf.

8. CARE International, *Basic and Girls' Education*, organizational pamphlet.

9. "Rural Women and Agricultural Extension in the Sahel," World Bank, *Findings: Africa Region* no. 46 (August 1995), www.worldbank.org/afr/findings/english/find46.htm.

10. The World Bank, http://genderstats.worldbank.org.

11. The Economist Intelligence Unit, *The EIU Country Report: Burkina Faso, Niger, Mali* (June 2002), available online to subscribers only (libraries).

12. World Bank, http://genderstats.worldbank.org.

13. Ibid.

14. Ibid.

15. United Nations, "The World's Women 2000: Trends and Statistics," http://unstats.un.org/unsd/demographic/ww2000/table2a.htm.

16. Salif Coulibaly, F. Dicko, S. M. Traoré, O. Sidibé, M. Seroussi, and B. Barrère, *Enquête démographique et de santé, Mali 1995–1996* (Calverton, ND: Cellule de Planification et de Statistique du Ministère de la Santé, Direction Nationale de la Statistique et de l'Information et Macro International, 1996), 89.

17. World Bank, "Mali: Summary Gender Profile."

18. *Women's Voices, Women's Lives: The Impact of Family Planning—A Synthesis of Findings from the Women's Studies Project*, www.fhi.org/en/wsp/wssyn/index.html.

19. Ibid.

20. *Women of the World: Laws and Policies Affecting Their Reproductive Lives* (New York: Center for Reproductive Law and Policy, 1999), 145.

21. Ibid., 149.

22. UNICEF, *The State of the World's Children, 2000*, www.unicef.org/sowc00.

23. UNICEF, "Mali: Prise en charge rapide des urgencies obstétriques," www.unicef.org/french/safe/10.htm.

24. UNICEF, 2000.

25. UNDP, *Human Development Report 2001*.

26. www.afrol.com/news2002/mal002_togo_gui_worm.htm.

27. World Bank, "Mali Summary Gender Profile."

28. Synergy Project/USAID, "Mali and HIV/AIDS" (June 1999), 1, http://synergyaids.com/documents/592_mali.pdf.

29. Ibid., 2.

30. Ibid.

31. There are different forms of this practice. They include clitoridectomy (removal of part or all of the clitoris); excision (removal of inner labia as well as clitoris); infibulation (removal of clitoris, prepuce, inner labia, outer labia and closure of vaginal opening). I will refer to excision as this is the term used by French-speaking Malians.

32. Coulibaly et al., cited in Claudie Gosselin, "Feminism, Anthropology, and the Politics of Excision in Mali: Global and Local Debates in a Postcolonial World," *Anthropologica* 42 (2000).

33. Synergy Project/USAID, "Mali Summary Gender Profile," 2.

34. Coulibaly et al., cited in Gosselin, "Feminism."

35. Ibid., 53.

36. Ibid., 54.

37. Ibid., 52.

38. Ibid.

39. Susanna D. Wing, "Women Activists in Mali," in *Women's Activism and Globalization: Linking Local Struggles and Transnational Politics*, ed. Nancy A. Naples and Manisha Desai (New York: Routledge, 2002), 179.

40. Ibid.

41. See www.malimuso.org/equite.htm.

42. U.S. Department of State, *Country Reports on Human Rights Practices: Mali, 2001*, www.state.gov/g/drl/rls/hrrpt/2001/af/8391.htm.

43. Joan Baxter, "Hero Worship," *Focus on Africa Magazine*, 2002, www.bbc.co.uk/worldservice/africa/features/focus_magazine/mali.shtml.

44. Ibid.

45. Gosselin, "Feminism," 53.

46. *Women of the World: Laws and Policies Affecting Their Reproductive Lives* (New York: Center for Reproductive Law and Policy, 1999), 148.

47. U.S. Department of State, *Country Reports: Mali*, sec. 6f.

RESOURCE GUIDE

Suggested Reading

Center for Reproductive Law and Policy. *Women of the World: Laws and Policies Affecting Their Reproductive Lives, Francophone Africa*. New York: Center for Reproductive Law and Policy, 1999. Overview of laws concerning marriage and reproduction in francophone African countries.

Gosselin, Claudie. "Feminism, Anthropology, and the Politics of Excision in Mali: Global and Local Debates in a Postcolonial World." *Anthropologica* 42 (2000): 43–60. Discusses the politics of the debate regarding female genital cutting.

———. "Handing over the Knife: *Numu* Women and the Campaign Against Excision in Mali." In *Female "Circumcision": Culture, Change, and Controversy*, edited by Bettina Shell-Duncan and Ylva Hernlund. Boulder: Lynne Rienner, 2000. An analysis of the campaign against excision, includes an important analysis of women's associations and donor agencies involved.

Imperato, Pascal James. *Mali: A Search for Direction*. Boulder: Westview Press, 1989. This book provides an excellent overview of all aspects of Mali's social, economic, and political development.

Poulton, Robin-Edward, and Ibrahim ag Youssouf. *A Peace of Timbuktu: Democratic Governance, Development, and African Peace-Making*. New York: United Nations, 1998. An important discussion of the conflict between the government and the Tuareg and the peace process.

Wing, Susanna D. "Women Activists in Mali." In *Women's Activism and Globalization: Linking Local Struggles and Transnational Politics*, edited by Nancy A. Naples and Manisha Desai, 172–85. New York: Routledge, 2002. This article addresses women's rights in Mali and the struggle between traditional practices and universal human rights.

Videos/Films

Faraw (Mother of the sand). 1997. Abdoulaye Ascofare. Bamako, Mali: Film de la Dune Rose. A Songhai woman in desperate poverty refuses to prostitute her young daughter to European men.

Finzan (A Dance for the Hero). 1990. Cheick Oumar Sissoko. Bamako Kora Films. The stories of a woman who refuses to be inherited by her brother-in-law and a young city girl who resists circumcision.

Tuufl Fanga (Skirt Power). 1997. Directed by Adama Drabo. This farce set in an eighteenth-century Dogon community concerns sexual politics and the status of African women today.

Yeelen (Brightness). 1987. Souleymane Cissé.

Web Sites

Afribone.com, www.afribone.com.
Includes diverse information on Malian economy, education, tourism, and news (in French).

MaliNet, www.malinet.ml.
This general site on Mali has links to associations and newspapers (in French).

Ministry for the Advancement of Women, Children, and the Family, www.malimuso. org.
Malian government web site (in French).

U.S. Department of State, *Country Reports on Human Rights Practices: Mali, 2001*, www.state.gov/g/drl/rls/hrrpt/2001/af/8391.htm.

Organizations

Association for the Progress and Defense of Women's Rights, APDF (Association pour le Progrès et la Défense des Droits des Femmes Maliennes)
Contact: Fatoumata Siré Diakité, President
B.P. 1740
Bamako, Mali
Phone: 223-232362
Fax: 223-232362
Email: apdf@datatech.toolnct.org
Web site: www.famafrique.org/apdf/apdf.htm

Association of Women Lawyers, AJM (Association des juristes maliennes)
Contact: Madina Diallo, President
Niarela, Rue 422, Porte 537
Boite Postale, M.A. 143
Bamako, Mali
Phone: 22-51-93
Email: ajm@afribone.net.ml

Coordination of Women's Associations and Nongovernmental Organizations, AFO
  (Coordination des Associations et ONG Feminines)
Dravela, Rue Cheick Zayed, Porte 103
Contact: Madame Traore Oumou Touré, Executive Secretary of CAFO
B.P.E. 194
Bamako, Mali
B.P. 2774
Bamako, Mali
Sogoniko, Rue 114, Porte 590
Bamako, Mali
Phone/Fax: 223-20-06-51
Email: woiyo@hotmail.com, woiyoo@yahoo.fr

Ministry for the Advancement of Women, Children, and the Family
Parehf-Pnud-Mli/00/002, Avenue Cheick Zayed
Hamdallaye (face à l'Imacy)
B.P. 120
Bamako, Mali
Phone: 223-29-25-04
Fax: 223-29-23-16
Email: parehf@afribone.net.ml
Web site: www.malimuso.org

SELECTED BIBLIOGRAPHY

Baxter, Joan. "Hero Worship." *Focus on Africa Magazine*, 2002. www.bbc.co.uk/
    worldservice/africa/features/focus_magazine/mali.shtml.
CARE International. *Basic and Girls' Education*. Organizational pamphlet.
Economist Intelligence Unit (EIU). *The EIU Country Report: Burkina Faso, Niger,
    Mali*, June 2002. www.eiu.com.
UNICEF. "Mali: Prise en charge rapide des urgencies obstétriques." www.unicef.org/
    french/safe/10.htm.
United Nations. *UN Human Development Report 2001*. www.undp.org/hdr2001/
    indicator/cty_f_mLI.html.
———. "The World's Women 2000: Trends and Statistics." unstats.un.org/unsd/
    demographic/ww2000/table2a.htm.
Women's Studies Project. *Women's Voices, Women's Lives: The Impact of Family Plan-
    ning: A Synthesis of Findings from the Women's Studies Project*. www.fhi.org/en/
    wsp/wssyn/index.html.
World Bank. *Gender Statistics*. http://genderstats.worldbank.org.
———. *Mali Summary Gender Profile*. www.worldbank.org/afr/gender/mali.pdf;
    www.worldbank.org/data.
———. "Rural Women and Agricultural Extension in the Sahel." *Findings: Africa
    Region*, no. 46 (August 1995). www.worldbank.org/afr/findings/english/find46.
    htm.

10

MOZAMBIQUE

Kathleen Sheldon

PROFILE OF MOZAMBIQUE

Mozambique is located on the southeastern coast of Africa, bordered by South Africa on the south, by Tanzania to the north, and by Swaziland, Malawi, and Zimbabwe on the west. The official name of the country is the Republic of Mozambique, or in Portuguese, República de Moçam-bique. Mozambique was a Portuguese colony until independence was won in 1975 following a fourteen-year war to end the colonial relationship. The primary group fighting for liberation was Frelimo (Frente de Liberta-ção de Moçambique, the Mozambique Liberation Front), which became the ruling party in a one-party state that promoted a socialist development program. During the 1980s Mozambique suffered from an internal war with Renamo (Resistência Nacional de Moçam-bique/Mozambique National Resistance) that had support from white-ruled South Africa for its opposition to Frelimo's socialist policies. Following years of destruction, famine, death, and millions of refugees, a peace accord was signed in 1992. In 1990 the constitution was revised, allowing for a greater role for a capitalist-oriented market economy and for multiparty elections. Frelimo has continued as the majority party in two elections since then.

From the coastal plain along the Mozambique Channel the country rises in low hills to the interior. The coast is home to several deep-water ports, notably at Maputo, the capital city located in the south, and at Beira in central Mozambique. The economy is dominated by agriculture, especially by individual family plots where people grow the food they consume. Exports have also been primarily agricultural crops such as cashews, sugar, tea, rice, and cotton; fish and prawns have also been major exports.

The 1999 population totaled 17,242,240 people, divided between 8,083,000 men and 8,757,600 women (52 percent). The vast majority, 70 percent, lived in rural areas. The overall life expectancy at birth was just 42 years in 1997, a partial result of high infant mortality. While infant mortality has ranged up to 200 deaths before the first year for every 1,000 births, in 1997 the rate was judged to be 135 infant deaths per 1,000 births. Fertility remained high, even when compared to neighboring countries in southern Africa, with estimates between 5.6 and 5.9 children for every woman, and an overall annual population growth rate of 2.3 percent.[1]

There are several ethnic groups, none of which is dominant. The most widely spoken language is Makua, with 26 percent of the population speaking that as their mother tongue. Shangaan, spoken in the southern provinces, is spoken by 11 percent of the population, and all other languages, including Sena, Ndau, Bitonga, Makonde, and others, are spoken by small segments of the population. Portuguese is the official language.

OVERVIEW OF WOMEN'S ISSUES

Mozambique is one of the poorest countries in the world, and this fact is essential to understanding the key women's issues. The national women's organization, Organização da Mulher Moçambicana (OMM), or the Organization of Mozambican Women, has been involved in programs that have focused on issues that are of concern to women. For example, OMM has raised awareness around domestic violence. Along with the government it has also long encouraged improved access to literacy for women and greater access to health care, particularly during pregnancy and for newborns. Nearly all women work as agricultural laborers for their families. Thus one of the main organizations is the União Geral das Cooperativistas (UGC/General Union of Cooperatives), which has organized cooperatives for women performing farm labor in the periphery of Maputo. The UGC's membership is over 90 percent female, and it has evolved into a potent voice for women as well as a visible and well-known development initiative that benefits women.

EDUCATION

Opportunities

In 1950 the British African colonies had 21.4 percent of school-age children enrolled in primary school, the Belgian colonies had 15.7 percent, the French 9.6 percent, and the Portuguese 5.7 percent.[2] Portuguese is the official language, but only 6.5 percent of the population states that their maternal language is Portuguese.

Adult women have mentioned the difficulties they have in attending classes, as they often do not have time to devote to such studies. Attention to the particular obstacles that girls encounter, such as family expectations that they will leave school to work in family agriculture, or the still common experience of early marriage that means an end to their schooling, have also been the subject of public education campaigns. In 1991 girls made up only 43 percent of students in the first level of primary schooling, and that figure dropped with each subsequent grade, with girls making up only 34 percent of secondary students.[3]

Literacy

Mozambicans had very limited access to formal education during the colonial period, resulting in extremely low literacy rates even when compared with other colonial societies. In the 1970 census, the last one before independence in 1975, 93 percent of Mozambican women and 86 percent of men were considered illiterate in Portuguese. Only 6 percent of women and 12 percent of men had completed a primary education, which is taught in Portuguese.[4]

Although one of the major efforts of the government since independence has been to expand opportunities for education for all, including literacy classes for adults and increased numbers of schools and classes for children, 60 percent of the population was illiterate in 1997. That figure disguises the gaps between urban and rural people and between men and women, as 85 percent of rural women could not read or write.

EMPLOYMENT AND ECONOMICS

Farming

Mozambique is primarily an agricultural country, with 80 percent of the population involved in farming or fishing. As with other African countries, women have a greater responsibility for agriculture than do men. In Mozambique in 1991, 92 percent of women were performing agriculture labor, whereas 63 percent of men were doing such work. Agricultural labor typically includes hoeing, weeding, planting, harvesting, marketing of produce, transporting crops from the fields home and storing them, and food processing. There were some commercial farming ventures, but the vast majority of that work was done within the family, with the crops destined for family consumption rather than the market.

Paid Employment

Other sectors of work employed more men than women; for example, 5.6 percent of men were in industry, while only 0.6 percent of women were found there. Men also dominated the government administrative sector, where 16 percent of men were employed and 4.9 percent of women.[5] Men were four times as likely as women to hold a wage-paying job, while 95 percent of the vegetable traders in the survey were women.

Informal Economic Activities

A study of over 500 families near Pemba in the northern province of Cabo Delgado found that the poorest families were those that relied exclusively on agriculture. Nearly 60 percent of families relying on agriculture had an annual income of under 10,000 meticais (approximately U.S.$12.50; 800 meticais then equaled U.S.$1.00), and only 6.3 percent had an income over 30,000 meticais (U.S.$37.50), which was equivalent to the minimum wage. The families who experienced a better standard of living depended on a mix of income sources, including salaried jobs in Pemba, involvement in market trade, fishing, and other self-employed activities such as carpentry, pottery-making, brewing, and production of other items for sale. Families tended to produce comparable amounts and varieties of crops whether they had another source of income or not, so that the nonagricultural income source was key to rising above levels of absolute poverty. At the same time men were more likely than women to be involved in nonagricultural activities, and they tended to keep their income for themselves while women were responsible for household expenses.[6]

Women selling shrimp at market, Mozambique. Photo © TRIP/B. Seed.

Entrepreneurship

During the 1990s more women in urban areas began to sell produce and other supplies in the markets. One study estimated that over half of all households in Maputo had at least one member involved in trading, partly in response to the reduced monetary value of salaries received for employment in the formal sector. A study in Beira (population 350,000) suggested that while "the overwhelming majority of street traders are women," more men were entering market trading in the 1990s. Those men tended to sell nonperishable items such as sugar, cigarettes, clothing, and soap, while women both on the street and in market stalls sold vegetables, fruit, and dried fish [7]

Between 55 and 75 percent of women in Maputo traded, though few of them could afford to pay rent for a cement stall in the formal market. Some of the overhead costs incurred by traders included transport, license fees, and contributions to security and maintenance of the market. During the late 1980s most traders were still located in the formal markets, but by the early 1990s the numbers of traders selling from the curbsides had grown to three times those in the established markets.[8] Many of the street vendors set themselves up adjacent to or inside the markets, though not in the stalls that were provided. They paid only a tiny symbolic fee to the city for the right to sell goods in vacant lots rather than the more expensive cement markets.[9] That was not always acceptable to authorities, who periodically tried to move vendors off the streets and into designated stalls in locations determined by government officials. This resulted in people calling the unregulated vending practices *dumba nengue*, which literally means "rely on your legs," implying that the vendor should be prepared to run away when police or other officials arrived.

Market women were not a homogenous group, but varied according to whether or not they had a stall, what kinds of goods they sold, how they obtained those goods, and whether they worked on their own account or for others.[10] The group of traders who had the highest income were those who sold prepared food, and that group also claimed the most male traders (about one-third of those interviewed in one 1992 survey).[11]

The street vendors in general were younger, more apt to be recent migrants to the city, and less likely to belong to a revolving credit association, which probably meant they were not sufficiently established to save their profits on a regular basis. In general the street sellers had a much lower income, as little as one-half the meager income earned by cement-market traders.

Very few women were found as business owners. An investigation into the ownership of microenterprises in central and northern Mozambique found that women-owned businesses were primarily involved in the sale of alcoholic beverages and beer brewing, as well as some commerce in selling fish or vegetables.

Lucrative fields such as construction had no women business owners at all, and women's income averaged $61 to men's $101. In the construction industry, "overall, single male owners outnumber single female owners (79.7 percent to 17.8 percent). The remaining 2.5 percent are owned by multiple owners."[12]

Support for Mothers/Caretakers

Maternal Leave

At the time of independence Mozambique introduced laws that gave sixty days' maternity leave following the birth of a child, and thirty minutes each morning and afternoon for nursing. Because most women do not work in the formal sector, however, they are not able to take advantage of these supports.

Child Care

The government also supported the development of child care centers. Originally neighborhood-based child care centers, called creches were to be built, but the local political structures often did not have the resources to support the centers. While the Social Action Department of the Ministry of Health coordinated and encouraged child care programs, they did not have the budget to fund them. Thus local businesses and work places came to play a prominent role in developing child care centers.

Typically the company provided the space and material such as beds, bedding, and utensils, while a small fee was deducted from the wages of workers whose children attended the creche. Those companies with many female employees were most likely to provide daycare. Of fifteen companies surveyed in 1979, the six with creches included three cashew factories and two garment factories, all with many women in their workforces.[13]

There was a substantially increased demand for access to child care in the 1980s, as more women sought waged work, as more people moved into the cities in response to deteriorating rural conditions, and as government funding was restricted under International Monetary Fund (IMF) guidelines. The presence of hundreds of abandoned children living on the city streets was regularly reported and readily observable.[14]

The need for child care in Maputo was far larger than could be met, and rural creches suffered even greater difficulties and shortages of educational supplies. The government plans for providing child care were derailed by political circumstances in the 1980s and 1990s.

Inheritance, Property, and Land Rights

Women's access to land was governed by a variety of structures and policies. Prior to independence local chiefs designated land for use by particular families, sometimes incorporating colonial government desires for the cultivation of certain crops or otherwise following colonial agricultural programs. After independence local Frelimo officials took control over some aspects of land provisioning, though the connection of women's access to land through their marital and kin relations persisted. The internal war with Renamo in the 1980s disrupted people's land holdings, as some fled the rural areas and new people moved into villages. The layers of complexity were evident in studies of local areas, where land was variously under the control of local authorities, colonial rulers, Frelimo officials, and most recently government representatives. The land law itself as well as the structure of local communities had changed. In most areas people had access to a variety of scattered small plots, so that they had wet lands and drier lands, some close to their homes and others more distant. The attempts to regularize access to land meant confronting layers of privilege and poverty in all regions of the country.

In the earlier law (in force until 1990) land was allocated to the "head of the family," who was assumed to be a man. In families headed by women there were impediments to those women gaining a legal right to farm their land, even though the constitution stated that women and men would have equal rights concerning land ownership and use. Women's lack of literacy often meant they did not know their rights and did not have the ability to collect the documentation necessary to prove land rights. Women also faced difficulties in acquiring a legal right to land in urban areas as statistics from 1993 suggest, when 2,447 men filed claims for land use in Maputo, compared to 746 women.[15] In northern Mozambique women sometimes reported that they had no problem in controlling their land because the region operates under a matrilineal system of kinship and inheritance that has maintained women's rights to land.

One study of Ndixe in southern Mozambique's Maputo province demonstrated how women had been unable to assert their personal rights to land throughout decades of changing land allocation systems. Land use there was investigated in detail, including agricultural labor inputs, ownership of fruit trees, and a growing demand for firewood in the nearby urban areas that led to serious deforestation. By the 1990s it was evident that most of the village men were working in urban areas or neighboring countries, while women remained in the village performing most of the agricultural labor and had almost no other options for supporting themselves. Yet the process of regularizing individual land rights was cumbersome and costly with multiple obstacles.

There was nationwide discussion of proposed revisions in the land law in 1997, with the initial law calling for increased privatization of landownership. The majority of rural people opposed privatizing land. The law that was eventually passed maintained land as being owned by the state, and prevented private ownership and mortgaging of land. People would have rights to land use, based in part on their history and their family history of living on and cultivating a particular parcel of land. Though land sales were forbidden, people and corporations could obtain 100-year leases for the use of land. The land law stressed the equality of men and women in their access to holding title to land. The new law, passed in July 1997, stated that inheritance must be "independent of sex." The land law affirmed that customary practices of land allocation cannot counter the constitution, which guaranteed that "men and women are equal before the law in all aspects of political, economic, social and cultural life" (Article 67). A further provision stated that communities or individuals who occupied land for ten or more years could acquire permanent rights to that land and did not need documents, a potential benefit for women who wished to gain title to land they cultivated.

Social/Government Programs

Structural Adjustment

In 1987 Mozambique implemented an economic restructuring program based on conditions imposed by the World Bank and IMF for acquiring loans. In order to repay its foreign debt, local currency was devalued and austerity measures introduced. The program emphasized privatizing many government services such as health care. The impact of such policies suggested to some observers that these outside agencies were actually setting priorities for Mozambique, and overriding governmental structures and policies.[16] The restrictions on the government's ability to provide services meant that many sectors that had supported women, such as child care centers and health services, were adversely affected and faced new limitations.

One of the most visible results of the adjustment program in Mozambique was an increase in food prices, a result of attempts to adjust prices that were set abnormally low by the government prior to structural adjustment. During the immediate postindependence period the government rationed basic foods and subsidized prices, so that nearly everyone had access to some food on the urban markets. Under structural adjustment not only did prices rise, but the rationing system was gradually eroded until it ended in 1993.[17]

New private shops began selling expensive consumer goods as well as imported food items. Because wages and salaries did not keep pace with rises in prices, the net impact on families was less money available to purchase food and other necessities. Women in rural and urban areas had to find more sources of income and they also had to make do with less food, which meant more work on a daily basis for the poorest women. By 1989, after only two years of structural adjustment, over 60 percent of the total population was living in absolute poverty.[18]

Women felt the effects of decreased access to health care and education for their children. While some of these losses, especially in the rural areas, were a result of the war, urban women were suddenly faced with higher fees when they needed health care. Likewise, textbooks required for school became more expensive, and families were more likely to keep children, especially girls, out of school when they could not afford the new, higher fees. In 1986 the Mozambican government had allocated 17 percent of its budget for education and 7 percent for health. By 1991 both sectors combined only claimed 3.2 percent of the budget, as the private sector was made more responsible for providing those services.[19]

FAMILY AND SEXUALITY

As Jancte Assulai, a lawyer with ORAM (Organização Rural de Ajuda Mútua, Rural Organization for Mutual Help), commented, "Our society is accustomed to putting women in second place. We must shift the mentality. It is important to repeat gender equality in all new laws to accustom people to the new thinking."[20] In spite of these changes, there is little evidence that women have, in fact, been able to exercise their new rights.

The debate in the legislature and the wider society raised a number of issues related to marriage, inheritance, "custom and tradition," and access to land for women. Gender issues and disagreement about the interpretation of women's place in Mozambican rural society, in particular, continued to be hotly contested in 1990s political debate.

Marriage

Mozambique is home to a variety of marital practices, including traditional rites and customs, church ceremonies, and (the least common) civil proceedings in a state marriage bureau. Although it appears that the practice of temporary relationships without formal recognition is increasing, many people practice some form of acknowledging a newly married couple, most often through the exchange of bridewealth, called *lobolo*. Historically this was most common in southern Mozambique, where patrilincal societies were found. The amount of *lobolo* and the ceremonies surrounding the initiation of a marriage have changed over time. Government campaigns have targeted *lobolo* and other practices. They have targeted polygyny (where a man may have more than one wife), early and arranged marriages, especially where parents promise their young daughters to older men, and the expectation that a widow will remarry within her deceased husband's family, preferably to his brother. These have not been made illegal, and many Mozambicans continue to marry polygynously, though there have been government-sponsored propaganda efforts to encourage people to change their behavior.

Although Westerners may interpret *lobolo* as the sale of women, people in Mozambique value the way such an exchange fosters networking and connections between families who are bound by marriage. Mozambican women do not universally condemn polygyny, as some women see advantages in having a cowife to share the burden of household and agricultural work and child care. There have been a wide range of experiences, from desperate jealousy and hatred between cowives, to families where the first wife has helped her husband choose a second wife, and the men complain that the wives band together in opposition to the outnumbered husband.

Reproduction

Sex Education

Education about sexuality and marital responsibilities was historically part of the initiation rites, held when young people reached puberty. Initiation rites have also been a source of controversy, as the government condemned them in the years immediately following independence. While there have been aspects of the rites that teach women to subordinate themselves to their future husbands, there are also songs that celebrate adult female sexuality in a positive way. Though these varied from place to place in Mozambique, they shared some general characteristics, including teaching girls about adult sexuality and preparing them for household responsibilities.

Contraception and Abortion

Mozambican women on the whole desire children, and the expectation is that all women will bear at least one child. Yet due to the high birthrates there is growing discussion about using family planning to control the timing and number of children born to a couple. In Maputo it appeared that women with more education and who had lived in the city longer and were more urbanized, were more likely to rely on Western methods of contraception available from health clinics.

But many women continued to use methods involving herbs and amulets, which they believed had been effective in preventing unwanted births. Women also relied on such methods to increase fertility when they had difficulty becoming pregnant. A further element was women's work environment, as women who were in groups or collective organizations were found to be more likely to rely on modern methods of contraception than women working alone.[21]

Although abortion was not legal, there were ways in which women could gain access to doctor-assisted abortions. The Ministry of Health published regulations in 1991 governing the provision of abortions, so that hospital abortions were legal in practice though not in a strict judicial sense.[22] Hospital access was better for women who were more highly educated, while poorer women turned to herbal and mechanical methods that they administered themselves. The most common reason given for seeking a hospital abortion was poverty, followed by students who wished to continue their studies, and then by mothers who were concerned over births that were too numerous or too closely spaced.[23]

The tragedy of women dying as a result of their attempts to end unwanted pregnancies was recognized by many women, though the issue of legalizing abortion was not a priority for OMM. As OMM leader Paulina Mateus commented, it was still "not discussed" widely among Mozambicans, and there was no strong public interest in legalizing access to abortion.[24]

Another tragic result of the legal situation was the abandonment of newborns. In the first half of 1999 five infants were abandoned in Beira and had to be placed in the provincial orphanage. Observers believed the actual numbers of cast-out infants was much higher.[25] That response to unwanted babies also reflected male refusal to take responsibility for the children they fathered and a lack of family support for mothers in difficult situations.

HEALTH

Health Care Access

Improved access to health care was another of the major efforts of the independent government after 1975. In ending the strictly segregated colonial system, the hospitals were opened to everyone at minimal cost, clinics were established in areas that previously had not been served, and people were trained to provide medical care within that system. Since then health care, like education, has suffered, as many hundreds of clinics were destroyed during the war with Renamo in the 1980s, and the implementation of structural adjustment programs in the 1990s greatly reduced the level of government support and encouraged more expensive private clinics. The result was a system that was overburdened and unable to provide care for all that need it.

Diseases and Disorders

The primary diseases in the 1980s and 1990s were malaria, cholera, chronic tuberculosis, and the spread of HIV/AIDS.

AIDS

Only at the end of the 1990s did Mozambique acknowledge that AIDS was a serious problem, with various studies indicating that many Mozambicans continued to rely on a combination of Western-style health care and more traditional remedies when they found they were HIV-positive or suspected they had the disease.

Increasing numbers of people were diagnosed with HIV/AIDS by the late 1990s, and it was clear that the numbers were growing with perhaps 10 percent or more of the Mozambican population carrying the virus. Statistics had not been collected in a rigorous way, however, so that the reality was impossible to discern. One study of rural pregnant women in Zambézia found that while over 12 percent of those women had syphilis, only 2.9 percent tested positive for HIV. A speech by Deputy Health Minister Aida Libombo reported that in early 2001, 1.4 million Mozambicans were living with HIV. Another study found that twenty out of every one hundred women visiting maternity clinics were infected with HIV. Some leaders recommended that information about AIDS be incorporated into sex education, including initiation rites, a suggestion that OMM seconded.[26]

Female Genital Cutting

By the end of the nineteenth century there was no evidence of genital cutting as part of initiation ceremonies, though women continued to practice other types of genital manipulation, including pulling on the labia to lengthen it to enhance pleasure during sexual intercourse. Women have also frequently been healers and spiritual leaders in their communities. Many women have also valued the rites as a time when women can gather and rejoice as women, strengthening ties between female neighbors and kin. In the 1980s people argued that there was no other venue to teach issues about sex to young people, and they resented the government attitude that denigrated the rites.

POLITICS AND LAW

Political Participation

In October 1994 Mozambique held its first multiparty elections for president and National Assembly representatives.[27] The process of registering voters and preparing for the election lasted over a year prior to the actual election. Gender issues were prominent in the civic educational materials and workshops held to teach Mozambicans about the mechanics of voting, with a clear emphasis on getting women out to vote. At the same time, only two of the twenty-one members of the CNE (Comissão Nacional de Eleições/National Elections Commission) were women, and women were much less likely to be members of the local teams registering voters. One of the restrictions, that team members have at least six years of education "or the equivalent," certainly limited the number of eligible women, although clearly the demands of registering people required some level of literacy. The materials, while containing information on women's rights in the elections and in society more broadly, also noted assumptions about women as being oppressed. These included articulating worries that women might not vote independently but be forced to vote the way their husbands or other male family members told them, and concerns that women were more susceptible to the influence of magic and bewitching, which might sway their vote.[28]

An important turning point in national politics was Frelimo's fifth party congress, held in August 1989. At that meeting delegates decided to end the definition of the party as a Marxist-Leninist organization, establish a clearer division between party and government, make provisions for multiparty elections, and shift to a mass party rather than a vanguard party formation.

Women's representation at the 1989 party congress, 29 percent, was double their presence at the 1983 congress. Many women joined OMM without also being members of Frelimo, as seen in the 281,000 members claimed by OMM in 1989, while there were only 51,659 women members of Frelimo that year. This was an increase in numbers from 33,000 members in 1983, but Frelimo itself had grown at a faster pace as more men joined, so the percentage of female members decreased. A Frelimo document prepared for the 1989 congress expressed concern at the low percentage of female members, reflecting the fact that in 1989 women accounted for only 25 percent of Frelimo members, a decrease from 30 percent in 1983.

Though some OMM members had hoped that a woman would be elected to the Political Bureau, the ruling body of Frelimo that was elected at the 1989 congress, was still all men. That situation was finally changed at Frelimo's sixth party congress in August 1991. Deolinda Guezimane, a longtime activist and veteran of the anticolonial struggle, was the first woman elected to the Political Bureau. The sixth congress also marked the first time that secret ballots were used in electing members of the Central Committee. In combination with what was called "positive discrimination" for women, members were obliged to vote for a minimum number of female candidates, and the number of women on the Central Committee rose to an unprecedented level. Fifty-seven women became Central Committee members, a full 36 percent of the total 160 members.[29]

Although Frelimo and Renamo were the main contenders in the 1994 election, many other smaller parties also emerged. It was difficult to discover the political platforms of some parties, as clarifying statements and publications were scarce. Most of these parties were quite small and experienced a bewildering number of splits and coalitions, often the result of personality conflicts and political experiences rather than actual ideological positions.[30]

The new parties generally did not mention women's issues in their platforms, or they included only the most general platitudes with no actual program of action. Essentially, as one observer commented, women were invisible in Mozambican party politics.[31] After the elections, the nascent women's leagues that many parties had established faced serious problems of organization and activity, and continued to be overshadowed by OMM.

In the 1994 election there were twelve presidential candidates (ten backed by parties and two running as independents) and twelve parties and two coalitions of parties fielding candidates for the National Assembly. Candidates for the National Assembly were selected on a provincial basis, and voters chose the party they supported rather than voting for an individual. There was a total of 3,115 candidates nationwide, of which 548 (17.59

percent) were women. The highest percentages were in the south, for Maputo City (27.87 percent female candidates) and Gaza province (24.06 percent), and the lowest was in the northern province of Niassa (12.78 percent).[32] Frelimo nominated women for 37 percent of the potential legislative seats, in comparison with Renamo's 9 percent. That was a deliberate decision, as Frelimo opted to allocate one-third of its available slots to women, which resulted in a high ratio of women in the National Assembly, almost all of them Frelimo members.[33]

In 1997, 28 percent (62 of 250 delegates) of the National Assembly was female. In the 1999 elections for presidency and assembly representatives, Frelimo continued its support of female candidates, with over one-third of those on the lists being women. Renamo counted only ten women out of fifty candidates on their list.[34] As a result of Frelimo's prioritizing of female candidates, 30 percent of the legislature seats were held by women.

In January 2000 newly reelected president Joaquim Chissano named the latest ministers to his cabinet and reformed some of the ministries. Among those appointed were three women, Luisa Diogo as minister of planning and finance, Lidia Brito as minister of higher education, science, and technology, and Virginia Matabele as minister of the reconfigured Ministry of Social Action, now the Ministry of Women and Social Action. The creation of a ministry devoted to women's issues fulfilled a longtime goal of Mozambican women involved in politics, and though there might be problems if women's issues are relegated only to one ministry, many believed its formation brought a long-deserved recognition to women in government.

Women's Rights

Women's rights are guaranteed in the constitution, which states that "men and women are equal before the law in all aspects of political, economic, social and cultural life" (Article 67). New laws, such as those concerning landownership, reiterate that men and women are equal in that specific instance in order to reinforce the principle of equality. Nonetheless, there have been sectors where strict equality has not been observed, such as obligatory military service, which will include women for the first time in 2002.

A controversy over nationality indicates some of the public debate over women in modern Mozambican society. At independence, the nationality law decreed that women who married foreigners would lose their Mozambican citizenship, while men married to foreigners would not. Many people felt that the law was patently unfair. The issue was raised at an OMM conference in 1984 only to be dismissed by then-president Samora Machel. In 1988, however, the national legislature changed the law to remove the discrimination against women. Women who had been affected in the past could simply declare their situation to the authorities in order to regain Mozambican citizenship.[35]

The problem of women and citizenship reemerged two years later, when the draft of the new constitution allowed a non-Mozambican woman who married a Mozambican man to acquire Mozambican citizenship through naturalization, but denied that right to a foreign man who married a Mozambican woman. Although the proposal of a nonsexist version of the law, allowing foreign men and women equal access to citizenship, did not succeed in obtaining the two-thirds majority needed to become part of the constitution, it did receive a majority of representatives' votes.[36]

Women activists continued to contest their legal situation at the end of the 1990s, as shown in a pamphlet that was published by the Women's Program at the university on "The Struggle to Defend Gender Equality in the New Family Law." Many laws from the Portuguese colonial era remained on the books, though they were not uniformly enforced. For example, de facto marriages and polygynous marriages were not included in written laws, and men were still assumed to be "head of the family." In 1992 the Supreme Court decided that "rulings on questions of the family are based on the Civil Code of 1967, which contains flagrant discrimination in relation to women." Minimum requirements for a fair family law would include a broad definition of marriage; would give both spouses autonomy in control of household goods; would allow either husband or wife to be head of the family; would set the minimum age at marriage as the same for men and women; and would recognize unregistered and polygynous unions with respect to paternity, guardianship of children, and inheritance.[37]

Discussion of the law brought out dissension in the Muslim community, as Muslim men expressed their support for polygyny, marriage between first cousins, and a younger marriage age than the proposed 16 years.[38] Muslim women spoke out in opposition to the formal recognition of polygyny, and others raised concerns about the imposition of Islamic law on all Mozambicans.[39]

Women's Movements

After the 1990 changes in the constitution allowing independent organizations to form, there was a proliferation of groups focused on issues of concern to women. OMM, along with other organizations, was proclaimed an autonomous organization, no longer dependent on Frelimo for its political direction. At an OMM conference in 1990, the delegates adopted a set of statutes that established OMM as an independent organization with membership open to all women, whether they agreed with Frelimo's politics or not. The organization would no longer focus on implementing Frelimo policy, but planned to emphasize legislation that would extend women's rights. While the new formulation allowed for greater political freedom, OMM faced serious problems in funding. Previously Frelimo supported OMM's daily operations. New possibilities for political organ izing autonomously of Frelimo might have made it easier for OMM to raise questions of gender equality, but the organization would not have the resources to exploit them effectively.[40] The financial issue was discussed at length at the 1990 meeting, with OMM leaders arguing for more self-funding efforts and a greater reliance on volunteer staff.[41]

The situation changed dramatically once again in 1996 when OMM leadership abruptly decided to return to their earlier affiliation with Frelimo. During a national OMM congress a delegate from Nampula commented in a speech from the floor that people should remember that "OMM is the fruit of Frelimo." The delegates reacted with wild support and broke into pro-Frelimo chants. With no discussion or formal motion, it then was simply announced that OMM had returned to its prior affiliation with Frelimo. Paulina Mateus was elected secretary-general of OMM at that congress. She explained that the decision to return to Frelimo was based on the idea that everyone always thought OMM was part of Frelimo, so the resolution simply ratified that perception.[42]

Women in a number of professions and with a variety of interests began forming their own organizations including women in business and in the public sector.[43] A more political approach was seen in the Movement of Mozambican Women for Peace (Movimento das Mulheres Moçambicanas pela Paz), which was founded in 1994 and began calling itself the Association of Mozambican Women for Peace in 1997. That organization participated in a meeting on peace, gender, and development in Kigali, Rwanda, which created the Federation of African Women for Peace.[44] Associação das Donas de Casa (ADOCA) was another group involved in development projects. Its name could be translated as "Housewives' Association," but that does not disclose the projects in which it is involved, such as helping build houses and settling families in the Matola-Rio area outside of Maputo.[45]

Women also continued older forms of organization, such as dance groups. In Cabo Delgado, Muslim women in the 1990s wore matching *capulanas* (Sarongs or wraparound cloths) for their dance contests, which involved extensive planning and travel to different locales. These groups had roots in Swahili coastal culture, but modernized their song lyrics, sometimes incorporating critiques of government policies. The group membership was very stable, and appeared to be a constant fixture in women's lives, even more than marriage in that region, where there was a particularly high divorce rate.[46]

Military Service

Obligatory military service included women for the first time in 2002.

RELIGION AND SPIRITUALITY

There is no dominant religion in Mozambique, and the constitution guarantees religious freedom. Half of the people told the 1997 census that they followed local religious practices, usually considered to be indigenous.

The main organized religions are Catholicism, with 30 percent of the population, other Christian churches, also with 30 percent, and Islam, with 20 percent of the population. The fastest growing segment is found in "Zionist" congregations, which are independent outgrowths of more established Protestant churches.

Rituals and Religious Practices

Historically women have had important roles in local religions, particularly in the practice of initiation rites. Some of these churches acknowledged traditional practices, such as purification rites for widows and birth rites for newborns, though these rituals were not necessarily incorporated into the Christian activities in the church. A recent study of Zionist churches in Maputo indicated their increasingly important role as a community of and for women, as a place to find respite from disease, and as an institution on the cusp between rural and urban life.[47]

VIOLENCE

Domestic Violence

A study of domestic violence in rural southern Mozambique found that although OMM had given women a public voice, relations within the household had not changed. Men still believed that the exchange of *lobolo* gave them rights over their wives. The women talked about all kinds of oppression, not just physical beatings. One woman told how her husband had sent his second wife to harvest and sell the beans she (the first wife) had cultivated, and had not given her a penny from the sale. The site of the study, Aldeia Machel, had been a communal village. The men were often absent at work in South Africa, and the women were active in local politics and held land in their own names, yet they testified to the prevalence of male violence against women.[48]

When Mozambicans began to rebuild and recover after the peace accord was signed in 1992, an important campaign to raise awareness about violence against women was organized. It was begun initially by the umbrella organization Fórum Mulher in 1995, and expanded in 1997 by OMM, Muleide (Mulher, Lei, e Desenvolvimento; Women, Law, and Development), and Mozambican Women in Education. There was no law that specified that domestic violence was illegal, though rape was deemed criminal. Court cases dealt with these as with other assault and battery cases, but awareness of the issue was low, and hospitals did not report cases that came to their attention.[49] Muleide operated with volunteer labor and a minimal budget, and developed a neighborhood-based program of legal clinics.[50]

One of their first tasks was to open up discussions regarding cultural ideas about men beating their wives. Although women had long complained about domestic violence, it was seen as "normal" male behavior.[51]

One study done under Muleide auspices documented violence against girls and young women, who were subject to beatings from their fathers as well as from lovers or husbands. Fathers often believed they had a right to use such brutality in order to teach their daughters obedience and respect.[52]

War and Military Repression

Renamo was responsible for widespread rural devastation and a near total breakdown of rural production and distribution in the 1980s. The war made organized agricultural production difficult if not impossible, and was also responsible for a surge of immigrants to the cities. Women in the rural areas were particularly affected due to their responsibility for food cultivation and preparation and their continuing primary role in child care.[53]

In southern Mozambique many of the men were absent doing wage labor in Maputo or in South Africa, leaving women and children to face the wartime hardships on their own. The large numbers of refugees and the disruption of basic agricultural production in many parts of the country made it clear that women were suffering the brunt of the destabilization.[54]

Women were frequently victims of the spread of war, as rural areas were overrun and families were forced to seek refuge in neighboring countries or urban areas. Women still were the primary agricultural workers, and when war came to their villages they had to leave unharvested crops and risk losing access to land. Many women who did stay in their villages did not sleep in their homes but stayed with their families, hidden in the bush at night in order to avoid encounters with Renamo. Often they tried to continue their work even after attacks that resulted in the loss of their houses and household goods and perhaps death or injury to family members. In some areas nearly every family experienced such losses.

The destruction of hundreds of schools and health posts by Renamo meant that women had to spend more time caring for children and trying to keep their families healthy. The danger of unexpected Renamo attacks meant that people did not practice social rituals such as funerals, rites of passage for adolescents or widows, or other religious activities, and they were unable to follow such practices if they were captive in Renamo camps. One woman told an interviewer, "We are afraid to dance."[55]

Hunger and starvation were widespread, with many stories of rural people trying to survive by eating tree bark and leaves that were not normally considered edible. The extreme disruption to daily life, health, and family relations cannot be overstated. Women experienced a wide range of traumatic events as a result of the war, including torture, violence, and rape. A study of 110 refugee women in a camp in Zambia found that 87 of them had been a victim of at least one attack or violent episode, including nearly half (44 percent) having witnessed a murder.[56]

The public nature of such crimes, for instance, the presence of witnesses to a woman being raped, contributed to "undermin[ing] social stability" and to community disintegration. Simultaneously, the intimate nature of rape made the victim an unwitting collaborator in her own violation. The psychological anguish for women of being forced to endure sexual relations with men whom they had seen murder their family members and destroy their homes is difficult to imagine.[17]

OUTLOOK FOR THE TWENTY-FIRST CENTURY

In the years ahead, Mozambican women face the daunting task of overcoming poverty as an integral part of improving women's lives. At the beginning of the new century they continue to enjoy governmental support and organizations that will help in the work of improving women's access to education, control over their land, and expanding their economic opportunities. Despite setbacks since independence, the current peaceful situation should bring improvements.

NOTES

1. Victor Agadjanian, "Negotiating Through Reproductive Change: Gendered Social Interaction and Fertility Regulation in Mozambique," *Journal of Southern African Studies* 27, no. 2 (June 2001): 291–309, statistics on 292, drawn from the 1997 official census, other official censuses, and from Demographic and Health Survey materials.

2. Based on UNESCO statistics as reported in Claire Robertson, "Women's Education and Class Formation in Africa, 1950–1980," in *Women and Class in Africa*, eds. Claire Robertson and Iris Berger (New York: Holmes and Meier, 1986), 106.

3. Ana Elisa de Santana Afonso, "Contribuição para uma reflexão sobre a excolarização da mulher e da rapariga em Moçambique," in *Eu Mulher em Moçambique*, ed. Ana Elisa de Santana Afonso (Maputo: CEGRAF, 1994), 173–87.

4. Anton Johnston, *Education in Moçambique 1975–84* (Stockholm: Swedish International Development Authority, 1984), 21.

5. Instituto Nacional de Estatística (INE), *Moçambique em números* (Maputo: INE, 1998), 6.

6. Ann Wigglesworth, "Invisible Farmers and Economic Adjustment in Mozambique: A Study of the Survival Strategies of Subsistence Farmers" (M.A. thesis, Monash University, 1983), 22, 30.

7. Jørgen Billetoft, "Coping with Uncertainty, Petty Producers in Postwar Mozambique: Small Business in the Course of Political and Economic Change," CDR Working Paper no. 98.4 (Copenhagen: Centre for Development Research, 1998), 14.

8. Peter D. Little and Irae Baptista Lundin de Coloane, "Petty Trade and Household Survival Strategies: A Case Study of Food and Vegetable Traders in the Peri-Urban Areas of Maputo, Mozambique," IDA Working Paper no. 90 (Binghamton, NY: Institute for Development Anthropology, 1992), 1, 8.

9. Rosemary Galli, "Women and Poverty in the Greater Maputo Area: Some Policy Considerations" (Maputo: typescript report for AID, 1992).

10. Emília Machaieie, "Algumas considerações sobre a mulher no sector informal: A caso do mercado bazuka, cidade de maputo, 1987/1997," in *Relações de Género em Moçambique: Educação, trabalho e saúde*, eds. Ana Maria Loforte and Maria José Arthur

(Maputo: Departamento de Arqueologia e Antropologia, Universidade Eduardo Mondlane, 1998), 39–46.

11. Little and Coloane, "Petty Trade," 8–13.

12. Rui M. S. Benfica, "Analysis of the Contribution of Micro and Small Enterprises to Rural Household Incomes in Central and Northern Mozambique" (M.S. thesis, Michigan State University, 1998), 85, 107.

13. Barbara Isaacman and June Stephen, *Mozambique: Women, the Law, and Agrarian Reform* (Addis Ababa: United Nations Economic Commission on Africa, 1980), 124.

14. Alfredo Tembe, "Crianças de rua: Algumas mãos remam contra a maré," *Tempo* 995 (November 5, 1989): 12–15; Gabriel Simbine, "Crianças da Rua: Quantas São?" *Tempo* 1004 (January 7, 1990): 22–27.

15. Fórum Mulher, "A situação da mulher em Moçambique," document prepared for the Fourth World Conference on Women in Beijing (Maputo: Fórum Mulher, 1994), 14–16.

16. Joseph Hanlon, *Mozambique: Who Calls the Shots?* (Bloomington: Indiana University Press, 1991); and Judith Marshall, "War, Debt, and Structural Adjustment in Mozambique: The Social Impact" (Ottawa: North-South Institute, 1992).

17. Bridget O'Laughlin, "From Basic Needs to Safety-Nets: The Rise and Fall of Urban Food Rationing in Mozambique," *European Journal of Development Research* 8, no. 1 (June 1996): 200–23, discusses the economic ideas behind such shifts in policy, and the resulting decrease in access to food that was felt by many in the urban areas.

18. R. H. Green, "Mozambique: Into the 1990s," in *Child Survival on the Frontline*, ed. Association of West European Parliamentarians for Action Against Apartheid (Amsterdam: African-European Institute, 1990), 49–52, information on 50.

19. Merle L. Bowen, "Beyond Reform: Adjustment and Political Power in Contemporary Mozambique," *Journal of Modern African Studies* 30, no. 2 (1992): 255–79, information on 267; see also Julie Cliff, "Destabilisation, Economic Adjustment, and the Impact on Women," *Agenda* 14 (1992): 25–38.

20. All quotes taken from "Land Law Increases Peasant Rights," *Mozambique Peace Process Bulletin* 19 (September 1997): 3–6.

21. Victor Agadjanian, "Women's Choice Between Indigenous and Western Contraception in Urban Mozambique," *Women and Health* 28, no. 2 (1998): 1–17; and Victor Agadjanian, "Women's Work and Fertility in a Sub-Saharan Urban Setting: A Social Environment Approach," *Journal of Biosocial Science* 32 (2000): 17–35.

22. Kajsa Pehrsson, "Country Gender Analysis for Mozambique" (Stockholm: Swedish International Development Authority, 1994), 21.

23. Victor Agadjanian, " 'Quasi-Legal' Abortion Services in a Sub-Saharan Setting: Users' Profile and Motivations," *International Family Planning Perspectives* 24, no. 3 (September 1998): 111–16.

24. Conversation by author with Paulina Mateus, secretary-general of OMM, September 14, 1998, Maputo OMM headquarters.

25. Untitled article, *Tempo* 1450 (August 29, 1999): 5.

26. H. A. Cossa et al., "Syphilis and HIV Infection Among Displaced Pregnant Women in Rural Mozambique," *International Journal of STD and AIDS* 5 (1994): 117–23; "At Least 1.4 Million Mozambicans Live with HIV," *Panafrican News Agency*, posted electronically March 27, 2001; "Twenty Per Cent of Pregnant Women HIV+," *AIM Reports* 208 (June 1, 2001, distributed electronically); and "AIDS Poses 'Terrible Challenge,' " *Mozambiquefile* 277 (August 1999): 15–16.

27. For detailed information on all aspects of the elections, see *Mozambique: Elections, Democracy, and Development*, ed. Brazão Mazula (Maputo: Embassy of the Kingdom of the Netherlands, 1996), especially Alcinda de Abreu and Angélica Salomão, "Women on the Path of Democracy," 509–37.

28. Ruth Jacobson, "Women's Political Participation: Mozambique's Democratic Transition," *Gender and Development* 3, no. 3 (October 1995): 29–35.

29. "Frelimo Sixth Congress," *Mozambiquefile* 182 (1991): 4–9. In 1997 at Frelimo's seventh congress, three women, Laurinda Kanji, Veronica Macamo, and Margarida Talapa, were elected to the Political Bureau. "Renewal and Continuity? Frelimo's Seventh Congress," *Mozambiquefile* 251 (June 1997): 4–9.

30. For a thorough guide, see Rachel Waterhouse, "Seventeen Parties Registered," *Mozambique Peace Process Bulletin*, special political parties supplement (August 1994).

31. Sabine Fandrych, "A mulher é invisível: Breve análise dos programas de alguns partidos políticos em relação à mulher," in *O espaço da mulher no processo multipartidario*, eds. Luis de Brito and Bernhard Weimer (Maputo: Universidade Eduardo Mondlane and Fundação Friedrich Ebert, 1994), 45–48.

32. Abreu and Salomão, "Women on the Path of Democracy," 526.

33. Jacobson, "Women's Political Participation."

34. "Candidates Register, Campaign Starts," *Mozambiquefile* 280 (November 1999): 7–10.

35. "New Legislation Approved," *AIM Information Bulletin* 138 (1988): 4.

36. "People's Assembly Approves New Constitution," *Mozambiquefile* 172 (November 1990): 4–10.

37. "Luta pela defesa da igualidade de género na nova lei da familia" (Maputo: Programa Mulher, Centro de Estudos Africanos, 1999); this is a two-page pamphlet and call to action.

38. "Lei de família em debate público interesante," *NotMoc* (electronic news digest) 2, 14 (April 17, 2000), reporting on public debate in preparation for bringing a new family law to the assembly by August 2000.

39. "Mozambique's Moslem Women Oppose Polygamy," Pan African News Agency, posted online May 18, 2000, and Marcelo Mosse, "Novo lei de matrimónio: A charia para Moçambique?" *Publico* (online news) (March 9, 2000).

40. "Relatório do Gabinete Central á IV Conferência Nacional da O.M.M." (Maputo: typescript, 1990). In this report about the preparations for OMM's fourth national conference, the primary difficulty mentioned was "a lack of financial and material means" to complete their work (13).

41. "Mozambican Women at the Crossroads," *Mozambiquefile* 174 (1991): 4–6. OMM relied on financial help from non-governmental organizations to fund their projects on women's health, social education, family planning, and educating mothers about the importance of children's immunization; "Políticos questionam carácter apartidário da OMM em Nampula," *Notícias* (November 28, 1995): 4.

42. "OMM Returns to Frelimo," *Mozambiquefile* 241 (August 1996): 4–5.

43. "Mulher na função pública também quer associação," *Notícias* (August 22, 1995).

44. Notices in online news digest *NotMoc* 97 (March 17, 1997) and 101 (May 3, 1997).

45. "ADOCA Está a Dar Novo Visual a Matola-Rio," *Notícias* (July 4, 1998): 9.

46. Signe Arnfred, "Female Identity Politics in a Period of Change? Muslim Women's Dance Associations in Northern Mozambique," presented at the annual meeting of the African Studies Association, Philadelphia, 1999.

47. Victor Agadjanian, "As igrejas ziones no espaço sóciocultural de Moçambique urbano (anos 1980 e 1990)," *Lusotopie* (1999): 415–23.

48. Marta Isabel Dominguez, "Género e violência doméstica: Análise comparativa numa zona rural do sul de Moçambique: Relatório final" (Maputo: Universidade Eduardo Mondlane Centro de Estudos Africanos, 1996).

49. U.S. Department of State, *Mozambique Country Report on Human Rights Practices for 1997*, www.state.gov/www/global/human_rights/1997_hrp_report/mozambiq/html.

50. Eulália Temba, "Experiência de trabalho da MULEIDE com a comunidade," paper presented at the IV Congresso Luso-Afro-Brasilieira, 1996.

51. "Shabby Office a Ray of Hope for Mozambique's Battered Women," *African Eye News Service* (accessed via *Africa News Online*, September 23, 1998); see also the information and individual stories in *Women and the Law in Southern Africa: The Justice Delivery System and the Illusion of the Transparency* (Maputo: Women and Law in Southern Africa Research Trust, 2000).

52. Conceição Osório, "Violência contra a jovem e construção da identidade feminina" (Maputo: Muleide, 1997), 21.

53. The impact of the war on women is discussed in Stephanie Urdang, *And Still They Dance: Women, War, and the Struggle for Change in Mozambique* (New York: Monthly Review, 1989).

54. Hilário Matusse, "Guerra e fome retardam libertação da mulher," *Tempo* 860 (April 5, 1987): 27–31; and "7 de Abril: Data assinalada com espírito de luta," *Tempo* 861 (April 12, 1987): 4–8.

55. Ivette Illas Jeichande, "Mulheres deslocadas em Maputo, Zambézia e Inhambane (Mulher em situação difícil)" (Maputo: OMM/UNICEF, 1990), 68; other information in this paragraph is also drawn from this study.

56. Margaret McCallin, "Psychological Needs of Mozambican Refugees; A Community-Based Approach," *Tropical Doctor*, supplement 1, vol. 21 (1991): 67–69.

57. Tina Sideris, "Rape in War and Peace: Some Thoughts on Social Context and Gender Roles," *Agenda* 43 (2000): 41–45.

RESOURCE GUIDE

Suggested Reading

Isaacman, Barbara, and June Stephen. *Mozambique: Women, the Law, and Agrarian Reform*. Addis Ababa: United Nations Economic Commission on Africa, 1980. A thorough overview of women in the immediate postindependence period.

Sheldon, Kathleen. *Pounders of Grain: A History of Women, Work, and Politics in Mozambique*. Portsmouth, NH: Heinemann, 2002. A history of women in the country as a whole, from the mid–nineteenth century to the end of the twentieth century.

Urdang, Stephanie. *And Still They Dance: Women, War, and the Struggle for Change in Mozambique*. New York: Monthly Review Press, 1989. A journalist's account of the situation in the 1980s.

Web Sites

A Bibliography of Lusophone Women Writers, www.arts.uwa.edu.au/aflit/femecalirelu.html.

A bibliography of Portuguese-speaking women writers, part of a larger web site on

African literature by women based at the University of Western Australia, it contains a useful essay by Tony Simoes da Silva (in English). The bibliography includes occasional links to pages about individual women writers, sometimes with text of their writings.

International Labour Organization, www.ilo.org/public/english/employment/skills/training/publ/pub7.htm.
"Post-Conflict Mozambique: Women's Special Situation, Issues, and Gender Perspectives to Be Integrated into Skills Training and Employment Promotion," 1997 ILO report by Sally Baden.

Ministry for Women and Social Action, www.mimucas.org.mz/documentos.html.
Report on their June 2000 meeting on violence against women.

Moçambique on-line, Mulheres em Moçambique, www.mol.co.mz/mulheres.
A Portuguese-language network.

Mozambique, www.mozambique.mz/eindex.htm.
Mozambique's official home page.

United Nations, www.un.org/ccosocdev/geninfo/afrec/vol12no4/women.htm.
A brief 1999 article by Ernest Harsch, from United Nations publication *African Recovery*.

University of Bradford, www.brad.ac.uk/research/ijas/rjijasel.htm.
Ruth Jacobson's paper "Gender and Democratisation: The Mozambican Election of 1994," complete text in English.

Women and Law in Southern Africa, www.mulher.org.mz/women_and_law.htm.
English-language home page for Women and Law in Southern Africa, includes list of all of their publications for the region.

Women in Mozambique home page, www.mol.co.mz/mulheres/index.html.
Includes links to other sites on women and to documents in Portuguese and English.

Organizations

COMUTRA (Comité das Mulheres Trabalhadoras, Working Women's Committee)
Departamento da Mulher
Rua António Manuel de Sousa 36
Maputo, Mozambique
Phone: 258-1-428300
Fax: 258-1-494571
Email: comutra@virconn.com

Organização dos Trabalhadores de Moçambique. Founded in 1995, this organization is a network of women's committees in a variety of trade unions and the national umbrella, the Organization of Mozambican Workers (OTM, Organização dos Trabalhadores Moçcambicanos).

Forum Mulher (Women's Forum)
C.P. 3632
Maputo, Mozambique
Phone: 258-1-49347
Fax: 258-1-493137

Fórum Mulher was formed in 1993 as a coalition of nongovernmental organizations concerned with women's issues.

Mozambican Association of Women and Education
Praceta Herois de Mocuba, 130-A
Maputo, Mozambique

Mozambican Women's Organization (OMM: Organização da Mulher Moçambicana)
Rua Pereira do Lago, 147, 2 andar
Maputo, Mozambique
Phone: 258-1-491821

The primary national organization of women, affiliated with the ruling party, Frelimo.

Muleide: Mulher, Lei, e Desenvolvimento (Women, Law, and Development)
Ave. Paulo Samuel Kankhomba, No. 2150
Maputo, Mozambique
Fax: 258-1-425714

Nucleo Mulher e Meio Ambiente (NUMMA, Women and Environment)
P.O. Box 1993
Universidade Eduardo Mondlane
Maputo, Mozambique
Phone: 258-1-490828
Fax: 258-1-491896

União Geral das Cooperativistas (UGC), General Union of Cooperatives
Rua Valentim
Sit: no. 39 — R/C
Caixa Postal no. 4488
Maputo, Mozambique
Phone: 258-1-3067371/430229
Fax: 258-1-306738

Women and Law in Southern Africa (WLSA), Mozambique chapter
P.O. Box 1993
Maputo, Mozambique
Phone: 258-1-490515
Fax: 258-1-491896
Email: wlsamoz@mail.tropical.co.mz

WLSA has promoted regional awareness of legal issues pertaining to women and has published a variety of reports, several specifically about Mozambique.

SELECTED BIBLIOGRAPHY

Agadjanian, Victor. "Negotiating Through Reproductive Change: Gendered Social Interaction and Fertility Regulation in Mozambique." *Journal of Southern African Studies* 27, no. 2 (June 2001): 291–309.

———. "Women's Choice Between Indigenous and Western Contraception." *Journal of Biosocial Science* 32 (2000).

———. "Women's Work and Fertility in a Sub-Saharan Urban Setting: A Social Environment Approach." *Journal of Biosocial Science* 32 (2000).

"AIDS Poses 'Terrible Challenge.' " *Mozambiquefilei* 277 (August 1999): 15–16.

"At Least 1.4 Million Mozambicans Live with HIV." *Panafrican News Agency.* Posted electronically March 27, 2001.

Billetoft, Jørgen. "Coping with Uncertainty, Petty Producers in Postwar Mozambique: Small Business in the Course of Political and Economic Change." CDR Working Paper no. 98.4. Copenhagen: Centre for Development Research, 1998.

Bowen, Merle L. "Beyond Reform: Adjustment and Political Power in Contemporary Mozambique." *Journal of Modern African Studies* 30, no. 2 (1992): 255–79.

Cliff, Julie. "Destabilisation, Economic Adjustment, and the Impact on Women." *Agenda* 14 (1992): 25–38.

Cossa, H. A., et al. "Syphilis and HIV Infection among Displaced Pregnant Women in Rural Mozambique." *International Journal of STD and AIDS* 5 (1994): 117–23.

Galli, Rosemary. "Women and Poverty in the Greater Maputo Area: Some Policy Considerations." Maputo: typescript report for AID, 1992.

Green, R. H. "Mozambique: Into the 1990s." In *Child Survival on the Frontline*, edited by Association of West European Parliamentarians for Action Against Apartheid, 49–52. Amsterdam: African-European Institute, 1990.

Hanlon, Joseph. *Mozambique: Who Calls the Shots?* Bloomington: Indiana University Press, 1991.

Isaacman, Barbara, and June Stephen. *Mozambique: Women, the Law, and Agrarian Reform*. Addis Ababa: United Nations Economic Commission on Africa, 1980, 124.

Jacobson, Ruth. "Women's Political Participation: Mozambique's Democratic Transition." *Gender and Development* 3, no. 3 (October 1995): 29–35.

Johnston, Anton. *Education in Moçambique 1975–84*. Stockholm: Swedish International Development Authority, 1984, 21.

"Land Law Increases Peasant Rights." *Mozambique Peace Process Bulletin* 19 (September 1997): 3–6.

Little, Peter D., and Irae Baptista Lundin de Coloane. "Petty Trade and Household Survival Strategies: A Case Study of Food and Vegetable Traders in the Peri-Urban Areas of Maputo, Mozambique." IDA Working Paper no. 90. Binghamton, NY: Institute for Development Anthropology, 1992, 1, 8.

Marshall, Judith. "War, Debt, and Structural Adjustment in Mozambique: The Social Impact." Ottawa: North-South Institute, 1992.

McCallin, Margaret. "Psychological Needs of Mozambican Refugees: A Community-Based Approach." *Tropical Doctor*, supplement 1, vol. 21 (1991): 67–69.

"Mozambican Women at the Crossroads." *Mozambiquefilei* 174 (1991): 4–6.

"New Legislation Approved." *AIM Information Bulletin* 138 (1988): 4.

O'Laughlin, Bridget. "From Basic Needs to Safety-Nets: The Rise and Fall of Urban Food Rationing in Mozambique." *European Journal of Development Research* 8, no. 1 (June 1996): 200–23.

Pehrsson, Kajsa. "Country Gender Analysis for Mozambique." Stockholm: Swedish International Development Authority, 1994, 21.

"People's Assembly Approves New Constitution." *Mozambiquefilei* 172 (November 1990): 4–10.

Robertson, Claire. "Women's Education and Class Formation in Africa, 1950–1980." In *Women and Class in Africa*, edited by Claire Robertson and Iris Berger, 92–113. New York: Holmes and Meier, 1986.

"Shabby Office a Ray of Hope for Mozambique's Battered Women." *African Eye News Service*. Accessed via *Africa News Online*, September 23, 1998.

Sideris, Tina. "Rape in War and Peace: Some Thoughts on Social Context and Gender Roles." *Agenda* 43 (2000): 41–45.

U.S. Department of State. *Mozambique Country Report on Human Rights Practices for 1997*. www.state.gov/www/global/human_rights/1997_hrp_report/mozambiq/html.

II

NAMIBIA

Gretchen Bauer

PROFILE OF NAMIBIA

Namibia is a large, arid country in southern Africa that only gained its independence in 1990. First colonized by the Germans in the mid-1880s, Namibia became a de facto colony of South Africa when Germany lost its colonies in Africa during World War I. Like South Africa, Namibia had a small but significant white settler population that largely cooperated with the South African authorities and acquiesced in the imposition of the same apartheid policies as in South Africa. From the mid-1960s onward Namibians fled their country in ever increasing numbers to wage a war of independence from exile bases in neighboring countries in an effort to wrest their country from South African control. At the same time, because of Namibia's de jure status as a mandate of the United Nations, international diplomatic efforts were also undertaken to end South Africa's illegal occupation of Namibia. In the late 1980s, in part as a result of the end of the Cold War and efforts to end the civil war in neighboring Angola, a settlement was reached and South Africa agreed to leave Namibia. In April 1989 a yearlong United Nations supervised transition to independence com-

menced, tens of thousands of exiled Namibians were repatriated to their homeland, and on March 21, 1990, Namibia finally obtained its long-sought independence.

At independence a new constitution, considered one of the most liberal and democratic in the world, was adopted. Today, Namibia is a parliamentary democracy that regularly holds elections at the local, regional, and national levels. Local councils (known as local authorities) govern villages, towns, and municipalities, while regional councils and regional governors govern Namibia's thirteen regions. At the national level, a bicameral parliament—comprised of a National Assembly (directly elected) and National Council (elected from the regional councils)—promulgates the laws of the land. Since independence, the government has been led by the South West Africa People's Organisation (SWAPO), the nationalist organization that brought the country to independence and black majority rule. Namibia has a mixed economy, one that privileges the private sector and allocates to government the primary role of creating an enabling environment for the private sector. The economy is dominated by its primary sectors—mining, commercial agriculture, and fishing—with a small manufacturing base and a growing tourist industry. Though considered one of the richest countries in sub-Saharan Africa, Namibia is also marked by a highly unequal distribution of income, with most of the wealth concentrated among the small white minority.

With a population of only 1,797,677 (2001 estimate), Namibia is a very sparsely populated country. Like most African countries, Namibia is ethnically diverse. The largest ethnic group are the Ovambo, who make up just over half the population and reside primarily in northern Namibia and urban areas in central and southern Namibia. Other ethnic groups include the Herero, the Nama-Damara, and the Kavango. There are small populations of white (primarily German and Afrikaans speaking) and mixed-race people known as "Coloureds" as well. Since independence, English has been the national language in Namibia although it is the first language of only a small minority of Namibians. Most Namibians speak one of several African languages as their first language. In the past, Afrikaans (first language to most whites and Coloureds) served as a lingua franca in Namibia, though over the last decade English has gained widespread use.

In 1998, the life expectancy rates at birth for women and men were about the same, 50.6 and 49.5 years, respectively. The infant mortality rate in 1998 was 57 per 1,000 live births and the maternal mortality ratio reported for 1990–1998 was 230 per 100,000 live births. The total fertility rate for the years 1995–2000 stood at 4.9.[1]

OVERVIEW OF WOMEN'S ISSUES

In order to comprehend the status of women in Namibia today, it is necessary to acknowledge the historical legacies of colonialism and apartheid. One hundred years of colonial rule, in particular seventy-five years of

South African white minority rule, created enduring racial and ethnic categories within the small Namibian population. Moreover, a migrant labor system first founded by the Germans, combined with apartheid policies imported from South Africa, ensured that these racial and ethnic categories largely coincided with clear class distinctions. Thus, race and ethnicity formed the basis for significant social, political, and economic discrimination against the majority of Namibians, who were black and lived in the rural areas. Most women in Namibia have suffered from race and class based discrimination as well as gender based discrimination.

With independence, concerted efforts have been undertaken to improve the social, political, and economic position of Namibian women. The Namibian constitution makes special reference to women and their concerns in an independent Namibia mandating, for example, that all persons shall be equal before the law and no persons shall be discriminated against on the grounds of sex, race, color, ethnic origin, religion, creed, or social or economic status. Moreover, the constitution also provides for the enactment of affirmative action legislation as it recognizes that women have suffered special discrimination and need to be encouraged and enabled to play a full, equal, and effective role in the political, socioeconomic, and cultural life of the nation.

EDUCATION

Before independence in Namibia, the education system was administered on an ethnic basis with schools for the black majority generally poorly funded, ill equipped, and lacking in qualified teachers. Since independence efforts have been underway to rectify this situation. Changes have included the establishment of a national education system, a transition from Afrikaans to English as the medium of instruction and a new curriculum at the secondary school level. Education has consistently received the highest share of government revenue in the annual budget. While school enrollments have increased by 20 percent since independence, dropout rates remain high.

Opportunities

In Namibia today, girls make up slightly more than half of all students at all levels.[2] They are less likely than boys to drop out of school at the primary level, although they are more likely than boys to drop out at the secondary level, frequently due to pregnancy and family work demands. At the secondary level, girls are less likely than boys to be promoted to the next grade. At both the secondary and tertiary levels the curricula have remained gender biased. Girls are typically steered into programs for training in careers such as primary school teaching and nursing. Still, women greatly outnumbered men as registered students at the University of Namibia in 1998 (female-male ratio was 1,990 to 1,464), although there were many more men than women (871 men compared with 193 women) enrolled at vocational training centers around the country.[3]

Literacy

Older women in Namibia are taking advantage of adult literacy programs to increase their skill base. Overall, the literacy rates for women and men in Namibia were about the same in 1998, 79.7 and 81.9 percent, respectively.[4]

EMPLOYMENT AND ECONOMICS

Farming

About half of all Namibians earn a living from the land—most eking out a meager existence from small plots of land in the communal areas in northern Namibia—while a much smaller number own or work on large commercial livestock ranches in central and southern Namibia. About 60 percent of those Namibians engaged in subsistence agriculture in the communal areas (usually producing maize, sorghum, or millet) are women. Typically, land in the communal areas is not owned, but is allocated by local leaders to male heads of households, thereby conferring women "usufruct" rights—that is, rights to use the land without legally owning it. In general, women's access to land in the rural areas is based on their relationships with men—husbands, brothers, and uncles. Moreover, discriminatory marriage customs and inheritance systems that favor men imperil women's continued access to land. For example, it is possible for women to lose access to the land that they have farmed once their husbands die. Upon being widowed, they may be forced to return to the home of their relatives. Moreover, women are often less likely than men to be able to take advantage of extension services in the rural areas due to lack of transport or cultural constraints that restrict their activities.[5]

Women who work on commercial farms or who live in households headed by commercial farm workers find themselves in particularly precarious positions. The wages of those employed on commercial farms are very low and the work is often on a casual basis, making for very little job security. In addition, farm workers often face heightened food insecurity and the threat of eviction from their homes at the whim of the commercial farm owner. The threat of abuse and exploitation by employers is also greater on isolated commercial farms.

Paid Employment

As everywhere, women in Namibia are economically active. However, since they are primarily active in subsistence agriculture, domestic service, and the informal sector, their contribution to Namibia's economy is greatly undervalued. As for formal-sector employment, about one-third of those working in the private sector or for government are women. This category includes some women with a secondary school education as well as those with postsecondary education. Though some women with a secondary school education work in agriculture or domestic service (about 36 percent), the rest work in wholesale and retail trade (17 percent), education (12 percent), health and social services (9 percent), and public administration (6 percent), with the remainder in other industries. Highly educated women are mainly employed in the education field, in health and social work, and in community, social, and personal services.

Informal Economic Activities

It is estimated that about one-third of urban households in Namibia resort to informal-sector income-generating activities. As in the formal sector, men in Namibia tend to dominate the high-income-generating occupations while women work in the lower-income-generating activities. So, men drive taxis, repair cars, and run shops while women cook food, brew beer, and make handicrafts, selling all of their wares out of their homes or in the streets or open air markets. Moreover, there are constraints to women's informal sector activity, including lack of access to credit, markets, and raw materials and competition from cheap manufactured goods imported from South Africa.

Pay

Large wage differentials between men and women exist in Namibia. Even women working in formal-sector jobs are concentrated in low-paying occupations.[6] While about half of all economically active women are involved in agriculture, another 10 percent perform domestic service. Alongside farm workers, domestic workers earn the lowest wages in the country and, because they work alone in their employer's home, are susceptible to intimidation from their employers. Domestic workers typically lack basic literacy skills, work long hours, and have no access to the benefits of formal sector employment. Because of the low wages, many domestic workers are forced to turn to the informal sector to supplement their income.

Support for Mothers/Caretakers

Since independence several new laws have been passed that attempt to improve conditions of employment for Namibian workers. A number of these have provisions that affect women in particular. For example, the Labour Act of 1992 prohibits employers from practicing unfair discrimination or harassment on the basis of sex, marital status, and sexual orientation, among other factors.

Maternal Leave

The Labour Act guarantees female employees who have been working for the same employer for one year the right to twelve weeks of maternity leave. The Social Security Act of 1994 provides for the extension of maternity benefits to women employees. The act establishes a Social Security Commission charged with administering a number of funds, including a Maternity Leave, Sick Leave, and Death Benefit Fund. Membership in the fund is mandatory for all employees. Benefits paid by the fund include up to 80 percent of basic pay for a woman on maternity leave.

The Labour Act further requires that women receive pension and health insurance benefits while on maternity leave and that they not lose seniority or promotion rights while on maternity leave. Of course maternity leave and maternity benefits are only available to formal sector employees, the majority of whom are not women. The Labour Act makes no provision for paternity leave and very few employers voluntarily offer paternity leaves or benefits in Namibia.

Child Care

As in many societies, child care is a formidable obstacle for Namibian women who work outside the home. Very few employers offer child care facilities on their premises. While privately run nurseries and child care centers do exist, they tend to be prohibitively expensive for many working Namibian women and the quality varies sharply from place to place. In general, the solution to the child care challenge in Namibia is for women to rely on members of their extended family, in particular grandmothers or other female relatives. An important implication of this pattern is that females have "little or no time to participate in income generating activities, literacy classes, or any other developmental activities."[7] A 1992 study found that 37 percent of Namibian households included children under the age of fifteen living with relatives apart from both parents. Older siblings also often provide child care for working mothers.[8]

Social/Government Programs

In 1998 the Affirmative Action (Employment) Act was passed; the goal of this act is to ensure that racially disadvantaged people, women, and individuals with disabilities enjoy equal opportunities at all levels of employment and are equitably represented in the workforce. The act focuses on the elimination of employment barriers and the institution of positive measures to increase employment opportunities for these groups.

FAMILY AND SEXUALITY

Gender Roles and Division of Labor

The overall ratio of males to females in Namibia is 95 to 100, although there are significant regional variations. For example, in some of the central and southern regions of the country there may be as many as 125 males per 100 females while in some northern regions there may be as few as 79 males per 100 females.[9] Historical factors largely account for these skewed gender ratios. In particular, the early establishment of a contract migrant labor system meant that men migrated to centers of formal economic activity: to mines in central and southern Namibia, the capital city of Windhoek, and the fishing industry on the coast.

For women in the rural areas, the continued migration of their men to jobs in cities and towns has meant that they are responsible for maintaining the rural homestead, producing the agricultural crops and caring for the children and the elderly. Women are further disadvantaged by remaining behind in the rural areas because there is less access to health care, education, and employment opportunities than in the urban areas. As a result of the migrant labor system, nearly 40 percent of households in

Namibian woman in the kitchen of a tin hut in the desert. Photo © TRIP/B. Crawshaw.

Namibia are female-headed. Such households offer a worse standard of living for members than do male-headed households. Female-headed households are less likely to own durable goods or have access to electricity, water and sanitation facilities, and health care than male-headed households.

Marriage

At any given time, about half of the women in Namibia are married. According to a 1992 health and demographic survey conducted in Namibia, 42 percent of women between fifteen and forty-nine years were married or living with someone in an informal union. An additional 7 percent of respondents were widowed, divorced, or separated. In Namibia there are two types of marriages—customary and civil.

In Namibia, customary law continues to exert at least some influence in the rural areas, where most Namibian women live. Officially, customary law may still be practiced in Namibia, so long as its provisions do not contradict those of the constitution of Namibia.

Customary marriages are not necessarily registered, may be polygamous, and vary in nature from community to community. According to some, customary marriages may be seen as alliances between two kinship groups rather than just between two individuals. The paying of a brideprice may also be involved.

Civil marriages are registered and governed by the 1996 Married Persons Equality Act. Civil marriages appear to be growing in popularity in Namibia, partly due to the strong influence of Christianity in the country. It is not unusual for people to marry according to both civil and customary law.

The Married Persons Equality Act made men and women equal before the law in marriage. The act invalidates marital powers that had made the husband the head of the household. It also provides for women in common-law marriages to have equal access to bank loans and ownership of property. The act also provides for equal guardianship over minor children of a marriage. Divorce in Namibia may still be granted on the assumption of one or the other parties being guilty or innocent. A larger share of communal assets is usually awarded to the innocent party, all the more so if the innocent one is the man.

Reproduction

The average number of children born live per woman in Namibia is 6.1. This rate is lower in urban areas (4.7) than in rural areas (6.8). The main reasons for the discrepancy between urban and rural areas are the availability of contraception and the high cost of living in urban areas. The average age that a woman in Namibia has her first child is twenty-one, with many women having their first child before marrying. As everywhere, the fertility rate for women in Namibia falls as education levels and employment opportunities rise. The total fertility rate for women with no formal education is almost nine children as compared with about three children for women who have completed grade twelve. The total fertility rate for self-employed and unpaid family workers is about eight compared to about three for government workers.[10] Most women consider five to be the ideal number of children for one family.

Sex Education

Sex education is not available in Namibian schools because most parents and educators believe it makes students more sexually active.

Contraception and Abortion

Knowledge about contraception and family planning options in Namibia is high, though their use is low. About 90 percent of all women know of at least one family planning method although only 23 percent of women currently use some form of contraception. The most widely known methods are the injection, the pill, condoms, and female sterilization.[11] Urban women are four times more likely to use contraception than are rural women. Contraceptive use is also higher among educated women and those living near health facilities that provide family planning services. Reasons given by women for not using contraceptives include cost, lack of information, negative attitudes, perceived side effects, religious or moral objections, and fear of partners' disapproval.[12] At the same time, the 2000 National Gender Study revealed that many women see reducing the number of children as a good way to combat poverty.[13]

Abortion is legal in Namibia under very limited circumstances, including danger to a woman's mental or physical health or to the fetus, rape, incest, and HIV infection. Attempts to liberalize the abortion law in Namibia were defeated in April 1999, when legislators abandoned a draft Abortion and Sterilisation Bill, claiming pervasive opposition to the bill from the populace.

Obtaining permission for a legal abortion is costly, time consuming, and complicated with the result that many women, especially girls, seek illegal abortions. Resorting to illegal and self-induced abortion clearly poses a danger to the health and lives of girls and women in Namibia. Infanticide is another increasingly common method by which young women, especially, avoid unwanted children. Many newly born babies are simply discarded, dying of exposure, though others are actually killed.

Teen Pregnancy

Teenage pregnancy is a growing problem in Namibia. In 1992, 45 percent of nineteen-year-olds were either pregnant or had already given birth to a baby.[14] As noted earlier, a significant number of girls are likely to leave school early as a result of pregnancy. In some cases, girls simply drop out of school because they are pregnant; if they do not, they are expelled because pregnant girls are not allowed to attend school. While the phenomenon is widespread, teenage pregnancy is not socially accepted and girls rather than males usually take the blame for their condition. Typically, those who impregnate the girls are teachers and other older men, rather than their male classmates. The high teenage pregnancy rate in Namibia has been linked to high rates of illegal abortion and infanticide. Schoolgirls even attempt to induce miscarriages on their own, for example, by drinking bleach or taking certain medications. Many girls cite the desire to return to school as a reason for hiding a pregnancy and discarding a baby.[15]

HEALTH

Health Care Access

At independence in 1990 Namibia's health care system was biased toward the white population and urban areas and emphasized curative services over preventive services. Since independence, the government has sought to change this situation through the adoption of a community-based primary health care strategy for the majority population in the neglected rural and urban areas. According to the Department of Women Affairs (DWA), this strategy has increased women's access to health care in Namibia.

Nonetheless, discrepancies still exist: women in urban areas in Namibia today have far better access to health facilities than do rural women. On average, women take about forty minutes to travel to a health facility in Namibia, with women in northwest Namibia traveling well over an hour. Women complain that health care facilities need to be more conveniently located and open for longer hours. Moreover, though most health facilities charge only nominal fees, the fees, combined with travel costs and the opportunity costs of lost work time, mean that health care costs can be high. About 56 percent of women in Namibia have access to prenatal health care, 48 percent to maternity care, 72 percent to immunization services, and 49 percent to family planning services within ten kilometers of their homes. The services most available at health facilities around the country include immunization, education on HIV/AIDS, use of condoms, family planning, and child care.[16]

Diseases and Disorders

AIDS

Along with other countries in southern Africa, Namibia has one of the highest HIV infection rates in the world. In 1999, UNAIDS estimated that 9.4 percent of the adult population was HIV positive, though many consider this figure to underestimate the true prevalence of HIV infection (more likely around 20–25 percent of the adult population). In 1998, 12,700 new cases of HIV infection were reported, an increase of 1,100 over the previous year. Although more men than women are infected with the virus in Namibia, in recent years (since 1998) women have accounted for 53 percent of all new reported HIV cases; thus women are being infected at a higher rate than men. Women are also diagnosed at a younger age than men, with the median age being thirty for women and thirty-four for men.

A number of factors are thought to account for the high HIV infection rate among women. Women may be more susceptible to infection if exposed. Other factors include early marriages, illiteracy among women,

women's lack of control over their own fertility, teenage pregnancies, rape, alcohol and drug abuse, prostitution to meet economic needs, culturally accepted promiscuity among men, and unequal sexual relationships between men and women even within marriage.[17]

HIV/AIDS is the greatest health threat to women and men in Namibia and other countries in southern Africa today. The government of Namibia has responded to the AIDS crisis with a five-year national strategic plan to combat HIV/AIDS in Namibia (1998–2003), following two previous plans (1990–1992 and 1992–1997). Among other things, the plan focuses on the mobilization of women, youth, and workers in the fight against AIDS. The plan includes, as well, a campaign to raise public awareness of the epidemic, the distribution of free condoms, and counseling, care, and support for those affected by the virus.

Female Genital Cutting

Female genital cutting is rarely practiced in Namibia. Some ethnic groups perform minor cutting of the vaginal lips, but there is no radical female genital cutting as is found elsewhere in Africa, where the clitoris or labia are removed.

POLITICS AND LAW

Leadership and Decision-making

With its independence in 1990, Namibia faced an unique opportunity to remake its polity and society. Among other things, this has offered the chance to begin to transform gender relations in Namibia. The first point at which this opportunity presented itself was in the writing of a new constitution. As noted earlier, the constitution of the Republic of Namibia makes special reference to the status of women in Namibia and the need to redress past discrimination against women. Indeed, legal scholars and women activists in Namibia have spent much of the first decade of independence attempting to operationalize these constitutional provisions. They have sought to reform past gender discriminatory legislation and to promote gender sensitive public policies.

In a relatively short period, considerable progress has been made. For example, in August 1990 a Department of Women Affairs was established within the Office of the President. The DWA played a key role in bringing gender issues onto the national agenda, facilitating communication between women and the government, and helping to identify priority areas for action on issues related to women. In 2000 the DWA was upgraded to a Ministry of Women Affairs and Child Welfare. For some women activists in Namibia, none of whom called for the creation of a separate ministry, this move represents a step backward. In their view, women's affairs are now much more likely to be marginalized and confined to one ministry rather than dispersed throughout ministries and sectors of government.

Quota Laws

Another goal of legal scholars and women activists in Namibia has been to facilitate the election of more women to political office. All citizens eighteen years of age and older have the right to vote. Since independence, considerable progress has been made on this front as well. In 2001, women made up 40 percent of local councillors in local governments around the country and in 2003 they made up 26.4 percent of parliamentarians in the National Assembly. By contrast, only 4 percent of regional councillors are women and, as a result, only two members out of twenty-six who are elected from regional councils into the National Council are women. This relatively high percentage of women elected to political office at the local and national levels can be attributed to the electoral system employed and to the use of electoral quotas. In Namibia, a closed list proportional representation system is employed in local council and National Assembly elections. In regional council elections in Namibia, by contrast, where women have fared very poorly, the plurality or winner-take-all method is utilized.

In Namibia, the law in local elections requires quotas. The Local Authorities Act of 1992, amended and strengthened in 1997, mandates that approximately 25 percent of candidates in local elections be women, although the law does not specify what positions must be given to women on party lists.[18] The Directorate of Elections, however, has recommended that parties arrange their lists in a "zebra manner," meaning that women be dispersed throughout the list, alternating with men, rather than grouped at the end of the list. Political parties in Namibia have largely complied with this voluntary request, as is evident by the fact that significant numbers of women have been elected at the local level.

As a result of these institutional changes, increasing numbers of women have been elected with each election. In the 1992 local authorities elections women won 31 percent of the seats, and in the 1998 elections women won 40 percent of the seats. The percentage of candidates who were women increased markedly in 1998—up to 47 percent from 38 percent in 1992. Moreover, nearly every party came close to the ideal of 50 percent representation of women on its party list, though fewer women were placed in positions one and two in the 1998 election than in the 1992 election.[19]

For the regional and national levels in Namibia, however, no such laws exist. By 2003, 26 percent of the parliamentarians were women, up considerably from the 1989 (7 percent) and 1994 (18 percent) elections. Several political parties can attribute these "relatively" high figures for female political representation to their voluntary adoption of informal quotas. In advance of the 1999 National Assembly elections, the Women's Manifesto Network, a coalition of women's, nongovernmental, and community organizations, challenged political parties to draw up party lists in which 50 percent of the candidates were women. Within a month of the network's challenge, several political parties proclaimed publicly their support for including more women on their party lists. As a result eighteen women gained seats in a parliament of seventy-two members. This shows evidence of some commitment on the part of political parties to meeting the challenge of the Women's Manifesto Network.

Political Participation

Outside of elected political office, however, women do not fare so well in high government positions in Namibia. As of September 2001, only two of nineteen ministers were women: predictably, the minister of women affairs and child welfare and the minister of health and social services. As of mid-June 1999 there were no female judges on the High Court in Namibia. Two of six members of the Public Service Commission were women and the Ombudsman was a woman. Only one of twenty permanent secretaries and three of twelve deputy permanent secretaries were women. Further down the hierarchy, twenty-three of eighty-nine directors within ministries were women as well as twenty-nine of 173 deputy directors. Only two of nineteen ambassadors or high commissioners were women.

Women's Rights

In 1992, a Law Reform and Development Commission (LRDC) was established to oversee the bringing of new and existing laws into compliance with Namibia's constitution. The LRDC established a Women and Law Committee to focus attention on the need to eliminate gender-related legal disparities between women and men in Namibia. Several of the new laws promulgated since independence were initiated or influenced by the LRDC. Also in 1992, the Namibian parliament ratified the United Nations Convention on the Elimination of All Forms of Discrimination Against Women. In 1995 the Legal Practitioners Act was passed to promote greater access to the legal profession and to legal representation for all sectors of society.

In 1997, following the recommendations of the Fourth United Nations World Conference on Women, a National Gender Policy (NGP) was launched by government and adopted by parliament in 1999. The NGP aims, ultimately, to end all forms of gender discrimination. It addresses ten critical areas of concern identified in the Beijing Platform of Action, including gender and economic empowerment, the girl child, and gender and legal affairs. The policy provides for the creation of monitoring mechanisms to oversee its implementation. These include a Gender Commission, Gender Focal Points, a Gender Sectoral Committee, and a Gender Network Coordinating Committee. The NGP was complemented by a plan of action in 1998, "which aims at translating policy into practice."[20]

Women's Movements

A number of women's organizations exist in Namibia, though it may be somewhat premature to speak of a unified women's movement. Most of the political parties have women's wings that serve primarily to mobilize women for elections and to advance women within the party hierarchy. In most cases, every female member of a party automatically becomes a member of the women's wing of the party. Of these, the SWAPO Women's Council, formed early on in the liberation movement's exile days, is the most significant. Similarly, other national organizations, such as the Namibia National Students' Organisation, have gender subcommittees or women's sections to promote gender equity among their members and peers.

The major trade union federation, the National Union of Namibian Workers (NUNW), runs leadership training programs for women and requires that all member unions work toward the better integration of women into their structures. About 40 percent of signed up members of the NUNW unions are women, with women predominating in certain unions such as the domestic workers union, the teachers union, and the food and allied workers union. The NUNW seeks to have women constituting 40 percent of the delegations to national and international meetings. Female secretary generals and other officeholders are not uncommon.

Apart from the women's wings of political parties and women's sections of national federations, a range of other groups exists that focus more explicitly on women's issues. Several high-profile national organizations are based in Windhoek. For example, the Namibian National Women's Organisation (NANAWO) was originally formed as an umbrella organization for Namibian women's groups but was later changed to be a group of individual rather than organizational members. NANAWO members include many black female civil servants as well as large numbers of women in the rural north. NANAWO has been active in law reform and health and social sector policy development.

Sister Namibia is an organization formed just before independence that engages in advocacy work on issues such as violence against women, women's health, and reproductive rights. Sister Namibia tends to reach the limited audience in Namibia of highly educated, urban women. Women's Action for Development provides basic training in income generation and other skills for women in rural areas, and in 1997 launched the nonpartisan Women's Voice with the goal of encouraging more women to stand for elective office.

Finally, Women Solidarity, another Windhoek-based group, provides counseling services and works with community organizations around issues of rape and violence against women. Beyond the Windhoek-based national-level organizations, the mobilization of women tends to revolve around local churches and self-help associations. At the same time, many of the national organizations have realized that such locally based groups provide an entry point for the further mobilization and engagement of women.

Women in Namibia clearly realize the need to mobilize in order to strengthen their position in Namibian politics and society. For example, in 1996 women in parliament united across party lines to form a Women's Caucus to increase their influence in parliament. As noted earlier, in 1998 a Namibia Elected Women Forum emerged to develop strategies for increasing the number of women on regional councils. Women's groups have occasionally organized demonstrations around the country in support of particular legislation or, more frequently, to protest rising levels of violence against women in Namibia.

Many groups are urban based and have failed to attract large numbers of younger women. Moreover, there is still not enough cooperation among women's groups that would make the women's movement a strong force to be reckoned with. Women in Namibia remain divided by race, class, and party political affiliations. As a result, it is argued, women and their organizations still do not lobby enough as a united front on issues such as women's representation in government, women's role in the AIDS crisis, gender equity in education and the economy, access to social services, and the power of customary law.

Women activists in Namibia are also actively involved in regional and international organizations working to promote women's interests and improve women's positions. There are a number of organizations in southern Africa that represent both grassroots level women's organization and national level women's organizations. Groups such as Women in Development Southern Africa Awareness Program, the Southern African People's Solidarity Network, and the Southern African NGO Network include Namibian women and their grassroots level organizations. Regional members of parliament belong to a Working Group to Enhance Women's Representation and Promotion of the Consideration of Gender Issues within Parliaments in Southern Africa. The Southern African Development Community, to which Namibia belongs, has issued a gender declaration.

For Namibian women activists and their organizations, participation in the Fourth United Nations World Conference on Women in Beijing in 1995 was a pivotal experience. Namibia sent a fifty-six-person delegation, headed by then–deputy foreign affairs minister Netumbo Nandi-Ndaitwah, who served as the rapporteur for the conference. The Namibian delegation was particularly concerned to learn about the experiences of women in other countries around a core set of issues including violence against women, alcohol and drug abuse, teenage pregnancy, the girl child, and poverty and illiteracy among rural women. Following the Beijing conference, southern African conference participants, with the goal of implementing a regional Gender Plan of Action, established a regional Gender Task Force.

Military Service

In Namibia today women and men are free to join the Namibian Defense Force (NDF) on a volunteer basis. The NDF numbers about 6,000; and as of mid-June 1999, however, there were no female officers in the NDF. At the same time, women in Namibia have a long history of involvement with the military, primarily through their role as combatants in the war for independence.

Among the very first exiles to leave Namibia for Tanzania in the early 1960s, only three were women. But by the early 1970s the percentage of women fleeing the country reached 20 percent and by the time of the repatriation of exiles in 1989 about 40 percent were women. From 1974 onward all young women exiles who were unmarried and had no children received military training. Male and female recruits received the same military training and were supposed to carry out the same tasks within the People's Liberation Army of Namibia (PLAN), the armed wing of the movement for independence from South Africa. The full integration of women into the PLAN was the result of pressure from the SWAPO Women's Council. The extensive presence of women in the NDF today is a result of their early involvement in the armed wing of the exiled liberation movement.

RELIGION AND SPIRITUALITY

Namibia is a highly Christianized country. It is estimated that 90 percent of the population belongs to a Christian denomination. Nearly half (48 percent) identify themselves as Lutheran, 32 percent as Roman Catholic, 10 percent as Dutch Reformed, 8 percent as Anglican, and 2 percent as Methodist.[21] In addition, there are a number of smaller, independent African churches. Christian missionaries first arrived in Namibia in the mid-1800s. For Namibian men and women, the missionary presence and conversion to Christianity meant abandoning many aspects of traditional culture. At the same time, though many women found themselves as servants of missionaries, others found that fleeing to the missions could be a liberating experience, removing them from an otherwise restrictive life. For many, especially women, the missions were critical in offering otherwise unavailable services such as schools and clinics. Over time, as some churches became Africanized, they became involved in the struggle for Namibia's independence and became some of the strongest voices against the continued South African occupation of the territory.[22]

In 1978 a number of black churches in Namibia formed a national federation, the Council of Churches of Namibia (CCN). In its early years, the CCN offered a range of social service programs to a needy population At independence the CCN, in particular its women members, played a critical role in the repatriation of the tens of thousands of Namibian exiles. Since independence, the CCN has been seen by many as a key organization of civil society, paying close attention to government initiatives and policies, and attempting to hold the ruling party accountable for its actions before independence and after. For more than a decade the CCN has had an active Women's Desk, which was an articulate voice for the needs of the churches' mostly women members.[23]

Women's Roles

Women in Namibia have held some leadership roles within their churches, although the ordination of women is a fairly recent phenomenon. The Evangelical Lutheran Church, the black Lutheran church in central and southern Namibia, decided to begin ordaining women in the early 1970s. However, by 1992 there were still only three women pastors. The Evangelical Lutheran Church in Namibia, the main church in northern Namibia, only approved the ordination of women in late 1991. By 1997, however, eighteen women had been ordained in the Lutheran Church and two in the Anglican Church.

In addition to the social services provided, organized religion in Namibia has been critical to women in another important respect. To the extent that women in the rural areas have organized themselves, they join local church groups. In fact, women's groups have been described as the "backbone of the church" in Namibia and women constitute the majority of its members. Before independence, rural church groups provided opportunities for women to meet and experience female solidarity in communities that had largely disintegrated as a result of war and repression.[24] Such groups were usually the sole basis for mutual help in the rural north, a help that was sorely needed during the decades of war. Neither "women's emancipation" nor "politics" were ever explicit objectives of these groups, however. Rather, the church groups confined themselves to conventional religious activities and social support.

As elsewhere, some religious leaders in Namibia have used religion as the basis for opposition to the adoption of new legislation or social policy favorable to women. For example, many religious leaders took a public stand against the proposed Abortion and Sterilization Bill and others have cited religious reasons for their opposition to AIDS education or more liberalized family planning policies. In response to such efforts to undermine the adoption of policies integral to women's well being, the Department of Women Affairs organized a group called the Ecumenical Women of Namibia and held a conference in 1992 to address some of the pressing issues facing women. It was at this event that Namibian president Sam

Nujoma signed the Convention on the Elimination of All Forms of Discrimination Against Women.[25]

VIOLENCE

Domestic Violence

Violence against women in Namibia is widespread. Domestic violence, in particular, may be even more prevalent in Namibia than in the past. One study suggests that half of all Namibian women and children have been or will be victims of domestic violence at some time in their lives.[26] In March 2001 it was reported that about 2,000 cases of domestic violence are reported each year in Namibia, making up one-fifth of all criminal cases. Despite its prevalence, domestic violence is not widely reported, in part because it is perceived as a family affair and in part because police lack legal remedies.

Rape/Sexual Assault

The incidence of rape also appears to be on the rise in Namibia. Before independence, in 1988, 352 rapes were reported to police; by 1994, 740 rapes were reported. This may reflect either a growing number of rapes or a higher percentage of rapes reported. In any event, it is assumed that the number of rapes reported is far fewer than actually occur.[27]

A number of proactive measures are being taken to try to combat the high levels of violence and rape against women. In November 1996 the Women and Law Committee held a series of regional hearings on violence against women in an effort to gain a better understanding of the issue.[28] Centers for abused women and children in major towns such as Oshakati, Windhoek, Keetmanshoop, Walvis Bay, and Rehoboth are staffed with specially trained female police officers able to assist victims of sexual assault and abuse. A newly established national police training center now offers a special training unit on gender sensitivity and safe houses for women and children have been opened in Mariental, Swakopmund, and Tsumeb. Indeed, the government continues to expand its network of woman and child protection units, just as many government officials and community leaders are strongly voicing opposition to violence against women and children.

In addition, two important pieces of legislation—the Combating of Rape Act and the Combating of Immoral Practices Amendment Act—came into effect in June 2000. A first draft of a third—a Domestic Violence Bill—was sent to parliament for public discussion in April 2001. The Combating of Rape Bill makes it illegal to commit a sexual act under a variety of coercive circumstances. It also prescribes minimum sentences for convicted rapists and precludes marriage or any other relationship from being a defense to a rape charge. The act also widens the definition of rape to include men as potential victims and places greater emphasis on the rights of rape victims.

The Combating of Immoral Practices Amendment Act makes it an offense for a person to commit or try to commit a sexual act with a child less than sixteen years of age.[29] The draft Domestic Violence Bill seeks to broaden the definition of domestic violence to include sexual, economic, emotional, verbal, or psychological abuse as well as intimidation and harassment. The draft bill also provides for any interested party to lay a charge of domestic violence on behalf of the victim, for the mandatory arrest of perpetrators in certain cases, and for the police to have enhanced powers of arrest without a warrant.[30]

War and Military Repression

Primarily as a result of the decades of war and repression (from the mid-1960s through the late 1980s), violence against women has a long heritage in Namibia. Indeed, in northern Namibia where the war for independence was fought, the South African forces of occupation considered everyone an accomplice to SWAPO and they carried out an open policy of violent intimidation and torture of civilians. The population, two-thirds of whom were women and children, lived under martial law, including a dusk-to-dawn curfew and the constant threat of detention. There were frequent incidents of torture, rape, beatings, murder, and other forms of harassment.

In response to the curfew and conditions of martial law, women armed themselves with certain skills. They also learned first aid and midwifery to assist those unable to travel to a clinic. They learned reading skills and English to stay informed of what might be happening with relatives or children outside the country. And they assisted in the resistance against South Africa by playing a supportive role to the PLAN combatants or to Namibian men wanted by the authorities. They carried messages, housed and fed combatants, and stored and transported arms and ammunition. But they paid a heavy price in terms of the brutal treatment meted out on them by the South African Defense Forces and their Namibian counterparts.[31]

Today Namibia is no longer at war, but violence against women persists. That violence against women includes physical, psychological, sexual, and financial abuse. Violence against women is made worse by poverty, unemployment, and high rates of alcoholism and drug abuse among men, and cultural norms and women's perceived low social status. Indeed, setting aside the war-induced violence of the 1970s and 1980s, violence against women in Namibia has increased dramatically since independence in 1990. This is attributed to the fact that although women's legal status has changed considerably since independence, their social status, for the most part, has not changed. At the same time, the changes that have occurred have also threatened male social status and men's positions as heads of households. Others attribute the high incidence of violence against women to "the problem of a strong culture advocating the superiority of men."

OUTLOOK FOR THE TWENTY-FIRST CENTURY

In the years since independence in Namibia, significant strides have been made toward creating a more equitable environment for women in Namibia. In particular, the use of the proportional representation electoral system and electoral quotas has helped to bring many women into political office, at least at the local and national levels. Moreover, through the enactment of a whole new body of laws, considerable progress has been made in establishing a more just legal framework in the country. Regional and international institutions and a nascent women's movement are reinforcing these developments. All are geared toward transforming gender relations at all levels. But while bringing more women into politics and adopting progressive new laws must be applauded, the more formidable challenges of changing attitudes, cultures, customs, and traditions remain. Given the history of race-, class-, and gender-based discrimination against women in Namibia, and their courageous responses to it, there seems little doubt that women in Namibia will continue to rise to these and other challenges.

NOTES

1. United Nations Development Programme (UNDP), *Human Development Report* (New York: Oxford University Press, 2000), 163, 188, 225.
2. Eunice Iipinge and Debie LeBeau, *Beyond Inequalities: Women in Namibia* (Namibia: Gender Training and Research Programme, Social Sciences Division, University of Namibia, 1997), 55.
3. Department of Women Affairs (DWA), *Namibia National Progress Report on the Implementation of the Beijing Platform for Action* (Windhoek: DWA, Office of the President, 1997), 26.
4. UNDP, *Human Development Report*, 163.
5. Iipinge and LeBeau, *Beyond Inequalities*, 38.
6. DWA, *CEDAW: First Country Report—Republic of Namibia* (Windhoek: DWA, Office of the President, 1995), 91–92, 94.
7. E. M. Iipinge, F. A. Phiri, and A. F. Njabili, eds., *The National Gender Study*, vol. 1 (Windhoek: University of Namibia, 2000), 270.
8. DWA, *CEDAW*, 99–100.
9. Iipinge and LeBeau, *Beyond Inequalities*, 45–46.
10. Ibid., 73.
11. DWA, *CEDAW*, 107.
12. Iipinge and LeBeau, *Beyond Inequalities*, 74.
13. E. M. Iipinge, F. A. Phiri, and A. E. Njabili, eds., *The National Gender Study*, vol. 1 (Windhoek: University of Namibia, 2000), 265.
14. DWA, *CEDAW*, 107.

15. DWA, *CEDAW*, 107.

16. Iipinge and LeBeau, *Beyond Inequalities*, 70, 71, 159.

17. DWA, *Namibia National Progress Report*, 35–37.

18. Kapena Tjihero, Doufi Namalambo, and Dianne Hubbard, *Affirmative Action for Women in Local Government in Namibia: The 1998 Local Government Elections* (Windhoek: Legal Assistance Centre, 1998), 2.

19. Ibid., 18–19.

20. Heike Becker, "A Concise History of Gender, 'Tradition,' and the State in Namibia," in *State, Society, and Democracy: A Reader in Namibian Politics*, ed. Christiann Keulder (Windhoek: Gamsberg Macmillan, 2000), 189.

21. Iipinge and LeBeau, *Beyond Inequalities*, 51.

22. Tessa Cleaver and Marion Wallace, *Namibia Women in War* (London: Zed Books, 1990), 103–8.

23. Ibid., 109–20.

24. Becker, "Concise History of Gender," 195.

25. Iipinge and LeBeau, *Beyond Inequalities*, 51.

26. Ibid., 78.

27. Ibid., 80.

28. Ibid., 77.

29. *The Namibian*, June 19, 2000, www.nambian.com.na.

30. *The Namibian*, February 20, 2001.

31. Iina Soiri, *The Radical Motherhood: Namibian Women's Independence Struggle*, Research Report no. 99 (Uppsala: Nordiska Afrikainstitutet, 1996), 59; Cleaver and Wallace, *Namibia Women in War*, 1–5.

RESOURCE GUIDE

Suggested Reading

Becker, Heike. *Namibian Women's Movement 1980 to 1992: From Anti-Colonial Resistance to Reconstruction*. Frankfurt: Verlag fuer Interkulturelle Kommunikation, 1994.

Cleaver, Tessa, and Marion Wallace. *Namibia Women in War*. London: Zed Books, 1990.

Cooper, A. D. "State Sponsorship of Women's Rights and Implications for Patriarchism in Namibia." *Journal of Modern Africa Studies* 35, no. 3 (September 1997): 469–83.

Hubbard, Dianne, and Colette Solomon. "The Many Faces of Feminism in Namibia." In *The Challenge of Local Feminisms: Women's Movements in Global Perspective*, edited by Amrita Basu. Boulder: Westview Press, 1995.

Schlyter, A. *Beyond Inequalities: Women in Namibia. Journal of Modern Afica Studies* 37, no. 3 (September 1999): 570–71.

Soiri, Iina. *The Radical Motherhood: Namibian Women's Independence Struggle*. Research Report no. 99. Uppsala: Nordiska Afrikainstitutet, 1996.

Web Sites

Africa Online Women, http://lagos.africaonline.com/site/africa/women.jsp.
Africawide source on women around the continent.

All Africa Women and Gender, http://allafrica.com/women/.
Useful site for recent news reports on women around Africa.

Government of the Republic of Namibia, www.grnnet.gov.na.
The official website of the Namibian government.

The Namibian, www.namibian.com.na.
Namibia's most popular daily newspaper; provides comprehensive coverage of women's and gender related issues.

Women Watch, www.un.org/womenwatch/daw.
The United Nations gateway to information on women's issues worldwide.

Women's Net, www.womensnet.org.za.
South African–based women's networking program designed to enable southern African women to use the web to find the people, issues, resources, and tools needed for women's social action.

Organizations

Council of Churches of Namibia
Women's Desk
P.O. Box 41
Windhoek, Namibia
Phone: 264-61-217621

Gender Training and Research Programme
Social Sciences Division
University of Namibia
Private Bag 13301
Windhoek, Namibia
Phone: 264-61-2063951

Legal Assistance Centre
Gender Research Unit
P.O. Box 604
Windhoek, Namibia
Phone: 264-61-223356

Namibian National Women's Organisation
P.O. Box 2359
Windhoek, Namibia
Phone: 264-61-217621

Sister Namibia
P.O. Box 40092
Windhoek, Namibia
Phone: 264-61-230618/230757

SELECTED BIBLIOGRAPHY

Becker, Heike. "A Concise History of Gender, 'Tradition,' and the State in Namibia." In *State, Society, and Democracy: A Reader in Namibian Politics*, edited by Christiann Keulder. Windhoek: Gamsberg Macmillan, 2000.

———. *Namibian Women's Movement 1980 to 1992: From Anti-Colonial Resistance to Reconstruction*. Frankfurt. Verlag fuer Interkulturelle Kommunikation, 1994.

Cleaver, Tessa, and Marion Wallace. *Namibia Women in War*. London: Zed Books, 1990.

Department of Women Affairs (DWA). *CEDAW: First Country Report — Republic of Namibia*. Windhoek: DWA, Office of the President, 1995.

———. *Namibia National Progress Report on the Implementation of the Beijing Platform for Action*. Windhoek: DWA, Office of the President, 1999.

Hubbard, Dianne. "Gender Scorecard 2000." www.lac.org.na/html/gscore00.htm.

Hubbard, Dianne, and Colette Solomon. "The Many Faces of Feminism in Namibia." In *The Challenge of Local Feminisms: Women's Movements in Global Perspective*, edited by Amrita Basu. Boulder: Westview Press, 1995.

Hubbard, Dianne, and Kaveri Kavari. *Affirmative Action for Women in Local Government in Namibia*. Windhoek: Legal Assistance Centre, 1993.

Iipinge, Eunice, and Debie LeBeau. *Beyond Inequalities: Women in Namibia*. Namibia: Gender Training and Research Programme, Social Sciences Division, University of Namibia, 1992.

Iipinge, E. M., F. A. Phiri, and A. F. Njabili, eds. *The National Gender Study*. Vol. 1. Windhoek: University of Namibia, 2000.

Labour Resource and Research Institute (Larri). *Still Fighting for Social Justice: A Survey of Trade Unions, Women's Organisations, Communal Farmers, and Service Organisations in Namibia*. Windhoek: Larri, 1998.

Soiri, Iina. *The Radical Motherhood: Namibian Women's Independence Struggle*. Research Report no. 99. Uppsala: Nordiska Afrikainstitutet, 1996.

Tjihero, Kapena, Doufi Namalambo, and Dianne Hubbard. *Affirmative Action for Women in Local Government in Namibia: The 1998 Local Government Elections*. Windhoek: Legal Assistance Centre, 1998.

United Nations Development Programme (UNDP). *Human Development Report*. New York: Oxford University Press, 2000.

U.S. Department of State. *Human Rights Reports for 1999: Namibia* (2000). www.state.gov/www/global/human_rights/1999.

12

NIGER

Ousseina Alidou

PROFILE OF NIGER

The Niger Republic is a former French colony located in central West Africa and extends over 2,687,000 square kilometers,[1] of which more than 60 percent is covered by the Sahara desert. The country shares borders with Burkina Faso and Mali to the west, Algeria and Libya to the north, Chad to the east, and Nigeria and Benin to the south.

The Niger Republic acquired its independence from France on August 3, 1960. The country is divided into seven administrative regional departments and thirty-five districts, and its capital city, located on the south bank of Niger river, is Niamey.

Niger's population is estimated to be 10,400,000 inhabitants. Of the overall population 50.4 percent are Nigerien women, of whom 42 percent are between fifteen and forty-two years old. Life expectancy is 44.9 years for male and 48.1 years for female.[2] Niger's population growth is estimated at 3.4 percent and one out of two Nigeriens is less than fifteen years old, of whom 75 percent are concentrated in the main urban centers.

Niger's population is multiethnic, with more than 50 percent Hausa, 22.8 percent Zarma-

Songhay, 10.4 percent Fulani, 8.5 percent Kanuri, 3 percent Tuareg, 0.5 percent Tubu, and 1.8 percent other ethnic minorities including the Schwa Arabs, the Gurma, and the Buduma. The language of each ethnic group has been promoted to a national language status although French is the only official language.

Niger is overwhelmingly a Muslim country (95 percent) and the other practiced religions include traditional beliefs and Christianity. Although the state is proclaimed secular, the Islamic ethos remains a powerful force in policy formulation and implementation.

A landlocked Sahelian country, the Niger Republic is one of the poorest countries of the world and experiences numerous economic and social hardships as a result of severe cyclical droughts leading to famine, desertification, massive rural-urban migrations, and exodus to foreign countries.

In the 1970s to early 1980s, Niger's depressed economy that had previously relied on subsistence agriculture and pastoralism—35 percent of its gross national product (GNP)—was revived due to the high demand for uranium on the international market. However, by the mid-1980s the decline in the demand for uranium in the world market, the structural adjustment programs (SAP) imposed by the World Bank and International Monetary Fund, followed by the 50 percent devaluation of the currency in 1994 put the country into a severe state of economic, social, and political depression. In 1994, 6.9 percent of Niger's gross domestic product (GDP) was derived from mining, which according to 1998 figures absorbed only 0.2 percent of the labor force.[3] In addition to the formal economy, there is an informal sector that contributes about 28.5 percent to the economy.

After fifteen years of civilian rule under the presidency of Diori Hamani, Niger experienced military rule from 1974 to 1991. However, like many third world countries, internal as well as external pressures forced the country to opt for democratization beginning in the early 1990s, leading eventually to the formation of a multiparty system of governance.

OVERVIEW OF WOMEN'S ISSUES

In spite of the numerous well-intended declarations about gender equity in the speeches of politicians, there is still strong patriarchal resistance against the implementation of policies that confer the equitable treatment of women via the national developmental agenda. This is true not only in the developmental areas where women have made overwhelming and effective contributions (as for example in agriculture and grain trade), but also in areas dealing with resource allocation such as in women's public health, women's education, and employment. Internal and external hegemonic patriarchal structures, extreme economic poverty, political instability, in addition to the various contradictions internal to women's social movements in the country, are factors that mostly account for the problems confronting Nigerien women today.

In spite of their demographic proportion, women in Niger are not accorded significant roles in development policymaking and implementation in the nation governed by successive patriarchal state regimes, often financed by international agencies. Since the 1990s, however, the discursive space opened by the democratization momentum has created new avenues for women to inscribe themselves in the national agenda and to popularize their cause internationally.

EDUCATION

Opportunities

From independence to the economic crisis of the mid-1980s, primary education was compulsory for both girls and boys from age seven. In 1999, education expenditure was 33,500 million francs CFA, which represents 15.2 percent of the total national spending.[4] However, from 1996 to 1998, figures indicate that female enrollment was about 38.6 percent in the primary level, 35.5

Woman carrying load on head, Niger. Photo © TRIP/TRIP.

percent in the secondary level, 27 percent in high school, and less than 10.8 percent in technical vocational schools.

There is a high dropout rate of female students in elementary school, with the rural areas being the most affected by scoring as high as 85 percent of the dropout rate. This phenomenon is caused by several factors, including the general paralysis of the country's educational system as a result of the economic crisis and lack of parental appreciation of the value of female educational pursuit in Western-style education.

In 1991 the proportion of female enrollment was 20 percent of the total student body at Abdou Moumouni University. Of these women only 1 percent graduated. Female students were and continue to be most visible in the school of education and medical school. This gender enrollment pattern coincides with the traditional gender distribution of professional fields. From 1987 to 2001, the Islamic University of West Africa located in Say (a town less than 100 kilometers to the south of Niamey) did not welcome female students who graduated from Islamic high schools. As a result, female graduates from the Islamic school track either enrolled in the mainstream secular Abdou Moumouni University or had to interrupt their educational pursuit altogether if their parents could not afford to send them to Islamic universities in foreign countries or if they failed to get state or international funding support from Islamic organizations.

The low rate of female students remaining in education has had a negative impact on women's access to training in professional fields such as administration, management, and telecommunications. But more recent pressure by women's organizations for gender equity has improved the enrollment of women in police training and in military and paramilitary fields.

Literacy

According to 1995 figures from the United Nations Educational, Scientific, and Cultural Organization (UNESCO), illiteracy affects 86.6 percent of the overall population, of whom women constitute about 93.4 percent. This means the literacy gender gap is 14 percent. There is evidence that even though the national literacy rate is increasing, the gender literacy gap is also widening.[5] All these figures, however, are not likely to include literacy in Arabic and Ajami (localized version of the Arabic script). If the latter is taken into account, especially in light of its growing popularity, and the parental preference of it for female children a different national literacy profile and a different female-male literacy ratio is likely.

EMPLOYMENT AND ECONOMICS

Farming

In addition to their contribution to household management, Nigerien women participate a great deal in economic production in sectors such as agriculture and husbandry (29 percent). In spite of their active participation in agricultural activities, however, Nigerien women confront numerous problems tied to their lack of adequate technical and business training, as well as a lack of access to agriculture loans. These limitations have impeded their productivity and affected the quality of their working conditions.

Paid Employment

In 1999 there were 490,350 employed women, which is less than a quarter of the number of employed males. Given their low educational and literacy background as well as the lack of access to professional training,

Table 12.1
The Percentage of Female Civil Servants in Various Professions, 1989

Occupation	Apprentice	Laborer	Skilled Laborer	Qualified Laborer	Office Clerk
Agriculture		3	19	46	84
Industry				2	19
Electrician		7	19	29	117
Construction			7		50
Hotel bars	69	9	47	77	879
Transport			78	31	110
Bank insurance	46	143	8	53	70
Social service	46	143	60	53	591
Total	46	174	243	247	1,969

Source: Abdou Hamani, *Les Femmes et la Politique au Niger* (Niamey: Democratie, 2000), 149.

Nigerien women are also underrepresented in the public as well as private professional sectors. In 1988, for example, women represented only 8.1 percent of wage labor compared to 91.9 percent of men. Out of 25,974 listed jobs in 1988, women held only 1,950, which equals 22.8 percent, clearly indicating their low participation in the formal sector. The distribution of female civil servants in various professional fields in 1989 is shown in Table 12.1.

There are almost no women in high-ranking positions in the private sector. In 1989 the overall number of workers in this sector was estimated to be about 28,034, of whom women counted about 3,554, that is 9.11 percent, all qualifications included.[6] In 1993, of the 39,236 civil servants, there were 9,226 female civil servants, which represents 23.5 percent of the labor force. Among these, there were 1,215 female clerks, 282 skilled laborers, 175 advanced skilled laborers, and 167 technocrats.[7]

Informal Economic Activities

Cultural factors for most ethnic groups prevent women from engaging in certain types of occupations, such as operating a barber shop, butchery, and traditional metal work, which are associated with men even within the caste professional system. However women participate heavily in the processing and trading of food and dairy products, as well as craft-making (weaving, pottery, tie-dying, braiding, sewing) and selling goods.

Because women providing domestic service are not employed through the labor offices, they do not receive any benefits or protection against unfair treatment by their employers. The meager wages obtained through domestic service are vital incomes that sustain the welfare of numerous households headed by women as a result of short or long term absence (due to rural-urban migrations) of male heads of households.

As far as the employment law is concerned, the legal stipulation is equal payment for equal work and for equal qualification across gender. However, the document presented by the Nigerien women representatives at the 1995 Women's World Conference in Beijing suggests that although there is no discrimination based on sex in the public labor sector, women experience overt discrimination in positions of responsibility. In addition, within the same sector, family allowances are granted to men even though women are the primary caregivers of children.

As for the private sector, the Nigerien women's document at Beijing also contends that the employers are often more inclined to recruit men over women in order to avoid the cost of pre- and postnatal paid maternity leaves. In addition, because women are said to possess lower qualifications than men, employers tend to avoid recruiting them because, supposedly, they cost more in training investment.

By the year 2000, far from closing this gender gap, there is evidence that in fact the gap has been growing as the labor force becomes increasingly masculinized. Furthermore, it has been shown that there is an obvious, though not pervasive, discrimination in wages, which can be overt or covert. Overt discrimination involves a disparity in employment remuneration with women earning less than men. In the nonovert case of discrimination, women and men are assigned to different types of jobs, of which the ones with less pay go to women.[8]

Support for Mothers/Caretakers

The majority of women from the rural areas help each other out with babysitting, cooking, and attending to the elderly, sick, and expectant mothers.

Maternal Leave

In both public and private sectors, women are granted paid maternity leave from the seventh month of pregnancy to forty days after delivery. Before the implementation of Structural Adjustment Programs (SAPs), in the mid-1980s the government took care of the cost of both maternal and infant care. Today, however, most individuals cover the cost of their own medical bills and, in most cases, the fate of unemployed women's care is in the hands of their husbands.

Inheritance, Property, and Land Rights

For the majority of ethnic groups in Niger, women are culturally denied land rights in spite of their tremendous contribution in labor for the cultivation of their husbands' farmlands. The 1993 rural code, which concerns, in particular, landownership, has yet to be implemented. This code allocates several rights to women, including equal access to natural resources, equal protection of rights, and equal access to parcels of land and to re-possessed and exploited lands.

Social/Government Programs

Structural Adjustment

Through the 1970s to early 1980s, Niger had begun to rely more on its uranium mining industry and less on subsistence agriculture and pastoralism. The fall of uranium prices in the mid-1980s, followed by the World Bank and International Monetary Fund's enforced SAPs, and the 50 percent devaluation of the franc CFA in 1994, led to the worst inflation and unemployment rate in the country's history. Women experienced (and continue to experience) its devastating impact in the form of discrimination in the labor market, unequal wages compared to male workers, and loss of tenure security in employment. Though migration is still most prevalent in the rural areas, it is increasingly becoming a feature of the urban space, even among civil-servant households since the imposition of SAPs.

FAMILY AND SEXUALITY

Gender Roles and Division of Labor

Nigerien women's role and place within and outside the household is to a large extent governed by traditional sociocultural and religious (Islamic) factors. Thus men are considered heads of household and bread-winners while women are treated as caregivers and homemakers. Rural women work an average of fourteen hours a day, fetching water and fire-wood, transforming millet grains into food, and assisting in farming.

Women are also involved in other forms of income-generating activities, such as the selling of cooked food, buying and selling goods (peanut oil, soaps, and dairy products), and contributing to supporting family needs. Most women participate in traditional forms of savings activities such as merry-go-rounds, which are more commonly known as rotating credit and savings associations in which a group of women pool their savings and draw from the pool in turns. Most often men participate in the cyclic rural-urban migration after harvest seasons and work hard to provide for the material needs of their families.

In Niger, women's and men's social status and acceptance depend on being married and having children. Female virginity is fundamental to family honor. In order to avoid shame as a result of female children engaging in premarital sexual activity, many parents impose early marriage, at twelve to fourteen years of age, on their daughters. Given that Islam as well as pre-Islamic traditional practices permit polygamy, 36 percent of women live in polygamous unions and each woman competes for an average birth of 8.5 children.

Reproduction

Sex Education

The religious *'ulama* have always opposed the introduction of sex education in the school curriculum, fearing that such endeavor would infuse Nigerien culture with the notion of sexual liberty, which is considered a moral sin in Islam.

Contraception and Abortion

The combination of religious factors as well as patriarchal conservatism have made any attempt to implement a widespread family planning program a volatile social and cultural issue in the nation. As a result, availability of contraception and family planning services have been limited mainly to a few urban health care centers in the capital city of Niamey and other cities in Niger. However, even in these centers outside of Niamey, medical personnel are required by law to request written consent from husbands before prescribing any contraceptive method to married women. Whereas adult sex workers have easy access to contraceptives, this is not the case for other single women, who often resort to illegal abortion in cases of "unwanted pregnancies."

Teen Pregnancy

Religious conservatism accounts for not only the rise of teen pregnancy in the country, but also the increase of HIV/AIDS infection and clandestine, often fatal, abortions among teens.

HEALTH

Health Care Access

In 1993, Niger had only three national hospitals.[9] The World Health Organization reported that there were 3.5 physicians, 22.9 nurses, 5.5 midwives, and 0.2 dentists per 100,000 people in 1997.[10] The state of the medical infrastructure catering to women's health care can be summarized as follows: 310 midwives, 983 certified nurses and 107 nurses aides, 158 doctors, of whom 18 percent are women, 22 maternity hospitals, and 40 maternal and infant health care centers.[11] The overall cost of national health care amounted to 1.2 percent of the GDP in 1998.

Between 1972 and 1992, two out of five women died as a result of lack of appropriate health care conditions during child delivery, maternal mortality approximated 6.5 deaths per 1,000 births, and fertility was estimated at 7.4 children per woman throughout the country.[12]

Fertility intervals numbered two years or less between pregnancies, which accounts quite often for early mother and infant mortality. It is estimated that 134 infants out of 1,000 die before their first birthday. By the fifth birthday, 334 infant girls die per 1,000 as opposed to 318 infant boys per 1,000. A similar gendered disparity accounts for all deaths related to adolescents with a ratio of 231 girls per 1,000 against 211 boys per 1,000.

Diseases and Disorders

The major causes of death among women of Niger include malaria, respiratory problems, dracunculosis (*ver de Guinée*), infectious diseases, and intestinal parasites. Maternal mortality is at a rate of 7 deaths per 1,000 mothers: obstetrical causes that lead to 75 percent of maternal deaths are tied to pre- and postpartum hemorrhaging (21 percent), rupture of the uterus (20 percent), intoxication (13 percent), abortion (3 percent), and infectious diseases (18 percent), of which 1.3 percent are HIV/AIDS.

Female Genital Cutting, Other Traditional Practices, and New Stressors

Although not widespread, a number of ethnic groups in Niger, including the Fulani, Kanuri, and Wogo fishermen, still continue to perform some ritual practices that are harmful to women's bodies and minds. These practices include female genital cutting, body scarification, physical seclusion, and forced fattening rituals. These customs prevail in spite of the tremendous effort of nongovernmental organizations to educate the population about their consequences. Other types of violence inflicted upon women are forced early marriage, wife-beating, and forced separation of mother and her children in case of divorce.

Prolonged male rural-urban migration leading to the abandonment of wives and children has increased the number of female divorcees and shifted gender roles by making women heads of household, which burdens women with the responsibility to cater to both material and other needs of an extended large family. The weight of this shift in gender roles partly accounts for the increased cases of infanticide and suicide among women. The various types of violence and humiliation that women are subjected to in Niger account often for women's mental health issues. Much of the literature dealing with women and health does not address this latter aspect.

POLITICS AND LAW

Political Participation

The first Nigerien women's union, called Union des Femmes du Niger, emerged in 1959 in preparation for the negotiation of the country's independence from France. It was affiliated to the Union of Popular Forces for Democracy–Sawaba political party. When the Rassemblement Democratic Africain, a political party headed by Diori Hamani, won the election in 1960, this association became integrated into the ruling party's women's wing with no ministerial, parliamentary, or executive appointments of its female members. In this civilian regime, in fact, there was not a single woman who had an executive post in the nation.

From 1974 to 1988, in spite of the U.N. declaration of 1975 as the International Year of the Woman, the military regime, headed by Lieutenant Seyni Kountché, was again characterized by the total absence of women in all institutions of decision making. Given the autocratic nature of the regime, the creation of the association of Nigerien women known as Association des Femmes du Niger (AFN) that year did not bring a fundamental change to the assignment of women to executive leadership positions, which in the view of the president were less "emancipatory" than their grassroots role as agents of economic and social mobilization.

The death of President Seyni Kountché in 1988 brought an end to autocracy in the Niger Republic, leading to constitutional, legislative, and electoral reforms under the leadership of General Ali Chaibou. Madame Aissata Moumouni, holding a Ph.D. in mathematics, became the first woman to hold a ministerial position in Niger in 1989. Furthermore, the law intended to protect women against discrimination on the grounds of sex and to guarantee them fair appointment in executive administrative and political positions was passed on December 8, 1989.

In 1991, Niger held a national conference to determine the democratic future and structure of the country. The body appointed to organize this event, however, did not include a single woman. On May 13, 1991, women nationally went on a protest march against their exclusion in this critical national process. This march served to stimulate greater gender awareness and better female representation in political and other organizations of the country. By 2000, Niger could count 2.72 percent of women in ministerial positions, 12.2 percent of women in political parties, and 2.5 percent of women in parliament.[13] Since then, however, there has been evidence of declining women representation in the legislative branch of the government to one seat in 2003.

From the 1990s to the present, there has been an increased visibility of women in executive leadership positions in administration as well as in politics, in addition to their continuing public activism especially in political parties, various labor unions, and secular or religious-based women's nongovernmental organizations.

Women's Rights

At the international level, Niger has not ratified the International Convention for the Elimination of all forms of Discrimination Against Women as well as the convention regarding the nationality of married women. But from independence to the present, all of the successive five regimes signed the 1981 African Charter on Human Rights, which advocates the equality between men and women. However, women's legal status in the Niger Republic is dependent on three legal systems, all of them with a strong patriarchal hold: a modern civil code, which partly draws from the French legal family code, a customary code based on ethnic tradition, and an Islamic code. The latter code unequally favors men over women on, for example, issues related to repudiation/divorce, the custody of children in cases of divorce or death of the father, and inheritance law (double share for male heir). The customary law varies from ethnic group to ethnic group and, as a result, is supposed to take into account primarily the women's ethnic origin and the cultural understanding of family law. Women's low rate of literacy represents a major handicap in achieving an understanding of the various laws and how to (re)claim their rights as well as understand their violations.

While the constitutions adopted by the successive governments in Niger affirm the equality of women and men before the law in accordance to the U.N.'s 1948 Universal Declaration of Human Rights and Citizenship, deviations resulting from societal conservatism have been observed in the application of the text law. A prime illustration of the violation of democratic liberty involves the right to vote as applied to the secluded married women who cannot exercise their right to vote personally. Their vote is cast for them by the husband who controls their right of movement within and outside the domestic space.

Another sphere of legal discrimination against women relates to the legal text on allocation of social benefits (health, retirement, etc.). According to the stipulation of the text, benefits are granted solely to heads of household. And since women in the Nigerien context are culturally not conferred the status of head of family, they are denied, as civil servants, the right to collect benefits even when their husbands are unemployed. Furthermore, in spite of the fact that women are increasingly assuming the responsibility of head of family, especially in contexts of divorce, prolonged absence, and illness or unemployment of husband, the finance law, which defines male's and female's incomes, takes into account the number of children who are counted as solely the husband's dependents.

Women's Movements

The U.N.'s declaration of 1975 as the International Year of the Woman had a major impact on women throughout the world and most especially in the third world countries. The participation of Niger's women in the various international and national forums organized and sponsored by various internal and external sociopolitical bodies seeking to empower women created a terrain for the AFN to begin to act openly on issues pertaining to the violation of women's and children's rights in the nation. The military regime, under local and international pressure, allowed the AFN and the AFJN, other jurist experts in Islamic law, and the leaders of the Islamic Association of Niger (AIN) to form a committee to work on formulating a new Family Code that would protect and respect individual rights within the family. During its tenure, from 1975 to 1990, the work of the committee was never really taken seriously. Moreover, the Family Code elicited vigorous resistance from patriarchal religious and secular bodies as well as politicians, making its legal implementation difficult. Consequently, patriarchal conservatism has resisted the adoption of an equitable family code that will ensure gender equality in the nation.

A few of the most active women's organizations include the previously mentioned AFN, the Democratic Assembly of Nigerien Women (Rassemblement Democratic des Femmes du Niger), the AFJN, and the Association of Muslim Women of Niger (Association des Femmes Musulmanes du Niger).

Military and Police Force Service

The proportion of women in institutional organs in charge of national and international security is extremely insignificant. Only 2 percent of gendarmes are female, of whom 37 percent are graduates and 8 percent are students. In 1994, there were seventy-eight females recruited into the police force, which is less than 5 percent of the overall police agents, and only one woman holds the rank of commissaire. As for the military, the 31 females enrolled do not fulfill any military role in reality. These figures clearly illustrate the patriarchal power over institutions responsible for ensuring peace and security in the nation.

RELIGION AND SPIRITUALITY

Ninety-five percent of Nigeriens are Muslim. The rest of the population practice indigenous beliefs or Christianity. Although Niger professes itself to be a secular nation, the Islamic perspective strongly influences governmental policy. Religious intolerance has grown to an alarming degree as evidenced in violent demonstrations against women's international fashion shows, or even women deemed inappropriately dressed.

Religious Law

As one of the three codes governing the lives of women, the Islamic law favors men over women on all aspects of life: wife repudiation, the custody of children in cases of divorce or death of the father, and inheritance law.

Minority Christians tend to use the modern civil code for matters related to personal law. In spite of its seemingly more liberal parameters, this law too is often subjected to patriarchal interpretations in its application. This small Christian constituency has voiced strong opposition to any suggested move towards the Islamic *shari'a* system of law in Niger.

VIOLENCE

Domestic Violence

Another significant women's protest took place on May 13, 2001, when women marched to protest against pedophilia, which in most cases involved sexual molestation of female children by adult males. Other types of human rights violations, including the persecution of homosexuals and marital rape, are neither debated nor punished.

Trafficking in Women and Children

Since the mid-1980s, Niger has experienced a fall in uranium prices that triggered the subsequent economic crisis. The government has neglected publicly run boarding schools. It also succumbed to the imposition of World Bank and IMF's Structural Adjustment Programs. These and other factors have led to an increase in poverty and have given birth to the phenomenon of child prostitution in urban and semiurban centers, especially among schoolgirls, who become easy victims of sexually transmitted diseases and drug abuse in the streets. Prostitution is legal in the Niger Republic and sex workers are required by law to register with the Ministry of Interior and to attend regular medical checkups at the appropriate health centers.

War and Military Repression

During the 1990s armed conflicts between national armed forces and the Tuareg and Tubu armed groups, Nigerien northern women, especially the Tuareg and Tubu women, experienced the brutalization of the state. The conflicts forced groups of women and children to choose between living in exile, remaining at the mercy of the state, or participating in the struggle. Unfortunately, the number of women who died in these "ethnic" or regional conflicts is still not specified for political reasons. Moreover, sisterhood among women in Niger was betrayed during these conflicts as a result of identity politics that led a great number of women in nonconflict regions or of nontargeted "ethnic" groups to pay blind allegiance to the state or political parties. Class-specific agendas and interests constrained Nigerien women's ability to arrive at a common vision of how to confront patriarchal authoritarianism, political manipulation of identity, and international and local forces that profit from the conflicts to the detriment of women and children.[14]

Furthermore, women in Niger have suffered and continue to suffer from armed conflicts between agriculturalists and pastoralists in various parts of the country. One of the most brutal conflicts of this kind, nationally referred to as *"le drame de Toda in Maradi,"* occurred in October 1991 and caused the death of 103 people, of whom 70 were women.

The rise of religious intolerance also has led to aggressive attacks against women and girls judged "unfit" in various main cities in Niger. In July 1992, for example, many young females were stripped of their clothes publicly and beaten by thugs sponsored by some mosque leaders. On July 17, 1992, the national association of human rights and most national unions extended their solidarity to more than 2,000 women who marched nationally to protest this intolerant religious aggression against young females. The women's protest led the government to take legal action against the perpetrators of these violent acts.

OUTLOOK FOR THE TWENTY-FIRST CENTURY

Women in Niger continue to be repressed and disadvantaged in spite of the modest reforms in the legal domain. The democratization momentum has indeed created new spaces for women to act on their new spaces for their situation and foster better their conditions in their lives. But globalization and the socioeconomic crisis in the country have also unleashed new patriarchal forces, some religious and some secular, which continue to undermine women's efforts for self-empowerment and to achieve parity with the men. At the same time, however, women in the Niger Republic are becoming more conscious and engaged in the struggle for the respect of their rights in the nation.

NOTES

1. One kilometer equals 0.6 miles.
2. UNESCO, *World Population Prospects* (1988), http://esa.un.org/unpp/p2k0data. asp.
3. *The Europa World Year Book*, vol. 11 (2002), 2984.
4. Ibid.
5. Abdou Hamani, *Les Femmes et la politique au Niger* (Niamey: Democratie, 2000), 137–38.
6. Ibid., 148.

7. *Rapport National 2000: Conference Mondiale sur Femmes et Developpement*, Ministere du Developpement Social de la Population et de la Promotion de la Femme, 31.

8. Hamani, *Les Femmes et la Politique au Niger*, 153.

9. *The Europa World Year Book*, 2985.

10. Human Development Report, http://hdr.undp.org

11. Ibid.

12. 1992 national census data.

13. Hamani, *Les Femmes et la politique au Niger*, 69, 127–32.

14. Ousseina Alidou, "Womanhood, Gender Politics, and Armed Conflict in Niger Republic," paper presented at the Thirty-first National Conference of Black Political Scientists, Washington, DC, April 2000.

RESOURCE GUIDE

Suggested Reading

Alidou, Ousseina. "A 'Cinderella' Tale in the Hausa Muslim Women's Imagination." *Comparative Literature* 54, no. 5 (Summer 2002): 242–55.

Cooper, Barbara. *Marriage in Maradi: Gender and Culture in a Hausa Society in Niger, 1900–1989*. Social History of Africa Series. Portsmouth, NH: Heinemann, 1997.

———."The Politics of Difference and Women's Associations in Niger: Of 'Prostitutes,' the Public and Politics." *Signs* 20, no. 4 (1994): 851–82.

Dunbar, Roberta Ann. "Islamic Values, the State and 'the Development of Women': The Case of Niger." In *Hausa Women in the Twentiety Century*, edited by Catherine Coles and Beverly Mack, 69–89. Madison: University of Wisconsin Press, 1991.

Masquelier, A. "Consumption, Prostitution, and Reproduction: The Poetics of Sweetness in Bori." *American Ethnologist* 22, no. 4 (November 1995): 883–906.

Sidikou, Aissata G. *Recreating Words, Reshaping Worlds: The Verbal Art of Women from Niger, Mali, and Senegal*. Trenton, NJ: Africa World Press, 2003.

Web Sites

Focus on Niger, www.txdirect.net/users/jmayer/fon.html.
Provides weekly news of Niger as well as a list of net resources on the country.

Jenda: A Journal of Culture and African Women's Studies, www.jendajournal.com.

Political Resources: Niger, www.politicalresources.net/niger.htm.

UNDP Human Development Report 2001, www.undp.org/hdr2001.

UNIFEM Progress of the World's Women 2000, www.unifem.undp.org/progressww/index.html.

United Nations: Women Watch, www.un.org/womenwatch.

University of Pennsylvania, Niger page, www.sas.upenn.edu/african_studies/country_specific/niger.html.

World Bank Group, www.worldbank.org/data/countrydata/aag/ner_aag.pdf.

World Bank Group: Gender Statistics, http://genderstats.worldbank.org/genderRpt. asp?rpt=profile&cty=NER,Niger&hm=home.

Organizations

Association des Femmes Comercantes et Entrepreneurs du Niger
B.P. 10602
Niamey, Niger
Phone: 227-74-02-83

Association des Femmes du Niger (AFN)
B.P. 2818
Niamey, Niger
Phone: 227-75-37-17/74-00-34

Association des Femmes Nigierennes Face au SIDA
B.P. 13406
Niamey, Niger
Phone: 227-72-22-24
Fax: 227-72-32-33

Comite Nigerien Sur le Practiques Traditionnelles
B.P. 11631
Niamey, Niger
Phone: 227-75-34-72

Rassemblement Democratic des Femmes du Niger (RDFN), the Democratic Assembly
   of Nigerien Women
B.P. 11933
Niamey, Niger
Phone: 227-73-24-65

SELECTED BIBLIOGRAPHY

International Monetary Fund. Niger General Data Dissemination System Site (GDDS). http://dsbb.imf.org/gddsweb/country/ner/ners2.htm.
Ministère du Developpement Social de la Population et de la Promotion de la Femme. *Rapport National 2000: Conference Mondiale sur Femmes et Developpement.* 2000.
United Nations. *Statistical Year Books.*
———. *World Population Prospects: The 1998 Revision.* http://esa.un.org/unpp.

13

NIGERIA

Nwando Achebe

PROFILE OF NIGERIA

Nigeria is the most populous nation in Africa and is named after the River Niger. With over 129 million people, it has been estimated that one out of every four Africans is a Nigerian. Nigeria has over 350 ethnic groups or nations of people who speak different languages and have different cultural beliefs. The three main ethnic groups in Nigeria are the Igbo in the southeast, the Yoruba in the southwest, and the Hausa-Fulani in the north.

Nigeria attained independence from Britain on October 1, 1960, and has since endured a succession of military governments and dictatorships, which have controlled the country's political and economic affairs for twenty-eight out of forty-three years of independence. In June 1998, General Abdulsalami Abubakar became head of state following the sudden death of one of Nigeria's most ruthless dictators, Sani Abacha. He ruled for a little under a year. On May 29, 1999, the democratically elected government of President Olusegun Obasanjo assumed power.

Since 1960, Nigeria has transformed itself from an economy dependent upon cash crop production to one almost solely based on oil. The oil sector ac-

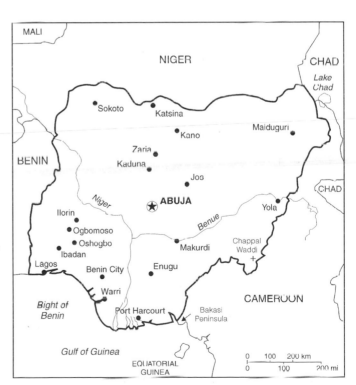

counts for approximately 40 percent of Nigeria's gross domestic product (GDP) and for about 85 percent of foreign exchange earnings.[1] In 1958, Nigeria produced 5,000 barrels of oil per day, and this production peaked at 2.3 million barrels a day in 1979. Between 1970 and 1983, Nigeria's overall exports (derived mainly from oil) grew at an average of 30 percent annually. Earnings from oil alone over this period stood at over $140 billion. During the 1970s, Nigeria was OPEC's sixth largest producer, contributing an average of 7 percent of the organization's total production.

Nigeria is the world's second largest exporter of cocoa, producing 172,000 tons in 1981. Other Nigerian exports include groundnuts, kola nuts, tobacco, palm oil, kernels, and rubber. Nigeria also produces crude oil, tin, hard and soft woods, hides, skins, and columbites (a black mineral compound of iron and niobium).[2]

Despite oil wealth, poverty is widespread in Nigeria and basic indicators place Nigeria among the twenty poorest nations in the world. President Obasanjo's administration has identified corruption and poor governance as realities that must be tackled in order to begin to reverse Nigeria's economic decline. To this end, an anticorruption bill was recently passed by the National Assembly and signed into law by President Obasanjo.

Women account for over half of Nigeria's population. There are approximately 102 Nigerian women to 100 men. Nigeria's infant mortality rate in 2000 was 84 deaths per 1,000 live births. The under-five mortality rate was 153 deaths per 1,000 live births.[3]

A number of factors can greatly increase the risk of death for women during pregnancy and childbirth. These include the age and health of the mother, how may children she has had, the intervals between births, poor antenatal care, as well as poor care during and after childbirth. In Nigeria the maternal mortality rate per 100,000 live births between 1990 and 1999 was 1,000. Conversely, the total fertility rate (i.e., births per woman) was estimated at 5.5 births in 1995 and declined slightly to 5.0 in 2000. In 1995, Nigeria's life expectancy rate at birth was estimated at 49.9 years, but this has since declined to 47.0 years for 2000.[4]

OVERVIEW OF WOMEN'S ISSUES

Historically, the Nigerian woman has been, and remains, the backbone of the Nigerian family and, by extension, Nigerian society. But for the most part, her story has been left untold by researchers. Most general texts have failed to incorporate women's concerns or gender relations into their editions, referring to Nigerian women only in passing. These studies have relegated her to the background, focusing only on her nurturing role as mother and wife and by so doing obscuring her other contributions to society.

Igbo women of southeastern Nigeria were among the first group of

Nigerian women to gain recognition as a group distinct from their men. This recognition was due in part to their mass demonstration against the colonial government in 1929. Unsettled by the aftermath of the 1929 women's war, Ogu Umunwanyi, the colonial government sent their officials and ethnographers into the field to study Igbo political systems. The vast majority of these ethnographers were European men who sought out and exclusively interviewed Igbo men for their studies. These histories thus ignored women's initiatives and concerns for change while concealing colonialism's deleterious effect on women's status and their protests against economic and cultural interference. Moreover they ignored Nigerian women's function in creating a new political tradition.

Nigerian women exercised political power more frequently than was previously assumed and although symbolic expressions of women's power differed from those of men, women were no less powerful. In some societies, a system of joint sovereignty existed whereby leadership responsibilities were shared between a king and a female counterpart. In these systems, women held power because of their relationship to the ruler in question, especially as mother, wife, daughter, or sister. Among the Yoruba of southwestern Nigeria, the Queen Mother, *Iyaoba*, the head wife of the *Oba* (king), known as *Olori*, and the *Iyalode* (ceremonial minister of social affairs) held significant political power, exerting considerable influence over men's offices, while participating actively in policymaking and traditional government.

In the ancient kingdom of Benin, the biological mother of the king, the Queen Mother, played a prominent political and religious role in administering her kingdom. Among the egalitarian Igbo, authority was dispersed between men and women in a dual-sex political system, which allowed each sex to manage its own affairs in an efficient and orderly manner. In this system of government, the *umuada* (daughters of the lineage) and *inyomdi* (wives of the lineage) emerged as supreme bodies of arbitration.

Islam was a central force in the lives of Hausa women of northern Nigeria. Contrary to popular belief, Islam did not prevent its female practitioners from occupying leadership positions in precolonial northern Nigeria. In Kano for instance, the power and authority that accrued to royal wives increased with age, and women elders often exercised authority over hundreds of women and men inside the palace. The senior wife of the emir was most revered and consequently was able to assume a lot of influence over him. It is important to note however that whatever power these women assumed was largely restricted to the royal harem, and this can be explained by the doctrine of Islam, which mandated that its female members be secluded and confined primarily to the privacy of the home. Also in these parts, the chador or *abayah*—long black cover garment—was not viewed as a mark of female oppression, but rather as

Women cleaning cassava root, Ossomalla, Nigeria. Photo © TRIP/J. Okwesa.

a symbolic indicator of women's entry into the public sphere. Muslim women in Nigeria today are increasingly adopting the chador as a political and religious statement.

British colonialism resulted in the deterioration of the status of Nigerian women relative to men. Western colonialism subjected Nigerian women to new forms of sexism, which were often times far more oppressive to women than previously existing relationships. Colonial rule marked the beginning of the end of any equality between the sexes in village life as well as politics. Nigerian women were confined to the background and could no longer take part in the decision-making processes that they were used to participating in during the precolonial period. Their power was further eroded as opportunistic young men who befriended the colonial masters were chosen to fill chief's positions. Disputes that previously went before women's organizations were now taken to the British courts.

Women's experiences in Nigeria today are integrally tied with their past. It is almost impossible to identify one monolithic or representative Nigerian woman, because her issues tend to be shaped by a multiplicity of variables—ethnicity, class, educational background, and whether or not she resides in the rural or urban areas, to name but a few. However, despite these differences, certain threads of commonality have emerged amongst women. The fight for educational and economic independence are issues that Nigerian women have overwhelmingly identified, irrespective of location. Closely related to these issues is women's struggle to provide food, pipe-borne water, and electricity, and to secure proper health care in order to sustain all members of the household. These are only a few of the issues that confront Nigerian women today.

EDUCATION

Opportunities

Since the 1980s public expenditure on education in Nigeria has been about 6 percent of the gross national product (GNP). In 1976 the Nigerian government instituted a system of free primary education for its citizens.

The educational program, called the 6-3-3-4 system, included six years of primary education followed by three years of junior secondary school, an additional three years of senior secondary school, and then a final four years in university.

In northern Nigeria, Muslim communities often favor boys over girls in deciding which children to enroll in primary and secondary schools. In the Christian south, economic hardship plays a role in restricting many families' ability to send girls to school, and many of them elect instead to direct their daughters into commercial activities such as trading and street vending. This notwithstanding, a number of regional initiatives have been put in place to help correct this female imbalance. Some Nigerian states have established scholarship funds for female students and made school attendance mandatory for them and at the same time prohibited the withdrawal of female students from school for purposes of marriage. In Calabar, for instance, a nongovernmental organization called Girls Power Initiative was formed in 1994 to promote the rights of girls and to mobilize them through education.

The number of female students in Nigerian primary schools has been increasing steadily. In 1980 females in Nigerian primary schools composed 43 percent of pupils. By 1990 this number increased to 67 percent. The figures drastically declined by secondary school, with the total female enrollment being estimated at about 30 percent for 2000.[5]

Literacy

The adult literacy rate for Nigerian women (i.e., women over the age of fifteen) has been rising steadily. Female adult literacy rates in 2000 had reached 55.7 percent, while the male adult literacy rate was 72.4 percent. This meant that women's rate of literacy was 77 percent that of men's.[6]

EMPLOYMENT AND ECONOMICS

Farming

Nigerian women participate in both the public and private domains and act as links between the two. Women in Nigeria are involved in three main areas of economic activity: farming, trading and manufacture. Over 70 percent of Nigeria's labor force is involved in agricultural production, and women are the chief cultivators. It has been estimated that over 44 million Nigerian women are actively involved in agricultural production. They till the communally owned land for their subsistence needs and sell their surpluses in the market.

Paid Employment

Nigerian women have made considerable progress in both the professional and business world. Between 1980 and 1996 the ratio of female teachers in Nigerian secondary schools increased from 29 percent to 36 percent.[7] There are numerous female university professors and an increasing number of heads of departments, university deans, and vice chancellors as well. Dr. Bene Madunagu, a biologist by profession, is the head of the Department of Botany at the University of Calabar in Nigeria. She joins the ranks of numerous other Nigerian female heads of departments. In February 2000, fifty-three-year-old physiology professor Olayombo Bolarinwa became the first female dean of the University of Ibadan's College of Medicine and the second woman dean at Nigeria's oldest and most prestigious university. Professor Grace Alele Williams became the first Nigerian female vice chancellor of the University of Benin in 1985 and there have since been three Nigerian women vice chancellors in universities in other parts of Nigeria. The vice chancellor is the chief administrative position in African universities in former British colonies because the national president is chancellor.

Women have also made important strides in the fields of law and medicine. A large number of Nigerian women have specialized as doctors, while still many more are nurses. Nigeria boasts numerous female lawyers and many female High Court judges. The number of women employed in the business sector in Nigeria has also been increasing steadily every year.

Informal Economic Activities

The market place is the Nigerian woman's domain. They oversee it, define its rules and regulations, fix market prices, and determine market taboos. A female-run market government and court establish market rules and regulations, which are enforced by a policewoman. In the open market place, Nigerian women and men trade in foods, crafts, hairdressing products, and cloth goods.

Nigerian women play two main roles in trading. First, they monopolize local trade and play a key part in distribution. Second, because most Nigerian women marry outside their natal villages, they help create vital links and contacts, which benefit trade. Some Nigerian women, mainly Igbo and Yoruba women, also excel as long distance traders. They are able to participate in this male dominated sector, partly as a result of traditional institutions like polygamy, which create female support networks that serve to encourage female entrepreneurship.

In the Hausa Islamic north, women are active in trade and have maintained their activity, even though the vast majority of them operate within the confines of *purdah* (seclusion). In some areas of northern Nigeria, however, pre-Islamic and Islamic cultural elements have been blended in a way that precludes many women's activities beyond reproduction and the performance of domestic chores.

While manufacture remains essentially a part-time occupation, an estimated 3.3 percent of all Nigerian women are involved in the industry. Nigerian women manufacture a variety of crafts including pottery, woodcarvings, calabash decorations, woven cloth and raffia, ropes, nets, baskets, bags, easy chairs, stools, brooms, sleeping mats, and fishing implements. Manufacturing techniques were traditionally passed down from mother to daughter during the precolonial period. During the colonial period, however, a system of apprenticeship developed, and still remains, whereby skilled craftswomen train female students for a small fee.

Pay

In terms of earning potential, women in Nigeria who work in the formal job sector are supposed to earn the exact same amount as men; however, in reality, their earnings averaged 42 percent of men's in 2000.[8]

Support for Mothers/Caretakers

Maternal Leave

By law, all Nigerian women are entitled to twelve weeks of maternity leave, during which time they must receive a minimum of 50 percent of their regular wages. The Nigerian labor law also requires employers to provide nursing working mothers with a least one hour of nursing time on each workday. However, employers in the private sector are permitted to formulate their own policies and entitlements with respect to maternity benefits, as Nigerian labor laws are not enforced in privately owned enterprises. It has been estimated that in this sector, Nigerian women receive an average of eighty-four days away from work; this includes time off for annual leave as well as maternity leave. The benefits, however, are not as generous in the predominantly Islamic north. In Kaduna for instance, unmarried mothers must take maternity leave without pay and in some cases, pregnancy can result in outright dismissal.

Child Care

Female traditional support networks typically provide child care relief and assistance to working mothers in Nigeria. These female networks consist primarily of extended family members and have been in place since the precolonial times. Women in Nigeria today still tap into these resources.

Inheritance, Property, and Land Rights

In much of precolonial Nigeria, land was owned communally and assigned to men and women for farming purposes. There has been some dialogue about the constraints and limitations that have traditionally discouraged Nigerian women from owning land. However, what is more telling is that in most of precolonial Nigeria, men did not own land either. Traditionally, communities owned land. With colonialism, however, the nature of landownership in Nigeria changed. The British government laid claim to Nigerian land, privatizing and commercializing it, thereby obstructing the traditional system of communal land ownership, usually to the detriment of women. They introduced crown grants, which allowed individuals, mainly men, who wanted to purchase or own land individually the right to do so, ignoring Nigerian women's long recognized and standing rights as land users. This new system not only made ownership of land by Nigerian women virtually impossible, but it also restricted their access to land for farming purposes.

The colonial ideal of individualized male ownership of land would solidify in patrilineal societies where inheritance was historically administered through the male line. In much of precolonial Nigeria, wives never really belonged to their husband's lineage, but were merely long-term visitors who did not have any real roots in their husband's homelands. This explains why a Nigerian daughter was more powerful than a wife and why Nigerian women until recently were transported back to their natal villages to be buried when they died. It did not, therefore, make sense for wives to inherent land in their husband's lineage, only to have to abandon it once they died. Neither did it make sense for daughters to inherit land in their natal villages for that matter, because they would have to give it up as soon as they got married. In fact, among the Igbo of eastern Nigeria, unmarried daughters often inherited land and property from their fathers.

Ironically, the colonial policy of land privatization dramatically changed the nature of landownership in present-day Nigeria by embracing the very women that it had previously sought to exclude. Although the basic principle of land inheritance through the male line remained unchanged, the determinant of landownership became financial, rather than gendered, for the most part. In other words, women who could afford to buy land, purchased land, and those who could not were often denied bank loans without written consent from their husbands. In northern Nigeria, however, women do inherit property, but they only inherit one half of what male children are entitled to.

Social/Government Programs

Between 1981 and 1982, the Nigerian economy was in a serious crisis due to a sharp fall in petroleum revenues. Nigeria was forced to appeal to international financial institutions—the International Monetary Fund (IMF) and the World Bank—for assistance. As a condition for providing Nigeria financial assistance, these institutions insisted that the government adopt a structural adjustment program (SAP). The federal governments of President Shehu Shagari (1979–1983) and Major-General Mohammadu Buhari (1984–1985) successfully resisted the institution of SAP in Nigeria. But military dictator General Ibrahim Babangida succumbed to international pressure to have a SAP instituted in 1986. Since then, directives from these agencies have played a major role in the management of the Nigerian economy.

Women have been especially hard hit by the negative consequences of structural adjustment, especially in terms of reduced public and social services, layoffs, and depressed wages.

One response to structural adjustment has been the development of credit schemes targeting women by government and nongovernmental agencies.

The Ministry of Women Affairs, for instance, has set aside funds for specific gender projects including: microcredit schemes, daycare/nursery schools, which are being established in the open marketplaces, and the building of women's development centers. It is, however, difficult to critically assess the impact of these government initiatives on women in Nigeria today. Undisputable, however, is the fact that strides have been made in the right direction. The Nigerian government also recently budgeted and built a multimillion dollar women's hospital in the federal capital territory, Abuja. In addition to this, the Nigerian federal government has been spending more on the education of young girls since the early 1970s.

Women's own strategies have been even more important than government efforts in dealing with economic hardships. Nigerian women have adopted precolonial strategies to guarantee their success in present-day Nigeria. A number of self-help groups (including cooperatives called *esusu* or *isusu*) have emerged in both the rural and urban areas in Nigeria. In Yorubaland, for instance, Chief Bisi Ogunleye has helped organize women in her community by having each donate one month's salary to a group of rural women so that they could start their own businesses. When the loans were repaid, the money was reinvested in other women's groups. In 1982 she founded the Country Women Association of Nigeria (COWAN), with six cooperatives of 150 members. The association has since grown to over 1,400 groups with over 31,000 active members across numerous states in Nigeria. In 1993, COWAN incorporated the Center for Development and Self-Help Activities for young women and rural women. The next year, the group partnered with the Center for Development and Population Activities to aid with health and family planning issues. Through COWAN, Chief Bisi Ogunleye established the Network of African Rural Women Association, which has instituted credit and agriculture programs as well as been involved in small business development.[9] These associations join the vanguard of other Nigerian women's organizations in collecting and disseminating information relating/affecting women, as well as organizing and participating in various solidarity and training programs. The focus of these women's groups for the most part center on training, outreach, and leadership methods.

FAMILY AND SEXUALITY

Gender Roles and Division of Labor

Gender roles within the Nigerian household and family raise interesting parallels for understanding of the importance that gender and other social constructs play in determining economic and, to some extent, political roles in the nation at large. Just as work within the public arena in Nigeria is gendered (for instance, 70 percent of Nigerian women are involved in the cultivation of "women's crops" including cassava, cocoa yams, tomatoes, greens, beans, etc.), unpaid work and roles within the Nigerian family are equally gendered. Consequently, Nigerian wives fulfill the unarticulated role of household caretakers, making certain that all the family cooking and cleaning are provided for. In most Nigerian families, the wife supervises services provided variously by female relatives or household maids. The husband on the other hand is expected to provide all of the economic needs of his family,[10] and as such does little in terms of day to day household responsibilities.

Marriage

There are four types of marriage in Nigeria—marriage by native law and custom (also referred to as customary or traditional marriage), and Christian, Islamic, and civil marriages. Most Nigerians actually adopt a combination of at least two forms of marriage, customary and Christian, or customary and Islamic, for instance. Customary and civil law marriages are legal and binding throughout Nigeria. In the northern Islamic states, marriage according to Islamic law is legally recognized. Polygamy (in which a man marries more than one wife), polyandry (marriages in which a woman marries more than one husband), and "woman marriage" (nonlesbian marriages in which a woman becomes a *female* husband, thereby assuming the social responsibility of husband by marrying a wife) are legal in Nigeria. They can be legitimized through Islamic or customary law without registration.

Islamic law permits a man to marry as many as four wives as long as he can afford to provide for them and love them equally. In contrast, civil-law marriages are monogamous. A 1999 National Demographic and Health Survey found that more than one-third of female respondents and one-quarter of male respondents were in polygamous unions. These numbers reflect a slight decline from 41 percent in 1990.[11]

Nigerian cultures regard marriage as a family rather than an individual matter. Thus Nigerians believe that families marry families. This in no way suggests that traditional marriages are arranged, but rather these marriages often involve long and drawn-out processes that include the paying of bridewealth or service and a period of "asking questions." The latter period can stretch into a number of months. Each family usually makes inquiries about the kind of family that their children are going to be marrying into, whether or not they have a history of incurable illnesses like sickle cell anemia, and whether there is a history of infidelity or violence in the family. The bridewealth is a token that is paid to the bride's family in order that the future husband be granted rights over his future children and that they bear his name. If the bridewealth were not paid, then any children born out of the marital union would belong to their mother's lineage and bear her name.

Under Islamic law, however, a father retains the customary right, *ijbar*, to arrange his daughter's marriage without her consent and regardless of her age. The customary marriage thus instituted involves a seclusion of the wife-to-be, in such a way that her movement is rigorously restricted to the home, and she cannot expect to leave these confines even in emergency situations. Muslim women in Nigeria seemed resigned to this fate, with many looking eagerly ahead to a time when they could remarry for love.

In 1999 the median marriage age for women in Nigeria was eighteen years. In contrast, men generally marry at the age of twenty-six.[12] Child marriage is common in the northern Islamic part of Nigeria, where girls typically marry between the ages of twelve and fifteen. In response to this crisis, the northern Nigerian state of Bauchi has implemented legislation called the Prohibition of Withdrawal of Girls from School for Marriage Act, but its enforcement has been lax and as a result the incidence of child marriages in this Islamic state continues unabated.

Various laws regulate divorce in Nigeria. The dissolution of customary and Islamic marriages are granted in accordance with the precincts of customary law and *shari'a*, an extreme interpretation of which has been practiced primarily in the northern states of Nigeria since 2000. Civil marriages are governed by Nigeria's 1970 Matrimonial Causes Act, which stipulates that civil divorce may only be granted if the marriage in question is deemed to have been irretrievably broken. In northern Nigeria, a man married according to Islamic law may divorce his wife by three times uttering, "I divorce you." This action, called the *talaq*, is not available to women. The plight of divorced women in Islamic Nigeria leaves much to be desired. On November 19, 1999, in the northern Islamic state of Zamfara for instance, the governor Ahmed Sani directed that all single women and divorcees in his state get married in line with Islamic *shari'a* principles or risk being fired from their jobs. To support this decree, the state initiated several incentives to encourage single women and divorcees to get married, some of which included buying beds, mattresses, and household utensils for women who got married.

Reproduction

Contraception and Abortion

The sale and use of contraceptive drugs or other devices in Nigeria are unregulated. The national population policy charges national family planning programs to make available to Nigerian couples a variety of contraceptive methods in order to ensure choice amongst these couples. The total contraceptive prevalence in Nigeria is 7.5 percent and the use of modern contraceptive methods is 3.8 percent. Among married Nigerian women who use contraception, the most common methods of contraception are the pill (29.7 percent) and injectables (24.3 percent). Most Nigerian women buy their contraceptives from private pharmacies. The Nigerian government, which does not favor one contraceptive method over the other, supplies approximately 37 percent of all modern contraceptives used by Nigerian couples, including condoms, spermicides, intrauterine devices, injectables, and the pill.[13]

The use of contraceptives has risen in recent years partly due to the economic hardships in the country. In 1999, for instance, about 65 percent of all women and 82 percent of all men were reported to have heard of at least one method of contraception. The pill was the best-known method among women, while the condom was the best-known among men.[14]

Abortions are illegal in Nigeria. The legal system prohibits all forms of abortion performed at all stages of fetal or embryonic development unless it can be proven that an abortion is required to save the life of a pregnant woman. Though abortions are illegal in Nigeria, they can be procured in private hospitals for the right price. Consequently, clients from very wealthy families take advantage of this provision. However, young girls and women who come from low-income families are often forced to undergo unsafe procedures with unqualified individuals, and by so doing expose themselves to complications, which may in turn result in death. A community-based study in 1998 revealed that 25 out of 1,000 women between the ages of fifteen and forty-four undergo an abortion each year, a rate higher than most Western European countries and on par with the United States, where abortion is legal. The study also reveals abortion procedures performed by nonphysicians—pharmacists, paramedics, nurses, midwives, women themselves, and individuals with no formal medical training—average 366,000 abortions each year. Of this number, the rate of abortion is highest in southwestern Nigeria, where as many as 46 per 1,000 abortions are performed on women between the ages fifteen and forty-four. These numbers are somewhat lower in southeastern Nigeria (32 per 1,000 abortions), and much lower in the northern states of Nigeria (10–13 per 1,000 abortions).[15]

Teen Pregnancy

Nigeria's 1999 National Demographic and Health Survey reported that half the women surveyed started having sexual intercourse by the age of eighteen, while one-quarter started before the age of fifteen. The median age at first sexual intercourse for men was twenty.[16]

Cultural restrictions on premarital sex and difficulties in discussing sexual matters openly with their parents invariably limit contraceptive use by these youngsters, although there are no legal restrictions to procuring contraceptives. Moreover, preventive sex education and instruction are not included in the public school curricula to educate young women and men about the dangers of early and unprotected sex.

Lack of knowledge about sexual precautions and health has invariably contributed to the rise in teenage pregnancy in Nigeria today. In fact, teen pregnancies account for about 80 percent of hospitalized cases of abortion in the country.[17] Nonetheless, a number of nongovernmental organizations (NGOs) have begun to offer sex education and have also opened up counseling clinics all over the country.

HEALTH

Health Care Access

In 1988 the Nigerian government adopted a National Health Policy, which aimed at finding strategies for enabling all Nigerians to access affordable heath care in one of its over 12,000 heath care institutions. Since Nigeria has no social security system, under the National Health Policy all states and local governments in Nigeria are required to provide health subsidies for preventive care and additional public assistance to low-income families. Nigeria has also enacted policies to help ensure quality heath services by protecting the rights of patients. For instance, the Medical and Dental Council of Nigeria has published ethical guidelines governing professional conduct, violations of which may result in disciplinary action by the council or suspension from practice. The guidelines prohibit the public disclosure of patients' information relating to abortion services, venereal diseases, attempted suicides, and concealed birth and drug dependence, unless the information is otherwise required by law.

However, the reality in the rural areas of Nigeria leaves much to be desired. There are not enough health facilities in the rural areas and most women, particularly pregnant women, cannot afford health services. Likewise, many of the local health centers in the rural areas are not functional and those that are open are poorly equipped and staffed. Not more than one nurse runs a typical health clinic in the Nigerian rural area at any given time and there are no doctors. In the event of a serious medical problem, patients are referred to bigger hospitals. Specialist care is very costly and most public hospitals are general hospitals. If it is necessary that patients be given laboratory tests, drugs, or first aid services, they are required to pay for these services, resulting sometimes in avoidable deaths because they cannot afford to pay. However, most low-income Nigerian women do have access to traditional medical health care, which is affordable and readily available in the villages.

Diseases and Disorders

Sexually Transmitted Diseases and AIDS

The most common sexually transmitted diseases (STDs) in Nigeria are nonspecific genital infection (59.4 percent), gonorrhea (19.2 percent), candidiasis (10.5 percent), and trichomoniasis (10.5 percent). In 1994, seroprevalence rates for HIV were estimated to be 3.8 percent of the general population. As of June 1996 there were 5,500 reported cases of AIDS. By 2000 the prevalence of HIV amongst girls and women between the ages of fifteen and twenty-four was 5.1 percent. About 67 percent of the total number of Nigerians who test positive for HIV are males.[18]

While the Nigerian government has not been able to address the AIDS epidemic in a significant manner since 1986, it has attempted to coordinate governmental responses to the epidemic and has implemented HIV/AIDS and sexually transmitted infection (STI) prevention activities through its National AIDS and STI Control Program (NASCP). Under the umbrella of NASCP, Nigeria has set forth four strategic objectives: (1) the prevention of HIV infection in the country, (2) education, which would in turn reduce the negative attitude towards HIV/AIDS-positive individuals and their families, (3) education to remedy the negative attitude towards HIV and AIDS in the society as a whole, and (4) the mobilization of efforts and resources to combat HIV/AIDS.

Health-education efforts for controlling AIDS in Nigeria have largely relied on the use of mass media, both print and electronic, and have concentrated their efforts primarily in the urban areas. A number of NGOs have emerged in Nigeria that are dedicated to the dissemination of information concerning AIDS. One such group is the Society for Women and AIDS in Africa, which is headed by Dr. Eka Esu-Williams and operates out of the University of Calabar.

Even though there have been efforts to increase awareness of AIDS in Nigeria, there still remains a significant amount of discrimination against individuals who are believed to be HIV positive or to have AIDS. In February 2001, for instance, a former nurse, Georgina Ahamefule, who had worked at the Imperial Hospital in Ebute Metta, a suburb of Lagos, for five years, sought damages from the High Court for being fired for her HIV-positive status. She was however barred from the courtroom because the presiding judge said that the disease made her presence in court too risky for other people. Judge Caroline Olufawa's decision, which is being appealed, was quickly criticized as misguided and prejudicial by many human/health rights groups such as the Society for Family Health, Women in Nigeria, and the Social and Economics Rights Action, an NGO. In her lawsuit, Ahamefule argued that her firing violated both the African Charter on Human and People's Rights and also Nigerian law. She is seeking $100,000 in damages for wrongful termination and denial of medical care. Ahamefule's case has generated considerable interest in a nation where HIV has infected an estimated 5.4 percent of Nigeria's 126 million population.

Female Genital Cutting

Grassroots efforts to educate women about the dangers inherent in the procedure and to help eradicate the practice altogether have been implemented at the Nigerian village level. Local NGOs and medical practitioners have been closely involved in this effort by introducing female practitioners of this ritual to safer and more sanitary methods of performing this rite. These education efforts have primarily focused on introducing proper methods of sterilizing implements, so that this might in turn go a long way in preventing the spread of disease.

Men and women both practice coming-of-age ritual circumcision in some parts of Nigeria. The most common form of female genital cutting that is practiced by women is clitoridectomy. In this procedure the foreskin of the clitoris is scraped off, much as the foreskin of the penis is during male circumcision.

Despite advances in making the procedure more sanitary, several women's groups in Nigeria have nevertheless been vocal in their outright disapproval of this practice and have organized protest marches, seminars, and symposia. In 1999, for instance, the Edo House of Assembly passed a law prohibiting clitoridectomy. The government of Nigeria has taken this a step further and promulgated a national decree that makes female genital cutting punishable in all of Nigeria.

POLITICS AND LAW

Suffrage

Nigerian women in the south were granted the right to vote in 1954; women in the north were not permitted to vote until 1978.[19] All citizens can vote as of eighteen years of age.

Political Participation

A repeat of the political marginalization of women in Nigeria, which has its roots in the introduction of British formal rule, is being witnessed in present-day Nigeria. Post independence Nigerian governments have attempted to reverse this situation by including a limited number of women in government, but this tokenism has neither met the need for gender equality of representation in government, nor has it ensured stability through a diversified distribution of power. Progressive action and more serious thought must be given to the problem of the elimination of gender biases in the Nigerian political system.

While there are no legal impediments to political participation or voting by women, men dominate the political arena. In President Olusegun Obasanjo's new civilian government, women are underrepresented. Additionally, Nigeria boasts only six female members of its Senate body; this number incidentally represents a dramatic cut in female representation in the Senate of the last government. Women have not fared any better in the National Assembly. Of the 366 elected members, only 12 are women.[20] What is more, there are no female governors in any of the country's thirty-six states and only one deputy governor is female. Women's rights groups in Nigeria have not taken this sitting down. They continue to protest what they feel is an underrepresentation of women in the political process. They have been particularly vocal in demanding constitutional reform, which they feel will create a "gender sensitive and sustainable democracy." To this end, they have specifically challenged the local, state, and the federal governments to adopt a 30 percent affirmative action program for women.

The Nigerian government, perhaps in response to women's grievances over female underrepresentation in politics as well as other spheres of life, has taken actions to increase women's access to productive resources and technical services. It has established a family economic advancement program. Additionally, individual Nigerian states have designed and implemented many programs to increase female enrollment in primary schools and more girls' schools are being established in the northern region of the country.

Women's Rights

Nigeria has had the unenviable position of being one of the world's greatest human rights and women's rights offenders. This notoriety is not a characteristic of the present government of President Obasanjo. Rather, Nigeria has had a long history of human rights violations that can be traced as far back as 1967, when mass ethnic cleansing was initiated during the Nigeria/Biafrian war. Human rights violations remained an ever-present reality in the country, especially during the tenures of two of Nigeria's most vicious dictators, Major-Generals Ibrahim Babangida and Sani Abacha. On October 19, 1986, for instance, *Newswatch* editor-in-chief Dele Giwa was killed by a letter bomb. Even though the perpetuators of the crime were never found and no one has been prosecuted or punished, it was widely believed that agents of the then military dictator General Ibrahim Babangida planted the bomb.

Nigeria was again thrown into the public limelight as many human rights groups the world over protested the hanging on November 10, 1995, of Nigerian playwright and environmental rights leader Ken Saro-Wiwa, an execution that was sanctioned by the government of Major-General Abacha.

Nigeria's human rights violations have continued unabated and in recent years have taken on a new face. This time, these violations have been fueled by the decision of a number of northern states in the country to institute *shari'a*, or Islamic law. The adoption of this particularly harsh interpretation of Islamic law in twelve of the country's nineteen northern states has brought the ever-present religious and ethnic tension to the surface once again. Many Christian groups and some women's groups have strongly voiced their opposition to the institution of *shari'a* law.

The January 26, 2001, flogging of an eighteen-year-old teenage mother in the northern Islamic state of Zamfara for having sex outside marriage has once again plummeted Nigeria into international limelight as human/women's rights groups the world over have voiced their public condemnation of the sentence. The young woman in question, Bariya Magazu, received 100 lashes for having sex with three men whom she claimed forced themselves on her. Her punishment was pronounced and carried out by a *shari'a* court in her home state. The Nigerian women's human rights group BAOBAB was particularly vocal in its condemnation of Bariya Magazu's sentence, calling it a clear misuse of religion carried out in the name of Islamic law. The negative publicity surrounding the flogging sentence, unfortunately, has not deterred *shari'a* courts in the rest of the nation from pronouncing equally sexist sentences.

On October 10, 2001, thirty-year-old Safiya Tungar-Tudu was sentenced to death by stoning after she pled guilty to adultery before an upper *shari'a* court of Sokoto state. Even though Tungar-Tudu's death sentence was commuted many months later, in early March 2002 another woman was sentenced to a similar fate. This time a *shari'a* court in the state of Katsina sentenced thirty-year-old Amina Lawal to death for having engaged in sex outside marriage.

Government authorities in Zamfara State have banned Nigerian women's football. The state director of sports, Alhaji Shehu Gusau, was quoted as saying that women playing football was "un-Islamic" and that the sport was against the teachings of Islam. He also indicated that Zamfara state officials were going to build a new sports stadium with separate stands for male and female spectators.[21]

These abuses in the name of religion have unfortunately not been restricted to practitioners of the Islamic religion. In the months preceding and following the institution of the *shari'a* law in northern Nigerian states in 2000, some Muslims engaged in the widespread killing of eastern Igbo

Christians in the northern states of the country. Igbo Christians then retaliated by killing a number of Hausa Muslims residing in the eastern part of the country. The violence got so out of hand that President Obasanjo had to employ the national military forces to abet the violence.

On a more positive note, the Edo state government has proposed a law abolishing the "inhuman treatment of widows." It states that it will be a punishable offence to subject or coerce a widow to participate in "inhuman treatments," such as the shaving of a woman's hair, swearing on the dead body of the husband, or sleeping on the bare floor or a mat for the period of mourning. Inhuman treatments also include forcing the woman to marry a relative of her deceased husband.

Women's Movements

Nigerian women insist that they be allowed to name and define the Nigerian woman's movement on their own terms, rather than be forced to define it within the context of Western feminism. To this end, many women have continued to resist what they perceive as an overtly radical Western feminism that among other things downplays the institution of motherhood, an institution that in the Nigerian context has historically had explicit feminist overtones. Drawing on their historically derived forms of protest, thousands of Warri women "made war" for ten days on two oil companies, Chevron Texaco and Shell. They demanded that the companies employ more local people, invest in electricity supply and other infrastructure projects, as well as assist the villagers in setting up poultry and fish farms. The priorities put forth by Nigerian women in such a movement are also radically different from those set by Western women. Discourse on class, race, and sexual orientation do not have as much urgency in the Nigerian women's movements as it would in the West. Instead, Nigerian women concern themselves with issues of everyday survival. Given these preferences, the Nigerian women's movement has aimed to be an inclusive movement that acknowledges and celebrates the involvement of men in their struggle for empowerment.

Lesbian Rights

In a country where religion—both Christianity and Islam—is deep-seated, homosexuality is publicly shunned. In keeping with this national sentiment, a number of women's groups have indicated their intense displeasure with lesbianism, claiming that lesbians should be crucified for wanting to elevate lesbianism to a respectable lifestyle. The general sentiment of these groups is that lesbianism is a hormonal imbalance, a genetic and chromosomal problem. In 1997 one of the foremost female gynecologists, Dr. Edidiong Usena, was barred from speaking at the Christian-organized Family Seminar for Reproductive Health in Jos because of her so-called support for lesbian causes. Between 1995 and 1996 a number of Nigerian lesbians were raped at gunpoint in the Women's Resource Centre in Eket, Cross River State. What is more, the Women Alive Society organized a protest against lesbianism in Nigeria's capital city, Abuja, in November 1998. The demonstration, which cost them over 2 million naira (over $25,000), was donated by Nigerian churches and government-owned women's organizations.

These negative actions notwithstanding, a number of lesbian groups have emerged, albeit underground, in some Nigerian cities. In Calabar, for instance, the Lesbian Sisters in Nigeria, under the leadership of Sarah Bassey, launched a newsletter called *Umani Defender* in October 1999. The newsletter's name is taken from the Ibibio word for "vagina." The Ibibios also have a goddess named *Umani*, whom they believe is invoked to protect the chastity of women in Ibibioland. During the launching of the newsletter, the editor vowed to tackle issues relating to the plight of lesbians in Nigeria. The lesbian newsletter has since published numerous articles of the dangers of genital cutting and rape.

RELIGION AND SPIRITUALITY

Women's Roles

Women and the female goddesses, medicines, diviners, priestesses, prophetesses have always been featured prominently in society. In fact, many indigenous Nigerian cultures believe that the divinities are the real rulers of their towns. Some of the most powerful deities in Nigeria are female. For instance, in most Nigerian groups the divinities in charge of water, land, and fertility are always female; and one cannot survive without water or the fruits of the lands.

Rituals and Religious Practices

Practitioners of traditional religion in Nigeria believe in the presence of a visible universe of human beings, natural forces, and phenomena. They also believe in an invisible universe of divine beings—good and bad spirits and departed ancestors. The spiritual universe is unfathomable and therefore terrifying. Nigerian deities represent personifications of natural phenomena, like the earth (*Ani* [Igbo]), the sun (*Anyanwu* [Igbo], *Olodumare* [Yoruba]), the river (*Ebe* [Igbo], *Oya* [Yoruba]), and thunder (*Amadiora* [Igbo], *Sango* [Yoruba]). Other spirits are deified medicines (*ogwu* [Igbo], *orisa* [Yoruba]); the great goddess Adoro of eastern Nigeria is a good example of this apotheosis. *Agwu* (Igbo) or *Obatala* (Yoruba) is the medicine deity who also advances spirit possession, prophecy, and divination.

At the zenith of the spiritual world is God, variously called *Chukwu*,

Ezechitoke (Igbo) or *Oluwa, Olorun* or *Olodumare* (Yoruba). God is neither male nor female. God is too great a force to behold and is therefore assisted by a pantheon of more accessible lesser gods and goddesses who are autonomous yet interdependent. The oracles also inhabit this world and administer their will through their physical agents. The ancestors (*ndi-iche* [Igbo], *iya iya* [Yoruba]) are the dead mothers and fathers of the clan who maintain a close link between the human and nonhuman worlds. They live in the invisible world, but are called upon to be present during everyday meetings and important events. In between these worlds are the priests and priestesses (*Attamas* [Igbo], in Yorubaland they are referred to as *Babalawo* [male] or *Iya Orisa* [female]) who embody idiosyncrasies from both worlds.

In many of the noncentralized precolonial Nigerian societies, women's religious and political groups like the association of daughters and wives took charge of the religious life of the community. They performed rituals for the general wellness of their communities and performed purification rituals. During the colonial period, however, a lot of these female religious and political organizations lost their prestige as colonial rule and Christianity began to replace their political and religious functions. Clinics and foreign drugs started to displace the need for the rituals and sacrifices these women's organizations undertook for the welfare of the village.

The Christian Church attacked the goddess religion and those customs that enhanced women's status. Church and school were synonymous, with classes being held in the church building. Girls had less access than boys to missionary education. These schools generally provided opportunities for education in vocations that were considered male like carpentry and printing thus excluding women in the process. The few girls who attended missionary schools were confined entirely to the private life of the family. They were taught cooking, cleaning, child care, and sewing, which were considered the necessary domestic skills for Christian marriages and motherhood, unlike the preparation in precolonial cultures that enabled women to be involved in both the private and the public domain. These prejudices against women by these missionaries were in keeping with the Victorian ideology that "a woman's place was in the home." Christian marriage also brought the title of "Mrs.," which replaced the Nigerian tradition of going by one's mother's first name, further diffusing the validation of women.

There were some exceptions to this general rule. In colonial Lagos, for instance, British expansion of girls' education allowed many women to become teachers and educational officers. Specialized training in domestic science during this period also helped increase the number of women involved in small-scale businesses such as tailoring, baking, and catering— businesses that allowed these entrepreneurial women to become quite influential. However, in the modern period, the patriarchal tendencies have continued and intensified and Nigerian women's power and status have continued to deteriorate.

Religious Law

Since the end of Abacha's military dictatorship, the controversy surrounding the institution of *shari'a* law in Nigeria has taken center stage, with violent civil unrest erupting in different parts of the country. Considerable concern was prompted in 1999 when the northern Nigerian state of Zamfara declared *shari'a* law, thus signaling its intent to make Islam the central course of state governance. Zamfara's announcement was followed by similar statements by other northern Nigerian states indicating their desire to adopt Islamic law, thus raising immediate concern and disquieting questions about the non-Muslim populations in those states. Many wondered whether Nigeria's constitution would continue to be operational, especially in regard to the rights of non-Muslims in these Islamic states; or whether they would be instead made subject to the legal, social, and cultural strictures of *shari'a*. A number of violent outbursts have ensued following these northern states' announcements. In Kwara state, for instance, declarations that *shari'a* law will be instituted have unleashed built-up resentment of Christians by Muslims, who have consequently attacked and destroyed a number of Christian churches, Christian-owned businesses, as well as Christian homes. The Islamic law has since been instituted in twelve of Nigeria's northern states since 2000.

VIOLENCE

Domestic Violence

Domestic violence is punishable under Nigerian law and women may cite domestic violence as grounds for divorce if their husbands have previously been convicted of seriously injuring them or attempting to do so. However, in the Islamic states of northern Nigeria, where *shari'a* law is operational, it is actually permissible for a husband to "correct" his wife's behavior with physical punishment. He may mete out such a punishment as long as it is not deemed "unreasonable in kind or in degree" and "does not amount to the infliction of grievous hurt."

Rape/Sexual Assault

According to the Nigerian penal code (enforced in the northern states of Nigeria) and the criminal code (enforced in the southern states of Nigeria), rape is a punishable crime. In these codes, rape is defined as involving the use of force, fraud, intimidation, and threats to life or physical harm to obtain sexual intercourse. Sodomy and the insertion of foreign objects into a woman's vagina are not defined as rape, but can be prosecuted under the country's criminal laws, which prohibit "unnatural" sexual offenses, assault, indecent assault, or acts of gross indecency. Under the provisions of the penal code of northern Nigeria, children under the age of fourteen are regarded as minors and therefore cannot consent to sexual acts.

Under the same law, children under the age of sixteen are incapable of consenting to any act of "gross indecency" with adults in positions of authority like teachers or guardians. Similarly, the southern Nigerian criminal code prohibits statutory rape and therefore sexual intercourse with minors under the age of thirteen is punishable by a sentence of life imprisonment, with or without caning. The sexual assault of a girl under the age of thirteen is punishable by imprisonment of up to three years. Likewise, sexual assaults committed against girls between the ages of thirteen and sixteen are punishable by imprisonment of up to two years.

Trafficking in Women and Children

There is an active market for trafficking of Nigerian women to Europe and elsewhere for illicit purposes. No one knows exactly how many women leave for Europe each year, but as many as 80 percent of the girls who are trafficked from Nigeria are thought to come from two states, Edo and Delta. While Nigerian society and government acknowledge that the trafficking in Nigerian women particularly to cities in Western Europe is a continuing problem, there is no national law making the trafficking of persons a crime in Nigeria.

In September 2000, 3,000 Nigerian girls were deported from Italian prisons for prostituting. Of the approximately 2,500 minors who worked as street prostitutes in Italy, it has been estimated that as many as 2,300 originally came from Nigeria and Albania. Another 403 Nigerian girls were deported from other countries for the same reason between January and July 2000. In neighboring Gabon, the Nigerian embassy has repatriated over fifteen girls between the ages of ten and fifteen who had been smuggled from Nigeria via Togo to Europe. Similarly, in January 2000, authorities of Côte d'Ivoire repatriated eleven 10–11-year-old girl "prostitutes" to Lagos, Nigeria from Abidjan.[22]

In response to this problem, the wife of the Nigerian vice president, Titi Abubakar, founded a group called Women Trafficking and Child Labor Eradication to counter the effects of this trade. The problem of women trafficking in Nigeria has also forced the midwestern state of Edo, where most of the girls originated, to enact an antiprostitution law to curb the practice. Governor Lucky Igbinedion signed the state's antiprostitution bill into law in 2000. The governor's wife, Eky Igbinedion, herself a keen crusader of the cause, had previously initiated the Idia Renaissance, to ensure what she termed the rebirth of social and moral values among Edo women. The state also reportedly paraded returnee prostitutes publicly in an effort to dissuade other women from traveling out of the country for prostitution. This act of shaming has done nothing to deter other women from experimenting with sex work abroad.

In northern Nigeria, the government of Zamfara state has declared its intent to offer money to any woman who gives up prostitution. The wife of the state governor, Karima Sani, told a Nigerian newspaper that each woman would receive 25,000 naira ($250). Twenty-seven women in her state had apparently already taken advantage of the offer. The Zamfara state government insists that the cash gifts are intended to help prostitutes abandon sex work and set up small-scale businesses instead. The monetary package that has been set aside for these purposes is equivalent to several months' salary for a typical Nigerian civil servant. Prostitution has officially been banned in Zamfara since *shari'a* law was instituted at the beginning of 2000. Many prostitutes have consequently been forced out of the region into neighboring states in northern Nigeria.

OUTLOOK FOR THE TWENTY-FIRST CENTURY

Nigeria has been wrought by ethnic and religious conflict as well as gendered discrimination. True progress in this young nation will depend on the implementation of a political agenda that not only respects but also takes into account the country's unique and rich character that includes its ethnic, religious, and gender diversity. While women in Nigeria have achieved a number of very progressive strides, in certain areas they have fallen short. The Nigerian government as a result has teamed up with local interest groups to address this oversight and right the situation. Of particular note is the federal government's National Policy on Women, which has been instituted to correct the "injustices and marginalization" that numerous Nigerian gender activists have complained about. The policy addresses issues like early forced marriages, female genital circumcision, and discrimination against women in the workplace.

NOTES

1. World Bank Group, *Nigeria Data Profile*, World Development Indicators Database, July 2000.

2. U.S. Department of State, *Country Report: Nigeria*, Bureau of African Affairs, August 2000.

3. World Bank Group, *Nigeria Data Profile*.

4. Ibid.

5. U.S. Department of Justice, Bureau of African Affairs, *Background Notes*, Nigeria, June 2002.

6. Human Development Reports, http://hdr.undp.org.

7. Population Reference Bureau, *Nigeria: Demographic Highlights*, 2002.

8. Human Development Reports.

9. www.thp.org/prize/96/ogunleye.htm, 1996 Africa Prize laureate Chief Bisi Ogunleye, founder, Country Women Association of Nigeria.

10. There is no such thing as a Nigerian housewife; all Nigerian women work outside the home.

11. Population Council, *Facts About Adolescents from the Demographic and Health Survey, Statistical Tables for Program Planning, Nigeria 1999*, tab. 8, "Marital Status" (percentage distribution), www.popcouncil.org.

12. Population Reference Bureau, *Nigeria: Demographic Highlights, 2002*.

13. Ibid.

14. Ibid.

15. Alan Guttmacher Institute, *The Campaign Against Unwanted Pregnancy*, 1998.

16. United Nations Population Fund, *Populi: The UNFPA Magazine* 28, no. 1 (April 2001).

17. Ibid.

18. Center for Reproductive Law and Policy (CRLP), "Women's Reproductive Rights in Nigeria: A Shadow Report 1998," www.reproductiverights.org. See also World Bank Group, *Gender Stats: Database for Gender Statistics, Nigeria, 2002*.

19. Women in Politics: Women's Suffrage, *A World Chronology of the Recognition of Women's Rights to Vote and to Stand for Election*, www.ipu.org/wmn-e/suffrage.htm; *Worldwide Guide to Women in Leadership*, www.guide2womenleaders.com/nigeria.htm.

20. U.S. Government, *Country Reports on Human Rights Practices for 1999*, February 2000.

21. "Women's Soccer Banned in Nigeria," *Islamic Voice* vol. 14-02, no. 158 (February 2000). www.islamicvoice.com/february.2000/news1.htm.#SOC.

22. Advocacy Project, *Nigeria: Trafficking in Women*, 2000, http://advocacynet.autoupdate.com/cpage_view/nigtraffick_deportation_6_36.html.

RESOURCE GUIDE

Suggested Reading

Amadiume, Ifi. *Male Daughters, Female Husbands: Gender and Sex in an African Society*. London: Zed Books, 1987.

Awe, Bolanle, ed. *Nigerian Women in Historical Perspective*. Lagos: Sankore Publishers, 1992.

Awe, Bolanle, Susan Geiger, et al. "Women, Family, State, and Economy in Africa." *Signs* 16 (1991).

Leith-Ross, Sylvia. *African Women: A Study of the Ibo of Nigeria*. London: Faber & Faber, 1938.

Mba, Nina E. *Nigerian Women Mobilized: Women's Political Activity in Southern Nigeria, 1900–1965*. Berkeley: Institute of International Studies, University of California, 1982.

Okonjo, Kamene. "The Dual-Sex Political System in Operation: Igbo Women and Community Politics in Midwestern Nigeria." In *Women in Africa: Studies in Social and Economic Change*, edited by N. J. Hafkin and Edna G. Bay, 45–58. Stanford: Stanford University Press, 1976.

Sudarkasa, Niara. *Where Women Work: A Study of Yoruba Women in the Marketplace and in the Home*. Ann Arbor: University of Michigan Press, 1973.

Van Allen, Judith. " 'Sitting on a Man': Colonialism and the Lost Political Institutions of Igbo Women." In *Women and Society: An Anthropological Reader*, edited by Sharon W. Tiffany, 163–87. St. Albans, VT: Eden Press Women's Publications 1979.

Videos/Films

Daura and Katsina and The Hausa Woman. 64 min. *Daura and Katsina* is a tour of two Northern Nigeria townships, renowned as ancient seats of Islamic culture and learning. *The Hausa Woman* documents how the Hausa women make themselves beautiful.

Mammy Water: In Search of the Water Spirits of Nigeria. 1991. 59 min. A look at Mammy Water (a water deity worshipped in Nigeria) rituals. Leaders and followers are interviewed. Uniquely Nigerian symbolisms of female power and authority are seen with devotees dancing themselves into trance.

Monday's Girls. 1993. 50 min. Two Nigerian girls experience a traditional rite of passage.

The Preferred Sex . . . The Desired Number. 1995. 53 min. The status of women in Nigeria and India is surveyed via interviews with couples, clergy, and family planning practitioners.

Web Sites

Country Brief, www.worldbank.org/afr/ng2.htm.

Country Data Profile, http://devdata.worldbank.org/external/dgprofile.asp?rmdk=82531&w=0&l=e.

Gender Statistics, http://genderstats.worldbank.org/.

Jenda: A Journal of Culture and African Women's Studies, www.jendajournal.com.

Nigeria Pathfinder, http://jolis.worldbankimflib.org/pathfinders/countries/nG/index.html.
To access data on gender issues, this database also allows you to run your own queries.

UNDP Human Development Report 2001, www.undp.org/hdr2001/.

UNIFEM Progress of the World's Women 2000, www.unifem.undp.org/progressww/index.html.

United Nations Women Watch, www.un.org/womenwatch/.

The World's Women 2000: Trends and Statistics, www.un.org/depts/unsd/ww2000/index.htm.

Organizations

BAOBAB for Women's Human Rights
P.O. Box 73630
Victoria Island, Lagos, Nigeria
Phone/Fax: 234-1-617134
Email: baobab@baobab.com.ng

Country Women Association of Nigeria (COWAN)
No. 2 Afunbiowo Street, PMB 809

Akure, Ondo State, Nigeria
Phone: 234-34-231945
Fax: 1-234-34-231633

Federation of Muslim Women's Associations in Nigeria (FOMWAN)
3, Karimu Kotun Street
Victoria Island, Lagos, Nigeria
Phone: 234-62-238278

International Federation of Women Lawyers (FIDA)
Anambra/Enugu zone
No. 9 Second Ave. Independence Layout
P.O. Box 1686
Enugu State, Nigeria

Women for Democracy and Leadership
25 Moremi Street
New Bodija, Ibadan, Oyo State
(with offices in Kwara, Edo, Oyo, Osun, Ekiti and Ondo)
Phone: 02-8102555/2411025
Fax: 02-2412199
Email: slawani@skannet.com.ng

Women Justice Programme (WJP)
37C Foresythe Street
Lafiaji, Lagos, Nigeria
Phone: 243-1-2632999
Fax: 243-1-2632811

Women's Consortium of Nigeria (WOCON)
No. 2 Arimokunri Street
Ijemo, Abeokuta
Phone: 039-242113/244758
Fax: 01-2635300
Lagos Office: 2nd Floor, Right Wing

SELECTED BIBLIOGRAPHY

Achebe, Nwando. *Farmers, Traders, Warriors, and Kings: Female Power and Authority in Northern Igboland, 1900–1960.* Portsmouth, NH: Heinemann.
Afonja, Simi. "Land Control, A Critical Factor in Yoruba Gender Stratification." In *Women and Class in Africa*, edited by Claire Robertson and Iris Berger. New York: Africana Publishing Company, 1986.
Amadiume, Ifi. *Male Daughters, Female Husbands: Gender and Sex in an African Society.* London: Zed Books, 1987.
Awe, Bolanle, ed. *Nigerian Women in Historical Perspective.* Lagos: Sankore Publishers, 1992.
Denzer, LaRay. "Domestic Science Training in Colonial Yorubaland, Nigeria." In *African Encounters with Domesticity*, edited by Karen Tranberg Hansen. New Brunswick, NJ: Rutgers University Press, 1992.

Ijere, Martin O, ed. *Women in Nigerian Economy*. Enugu: Acena Publishers, 1991.

Imam, Ayesha. "The WIN Document: Conditions of Women in Nigeria and Policy Recommendations to 2000 A.D." Presented at the NGO Forum, UN Conference on Women, Zaria, Nigeria, 1985.

———. *Women in Nigeria Today*. London: Zed Books, 1985.

Leith-Ross, Sylvia. *African Women: A Study of the Ibo of Nigeria*. London: Faber & Faber, 1938.

Mann, Kristin. "Women, Landed Property, and the Accumulation of Wealth in Early Colonial Lagos." *Signs: Journal of Women in Culture and Society* 16, no. 4 (1991).

Mba, Nina E. *Nigerian Women Mobilized: Women's Political Activity in Southern Nigeria, 1900–1965*. Berkeley: Institute of International Studies, University of California, 1982.

Nnaemeka Obioma, ed. *Sisterhood, Feminisms, and Power: From Africa to the Diaspora*. Trenton, NJ: African World Press, 1998.

Ogundipe-Leslie, Molara. "Women in Nigeria." In *Women in Nigeria Today*, edited by D. L. Baddejo. London: Zed Books Ltd., 1985.

Okonjo, Kamene. "The Dual-Sex Political System in Operation: Igbo Women and Community Politics in Midwestern Nigeria." In *Women in Africa: Studies in Social and Economic Change*, edited by N. J. Hafkin and Edna G. Bay, 45–58. Stanford: Stanford University Press, 1976.

14

RWANDA

Michele Wagner

PROFILE OF RWANDA

Rwanda is a small mountainous country in the Great Lakes region of eastern central Africa, bordered by Uganda, Tanzania, Burundi, and the Democratic Republic of Congo (formerly Zaire). Rwanda's total area is 10,186 square miles (26,338 square kilometers). The precursor to the modern nation-state of Rwanda was a precolonial kingdom ruled by a small aristocratic dynasty, the Banyiginya, and located in the south-central highlands, near modern-day Butare. In the nineteenth century, it was conquered by the Germans and administered as a district of German East Africa. Following World War I, it came under Belgian administration. Rwanda gained its independence in July 1, 1962, and appeared to outside observers to be well on the path of successful economic development.

In 1990, Rwanda underwent a rapid succession of challenges, including an economic crisis, a shift from single-party to multiparty politics, and an armed incursion from rebels in exile, sending it on a downward slide. Within four years, the country plunged into full-scale war, politically targeted massacres, and ethnic genocide—a complex set of catastrophes from which it has yet to recover. Today, the stress of these events and of the ongoing war Rwanda has fought in neighboring Democratic Republic of Congo (formerly Zaire) is borne by all Rwandans, but particularly by Rwandan women and girls. They comprise the majority of Rwanda's current population, estimated up to 70 percent, and a large percentage of the country's heads of households.[1]

Rwanda is in the tropics, one degree south of the equator but at relatively high altitude, with an average altitude of 5,200 feet (about 1,500 meters) above sea level. The high altitude is instrumental in modifying the climate. The average annual daily temperature is thirty degrees centigrade, but temperatures vary greatly by region and fluctuate considerably between day and night. Nighttime temperatures in the higher altitude regions can drop below freezing. Variation in altitude also affects the rainfall. Some of the highest elevations may receive an annual rainfall of more than seventy inches, and the lowlands less than thirty inches. The average annual rainfall in the country's hilly central region varies between forty and fifty-five inches. This climate allows the cultivation of a wide variety of tropical highland crops including coffee, tea, bananas, cereals, beans, and a variety of tubers.

Rwanda is one of the world's most densely populated countries. The average population density in Rwanda is 337 people per square kilometer, with an estimated growth rate of 2 percent per annum.[2] The population before 1994 was 7.3 million, and it had been projected that by the year 2000 the population would have reached 10 million. Following the massive violence of 1994, which claimed an estimated 800,000 to 1 million lives and induced at least 2 million people to flee the country,[3] the 2002 population was believed to be in the range of 7.3 to 8.7 million.[4] Demographic estimates regarding Rwanda should be treated with considerable caution, however, since no systematic survey of the population has been carried out since the catastrophic events of 1994. In addition to sustaining an enormous number of deaths, Rwanda has also undergone massive population turnover. The events of 1994 induced millions of citizens to flee, but it also motivated large numbers of Rwandans who had lived in exile for many years to return to the country, together with their families and other household members. This returning group, most of them Tutsis (often referred to as "returnees" or "old caseload refugees"), constituted a sizable population influx. In the aftermath of such turbulence, demographic information is highly politically sensitive. It is clear that pregenocide ethnic statistics (Hutu 85 percent, Tutsi 14 percent, and Twa 1 percent) may no longer be considered valid, but a thorough enumeration of who did or did not survive the conflict, at which stage they died, and the origins and ethnicities of both the living and the dead are controversial matters. Further complicating the issue of demography, a number of analysts have asserted that Rwanda's dense population was itself a cause of the nation's tragedy. They have argued that rapid rates of population growth, high population density, and intensifying land pressures, combined with negative rates of economic growth, gave rise to the internal stresses that propelled Rwandans toward war and genocide.[5]

As can be anticipated, Rwanda's population composition, life expectancy rates, and other demographic phenomena have been altered by conflict and a persistent state of crisis that has remained since 1994. By 2002, life expectancy rates stood at forty years of age for females and thirty-nine for males.[6] While the total fertility rate was relatively high at 5.8 percent among women of child-bearing age,[7] the infant mortality rate was also high at 100 per 1,000 live births, and the under-five mortality rate was quite high at 187 per 1,000 live births.[8] The overall composition of Rwanda's population was skewed toward youth: children under age five composed 16.8 percent of the population while those under fifteen comprised 44 percent of the total population.[9] Elders over sixty-five years were very few in number, comprising only 1.9 percent of the total population.[10]

Rwanda is a rural nation: it is estimated that 93 percent of Rwandans live in rural areas, where the main economic activity is subsistence agriculture. A high reliance on subsistence is reflected in its low per capita income of $220.[11]

OVERVIEW OF WOMEN'S ISSUES

Rwanda's women live in a highly ethnicized and politicized country that most recently suffered an ethnic genocide in 1994. The challenges that women face are inextricably linked to ethnicity and to the contours of their lives before and during 1994. Even women of the same ethnicity face different challenges depending on where they lived during the war. Tutsi women, for example, face different challenges if they are genocide survivors, that is, if they were living inside the country when the genocide broke out, than if they immigrated to Rwanda after the war in the flood of "Tutsi returnees" from exile. Hutu women face vastly different challenges depending on their own or their family's political position prior to the war, their family's prewar socioeconomic status, and whether or not they became displaced. Many Rwandans were or are members of ethnically mixed families, and have learned to maneuver with great subtlety in their nation's ethnically hypercharged milieu. Twa women face a unique set of challenges that relate to their extreme degree of marginalization; they are invisible in Rwanda's ethnically "bipolar" self-image. In addition, regardless of ethnicity, most Rwandan women bear responsibility in assisting the members of their extended family, so that even those women who have not themselves directly experienced physical violence may be caring for others who have.

The prevalence and long-term persistence of overt armed warfare, which has engaged Rwandan soldiers from 1990 until the present, and of massive internal human rights abuse, has left very few Rwandan families untouched to this day. More severely affected families have not survived intact, and today as many as 40 to 70 percent of Rwandan women of all ethnicities find themselves in the position of head of household. Although nearly all Rwandan families face distressingly complex problems and a frustrating lack of resources to address them, many of those families headed by women and girls find the challenges compounded by gender discrimination. This is because neither the administrative system nor the individuals who compose or interact with the system have until recently conceived of a Rwanda in which women would be filling roles previously regarded as "male."

Prior to 1994, the responsibility of representing the family in the larger society rested almost exclusively on male shoulders. Men conducted almost all transactions engaging the family with public institutions such as government agencies, banks, or even the police. Dealings with commercial enterprises, public offices in general, even marriage negotiations were automatically regarded as the domain of male family members, and especially the male head of household. It was sons, and normally not daughters, who were raised with the skills and the self-image required to represent the family in the larger community. This meant that the cultures of public institutions were largely shaped by men. Therefore, in the case of today's female-headed households, their skills and means to connect with public institutions and to use them to solve their family's problems—as well as their confidence to do so—are frequently insufficient. Women who may be highly competent at managing a household from within simply never anticipated that they would manage their family links to external institutions. Entering into this wider realm to advocate on behalf of their family's needs has been a daunting challenge for many Rwandan women, and one in which they feel the stress of their situation most keenly.

A particularly painful issue that has affected the lives of Rwandan women of all ethnicities is the gender-related physical and sexual violence that became widespread during and after the genocide. In 1994, an estimated 250,000 women were raped during the war and genocide.[12] This violence has continued, and it is often perpetrated in places that are meant to be safe, such as refugee camps, or by those who are meant to protect the women.

EDUCATION

Education is a sector that has recently attracted considerable attention and investment from both the Rwandan government and the international community. The 1994 conflict destroyed Rwanda's educational infrastructure, which prior to the war had been outstanding among its peers in the region. Schools were transformed into massacre sites and displaced persons camps. Teachers were killed or forced to flee. But since 1994, Rwanda's educational system had come under scrutiny for another reason: it has been identified as one of the genocide's causal factors. Education, or miseducation, the postwar government has asserted, sowed ideological seeds that germinated in genocide. To address these concerns, international groups have poured resources into peace education and conflict-resolution training, while international governments, particularly the European Union, have invested in physical repair. This massive international assistance and scrutiny with regard to education has had a perceptible impact on improving its accessibility to females.

Opportunities

Increasing educational accessibility has been a high priority for Rwandan governments since the era of independence. Education has undoubtedly been a focus of attention precisely because of the inattention given to it by Rwanda's colonial rulers. In 1963 when Rwanda attained its independence, very few of its citizens had ever had access to a formal education at any level, and nearly all of those who had were male. Moreover, government-sponsored public education has not been part of Rwanda's colonial experience because of a 1925 Belgian decision that education would be conducted by missionary orders. It was not until the 1950s that public schools run by the government and staffed by civil servants were created.

Colonial-era educational policy focused almost exclusively on the primary level, which was divided into "lower primary" (grades one and two) and "upper primary" (grades three through six). Primary school training concentrated on gardening, hygiene, vocational education, and simple literacy in the Rwandan language (Kinyarwanda). French, the colonial language, was compulsory for upper primary boys, but only optional for those girls who managed to enter primary school at all. Until the mid-1950s Rwanda had only one secondary school, the Groupe Scolaire, a Catholic institution founded in 1929. Its efforts were directed almost exclusively at Tutsi boys. No postsecondary educational institutions existed in the country until the late 1950s, except a theological seminary open only to males.

Rwanda's educational system began to open up around the time of independence. In the late 1950s, as independence loomed near, the colonial administration recognized that Rwanda lacked adequate personnel to function as an independent country and established a series of postsecondary facilities, including a teacher training school, a vocational school, and a preuniversity institution. At independence, Rwanda's first university was established in a partnership between the government and the Roman Catholic Dominican Order of Canada. However, the pool of secondary school graduates eligible to attend the university was so small there were hardly enough candidates to fill all the places. One of the reasons for this shortage was that a large majority of those who had completed secondary education were Tutsi males, the most likely group to be expelled during independence-era ethnic power struggles.

At independence, Rwanda invested heavily in education because the Hutu-led government desperately lacked educated personnel. Initially, it had neither the means nor the personnel to set up a nationwide educational system, so it relied heavily on the Catholic Church for assistance. Even by the end of the 1960s, 80 percent of primary and nearly all secondary schools were mission operated.[13] Nevertheless, more than a quarter of the national budget (27 percent in 1968) was invested in education.[14] In addition, policies were put in place to address the colonial-era educational ethnic imbalance. Access to school was allocated on a quota system, based on the percentage of the ethnic composition of the general population, in order to give Hutus the opportunity to "catch up" to Tutsis. Gender was never a consideration in this effort to overcome earlier educational discrimination: inequalities in access were framed on a Hutu-Tutsi grid, not a gendered one. But since Rwandan Hutus of the colonial era suffered discrimination when the primary-level educational system expanded in the 1970s–1980s, their daughters were similarly marginalized.

The postgenocide educational system is by all accounts a sector of considerable investment and national interest, but accurate statistics are hard to come by. Since the current national population includes significant subpopulations of Rwandans who have recently returned after living many years as refugees in countries with English-based educational systems (particularly in Uganda and Tanzania) as well as Rwandans trained in a French-based system (that had existed in Rwanda and Burundi), today's Rwandan students speak different languages—and perhaps more importantly, parents and policymakers have different concepts of the best approach to education. There has been a flourishing of private schools at all levels, including a private university, which serve primarily the returnee community. Public school enrollments are reportedly strong. The gross primary school enrollment ratio is 88 percent, while the net primary school enrollment ratio is 68 percent female (67 percent male).[15] A separate United Nations Development Programme (UNDP) study found 102 female primary students for every 100 male primary students.[16]

This strong showing of females in Rwanda's primary school system diminishes slightly at higher educational levels. At the secondary and tertiary levels, it is estimated that three out of every seven students are female.[17]

Literacy

Literacy statistics from a 1997 study demonstrated that the cohort of school-age girls from the 1970s through the early 1980s did attend school: 77 percent of young women and 83 percent of young men were literate by 1997.[18] Adult literacy rates are relatively high in Rwanda: the estimated adult literacy rate in 2000 for all adults was 69 percent (60 percent among women and 73.6 percent among men).[19]

EMPLOYMENT AND ECONOMICS

Farming

The dominant economic activity in Rwanda is farming: it accounts for the expenditure of most productive labor and the largest piece of the national gross domestic product, some 40.5 to 47 percent.[20] The vast majority of Rwandan women—immediately prior to the war, an estimated 98 percent—were farmers.[21] The basic unit of agricultural production is the household. Most rural households mix the production of crops and the raising of livestock intended for their own consumption with similar production intended for sale. The main consumption crops are bananas, sweet potatoes, cassava, sorghum, and legumes. The main export staples are coffee, tea, hides and skins, and pyrethrum.[22] The overwhelming share of agricultural labor is expended on crops destined for household consumption, rather than the export market. Among domestic food crops, however, the distinction between household-consumed food crop and cash crop blurs because what are generally considered as food or subsistence crops also bring cash to the household when traded in the market. Indeed, many of the crops conventionally identified as intended for subsistence bring more cash in the household than those conventionally identified as cash crops. The former crops are primarily under the management of women, although in postwar Rwanda, in many households women also manage cash crops.

Rwandan agriculture has been very labor intensive and has entailed a major initiative to open up farmland. This degree of labor input into the land means that within the issue of landownership, the question of which land is very important. Further, other kinds of household-owned fields, including banana and coffee plantations, also represent significant input. These and other factors have come into play in massive postwar land conflict. Prior to the war, land competition was a point of social tension, and an oft-cited causal actor in the political conflict of the 1990s. Since the war, competition for land has increased. With the influx of returning Tutsi "old caseload" refugees and recent "new caseload" refugees (Hutu), two different generations of refugees of acutely opposed ethnic groups have found themselves making competing claims for the same land. In many cases, the disputants have been female—particularly in the case of the new caseload refugees—and the stakes have been high, since land is the foundation of survival and well-being. The stakes have been high in another sense as well, as human rights monitors have found that among those detained in prison facing genocide accusations many have been accused by their codisputants in a land conflict.

Paid Employment

Apart from agriculture, the second largest sector of the national economy is the service sector, which accounts for nearly 38 percent of the gross domestic product, but only 2 percent of female labor. Industry and manufacturing, the third largest sector, accounts for some 31 percent of the national economy, but only one percent of female labor.[23] Rwanda's postcolonial development strategy never concentrated on developing industry. It instead concentrated on farming, since the majority of citizens (and particularly Hutus, its constituency) were farmers. Rwanda's small industrial sector concentrated on processing agricultural produce, manufacturing beverages (beer and soft drinks), cigarettes, shoes, plastics, and cement on small-scale basis. Rwanda has great industrial potential—including labor, energy, and natural resources. Its potential energy sources include methane from Lake Kivu (currently used in processing beer) and excellent conditions for hydroelectric power. It also has mineral resources including cassiterite (tin ore), uranium ores, wolframite (tungsten ore), beryllium ore, potassium compounds, and phosphate of lithium.

According to the ILO, Rwandan maternity leave policy states that women should receive twelve weeks of paid maternity leave at 67 percent of their regular wages from their employer.[24]

Inheritance, Property, and Land Rights

Most women in Rwanda live in the rural areas, where the main economic activity is subsistence agriculture. In this milieu, women's well-being is directly and indirectly linked to their access to land. Land is a source of food, wealth, status, and respect. Although gender discrimination is legally banned, established patterns of everyday life dictate that land and capital assets pass from fathers to sons. In preconflict Rwanda, women's access to land came from their husbands. In the case of the husband's death, the widow had usufruct (user) rights to his land as long as she cared for their young children (and particularly his sons). As the children grew into adulthood, their cooperation was vital for their mother to maintain usufruct rights to her land. In postwar Rwanda, the question of land rights is a knotty one in which human relationships and emotions, including jealousy and revenge, overlap or compete with law—and where the legal system has been so paralyzed by genocide accusations that questions about land rights have fallen far down the list of legal priorities. In this context, Rwandan women face the challenges of presenting their case before local administrators and learning to use the system to work on their behalf. These challenges have become victories for some women, and insurmountable barriers for others.

Social/Government Programs

Structural Adjustment

Economic policies of the early 1990s, notably the implementation of a structural adjustment program of the International Monetary Fund, are often cited as an aggravating factor leading toward the internal political conflict that ultimately provoked the genocide. Two large currency devaluations and the removal of official prices provoked an economic crisis in the early 1990s. This crisis especially affected salaried workers—particularly those employed in the civil service or in state-owned enterprises—precisely the group most active in the genocide.

FAMILY AND SEXUALITY

Gender Roles and Division of Labor

The 1994 genocide not only took some 800,000 lives, it destroyed families, particularly Tutsi and multiethnic families. Even those individuals who escaped with their lives did not survive with their deeper sense of themselves intact, for in Rwanda the family sits at the core of identity, and Tutsi families as collective entities were killed. Similarly, the massive abuses of the postwar government, including the more overt abuses such as the detention of at least 200,000 persons in the most inhumane and degrading of conditions for years on end, has destroyed Hutu families. And in both cases, it has been the role of Rwanda's women to form the fragments into new, often makeshift families and struggle to nurture those shattered by war. This process is not left solely to women, however. Many children, particularly girls, are raising siblings alone.

The extended family (*muryango*) was the fundamental unit of precolonial Rwandan society. These powerful collective structures negotiated with one another, thus forming the basis of local politics, but also negotiated internally, managing collective property, as well as the behavior and productivity of individual members. Many of the vital functions of modern civil society—from justice, mediation, and punishment to labor organization and education—were performed by and within the family. Individual members sought to fulfill their responsibilities toward the family and even submit to the collective will, not only because of the terrestrial consequences (tension, disfavor, abandonment) but also because of the punitive capacity of deceased senior relatives (ancestors). The continued importance of the family in independent Rwanda was explicitly articulated in the young nation's constitution, which stated that family was "the basis of Rwandan society." And what the constitution affirmed legally, Rwandan subsistence farmers, who relied on their families for fundamental survival, already understood practically. The family was the unit of survival, and of well-being.

Reproduction

Rwanda's focus on the family, and particularly on the notion that more members meant greater strength, placed tremendous emphasis on female fertility. Colonial policies did not discourage this, because the attractiveness of Rwanda to both Germany and Belgium lay in the density of its population. The lovely, fertile region held an enormous potential labor force, with mines and plantations relatively nearby. Germany had contemplated building a railway to Rwanda to tap into its labor potential. Belgium, too, examined programs to connect the vast population to mines and plantations in the nearby Congo.

The colonial-era introduction of Christianity, and Roman Catholicism in particular, further reinforced Rwandans' own emphasis on large families and female fertility. Catholic notions of motherhood as a fundamental Christian vocation reinforced ideas that merged "woman" with "mother" in Rwandan culture. The different and disparate ideologies the Rwandans encountered both before and during colonialism appeared to converge on the importance of female fertility. By the 1980s a new discourse introduced by the donors of international aid challenged the government and the church—the discourse of population control. Fertility, in this new set of ideas, generated not wealth but impoverishment. Rwanda was overpopulated, and overpopulation was a problem. This view about women's reproductive capacity remained important until 1994 when, in a new political milieu, it shifted again, particularly with regard to Tutsi women. Genocide was a political strategy that was meant to destroy the rebel movement called the Rwandan Patriotic Front (RPF) by destroying all persons who might possibly offer any potential support to that movement—even support in the distant future in the case of infants.

In the case of the Rwandan genocide, this mixing of the political and the demographic continued in the aftermath. It was expressed in a popular discourse that centered on the political responsibility of Tutsi women to rebuild the Tutsi people. In post-genocide Rwanda, motherhood became depicted as patriotic. In political rallies and in political meetings, Rwandan women took up the wearing of decorative headbands, popularly referred to as "the traditional crown of motherhood." Women had become the means of salvation in a predominant political discourse of genocide recovery.[25]

HEALTH

Health Care Access

The war-damaged health care system continues to recover. The active presence of humanitarian nongovernmental organizations and UN agencies has delivered care to certain regions and to specific sectors of the population, such as small children. In terms of infant and child health, the UN Children's Fund (UNICEF) has played an active role in coordinating and delivering medical treatment. While the under-five death rate remains high (187 per 1,000 live births), the youngest Rwandans are getting access to vaccinations: between 85 and 94 percent of children under one year of age had received their vital childhood vaccinations.[26] Others remain at risk: only 41 percent of Rwandans have access to safe drinking water.[27]

Nurse treating patient, Rwanda. Photo © TRIP/R. Vargas.

Health care is a highly politicized issue in Rwanda, since accessibility and quality entail choices about how to allocate limited resources to a sharply divided population. Rwanda's health care system was quite damaged in the events of 1994—hospitals and dispensaries, like other public places such as schools and churches, attracted terrified citizens seeking refuge. Some, therefore, became sites of massacre, others became shelters for internally displaced people, and others were used far beyond capacity in treating the enormous number of casualties from the 1994 massacres. The ability of Rwanda's hospitals and dispensaries to remain operational throughout the 1994 crisis and beyond was largely due to the United Nations and international emergency relief organizations, many of which still operate in Rwanda. Other medical organizations, having served during the genocide and reported the atrocities committed against Rwanda's Tutsi citizens, continued to report abuses in the post civil war context, this time against Hutu citizens. Several of these organizations were expelled from the country by the postwar government for reporting violations against Hutus. This sent a chilling message about the continued reporting of human rights abuses.

Diseases and Disorders

Pressing health concerns in postwar Rwanda include mental health trauma, resulting from the genocide and other political violence, HIV/AIDS, and upsurges of endemic diseases such as meningitis and malaria. Water-borne and sanitation-related diseases remain a problem, since only 41 percent of Rwandans have access to safe drinking water.[28]

During the genocide and war, many women were subject to physical and sexual violence, and torture. Women and girls of all ages were raped, raped and tortured with objects, repeatedly brutalized by groups of men, and held at length in sexual bondage.[29] Women and girls were subjected to the mutilation of their bodies, and particularly their sexual organs, including the pouring of boiling water into the vagina, the slashing of the pelvic area or vagina, and the disemboweling of pregnant women to attack the unborn child. Other women and girls were mutilated in order to disfigure them, including facial slashing, blinding, and the severing of fingers, noses, and breasts. In many cases, the attacks took place before witnesses, including members of the woman's own family. Limited statistical and more extensive anecdotal evidence shows that Rwandan women and girls suffer from a high rate of psychological and gynecological problems relating to sexual and other violence.

AIDS

Prior to the events of 1994, Rwanda had one of Africa's longer-established and larger HIV/AIDS-infected populations. At the end of 2001, an estimated 500,000 Rwandan were living with HIV/AIDS, and nationally, AIDS was one of the three leading causes of death.[30] Presently, HIV/AIDS infected persons constitute between 9 and 11 percent of the adult population, but among women the rate is significantly greater, and the rates of mother-to-child transmission are believed to be high. During the middle and late 1990s, several small studies were conducted focusing on specific sectors of the Rwandan population. A 1996 study conducted among pregnant women in Kigali, Rwanda's capital city, found an average HIV prevalence rate of 22 percent. A broader regional study, conducted in the same year (1996) also conducted among pregnant women found much lower rates existing in less urbanized areas, averaging about 8 percent. This study also found that the twenty-to-twenty-nine-year-old age group had highest infection among women, at 19 percent.[31] Another study conducted in Rwandan refugee camps found that among the group of women who reported being raped, more than 50 percent were HIV-positive.[32]

POLITICS AND LAW

Leadership and Decision-making

In eighteenth- and nineteenth-century Rwanda, at the court of the Banyiginya dynasty, who ruled the large areas of the south-central highlands, women were deeply engaged in the exercise of power and even ruled directly. Although the court centered on a king called the *mwami*, whose perceived embodiment of sacredness gave him the legitimacy to rule, in practical terms the *mwami* was chosen from among the youngest children of the previous king and was usually enthroned as a very small child. In this case, the primary regent was his mother (the queen mother), who ruled openly throughout his childhood, and coruled during his adulthood until her death. Each queen mother had her own royal palace, her own entourage, and her own means to exercise power and patronage. In ideological terms, she needed her link to the *mwami*, for his sacredness empowered her as well. But in practical terms, the *mwami*'s sacred nature could encumber him, while the queen mother remained unimpeded. Banyiginya rulers of the past engaged in dramatic and sometimes ruthless politics. Both *bami* (plural of *mwami*) and queen mothers are associated with having ordered individual killings and also massacres.[33]

Rwanda, the kingdom of the Banyinginya dynasty, was expanding when it came into contact with German colonizers in the 1890s. By trading nominal submission for German military assistance, *Mwami* Musinga was able to continue his kingdom's expansion throughout the German colonial period. This introduction of a new, external source of power, German troops, upset the configuration of power at the court, possibly to the detriment of the queen mother.

With Germany's defeat in World War I, Rwanda (then written "Ruanda") was placed under the authority of the League of Nations, which granted custodial administration to Belgium. Belgium then joined the small colony with its similarly small neighbor and governed them together as Ruanda-Urundi. This effort at administrative "streamlining" was soon followed by other moves to render Ruanda more "efficient," including the destruction of precolonial institutions that had limited and counterbalanced the *mwami*'s power. The precolonial power-sharing system, characterized by Belgians as impossibly complicated, was replaced with what they considered a more streamlined and "rational" system of indirect rule. It concentrated power in a small group of Rwandan partners who governed at the regional and local levels at Belgium's behest.

Women tended not to figure among the colonial administration's preferred political partners. Rwandan women were marginalized in the allocation of power by colonial administrators, whose notions of women's capability were influenced by European gender ideologies of the day. Indirect rule also aggravated and manipulated precolonial social divisions, particularly those between commoners and aristocrats, and between herders and farmers. Colonial legislation solidified these divisions into legally recognized "ethnic" groups (Tutsi, Hutu, and Twa), which administrators and policymakers used as the basis for allocating resources and opportunities, and for expropriating labor. Indirect rule marginalized and exploited members of the Hutu and Twa groups to the advantage of the Tutsi group, just as it marginalized all women to the advantage of certain groups of men.

The sustained injustice of indirect rule created simmering social tensions that burst out into the open immediately prior to independence. As Belgium, under considerable international pressure, grudgingly moved Ruanda toward independence in the late 1950s, the largest group of the politically marginalized ethnic groups, the Hutus, organized politically along ethnic lines intending to seize power through the ballot box. Having gained power by "democratic" means in the elections of the late 1950s, Hutu leaders explicitly set out to disempower, and in some cases to exact revenge on, members of the previously privileged Tutsi group. During what Hutus regarded as a populist revolution, Tutsi families were targeted for intimidation and even violence, and many fled into exile in neighboring countries. In this climate of tension and revenge, which Hutus regarded as a "revolution," Rwanda[34] attained independence in July 1962.

Using ethnicity as evidence of "majority" and hence democratic legitimacy, President Gregoire Kayibanda of the newly self-proclaimed Republic of Rwanda made efficient use of his citizens' revolutionary enthusiasm, but also high level of anti-Tutsi fear, to concentrate power under himself. Internal opposition did exist, particularly coming from the north, where residents accurately accused him of discrimination in favor of his home region, the south. Kayibanda deflected this and other criticism by raising anti-Tutsi paranoia. In 1973, however, the strategy backfired when army General Juvenal Habyarimana seized power precisely in the midst of a bout of such paranoia. He pledged to protect his Hutu countrymen. Capitalizing on this pledge, Habyarimana promoted the harassment of Tutsis, including Tutsi women, who were portrayed as beautiful and shrewd manipulators who advanced their ethnic agenda by seducing Hutu men.

While demonizing Tutsi, and particularly Tutsi women, Habyarimana quietly concentrated power in the hands of a very small group of close associates, informally called the *akazu*. The composition of this group, analysts have noted, seemed to center on the relatives of his wife, Agathe. The degree to which Agathe Habyarimana coruled with her husband is still a matter of speculation. She is believed to have been, at the very least, a leading member of the *akazu*, and one of the closest advisers of the president.

In the tumultuous year of 1990, the reintroduction of multiple political parties, which Habyarimana had banned, under international pressure, and an invasion of longtime Tutsi refugees from Uganda, stimulated the *akazu* to unleash a new wave of anti-Tutsi paranoia. In doing this, Rwanda's leaders resorted to clandestine tactics, which on the one hand undermined the nation's overt political structures, but on the other hand concentrated resources in a subversive, parallel system that they controlled. In this way, Habyarimana and his associates could appear to promote democracy and peaceful negotiations with Tutsi rebels, while quietly assassinating political opponents and training armed militia.

Political Participation

Despite the deadly underside to the politics of the early 1990s, the multiparty challenge to authority ushered in new actors at all levels, from local to national, and prominent among this group of new challengers were women. At the national level, Agathe Uwilingiyimana, a former schoolteacher, rose quickly in the ranks of the central leadership of the dominant opposition party. When international pressure compelled President Habyarimana to negotiate with the opposition and to form a new, multiparty cabinet, Uwilingiyimana was named to the post of minister of education. She subsequently became prime minister, the first female prime minister in Rwanda and in Africa. During her tenure in office, Uwilingiyimana advocated tirelessly for ethnic tolerance and human rights, a struggle that she carried out not only politically but also personally, for she herself faced gender and ethnic discrimination. As a woman and as a Tutsi in a primarily Hutu government, she confronted constant scrutiny and criticism. Indeed, her appointment was widely protested not only by Hutus but also members of her own party, and her term ended with her brutal torture, sexual assault, and assassination in April 1994.

The "openness" of the multiparty era also created the opportunity for women to play leadership roles in Rwanda's newly active civil society. Among Rwanda's most prominent leaders of the 1990–1994 era was Monique Mujawamariya, a human rights activist who was forced to flee as a result of the genocide. Conservative women also found new opportunities to participate in President Habyarimana's political party, the political "mainstream," such as Pauline Nyiramasuhuko, who became the minister of family and women's affairs.

Despite the apparently growing openness stimulated by Rwanda's new multiparty system, the *akazu* quietly pumped massive resources into a parallel system, which finally exploded in April 1994 with the assassination of President Habyarimana. A preplanned wave of massive killing erupted, targeting political opponents and other competitors, as well as their families. This politically focused killing rapidly transformed into a broader wave of killing targeting all "enemies of the people," whom Hutus understood as all ethnic Tutsi. To facilitate the expansion of killing, national and local leaders organized Hutu citizens into "civilian defense" teams, many of whom functioned as killing squads. Although much remains to be studied, it appears that those who played more active roles in organizing the killing in local settings were especially ambitious individuals who wished to demonstrate their "dynamism" to those above them in the political or administrative hierarchy. For these individuals, killing or organizing the killing was a means to "impress" a superior, and potentially a means of attracting patronage.

Since women as a group had remained marginal to the Rwandan political processes and generally outside the networks of political patronage, few women participated in the killing squads. The minister of family and women's affairs, Pauline Nyiramasuhuko, was one woman thus motivated. She participated publicly and actively in the planning and killing of Tutsis in politically liberal Butare, a region that had resisted ethnic extremism.

As this wave of killing swept across the country, the Tutsi rebel army launched a new offensive. Simultaneously, both a civilian genocide and a civil war erupted. Over the course of three months, more than 800,000 people died in these two events, and tens of thousands more died from revenge-inspired violence after July 1994, when the rebel group, the Rwandan Patriotic Front (RPF), took power.

As the RPF transformed itself from a guerrilla group to a government, many of those who had served the organization militarily moved into civil servant and administrative positions, including a number of women. Among the more prominent RPF leaders were Major Rose Kabuye, who became prefet (or governor) of the province of Greater Kigali, and subsequently a member of parliament. In 2002, as lieutenant-colonel, she chaired a national AIDS commission.

By 2002, women numbered among the senior functionaries of the Rwandan government, including three women ministers and four general secretaries. Women claimed nineteen out of seventy-four parliamentary seats, giving them 25.7 percent legislative representation—high by African and international standards. A woman was appointed to head a new participatory justice system called Gacaca. In the military, it was not clear to what extent women continued to function in command or combat roles in an army that remained continuously militarily engaged, first within Rwanda (including large-scale military campaigns conducted in rural community of the northwest) and subsequently in neighboring Zaire (now the Democratic Republic of Congo), which it invaded in 1996.

Women's Rights and Women's Movements

In the rebuilding of civil society, women's groups and individual women have stepped forward to play vital roles.[35] In rural areas, groups of women have joined to provide economic and social support to their members, some even working across ethnic lines. In the capital city of Kigali, women have rebuilt women's rights organizations that had existed prior the genocide, such as Pro-Femmes/Twese Hamwe, and have created new organizations to meet the critical needs of women and girls in the postgenocide setting. Pro-Femmes/Twese Hamwe is a collective of at least thirty-five women's organizations, including those that were formed before the genocide, such as the microcredit organization Duterimbere (Let's Move Forward); associations that had been founded by Rwandan women living in exile prior to the genocide, such as Amaliza; and new organizations founded to deal with the aftermath of the genocide, such as the widows association Avega and the Associations des Femmes Chefs de Famille (the Association of Women Heads of Families). As a group, these organizations meet a broad spectrum of urgent and specific needs. Working together as a collective, in 1995 the organizations cooperated in a unified Pro-Femmes Campaign for Peace, a comprehensive program for reconstructing Rwandan society. The Campaign for Peace developed a four-point blueprint for social reconstruction that emphasized developing a culture of peace, combating gender discrimination, promoting socioeconomic reconstruction, and reinforcing civic associations. The Campaign for Peace was an unprecedented attempt by Rwandan women to work collectively to reshape the national agenda, and its impact continues to be felt.

As a group, Rwanda's women have made a notable impact on recent national policy. Assisted by the lobbying efforts of numerous women's groups, parliament passed a revision to the inheritance laws that allows women to inherit property from fathers and husbands. Women activists succeeded in changing rape laws. They pushed for greater representation of women in all branches of the government, from local-level communal government, to the army and police, to the parliament. Although in Rwanda's ethnically contentious postgenocide climate the early beneficiaries of these new changes have tended to be Tutsi women, it is clear that a foundation is being established that will potentially benefit all women in the future.

RELIGION AND SPIRITUALITY

The simultaneous establishment of both Christianity and colonialism in Rwanda had a particular impact on women. Prior to colonialism, women of all strata, from the court to the countryside, played a wide variety of ritual and spiritual roles. At the royal court, for example, the cosmological framework for Rwandan kingship required that the king be ritually empowered and blessed on an ongoing basis by members of a group of royal ritualists, among whom particular personnages were ritually required to be female. In addition, female healers, divination specialists, and spirit mediums made use of their expertise in all regions and all strata of the kingdom. Divination or mediumship skills reinforced and enhanced the political power of royal women. Among rural women, such skills earned their practitioners' recognition, economic benefits, influence, and the ability to command considerable latitude in determining the direction of their own and their loved ones' lives.

By the mid-nineteenth century spirit mediums, both female and male, had successfully transformed spiritual authority into political authority along the northern borders of the Rwandan kingdom. They organized their followers into autonomous communities in which the mediums functioned as local political leaders, and even resisted encroachment from tribute-seeking agents of the Rwandan court. In the early twentieth century, the mediums participated actively in a broad regional campaign to resist German-backed Rwandan political expansion.

The most famous of the Nyabingi medium resisters was Muhumusa, a woman whose movement lasted from 1905 until the end of German rule. Although in pre-Christian spirit cults Rwandan women like Muhumusa had played active and open leadership roles in realms that drew together both genders, as Christian institutions took root, particularly during Belgian rule from the 1920s onward, women's access to formal leadership was much more limited, and became restricted to female-specific religious settings such as church-based women's groups, convents, and female religious orders. In general, these patterns persisted, surviving the transition to independence, until the mid-1990s.

The role of Rwandan women in their nation's contemporary religious life had been strongly influenced by its overwhelmingly Roman Catholic character. In the 1990s, more than half of all Rwandans had been baptized in the Catholic church, and the church's institutional infrastructure, including schools and development projects, reached all corners of the country. Of those Rwandans who were not Catholic, 28 percent belonged to other Christian denominations and 2 percent were Muslims.[36] Women played a variety of roles within the Rwandan Catholic Church but did not figure in the formal national leadership.

Since 1994, genocide has had a profound impact on the religious behavior and institutional participation of both men and women. In both Catholic and Protestant parishes, members have been divided by mutual suspicion and recrimination over what roles they were alleged to have played during the genocide itself, as well as during bouts of pillaging and postgenocide revenge. In the months of the genocide, parishes themselves were among the most prominent and grisly massacre sites—massacres took place inside church buildings where fearful citizens had gathered to seek sanctuary. Moreover, members of the clergy have been implicated in the genocide as passive accomplices and as active participants. However, it is important to point out that clergy have played a wide variety of roles in their communities' experience of national conflict; many have stood up to oppose all forms of violence, and many have lost their lives. Nevertheless, the generally quiescent and ambivalent response of Rwanda's religious institutions and religious leaders in reacting to shocking violations of the moral order has led many Rwandans to retreat from established churches. On the other hand, the need for healing following the trauma of the genocide and civil war has attracted others toward a plethora of new, charismatic evangelical Christian groups that have entered Rwanda in recent years. A number of these groups have already been present in English-speaking countries of the region and are expanding their ministries to Rwanda and promoting messages of reconciliation.

VIOLENCE

Rape/Sexual Assault

With the ending of the genocide and civil war, sexual violence against Rwandan women continued in refugee camps, in places of detention, and in the community at large. The prevalence of arms, the enormous number of traumatized and angry individuals, the presence of large numbers of soldiers or recently demobilized soldiers, including teenagers, the paralysis of the judicial system, and a relative disregard for crimes less serious than genocide itself, created a context conducive to rape.

Due to the efforts of many women's organizations since the genocide, rape is now legally considered a crime against humanity in the same category with murder, rather than a minor offense as it had been before. Regardless, although statistics are not available, rape continues to figure among the serious issues that Rwandan women and girls confront. Rape-related health problems, including sexually transmitted diseases, injury from sexual torture and mutilation, complications from nonprofessional abortion procedures, and pregnancies and childbirth among girls, number among women's health problems.

War and Military Repression

During the events of 1994, Rwandan girls and women were subjected to physical violence, including sexual violence and torture, by members of extremist Hutu militia groups, soldiers of the Rwandan armed forces, civilians, and soldiers of the Rwandan Patriotic Front.[37] Girls and women were wounded and killed in the course of combat. They were maimed by land mines, grenades, and other ordnance intended to disable enemy combatants. They were wounded or killed in their homes or in public gatherings during genocidal purges. They were hunted and killed while trying to escape. As females, Rwandan girls and women were specifically targeted for sexual violence. They were individually raped and gang raped. They were raped with objects such as gun barrels. They were raped before witnesses, including their parents, husbands, and children. They were sexually tortured and mutilated. Some were kidnapped and held by their rapists, many were killed immediately after being raped. During the genocide, sexual violence was used as a weapon to terrorize and degrade Rwandan females for political objectives. By degrading and dehumanizing individual women, assailants could by extension assault their victim's family, community, and in the context of Rwanda, their ethnic group.

OUTLOOK FOR THE TWENTY-FIRST CENTURY

Events over the past decade have dramatically transformed the image of Rwandan women. The "ideal" image of the calm and obedient mother (*muvyeyi*), an image that many women had been socialized to personify, has given way to other images—some uplifting such as prime minister, some deeply disturbing such as active participant in killing, and some that are simultaneously intimidating and empowering such as head of household. Now in a clear demographic majority and constituting a significant proportion of the heads of household in their country, Rwandan women have unprecedented demographic power. They are in a position to make a decisive impact in the rebuilding of their country's civil society.

NOTES

I would like to acknowledge the work of Colman Titus Msoka of the University of Minnesota Department of Sociology who provided much appreciated assistance for the research for this article.

1. E. Royte, "The Outcasts," *New York Times Magazine*, January 19, 1997; Jane Lampman "Women Lead in Effort to Rebuild Rwanda," *Christian Science Monitor*, February 15, 2001.

2. World Bank, 2000.

3. World Bank, September 2002.

4. CIA, *The World Factbook*, 2001, 7.3 million; UNICEF, *Rwanda*, 2002, 7.6 million; World Bank, *Rwanda Data Profile*, 2002, 8.7 million; Population Reference Bureau (PRB), *Women of Our World*, 2002, 8.11 million.

5. Proponents of this argument even include Rwandan scholars such as James Gasana, who published in *World Watch*, September–October 2002.

6. PRB, *Women of Our World*, 2002.

7. Ibid.

8. UNICEF, *Rwanda*, February 1, 2002.

9. Ibid.; UN Statistics Bureau, 2001.

10. CIA, *The World Factbook*, Rwanda, 2001.

11. World Bank, *Rwanda at a Glance*, September 18, 2002. U.S. Department of State, *Background Notes: Rwanda*, November 2001, U.S. $250.

12. Human Rights Watch/FIDH, *Shattered Lives: Sexual Violence During the Rwandan Genocide and Its Aftermath*, 1996.

13. *Area Handbook for Rwanda*, 1969.

14. Ibid.

15. UNICEF, 2002.

16. UNDP, 1998.

17. PRB, *Women of Our World*, 2002; "Women's School Enrollment Increasing in Rwanda," afrol.com, March 3, 2002.

18. UN Statistics Bureau, 2001, based on UNESCO 1997 study.

19. World Bank, September 18, 2002. This is an estimate for 2001; U.N. Statistics Division, 2000. UNICEF, February 1, 2002, female 61 percent and male 74 percent.

20. World Bank, 2001, 40.5 percent. U.S. Department of State, *Background Note: Rwanda*, 2001, 47 percent.

21. Rwanda Summary Gender Profile.

22. U.S. Department of State, *Background Note: Rwanda*, 2001.

23. ILO, 1998.

24. World Bank, *Rwanda at a Glance*, September 18, 2002; U.S. Department of State, *Background Note: Rwanda*, 2001, industry alone is 20 percent; World Bank, 2000,

industry alone is 21.6 percent and manufacturing alone is 9.8 percent; Rwanda Summary Gender Profile.

25. See Clotilde Twagiramariya and Meredeth Turshen, " 'Favours' to Give and 'Consenting' Victims: The Sexual Politics of Survival in Rwanda," in *What Women Do in Wartime*, eds. Turshen and Twagiramariya (London: Zed Books, 1998).

26. UNICEF, February 1, 2002.

27. UNICEF, Rwanda, February 1, 2002.

28. Ibid.

29. Human Rights Watch/FIDH, *Shattered Lives*.

30. USAID, *HIV/AIDS in Rwanda: A USAID Brief*, July 2002.

31. US Census Bureau, HIV/AIDS Surveillance Data Base, June 2000.

32. USAID, *HIV/AIDS in Rwanda*.

33. Alison Des Forges, "Defeat is the Only Bad News: Rwanda Under Musiinga, 1896–1931" (Ph.D. diss., Yale University, 1972); Jan Vansina, *Le Rwanda ancien: Le Royaume nyiginya* (Paris: Karthala, 2001).

34. At independence, Rwanda became the new spelling of the country's name.

35. Catharine Newbury and Hannah Baldwin, "Confronting the Aftermath of Conflict: Women's Organizations in Postgenocide Rwanda," in *Women and Civil War: Impact, Organizations, and Action*, ed. Krishna Kumar (Boulder: Lynne Rienner, 2001).

36. Timothy Longman, in "Christian Churches and Genocide in Rwanda" (http://faculty.vassar.edu/tilongman/Church&Genocide.html), cites the 1991 Rwandan government census findings: 89.8 percent of the 1991 population claimed membership in a Christian church, of which 62.6 percent identified themselves as Catholics, 18.8 percent as Protestants, and 8.4 percent as Seventh Day Adventists.

37. Human Rights Watch/FIDH, *Shattered Lives*.

RESOURCE GUIDE

Suggested Reading

Human Rights Watch/FIDH. *Shattered Lives: Sexual Violence During the Rwandan Genocide and Its Aftermath*. New York: Human Rights Watch and FIDH, 1996.

Jefremovas, Villia. *Brickyards to Graveyards; From Production to Genocide in Rwanda*. Albany: State University of New York Press, 2002.

Newbury, Catharine, and Hannah Baldwin. "Confronting the Aftermath of Conflict: Women's Organizations in Postgenocide Rwanda." In *Women and Civil War: Impact, Organizations, and Action*, edited by Krishna Kumar. Boulder: Lynne Rienner, 2001.

Twagiramariya, Clotilde, and Meredeth Turshen. " 'Favours' to Give and 'Consenting' Victims: The Sexual Politics of Survival in Rwanda." In *What Women Do in Wartime*, edited by Meredeth Turshen and Clotilde Twagiramariya. London: Zed Books, 1998.

Videos/Films

Chronicle of a Genocide Foretold. 1996. 141 min. Directed by Daniele Lacourse and Yvan Patry. Available from First Run/Icarus Films.

Forsaken Cries. 1997. 34 min. Produced by Andrea Torrice, Amnesty International. Available from http://store.yahoo.com/aipubs/forcriesstor.htm.

The Triumph of Evil. 1999. Produced by WGBH and PBS/Frontline. Related materials are available at the WGBH-PBS/Frontline website, www.pbs.org/wgbh/pages/frontline/shows/evil.

Valentina's Nightmare. 1998. Produced by WGBH and PBS/Frontline. Related materials are available at the WGBH-PBS/Frontline website, www.pbs.org/wgbh/pages/frontline/shows/rwanda.

The Weapon: The Untold Story of the Rwandan Genocide. 1997. Produced for ABC News.

Web Sites

AllAfrica.com—Rwanda News, http://allafrica.com/rwanda.
Includes PANA, the Dakar news agency. Has merged with the former *Africa News*, Durham, N.C.

Imvaho Nshya, Kigali, www.orinfor.gov.rw/docs/Imvaho70.htm.
The government paper published by the Office Rwandais d'Information (ORINFOR).

One World News Service, www.oneworld.org/africa/index.html.
Articles from Human Rights Watch, Inter Press Service, Amnesty International, among others. Has a keyword search facility.

Stanford University Africa Site: Rwanda, www-sul.stanford.edu/depts/ssrg/africa/rwanda.html.

Organizations

Association Rwandaise des Femmes Pour l'Environnement et le Developpement
P.O. Box 1364
Kigali, Rwanda
Phone: 250-77283
Fax: 250-76574

AVEGA—RWANDA
B.P. 1535
Kigali, Rwanda
Phone/Fax: 0171-460-0596

An association of the survivors of the genocide.

International Criminal Tribunal for Rwanda
P.O. Box 749
Kigali, Rwanda
Phone: 212-963-9906

National Revolutionary Movement for Development
B.P. 1055
Kigali, Rwanda

Réseau des Femmes Oeuvrant pour le Développement Rural
P.O. Box 2368

Kigali, Rwanda
Phone: 250-86350 or 250-86351
Fax: 250-86350
Email: alvera.mparaye@wfp.org

A women's network working for rural development.

Réseau des Femmes pour le Developpement Rural
B.P. 1295
Kigali, Rwanda
Phone: 250-72310

Natural resources management, training, institution building.

SELECTED BIBLIOGRAPHY

Africa Rights. *Not So Innocent: When Women Become Killers*. London: Africa Rights, 1995.
———. *Rwanda: Death, Despair, and Defiance*. Rev. ed. London: Africa Rights, 1995.
Human Rights Watch/FIDH. *Leave None to Tell the Story*. New York: Human Rights Watch/FIDH, 1999.
Jefremovas, Villa. "Loose Women, Virtuous Wives, and Timid Virgins: Gender and the Control of Resources in Rwanda." *Canadian Journal of African Studies* 24, no. 3 (1991): 78–95.
Modi, Renu, and Charlotte Karungi. *Gender and Armed Conflict: A Case Study of Rwanda*. Mumbai: Centre for African Studies, University of Mumbai, 2001.
UNICEF. *Situation Analysis of Children and Women in Rwanda*. Kigali, Rwanda: UNICEF, 1988.
———. *Situation of Children and Women in Rwanda: Survival Development and Protection*. Kigali, Rwanda: UNICEF, 2000.
"Violence Against Women and International Law: Rape as a War Crime." *Contemporary International Law Issues* no. 90 (1996): 605.
Women's Commission for Refugee Women and Children. *Rwanda's Women and Children: The Long Road to Reconciliation—A Field Report Assessing the Protection and Assistance Needs of Rwandan Women and Children*. New York: Women's Commission for Refugee Women and Children, 1997.
———. *You Cannot Dance If You Cannot Stand*. New York: Women's Commission for Refugee Women and Children, 2001. www.womenscommission.org/reports/womenscommission-rwi-assessment.pdf

15

SENEGAL

Erin Augis

PROFILE OF SENEGAL

A country of 9.9 million people, Senegal is located just south of the Sahara desert in the arid Sahelian region. Bordered on the north and east by Mauritania and Mali, and on the south by Guinea and Guinea Bissau, its western edge is 531 miles of coastline along the Atlantic Ocean. The Cape Verdian Peninsula juts outward into the sea, creating a natural port for the capital city of Dakar and making Senegal the westernmost country in Africa. Senegal's geographic and metaphoric location as the "door to Africa" has fostered a long history of cultural and political interchanges with peoples of East Africa, the Maghreb, and Europe. Centuries after the indigenous people of Senegal experienced waves of immigration from East Africa and engaged in religious and economic exchange with North Africans, they collaborated in and were subjugated by the European slave trade of the seventeenth, eighteenth, and nineteenth centuries. During and after this epoch, they were subjected to imperial domination by the Portuguese (1400s), Dutch (1600s), and French (1600s–1960). This multiplicity of contacts, some mutually voluntary and others brutally imposed, has created a

blended legacy of cultural, religious, and political-economic influences that have molded the society in which Senegalese women structure their lives, but that have also been reshaped by them.

Although Senegal terminated its official status as a French colony in 1960, a number of bureaucratic vestiges from the colonial era remain. Nonetheless, over the years the government has reformed other administrative structures. In 1985 it organized the country into ten regions: Saint-Louis, Kolda, Tambacounda, Louga, Fatick, Kaolack, Diourbel, Ziguinchor, Dakar, and Thiès. Whereas most of Senegal is rural hinterland, the latter two regions are highly urbanized. In fact, the regions of Dakar, Thiès, and Louga contain Senegal's three largest cities, which are, respectively, Dakar, Thiès, and Saint-Louis. Ziguinchor, whose large capital city bears the same name, is located in the Casamance, a lush, tropical area known for rice cultivation and geographically separated from the rest of Senegal by the Gambia, the former British colony that intersects Senegal's southern half. The Casamance is home to the separatist Movement of Democratic Forces in the Casamance, whose members contend that the national administration fails to address the economic and social needs of their region's population. Their history of violent clashes with government troops and a litany of human rights violations on both sides are in part the legacy of colonial borders drawn without regard for indigenous nationalisms.

Despite four centuries of French infiltration, only one-third of the Senegalese population speaks the former colonizer's tongue, which remains the country's official language. Furthermore, although a trend in "Wolofization" is occurring where all Senegalese are increasingly adopting the customs, language, and identity of the dominant Wolof ethnic group, people of other ethnicities have nonetheless maintained their indigenous traditions and languages. Besides the Wolof, who comprise 43.7 percent of the population, the most prominent ethnic groups are the Haal Pulaar (includes Peuhls and Tukulors) (23.2 percent), Serer (14.8 percent), Diola (5.5 percent), and Manding (4.6 percent). The Wolof are associated with the geographic areas of Louga, Diourbel, Sine Saloum, and Thiès, but they also share the Cap Vert (Dakar) with the Lebou, who are now classed in the national census as a Wolof subgroup. The Serer are linked to the Sine area, the Tukulor with the Fuuta Toro, and the Diola with the Casamance. Mandings and Peuhls are associated with the southern and northern regions of eastern Senegal, respectively. However, members of these ethnic groups are not physically bound to lands associated with their origins; representatives of each populate all the regions of Senegal, having participated in a constant flow of people and commerce throughout the area's history. A very small minority (approximately 1 percent) are of Lebanese or French origin. A few French remain from colonial times, and the Lebanese have infiltrated the electronics and clothing market in Dakar. Although both groups have adopted Senegal as their home country, they live largely apart from indigenous Senegalese.

Ninety-three percent of Senegalese are Sunni Muslims (including Brotherhood adherents and fundamentalist reformers in the "Sunni" movement), between 2 and 5 percent are Christian (the majority of whom are Catholic), and the rest practice solely indigenous traditions. It is important to note, however, that the vast majority of Christian and Muslim Senegalese still blend their faiths with indigenous spiritual beliefs. The Senegalese were Islamicized in three waves, the first beginning in the eleventh century and the most recent at the turn of the twentieth century, when indigenous leaders such as Cheikh Ahmadou Bamba converted tens of thousands. Catholicism was imported to the Senegalese region by Portuguese and French colonizers, and the Manjak ethnic group, who are a small minority in Senegal, are almost entirely Catholic. Other ethnic groups such as the Wolof and Tukulor are almost entirely Muslim. Numerous Islamic doctrines have shaped Senegalese culture and society; nonetheless, many indigenous influences have remained, mixing with imported religions.

One of the most pervasive divisions, particularly for Wolof, Tukulor, and Serer peoples, is based on caste, which is tied to professions. While types of caste professions vary to a certain degree per ethnicity, people from each of these ethnic traditions are still separated into the *geer*, or the prestigious noncasted and casted artisans, such as iron workers, weavers, carpenters, and griots (laudatory singers, musicians, or oral historians). While some mobility has arisen through urbanization, intermarriage between members of different castes rarely occurs in cities or rural areas.

Despite their cultural and economic differences, relatively little political strife occurs between members of ethnic and caste groups on a national level. Senegal's government is a de jure multiparty democracy, with a strong presidency, a 24-minister cabinet, and a 120-seat legislature (the National Assembly). The Parti Socialiste remained the party in power since independence in 1960 to 2000. Despite the presence of multiple, popularly supported challengers from opposition parties, only Léopold Sedar Senghor and Abdou Diouf of the Parti Socialiste held the office of president during those years. However, the party's inability to resolve mounting economic crisis, in addition to a series of contested elections rife with rumors of nepotism and fraud, created immense problems of legitimacy for its administrations. Ultimately, in a March 2000 election highly scrutinized by national and international observation boards, the Senegalese elected Abdoulaye Wade of the opposition Parti Democratique Senegalais.

The state's crisis of legitimacy has been temporarily resolved. However, it remains to be seen whether Wade's administration can stem the tide of economic disaster that has increasingly plagued the country. Senegal is now the thirty-ninth least developed country in the world with a per capita gross national product of only $520, life expectancy at 52 years, an infant mortality rate of 67 per 1,000 live births, a maternal mortality rate of 567 per 100,000 live births, and a fertility rate of 5.4 children per woman.[1]

The roots of Senegal's contemporary economic difficulties lie in the country's enfeebled position in the world market, as well as in its dealings with international lending institutions. A drought that started in the late 1960s destroyed Senegal's monocrop peanut economy, causing rural exports to drop by more than half and instigating an exodus to the cities, which continues today. Whereas in 1960 only 20 percent of the population lived in urban areas, this statistic is now 47 percent. Dakar alone urbanized at almost 4 percent per year from 1988 to 1997, and over one-third of its population is composed of immigrants from Senegal's hinterlands or other African countries.[2]

In an attempt to repair its economic difficulties in the agricultural sector, which were compounded by external oil price hikes throughout the 1970s and 1980s, Senegal has borrowed increasingly from foreign financial institutions. As early as 1978, when it became clear that it would not be able to pay back these loans, the national administration agreed to a series of structural adjustment reforms with the International Monetary Fund. Ironically, these reforms not only increased Senegal's debt from $1.4 to $3.5 billion between 1980 and 1991 alone, but they have intensified economic hardship for the country's people. Throughout the 1980s, the government removed subsidies on imported staples such as food and gas, and imported other agricultural goods at lower prices than they could be locally produced, further devastating the economies of farm communities. Thousands of civil service jobs were eliminated, employers were given legal permission to fire employees at will, and government spending on education and health was drastically reduced. These changes brought about widespread unemployment, rising health care costs, the elimination of teachers, and the deterioration of educational and municipal facilities, such as schools, roads, and sewage, water, and electric services.

These problems were then compounded by the French decision in 1993 to devalue by 50 percent the currency of the Communaute Financière Africaine (referred to more commonly as the CFA), which was pegged to the French franc at the time. This caused the prices of staples such as rice, flour, cooking oil, gas, electricity, and transportation to rise by 33 percent.[3]

Although the Senegalese economy has rebounded in secondary and tertiary sectors with real growth in yearly gross domestic product averaging 5 percent, it is still not growing fast enough to absorb the economic needs of the population. Unemployment now stands at 63 percent. In fact, job opportunities are poorest for the youngest generation of workers; 82 percent of people ages fifteen to twenty-four are without work. Perhaps the most serious aspect of this trend is that the number of youths with education rises significantly every year. However, for the number of literate people to be absorbed into the labor market, the Senegalese economy would have to grow 7 to 10 percent annually.[4] Young women and girls, whose education rates continue to increase, are affected by these trends.

OVERVIEW OF WOMEN'S ISSUES

Senegalese women of every age and ethnicity devise creative solutions to cope with the social changes and economic difficulties brought about by rural degradation, urbanization, colonial legacies, and the country's thirty-year decline in the world market. Those who are financially able struggle to complete their postsecondary education in hopes of one day working to support themselves and their families, and those without such opportunity work in the urban informal market or continue cultivating land in Senegal's vast rural areas. In addition to participating in the economy, they strive to fulfill, and often reshape, their roles as mothers, daughters, and wives in families changed by urbanization, unemployment, and relatives' emigrations to other countries. They do not confine their social roles to the public economy or the home, however; they also remain active participants in Senegal's bustling civil society—in religious groups, politics, and neighborhood organizations.

EDUCATION

Opportunities

At the ages of four and five, the majority of Senegalese girls attend Qu'ranic schools, where they are taught about their religion by local *marabouts*; however, only a minority continue any formal education past Qu'ranic or public elementary school. Senegal's public education system has its origins in the late 1850s, when Louis Faidherbe was the colonial governor. Schooling is divided into primary, middle, and secondary levels. Students must pass qualifying exams to be awarded diplomas for each, the most prestigious of which is the baccalauréat (Bac), viewed as the termination of secondary education but which is equivalent to one or two years of college in the

Senegalese women, Dakar. Photo © TRIP/TRIP.

U.S. system. In the 1996–1997 school year, 53 percent of girls attended elementary school, but only 15.5 percent were enrolled in the middle grades and 6.4 percent in secondary education. Yet despite these small percentages, the number of Senegalese females in each level increases yearly.[5]

Between 1990 and 1999 alone, girls' enrollment in primary schools increased from 50 to 65 percent, while boys only increased from 68 to 78 percent.[6] Moreover, between 1970 and 1988, girls' enrollment in secondary education rose in half of Senegal's ten regions. While rates were still highest in the urbanized regions of Dakar and Thiès, average increases of 10 percent occurred in Ziguinchor, Saint-Louis, and Kaolack.

There are more girls enrolled in private Catholic schools than public schools. In Dakar, Saint-Louis, and Thiès, half of students in Catholic secondary schools are female, and girls compose approximately 35 percent of the population in these institutions for most other regions. These numbers reflect not only the willingness of Catholic parents to keep their daughters in schools, but also their relatively better financial means, compared to the majority of Muslim families in these cities.[7] Nonetheless, Muslim parents who have the means, often send their daughters to Catholic schools as well, and others enroll them at private Islamic schools run by organizations such as Al Falah and Jama'at Ibad ar-Rahman.

Young women who receive their middle school certificate may go on to study at technical schools and those with their Bac may choose to enroll in the university. In public universities like Dakar's Université Cheikh Anta Diop, female enrollment increased from 21 to 27 percent of the student body between 1987 and 1997, and growing numbers of young women are choosing to study in the university's faculties of economics, law, journalism, and education. Furthermore, women's enrollment in the medical and pharmacology faculties has remained at 36 percent of the student body.[8] Women have also been enrolling increasingly in a number of new, private training institutions that offer fields such as law, management, accounting, nursing, and laboratory work. Given that the labor market for those with postsecondary education has changed from functionary positions in the public sector to services, more and more young women with their Bac have been choosing technical and vocational training as opposed to university educations.

As might be expected, on the whole, educated Senegalese women fare better on the labor market than those with little or no education. Whereas women with no schooling compose 80 percent of females at the lowest income levels, those with education make up 41 percent of the highest income group.[9] Nonetheless, in the current labor market, the majority of women with education are still unable to find employment appropriate to their skills. Instead, they work in Senegal's massive informal sector, as do those women who never attended school.

Literacy

Although only 25 percent of Senegalese women over age fifteen can read and write in French, since 1980 the number of literate females ages fifteen to twenty-four has doubled to 40 percent. This growth reflects an overall increase in girls' education.

EMPLOYMENT AND ECONOMICS

Farming

Despite Senegal's rapid rates of urbanization, 75 percent of women still live in the countryside and they remain highly engaged in agricultural work. In 1990, 86 percent of the female labor force engaged in rural labor, outnumbering men in this sector by 15 percent. Traditionally, Wolof women have planted seeds and helped harvest peanuts and millet; however, they also have begun to grow vegetables such as tomatoes, chilies, and onions, as well as raising chickens and other small farm animals to compensate for economic losses during the long recession. Like their Wolof counterparts, Serer women also grow peanuts, although it is still Serer men's duty to grow millet. Of all Senegalese females, Diola women, who continue to grow rice as their principal crop, have the greatest agricultural autonomy from men, because they cultivate separate fields and have their own granaries. However, as the value of indigenously produced rice has decreased in the domestic market, Diola women's economic power and status in the home has declined.[10]

Haal Pulaar women's agricultural roles have changed the most during the last two decades; they have almost completely infiltrated men's farming tasks. For example, women villagers in the Vallée du Fleuve, who formerly had no involvement in family fields, only farmed bissap (dried red flowers of a hibiscus plant that is made into a juice), gumbo, beans, cotton, and indigo for sale or household consumption. Yet since the 1980s, more than half have begun working in irrigated rice fields formerly dominated by their male kin, who have since emigrated in search of urban labor.[11]

Paid Employment

Senegalese women have always been actively involved in economic production, not only in agriculture, but in urban markets as well. As early as the seventeenth century, wealthy businesswomen called *signares* capitalized on commerce in trading posts along the Atlantic coast, by acting as intermediaries between European traders and indigenous producers. Today, women compose 43 percent of Senegal's labor force and two-thirds of its commercial activity.[12] In fact, as economic opportunities for men have dwindled, forcing them into unemployment or to emigrate in search of work, women in rural areas as well as cities are increasingly undertaking a number of male tasks.

Informal Economic Activities

While rural women's new forms of labor have kept villages operating, it has been to their economic and physical detriment. Although women still cultivate individual gardens in addition to their increased work on family fields, they must now use most of the produce from these gardens to feed their own families instead of for spending money. Nonetheless, in order to cope with economic contraction, many still sell some agricultural products informally. They market agricultural goods along national roads, or travel to cities to sell their wares. With their earnings they then purchase manufactured goods such as toiletries, shoes, and cosmetics to sell in their villages.[13]

Like their rural counterparts, urban women also engage in informal commerce, but in even greater numbers, since city settings allow for more commercial opportunities. Fifty percent of urban Senegalese are estimated to carry out some form of informal market activity, and women participate equally if not more than men. Besides working as maids in middle- and upper-class households, women engage in a great deal of petty commerce. In front of their homes, in the street, at the market, or local taxi stands and bus stations, women sell vegetables, fish, cooked dishes, condiments, juices, syrups, frozen juices, and fried dough. Others market clothing and jewelry they have made themselves or purchased elsewhere. Some travel to North and Central African, Gulf, and European cities to buy women's apparel, accessories, jewelry, cosmetics, and leather goods to market at home.[14]

Entrepreneurship

A small number of businesswomen have become brokers or owners of large commercial enterprises, domestic as well as international. They engage in sales of construction materials, hardware, pharmaceuticals, manufactured goods, agricultural products, public works, and imports and exports. For instance, Adja Awa Ndiaye is the president and general director of the large construction company SENEMAC; Diouma Dieng Diakhate opened up the field of haute couture fashion design to Senegalese women; and Oumou Salamata Tall did the same for females in the textile industry. In fact, women have now monopolized cloth imports to Senegal.[15]

As in large commercial business, only small numbers of women are employed in management, technical work, the public sector, or the professions. Only 8.8 percent of managers, 26 percent of technicians, 15 percent of state employees, 12.8 percent of intellectuals, and 14 percent of lawyers are women.[16]

Pay and Working Conditions

Despite large gaps between the numbers of men and women employed in the professions and other relatively well-paid formal market jobs, several laws have been passed to protect women's rights in the workplace. The Labor Code (1961) and the Collective Convention on National Interprofessionals (1982) pertain to equal remuneration for equal work. While these function well in the public sector because adherence to them can be easily monitored, in the private-sector women are often paid by the task, whereas men are usually paid per day. Consequently, great differences exist in pay for males and females in these jobs. Even with just remuneration, married women pay higher taxes on their earnings because they are not officially considered heads of households.[17]

Despite their increased responsibilities in commercial farming, female cultivators say they feel dominated by village men, have little decision-making power, and have great difficulty obtaining credit from agricultural lending institutions, even when they participate in the women's economic cooperative groups introduced by the state in the 1980s.

In the urban environment, for example, hair braiders work under exceptionally difficult conditions, with poor lighting, overcrowding, long hours, and minimal pay, the majority of which they must often turn over to male salon owners. After working approximately fifty hours a week, hair braiders will only earn between $150 and $300.

An analysis of Senegalese women's labor must also include those who work abroad and remit part of their earnings to their families at home. Tens of thousands of Senegalese work outside their country, and an important part of these are female workers. Most often, they join male family members in large North American and European cities such as Paris, Milan, New York, and Washington, DC. Although some receive student or merchant visas, most Senegalese immigrant women work long hours in low-wage and often illegal jobs such as hair braiding, cleaning, cooking and serving in restaurants, operating cash registers in large grocery stores, or selling items such as purses, cosmetics, and tourist paraphernalia on the street. The amount of money female workers remit to their families in Senegal depends on their earnings.

It is often hotly debated among Senegalese immigrant men as to whether they should send for their spouses. These men often complain that women who emigrate to developed countries do not contribute enough of their earnings to local household expenses, nor time to their traditional roles as wives and mothers, but instead send too much money to their families at home.

Support for Mothers/Caretakers

Maternal Leave

The Labor Code provides women with a fourteen-week paid maternity leave, with one hour a day off for fifteen months for breast feeding.[18] The stipulation here, however, is that these women must have a job and salary recognized by the state. This of course excludes the vast majority of working women in urban and rural areas.

Inheritance, Property, and Land Rights

Rural women's access to land is still quite ambiguous. In 1964, the Law of National Domain was passed, which ruled that all farmers should have equal access to land, regardless of caste or gender. However, numerous customs prevent women from claiming this right. To begin with, powerful male rural council leaders still often disfavor small farmers and female cultivators in land allocation. Second, in the traditions of many Senegalese ethnic groups, women are not allowed to inherit land, and when Islamic customary laws are applied, their inheritance is at best one half that of male sons or one-eighth of their husband's property if they are widowed.[19]

Social/Government Programs

Women in small enterprises contend that it is very difficult to borrow capital from official lending institutions, such as the Caisse Nationale du Crédit Agricole du Sénégal and the Banque Internationale pour le Commerce et l'Industrie du Sénégal, which is the Senegalese branch of the Banque Nationale de Paris. In fact, they voice their distrust of banks, recounting stories of repossession and making comments such as *"banque dafa ñakk sutura"* (the banks respect no one). Instead, women have more often borrowed credit for small enterprises from nongovernmental organizations such as Oxfam and the U.S. Agency for International Development. Most others prefer to finance their businesses themselves or with the support of *tontines*, which are informal rotating credit unions organized by female friends or colleagues.

FAMILY AND SEXUALITY

Gender Roles and Division of Labor

The same economic and social changes that influence trends in Senegalese immigration also impact the organization of family life in Senegal. First, as a result of economic crisis and women's engagement in the labor force, not only do rural and urban women take on men's tasks, but in urban areas men increasingly assume household chores and child care duties while their wives work. Yet although their economic power has greatly diminished and they even assume some of women's traditional responsibilities, men maintain a high degree of moral authority in the household. Consequently, women still have less decision making power than male family members, despite the fact that the majority contribute 51 to 85 percent of household funds.[20]

Most Senegalese maintain that it is women's religious obligation to cede to men's judgment, and in everyday conversation the Wolof term *jeker*, or husband, is fully interchangeable with *khilifa* (lord) and *borom keur* (master of the house). Just as it is assumed that husbands must remain in charge of households, Senegalese women's primary role is still considered to be that of wife and mother.

Marriage

Marriage and childbirth are understood to be social and religious duties in local Christian as well as Muslim traditions, and a polite phrase commonly told to young women after an affirmative response to the question "*Am nga jeker?*" (Do you have a husband?) is "*Yalla na la Yalla may la doom*" (May God give you children). Furthermore, marriage is for the most part still understood to be a contract between two families. Traditionally, the wedding ceremony consists of the bridewealth exchange between the parents, and the couple rarely attends. This ceremony is usually practiced before civil proceedings in accord with the Family Code take place. Although the code requires all married couples to legally register their marriages, many families do not comply.

It is indeed difficult to enforce laws which protect women in the private sphere. The Family Code has legislated that sixteen is the minimum legal age for women to marry, and that they must give their consent. However, the average marriage age for rural Senegalese women is still fifteen, and 30 percent of women aged fifteen to nineteen in Senegal are married.[21] It follows that if women are married in violation of the Family Code before age sixteen, then their consent is not always sought. In fact, as late as 1999, new agencies were reporting that in rural communities in Eastern Senegal, Peuhl girls were still married and relocated to their husbands' homes as early as eleven years of age.[22]

Women's abilities to make choices in marriage depend greatly on their socioeconomic and educational status, including their decisions to participate in polygamous unions. The more educated or financially secure they are, the less likely they are to accept becoming a cowife. Sometimes, however, women still face difficult choices about polygamy. If couples adhere to the Family Code, men must sign a contract stating how many wives they intend to marry, with the choice between one to four. The wife is then asked to sign her consent. Yet if a man breaks this contract, he faces no legal punishment, and his wife's choice is simply to divorce and risk losing custody of her children, or accept becoming a cowife. Women at various levels of educational and socioeconomic status contend that they would not divorce their husbands for taking another spouse because they would not give up their place as first wife to another woman. However, a well-paid secretary in Dakar stated in an interview: "Sign monogamy? No. I told my husband to sign for four wives if he wants to. But my husband knows that if he *ever even thought* about taking a second wife, I would leave him immediately."[23]

The rate of polygamy is somewhat higher in rural areas than cities. Whether this is because of women's resistance or the financial constraints of maintaining two wives in an urban area is debatable. Whereas 49 percent of rural women are in polygamous unions, in Dakar only 11.6 percent of men have more than one wife. Overall, 62.4 percent of women are in monogamous unions, 26.5 percent have one cowife, and 11 percent have two.[24]

Religious and legal precepts have compounded indigenous cultural norms of patriarchy and removed the few bases of married women's traditional authority, which concerned matrilineal inheritance and child guardianship. For instance, in cases of divorce, the official guardian of the children in indigenous custom was the maternal uncle. However, Islamic law, which has eclipsed traditional norms as customary, dictates that children are the father's property. The Muslim allowance for repudiation was forbidden by the Family Code; therefore a husband cannot arbitrarily disown his wife simply by announcing it three times as is permissible under Islamic law. Nonetheless, the women's rights activists have criticized the code for leaving too much power in male hands. For example, even if the mother gains custody of the children, the father is still considered their sole legal guardian. Although both parties usually remarry rather quickly, the current divorce rate is approximately 50 percent.[25]

Reproduction

Whereas women's status in marriage has improved only marginally over time, childbearing has become easier. In addition to the drop in Senegal's birth rate from 6.8 children per woman in 1980 to 5.5 today, in the same two decades, infant mortality rates have dropped by nearly half, largely due to increases in prenatal care and birth assistance. Today, skilled health staff attend to 47 percent of women in childbirth, and 74 percent receive some form of prenatal care.[26]

Sex Education

Although there are no classes offered in public schools for family planning, nongovernmental organizations such as Projet Pour Jeunes (Project for Youth), Group pour l'Enseignement et l'Etude de la Population (Group for the Education and Study of the Population), and Association Senegalaise pour le Bien Etre Familal (Senegalese Association for Family Well-Being) offer courses as well as support family planning clubs in high schools and universities. These groups, or clubs for the Study of Family Life, are credited with increased awareness about sexually transmitted diseases as well as contraception.

Contraception and Abortion

Furthermore, since the 1980s, a number of state-run family planning clinics have been built in urbanized areas for counseling, contraception, preventing sexually transmitted diseases, and promoting birth spacing, yet there remains a serious dearth of these services in rural areas. Only 13.7 percent of women practice modern forms of birth control, and the majority of contraceptive users have secondary education or higher. Young urban women prefer condoms, while older urban women use the pill, IUDs, and injections.[27]

Abortion is only legal in cases of rape or endangerment of the mother's health. In a study of women in the Dakar suburb of Pikine, it was found that 30 percent had undergone illegal abortions, the highest rates being among women ages fifteen to nineteen. Women used drug overdoses of pharmaceuticals such as Nivaquine, which is a toxic antimalarial, traditional method such as mixtures of roots or bark, and mechanical or chemical means such as bleach or sharp wires.[28]

Teen Pregnancy

Despite the relatively high availability of contraceptives in urban areas, more young urban than rural women have children out of wedlock. In Dakar, 12 percent of unmarried women under age twenty have children.[29] This is due to the fact that a slightly higher percentage of urban than rural women engage in premarital sex, there are lower levels of social control over urban young people's personal lives, and women tend to get married later in urban areas.

Nonetheless, low levels of social control do not necessarily translate into higher societal acceptance of out-of-wedlock pregnancy or birth. Young women fear being told to leave the house if their pregnancy is discovered, and aside from Keur Yaakaru Jigeen Ni (House of Hope for Women), which is a small shelter for unwed mothers in Dakar, they have few options. For this reason, many turn to illegal means of abortion. Young women who are unable to care for their babies sometimes abandon them at birth; if the child is discovered, newspapers publish sensational articles on the event, often depicting the mothers as cruel, instead of as young women who believe they have little recourse. These regrettable situations, along with illegal abortions, are symptomatic of socioeconomic crisis and the absence of a health infrastructure designed to address the problems of out-of-wedlock pregnancy.

HEALTH

Health Care Access

Senegalese women's access to adequate health care, financially as well as geographically, is quite limited. Only 7.5 doctors, 22.1 nurses, 6.6 midwives, and 1.2 dentists are available for every 100,000 people, and most of these health care personnel are concentrated in Dakar, where conventional medical services are nearly impossible for most of the population to afford. In fact, 63 percent of urban women state that medicine is too expensive, and 54 percent of rural women say health services are geographically too far away, with only 20 percent having access to a public hospital.[30]

Diseases and Disorders

AIDS

Senegal is internationally renowned for its success in stemming the AIDS epidemic: only 1.77 percent of the population is infected. Women compose half this population, and an estimated 30 percent are sex workers. Although it has been argued that Islamic norms, which forbid premarital sex, have helped contain the spread of the virus, no accurate record of Senegalese sexual practices exists. In their study of Dakarois' sexuality and AIDS transmission, researchers for the Minstère de la Santé (1998) report that 87 percent of women and 60 percent of men have not had multiple partners or sexual relations outside of marriage; however, the authors qualify that respondents, particularly women, are likely to have underreported their experiences.

It is thus more likely that the low AIDS rate is attributable to the government's prompt attention to warnings from the international medical community about the virus. In 1986, the Programme National de Lutte Contre le Sida organized the screening of all blood supplies, initiated public information campaigns, and canceled the tax on condoms to encourage their use. Radio announcements were made, posters were hung on high school and university campuses about the importance of using condoms, and billboards warning about the virus were erected on major national roads.

Furthermore, Muslim and Christian religious leaders in conjunction with the Ministry of Health were quick to take up the cause in spreading public awareness. In addition to radio broadcasts, they published and distributed the books *Islam and AIDS* and *The Medical, Koranic, and Biblical*

Principles All Believers Must Read, Know, and Apply. This free literature explains the virus, its prevention, and moral stances on premarital sex as well as caring for infected friends and family members.

The state has introduced new programs to fight the HIV virus in the last several years. These include requiring all prostitutes to be registered and carry cards that verify regular health checks, making antiretroviral therapy available to HIV/AIDS patients, and the free distribution of antiretrovirals to pregnant women with the virus, which began in December 2000. Nongovernmental organizations have also supported group homes for people living with advanced stages of AIDS.

Female Genital Cutting

Although the Senegalese health infrastructure has also attempted to address the problems associated with female genital cutting, it has had less success than in its approach to AIDS. The practice ranges from *sunnah* (cutting off the tip and hood of the clitoris) to *pharaonic* (infibulation). Although the most systematic study reports that 20 percent of Senegalese women are circumcised, since the study was only carried out in 37 health clinics in western Senegal, rates are likely much higher in other regions.

In many Senegalese communities, the practice of female genital cutting is understood as a rite of passage for girls that renders them fertile. Ethnic groups are estimated to practice female genital cutting in the following percentages: 75 percent of Mandé, 53 percent of Hall Pulaar, 53 percent of Diola, 25 percent of other Casamançais ethnic groups, 4 percent of Serer, and 0.5 percent of Wolof women.[31]

For over a decade, representatives from several international development organizations have supported grassroots projects that work to end the practice, and some have been successful. In conjunction with TOSTAN (Wolof for "breakthrough"), the United Nations Women's Fund (UNIFEM), and the United Nations Children's Fund (UNICEF), leaders of twenty-nine villages declared an end to the practice in 1998, stating that Islam contains moral prescriptions which protect the chastity of young women.[32] Likewise, several Islamic leaders like Imam Serigne Madior Cissé have spoken publicly against the practice.

Furthermore, on January 29, 2000, the Senegalese government passed a law forbidding female genital cutting. It condemns anyone who carries out or recommends the process to up to five years in prison. The law stipulates that if a female child dies from circumcision, any parties involved will be required to carry out forced labor. Thus far, only three people have been convicted under the law. The low rate of reporting female genital cutting, despite its high incidence, indicates its widespread acceptance among the majority of Senegalese. Groups of women in southern Senegal have protested against the law forbidding the practice, and one village chief organized the excision of 121 girls on the evening before it was passed.[33]

POLITICS AND LAW

Political Participation

Senegalese women are active in making their voices heard about government decisions that affect their lives. Despite the problem that their representation in political offices is far from having parity with men, the fact the Senegalese women hold 19 percent of legislative seats is quite promising, compared to a rate of 15 percent globally.[34] Nonetheless, these improvements have been slow in coming. Although Senegalese women have been voting since 1945, it was not until 1978 that President Senghor established the office of the Secretary of Women's Condition. Finally, in 1990 the Ministry of Women and Children was established.

Before the legislative elections in April 2001, a federation of women's organizations called the Group of Five announced in a press conference that the lowest acceptable level of women in leadership positions was 30 percent. The Group of Five includes the Association of Women Professionals in Communication, the Association of Female Jurists, the Siggil Jigeen Network, the Senegalese Women's Council, and the Women's Collective for Defense of the Family. As they explained:

> The minimum we are entitled to ask for is 30 percent. The issue of women's representation should stop being used just to gain popularity. It should be based on a real political commitment. . . . The disparity existing between the real contribution of women in development and their representation in decision-making bodies is striking.[35]

Perhaps the most recent and significant change affecting the potential for Senegalese women's political engagement has been President Abdoulaye Wade's March 2001 appointment of Madame Mame Madior Boye as Senegal's first female prime minister, who served in this capacity until November 2002. Currently there are seven women ministers, five of whom were appointed by Boye.

These seven appointments represent 25 percent of the cabinet's twenty-eight seats, which is an improvement over the previous government, in which there were five women ministers out of thirty-one posts. Yet despite the fact that women make up 50.5 percent of Senegal's 2.8 million registered voters, relatively few hold even local leadership positions. Only 6 percent of mayors, 12 percent of judges, and 7.6 percent of grassroots organizers are women.[36]

Women's Rights and Women's Movements

While the first organization to fight for the political rights of women was Yewwu Yewii (Wake Up!) in the 1980s, there are now numerous small organizations with varying goals and political orientations. Other organizations that work to promote women's welfare are economic and professional associations, such as the Association of Female Jurists, the African Network for the Support of Women's Entrepreneurship, and the Association of Women in Business and Commerce, which is 5,000 members strong.

The organizations that comprise the Group of Five are part of a large and multidirectional women's movement in Senegal. The Conseil Senegalais des Femmes (COSEF), led by Marema Touré, is a nonpartisan organization concerned with promoting the economic and political empowerment of women, as well as their status within the family. However, a number of women's groups attached to political parties also exist. The National Movement of Women of Senegal, for example, is an auxiliary of the Parti Socialiste; the Democratic Movement of Women is associated with the Democratic League-Labor Party Movement; the Democratic Union of Women of Senegal with the Independence and Labor Party; and the National Movement of Women with the Parti Democratique Senegalais. Yet as COSEF member Katy Cissé Wone has pointed out, it is the diverse political orientations of these groups that have been detrimental to a unified movement. She cites the example of the Union of Women of Senegal, a multiparty group that eventually split along political lines.[37]

Additionally, women's organizations associated with research and academic institutions contribute to the movement, such as the Association of African Women for Research on Development and the Group for Research on Women and Law in Senegal.

RELIGION AND SPIRITUALITY

At the same conference where the Group of Five declared its goals for women's leadership, members proclaimed that they would also continue to fight for girls' education, since they are not brought up to become leaders "in this dominant patriarchal culture reinforced by religious precepts."[38] Yet ironically, it is through religion that many young women find social support and fight for their understanding of their rights.

In the past it has been observed that Senegalese politicians have been highly dependent on the power of Muslim brotherhoods because they rely on influential *marabouts* (spiritual leaders) to persuade the electorate. However, it is also the case that women, who are so poorly represented in national and local politics, turn to religious institutions to garner moral support and material power in their daily lives. This is true for Muslims as well as Christians, in addition to those who engage solely in traditional indigenous spiritual practices.

Whereas the overwhelming majority of Senegalese are Muslim, between 2 and 5 percent are Christian, the majority of whom are Catholic. Catholicism was imported to Senegal by the Portuguese and later the French.

The French clergy remain highly involved in Catholic institutions in Senegal. Many Catholic women, particularly those in urban areas, benefit from a long tradition of Western-oriented education, which has lent itself to increased economic opportunity.[39] A smaller number of women are in Protestant groups such as the Lutheran and Presbyterian Churches, as well as Evangelical Lutheran and Methodist missions, Campus for Christ, and the Jehovah's Witnesses. Women involved in these congregations and their affiliated aid organizations often receive access to schooling, medical care, food, and sometimes employment or the opportunity to travel abroad.

On the other hand, Muslim women also participate in a number of religious organizations, both formal and informal, through which they too address moral, economic, and educational issues. Although a significant number of women remain independent of Muslim brotherhoods, most declare an affiliation to one of the brotherhoods: the Mourides, Tijans, Layennes, or Khadirs.

However, in reformist Islamic organizations, which strive to move beyond the hierarchical structure and influence of the brotherhoods, other leadership possibilities have opened for women. For instance, in the Moustarchidine wal Moustarchidaty, an organization that is a blend of reformism and Tijanism, leaders emphasize the group's female membership of 60 percent.[40] The group is led by a set of women leaders who refer to themselves as Synérgie. Besides leading neighborhood chapters of Moustarchidat women, Synérgie members organize conferences for the public related to politics, women's health, religious responsibilities, education, and job training.[41]

Fundamentalist Sunni organizations are also reformist in that they oppose the cultural, economic, and political influence of the brotherhoods, which, they argue, defy orthodox interpretations of the Qu'ran and the Sunna. Sunnis advocate Qu'ranic literacy in Arabic, and have affiliated schools, child care centers, and medical dispensaries that are funded largely by Gulf countries. Followers participate in a pan-Islamic reform movement, whose goal is to return Islam to its original state during the lifetime of Mohammed and his first four predecessors, in addition to replacing Senegal's secular government with an Islamic state. Members and leaders engage in a global exchange of information, education, and finances with similar groups all over the world, but particularly in the United States, North Africa, and the Gulf countries. Sunni women choose to don the veil and discontinue any physical contact with men, including shaking hands. They advocate a return to traditional relationships between men and women in the home, and argue that a woman may work only if it is economically necessary for her family, and as long as she places her duties as wife and mother first. Since the mid-1990s, the movement has attracted a number of young urban women from multiple class and ethnic backgrounds.

Whereas the Mourides and Layennes are indigenous to Senegal and the

Tijans and Qadirs originated in North Africa and the Middle East, all four brotherhoods represent a blend of traditional belief systems, Qu'ranic doctrine and practice from Sunni Islam that form their religious styles. Consequently, women adherents of various religious practices differ according to the specific history and doctrine of their brotherhood. For instance, Mouride women refer consistently to the piety, wisdom, and obedience of Maam Diarra Bousso, the mother of their spiritual leader, Cheikh Ahmadou Bamba (c. 1850–1927), who was founder of the Mouride brotherhood in Senegal and regarded by many as Senegal's most important national hero. On the other hand, many Layenne women, who are of Lebou ethnicity, blend their faith with their ancestors' traditional relationship to the sea.

Brotherhood women follow a *marabout* whom they tithe and from whom they seek spiritual guidance. It has been commonly assumed that when they marry, they become followers of their spouse's *marabout*. However, many women interviewed by the author stated that after marriage, they continue to follow their own *marabouts*. Urban brotherhood women also maintain religious autonomy from their husbands by participating in sex-separated religious meeting groups called *daairas*, where they collectively pray, chant, and attend religious pilgrimages, in addition to supporting each other financially for commercial endeavors, births, weddings, and funerals.

In rare cases, women achieve *marabout* status with brotherhoods; for instance, Sokhna Magat Diop in Thiès, the only heir of the famous Mouride spiritual guide Abdoulaye Yakhine, has her own following of thousands. In addition, Sokhna Maye Mbacké, perhaps the most revered daughter of Cheikh Amadou Bamba, also held the status of *marabout*. These examples are largely exceptions, however; most brotherhood women gain authority by leading *daairas* and teaching the Qu'ran to other women, or holding offices in student brotherhood groups, such as the women's section of the Mourides' Hizbut Tarquiyya.

VIOLENCE

Domestic Violence

While no accurate count of conjugal violence on women in Senegal is available, spousal abuse exists. In 1992, women organized a march in Kaolack when a young wife was beaten to death by her husband, and scandalized newspaper headlines reported the savage killing of a seventeen-year-old female at the hands of her spouse. However, less brutal instances of domestic violence are seen as commonplace. In addition to stories of physical conflicts between cowives, it is popularly accepted that husbands may occasionally beat wives who are thought to be unruly. Although men found guilty of domestic violence can be fined $833 and sentenced to up to five years in prison, few incidents are reported to the police. One Islamic recommendation repeatedly cited by Senegalese is that men may physically punish their wives, if convincing them verbally and banishing them from the bedroom have failed as tactics.

Rape/Sexual Assault

In addition to domestic violence, Senegalese law recognizes extramarital rape and sexual harassment as crimes. Rapists can be imprisoned for up to ten years, and rape trials often result in convictions. Furthermore, sexual harassment was made a crime in 1999; it is punishable by a fine of $88 and up to three years in jail. However, given the already precarious position of women in the formal labor market, it is unlikely that the actual number of sexual harassment infractions are reported.

Though the Ministry of Women asserts that more and more women come to court with claims of domestic violence, rape, incest, and sexual harassment, it recognizes that a kind of violence even more difficult to combat is the fear of physical and moral violence imposed on women by men. Cultivating this fear involves intimidation, physical and psychological threats, sexual aggression, and economic deprivation. The Ministry of Women states that this terror inhibits women from making claims on their human rights, and that "violence against women is what the Centre de la Tribune Internationale de la Femme calls, justly, an 'invisible' obstacle to development."[42]

Trafficking of Women and Children

Trafficking of girls and young women for sex work can be considered another such obstacle. In 2001 the prominent female fashion designer Oumou Sy was arrested for attempting to transport 100 young women to Libya for prostitution. Women and girls are trafficked regularly to Europe as well as resort areas in Senegal and the Gambia for sex work during the tourist season. In addition to this type of labor, thousands of women and girls are sent within Senegal as well as to neighboring countries to work as domestic servants.[43]

OUTLOOK FOR THE TWENTY-FIRST CENTURY

Young women involved in Senegal's fundamentalist Islamic Sunni movement argue that change must occur in Senegal. For them, political corruption, poverty, urban crime, and the degradation of traditional values in the home, religion, and mutual aid must come to an end. For these young adherents, answers can be found in strict adherence to Islamic precepts. Yet at the other end of the spectrum of Senegal's female activists are those in feminist organizations such as the Group of Five, which calls for an end to the patriarchal norms of religion which oppress women, and which rallies for increased female political leadership. Members of such groups, in addition to those in organizations ranging from the prolific Association of Women in Business and Commerce to the smallest neighborhood *tontine* savings club, struggle daily to improve Senegalese women's lives. Yet solidarity alone may be insufficient, "for women to be able to influence the directions of . . . social politics. . . . Economics imposes itself as the major point of entry."[44] Women must have access to new resources to gain autonomy in decision-making, regardless of whether they choose to militate for a fundamentalist Islamic movement or to run for president of the Republic.

NOTES

1. United Nations, *The Least Developed Countries 2000*, report of the Third United Nations Conference, 2001.

2. Republic of Senegal, *Recensement sur la population générale, région du Dakar* (Dakar: Ministry of Health, 1992–1993). *Enquête sur les comportements de preventions en matière de MST/SIDA dans la population général à Dakar* (Dakar: ONUSIDA, 1998).

3. Karen Somerville, "Reaction and Resistance: Confronting Economic Crisis: Structural Adjustment and Devaluation in Dakar, Senegal," in *Globalization and Survival in the Black Diaspora*, ed. Charles Green (Albany: State University of New York Press, 1997); Nii K. Bentsi-Enchill, "Devaluation Hits the African Franc Zone," *Africa Recovery* 7 (1993 1994): 3–4.

4. Donal Cruise O'Brien, *The Mourides of Senegal* (Oxford: Clarendon, 1971).

5. Ministry of National Education, 1998.

6. World Bank, *Gender Stats: Senegal*, 2001, http://genderstats.worldbank.org.

7. Barbara Callaway and Lucy Creevey, *The Heritage of Islam* (Boulder: Lynne Rienner, 1994).

8. Ministry of National Education, 1998.

9. Callaway and Creevey, *The Heritage of Islam*.

10. Ibid.

11. Fatou Sow, "Les Initiatives féminines au Sénégal: Une réponse à la crise?" *Africa Development* 18, no. 3 (1993): 89–115; Callaway and Creevey, *The Heritage of Islam*.

12. Fatou Sarr, *Femmes et pouvoir economique: COSEF infos* (Dakar: Sénégalaise de l'Imprimicrie, 1996).

13. Sow, "Les Initiatives."

14. Ibid.

15. Ibid.; Sarr, *Femmes et pouvoir economique*.

16. U.S. Department of State, 2000.

17. Ministry of Family, 1993.

18. *Women in Development 1992*.

19. Sow, "Les Initiatives."

20. Ibid.

21. Fatou Sow, "Famille et loi au Sénégal. Permanences et changements," *Women Living Under Muslim Laws*, dossier special no. 1.

22. Reported November 1999, www.sudonline.sn, official web site of the independent national *Sud Quotidien* newspaper and radio station.

23. Interview conducted by the author.

24. Salif Ndiaye and Ibrahima Sarr, "Evolution récente de la nuptialité (1978–

1986)," in *La Population du Sénégal*, eds. Salif Ndiaye and Yves Charbit (Paris: Imprimerie Jouve, 1994); Ministry of Health, *Enquête sur les comportements de preventions en matière de MST/SIDA*.

25. Callaway and Creevey, *The Heritage of Islam* Sow, "Famille et loi au Sénégal."

26. World Bank, *Gender Stats*.

27. Ndiaye and Charbit, *La Population Sénégal World Development Indicators 1999*.

28. Makhtar Diouf, *Senegal: Les Ethnies et la nation* (Geneva: UNRISD, 1994).

29. Centre d'Études et de Recherches sur la Population pour le Développement, *Les Jeunes en danger: Resultats d'une étude regionale dans cinq pays de l'afrique de l'oeust* (Dakar: n.p., 1996).

30. Republic of Senegal, *Enquête demographique et de santé au Sénégal* (EDS-II), Dakar 1992–1993; World Health Organization, *Who Estimates of Health Personnel*, 1995, http://www3.who.int/whosis.

31. Marie-Hélène Mottin-Sylla, *Excision au Sénégal*, ENDA-Tiers Monde, 1990; Fatou Sarr, "De la survivance d'un mode de pensée archaïque au contrôle de la sexualité féminine: La Quetiosn de l'excision," *Présence Africaine* 160 (2000).

32. Gerry Mackie, *Abandon collectif de l'excision: Le Debut de la fin* (Dakar: UNIFEM, 1999).

33. Amsatou Sow Sidibé, "Les Mutilations génitales féminines au Sénégal," *Présence Africaine* 160 (2000); Fatou, "De la survivance d'un mode de pensée archaïque."

34. Interparliamentary Union, 2002.

35. COSEF spokesperson Aminata Touré, in Aida Soumare Diop, *Senegalese Women Want to Be Elected, Not Electors*, Pan African News Agency, February 12, 2001, http://allafrica.com.

36. Florence Dini, interview with the president, *Amina* no. 563 (2001); Diop, *Senegalese Women*.

37. Katy Cissé Wone, "Femmes et pouvoir politique," in *Femmes et processus de prise de decisions* (Dakar: Conseil Sénégalais des Femmes, 1996).

38. Diop, *Senegalese Women*.

39. Callaway and Creevey, *The Heritage of Islam*.

40. Leonardo Villalón and Ousmane Kane, "Entre confrérisme, réformisme et islamisme: Les Mustarchidin du Sénégal," in *Islam et Islamismes au sud du Sahara*, eds. Ousmane Kane and Jean-Louis Triaud (Paris: Karthala, 1998).

41. Ibid.

42. Ministry of Women, Children, and Family, *Femmes sénégalaises à l'horizon 2015* (Dakar: Population Council, 1993), 22.

43. ECPAT International, *Child Prostitution and Trafficking*, 2002, www.ecpat.net; Afrol News, *Senegal Source of Women Trafficked to Europe*, 2002, www.afrol.com.

44. Sarr, *Femmes et pouvoir economique*, 13–14.

RESOURCE GUIDE

Suggested Reading

Ba, Mariama. *Une si longue lettre*. Dakar: Nouvelles Editions Africaines, 1981. A famous African novel on the complex problems of polygamous families in Senegal.

Beck, Linda J. "Democratization and the Hidden Public: The Impact of Patronage Networks on Senegalese Women." *Comparative Politics* (January 2003): 147–69.

Callaway, Barbara, and Lucy Creevey. *The Heritage of Islam*. Boulder: Lynne Rienner,

1994. A general study on the living conditions of Muslim women in Senegal and Northern Nigeria.

Cruise O'Brien, Donal. *The Mourides of Senegal*. Oxford: Clarendon, 1971. A history of brotherhood Islam in Senegal.

Diop, Abdoulaye Bara. *La Famille wolof*. Paris: Karthala, 1985. Two sociological discussions of the historical and contemporary structures of Wolof families and society in Senegal.

——. *La Société wolof*. Paris: Karthala, 1981.

Loimeier, Roman. "The Secular State and Islam in Senegal." In *Questioning the Secular State*, edited by D. Westerlund. London: Hurst, 1996. An overview of the history and characteristics of the burgeoning fundamentalist Islamic movement in urban Senegal.

Mbodj, Mohammed, et al. "The Senegalese Student Movement from Its Inception to 1989." In *African Studies in Social Movements and Democracy*, edited by Mahmood Mamdani. Dakar: CODESRIA, 1995. An analysis of student political activism and stagnation over several decades.

Perry, Donna. "Rural Ideologies and Urban Imaginings: Wolof Immigrants in New York City." *Africa Today* 44, no. 2 (1997): 229–60. Describes the life trajectories and labor of Senegalese immigrants.

Somerville, Karen. "Reaction and Resistance: Confronting Economic Crisis, Structural Adjustment, and Devaluation in Dakar, Senegal." In *Globalization and Survival in the Black Diaspora*, edited by Charles Green. Albany: State University of New York Press, 1997. A comprehensive explanation of Senegal's economic decline since independence.

Villalón, Leonardo. "Generational Changes, Political Stagnation, and the Evolving Dynamics of Religion and Politics in Senegal." *Africa Today* 46, nos. 3–4 (1999).

——. *Islamic Society and State Power in Senegal: Disciples and Citizens in Fatick*. New York: Cambridge University Press, 1995. Political analyses of civil society, religion, and political activism in Senegal.

Videos/Films

Faat Kine. 2000. Directed by Ousmane Sembane. San Francisco: California Newsreel.

Heroisme au Quotidien. 1998. Directed by Ousmane Sembane. Part of the eight-film series *Women Hold Up the Sky*, executive producer Shulamith Koenig. New York: People's Movement for Human Rights Education.

Karmen Geï. 2001. Directed by Joseph Gaï Ramaka. San Francisco: California Newsreel.

Rassemblage. 1982. Directed by Trin T. Minh-ha. New York: Women Make Movies.

Tableau Ferraille. 1997. Directed by Moussa Sène Abda. San Francisco: California Newsreel.

Web Sites

Metissicana, www.metissacana.sn,
Commercial web site linked to numerous research, email, tourist, artistic, news, and shopping resources in Dakar (in French).

Obeservatoire sur les Systèmes d'Information, les Reseaux et les Inforoutes au Sénégal, www.osiris.sn.
A comprehensive list of all websites in Senegal (in French).

Republic of Senegal, www.primature.sn/mfef.
Official web site of the Ministry of Women, Children, and Family (in French).

Le Soleil, www.lesoleil.sn.
Official web site of the state-managed newspaper *Le Soleil*.

Sud Quotidien, www.sudonline.sn.
Official web site of the independent national *Sud Quotidien* newspaper and radio station.

University Cheikh Anta Diop, www.ucad.sn.
Official web site of the University Cheikh Anta Diop of Dakar, with links to scholarly and research organizations around the city.

Walfadjri, www.walf.sn.
Official web site of the national Islamic newspaper and radio station *Walfadjri*.

Organizations

Association of African Women for Research and Development (AAWORD)
B.P. 15367
Dakar-Fann, Senegal
Phone: 221-824-20-53
Fax: 221-824-20-56
Email: aaword@telecomplus.sn

Centre de Recherche Ouest African (West African Research Association—Dakar office)
Rue E x Leon G. Damas
Fann Residence, Dakar
Phone: 221-865-22-77
Fax: 221-824-20-58
Email: assist@mail.ucad.sn

The West African Research Association is an excellent facility for foreign researchers. For an affordable membership fee, members receive access to computer/study rooms, as well as regular meetings with Senegalese and visiting scholars. Staff can facilitate housing, research projects, and government research clearance.

ENDA-SYNFEV (Environment and Development in the Third World–Synergy, Gender, and Development)
B.P. 3370
Dakar, Senegal
Phone: 221-821-60-27 or 221-822-42-29
Fax: 221-822-26-95
Email: mhms@enda.sn

While ENDA's headquarters are based in Dakar, it is an international nongovernmental organization. SYNFEV works mainly in Francophone Africa to improve living conditions for women and to promote development in electronic communication for women.

Reseau Siggil Jigeen
B.P. 10137
Dakar Liberté, Senegal
Phone/Fax: 221-825-00-56
Email: sjigeen@sentoo.sn

Reseau Siggil Jigeen is an umbrella organization for a number of women's aid groups located in Dakar.

UNIFEM Senegal
B.P. 154
Immeuble Fayçal
19 Rue Parchappe
Dakar, Senegal
Phone: 221-823-52-07
Fax: 221-823-50-02
Email: unifsen@telecomplus.sn

UNIFEM Senegal is the Senegalese office for the United Nations Women's Agency. It is directed by Madame Yassine Fall.

SELECTED BIBLIOGRAPHY

Afrol News. *Senegal Source of Women Trafficked to Europe.* 2002. www.afrol.com.

Centre d'Études et de Recherches sur la Population pour le Développement. "Les jeunes en danger: Resultats d'une étude regionale dans cinq pays de l'afrique de l'oeust." Dakar: n.p., 1996.

Diop, Aida Soumare. *Senegalese Women Want to Be Elected, Not Electors.* Pan African News Agency, February 12, 2001. http://allafrica.com.

Diouf, Makhtar. *Senegal: Les Ethnies et la nation.* Geneva: UNRISD, 1994.

ECPAT International. *Child Prostitution and Trafficking.* 2002. www.ecpat.net.

Kane, Ousmane, and Jean-Louis Triaud, eds. *Islam et Islamismes au sud du Sahara.* Paris: Karthala, 1998.

Mackie, Gerry. *Abandon collectif de l'excision: Le Debut de la fin.* Dakar: UNIFEM, 1999.

Ministry of Health. *Enquête sur les comportements de preventions en matière de MST/SIDA dans la population général à Dakar.* Dakar: ONUSIDA, 1998.

Mottin-Sylla, Marie-Hélène. *Excision au Sénégal.* ENDA-Tiers Monde, 1990.

Ndiaye, Salif, and Yves Charbit. *La Population du Sénégal.* Paris: Imprimerie Jouve, Ministry of Health, 1998.

Population Council. Ministry of Women, Children, and Family. *Femmes sénégalaises à l'horizon 2015.* Dakar: Population Council, 1993.

Republic of Senegal. *Enquête demographique et de santé au Sénégal (EDS-II).* Dakar, 1992–1993.

———. *Recensement sur la population générale, région du Dakar.* Dakar, 1992–1993.

Sarr, Fatou. "De la survivance d'un mode de pensée archaique au contrôle de la sexualité féminine: La Quetions de l'excision." *Présence Africaine* 160 (2000).

———. *Femmes et pouvoir economique: COSEF infos.* Dakar: Sénégalaise de l'Imprimierie, 1996.

Sidibé, Amsatou Sow. "Les Mutilations génitales féminines au Sénégal." *Présence Africaine* 160 (2000).

Sow, Fatou. "Famille et loi au Sénégal: Permanences et changements." *Women Living Under Muslim Laws,* dossier spécial no. 1 (1996).

————. "Les Initiatives féminines au Sénégal: Une réponse à la crise?" *Africa Development* 18, no. 3 (1993): 89–115.

United Nations. *The Least Developed Countries 2000*. Report of the Third United Nations Conference, 2001.

Wone, Katy Cissé. "Femmes et pouvoir politique." In *Femmes et processus de prise de decisions*. Dakar: Conseil Sénégalais des Femmes, 1996.

World Bank. *Gender Stats: Senegal*. 2001. http://genderstats.worldbank.org.

World Health Organization. *Who Estimates of Health Personnel*. 1995. www3.who.int/whosis.

16

SOMALIA

Ladan Affi

PROFILE OF SOMALIA

Somalia is located in the Horn of Africa and is surrounded by Ethiopia, Kenya, Djibouti, and the Indian Ocean. It has a land area of 637,540 square kilometers (106,233 square miles). The land is mostly savannah with some mountains in the north. The two major rivers in the country—the Jubba and Shebelle—are in the south, making that region more fertile.

The population of Somalia is estimated at 7 million. Somalia is one of the few countries in Africa in which its citizens share, for the most part, one common language (Somali), ethnicity (Somali), culture (Somali), and religion (Islam). Most Somalis trace their origins from two brothers—Samaale, also known as Soomaali, and Sab. The descendants of Samaale are divided into four clan families, which are Dir, Darod, Hawiye and Isaaq, while the descendants of Sab, living predominantly in the south, are divided into Digil and Mirifle. Minority groups include the Reer Hamar, who are of Somali and Asian origin, the Reer Barawe, the Bantu Somalis, and the Baajuun, who are Swahili-speaking. The most marginalized groups include the Tumaal, Midgaan, and Yibir.

Somalia is a patriarchal society

where the primary form of identification and loyalty is towards the clan.[1] With the collapse of the Somali state in 1991, the clan has become even more important as a source of protection and participation—socially, economically, and politically. The majority of Somalis are pastoral nomads who make their living herding camels, sheep, and goats, and in favorable regions cattle, while others engage in farming, fishing, or urban trade.

In the late 1880s, the British and Italians, followed by the French, arrived in Somalia, dividing the country into five different spheres of influence.[2] In 1960, British and Italian Somalilands gained their independence and united, forming the Somali Republic and establishing a democratic government.

In 1969, after a disgruntled military officer assassinated President Abdirashid Shermarke, a bloodless coup d'état was staged, bringing in the military dictatorship of Siad Barre. The Barre reign lasted for twenty-one years and was marked by numerous human rights violations. In 1991 a coalition of opposition clans ousted Barre from power. But they were then subsequently unable to agree on the formation of a government, plunging the country into civil war. Since then, Somalia has not had any internationally recognized central government.

In 1992, the United Nations and the United States intervened in Somalia in a humanitarian mission to stop the famine and to attempt to bring peace and order back into the country. The joint UN/U.S. mission also made an effort to help create a government for Somalia. Having failed to bring peace or create a government, the UN/U.S. peacekeepers pulled out of Somalia in 1995. Meanwhile, various parts of Somalia have declared independence such as Somaliland, or declared regional autonomy, such as Puntland, although none have received international recognition.

In 2000, Somali civil groups meeting in Djibouti agreed to create a government and formed a Transitional National Government (TNG), which has been internationally recognized but exercises little power over the country.[3] Although the TNG was mandated for three years to lay the groundwork for the creation of a permanent government, it had not been able to accomplish its mandate as of 2003.

Somalia is one of the poorest and least developed countries in the world.[4] However, even though during the civil war much of the infrastructure was destroyed and the resulting insecurity has hampered trade, business continues to thrive in some areas of Somalia.[5] Livestock export remains the most important sector, accounting for 40 percent of the gross domestic product (GDP).[6] But the livestock ban imposed by the Gulf States in 1998 has negatively impacted on the Somali economy. Additionally, remittances from Somalis abroad to their families in Somalia estimated at close to U.S.$1 billion a year have been reduced due to the recent closing of the U.S. operations of the largest remittance company in Somalia, Al Barakaat, by the U.S. government on allegations of terrorist links.[7]

According to 2001 estimates, the ratio of male to female in Somalia is

1.01 males per female, although women have higher life expectancy, 48.25 years compared to 44.99 years for males. Total fertility is calculated at 7.11 children for each woman, infant mortality is at 123.97 deaths per 1,000 live births, and maternal mortality is at 1,600 per 100,000 women.[8]

OVERVIEW OF WOMEN'S ISSUES

Because of their crucial role in the political, economic, and social domain, women are the backbone of Somali society. They do much of the country's physical work but receive little or no recognition. This view was drastically reinforced after the fall of the government in 1991, when Somali women were forced to take on male responsibilities. Many of them became primary income earners and heads of households, despite the fact that throughout the civil war, Somali women were raped, tortured, and sometimes killed.

EDUCATION

During the civil war in Somalia, the warring factions destroyed Somalia's infrastructure, including government buildings such as public schools, technical schools, and universities. Those buildings that were not destroyed have now become home to displaced refugees. Despite the lack of a nationally organized educational system, the relatively peaceful parts of the country have organized public schools, while other parts of the country have managed to retain private schools, technical schools, and in some instances universities.[9] Most of those schools are located in the urban areas, and for the majority of Somalis who live in the rural areas, the only education available is through Qur'anic schools. Some international organizations and regional bodies such as the UNESCO and the European Union have made the effort to rehabilitate the educational system but they have not been entirely successful.[10]

Opportunities

Without a government to enforce girls' attendance at school, anecdotal evidence suggests that the level of school enrollment for girls remains less than that of boys, despite the increased number of primary and secondary schools in the last few years.[11] More Somali women are working outside the home. This has negatively affected the ability of girls to continue their education, as the responsibility for looking after younger siblings and doing the housework has fallen on them. It appears that until girls are relieved from family responsibilities, the gap in education between boys and girls will continue to increase. Although Somali society is more aware and perhaps appreciative of the role that women assumed since the start of the civil war, this has not necessarily translated into more opportunities for girls to advance academically. Instead, girls continue to be restricted to traditional roles and occupations.

Literacy

The UN estimated an adult literacy rate of 49.7 percent for men and 25.8 percent for women in 2001.[12]

EMPLOYMENT AND ECONOMICS

Farming and Herding

In the rural environment, most of the work falls to women. Nomadic women are responsible for caring for the smaller livestock such as sheep and goats. Nomadic women also are responsible for milking the animals, processing the milk, and feeding the family. Women collect the firewood, cook, and do other housework. In addition, women are the architects, because whenever the nomads move, it is the responsibility of women to dismantle and reassemble the house, load and tie all the possessions on the camels, and make sure that the family has enough supplies for the journey.[13]

In farming communities, women are concentrated in subsistence agriculture, performing over 60 percent of the labor using basic tools.[14] In Somalia, a woman's back is never free; she is carrying either a baby, a container of water or milk, or firewood. Among the agro-pastoralists, the division of labor varies depending on rainfall. During droughts, women are obliged to trek for days in search of water, while during the rainy season, women are responsible for the needs of the household.

Paid Employment

Before the outbreak of the war, Somali women, particularly those who were educated and in urban areas, worked for the government as public servants, teachers, nurses, and the like, while others were housewives. As heads of households, women have been left with little choice in what kind of employment they take up.

Informal Economic Activities

As women have taken on traditionally male responsibilities, more and more are becoming the primary, and sometimes the only, income earners for their families. Many of these women, often having little education, have turned to business as a means of supporting themselves and their families.

Entrepreneurship

Statelessness in Somalia has increased the number of private businesses. Due to the absence of government regulations, Somalia has been described as having a laissez-faire economy where development is market driven. This sector has also been key in providing services, such as education and health care, normally provided by government. Unfortunately, because these basic services are profit oriented, poor people are unable to afford them.

The evidence suggests that urban women own many of the small businesses, with most engaging in petty trade in foodstuff and clothing, while women in the rural areas engage in small-scale production of pottery, basketry, leather goods, and containers for milk and storage.[15] Some women have crossed into large businesses such as the *khat* trade (a stimulant chewed in the form of a leaf or a small bud),[16] although many women still continue to be excluded from the more lucrative livestock export business.

To attempt to overcome lack of access to large amounts of funds, some women have formed cooperatives, pooling their money together and often sending one woman overseas to buy large quantities of merchandise on their behalf.[17]

Support for Mothers/Caretakers

Maternal Leave

In traditional Somali culture, a woman having a child receives a great deal of support from family, friends, and neighbors. Often, mothers stay at home for forty days after having a child to receive special care. Since there is no national government in Somalia, maternal leave and other associated benefits provided by government are not available or even relevant.

Child Care

Somalis live in extended families, as children are considered to be the responsibility of all adults. Since Somali women tend to have many children, they are often helped in their care by other female relatives such as sisters, mothers, and grandmothers, as well as neighbors.

Inheritance, Property, and Land Rights

In Somalia, inheritance laws are based, at least in theory, on Islamic law, although in practice, customary law often supersedes it. In Islam, men are responsible for the financial maintenance of the household.[18] Women therefore inherit from their parents only half of what their brothers inherit. Upon the death of the father in Somalia, the family livestock, particularly camels (considered the most prestigious animal), are not divided up, but rather are kept together and ownership belongs to the entire family. As a result, women rarely get their share.[19] However, it is quite common for women to inherit smaller livestock such as sheep and goats as well as land. In accordance with both Islamic and Somali customary law, women maintain ownership over their wealth and property even after marriage and it does not go to the husband or become part of the common marital property.

Social/Government Programs

Since the 1991 civil war, Somalia has not had any internationally recognized central government. When the joint UN/U.S. mission pulled out in 1995 after having failed to stem the onslaught of famine or to instill order, various parts of the country declared independence. None are recognized internationally and as of 2003 there are still no quantifiable data to determine any programs from the various governments—including the TNG—to help the country recover. Somalia remains one of the poorest and least developed countries in the world.[20]

FAMILY AND SEXUALITY

Gender Roles and Division of Labor

Women perform a significant role in Somali society, where the division of labor is clearly defined and allocates women a heavy workload. Somali culture is publicly patriarchal, although women play important economic roles in both the nomadic and farming communities and in business in the cities. Women are valued for their productive as well as reproductive capabilities. Due to the civil war, women's responsibilities have increased as men have been killed in the conflict or have migrated abroad. Some men who used to work for the government are unable to find employment now that government jobs are defunct;

Somalian woman and children. Photo © Claver Carroll/Painet.

others have become addicted to chewing *khat*[21] and are uninterested in working.

Marriage

Both Somali culture and Islam place a great deal of emphasis on the importance of marriage. Within Somali culture, marriage is viewed as an opportunity to increase and expand networking by making alliances with other families, while Islam views marriage as the completion of half of the believer's faith.

The usual marital age for girls in the rural areas is fifteen, which is younger than that of urban girls, who often get married around eighteen. Men's first marriages often occur when they are between eighteen and twenty-five. Parents or other senior relations usually have an important say in the choice of the first marriage partner.[22]

Among Somalis, bridewealth or *mehr* is given to the bride herself and, if the marriage ends, she is ordinarily entitled to keep it. The bridewealth primarily consists of livestock in the nomadic environment or money or gold and other objects in the urban areas, provided by the husband and his family.[23] Newly married women often use their bridewealth to start a business.

Reproduction

Contraception and Abortion

Islam views marriage as a means of attaining tranquility and protection for men and women as well as a source of procreation. Islam, as practiced in Somalia, does allow for the use of contraception in order to control the timing of births with the intent of distancing the occurrences of pregnancy or to delay it for a specific amount of time. However, most Somali women do not use Western methods of contraception due to cultural unfamiliarity or the scarcity and expense associated with it.[24] Instead, women rely on traditional methods of contraception such as withdrawal, while other women breast-feed children for up to two years in an attempt not to get pregnant.

There are differing views on abortion in Islam. Most Muslim scholars agree that abortion is allowed at any point during the pregnancy if the mother's life is in danger, whereas some scholars allow abortion if there is a legitimate reason such as rape. Other scholars discourage it, while a fourth group prohibits abortion in all cases, except if the mother's life is in danger. As Muslims, Somali women would consult with a religious scholar about their specific cases. However, even if a Somali woman wanted to get an abortion, lack of access to health care facilities would be a hindrance to actually doing it. Most Somali women are unlikely to seek abortion, because of the traditional positive view toward having many children.

Teen Pregnancy

Girls in rural areas marry at approximately fifteen years of age, whereas urban girls get married around eighteen years of age. Teen pregnancy out of wedlock is rare but is more common in urban areas. If the father is known, then a marriage is forced between him and the pregnant girl. Somalis, as Muslims, view pregnancy out of wedlock as shameful, but if it occurs the family of the girl often raises the child.

HEALTH

Health Care Access

Before the collapse of the state in Somalia, the government provided free health care. Although most of the hospitals and health clinics had been located in urban areas, the number of health care facilities and professionals had been increasing. The fall of the government led to further deterioration of the health system and the provision of health care fell to the private sector, becoming a for-profit enterprise and remaining largely urbanized. So, in addition to health care being expensive for the majority of Somalis, it also became out of reach for the poor. According to UNICEF, the inability to access health care is a significant factor in maternal mortality and in the deaths of infants and children under five years of age.[25]

Diseases and Disorders

Major diseases prevalent in Somalia include pulmonary tuberculosis, malaria, and a host of infectious and parasitic diseases. Many of those diseases are aggravated by the lack of hospitals. Additionally, large numbers of educated Somalis including doctors and nurses fled the country due to the civil war.[26] High rates of malnutrition worsened by periodic droughts, famine, and unsanitized drinking water contribute to the alarming statistics of illness and death.

AIDS

According to the United Nations, the estimated number of people living with HIV in Somalia is 1 percent of the adult population. Although that is one of the lowest rates in Africa, Somalia shares borders with two countries, Ethiopia and Kenya, that have high rates of AIDS occurrence. Although there have been attempts to increase awareness among Somalis about this disease, the lack of a national government to coordinate programs and the absence of a health care system are detrimental to preventing the spread of AIDS among Somalis.[27]

Female Genital Cutting

Female genital cutting is widely practiced in Somalia. Although the practice was criminalized by the Siad Barre regime, the law has had little impact on its prevalence.

Cutting of children is commonly practiced. A majority of Somalis mistakenly link cutting to Islam, even though Islam only requires circumcision of boys as part of the covenant between God and Abraham. In reality, the practice of cutting girls is believed to predate Islam, and is thought to have originated in Pharaonic Egypt.

This confusion of a tradition with a religious requirement has resulted in the continuation of female genital cutting. The practice is particularly strong in rural areas, where the autonomous labor of girls is important because it is believed that the practice discourages premarital sex and prevents or minimizes rape. Often the strongest advocates and practitioners for female genital cutting are mothers and grandmothers. Many girls also look forward to this practice, viewing it as a part of a ritual in leaving childhood and becoming a woman.

Due to the civil war and the subsequent emigration to other countries, many Somalis have come into contact with other Muslims who do not practice female genital cutting, and as a result Somalis have become aware that Islam does not require girls to be cut. The practice appears to have decreased considerably among Somalis living in the diaspora.

POLITICS AND LAW

Leadership and Decision-making

Somalia has been without a central government since 1991. Various regions have either declared their independence (Somaliland) or set themselves up as autonomous regions, such as Puntland and the recently formed but already faltering southwestern Somalia. Since 2000 the Transitional National Government (TNG) attempted to set up a united government, without much success. Politics tends to be male dominated and runs along clan lines, with the result that women are often marginalized.[28]

Somali women have traditionally been excluded from leadership and decision-making processes, whether at the national level or at the clan level. Women's customary role in times of war and conflict has often been that of peacemaker; however, this is changing as more women realize that being politically active means being able to determine the course of their lives. Despite their traditional exclusion, Somali women played an active and positive part in the political process from the independence movement in the 1940s and 1950s, the revolution of Siad Barre in the 1970s, opposition to Siad Barre's tyranny, and the civil war.[29] Before the civil war, women were excluded from clan deliberations. The Barre regime, although it promised reforms to improve the position of women in society, in the end excluded women from meaningful political participation and did not appoint even one woman to a leadership position. However, during the civil war, women became increasingly active and have since taken part in the many reconciliation conferences, often bringing the different factions to a compromise agreement.[30] At the last reconciliation conference held in Arta, Djibouti, twenty-five women were appointed as members of parliament in the TNG, indicating a change in the traditionally male dominated politics. Women have also been appointed as ministers and deputy ministers within the TNG. A woman has even run as a presidential candidate in one of the elections in Somaliland.

Quota Laws

As part of the mandate of the TNG, women have been allocated twenty-five seats in the parliament. Within the cabinet, the appointment of women lies entirely with the prime minister and the president and so far there has only been one woman appointed as minister, while a few others have been named as deputy ministers. Although it is not known what will happen once the three-year mandate of the TNG is over, Somali women have fought for inclusion at the national political level and are unlikely to accept exclusion again.

Political Participation

Since colonial times, Somali women have been politically active, usually advocating for the interests of the society at large. Somali women have used a variety of methods to ensure their political participation, ranging from composing and reciting poetry and songs, and selling their gold jewelry to contribute to certain national causes, to taking part in demonstrations and other political activities. For their political activities, women suffered under colonialism and under the dictatorship of Siad Barre, both of which imprisoned and tortured women in order to silence them.[31]

Women's Rights

Women's Movements

As a result of the ongoing civil war, there is no national women's organization in Somalia.[32] However, many women have become active promoters of peace by either forming or joining nongovernmental organizations that are dedicated to meeting the needs of women or engaging in activities promoting a culture of peace. Some women's groups helped avert conflict between warlords through mediation, while other women's groups collaborated with each other across clan lines. During the last peace and reconciliation conference in Djibouti, women participated in the hundreds for the first time.

Women's groups also provide various social services ranging from skills training programs for women and demobilized youth militia as well as peace poetry and song contests creating a healing environment and promoting peace. Women's groups have also emerged among the strongest advocates for human rights, environmental protection, and the rule of law. It is for these activities that different Somali women have received international recognition and awards.[33]

Military Service

During the Barre regime, high school graduates—both male and female—wanting to continue to higher education or find employment with the government were required to undergo national service. Part of this national service included military training. Since there is now no government in Somalia, there is no required military training.

RELIGION AND SPIRITUALITY

Women's Roles

Almost all Somalis are Sunni Muslims and for many Somalis, Islam and Somali culture are so intertwined that it is difficult to tell where one ends and the other starts. Therefore in Somalia, attitudes, social customs, conflict resolution, and gender roles are based on combined Somali and Islamic traditions.

Various verses in the Qur'an, the Muslim holy book, explicitly outline the equality between men and women—morally and spiritually. In addition, Somali culture, while patriarchal, nevertheless values both the reproductive and productive role of women, seeing them as vital to the survival of the family.

In Islam, women do participate in religious activities such as prayers and Somali women often organize religious classes and celebrations for children and for themselves. Women also lead prayers for other women but not for men, due to the nature of the Muslim prayer.[34]

VIOLENCE

Historically in Somalia, clans and various groups often fought over resources. These fights tended to be short-lived and often the clan elders would convene a meeting to bring the warring groups together and work out a truce. Often, as part of the truce agreement, the warring clans would exchange women to prevent further hostilities, in the belief that those that are related through marriage are less likely to fight.[35] During the Barre era, the clans became politicized as Barre armed various factions in his attempt to maintain control. However, women were not specifically targeted during conflicts between groups.

Domestic Violence

A Somali proverb states that a woman who marries thirty times is better off than the one who lives in an abusive marriage, signaling that there was cultural acceptance for women to leave abusive relationships. As well, in the rural areas, families were often reluctant to agree to give their daughters in marriage to a man known as abusive. However, domestic violence did occur in Somalia and it was often accepted that a man could beat his wife.[36] Women who did not want to live in such a situation, and there were many, often asked their brothers or other male relatives for protection; some turned to the clan for protection, asking for a meeting of the elders; others often simply fled the marital home.

Rape/Sexual Assault

Within Somali society, particularly in the rural areas, rape was not very common. However, as a result of the breakdown of society and the mores governing it, rape became widespread during the height of the civil war. Both women and girls were targeted as clans fought for supremacy and often this violence against women was pursued as a means of demoralizing other groups. The women and girls who became pregnant as a result of the rape were often ostracized by society.[37] Women would leave areas where they were known and go to other parts of the country, passing themselves off as either divorcees or widows.

Prior to the formation of the TNG, women in the more unstable areas such as Mogadishu were supporters of the Islamic *shari'a* courts. These courts handed stiff sentences against violent offenders, particularly those who committed rape, making the streets a bit safer for women. Yet women still face many limitations as a result of the ongoing civil war in Somalia.

OUTLOOK FOR THE TWENTY-FIRST CENTURY

The famous contemporary Somali novelist Nuruddin Farah wrote that it requires a great deal of courage for Somali women to fight for equality and justice in these difficult times, yet it is more necessary than ever for women to fight these battles.[38] It appears that Somali people are coming to accept women's more open participation in society, with some political leaders even tentatively suggesting that since men have failed to bring peace to Somalia in the last twelve years, perhaps the political leadership should be handed over to women. Travelers since the ancient Egyptians have noted Somali women's dominant and extraordinary personalities. Despite living under patriarchy, Somali women will continue to play a positive role in helping lessen conflict by resisting war and other armed conflict, thus strengthening peace and promoting development.

NOTES

1. A clan is a collection of extended families that trace their lineage to a common ancestor. It forms a unit in a kinship-based segmentary society like Somalia. In Somalia, children inherit the clan of their fathers. The clan was the primary method of figuring out who your extended family was. Additionally, it sometimes acts as a welfare system, raising money, and providing other forms of help to its members.

2. Somalia was divided into five parts by the European powers France, Britain, and Italy, and two parts of Somalia were given by the British to Ethiopia (commonly called the Ogaden region) and one part was given to Kenya (formerly called the Northern Frontier District and now known as the Northeastern Province).

3. In 1999, Djibouti announced that it would hold a reconciliation conference for Somalia to see if a government could be formed. Somalis from a variety of socioeconomic background met in Arta, a resort village near Djibouti City, and deliberated for six months. The conference ended with the formation of the transitional national government, including a parliament, a prime minister, and a president. In August 2000 the transitional national government moved to Mogadishu to try to establish a government. For more information, see www.somalia-rebirth.dj.

4. In 1996, Somalia ranked 172 out of 174 on the United Nation's Development Programme's Human Development Index (HDI). Since then, Somalia has not been ranked due to lack of data. See www.unsomalia.org/infocenter/factsheets.htm. Most of the statistics used in this chapter were obtained from the online version of the *CIA World Factbook* for Somalia, available at www.odci.gov/cia/publications/factbook/geos/so.html. See the United Nations Somalia web site at www.unsomalia.org, and the United Nations web site at www.un.org.

5. See Peter Maass, "Ayn Rand Comes to Somalia: Economy of Mogadishu Thrives Despite Lack of Government," *Atlantic Monthly* 287, no. 5 (May 2001): 30–31; Hassan Barise, "Money Rules in Mogadishu," *UNESCO Courier* 54, no. 2 (February 2001): 21; and Peter Willems, "Somalia: Business Under the Gun," *African Business* no. 76 (May 2002). 44–45.

6. *CIA World Factbook*, www.odci.gov/cia/publications/factbook/geos/so.html.

7. Currently the UN estimates that annual remittances into Somalia at U.S.$700 million, while some scholars on Somalia estimate the foreign aid given to Somalia at U.S.$25 million per year. See Donald G. McNeil Jr., "A Nation Challenged: Sanctions; How Blocking Assets Erased a Wisp of Prosperity," *New York Times*, 13 April 2002.

8. *CIA World Factbook*.

9. Amoud University, www.amoud-university.borama.ac.so/; University of Hargeisa, www.universityofhargeisa.org/.

10. UNESCO, www.unesco.org.

11. The overall enrollment for primary school is estimated at 13.8 percent. For boys it is 14.9 percent and for girls it is 12.1 percent. For more information, see www.unsomalia.org.

12. See www.unsomalia.org.

13. Ibrahim Rhoda, "The Changing Lives of Somali Women," in *Changing Per-*

ceptions: *Writings on Gender and Development*, eds. Tina Wallace with Candida March (Oxford: Oxfam, 1991).

14. *Somalia: Country Gender Profile* (Washington, DC: World Bank, n.d.).

15. A report released by the International Labour Organisation found that the labor force participation of Somali women was relatively high when compared to many other African nations. This same report found that almost two-thirds of working women were self-employed, while another 15 percent and 20 percent were employees and family helpers respectively. See International Labour Organisation, *Generating Employment and Income in Somalia: Jobs and Skills Programme for Africa* (Geneva: ILO, 1989).

16. Khat, also known as Qat, Mirra, Abyssinian/African tea, and African salad, commonly grows in East Africa and southern Arabia. It liberates the user from daily realities and produces feelings of euphoria, excitement, clarity of thought, loss of appetite, and insomnia. In Somalia, most users of khat are men and it is thought to contribute to their unemployment, although many of its sellers tend to be women because it is a very lucrative business. Somalia imports khat from Kenya and Ethiopia and the costs associated with its consumption are millions of dollars annually. It was illegal in Somalia but its use skyrocketed after the fall of the government. It is illegal in the United States and many other western countries such as Canada, Sweden, and Denmark. For the negative socioeconomic and health costs of this drug, see Reginald Herbold Green, "Khatt and the Realities of Somalis: Historic, Social, Household, Political, and Economic," *Review of African Political Economy* 26, no. 79 (March 1999): 33–49. See also www.sas.upenn.edu/african_studies/hornet/qat.html.

17. In Somalia, in an effort to collect large sums of money at one time, women often form groups called Hagbad or Shaloongo. In these groups, each woman pays a certain share of money every month, which is collected by each member in turn.

18. In Islam, men are responsible for taking care of women (wives, mothers, sisters, etc.). Even if a woman earns or has more wealth than a man, she is not required to spend it on herself.

19. This is contrary to Islamic law, which states that everyone must receive his or her share of the inheritance. However, Somali nomadic culture supersedes Islamic law in this case.

20. See note 4.

21. See note 16.

22. Somali women choose their marital partners as indicated by this Somali proverb: "A woman talks with a thousand men but only marries one." Sometimes, if parents do not agree to the marriage, the man and the woman may elope.

23. In Islam the bride decides the bridewealth given by the groom. Within Somali culture, compensation is often offered to the family of the bride, since they will be losing her productive contribution, in addition to the bridewealth.

24. Some Somalis may also not know that Islam does allow the use of contraceptives for this purpose.

25. In Somalia only 1.5 children between the ages of one and two have been vaccinated against all childhood diseases. See www.unsomalia.org/infocenter/factsheets.htm.

26. The UN estimates that there are 0.4 doctors per 100,000 and 2.0 nurses per 100,000. See www.unsomalia.org/infocenter/factsheets.htm.

27. Previously, increasing awareness of AIDS was limited to media outlets such as radio and television. However, recently there were attempts to educate people of the dangers of AIDS through demonstrations, which were held in southern Somalia. See

"Somalia: First-Ever AIDS Awareness Campaign," www.irinnews.org (accessed 16 July 2002).

28. In Somalia, interclan marriages are quite common and as such women are often not trusted in politics because women come from one clan and marry into another. Interestingly, it is this same situation that provides women with the abilities to be effective peacemakers because they are able to relate to different clans.

29. For their activities in opposing the dictatorship of Said Barre, see Nuruddin Farah, "The Women of Kismayo," *Times Literary Supplement* no. 4885 (November 15, 1996). For their role after the civil war, see Hassan Keynan, "Somalia: The Great Escape," *UNESCO Courier* no. 9 (September 1995): 26–27. See also Amina H. Aden, "Somalia: Women and Words," *Ufahamu* 10, no. 3 (1989): 115–42.

30. For example, during the Borama conference held in Somaliland, women played a crucial role indirectly in its success by influencing their male relatives to compromise and agree to peace. Some women who disagreed with their male relatives' decisions would retaliate by "burning the dinner," among other things.

31. On Somali women's political participation during colonialism, see Zeinab Mohamed Jama, "Fighting to Be Heard: Somali Women's Poetry," *African Literature and Cultures* 4, no. 1 (1991): 43–53. On their opposition activities during the Barre regime, see Nuruddin Farah, "The Women of Kismayo," *Times Literary Supplement* no. 4885 (15 November 1996). On their activities during the civil war, see Matt Bryden, *Somalia Between Peace and War: Somali Women on the Eve of the Twenty-first Century* (Nairobi: UNIFEM, 1998).

32. Barre created the Somali Women's Democratic Government as a mean of mobilizing women, using them in his efforts to undermine Somali culture and particularly the clan but doing little for women aside from passing superficial laws.

33. Just within 2002 alone, two Somali women, Mariam Hussein and Fatima Jibrell, won awards in the United States for promoting human rights and fighting environmental degradation respectively.

34. The Muslim prayer includes bowing and prostrations; women often pray beside or behind men, not in front.

35. Women from each clan would be asked to volunteer to marry men from the other clan.

36. Interestingly, it was considered shameful for a man who beat a woman who was not related to him.

37. Some Somali women were raped in the refugee camps after fleeing the chaos in Somalia. See "Somali Refugee Women Face Rape," *Off Our Backs* 23, no. 10 (November 1993).

38. See "The Women of Kismayo," *Times Literary Supplement* no. 4885.

RESOURCE GUIDE

Suggested Readings

Bryden, Matt. *Somalia Between Peace and War: Somali Women on the Eve of the 21st Century*. Nairobi: UNIFEM, 1998.

Farah, Nuruddin. *Gifts*. New York: Arcade, 1999.

Kapteijns, Lidwien, and Maryan Omar Ali. *Women's Voices in a Man's World: Women in the Pastoral Tradition in Northern Somali Orature c. 1899–1980*. Portsmouth, NH: Heinemann, 1999.

Lewis, I. M. *Understanding Somalia: Guide to Culture, History, and Social Institutions*. London: HAAN, 1993.
Ramsey Marshall, Donna. *Women in War and Peace: Grassroots Peacebuilding*. Washington, DC: U.S. Institute of Peace Press, 2000.
Sheikh-Abdi, Abdi. *Tales of Punt: Somali Folktales*. Macomb, IL: Dr. Leisure, 1993.

Web Sites

AllPuntland.com, www.allpuntland.com.
A news web site that provides information in primarily Somali and some English, focused on the Puntland region of Somalia.

Arlaadinet, www.arlaadinet.com.
Provides news in English and Somali, focusing on the south of Somalia.

Banadir, www.banadir.com.
A popular web site providing daily news in English and Somali on what is happening within Somalia and in the diaspora, with extensive archived news.

Hiiraan Online, www.hiiraan.com.
A well-known web site providing news in English and Somali.

Pan-Somali Council for Peace and Democracy (ISRAACA), www.israaca.org.
An advocacy organization promoting Somali unity.

Somaliland Net, www.somalilandnet.com.
Somaliland web site provides news and commentary in Somali and English, on Somalia and Somaliland.

SomaliNet, www.somalinet.com.
SomaliNet is one of the most popular web sites, providing information on a variety of topics ranging from news, culture, and current happenings within the Somali community.

UN Office for the Coordination of Humanitarian Affairs, www.irinnews.org.

United Nations Somalia, www.unsomalia.org.

Organization

Pan-Somali Council for Peace and Democracy (ISRAACA)
1201 Pennsylvania Ave.
NW #300, PMP #49
Washington, DC 20004

SELECTED BIBLIOGRAPHY

Aden, Amina H. "Somalia. Women and Words." *Ufahamu* 10, no. 3 (1989): 115–42.

Barise, Hassan. "Money Rules in Mogadishu." *UNESCO Courier* 54, no. 2 (February 2001): 21.

Bryden, Matt. *Somalia Between Peace and War: Somali Women on the Eve of the 21st Century*. Nairobi, UNIFEM, 1998.

Farah, Nuruddin. "The Women of Kismayo." *Times Literary Supplement* no. 4885 (15 November 1996).

Herbold Green, Reginald. "Khatt [*sic*] and the Realities of Somalis: Historic, Social, Household, Political, and Economic." *Review of African Political Economy* 26, no. 79 (March 1999): 33–49.

Ibrahim Rhoda. "The Changing Lives of Somali Women." In *Changing Perceptions: Writings on Gender and Development*, edited by Tina Wallace with Candida March. Oxford: Oxfam, 1991.

International Labour Organisation (ILO). *Generating Employment and Income in Somalia: Jobs and Skills Programme for Africa*. Geneva: ILO, 1989.

Jama, Zeinab Mohamed. "Fighting to Be Heard: Somali Women's Poetry." *African Literature and Cultures* 4, no. 1 (1991): 43–53.

Keynan, Hassan. "Somalia: The Great Escape." *UNESCO Courier* no. 9 (September 1995): 26–27.

Maass, Peter. "Ayn Rand Comes to Somalia: Economy of Mogadishu Thrives Despite Lack of Government." *Atlantic Monthly* 287, no. 5 (May 2001): 30–31.

McNeil, Donald G., Jr. "A Nation Challenged: Sanctions; How Blocking Assets Erased a Wisp of Prosperity." *New York Times*, 13 April 2002.

Somalia: Country Gender Profile. Washington, DC: World Bank, n.d.

Somalia: First-Ever AIDS awareness campaign. www.irinnews.org (accessed 16 July 2002).

"Somali Refugee Women Face Rape." *Off Our Backs* 23, no. 10 (November 1993).

Willems, Peter. "Somalia: Business Under the Gun." *African Business* no. 276 (May 2002): 44–45.

17

SOUTH AFRICA

Hannah Britton

PROFILE OF SOUTH AFRICA

South Africa is a vibrant nation that has been at the forefront of international news and politics since the 1950s. Only in 1994 did South Africa have its first free and fair democratic elections. Europeans began settling the area in the mid-1600s, disregarding the indigenous people's control of the land and bringing disease, conflict, and slavery. Early in the 1900s, South Africa was formally ruled by a white minority government that implemented the policy of apartheid in 1948, which enforced racial segregation and discrimination. Non-whites were excluded from owning land, participating in elections, or having freedom of movement. Today, South Africa is transitioning from this minority-ruled authoritarian government into a democracy. Each of South Africa's eleven ethnic groups participates regularly and equally in the processes of government and civic life.

Located at the southern tip of the African continent, South Africa's land is as diverse as its people. The nation has a combination of lush tropical regions, productive coastlines, agriculturally fertile plains, and mineral-rich soils. Currently, South Africa's constitutionally ruled government

is a parliamentary system with three coequal branches of government: executive, parliament, and the judiciary. Provincial and local governments manage many critical resources, but ultimate authority lies with the national government in this unitary system. The economy is one of the strongest in Africa; however, the new government has several pressing challenges, including vast inequalities of opportunity between the former white minority elite and the majority indigenous population. According to the 1996 census, 76.7 percent of the population classified themselves as African, 10.9 percent as white, 8.9 percent as Colored,[1] and 2.6 percent as Indian/Asian. South Africa has a mixed economy, which is primarily a combination of agricultural and mining activities but also contains fairly advanced levels of industrialization within the urban settings.

Because of the vast inequalities enforced by apartheid, notable differences in the quality of life continue today based on citizens' race, class, and gender. For example, women of African origin face a maternal mortality rate of 58 per 100,000 live births, whereas white women face only 3 per 100,000. Similarly, the rate of death at birth for African babies is 54 out of every 1,000, whereas the figure drops to 7 of every 1,000 for white babies.[2] The fertility rate per woman from 1995 to 2000 was 3.1, which is a significant reduction from 1970 to 1974, when the figure was 5.4.[3]

South Africa's population is 52 percent female, and on average women of all population groups live longer than men of the same ethnic groups. The average life expectancy for all South Africans is 56.2 years for women and 50.3 years for men.[4] But these averages again hide the impact of the historical discrimination against the nonwhite population. The average life expectancy for white men is consistently higher than the average life expectancy for women of African origin.[5] African men's life expectancy is 60 years; women's is 67 years. Indian men's average life-span is 64 years; women's is 70 years. White men's life expectancy is 69 years, women's 76 years. The Colored population has the lowest expectancy, with men at 59 years and women at 65 years.[6] Women's per capita income stands at 44 percent of men's—one of the clearest indicators of inequality between men and women.

OVERVIEW OF WOMEN'S ISSUES

Just as South Africa's political system is currently in flux, so too are the cultural practices and social norms affecting women's status and power in society. The first democratically elected government in South Africa made significant symbolic and legislative strides toward improving the legal and constitutional status of women. Similarly, the number of women in high political office increased dramatically, from less than 1 percent during apartheid to over 26 percent in 1994 and to 30 percent in 1999.

Translating these critical promises and goals into reality for the citizens of South Africa has remained one of the most vexing problems facing the new government. For example, while South Africa was ranked seventh in the world in terms of the number of women in national office, the nation was simultaneously ranked first in the world for the number of women reportedly raped. High levels of violence against women are only one piece of the problem facing women in South Africa. Despite the fact that women are legally considered equal citizens and economic participants, the majority of South African women remain trapped within inferior educational opportunities, constrained by customary law and practices, and ensnared by limited economic roles. While this is the current reality for the majority of women, South Africa has the possibility of becoming a highly progressive state. Unlike many more industrialized governments, South Africa has the constitutional and legislative framework in place for a highly egalitarian society. Just as women had to struggle against apartheid, they will need to continue their struggle to ensure that the country begins to foster a legitimate democracy and a progressive society.

EDUCATION

Opportunities

There are historic and contemporary obstacles to educational access, opportunity, and achievement for all nonwhite peoples in South Africa. Historically, the apartheid system depended on the Bantu educational system to create and maintain racial divisions in lifestyle and employment. It was used by the Afrikaners to refer to people of African origin. The minister of native affairs, Hendrik Verwoerd, designed the 1953 Bantu Educational Act to ensure that black children "knew their place" in South African society. They were to be trained specifically to fill the service jobs needed by white society and that their educational achievement would be intentionally limited. White children would receive the opposite treatment, and they would grow to expect to be managers and leaders. Colored children would be given slightly better opportunities than blacks, but they would not see the same level of possibilities as whites.

Women's groups, like the Federation of South African Women, mobilized to combat the Bantu educational system. Apartheid's educational policies prompted the Soweto uprising, which led to widespread international condemnation of the apartheid government. On June 16, 1976, children in Soweto gathered to protest a policy that mandated that African children could no longer be taught in their indigenous language. Instead they would be taught in Afrikaans, which was seen by the African population as the language of the white oppressor. No African was allowed to vote on this or any other issue. The children's peaceful protest was met by violent and deadly police repression. The sparks of Soweto spread rapidly throughout the nation, and youth continued to rebel against the system. The townships became ungovernable until the following December.

The 1994 democratically elected government abolished policies of racial division. All South Africans in theory should have equal access to education. However, apartheid created essentially three completely separate national education systems: one for blacks, one for whites, and one for Colored/Indians. Each had vastly different resources, with the black schools often facing a complete lack of educational materials and almost always facing overenrollment and understaffing. Colored and Indian schools were also underresourced as compared to white school systems, but they consistently were better funded in comparison to the black system.

With the 1994 elections, the African National Congress–led government decided to pursue a plan of consolidation and rationalization of the three systems into one unitary and equal educational system. This meant at the very least moving teachers, resources, and materials from the white and Colored systems into the former black systems. It also called for the construction of new schools in the former black areas. There was a prolonged uproar among teachers, parents, and students in the Colored and white systems, arguing that the new policies were not raising the standards of the former black systems but instead were lowering the standards of the former white and Colored systems. Many white teachers refused to transfer to black schools. They were offered hefty severance packages and were replaced.

Progress has been made, and schools are now more diverse than before—with the principle of diversification occurring in former white schools and not in former black schools. New facilities and resources have been successfully channeled into the former black schools, but the apartheid inequities were so vast that it will take several generations to begin to measure any impact. There have also been notable changes in public expenditures on education, which have increased from 6.1 percent of the gross national product (GNP) in 1985–1987 to 7.6 percent in 1995–1997.[7] The 2002 South African budget projects a consolidated national and provincial spending on education of 20 percent. The government's commitment to education remains clear, especially when compared with the military budget, which is only 7 percent of the consolidated national and provincial spending. Although legal racial divisions have ended, practical divisions persist. There no longer are legally mandated white and black living areas; however, the reality is that most families still live within the previous designations. Blacks do not have the resources and whites do not have the desire to change their living arrangements.

Gender differences also block full educational achievement. Both men and women list lack of finances as the single biggest reason for not completing their education. Women's second reason for not completing school was pregnancy, which was highest for African women (23 percent), followed by Colored women (10 percent) and Indian women (9 percent), and lowest for white women (4 percent). Conversely, men listed pregnancy as their last reason for ending an education. The third reason women cited for ending their education was family concerns, followed by distance to school and then health reasons. Men's second reason was family concerns, followed by health, distance to school, and finally by pregnancy.[8]

The statistics are notably more favorable for females in terms of current educational enrollment. The combined primary, secondary, and tertiary gross enrollment ratio for 1999 was 96 percent for females and 89 percent for males.[9] There are noticeable racial differences in preschool attendance but not gender differences. White children are the most likely to attend preschool. At the other end of the educational spectrum, women compose the majority of the students in universities, but they are the minority at technikons, or technical schools.[10] While there are many possible reasons for this trend, it is certainly reflective of the end of apartheid's restrictions on females and the black population. With the end of the discriminatory Bantu Educational System, education is now widely recognized as the means for personal advancement. The fact that more females are enrolled than men is indicative both of the higher percentage of females in the population and of the widespread pattern of females entering school at various stages, including a group of women returning to school after child rearing.

In terms of educational achievement, white men have secured the most advanced degrees (15 percent), followed by Indian men and white women (8 percent). Indian women receive degrees one-half as often as men (4 percent). Only 2 percent of African and Colored men receive advanced degrees, and this figure is even smaller for both African and Colored women (0 percent).[11]

Literacy

The legacy of these educational policies is several generations of racial divisions in educational opportunity and access. For example, 16 percent of African men and 23 percent of African women have never received any formal education. Ten percent of both Colored men and women have never received any formal education, whereas 11 percent of Indian women and only 2 percent of Indian men have not. The biggest contrast among the races is seen with the white population, where *all* white men and women have received some form of formal education.[12] The adult literacy rate is slightly lower for women, at 84.2 percent, than it is for men, at 85.4 percent.[13]

EMPLOYMENT AND ECONOMICS

Gender and race biases are clearly evident in employment rates, pay, and occupation. White South Africans face significantly lower rates of unemployment than black South Africans. Similarly, women face higher rates of unemployment than men in each racial category.[14] For example, employment statistics from 1995 indicate that the unemployment rate for white

Microsoft support staff, Johannesburg, South Africa. Photo © TRIP/R. Spurr.

men was only 4 percent and for white women it was 8 percent. The unemployment rate for African men was 29 percent and for African women it was 47 percent.[15] This pattern continues regardless of educational level, as 69 percent of African men with a degree and only 60 percent of African women with a degree were employed. For those without a degree, 44 percent of African men and only 17 percent of African women were employed.[16]

Farming

Farming has always been a central part of the lives of rural women, and more women than men are engaged in subsistence farming that is "unskilled" and unwaged. In recent years, the number of women in cash-crop farming has actually increased because of employers' desire for cheap labor. This increase of women in agriculture has simultaneously increased women's vulnerability, because agricultural workers have only recently been covered by the national labor laws and are still not under the minimum wage law.

Paid Employment

There are also gender and racial differences in types of jobs people hold. Women are disproportionately found in undervalued jobs such as textiles or domestic labor. About 38 percent of women of all races occupy these low-income jobs, while men occupy only 27 percent of them. This figure is exaggerated further by race, with 51 percent of African women employed in "unskilled" labor and 36 percent of African men.[17] Domestic labor is almost exclusively the occupation of African women or Colored women. Women also make up the majority in the service sector, such as teaching and nursing, and they comprise a considerable portion of the trade sector. Men predominate in manufacturing, cash-crop agriculture, utilities, and transportation.[18] However, men overwhelmingly predominate in construction and mining jobs.[19]

Pay

Within the field of employment and economics, there is a division between the protections provided by the constitution and the reality faced by the majority of the population. Even though sex-based pay inequities are illegal, pay rates are marked by the same discriminatory patterns due to cultural and social pressures that have pushed men and women/whites and Africans into different types of employment. On average, women consistently earn 72–85 percent of what men earn.[20] White women earn only 60 percent of what white men earn; African women earn 89 percent of what African men earn. African women's discriminatory position is further revealed when comparing racial differences in pay. African women earn 43 percent of what white women earn and only 26 percent of what white men earn. These inequalities are tempered but still persist when you control for educational achievement.[21]

Working Conditions

The postapartheid government has worked diligently to ensure workers' rights are respected. But these laws are often difficult to enforce because of the lack of government resources and because of the remote location of many places of employment.

Domestic workers, a sector almost completely filled by African women, is also a highly vulnerable occupation for women. Historically difficult to organize, domestic workers have lacked the traditional bargaining power utilized by industrial workers and textile unions. Domestic workers also lack a minimum wage and are not covered by many key labor protections, such as the Unemployment Insurance Act, and therefore do not have maternity leave.

Support for Mothers/Caretakers

Maternal Leave

Maternity leave is particularly important for black South African women because many depend on consistent wage labor for their families' survival. The 2000 Unemployment Insurance Act is an important step forward for women, as it provides up to 45 percent of workers' wages. However, not all workers are covered by the act. The act also does not cover those persons who had previously been working and it excludes many South Africans who have never been involved in waged labor.[22]

Inheritance, Property, and Land Rights

Land rights are critical economic and political resources for women, and the recent land reform conflicts in Zimbabwe have been particularly destabilizing for land reform movements in all of southern Africa. While equality of men and women is protected in the South African constitution, many individuals are living in areas governed by customary law and that are subjected to the authority of chiefs and traditional leaders. Within customary law, women often cannot own land, may not inherit land, and cannot maintain control over their land when their husband dies. This leaves many women who are dependent upon the land for their families' survival particularly vulnerable to the attitudes and feelings of traditional leaders or male patriarchs in their families. Attempts at land reform are particularly complex for the postapartheid government. Committed to avoiding the problems Zimbabwe faced, the government continues to make tentative steps toward redistribution or reparations to families whose land was taken. Much of this land was taken from African families only a few decades ago by white families or the apartheid government. These reforms are not generally supported by white families who may lose their land, by traditional leaders who lose political control over a valuable resource, and by many men who want to be the sole proprietor of their families' land.

Social/Government Programs

Structural Adjustment

Land reform is only one of many national programs focused on reconstructing South Africa following apartheid's years of discrimination and exclusion. In 1994, the government began the Reconstruction and Development Program (RDP), designed to channel public resources into national construction projects, employment strategies, and development initiatives. The philosophy guiding the RDP was one of participatory development and sustainability, in which local communities initiated, planned, and implemented projects that they needed. Following Keynesian economic principles, the goal was to inject public funds into social spending by increasing basic services, education, and health care. This spending would in turn create jobs and increase production, expand the economy, and improve the business infrastructure. For example, one governmental goal was to build one million new houses in five years.

The RDP was fraught with administrative and financial difficulties. However, many believe that pressure from Western policy advisers to attract foreign investment led to its demise. The Growth, Employment, and Redistribution (GEAR) program quickly replaced the RDP. Government officials assert GEAR is a policy similar to the RDP in its *outcomes* but not its *means*. Unlike RDP, which prioritized social spending as the engine of growth, GEAR prioritizes export-led growth by increasing trade in order to stimulate the economy. GEAR is a form of self-imposed structural adjustment, which attempts to jump-start the economy by reducing government services, devaluing the currency, and decreasing business taxes and regulations. The idea is that such structural adjustment policies would attract foreign investment, which would then theoretically increase business spending, strengthen production, and stimulate employment. It is called a self-imposed structural adjustment program because South Africa has never received funds from the International Monetary Fund or the World Bank and is not subject to their economic dictates. However, for all intents and purposes, South Africa has been following their guidelines and suggestions voluntarily since the end of apartheid. Therefore, the liberalizing policies have not been as rigid, but neither have they been as consistent or stable.

Many women's groups and public interest organizations have questioned the short-term and long-term impact of the GEAR policy on women. As women are the most expendable workers, they are often the first to lose their jobs. Since businesses have fewer government regulations, labor standards are not necessarily enforced, leaving women vulnerable to low wages, long hours, and mistreatment. The cuts in government programs also most directly affect women, who are responsible for their families' health, education, and welfare. The government's austerity programs force women to take on more responsibility with fewer resources and a shrinking support structure.

GEAR had several clear goals: to reduce the budget deficit from 6.9 percent to 3 percent, decrease inflation from the double digits to 8 percent, decrease unemployment by creating 1.3 percent jobs, and foster an annual growth rate of 6 percent. The results of GEAR have been mixed. The budget deficit has stayed relatively on track and has not worsened. But GEAR promised a 1.3 percent increase in jobs and has instead seen a 1.3 percent *decrease* in jobs. The growth rates have been much lower than the predicted 6 percent and much lower than needed to maintain government programs and projects. Growth rates fluctuated from 1.5 to 3.4 percent between 1994 and 1997, declined to 0.5 percent in 1998, and slowly rose to 2.5 percent by 2001, falling after the terrorist events in the United States on September 11. Most positively, inflation rates have improved, falling to 6 percent in 1999 for the first time in twenty years and remained within the 3 to 6 percent range for 2001.

Supporters of GEAR claim that the program is too new to criticize and that the growth rates were negatively affected by the Asian financial crisis of the late 1990s, bad weather that hurt agricultural production, and the global economic slowdown of 2001. Opponents claim that GEAR has failed by increasing both poverty and unemployment, which directly led to increasing crime, decreasing social services, and decreasing foreign investment and productivity. Members of the Women's National Coalition (WNC), a coalition of over 100 women's groups, are calling for a return to the earlier RDP. The GEAR program is "not enough" because it has most clearly affected the areas of the economy that involve women, such as social services, health, education, housing, and employment—all of which were elements of RDP. The cuts in housing and public works especially hurt women, and the WNC argued this was not the answer to the budget crisis.[23] Similarly the Commission for Gender Equality voiced concerns that the GEAR program has slowed or reversed progress toward gender equality, but as of yet there are no reliable sources marking this differential impact.

Gender Budgets

While women's economic status has been slipping, the government is taking positive steps to strengthen women's position in the long term. One such step has been the successful creation and implementation of the Women's Budget Initiative. The Women's Budget is a cooperative venture among nongovernmental organizations (NGOs), members of the Joint Standing Committee of Finance, provincial legislatures, and academics. The initiative, started soon after the 1994 elections, is based on a similar mechanism in Australia, and it identifies, monitors, and tracks all the budget votes and the budgetary expenditures of government departments from a gender perspective. As members of the initiative recognize, "the budget is the most important economic policy instrument of any government," and this budget looks at how much or how little money is being spent on women in all sectors.[24] The South African Women's Budget Initiative is not a separate budget for women, it is an analysis of government spending on women. Debbie Budlender, a leading analyst of the Women's Budget, emphasizes that the South African initiative is "concerned with women to the extent that they are disadvantaged," and therefore takes into consideration not only gender but also race and geography.[25] While the Women's Budget is a critical tool for monitoring spending, as yet there are no mechanisms in place for assessing the impact of such spending.

The South African Women's Budget Initiative has been heralded internationally by women's movements and has been duplicated throughout Africa, the Caribbean, and Asia.[26] Attention to the South African initiative is not restricted to the developing world. There have been workshops, training exercises, and discussions of similar initiatives in Canada, the United Kingdom, and the United States, indicating that gender-analyses are also important for developed nations.[27] Yet domestically the WBI has been limited in both its scope and its longevity. While the WBI was a critical tool for monitoring spending, there were no mechanisms in place for assessing *the impact* of such spending. The WBI was also a pilot project that ended in 1999, and "in 2000 and 2001, gender budgeting has no longer been reflected in the national budget."[28] While the initial project was highly successful in completing its mandate of tracking government's gender spending, the project may have been too short to ensure the institutionalization of a gender analysis of the national budget. A promising outgrowth of the WBI domestically is that several local governments and two provincial governments, Guateng and Western Cape, have started their own gender budgets.

FAMILY AND SEXUALITY

Gender Roles and Division of Labor

Verifiable research concerning women's status in precolonial southern Africa is scarce at best. While the exact status of women in precolonial Africa will remain cloudy, it is reasonable to assume their status was markedly greater before colonization because of the changes in the socioeconomic, religious, and political systems brought about by the colonialists. Many precapitalist societies were not organized around the accumulation of material wealth, as we find in capitalism, but rather the accumulation of productive potential, specifically in terms of agricultural production and reproductive labor. Women were vitally important in this society because of the agricultural labor they could offer and the powerful reproductive potential they represented.

It was only with the introduction of colonialism and its various religious, educational, and economic trappings that women were stripped of their pivotal societal status and became akin to property and merchandise. Colonial Christianity lessened women's status and power through missionary organizations established to ensure the predominance of Western notions of ideal female behavior, making women essential as mothers and wives and constricting them to the domestic sphere. The colonial education system almost exclusively trained males to become clerical and administrative cheap labor. Women's education, when it occurred, emphasized skills needed to be efficient homemakers and mothers.

This gendered division of labor was reinforced with the introduction of the migrant labor system. The migrant labor system extracted young, productive males from the rural society and left women and children behind in the undeveloped rural areas. Women in the rural areas then had to take on responsibilities typically shared with men, including management of the household, production of all food and necessities, and negotiations with local governments and communities. One particularly negative outcome of this system was that a large portion of the productive labor force had left for the cities, and the already poor rural infrastructure began to deteriorate. This established a pattern of impoverishment and a pattern of female-headed households.

Soon industrialization and capitalist progress created a demand for labor that exceeded the African male population. South African women were brought into the industrial and domestic labor force. But again the apartheid government tightly controlled their movement, and employers sought women's labor because it was cheap and plentiful. These gender differences were further entrenched within the household division of labor. National labor statistics indicate that men work on average slightly more than women. However, these statistics do not take into account the hours of unpaid labor performed by women in the household. Women in all population groups continue to be the primary caregivers for children, the elderly, and sick family members. They are also responsible for the majority of domestic chores and duties. For example, one of the most important national women's issues is access to clean water, because maintenance of the family water supply for cooking, drinking, and cleaning falls almost exclusively on women. Over 70 percent of black women have to gather water from outside their homes, whereas 28 percent of Colored women do so, and only 3 percent of Indian and white women must do so. These figures increase when looking only at rural areas, which are primarily occupied by black households. Obtaining water from a remote location is a time-consuming process, with the average household spending approximately an hour and a half a day fetching water.[29] This labor is unwaged and is therefore not included in any national labor statistics.

Obtaining wood for fuel and heat is also almost exclusively a woman's obligation, and this labor again is not included in wage-labor studies. Females comprise 86 percent of those fetching wood while males comprise only 14 percent. This survival activity is also disproportionately found in the black and Colored populations, with 41 percent of African women and 19 percent of Colored women involved in gathering wood for fuel. Contrast these statistics with those of only a mere 1 percent of Indian and white women dependent on gathering wood for fuel. The time spent on this activity between men and women also differed greatly, with men spending on average 2.5 hours and women spending 5.5 hours a day fetching wood.[30]

The gendered division of labor is therefore more visible when it comes to the unpaid work of men and women. Men may work more hours in the waged economy, but on average women spend 1.5 more hours than men collecting water and 3.5 more hours than men collecting wood. These figures also do not include the hours women spend on food preparation, child care, elderly care, and cleaning.

Marriage

Marriage is a complex topic, as it is manifested in different ways within each population group. Generally, South African men first marry at an older age than most women do; 29 percent of women between the ages of twenty and twenty-nine are married but only 18 percent of men are married in the same age group. Most South Africans do marry, as the percentage of women over age sixty who never married is only 6 percent and of men only 4 percent; this would include common-law marriages and traditional ceremonies. Because of the difference in the life-span, there are more widows than widowers in South Africa. Within the African population, marriage often consists of two types of ceremonies, a traditional ceremony and, if funds permit, a civil ceremony as well. Of the traditional ceremonies performed, over 90 percent of them are performed for African weddings. Whites comprise over 30 percent of the civil rites performed, far outnumbering their percentage of the population.[31]

These traditional ceremonies are a potent example of African women's changing status, as seen in the institution of *lobola* or bridewealth. During the precolonial era, the groom's family provided the bride's family with a negotiated number of cattle, livestock, or household goods that represented and replaced the loss of productive and reproductive power of the bride. This symbolic value was undermined by the introduction of a cash economy. In a cash economy, money replaced livestock, and the *lobola* became more of a financial negotiation rather than a way to honor women's productive and reproductive worth. The cash payment gives the impression a husband is purchasing a wife rather than honoring her importance. For this reason, many South African women now advocate the elimination of *lobola*. Political scientist and a former leader of the African National Congress (ANC) Women's League, Mavivi Manzini, asserts that "we live in a different era now. . . . I don't think it is possible to go back to the traditional way of life where *lobola* used to be respected and where the men used to respect their wives. If we want equality, *lobola* has to be scrapped."[32] Black South African women more generally are willing to stop this practice because colonialism and capitalism have stripped the practice of its earlier purpose and power.

Lobola is an extended process that continues today. *Lobola* originally involved a negotiation between the families of the prospective groom and bride. Celebrations marked various stages of this negotiation. Today for women of some professional and educational status, the institution can be quite cumbersome. As couples court one another, these women desire more of a role in the selection of their mates and the pace of their relationships. This independence in relationships often comes into conflict with traditional rituals imposed by the *lobola* process. Daughters may be forced into the first stages of the *lobola* process by their parents, often involving a significant financial down payment, before they have decided to marry. If these women decide later to break their engagements, the money must be repaid. Unlike cattle, money flows quite quickly through impoverished families, thus trapping women into engagements because they lack the funds to repay the initial *lobola* payment.

Reproduction

Sex Education and Teen Pregnancy

Since the end of apartheid, health rights have been protected in South Africa's progressive constitution. Health rights in the constitution include access to sex education and protection against discrimination related to pregnancy. However, translating these impressive rights into reality continues to be a major struggle for the democratic government, primarily, due to a lack of resources and funds. Government statistics find that sexual activity begins for most South Africans during their mid-teens, and this age group is particularly uninformed about sexual and reproductive health. Over one-half of all reported instances of sexually transmitted diseases in South Africa occur in young adults and teens, with young women having the highest number of HIV infections. Teenage pregnancy rates have been going down in recent years, but still remain remarkably high. Thirty-five percent of all teenagers have been pregnant or have had a child before they reach the age of twenty. In 1996, 78 out of every 1,000 women between the ages of fifteen to nineteen gave birth. In 1999, 11 percent of abortions in South Africa were performed for women under the age of eighteen. Continued societal discrimination against teen pregnancy is rampant, with approximately 75 percent of schools expelling pregnant girls in 2001, stating that the schools cannot accommodate the needs of pregnant learners. Only 25 percent of schools expelled the fathers. These policies have come under government review because they are in direct violation of the constitution.

Given these startling figures, several initiatives and programs have been undertaken by government and nongovernmental agencies. These programs range from multimedia programming specifically targeting young people to distribution of information in schools and community workshops. Peer education continues to be one of the most successful attempts at sex education; however, those most often benefiting from the programs are the peer educators themselves. There continues to be an emphasis on school education, and there are fewer programs targeting health clinics or the streets. Overwhelmingly, the government and the nongovernmental organizations have shaped the programs and their message in ways that are especially appealing and applicable for young people.

Contraception and Abortion

Reproductive issues remain at the forefront of national political debate. Contraceptive use is heavily skewed by gender, and it is used primarily as a means of preventing pregnancy and not as a way to prevent the spread of the AIDS virus. Indian women have the highest percentage use of contraception, at 77 percent, followed by Colored women, at 75 percent, and white women, at 74 percent. Black South African women have the lowest contraceptive use, at only 61 percent. The usage statistics for men are vastly lower, with white men at 45 percent, Colored at 22 percent, Indian at 21 percent, and African at only 15 percent.[33]

Abortion has been legal in South Africa since 1975 but only under special circumstances, such as rape, incest, or risk to the mother's health. The requirements for obtaining such abortions were very expensive, as women had to consult three different doctors to verify the cause and the need for an abortion. Such financial burdens excluded legal abortions for the majority of South African women. The 1975 legislation made no provision for abortion on demand and no provision for a woman financially unable to care for a child. Back-street abortions, estimated between 300,000 and 400,000 a year, were thought to result in hundreds of deaths per year.[34]

The 1996 Termination of Pregnancy Act eased the requirements for obtaining a legal abortion. The act recognized that "the decision to have children is fundamental to women's physical, psychological, and social health and that universal access to reproductive health care services includes family planning and contraception, termination of pregnancy, as well as sexuality education and counseling programmes and services." The act legalized terminations on demand up to and including the thirteenth week and allowed terminations up to and including the twentieth week for risk to the mother's health, an abnormal fetus, rape, or incest. Most significantly, abortion may now be granted up to the twentieth week if the "continued pregnancy would significantly affect the social or economic circumstances of the women." This provision eased the financial hardships for poor women. This act, therefore, widely extends both the access and legality of abortions to the majority of women.

Heralded as a triumph for women's rights by many progressive party leaders, the debates and outcomes of the act were not a unifying process for South African women. Journalist Jenny Viall of the *Cape Argus* comments, "The passage of the abortion law was a stormy one, marked by religious, cultural, and moral arguments as the pro-choice and anti choice activists made themselves heard."[35] Abortion rights' activists now face the challenging problem of abortion education. Informing women about the option of abortion and finding physicians willing to perform them may prove to be more difficult than enacting the legislation. Further, a growing antichoice movement, supported in part by United States' lobbyists, continues to pressure for legislative reform and to disseminate antiabortion information. The antichoice lobby in South Africa, however, professes a commitment to nonviolent resistance, having observed the problems of abortion-clinic bombings and doctor assassinations in the United States. The South African antichoice movement intends to oppose abortion through litigation, prayer, education, demonstrations, and lobbying.

HEALTH

Health Care Access

Lack of access to both health services and to adequate living standards is the greatest obstacle to good health facing most South African women. The availability of medical aid is lower for women than men generally, but the largest inequality may be found among population groups. Only 8 percent of African women and 11 percent of African men have access to medical aid. Contrast these figures with those of the white population, in which 72 percent of women and 73 percent of men have medical aid.[36] This inequality, which was created during apartheid and which is perpetuated by the legacies of discrimination, will continue to compound racial and class differences in maternal mortality, infant mortality, life expectancy, and quality of life.

There are vast inequalities of access to proper health facilities among the South African population. Many black households have to travel great distances to obtain medical care, with over 42 percent traveling over five kilometers or more to the nearest facility. Access to hospitals is of critical importance to women, especially during childbirth. At least 94 percent of white women give birth in a hospital as compared to 91 percent of Indian women, 80 percent of Colored women, and only 68 percent of African women. Eighteen percent of African women and 14 percent of Colored women give birth somewhere other than a hospital or clinic, whereas only 5 percent of Indian women and 2 percent of white women do so. African women are more likely than any other population group to use a health clinic for births.[37]

Diseases and Disorders

Given the pattern of inadequate resource distribution to the African population, most South African women do not have the basic resources to sustain a healthy lifestyle, including proper housing, nutrition, sanitation, and water. Because of this, women are also exposed to high rates of poverty-related diseases.[38]

AIDS

The inadequate standard of living faced by the majority of the population has greatly exacerbated the HIV/AIDS epidemic in South Africa, which ranks at the top of the global infection statistics. The percentage of the adult population with HIV/AIDS is 13 percent, and the total number of adults and children living with HIV/AIDS is 2,900,000. However, figures for women alone are much higher. These figures indicate that the HIV infection rate is 22 percent for women in 1999. The South African epidemic has been exacerbated by the labor migration patterns established during apartheid, which increased the mobility of the population and the spread of the disease. Family patterns and social norms were also changed by these labor patterns. The separation of spousal partners for 11 months a year increased the use of sex workers and the number of sexual partners. This pattern, combined with high poverty rates and low education rates, has limited the availability of AIDS-prevention education. The traditionally low status of women in the society is another contributing factor, as women do not feel they have the power to control their sexuality or their sexual practices.[39]

Creating international controversy, President Thambo Mbeki publicly questioned the link between HIV and AIDS. He initially blocked the distribution of foreign-produced AIDS treatments, because he saw them as potentially more toxic than the disease and because he felt the medical community in South Africa was unprepared to distribute, control, and manage the treatments. Despite these intentions, these official government acts have sent a mixed message to people and increased the resistance to condom use and changing sexual practices.

POLITICS AND LAW

Political Participation

In the antiapartheid movement, women were vital for every aspect of the struggle for liberation and were widely knows as "the backbone of the struggle." Perhaps most significantly, women pushed the resistance movement toward mass action with their protests of the pass laws in 1913 and the 1950s. Women were active inside South Africa during the antiapartheid struggle, and they mobilized within the ranks of the African National Congress in exile. Many of the women in exile used their international status to pursue higher education or to seek military training, which earned them substantial power within the external party structures. In many ways, women were both leaders in the forefront of the movement and followers serving as the backbone and the "silent strength" of the movement. Women's resistance to apartheid pushed the antiapartheid struggle into national mass action long before the male leaders were prepared to do so. Women unified across race and class lines because they desired to change the system and "save the nation for their children." This emphasis on their maternal identity enabled women to come together in ways men had not. Official leadership positions within all political parties, however, were almost exclusively male.

The path of women to political office included a period of multiparty coalition building, a stage of revising the electoral system to facilitate the election of women candidates, and a phase of pressuring the leadership of political parties to advance the status of women through the use of affirmative action measures and gender quotas. One of the major victories of recent years has been the successful push to national office achieved by women in South Africa. In a span of four years, from 1991 up to the 1994 elections, the women of South Africa moved from the "silent backbone" of the nation to a force of considerable political power and public influence. With the 1994 elections, South Africa moved from 141st to 7th in the world in terms of the number of women occupying seats in the national parliament, with over 26 percent of the seats held by women. This impressive gain was further enhanced with the 1999 elections, bringing the number of women to 29.8 percent.

South Africa adopted the system found most likely to enhance women's representation cross-nationally. When people are voting for a party list of candidates, party leaders are more apt to provide a diverse candidate pool so as to attract an equally diverse number of voters. In the alternative system, which involves voting for a single individual for a specific seat, party leaders are less likely to support a female candidate. She may seem like a political risk or, in any case, will occupy the only seat the party wins. Therefore, a party will run a greater number of women candidates if there is a large number of seats in question. South Africa therefore adopted the multimember district electoral system that utilizes party-list proportional representation.

Having secured the election rules that would likely produce more women candidates and office holders, women then turned their attention to internal party politics. South African women again utilized the ground-swell of the emerging women's movement to pressure their parties for internal affirmative action measures. By making the argument that more women on the party lists equal more votes, women were strategically able to demand quotas and/or the recruitment and training of women candidates.

The ANC Women's League is perhaps the most successful and notable example of this process of advancing women candidates within the party. The ANC Women's League secured a commitment to have a third of the ANC seats in parliament reserved for women. The ANC's commitment of having one-third of its seats filled by women has accomplished two important objectives. First, it has greatly increased women's numerical representation in national government, which has and will continue to bring international support and approval. The second and more lasting impact of the quota is that it has successfully pressured other political parties to increase the number of women on their party lists. Women in the opposition parties have been advocating for increased numbers, and the ANC's success has assisted this call.

The Women's National Coalition (WNC) became one of the main vehicles through which women mobilized for action during the negotiation period. Formed in 1991, the WNC is a coalition of over 100 women's organizations that united to ensure women's voice in shaping the new South African society. The WNC is composed of women of all races, classes, and political parties and has a broad agenda focused on women's place in both formal and nonformal politics, in national development efforts, and in personal empowerment activities.

With the participation of women in political office secured and accepted, attention now focuses on the participation of women in civic life, including electoral voting, social movements, and interest groups. Before the 1994 election, nearly 80 percent of the population had never been allowed to vote. Therefore, voter education was central to informing people about both the significance and the process of voting. The main obstacles facing women's electoral participation occurred before the elections, not during them. Prior to the elections, women had to overcome traditional cultural attitudes and contemporary media stereotypes, both of which portrayed women as the lesser to men in politics. Poor African women faced two additional obstacles. First, illiteracy rates among African women created significant problems of understanding the processes of voting. Second, many had difficulty securing the proper identity documents because their fingerprints had been damaged by years of heavy labor.[40]

While the exact number of women voting in the national elections is not known, it was generally assessed that both men and women equally attended the polls. The elections were found by the national and international election monitors to be open and free. The main problems facing women came from within the household in the form of spousal intimidation.

As the new parliamentarians struggle to find their identities in office and meet the challenges of reconstruction and development of South Africa, the numerous women's organizations on the ground are also struggling to redefine their mission and to secure effective leadership. During apartheid, most women's groups were focused on challenging or toppling the government. Now that apartheid has ended and democracy has started to function, these same women's groups have to change their mission from resistance to government to collaboration with government. Similarly, many of the former leaders of women's groups were elected into parliament, leaving a leadership gap. While women's groups are struggling to redefine their mission they must also attempt to select, train, and recruit a new set of leaders.

The agenda and tactics of the groups are also in flux, and they are faced with new challenges of collaboration, time, and funding. The groups originally worked as antiapartheid resistance organizations. While being comfortable with direct confrontation of the former apartheid regime, many of these women's groups are struggling to work with the new democratic government and simultaneously critique, monitor, and challenge the new government.

Women's Rights

The impact of the activities of women's organizations on the democratization process was significant. The Women's National Coalition's Women's Charter ensured that women's interests were recognized in the constitution. South Africa's constitution has one of the broadest and most inclusive anti-discrimination clauses internationally. The equality clause establishes that neither the state nor a person may "unfairly discriminate directly or indirectly against anyone on one or more grounds, including race, gender, sex, pregnancy, marital status, ethnic or social origin, colour, sexual orientation, age, disability, religion, conscience, belief, culture, language and birth." The constitution also promises to promote affirmative action measures, basic education, reproductive choice, and access to basic needs and land resources. Although there is recognition of customary law, when customary law and the constitution are in conflict, the constitutional rights predominate.

Lesbian Rights

The equality clause in the constitution made South Africa one of the first and only nations to ensure constitutional protection for gays and lesbians.

RELIGION AND SPIRITUALITY

According to the 1996 Census, approximately 75 percent of the South African population defines themselves as Christian, which also includes those who combine the elements of traditional African religions with Christianity. Only 1.39 percent of the population identifies themselves as followers of Islam, but Muslims are an increasingly visible political force in South Africa, especially in Durban and Cape Town. Hindus comprise about 1.35 percent of the population and Jews only 0.17 percent.

Women's Roles

Christianity and colonization went hand in hand to disrupt traditional African patterns of governance, family life, and spirituality. Women were perhaps most affected by the advent of Western Christianity, which diminished the pivotal role women had in the family, in agriculture, and in society. The form of Christianity extended by the early church relegated women to the household and to a subordinate political status in the eyes of the law and in the eyes of their families. Colonial Christianity also paved the way for the religious nationalism that was to be the foundation and sustenance of apartheid. During the apartheid era, the teachings of the Bible were used regularly to justify the separation of the races, to reify the power of the government as one chosen by God, and to distinguish the Afrikaner population as divinely created.

During apartheid, South African churches experienced almost universal self-segregation, which began to work to the advantage of the resistance movement. As political organizations and labor unions were banned, the black churches became a safe haven for political activity. Women, who had long been the most active group among the laity, were quickly and quietly able to organize support systems for activists, prisoners, and freedom fighters. While no government official would condone women organizing for a political rally, no one could argue with women going to church meetings. Since most religious and political leaders were male, government officials easily dismissed women's activities in churches.

White churches also had a role in the resistance. As early as 1948, several white religious leaders openly censured the apartheid government, and the multiracial South African Council of Churches condemned apartheid anti-Christian in 1968. In 1985, 152 religious leaders from several religious traditions joined together to oppose apartheid and its manipulation of religious teachings. They issued the Kairos Document in 1985, which stated that the Bible could not be used to support the policies or actions of apartheid. The Document advocated that all Christians, regardless of race, join in non-violent protests, boycotts, and mass action against the government. While many did so, several leading white churches resisted this call. Although most Afrikaner religious leaders quietly or openly supported apartheid, the religious movement against the system persuaded some of the Afrikaner population about the unbiblical nature of apartheid. Eventually even the Dutch Reform Church, the mainstay of Afrikaner religious identity, split over the issue. Today, most churches remain racially segregated, though a few churches are beginning to see limited integration.

Women are still the rare exception as ministers or priests leading the church or religious societies; however, they remain the most vital group within most faith traditions in terms of lay work, support structures, and community outreach. In spite of the pronouncements of the churches about the proper role of women in spirituality, women have continuously been involved in the spiritual life of their communities in a variety of ways. Some of the most vibrant and essential women's grassroots organizations are found within the church. These groups often are the only social safety net for the African communities. Women's funeral societies are key examples that are found in almost every church in the former black areas. Events surrounding funerals may last several days and involve numerous meals for the entire community. The vast majority of black South African families do not have the resources to cover the expense of such events individually. Upon the death of a family member, the members of a funeral society pool their labor and financial resources to cook the meals, host the out-of-town family members, and defray funeral costs.

Women's organizations are mounting increasing pressure on religious groups to re-examine and alter their attitudes toward women and women's roles. A recent documentary, *The Other Voices*, by the World Conference on Religion and Peace, carefully traces how the dominant religions in South Africa promote the subordination of women and perpetuate patterns of domestic violence. The people who worked on the film have now launched a national organizational focus on women and religion in South Africa. The organization has become a network for women who are rejecting the view that they should be obedient of their husbands and that battered women should remain with their abusers.[41]

VIOLENCE

Domestic Violence

Violence against women is an epidemic internationally, and South Africa is no exception. South African levels of domestic violence and rape are some of the highest in the world. Some estimate that rape, for example, occurs in as many as 60 percent of marital relationships.[42] There are several problems in assessing the level of violence, including the dramatic under-reporting of crimes and the constraints of a patriarchal society. The South African government passed the Domestic Violence Act in 1998 and began implementing the act in 1999. The legislation is a good step forward for victims and their advocates, because it expands the definition of domestic. As outlined in the act, domestic violence now includes physical abuse, sexual abuse, emotional, verbal, and psychological abuse, economic abuse, intimidation, harassment, stalking, damage to property, entry into dwelling without consent, or "any other controlling or abusive behavior . . . where such conduct harms . . . the safety, health or well-being of the complainant."[43] The responsibilities of the officers of the courts have also been clarified and expanded, including arrest without warrant, issuing protection orders, seizure of arms and dangerous weapons, and the duty to inform and assist the complainant. To complement the 1998 act, the Gender Advocacy Project, a gender-based NGO, launched a domestic violence program that provides sensitivity training, education, and awareness to the police, politicians, and members of the judicial system.

Rape/Sexual Assault

South Africa consistently has the highest per capita rate of reported rapes internationally. According to Rape Crisis South Africa, the number of reported rapes in 1998 totaled 49,280, meaning there were 115.6 reported rapes for every 100,000 of the population. This figure has increased, with 52,000 reported rapes for 2000. There was a moratorium on the release of crime statistics in South Africa for eleven months in 2000, purportedly until the police service could improve their method of data collection. This moratorium was strongly criticized by women's groups in South Africa, as it was hindering their work and advocacy.

Even with the startlingly high level of reported rapes, South African police estimate that only three percent of all rapes are actually reported. Rape Crisis South Africa uses a slightly lower multiplier to calculate the actual figure of rape based on the reported figures, one out of twenty. Using this more conservative estimate, if only one out of every twenty rapes is reported, there would have been 985,600 actual rapes in 1998. Others in government and the media use a higher multiplier of one out of every thirty-five, estimating the actual number of rapes in 1998 to have been 1,724,800. As if these statistics alone were not troubling enough, the current definition of rape is very limited and excludes many forms of rape recognized elsewhere, including the rape of men and male children, rape using objects, and oral rape. There is a 4 percent conviction rate for the cases that actually make it to court.[44]

The ANC Women's Caucus initiated a parliament/NGO task force on violence against women in 1997. The task force has two goals: to raise awareness about the dramatically high level of violence against women in South Africa and to push for legislative change and political action around that issue. The task force is open to all political parties, although very few women from outside the ANC have participated. The task force is not elite driven or sustained, and it is not merely operated by members of parliament. The task force has representatives from NGOs concerned with women's issues, such as Rape Crisis, Gender Advocacy Project, Bush Radio, and RAPCAN (Resources Aimed at the Prevention of Child Abuse and Neglect). Black, Colored, white, and Indian women participate in the task force, as do women from both upper and lower socioeconomic classes.

Since its inception, the task force has organized several awareness-raising activities, including a march on parliament, a button campaign for members of parliament on the first day of the 1997 parliamentary session, and an International Women's Day observance on Robben Island. This observance involved survivors' testimonials, inputs from NGOs concerning legislative reform, and dialogue with government representatives. The task force has also lobbied for legislative change. These tactics and strategies are reminiscent of the methods women used in the antiapartheid struggle. This return to resistance politics has encouraged women from all backgrounds and experiences to participate and has rejuvenated members of parliament that had become alienated and dissatisfied with their legislative duties.

Rape Crisis undertook a major initiative in Cape Town to move the domestic violence and sexual assault cases into special Sexual Offense Pilot Courts. Leaders of Rape Crisis found that women who were brave enough to report their rape were often harassed or humiliated by the police, judges, or hospital workers. These courts are intended to reduce the secondary victimization of assault survivors by the courts and law enforcement officials, as well as provide a multitude of support structures and resources such as counseling and health care. Since such courts are a costly venture and would not be feasible in rural areas, there is a national push toward sensitivity training for police and doctors throughout the system.[45]

Trafficking in Women and Children

Although South Africa has not historically been either one of the main source countries or destination countries for sex trafficking, there have been increasing observations that trafficking does occur within South Africa, especially the trafficking of children for prostitution or forced labor. Since the end of apartheid and the opening of South Africa to the world, the Department of Social Development reports that Cape Town is rapidly becoming a destination site for sex tourism. Instances of local and domestic trafficking have also been increasing. However, as the country is not on one of the major sex trafficking routes, the issue has received relatively little media attention, with issues of HIV/AIDS, gender violence, and prostitution occupying most public discussion. The South African government has come under pressure from gender activists to have specific legislation against trafficking. While South Africa signed the UN's Convention Against Transnational Organised Crime, there is no specific policy to stop the trafficking of women and children. Those caught in these activities do in fact face charges of kidnapping and abduction. The problem of trafficking children, especially for prostitution and pornography, promises to increase given the national rates of poverty, domestic violence, and unemployment. Children are increasing forced to fend for themselves and many find themselves on the streets and are particularly vulnerable to traffickers.

War and Military Repression

The ravages of apartheid still lay claim upon the bodies and minds of South African women. Although no longer in a state of war, the long-term effects of the resistance struggle and brutal government repression will remain with the citizens of South Africa for generations. While many do not classify the antiapartheid struggle as open revolution, there was a protracted violent confrontation involving both men and women in armed conflict, military maneuvers domestically and abroad, and imprisonment and torture. While the apartheid government censored much of the information on these activities, additional reports involving women were silenced because of fear, sexism, and loyalty. South Africa's Truth and Reconciliation Commission (TRC) worked to bring such injustices to national attention by documenting the abuse, using the testimonies of both the perpetrators and the victims. By recording the truth about the conflict, South Africans hope to prevent such torture in the future and to dispel the myth that apartheid policies led to no harm.

Truth commissioners and women's organizations rapidly found, however, that the TRC's procedures were not conducive to stories by women about their own torture and victimization. Women were frequent representatives at the hearings, but almost exclusively they made their cases as the mothers, daughters, or spouses of male victims. The commissioners and women's groups worked together to create special "women's only" hearings. These hearings were successful in gathering and documenting the testimony of women's gendered repression.

During apartheid, women were victimized by political violence including the gross violations of human rights and loss of basic needs and resources. Female political prisoners often faced specific means of torture that targeted their gender, such as forced abortions, gang rape, and forced sterilization. Women in political exile or military training abroad often faced two types of sexual victimization: rape by white South African soldiers or rape by their own commanding officers. Often, women in the camps differentiated between these abuses. "Real" rapes were those committed by the white soldiers. Rapes by women's own officers or other freedom fighters were seen as part of their duty: satisfying their male officers and remaining silent. Apartheid has ended, but the scars remain. The pattern of sexual assault and gender violence established during the struggle for liberation clearly is connected to the continued high rates of violence against women. These abuses are compounded by the diffusion of light weapons from the West since the end of the Cold War. These weapons have destabilized all of Africa and are directly related to the increase in sexual violence against women, as even small boys are now capable of placing sexual demands on women of all ages.[46] Violence against women continues unabated.

OUTLOOK FOR THE TWENTY-FIRST CENTURY

Examining the contemporary landscape of women's issues in South Africa, one is faced with a complex picture of economic discrimination versus electoral success, physical insecurity versus political promise. South Africa has had many problems of under-representation resulting from a tragic history of discrimination and oppression. Questions of race and gender representation have been and will continue to be central to the legitimacy and stability of the democratic system in South Africa. Much like women throughout Africa, South African women are struggling to overcome years of resource inequality and racial division.

Many face undue burdens of poverty and depravation that make survival their first and only priority. Yet the political ideals, legislative accomplishments, and spending priorities of the government since the end of apartheid signal a dramatically new direction for the nation. Equality is promised in the constitution, and women see the results of their work in electoral outcomes, voting patterns, and government spending. Interest groups and women's organizations continue to work with the new government to shape a civil society that matches the goals and ideals of the constitution. The nation will need to combat poverty, sexual violence, racial discrimination, and AIDS to advance the cause of women, but the potential for growth and equality in South Africa is great, specifically because the constitutional and legislative framework is already in place.

NOTES

1. "Colored" is a term developed by the apartheid government to classify people of mixed ethnicity. The only major difference they have with the white population is racial, since both groups share languages, religions, and culture. The apartheid government further divided the Colored population into seven subcategories. When referring to the group as a whole, the population is known as Colored with a capital "C."

2. Sally Baden, Shireen Hassim, and Sheila Meintjes, *Country Gender Profile: South Africa* (Pretoria, South Africa: Swedish International Development Co-operation Agency, 1999), 18.

3. The average number of children a woman would bear if age-specific fertility rates remained unchanged. *Human Development Report* (2001), United Nations Development Programme (UNDP), www.undp.org/hdr2001.

4. Ibid.

5. Baden, Hassim, and Meintjes, *Country Gender Profile*, 18.

6. Debbie Budlender, *Women and Men in South Africa* (Pretoria, South Africa: Central Statistics, 1998), 32.

7. *Human Development Report* (2001).

8. Budlender, *Women and Men in South Africa*, 29.

9. *Human Development Report* (2001).

10. Budlender, *Women and Men in South Africa*, 26–30.

11. Budlender, *Women and Men in South Africa*, 27.

12. Ibid., 27.

13. *Human Development Report* (2001).

14. Ibid., 16.

15. Baden, Hassim, and Meintjes, *Country Gender Profile*, 21.

16. Budlender, *Women and Men in South Africa*, 16.

17. Ibid., 21.

18. Baden, Hassim, and Meintjes, *Country Gender Profile*, 22–23.

19. Budlender, *Women and Men in South Africa*, 20.

20. Baden, Hassim, and Meintjes, *Country Gender Profile*, 22.

21. Budlender, *Women and Men in South Africa*, 24.

22. Baden, Hassim, and Meintjes, *Country Gender Profile*, 23.

23. Pregs Govender, *Draft Committee Report on Women, the Budget, and Economic Policy* (Ad Hoc Joint Committee on Improvement of Quality of Life and Status of Women, Parliament of South Africa, 1998), http://womensnet.org.za/parliament/money2.htm.

24. Debbie Budlender, *The Women's Budget Initiative*, Institute for a Democratic Alternative in South Africa, 1996.

25. Debbie Budlender, "The Political Economy of Women's Budgets in the South," *World Development* 28, no. 7 (2000): 1366.

26. Colleen Lowe Morna, "Gender Budget on the Rocks?" *Mail and Guardian*, 4 August 2000, 1–2. http://archive.mg.co.za.

27. Budlender, *Women's Budgets*, 1372.

28. Pregs Govender, "Gender Budgeting Was Removed, Not Committee's Funding," *Mail and Guardian*, August 17, 2001, 1–2, http://archive.mg.co.za/.

29. Budlender, *Women and Men*, 11.

30. Ibid., 12.

31. Ibid., 6–7.

32. M. Manzini, "Women and the African National Congress," in *Lives of Courage: Women for a New South Africa*, ed. Diane Russell (Oakland: Basic Books, 1991), 131.

33. Budlender, *Women and Men*, 36.

34. Jenny Viall, "The Law That Lets SA Women Choose: Abortion Act Welcomed as Clinics and Hospitals Stand at the Ready," *Cape Argus*, 3 February 1997, 8.

35. Ibid., 8.

36. Budlender, *Women and Men*, 35.

37. Ibid., 33.

38. Baden, Hassim, and Meintjes, *Country Gender Profile*, 18.

39. AIDS Foundation of South Africa, www.aids.org.za.

40. Julie Ballington, *The Participation of Women in South Africa's First Democratic Elections*, Electoral Institute of South Africa, 1999, 4–12.

41. *The Other Voices* (2001), World Conference on Religion and Peace, Yeoville, South Africa, http://mandla.co.za/tov/aboutus.htm.

42. *The Rape Crisis Website* (2001), Cape Town, South Africa, www.rapecrisis.org.za.

43. Domestic Violence Act no. 116, *The Government Gazette* (Cape Town: Republic of South Africa, 1998).

44. *The Rape Crisis Website*, www.rapecrisis.org.za. If reported sexual assaults and incest cases are included, the 1998 figure jumps to 54,310.

45. Pregs Govender, *Draft Report on Violence Hearings: Ad Hoc Joint Committee on Improvement of Quality of Life and Status of Women, Parliament of South Africa* (Cape Town: Government Printing Offices, 1998).

46. Meredeth Turshen, and Clotilde Twagiramariya, eds., *What Women Do in Wartime: Gender and Conflict in Africa* (New York: Zed Books, 1998).

RESOURCE GUIDE

Suggested Reading

Berger, Iris. *Threads of Solidarity: Women in South African Industry, 1900–1980*. Indianapolis: Indiana University Press, 1992. Berger examines the role of women in industry and the importance of labor unions in South Africa.

Berger, Iris, E. Frances White, and Cathy Skidmore-Hess. *Women in Sub-Saharan Africa: Restoring Women to History*. Indianapolis: Indiana University Press, 1999. This historical overview examines the role of women in the political, economic, cultural, and social institutions in Africa.

Cock, Jacklyn. *Colonels and Cadres: War and Gender in South Africa*. Oxford: Oxford University Press, 1994. Cock uses interviews with soldiers and victims of violence to examine the relationship between gender and militarism within South Africa.

Kendall, K. Limakatso, ed. *Singing Away the Hunger: The Autobiography of an African Woman*. Indianapolis: Indiana University Press, 1997. Based in Lesotho and

South Africa, this memoir recounts one woman's struggle to survive poverty, racism, and violence.

Kuzwayo, Ellen. *Call Me Woman*. Johannesburg: Ravan Press, 1985. A South African classic, Kuzwayo's autobiography reveals what life was like for women in the townships under apartheid.

Perkins, Kathy A. *Black South African Women: An Anthology of Plays*. London: Routledge, 1998. This collection of ten plays provides the reader with a glimpse of what life is like for contemporary South African women.

Ramphele, Mamphela. *Across Boundaries: The Journey of a South African Woman Leader*. New York: Feminist Press, 1997. Ramphele tells her internationally known life story as an educator, a nurse, and an activist during apartheid and now in the transition to democracy.

Russell, Diana E.H. *Lives of Courage: Women for a New South Africa*. New York: Basic Books, 1989. Russell's text contains dozens of narratives of some of the most important women in the antiapartheid struggle. Based on reconstructed interviews, women explain the nature of oppression, feminism, and struggle.

Walker, Cherryl. *Women and Resistance in South Africa*. New York: Monthly Review Press, 1992. An overview of women's role in the antiapartheid movement within women's organizations and political parties.

Videos/Films

Cry Freedom. 1988. Directed by Richard Attenborough. Distributed by MCA Home Video.

Dry White Season. 1990. Directed by Euzhan Palcy. Distributed by CBS Fox Video.

Maids and Madams. 1985. Directed by Mira Hamermesh. Distributed by Filmakers Library.

Sarafina. 1993. Directed by Darrell James Roodt. Distributed by Buena Vista Home Video.

A World Apart. 1988. Directed by Chris Menges. Distributed by Media Home Entertainment.

Web Sites

Agenda, www.agenda.org.za.
The site for the national quarterly feminist journal. Run by a collective, Agenda publishes articles, opinion pieces, creative work, and original research by leading South African academics, politicians, and activists.

Commission for Gender Equality, www.cge.org.za.
This is a national commission charged with overseeing gender equity issues nationally, advising and monitoring governmental agencies and legislation, and responding to the needs of victims of gender discrimination.

Gay and Lesbian Archives of South Africa, www.wits.ac.za/gala.
This site provides links to historical and contemporary materials relating to gay and lesbian experiences in South Africa. It also is a forum for gays and lesbians to share their personal stories and to connect with one another.

Gender Advocacy Project, www.gender.co.za.
GAP is a nonprofit advocacy organization that lobbies government on behalf of women, provides links between women and government, and overseas legislation and policy from a gender perspective. GAP's projects are focused on issues such as reproductive rights, domestic violence, social policy and gender, and women and governance.

South African Government On-line, www.gov.za.
This site is a user-friendly reference tool for learning more about South African economics, politics, and culture.

Women in Parliament, http://womensnet.org.za/parliament/parliament.htm.
Part of the Women's Net page, this site is connected to government information, relevant bills and legislation, and parliamentary women's activities.

Women's Net, http://womensnet.org.za.
This is a first stop for any student of South African women. It is the hub for all women's activities in the nation and provides all the essential links to the relevant women's organizations, government information, and African resources.

Organizations

African Gender Institute
All Africa House
Middle Campus
University of Cape Town
Rondebosch, Cape Town, South Africa

Housed at the University of Cape Town, AGI works to link academics, politicians, and activists in their work to advance the status of women, to understand the theoretical implications of gender, and to promote gender equity.

Gender Advocacy Project
7th Floor, Ruskin House
2 Roeland St.
Cape Town 8001, South Africa
Phone: 021-465-0197;
Fax: 021-465-0089;
Email: genap@sn.apc.org

GAP is a nonprofit advocacy organization that lobbies government on behalf of women, provides links between women and government, and overseas legislation and policy from a gender perspective.

Women's National Coalition
P.O. Box 62319
2107 Marshalltown, South Africa
Phone: 011-331-5958

This coalition of over 100 women's organizations was formed in 1992 to ensure gender issues were incorporated into the new South African constitution. The WNC now works on national gender empowerment projects, maintains a national network for women's groups, and monitors the government's adherence to the promises of gender equity.

SELECTED BIBLIOGRAPHY

Budlender, D. "The Political Economy of Women's Budgets in the South." *World Development* 28, no. 7 (2000): 1365–78.

Cock, J. *Maids and Madams: A Study in the Politics of Exploitation*. Johannesburg: Raven Press, 1980.

Cope, J. *A Matter of Choice: Abortion Law Reform in Apartheid South Africa*. Pietermaritzburg: Hadeda Books, 1993.

Davies, R., D. O'Meara, and S. Dlamini. *The Struggle for South Africa: A Reference Guide to Movements, Organizations, and Institutions*. Vol. 2. London: Zed Books, 1985.

Ginwala, F. *Non-Racial Democracy—Soon; Non-Sexism—How?* Women's National Coalition, speech at national workshop, 25–26 April 1992.

Kadalie, R. "Women in the New South Africa: From Transition to Governance." In *The Constitution of South Africa from a Gender Perspective*, edited by S. Liebenberg. Cape Town: David Philip, 1995.

Liebenberg, S. *The Constitution of South Africa from a Gender Perspective*. Cape Town: David Philip, 1995.

Lodge, T. *Black Politics in South Africa Since 1945*. New York: Longman, 1983.

Lovenduski, J., and P. Norris. *Gender and Party Politics*. London: Sage, 1993.

Norris, P. "The Gender Gap in Britain and America." *Parliamentary Affairs* 38 (1985): 192–201.

———. *Politics and Sexual Equality*. Boulder: Lynne Rienner, 1987.

Rule, W. "Electoral Systems, Contextual Factors, and Women's Opportunity for Election to Parliament in Twenty-three Democracies." *Western Political Quarterly* 50 (1987): 477.

———. "Why Women Don't Run: The Critical and Contextual Factors in Women's Legislative Recruitment." *Western Political Quarterly* 34 (1981): 477.

Russell, D. *Lives of Courage: Women for a New South Africa*. Oakland: Basic Books, 1989.

Schapera, I. *Married Life in an African Tribe*. Evanston: Northwestern University Press, 1996.

Walker, C. *Women and Resistance in South Africa*. Cape Town: David Philip, 1982.

Wells, J. *We Now Demand: The History of Women's Resistance to Pass Laws in South Africa*. Johannesburg: Witwatersrand University Press, 1993.

18

SUDAN

Asma Mohamed Abdel Halim

PROFILE OF SUDAN

The Republic of Sudan, known as the Sudan, earned its independence from Anglo-Egyptian rule in 1956. It has a tri-city capital formed by the cities of Khartoum, Khartoum North, and Omdurman. The Sudan occupies an area of 2,505,813 square kilometers,[1] which is slightly more than one-quarter the size of the United States. This makes it the largest country in Africa. Its citizens are fond of calling it the one million square miles country. The Sudan is surrounded by nine countries: Egypt and Libya to the north; Ethiopia and Eritrea to the east; Chad and Central African Republic to the west; Kenya, Uganda, and the Democratic Republic of Congo (former Zaire) to the south. The Red Sea separates the country from the Arabian Peninsula.

The main body of water that runs through the country from the far south to the far north is the river Nile, which is the main source of fresh water. The Sudan is rich in natural resources: petroleum as well as small reserves of iron ore, copper, chromium ore, zinc, tungsten, mica, silver, and gold. The last census, in 1993, reported that the Sudan had a population of 25.5 million. The total population is 32.2 million as of

2003, based on the last count in 2001.[2] The average births to a woman is 5.8 children. Life expectancy is fifty-seven years for women and fifty-five for men. The maternal mortality rate is 550 per 100,000 live births, while the infant mortality rate is 55 per 1,000.[3] The infant mortality rate is expected to decrease because of the free immunization provided by the World Health Organization (WHO). The program was successful in covering a high percentage of the children. Immunization is provided for children in the war zone by UN organizations and other nongovernmental organizations (NGOs).

The Sudan is a federal state that comprises twenty-six states. The president is the head of state and the National Assembly is the legislative body. Each state has a governor, referred to as the *wali*, and a legislative body known as the State National Assembly. Despite the legal status of federation, power is concentrated in the hands of the central government. The current government rose to power through a military coup that overthrew the elected government in 1989.

The southern Sudanese have been resisting the central government since 1955, one year before independence from the Anglo-Egyptian rule in 1956. They have been resisting the subordination they face as a people and the underdevelopment of their region. The different central administrations have ignored these regions and paid attention only to the center. There had been a period of peace after an agreement between the southern fighting factions and the central government in 1972. This ended in 1983 when the government reneged on parts of the 1972 agreement. Once more southern leaders resorted to armed resistance.

Southern Sudan was locked and isolated by the British administration under the claim that it was being protected from the slave trade. The south was left without any development schemes and totally isolated from the north. The infrastructure left in the north was enough to sustain the colonial interests but not an independent Sudan. In 1947 a few years before independence the southern leaders were consulted on the issue of whether the south should be united with the north or not. There was an agreement to unite the country but the safeguards promised to southerners were ignored by the successive governments. In September, a few months after the break of the war in 1983, the then-ruling military junta declared Islamic law as the law of the land. Such a declaration set the north and the south further apart. In addition to the religious differences, ethnic differences between the northerners, who are mainly Arabized Nubians and Hamitic groups, and the southerners, mainly Bantu Africans, contributed to the tension between the two parts of the country. More southerners joined the war. Others in previously ignored peripheral areas such as the Nuba Mountains in the West joined the rebels to draw attention to their condition. By 1995 even the northern opposition joined ranks with the rebels and started its attacks on the Eastern region of the country. So far this relentless war has claimed an estimated 2.5 million lives and displaced over 4 million people. It is considered the longest continuing war in Africa and has claimed more lives than any African war in the twentieth century (with the possible exception of the conflict of the Democratic Republic of Congo), yet it attracts minimum international attention.

OVERVIEW OF WOMEN'S ISSUES

Sudanese women belong to different ethnic groups and religions. Their affairs are governed by various customary and religious norms. In the northern, central, eastern, and western parts, where the majority of the people are Muslims, a version of Islamic law, *shari'a*, has governed family affairs since the Islamization of those parts five centuries ago. Now *shari'a* governs all walks of life.

In the south the majority of the people live by traditional religions. An estimated 10 percent of the southerners are Christians, who mix traditions and religion in the same way their counterparts in the north mix Islam and traditions. The overall result is that Sudanese women are subordinated to men through either religion or tradition. During the past five decades women have been able to secure some of their rights, such as equal pay and paid maternity leave. Women form an active and important part of the work force in the agricultural areas. In 1997, 45 percent of teachers were women.[4]

EDUCATION

Opportunities

Opportunities for education are available for boys and girls; however, a little over 50 percent of girls have a chance to attend schools. Traditionally girls may be deprived of an opportunity for education if the family has no financial means to educate all of its children. Gender disparities make girls less valuable to the family than boys who are expected to take care of the family.

Education is segregated until high school. Many universities are co-educational, but some are strictly male or female. The Islamic

University students in Khartoum. Photo © TRIP/R. Spurr.

University, for instance, operates as one institution but has separate and different departments for women. Ahfad University for Women is a private institution and is the first female-only university in the country.

Literacy

Male literacy in the Sudan is 68 percent whereas female literacy is only 46 percent. The primary education rate for men is 48 percent compared to that of women at 37 percent. Twenty-one percent of the students in secondary education are male compared to 19 percent female.[5]

EMPLOYMENT AND ECONOMICS

Farming

The Food and Agriculture Organization (FAO) reports that 49 percent of the farmers in the irrigated sector of the Sudan are women. They form 57 percent of the farmers in the areas that depend solely on rainfall (rain-fed lands) to water their crops. Women's share of the work in the agricultural sector is best described in the FAO report:

Women carry out a major portion of agricultural activities and bear almost the entire burden of household work, including water and fuel wood collection and food processing and preparation. According to a Ministry of Agriculture baseline survey of the rain fed traditional sector in 1989, both men and women participate in land clearance and in the preparation, harvesting, transporting and marketing of crops, while women carry out most of the planting, weeding and food processing. In the livestock sector, men have the primary responsibility for cattle and sheep raising, while women participate in milking and processing milk products. Both men and women are involved in raising goats and poultry. In fisheries, women participate in processing and marketing. In the agro-forestry sector, women participate in all aspects of the work and have the major responsibility for seedling preparation and weeding. Men and women are sometimes responsible for different types of trees.[6]

Paid Employment

Despite the fact that women have been appointed as judges, have worked as lawyers and at the attorney general's offices, and get token representation in some key positions in various ministries, women are still denied equal opportunity in available jobs. They can only look through the "glass ceiling" and have never earned the right to be promoted to higher positions, especially in the armed and police service. In addition women are subject to the Islamic dress code in the workplace and have suffered dismissal for the "public good."

Although women are steadily forging their way into different occupations, they are hindered by certain laws, such as the Personal Law for Muslims Act of 1991, which clearly does not recognize work as a right for the woman. Work is a privilege to be granted and agreed to by a woman's guardian. The only limit on the guardian's or husband's authority is his sense of reasonableness in his decision to order the woman to stay at home. This standard of being reasonable is open to debate in court as the law does not even give examples of what could be an unreasonable or reasonable restriction. Women's employment is subject to many restrictions, social and legal, but they are eased and sometimes ignored as the need for women's income increases and as an increasing number of men seek employment in other countries as expatriates.

In October of 2000 the governor (*wali*) of Khartoum issued an order that caused an international outcry regarding women's rights. The order prohibited women from working in gas stations and hotels. Both places were ordered to dismiss women immediately. The governor deemed work at these places to be against the dignity of women.[7] Sudanese women mobilized against the order and filed a constitutional suit on the basis that the order discriminated against them by reason of sex. The Constitutional Court ordered a preliminary halt of the governor's order; however, the businesses named in the order rarely employ women for fear that their work may be interrupted by such orders or by family members (guardians) any time.

Informal Economic Activities

Many women generate income by starting their own small businesses as petty sellers of some goods or makers of food, tea, and coffee near places of work and markets. Women almost have a monopoly on making crafts such as straw baskets and food covers. In drought-affected areas such small industries have provided jobs for men as sellers and transporters of these products to the markets. Dress-making for women and other cloth household items such as drapes and curtains is another informal sector occupation in which women find jobs. Men are fierce competitors in the field of sewing and are more successful as they have access to public places in markets where they can practice tailoring. For women sewing is a home-based business only. Displaced women seek domestic jobs such as child care and cleaning and lately as messengers in government and private offices.

Entrepreneurship

Very few businesses are owned by women; therefore women entrepreneurs are rare. Through inheritance or purchase women may own shares in companies or parts of businesses but the affairs of such businesses are run by the men in the family.

Pay

Because of gender disparities, the huge amount of work contributed by women as subsistence farmers and workers in the cash crops areas is undervalued. Often women's agricultural contributions are unpaid because they are considered simply helping other members of the family, even if that family member is only hired to work on that land.

The Public Service Act (1994) and its predecessors stipulate equal pay for equal work. The constitution also prohibits discrimination by reason of sex. Nevertheless, according to the UNDP data from 2000, women make about 30 percent of men's earned income.[8]

Support for Mothers/Caretakers

Wherever women happen to work they still lack some of the vital support they need. Women's work as wives and mothers is not considered work. A woman who spends a lifetime as a mother and a homemaker may lose support upon divorce. The only support women find, and that the law enforces, is maintenance by their sons and/or daughters or the nearest of kin if they do not have children. Legally, religiously, and socially children are obliged to take care of all their parents' needs.

Maternal Leave

Sudanese law abides by the rules laid drawn by the International Labour Organisation and gives women a paid maternal leave of eight weeks. Sick leave is also provided by law and women are allowed a sick leave over and above the maternity leave if they fall sick after birth and cannot return to work after eight weeks. Although a widowed pregnant woman is entitled to a mourning leave as well as maternal leave, it can be terminated upon the child's birth.

Child Care

A major problem that faces working women is child care. Urbanization has to a great extent dismantled the extended family; therefore, the services of mothers, aunts, and other female members are not readily available for working women. Daycare centers are expensive and are a new addition to the Sudanese lifestyle. Women depend on live-in baby-sitters who are more trusted in taking care of children, especially infants, than daycare centers. Refugees from neighboring countries and displaced Sudanese women provide the live-in baby-sitter jobs. These women are comfortable with domestic work and child care as it gives them some security and they add to their income by securing some food and clothing from the employing family for their own families.

Family and Medical Leave

The law provides for family leave of up to one year (unpaid) for either the husband or the wife. A widowed woman is entitled to a mourning leave, which extends to four months and ten days for Muslim women. It may be more or less for a pregnant widow because the leave is terminated upon her giving birth.

Inheritance, Property, and Land Rights

Sudanese women own property through direct purchase, inheritance, or gifts. Inheritance is governed by the religious rules of the deceased person. For example, if the deceased is Christian, a Muslim sibling or parent may not inherit property from him/her. For the majority of women who are Muslims, different shares of inheritance are dependent on their relationship to the deceased. Male siblings inherit twice as much as their female counterparts. An only daughter with no male siblings would inherit half of the estate but the other half would go to her uncles or cousins on her father's side. A mother may inherit up to one third of her son's estate, depending on whether the deceased was survived by any offspring.

The women's share in inheritance is justified by the fact that they are not under any obligation to spend their money in the household. All their needs are to be met by their male relatives. Changing social and economic conditions have caused family members to take advantage of other Islamic rules that allow them to give or sell any of their property to whomever they like. A gift may be made to a daughter who stays to take care of a parent or any other relative, so as to secure a sufficient income in case of her parent's death. In addition to that gift she also inherits the prescribed portion of property. A childless wife may be protected by her husband and given a good share of his property in addition to what she would inherit.

In other parts of the country, especially the eastern states, women have no access to their inheritance despite the fact that they are Muslims. The male members of the family customarily take over the estate. In other parts, mainly in the South, women are resisting certain customs such as being deprived of the right to inherit property, but also the practice in which a woman herself may be inherited by the brother or cousin of the deceased and freed to marry them.[9]

Residential plots assigned by the government from time to time are a symbol of discrimination and gender disparity. A man may apply for a plot without obligation to share it with his wife, but a married woman is obliged to share property with her husband. Sometimes if the husband has a house the woman does not get a plot of her own even if she meets all the criteria for assignment of a plot.

Social/Government Programs

As Sudan is one of the poorest countries in the world and thus constrained by the International Monetary Fund and World Bank policies, the government has failed to provide the basic social services for women. Gender disparities have been intensified by the religious nature of the state.

FAMILY AND SEXUALITY

Traditionally the family is a priority in everyone's life. The extended family keeps close relations despite urbanization and the movement of mostly younger people to the cities. Nuclear families are gaining independence while continuing to maintain contact with their families in other parts of the country.

Gender Roles

The 1998 constitution of the Sudan stipulates equality of the sexes in vague terms. But it does address women as persons responsible for families and makes it clear that a woman's primary role is as wife and mother. Article 15 of the constitution has the short title "Family and Women" and stipulates: "The State shall care for the institution of the family, facilitate marriage and adopt policies to purvey progeny, child upbringing, pregnant women and mothers. The State shall emancipate women from injustice in all aspects and pursuits of life and encourage their role thereof in family and public life."[10]

Marriage

Whereas the constitution prefers that women be wives and mothers, it does not preserve their rights in the domestic sphere nor does it give attention to their reproductive rights. Laws governing marriage and divorce are a good example of that neglect. Men may divorce unilaterally and without resorting to any court proceedings; yet women have to resort to the courts and prove that a man is either absent from the matrimonial home, does not pay her maintenance, or mistreats her. While a man can finalize a divorce in a few minutes with minimum resort to authorities, a woman may take years to get a divorce through a court of law.

A woman's custody of her children ends when the male child turns seven years of age and the female child reaches nine years of age. A woman may sue to prove that it is in the interest of the children to have them continue living with her. Even if granted custody a woman is responsible for the physical well-being of the children while the father or the male guardian is responsible for their guidance. A woman who devoted her life to a family may very well end up divorced and with no means of subsistence except what her family may provide. Maintenance after divorce is for a limited period of time. In the south a divorced woman is a liability to her family since the family is obliged to return the bridewealth paid at the time of marriage.

Shari'a laws determine that sexual relations between people who are not married to each other constitute a crime, called *zina*. Despite the difficulty of proof of *zina*, a woman is more at risk of coming under this law if she gets pregnant. While a man can deny any engagement in the act that resulted in her pregnancy, that pregnancy is taken as prima facae evidence against the woman. Women have been able to rebut the presumption of *zina* by claiming rape. A man does not get punished for rape due to lack of evidence against him; a woman may evade punishment because there is no evidence to contradict her claim of rape.[11]

Reproduction

Women's sexuality is heavily guarded by the society. Premarital or extramarital relations bring about social disgrace and punishment by law.

Sex Education

There is no sex education in schools. Young people depend on each other for information but sometimes do go to their parents.

Contraception and Abortion

A very low percentage of women, mainly in urban areas, use contraceptives. About 7.2 percent of the population uses contraceptives according to the Population Reference Bureau's 2003 factsheet. Like all other medical supplies, contraceptives are expensive. There are NGOs such as the Sudan Family Planning Association that distribute contraceptives to poor women in urban areas and adjacent rural areas. These organizations have been under attack by the authorities for "illegally distributing contraceptives." The president of Sudan publicly urged people to ignore family planning and have as many children as they want.[12]

All the penal codes in the Sudan since 1925 have prohibited abortion, except to save the life of the mother. The latest criminal-law act, ratified in 1991, expanded the circumstances under which no punishment will be levied for abortion. These circumstances encompass the necessity to save the mother's life, the death of the baby in the womb, or a pregnancy resulting from rape or incest. While the law acknowledges the above circumstances there is no clear policy on making sure that the best or easiest ways to induce abortion are available.

HEALTH

Health Care Access

As one of the poorest countries in the world the Sudan lacks the basic infrastructure to provide universal health care for its citizens. Trained midwives and medical assistants or nurses provide care for the majority of the population. Women's health is greatly affected since a major part of their lives is spent in reproductive activities coupled with housework and, for many women, an outside job. Although midwives are provided throughout the country, they have had no training to deal with birth complications. Prenatal and neonatal care is available in cities but expenses are beyond the majority of the population's financial abilities. Since most government subsidies have been withdrawn from social services, which is part of the structural adjustment programs agreed to with the International Monetary Fund, people have to pay for services at government hospitals that previously provided free services.

Diseases and Disorders

AIDS

UNAIDS (Joint United Nations Programme on HIV/AIDS) estimates the total number of people with HIV/AIDS at 450,000 or 2.6 percent of the population. Of this number there are 230,000 adult women who are infected.[13] AIDS orphans are mainly cared for by women, especially in the refugee and displaced camps. Rates of HIV/AIDS infection are considered low compared to adjacent African countries but this is expected to increase as people move between Uganda and southern Sudan.

Female Genital Cutting

Female genital cutting[14] is one of the traditional practices that has proven to be a danger to women's health and a breach of their rights. Sudanese women have been trying for decades to eradicate this harmful practice but with little success. Female genital cutting is linked to issues of virginity, honor, and femininity in general. Many women take pride in being cut and they want their daughters to feel the same pride. Men believe that it protects virginity by reducing the sexual desire of a woman. One type of female genital cutting, infibulation, is practiced to make sexual relations difficult and therefore ensure virginity, which is essential for getting married. Both men and women attach great value to female genital cutting. Uncut women may be ridiculed and their chances of getting married may be minimized.

The majority of northern Sudanese practice one type or another of female genital cutting. The only region that does not practice it is the southern region. There are no dependable statistics or research about the reports that southern women who move to the north or those abducted during the war have been either voluntarily or forcibly cut. Recently urban areas that have a high percentage of education among both women and men started to abandon the practice.

The earliest attempts to eradicate female genital cutting started in the Sudan more than fifty years ago. The few educated women at that time started discussing the practice, as did British women who were in the formal educational system. The initial attempts were limited and were greatly hindered by the taboos connected to the sexual behavior of people in general. At that time there was tremendous difficulty in convincing the people to even send their daughters to school (let alone remain uncut). It was feared that the daughters would be exposed to a type of knowledge and education that was foreign to them, and that might adversely affect and disrupt the social life.

In the past, the Sudan was at the forefront of countries fighting the practice of female genital cutting. It hosted two international conferences organized by WHO on the eradication of female genital cutting, in 1979 and 1984. The Ahfad University for Women, the Physicians Association, the official Women's Union, and many professional and social organizations were active in both conferences. Fearing resistance by the people, the successive governments paid only lip service to eradication efforts. In May 2002 the Ministry of Guidance and Endowments held a conference, in collaboration with the female students of the Islamic university, in which it hosted speakers who supported female genital cutting. This conference caused an outcry within the medical profession and women's organizations in the country.[15] Official support of the practice will only further entrench the tradition of female genital cutting and give medical and religious reasons for continuing the practice.

POLITICS AND LAW

The constitution has created standards, rather than rules, in terms of women's place in society. Article 21 stipulates: "All people are equal before the courts of law. Sudanese are equal in the rights and duties as regards to functions of public life; and there shall be no discrimination only by reason of race, sex or religious creed. They are equal in eligibility for public posts and offices not being discriminated on the basis of wealth."[16]

This article is criticized because it recognizes equality before the courts of law, instead of the known general statement that people are equal before the law. It is vague enough to constitutionalize gender disparities and discrimination on the basis of sex. Discrimination is prohibited if it is only on the basis or race, sex, or religious creed. The word *only* makes discrimination possible if other reasons exist.

Leadership and Decision-making

The ancient history of the great Nubian Empire of Kush recorded the lives of women as strong queens and leaders. A matrilineal system governed all walks of life including inheritance. The lives of women changed as the country moved from ancient beliefs to Christianity and finally into Islam.

Women's participation in decision-making is hampered by the laws that treat them as minors. Token appointments as ministers or governors do not exempt women from regulations such as restrictions on movement. Women may not travel alone and have to have a male relative (who may not be married to the woman but rather a father, brother, or uncle) travel with her. Initially a woman leaving the country needs to produce the written notarized consent of her guardian. The written consent is not a guarantee that she can leave the country, for the responsible officer may decide that she should not. Women in higher positions are not asked to present such documentation mainly for fear of international embarrassment. However the rule remains effective and can be applied to all women leaving the country.

A woman's decision-making power in the home is greatly diminished by the fact that she is considered a ward of her husband, father, or brother and should obey him and abide by his orders.

Suffrage and Political Participation

All citizens of the Sudan can vote by the age of seventeen.[17] As provided by Article 67(b) of the constitution: "Twenty-five percent of its [the National Assembly's] members are elected by special elections or indirect election from among women, and the scientific and professional communities, in either states or nationally, as is determined by law."[18] The Assembly comprises 360 seats. Women have been assigned 20 seats in the indirect elections. In the 2000 elections, women claimed 9.7 percent (or 35) of the Assembly seats, according to the Inter-Parliamentary Union.[19] Local assemblies reserve 10 percent of their seats for women.

Women's Rights

Contemporary Sudanese women, like women worldwide, experience subordination under patriarchal systems. The struggle for women's rights in the Sudan started nearly fifty years ago. At that time, those few women who were educated lived mainly in the major cities. The Sudanese

Women's Union (the Union), was formed in the capital city in 1952. In 1965 the president of the union, Fatima Ahmed Ibrahim, became the first woman in parliament. The Union fought fiercely for women's rights and promoted women's education. Its effort to eradicate women's illiteracy put it among the winners of the 1993 United Nations award for human rights.

The struggle for women's rights continues today despite the dissolution of the Union and its replacement by a quasi-governmental union. The thrust of that movement was concentrated in central Sudan and was concerned with some women's legal and work issues. It developed with the increased education for women and better communications between the different regions of the country, and most importantly with linking up with the international women's movement.

Women's Movements

Women's nongovernmental organizations have been formed to address various issues but are under continuous scrutiny by the authorities. The organizations that exist today work in areas of legal aid, documentation of human rights, development health, and income generation. The short lived democratic eras (the Sudan enjoyed democratic governments in the periods 1956–1958, 1965–1969, and 1985–1989) gave women room to organize and network. Such organizations gave them strength to come back after dissolution during the long dictatorships.

Since the early 1990s women's organizations suffered closure, dissolution, interrogation of leaders, and in many occasions detention of some of the members. Search and seizure of documents is still practiced despite the breathing room offered since 2001. Funding for organizations is usually in minimal amounts provided by international organizations such as the Netherlands Organization for International Development Co-operation (NOVIB), the U.S. National Endowment for Democracy, and Sweden's Save the Children (Rädda Barnen). The Ford Motor Company was a main source of funding until the boycott by the U.S. government. The United Nations funds projects related to its programs such as family planning. Some nongovernmental organizations are supported by the government, so some of their projects are pro-government. International entities such as the International Muslim Women's Union are situated in the Sudan.

RELIGION AND SPIRITUALITY

An estimated 70 percent of the population is Muslim, residing mostly in the northern states. Twenty to twenty-five percent have indigenous beliefs and reside in the south. Christians are an estimated 5–10 percent and reside mainly in the southern states and the major cities.

Women's Roles

Women's role within the major two religions, Islam and Christianity, is mainly that of worshippers. Any teaching roles are limited to being school teachers or nuns. Engagement in public talks is limited to radio and television programs that rarely host women. Leading prayers and giving religious opinions (*fatwa*) are exclusively men's jobs. Women may be revered within the ranks of the Sufi Islamic sect tradition if they or their families are recognized as leading sufi figures, however their revered status is more often because of their male counterpart's status.

Rituals and Religious Practices

Women are usually precluded from public sufi sessions, where hymns praising Allah and the Prophet are recited with vigorous body movements. In such sessions women are only allowed in the audience. Within churches men are the leaders and women are nuns who may perform social acts encouraged by religion, such as teaching and nursing.

Women practice some spiritual traditions that survived both religions. *Zar* is one such practice in northern Sudan. *Zar* sessions include certain songs that are supposed to heal women who believe that they are sick because certain spirits are controlling them. During these rituals certain practices that are usually prohibited by religion may take place, such drinking wine. Women will dance to music, inviting the spirit to come through them to make certain demands for gifts such as clothes, jewelry, and anything else that may make the spirit happy. Such practices are discouraged and prohibited by the current religious state.[20]

Religious Law

Since 1983 the Sudan has been governed as a religious state: the military government that was overthrown in 1985 introduced laws based on *shari'a* to govern the whole country, except for personal or family laws for non-Muslims. The fundamental sources of Islamic law are the Qur'an, which is believed to be the literal word of God, and the *sunna*, the traditions of the Prophet Mohammed. Both the Qur'an and the *sunna* have been subjects of extensive interpretation and counterinterpretation since the death of the Prophet Muhammed in 632.[21] This process, known as *ijtihad* (learned opinions of knowledgeable individuals), has resulted in the *shari'a*, the comprehensive codes governing all walks of live. Individual rights are governed by the *shari'a*. Customary law governs the parts of the country where the people are adherents of traditional beliefs or of Christianity.

VIOLENCE

Domestic Violence

There are no dependable reports on the incidence of domestic violence. The presence of extended families has for years alleviated the incidence and consequences of domestic violence. Women found refuge with other members of the family such as uncles and aunts and also counted on the pressure of the elders to stop any violence against them. Urbanization, refugee and displaced situations increased economic pressures and dismantled both communities and extended families. Physical abuse is punishable no matter who inflicted it. However cultural standards still discourage women from filing charges against husbands and other male members of their family.

Rape/Sexual Assault

In Sudan a man does not get punished for rape because there is only the woman's word against his that the act occurred, therefore there is rarely evidence.[22] Pregnancy resulting from rape is considered evidence against the woman for pre- or extramarital sex. A woman can, however, defend herself against the charge of adultery or pre- or extramarital sex by claiming rape.

War and Military Repression

The conflict between the northern Khartoum government and the southern Sudanese has proven to be the most devastating to women and children not only in the south but in the whole country.[23] They suffered enslavement by the nearby ethnic groups, were displaced and scattered throughout the country and ended in refugee camps in adjacent countries such as Kenya, Uganda, and Ethiopia. The rights of these displaced and refugee women are ignored. Their disempowerment continues as they have lost their coherent communities, thus their stable lifestyle.

OUTLOOK FOR THE TWENTY-FIRST CENTURY

The Sudanese people have an optimistic outlook on the future. There are major obstacles to the progress of the country and its people. The biggest obstacle is the war between the central government and the rebels in the south. Women are part of the peace process and are very optimistic that they will play a vital role. Southern women's organizations are active and internationally connected. Northern Sudanese women are taking the peace process more seriously than they ever did before.

Poverty is another obstacle and unfortunately it is on the rise because of both the policies enforced by the International Monetary Fund and World Bank and also the economic boycott enforced by the United States on Sudan. However, the country's resources of oil and minerals are just beginning to be tapped and look promising. The Sudan is potentially a major source of food for the countries of the Horn of Africa because of its vast unused arable areas and Nile water. International interest in the Sudan promises to bring in much needed aid as well as transparency into the governance and human rights issues that include women's rights.

NOTES

The statistics available about the Sudan are mostly estimates; therefore, the reader may find different estimates in different sources.

1. One kilometer equals 0.6 miles.

2. *Human Development Indicators 2003*, www.undp.org/hdr2003/indicator/cty_f_SDN.html.

3. UNICEF statistics, www.unicef.org/statis/country_1page163.html; Mission of the Republic of Sudan in Geneva, www3.itu.int/missions/sudan/english/frame.html.

4. *World's Women 2000: Trends and Statistics* (New York: United Nations, 2000).

5. UNICEF statistics.

6. Food and Agriculture Organization.

7. See http://web.amnesty.org/web/ar2001.nsf/webafrcountries/sudan for a full report on the Sudan and this case.

8. *Human Development Reports*, http://hdr.undp.org.

9. Sonia G. Puente, "Sudanese Women: Trapped by Tradition and Religion," *Middle East Times* no. 24 (1997).

10. The official English translation of the constitution of the Republic of the Sudan, 1998, may be found on the web site of the Sudan Embassy in the United States, www.sudanembassy.org/default.asp?page=documentsreports_constitution.

11. See www.wluml.org/english/alerts/2002/sudan/abok-alfau-akok.htm for an alert to action by Women Living Under Muslim Laws regarding Abok Akok of Sudan. A report may be found at the Human Rights Watch web site, http://hrw.org/africa/sudan.php.

12. *Al Wan* (Sudanese newspaper), February 16, 1999; *Sudan Update* 10, no. 4 (21 February 1999).

13. Joint United Nations Programme on HIV/AIDS (UNAIDS), www.unaids.org.

14. For a detailed description of female circumcision and its consequences see the World Health Organization's *Fact Sheet*, www.who.int/frh-whd/FGM/index.htm. For information about specific countries see Dara Carr, *Female Genital Cutting: Findings from the Demographic and Health Surveys Program* (Calverton, MD: Macro International, 1997).

15. See the statement issued by women organizations at www.midan.net/nm/private/news/swrg18_6_02.htm.

16. Ibid.

17. *CIA World Factbook*, www.odci.gov/cia/publications/factbook/geos/su.html.

18. Official English translation of the constitution of the Republic of the Sudan, 1998.

19. www.ipu.org/wmn-e/classif.htm.

20. For more on *Zar* see, Janice Boddy, *Wombs and Alien Spirits: Women, Men, and the Zar Cult in Northern Sudan* (Madison: University of Wisconsin Press, 1989).

21. See generally Abdullahi Ahmed An-Na'im, "Problems of Universal Cultural Legitimacy for Human Rights," in *Human Rights in Africa: Cross Cultural Perspectives,* eds. Abdullahi An-Na'im and Frances Deng (Washington, DC: Brookings Institution, 1990), 359.

22. See www.wluml.org/english/alerts/2002/sudan/abok-alfau-akok.htm.

23. For detailed human rights abuses of this war, see Human Rights Watch, Africa Staff, *Civilian Devastation. Abuses by All Parties in the War in Southern Sudan* (New York: Human Rights Watch, 1994); and, *Civil War in Sudan*, ed. Martin W. Daly and Ahmad A. Sikainga (New York: St. Martin's Press, 1993).

RESOURCE GUIDE

Suggested Reading

Abusharaf, Rogaia Mustafa. *Wanderings: Sudanese Migrants and Exiles in North America*. Ithaca: Cornell University Press, 2002.

An-Na'im, Abdullahi Ahmed. "Problems of Universal Cultural Legitimacy for Human Rights." In *Human Rights in Africa: Cross Cultural Perspectives*, edited by Abdullahi An-Na'im and Frances Deng. Washington, DC: Brookings Institution, 1990.

Boddy, Janice. *Wombs and Alien Spirits: Women, Men, and the Zar Cult in Northern Sudan*. Madison: University of Wisconsin Press, 1989.

El Dareer, Asma. *Woman, Why Do You Weep? Circumcision and Its Consequences*. London: Zed Press, 1992.

Hale, Sondra. *Gender Politics in Sudan: Islamism, Socialism, and the State*. Boulder: Westview Press, 1997.

Hall, Marjorie, and Bakhita Amin Ismail. *Sisters Under the Sun: The Story of Sudanese Women*. London: Longman, 1981.

Human Rights Watch, Africa Staff. *Civilian Devastation: Abuses by All Parties in the War in Southern Sudan*. New York: Human Rights Watch, 1994.

Lobban, Richard A., Jr., Carolyn Fluehr-Lobban, and Robert S. Kramer. *Historical Dictionary of the Sudan*. 3rd ed. Lanham, MD: Scarecrow Press, 2002.

Petterson, Donald. *Inside Sudan: Political Islam, Conflict, and Catastrophe*. Boulder: Westview Press, 1999.

Web Sites

AllAfrica Global Media, http://allafrica.com/sudan.

Human Rights Watch, www.hrw.org/wr2k1/africa/sudan.htm.

Sudan.Net, http://sudan.net.

Sudan Embassy in South Africa, www.sudani.co.za.

United Nations Economic and Social Council, www.unhchr.ch/tbs/doc.nsf/(symbol)/e.c.12.1.add.48.en?opendocument.

Organizations

Babiker Badri Scientific Association for Women Studies (BBSAWS)
Ahfad University
P.O. Box 167
Omdurman, Sudan
Phone: 249-11-564401
Fax: 249-11-553363

Committee for the Eradication of Abduction of Women and Children (CEAWC)
CEAWC
Mek Nimir St.
Khartoum, Sudan

An entity established by the government of Sudan in May 1998 for the purpose of identifying abducted women and children and reuniting them with their families or with their local communities.

Mutawinat Group
P.O. Box 2348
Khartoum, Sudan 11111
Email: mutawinat@hotmail.com

Legal aid for women and development research.

Sudan Human Rights Organization
Web site: www.shro-cairo.org/contact.htm

Sudanese Women Voice for Peace
Email: swvp@africaonline.co.ke

A southern Sudanese women's group established to participate in peace efforts.

SELECTED BIBLIOGRAPHY

An-Naʿim, Abdullahi Ahmed, and Francis Deng, eds. *Human Rights in Africa: Cross Cultural Perspectives*. Washington, DC: Brookings Institution, 1990.

Carr, Dara. *Female Genital Cutting: Findings from the Demographic and Health Surveys Program*. Calverton, MD: Macro International, 1997.

Daly, Martin W., and Ahmad A. Sikainga, eds. *Civil War in Sudan*. New York: St. Martin's Press, 1993. www.midan.net/nm/private/news/swrg18_6_02.htm.

Human Rights Watch, Africa Staff. *Civilian Devastation: Abuses by All Parties in the War in Southern Sudan*. New York: Human Rights Watch, 1994. http://hrw.org/africa/sudan.php.

Mission of the Republic of Sudan in Geneva. www3.itu.int/missions/sudan/english/frame.html.

Puente, Sonia G. "Sudanese Women: Trapped by Tradition and Religion." *Middle East Times* no. 24 (1997).

World Health Organization (WHO). *Fact Sheet*. www.who.int/frh-whd/fgm/index.htm.

19

TANZANIA

Ruth Meena

PROFILE OF TANZANIA

The United Republic of Tanzania includes the mainland (formerly Tanganyika) and Zanzibar (made up of the Unguja and Pemba islands). The country covers 945,085 square kilometers[1] and is the largest in eastern Africa, estimated to be twice the size of France. It borders Kenya, Uganda, Rwanda, Burundi, Democratic Republic of Congo, Malawi, and Mozambique. Although Swahili is spoken by the majority of the Tanzanians, Tanzania is a multilingual country with approximately 120 ethnic groups with different accents, customary practices, and value systems that determine largely the position and condition of women.[2] Tanzania has a population of 33.7 million, of whom women make up 50.5 percent. Life expectancy is relatively low: for men it is forty-four years, while for women it is forty-six years.

Tanzania is considered one of the poorest countries in the world. More than 50 percent of its population have an average income that sits 16 percent below the national poverty line.[3] Poverty, inequality, and the legal and regulatory environment have been singled out as the most pervasive factors affecting the lives of

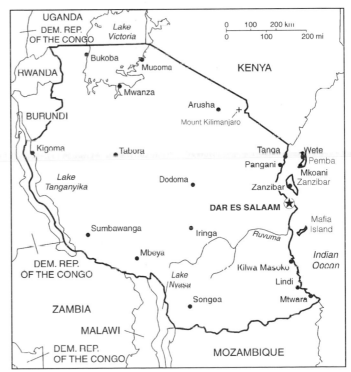

men and women in this country. The gross domestic product (GDP) per capita is U.S.$523 and the country's overall annual GDP stands at U.S.$9 billion. This is lower than the average for sub-Saharan Africa, which has a gross national product per capita of U.S.$1,831.[4]

About half of all Tanzanians live in poverty and 36 percent of all Tanzanians live in absolute poverty. Approximately 59 percent of the rural population is poor (10.9 million Tanzanians). About 85 percent of all the poor are found in rural areas. Approximately 39 percent of urban population, including those living in the capital, Dar es Salaam, are also poor. The urban population is growing rapidly at the rate of 6.8 percent every year, the fourth highest rate in eastern and southern Africa. Although the poor spend at least 75 percent of their minimal income on food alone, it is of low nutritional value (less than 2,100 calories per person). They spend only 2 percent of their income on health and 0.6 percent on education. It is estimated that 32 percent of all poor and 57 percent of absolute poor have never had any form of formal education at all. Women head more than 25 percent of Tanzania's households.[5] Women carry a disproportional burden of poverty due to customary laws and practices that preclude them from accessing property and other credit facilities.

Tanzania is considered to be a country in transition from a monolithic political system to a pluralist political system. In May 1992 parliament passed a constitutional amendment that ended one-party rule in Tanzania and provided for multiparty elections both at the national level and in local government. The transition, however, has been state engineered. Typical of state-managed transitions, the process of liberalization has been slow, as the state has not been willing to rewrite the political rules to make it possible for other actors to participate freely and fairly. The government is reluctant to guarantee too much freedom to the people and has a strong interest to control the media and associations. It is also hesitant to completely open up the system to fair and free competition. There is a tendency toward greater centralization of power at the local level rather than decentralization. Indeed, the state-engineered transition perpetuates the politics of social exclusion, undermines basic human rights and freedoms, limits freedom of association and expression, and often undermines the rule of law. Ultimately, there has been reluctance to rewrite the rules of the game to empower those citizens who have been socially excluded, particularly women and other historically disadvantaged citizens to take effective part in the political processes.

OVERVIEW OF WOMEN'S ISSUES

Women's economic position in Tanzania is largely a result of a combination of multiple factors. These include a dual legal system, which allows for the coexistence of customary law and civil law. Despite efforts by the government to improve the status of women, Tanzanian women own and control less property than men, have less access to credit facilities, have less educational and training qualifications, and enjoy fewer rights and privileges than their male counterparts. This is attributed to existing sociocultural norms, values, and customary practices, which position and locate women in low social status relative to men. The condition has been worsened by the economic development models that have been implemented from the period of independence to date and which failed to address the root causes of the structural gendered inequalities and the corresponding power relations between men and women. Such models included modernization strategies, which promoted growth without paying any attention to gendered inequalities inherited from the colonial state. This model was later criticized for having left out the poor and particularly women in the development process.

At the market, Arusha, Tanzania. Photo © TRIP/F. Good.

The gendered nature of poverty has affected women and men differentially. Women disproportionately carry the burden of poverty because of their social and biological roles in the birthing and raising of children and caring for the household. The negative consequences of economic crisis have disproportionately fallen on women rather than men, and strategies for "wealth creation" or for poverty reduction have not adequately addressed structural gender equalities in the areas in which women suffer the most deprivation. The United Nations Development Programme's Human Development Index ranks Tanzania 126th out of the 143 countries in the Gender Related Development Index. Overall, women are worse off economically and educationally than men although the gender gap is significantly narrower than in many African countries. Despite the narrow gap, income for the majority of the Tanzanian women remains in absolute terms lower than many other countries and the country is ranked 151th out of 173 countries with respect to average personal income.[6]

EDUCATION

Opportunities

Tanzania's education and training policy has defined gender equality as a main anchor of its policy. The 1999 Ministry of Education and Culture policy states that in order to raise the participation rate of women it will promote girls' education by maintaining seven years of universal and compulsory education for all children starting at age seven; promote coeducational and girls' secondary schooling in various ways; establish financial support initiatives for girls' and women's education; promote adult education for women; revise the curriculum to strengthen the performance of girls in math and sciences; seek to eliminate gender stereotyping in curriculum, textbooks, and classroom teaching; offer special training programs for women teachers; and build hostels for girls attending day schools in urban areas.

At both the primary and secondary level significant progress has been made to bridge the gender gap and remove stereotyping in the curriculum. Programs to improve the physical facilities to make the school more girl-friendly have been implemented. A special fund for girls' education has been piloted in the most deprived areas. Increase of physical space for girls has been done through a variety of initiatives. These initiatives have lead to improved access and retention at both the primary and secondary levels. By 1998, gender parity at the primary school level had been achieved, while at the secondary level near parity had also been achieved. The female-male ratio at the primary level stood at 103:100, 74:100 at the secondary level, and 26:100 at the tertiary level.

The main problem for girls and women at both secondary and tertiary levels has been quality of education, retention of students, and their performance. Although significant progress has been made to increase the level and amount of education for every citizen, access to higher levels of learning remains a particular problem for women. One of the national priorities for Tanzania is its firm resolve to provide higher education to as many people as possible. But access to university education is difficult for both sexes, with women having fewer opportunities than their male counterparts.

The University of Dar es Salaam remains the main university with three campuses with twelve faculties. As of 2002, 29 percent of the University of Dar es Salaam students nationwide were women, which represents a significant jump in recent years. However, of the faculty Ph.D. recipients on the main campus, only 8 percent were women.

Only 20 percent of all applicants are admitted to university education.

The gender ratio of applicants and the corresponding ratio of those who are selected are of particular interest. For instance, during the academic year 1995–1996, for the faculty of education, 532 males and 450 females applied, while 130 males and just 22 females were admitted. For the B.A. degree in the same year, 571 males and 393 females applied, while 357 males and just 51 females were admitted.[7] Only in recent years have the number of female students begun to increase, having reached 29 percent of the student body in 2001.[8]

The low university enrollment in Tanzania hinders the production of the high level human resources that is needed for self-sustainable development in government, trade, industry, agriculture, and other sectors. The gender gap at this level precludes women from accessing formal employment, particularly in those well-paid and decisionmaking positions.

Literacy

The female adult literacy rate as a percentage or male literacy was 79 percent. However at the level of youth, female literacy as a percentage of male literacy stood at the much higher rate of 94 percent.[9]

EMPLOYMENT AND ECONOMICS

Farming

The majority of Tanzanian women live in the rural sector and are engaged in agricultural production. Poverty in Tanzania has a rural and feminine character. Agriculture is the mainstay of the Tanzanian economy. The current agricultural policy acknowledges that the agricultural sector contributes to 60 percent of export earnings and 84 percent of employment. The policy further acknowledges the contribution made by women in agricultural production. It recognizes that women contribute about 70 percent of the food crops and bear substantial responsibilities for many aspects of export crops and livestock production.[10]

Even though the policy recognized the contribution of women in agricultural production, it did not highlight men's limited contributions. Similarly, the policy document is silent on those factors that hinder men from meaningful participation and contribution to the productive processes. The underuse of male labor and the corresponding overtaxing of women's labor in this sector are not adequately addressed.

Paid Employment

Women and men are subjected to the same working environment of low pay and the insecurity that has accompanied retrenchment policies currently being pursued. Women currently earn 71 percent of men's income according to the UNDP's 2000 statistics.[11] Women are relegated to low-paying jobs largely due to their low educational status. Of those in professions, 28 percent are women, while 22 percent of those in administrative positions are female. Women tend to be relegated to unskilled or semi-skilled jobs with little chance for advancement, on-the-job training, or increases in pay and benefits.[12]

As low-paid employees, women have often been the first to be laid off. They also suffer when their spouses are retrenched since it adds to their workload in the household, having to take care of an unemployed spouse. Women become potential victims of sexual harassment at the workplace as their employers sometimes have taken advantage of their vulnerability, either forcing them to provide sexual favors or even raping them. Figures for these occurrences are not easily available, as most women would rather keep quiet due to the social stigma they would have to face were they to make rape or sexual harassment public.

Entrepreneurship

Because women's access to resources such as land and water, let alone marketing services, information, credit, and labor-saving technologies, are severly limited, it is difficult for women to use land as collateral to access credit facilities and other financial facilities needed to improve their productivity. Women's lack of education and training relative to men's is yet another barrier to their ability to access credit facilities. It is no wonder that the majority of rural women farmers are concentrated in subsistence crops rather than cash crop farming, which is normally controlled by men. As a result, women continue to reproduce poverty, as they cannot break out of subsistence production due to lack of cash income.

The overworked Tanzanian women and the corresponding deprivations they suffer along with structural gender hierarchies affect agricultural productivity and particularly the food security situation of the country. The factors largely account for the high levels of malnourished children and adults, the poor living conditions of the majority of citizens and also for low life expectancies for both men and women. Improving productivity of the agricultural sector cannot be attained without improving the economic status of women, who constitute the bulk of the agricultural labor force in addition to being responsible for the reproduction of this labor force through the care of the household and its members.

Pay

The law provides for equal pay between the two sexes, but practices by employers discriminate against women in promoting and accessing high-paid jobs. For instance, one female judge was sworn in as the first woman district magistrate in 1972, but it took her twenty years to be promoted to the post of a judge in the court of appeal, which is the highest hierarchy in the Tanzanian court system.

Support for Mothers/Caretakers

Maternal Leave

Although the law provides for a paid maternity leave of three months, recent trends towards liberalization have lead to the erosion of this gain. Some foreign corporations, in particular, either discriminate against women in their reproductive years or refuse to adhere to the maternity leave laws.

Inheritance, Property, and Land Rights

Despite their contribution to agricultural production, women's access to productive resources (land, water, etc.), supportive services (marketing services, information, credit, labor-saving technologies), and income in agricultural production is severely limited by social and cultural factors. Studies have shown that women's land holdings in Tanzania do not exceed five hectares per woman. This is attributed to limited access to credit facilities and land inheritance patterns, as well as the lack of improved tools of labor.[13] This is despite the seemingly gender progressive Land Act and the Village Land Act of 1999. The acts provide women the right to acquire title and registration of land, hold, use, and deal with land and actively promote women's representation in decisionmaking bodies that administer and settle disputes relating to land issues. The Land Act prohibits the use of customary law in determining the right of occupancy if the law denies women their right to use, transfer, and own land.

Despite such provisions, women's right to access land continues to be governed by existing customary practices that discriminate against women's rights to own and control land, particularly clan land and matrimonial property. This underscores the need to provide legal and human rights education to complement the progressive laws.

Despite these gains, most of the decisions regarding women's accessing and controlling land particularly after the death of a spouse or parent are governed by customary law, which is legal under the new law. And yet most customary laws, which operate in the majority of communities in Tanzania, preclude women from accessing land like their male counterparts. In some parts of Tanzania where women traditionally had user rights to some of their husbands' or fathers' or brothers' land, reforms have transferred land to an almost exclusively male-oriented tenure system, hence relegating women to landlessness.[14]

Social/Government Programs

Structural Adjustment

In the 1970s, then-president Julius Nyerere's philosophy of *ujamaa na kujitegemea* (socialism and self-reliance) did lead to some significant gains for women, despite enormous constraints and challenges. A primary health care program enabled women to access health facilities. Universal and compulsory education bridged the gender gap in access at the primary school level. The Universal Clean Water Supply program reduced significantly the distance that women had to walk to fetch water. These successes were possible due to massive donor support in the social-service sector.

The gains were, however, offset by the 1980s Structural Adjustment Program (SAP) strategy that was and continues to be implemented under pressure from the World Bank and other western donor countries. The implementation of SAPs combined with effects of internal inefficiencies of the state apparatus, and the mismanagement of the economy landed Tanzania into poverty, dependency, and debt crisis. With less state funding for primary health care programs, basic education, water, and farm subsidies to small-holder farmers, women were left to be the "shock absorbers" of the crises that continued to characterize the Tanzanian political and economic scene.

FAMILY AND SEXUALITY

Gender Roles and Division of Labor

Tanzania has a young population due to high fertility rates. More than 45 percent of its population is under fifteen with an annual population growth rate of 2.3 and a total fertility rate of 5.5 percent.[15] This implies a heavy workload for women who are basically responsible for most of the domestic tasks at the household level. Planners and policy makers have yet to address the gender realities of social stratification and differentiation at the village and household levels. They have not paid sufficient attention to the imbalances in power relations that influence who gets access to the means of production and who controls the surplus or profits that result from the labor input of men and women in all sectors, particularly in the agricultural sector.

About 13 percent of households are headed by women and have an average size of 5.1 household members. Female headed households on average are poorer and less able to save money. Female heads of households also have lower educational levels (2.8 years compared to an average of 4.5 years for male household heads).

Tanzanian women contribute significantly to agricultural production, doing three-quarters or more of the work. They also are largely responsible for food crops. In addition to the farming activities, rural and urban poor Tanzanian women are also responsible for most of the social reproductive tasks that include child care, provision of water and domestic energy (which can involve walking daily for miles to carry heavy wood for cooking and buckets of water), food processing and preservation, as well as marketing. Women carry out most of these activities with the most rudimentary tools, without access to extension services, inputs, and credit facilities.

Marriage

The mean age of first marriage for mainland Tanzania is twenty-three for women and twenty-five for men. The law allows women to marry at the age of fifteen and men at the age of eighteen.[16]

Reproduction

Contraception and Abortion

Tanzania's high fertility rate is attributed to the low level of contraceptive use, particularly among rural women. Knowledge of family planning is high, yet only 24 percent of women use some form of contraception; only 64 percent of rural women are even aware of birth control methods.[17] There are no serious efforts to engage men in family planning programs; hence, women continue to shoulder this responsibility alone.

Teen Pregnancy

Teenage pregnancy is a problem, forcing a number of girls to terminate their schooling. It is believed that the number of maternal deaths is inflated by teenage pregnancy. Maternal mortality stands at approximately 530 deaths per 100,000 live births. It is estimated that the infant mortality rate is around 104 per 1,000 live births while the under-five mortality rate per 1,000 live births is 165.[18]

HEALTH

Health Care Access

The *ujamaa na kujitegemea* (socialism and self-reliance) model of the 1970s created a primary health program that enabled women to access health facilities. As of 1985, skilled staff attended to 58 percent of all births. This number has plummeted, however, to 35 percent in 1999, due primarily to changes caused by the SAPs of the 1980s that curtailed spending on health care.[19]

Diseases and Disorders

AIDS

The HIV/AIDS pandemic disproportionately affects women, who can infect their newborn babies. Women—particularly younger women—are infected at higher rates than men and are economically less able to care for themselves or family members who are ill, yet they are the ones who primarily take care of orphans or sick relatives. Many infected women are in their prime years of reproduction. The AIDS cases for girls and women under the age of twenty-five is estimated to be more than double that of men in the same age category.

POLITICS AND LAW

Political Participation

Tanzania was one among the first countries in the region to have introduced a quota system in favor of women political candidates. This quota system, which is also referred to as "positive discrimination," was introduced as a result of declining trends of women in the parliament since independence. Whereas the 1961–1965 parliament had 7.5 percent of women members, this percentage dropped to 3.5 percent during the 1970–1975 parliamentary elections. Tanzania introduced a quota system in 1992, which provided for 15 percent of parliamentary seats and 25 percent of local government seats to be held by women.

Low representation in parliament influences the percentage of women appointees as ministers, regional commissioners, or district commissioners. With the 2000 elections, out of the twenty-seven full cabinet ministers, there were only four women, and out of the seventeen deputy ministers, there were only four women. Also in the 2000 elections, thirty-seven women (15 percent of the overall parliamentary seats) were elected by their political parties on the basis of proportional representation of political parties represented in the National Assembly. The majority of the parliamentary seats for directly elected members are obtained by simple majority vote. In 2002, 22.3 percent of the seats were held by women (61 out of 274). While the numbers of women held seats in parliament has increased, it is argued that the electoral quota system has enabled a male-dominated parliament to elect a few women on whom they can count for their support. This has often meant that the elected women are more loyal to their political parties than to women's concerns.

Women's Rights and Women's Movements

As a response to the low level of political participation, the women's movement and gender activists have taken initiatives to support women candidates and to pressure for legal and constitutional reforms that will accommodate more women and other socially excluded groups. Tanzania Gender Networking Program (TGNP) and Feminist Activism Coalition (known as FemAct) members, for instance, carried out a number of activities that supported women candidates. They contributed to the constitutional debates, challenging exclusionary clauses in the constitution, and reviewed electoral roles from a gender perspective.

FemAct, created by the TGNP umbrella, works as a network to push for women's specific concerns as well as gender equality issues. Through the coalition, they have been able to push for gender progressive laws, such as the Land Act, the Sexual Offense Bill, and so forth. They also developed a gender checklist for free and fair elections, which has been adopted by the majority of Southern African Development Community member countries as part of the norms and standards for fair and free election in the region.

Up until the 1990s, women's organizations had tended to be localized, focusing primarily on developmental activities. In the 1990s, a new level of political activism took hold as new kinds of organizations emerged at the local district and national levels. The organizations took up advocacy, education, and struggles to advance women's rights in the areas of violence against women, health and reproductive rights, environmental issues, and land rights, among others. Women activists were also involved in broader networks and coalitions formed to promote the interests of pastoralists and other marginalized peoples around issues such as land. Women's associations, along with human rights organizations, sought legislative reform in the areas of women's inheritance, domestic violence, land reform, and children's rights, and fought government efforts to curtail and monitor nongovernmental organizations. The new organizations were characterized by the breadth of their agendas.

Military Service

The Tanzania Military service does not discriminate against women, but it continues to be dominated by men, particularly in the high-ranking positions. Although up-to-date data are not available, there is only one women brigadier, which is the highest rank in the army.

RELIGION AND SPIRITUALITY

Tanzania allows, in principle, for religious freedom. Islam and Christianity are the dominant religions but many people also adhere to traditional beliefs and religions. Christians make up 30 percent of the population, Muslims 35 percent, and adherents of indigenous beliefs over 35 percent, overlapping with the Christian and Muslim communities.

Women's Roles

Religious beliefs and institutions have contributed to women's subordinate social status, especially Christian and Muslim teachings that emphasize women's inferior status. These beliefs are reflected in the top leadership of both Christian and Muslim religious institutions, which are led primarily by men. When these are applied in combination with the African traditional customary laws, they indeed relegate women to a low social status.

VIOLENCE

Violence against women expresses itself in a variety of ways. Discrimination against women in the economy and in decisionmaking contributes to making women vulnerable to sexual violence, battery, and neglect. Women's organizations and gender activists have organized to challenge violence against women. The Tanzania Media Women Association as a FemAct member has played a leading role in the campaign to stop violence against women. Some of the gains that have been made in this area include: The passing of the Sexual Offense Bill, which increased the awareness of women and children of their rights; freedom from torture; and enhanced capacity to hold elected officials accountable for the increased levels of violence against women and children. A number of legal-aid clinics are provided by civil society organizations such as the Tanzania Women Lawyers Association, the Environmental and Human Rights Care Organisation, as well as the Legal and Human Rights Centre.

Domestic Violence

High rates of spousal battery have been one by-product of poverty, recession, and economic hardship in the household. A survey between 1986 and 1993 indicated that about 60 percent of Tanzanian women reported physical abuse by a male partner.[20] The problem is greatest among communities where wife-beating is seen as socially acceptable and not subject to social sanction. Traditional acceptance does not diminish the physical and psychological harm women suffer. Women who take their grievances to the police find that their statements fall on unsympathetic ears: they are frequently told to withdraw their complaints, which means that most instances of such abuse go unreported.

Rape/Sexual Assault

Similarly, statistics on rape are not available due to social stigma attached to rape. As with battery, gender insensitivity among law enforcers and in the courts discourages women from reporting cases of rape. Related to rape and resulting from rape is the voluntary spread of HIV/AIDS by partners and particularly male partners who are aware of their condition and who deliberately force their partners to have sex or who rape young girls. This is one reason women and girls are more vulnerable to the HIV/AIDS epidemic than men and boys. Tanzanian women also experience other forms of violence, including the killing of older women on allegations of witchcraft, especially in the northwestern regions of the country, and the genital cutting of young girls in several regions as part of initiation ceremonies bringing girls into adulthood.

OUTLOOK FOR THE TWENTY-FIRST CENTURY

Women activists are convinced that Tanzania needs a new generation of leadership that is politically committed and gender sensitive. The new leaders should have an interest in the development of women and men. They should have an understanding of the dynamics of the global economy so as to maximize opportunities and minimize the risks and vulnerability of Tanzanians. Women leaders are assessing and analyzing levels and patterns of poverty in terms of its gendered nature and strategizing about how to mobilize additional resources to rebuild the economy and alleviate the disproportionate burden, which women are carrying. They are trying to generate new ideas that will accommodate diversities, and particularly the perspectives of women and poor men. Moreover, they are working within the legal arena to reform laws that act as a barrier to the promotion of gender equality.

For them the Tanzanian government has the primary responsibility of facilitating a legal and regulatory environment that will promote growth, social justice, and gender equality. They see that the government is legally bound to ensure that all citizens enjoy basic and fundamental rights, that all women and men are free from want and have opportunities to develop their intellectual and human capabilities to the full. Women are especially cognizant of the importance of land to their general welfare.

Women activists are also keen to see that women and men hold the country's leaders accountable. They are working to use the existing political situation to recruit leaders whom they can trust, and hold accountable. Tanzanian intellectuals have a specific responsibility of analyzing the processes, patterns and levels of poverty, human injustice, gender, and other forms of inequalities that have cumulatively contributed to the abject levels of poverty in this continent and the corresponding burden, which women are carrying. Such information will be useful planning and policy making tools as well as tools for lobbying and advocacy activities for promoting gender equality, human rights, and people-centered development programs. Finally, progressive elements in the north are playing a complementary role in supporting the various initiatives that are being directed at liberating the country from abject poverty, social injustice, and gender oppression. The responsibility of the networks in the north is to unveil exploitative practices by their respective governments and multinational corporations.

NOTES

1. One kilometer equals 0.6 miles.

2. Fenella Mukangara and Bertha Koda, *Beyond Inequalities: Women in Tanzania*, Salaam and Harara, Zimbabe: Southern Africa Research and Documentation Centre (SARDC), 1997, www.tgnp.co.tz.

3. TGNP, gender analysis of elections for the year 2000.

4. Friedrich-Ebert-Stiftung (FES), http://tanzania.fes-international.de, *NGO Calendar* (1998–2000). The figures have been quoted from FES and were calculated using the Atlas method.

5. Mukangara and Koda, *Beyond Inequalities*.

6. United Nations Development Programme (UNDP), *2002 Human Development Report*, http://hdr.undp.org.

7. Basic statistics on higher learning institutions in Tanzania, 1997/98–2000/01.

8. Burton Bollag, "An African Success Story at the U. of Dar es Salaam: University Is Seen As a Model for Its Ambitions and Reforms," *Chronicle of Higher Education* 47, no. 30 (April 6, 2001).

9. UNDP, *2002 Human Development Report*.

10. *Agricultural and Land Policy* (ALP) 1998, 3, UNDP, *2002 Human Development Report*.

11. UNDP, *2002 Human Development Report*.

12. Mukangara and Koda, *Beyond Inequalities*, 25.

13. Mukangara and Koda, *Beyond Inequalities*.

14. A. Manji, "Gender and the Politics of the Land Reform Process in Tanzania," *Journal of Modern African Studies* no. 36, 4 (December 1998): 645–67.

15. UNDP, *2002 Human Development Report*.

16. Mukangara and Koda, *Beyond Inequalities*, 55.

17. UNDP, *2002 Human Development Report*.

18. Ibid.

19. World Bank gender statistics, downloaded December 2001, www.worldbank.org/gender/.

20. Naomi Neft and Ann D. Levine, *Where Women Stand* (New York: Random House, 1997), 154.

RESOURCE GUIDE

Suggested Reading

Baylies, Carolyn, and Janet Bujra. *AIDS, Sexuality, and Gender in Africa: Collective Strategies and Struggles in Tanzania and Zambia*. London: Routledge, 2000.

Geiger, Susan. *TANU Women: Gender and Culture in the Making of Tanganyikan Nationalism, 1955–1965*. Portsmouth, NH: Heinemann, 1997.

Mbilinyi, Marjorie. "I'd Have Been a Man: Politics and the Labor Process in Producing Personal Narratives." In *Interpreting Women's Lives: Feminist Theory and Personal Narratives*. Bloomington: Indiana University Press, 1989.

Neft, Naomi, and Ann D. Levine. *Where Women Stand*. New York: Random House, 1997.

Rwebangira, Magdalena K., and Rita Liljeström, eds. *Haraka, Haraka . . . Look before*

You Leap: Youth at the Crossroad of Custom and Modernity. Stockholm: Nordiska Afrikainstitutet, 1998.

Swantz, M. L. *Women in Development: A Creative Role Denied?* London: C. Hurst and Company, 1985

Wright, Marcia. *Strategies of Slaves and Women*. New York: Lilian Barber Press, 1993.

Videos/Films

From Sun Up. Maryknoll World Video (Swahili with English subtitles). 1987. 28 min. Filmed in Tanzania "From Sun Up" shows the hard work of black African women.

Marriage of Miriamu. Tanzania Film and Ron Mulvihill (Swahili with English subtitles). 1983. 36 min. Portrays a young woman's struggle to regain her health with traditional healing.

These Hands. Directed by Flora M'mbugu-Schelling, Tanzania (Swahili and Kimakonde with English subtitles). 1992. 45 min. Follows Mozambican refugee women in Tanzania working in a gravel mine.

Women's Human Rights Education—Tanzania 1995. (English/Swahili). 10 min. Human rights education in Tanzania, by the Tanzania Women's Media Association (TAMWA). Email: pdhre@igc.org. Web site: www.pdhre.org/videoseries.html.

Web Sites

AllAfricanews.com, http://allafrica.com/tanzania.

Ministry of Community Development, Women, and Children, www.tanzania.go.tz/community.htm.

Tanzania Gender Networking Programme, www.tgnp.co.tz.

United Nations Women Watch—Tanzania, www.un.org/womenwatch/world/africa/tanzania.htm.

Organizations

Tanzania Gender Networking Project
P.O. Box 8921
Dar es Salaam, Tanzania
Phone: 255-022-2443205/2443450
Fax: 255-022-2443244
Email: tgnp@tgnp.co.tz

Tanzania Media Women's Association (TAMWA)
P.O. Box 8981
Dar es Salaam, Tanzania
Phone: 255-51-29089
Fax: 255-51-44939
Email: tamwa@raha.com

Tanzania Women Lawyers Association
P.O. Box 9460, Zanaki Street (Avalon Cinema)
Dar es Salaam, Tanzania
Phone: 255-022-110758
Fax: 255-022-113200
Email: tawla@raha.com

Union of Tanzania Women/Umoja Wa Wanawake Tanzania (UWT)
P.O. Box 825
Dodoma, Tanzania
Phone: 22-903-21-853

Women's Legal Aid Centre
P.O. Box 10463
Dar es Salaam, Tanzania
Phone: 256-41-113177
Fax: 256-41-113177

SELECTED BIBLIOGRAPHY

Manji, A. "Gender and the Politics of the Land Reform Process in Tanzania." *Journal of Modern African Studies* 36, no. 4 (December 1998): 645–67.

Mbilinyi, Marjorie. "Agribusiness and Women Peasants in Tanzania." *Development and Change* 19, no. 4 (October 1988): 549–83.

———. " 'This Is an Unforgettable Business': Colonial State Intervention in Urban Tanzania." In *Women and the State in Africa*, edited by J. L. Parpart and K. A. Staudt. Boulder: Lynne Rienner, 1989.

Meena, Ruth. "The Impact of Structural Adjustment Programs on Rural Women in Tanzania." In *Structural Adjustment and African Women Farmers*, edited by Christina Gladwin, 169–90. Gainesville: University of Florida Press, 1991.

Mercer, Claire. "The Discourse of Maendeleo and the Politics of Women's Participation on Mount Kilimanjaro." *Development and Change* 33, no. 1 (January 2002): 101–27.

Rwebangira, Magdalena K. *The Legal Status of Women and Poverty in Tanzania*. Uppsala: Institute of African Studies, 1996.

Tripp, Aili Mari. "The Impact of Crisis and Economic Reform on Women in Urban Tanzania." In *Unequal Burden: Economic Crises, Persistent Poverty, and Women's Work*, edited by Lourdes Beneria and Shelley Feldman, 159–80. Boulder: Westview Press, 1992.

———. "Political Reform in Tanzania: The Struggle for Associational Autonomy." *Comparative Politics* 32, no. 2 (January 2000): 191–214.

———. "Urban Women's Movements and Political Liberalization in East Africa." In *Courtyards, Markets, City Streets: Women in Urban Africa*, edited by Kathleen Sheldon, 285–308. Boulder: Westview Press, 1996.

———. "Women and the Changing Household Economy in Urban Tanzania." *Journal of Modern African Studies* 27, no. 4 (1989): 601–23.

20

TOGO

Jennifer Seely

PROFILE OF TOGO

Togo is a thin strip of West Africa bordered by Ghana on the west and Benin on the east. The country ranges from a tropical climate in the south to semiarid in the north. As much as 65 percent of the population works in the agricultural sector, including subsistence and cash crop farming (cocoa, coffee, and cotton). Togo has deposits of phosphates, used in fertilizer, which are a valuable resource. The remainder of the country's productive capacity is in services, including trade; Togolese women are very active in this sector. Togo is a poor country, where more than 30 percent of the 5 million people live below the poverty line. The population is growing by an estimated 2.6 percent each year, as women bear on average 5.32 children, and infant mortality stands at 70.43 deaths per 1,000 live births. There are an estimated 97 men for every 100 women in Togo, and life expectancy is just over 52 years for men and just over 56 years for women.[1] Togo's president, General Gnassingbé Eyadéma, has ruled the country since 1967, though many in Togo and in the international community have pressured him unsuccessfully to hold free and fair elections. Since the early 1990s Togo has endured political upheaval and international sanctions that have reduced living standards considerably.

OVERVIEW OF WOMEN'S ISSUES

Women in Togo have a history of mobilizing for their rights, but many instances of discrimination remain. Togolese women are more likely to be poor and uneducated than men, and family and community structures may favor the advancement of males over females. National laws protect many rights of women, but the laws are incomplete and in practice may be subordinated to customary laws. In the wake of political liberalization in the early 1990s, many women's organizations were formed to create awareness of women's problems and lobby for women's rights. This situation of women in Togo is improving thanks to their efforts, but political and economic troubles threaten to undermine progress.

EDUCATION

Opportunities

Togo has a policy of universal primary education, but has been more successful in educating boys than girls. Enrollment figures for 2000 showed that 74 percent of eligible boys but only 70 percent of eligible girls were enrolled in primary school. Enrollment figures for secondary school are lower, with 52 percent of eligible males enrolled, while only 40 percent of eligible females were enrolled in 2000.

Literacy

Inequality in access to education for girls is reflected in lower literacy rates, though literacy has improved over time. Overall illiteracy in the population went from as high as 93 percent in 1970 to about 57 percent by 2000, but adult literacy for women is only about 38 percent.[2]

EMPLOYMENT AND ECONOMICS

Women at farming school, Togo. Photo © TRIP/ASK IMAGES.

Farming

The agricultural sector is the largest source of employment for people in Togo, and women are very active in this sector. Women make up 56 percent of the rural sector, in part because they do not have the same level of formal education as men and other employment opportunities are denied them.[3] Within the rural sector, women may also be at a disadvantage because they are often marginalized in family and village decision-making, and do not often have collateral required for loans. Some grassroots organizations have sprung up to support women in agriculture, but relatively few women benefit from these organizations.

Paid Employment

According to 2001 United Nations Development Programme estimates, Togolese women's nonagricultural wages on average amounted to 47 percent of men's earned income.[4] In manufacturing, women are close to 30 percent of employees.[5] For the most part, Togolese women are employed in sectors that are considered traditionally female: commerce and food production and preparation.

Informal Economic Activities

It is estimated that women contribute about 46 percent of gross national product (GNP) in Togo, in part because much of the work women perform is statistically invisible, or outside the formal sector. The informal sector, including cottage industries, unregulated trade, black market activities, artisan enterprises, and prostitution is largely in the hands of women, who make up as much as 70 percent of informal sector activity.

Entrepreneurship

Togolese women have historically been very active in trade and commerce, and Togo's strategic port and easy land access to nearby markets in countries like Ghana, Benin, and Nigeria have opened up the opportunity for wholesale and commercial traders to make considerable fortunes. Colorful cloth is very popular for making clothing for men and women in West Africa, and the voluminous Togolese trade in "wax" patterns and other material has given rise to the legendary class of the Nana Benz (Auntie Benz). These market women controlled large quantities of cloth in the city of Lomé's market, Asigamé, and their reputation for being dropped off for work each morning in chauffeured Mercedes Benz cars earned them their name. The volume of trade controlled by the Nana Benz made them important politically. They were know to have lobbied Togo's government for favorable trade terms, and in return supported the regime of President Eyadéma from the 1960s. The power and influence of the Nana Benz has waned since the 1980s, when political and economic changes in Togo and neighboring countries introduced more competition into the regional textile market. Some Nana Benz were forced to put their cars into service as taxicabs when Togo fell on hard economic times in the 1990s. The so-called daughters of the Nana Benz still preside over the trade in cloth in Togo, and are not shy to use their clout when their livelihood is threatened. A new market structure on the outskirts of Lomé, Xédzran-awoé, has been built to reduce congestion in the city center, but the market women have refused to move their operations to the location with poor access to international roads.[6] Most Togolese women do not enjoy such high-profile employment, however.

Pay

When women do attain salaried positions in the formal sector, Togolese law does mandate that they receive equal pay to men. The civil servant salary scale is a matter of public record, and employees at each level receive the same pay whether male or female. However, relatively few women have been able to attain supervisory positions in either the public or the private sector, which offers the highest pay. With the exception of entrepreneurs like the Nana Benz, most Togolese women are economically disadvantaged with respect to men, and suffer from poverty more often than do men.

Inheritance, Property, and Land Rights

The Family Code, passed in 1980, specified the rights of women to inherit property. Under the law, a widow may inherit her husband's property only if she officially renounces any claim to customary law, which is rare. Customary law is therefore more likely to be followed in inheritance claims, and women in some ethnic groups have little protection under such practices.

FAMILY AND SEXUALITY

Gender Roles and Division of Labor

The situation of women in Togo begins at home among family, where there are often many children who must contribute to the household as well as prepare for life as adults. Often financial constraints dictate that only some children can attend school, or can attend beyond primary school. The children chosen for continuing education are often male. Girl children may remain at home to help care for other children and work on the family farm in rural settings, and may hawk wares on the street or go to work as a domestic servant in urban settings. Lacking education, girls have limited opportunities for advancement from an early age, though many may enjoy the opportunity to earn an income from trade, and may continue to pursue commerce into adulthood.

Marriage

Other family structures may limit opportunities for women, including the propensity of girls to marry young (often before age twenty), to marry in a traditional rather than civil ceremony, and to marry into polygynous households. State law does not always protect women in such marriages, and customary laws tend to favor male claims over female ones.

Reproduction

Population growth is fairly high in Togo, and women on average bear more than five children. In part this is due to the cultural benefits of large families, as well as the contribution children may make to household labor and to the support of parents in old age. As infant mortality declines and women's education improves, women in Togo may bear fewer children.

Contraception and Abortion

Access to contraception, as well as information available to women about their options, is limited. Only an estimated 23 percent of married Togolese women use some form of birth control, and the majority of these use a traditional method, such as the rhythm method or traditional medicines. Only about 7 percent of married women use more modern methods, including injectables, condoms, or birth control pills. These methods are available from private clinics as well as government-sponsored programs, but the expense and lack of awareness may prevent some women who would like to use modern contraception from doing so.

Abortion has an uncertain legal status in Togo, as there is no explicit law that addresses the practice. Abortions seem to be performed if they are necessary to save the life of the mother, but women are not officially permitted to have abortions in cases of rape or incest, or for concerns about the health of the fetus or mother. However, abortions have been performed at medical facilities for these reasons without prosecution.

Back-alley abortions are also performed in Togo, particularly on unmarried teenage girls, whose rates of pregnancy seem to be on the rise. Most teenagers who seek abortions do so because they do not wish to drop out of school. The Togolese government passed a law in the 1980s designed to punish men who impregnate teenage girls enrolled in school.

HEALTH

Health Care Access

The availability of health care services throughout Togo is uneven. Though the Togolese government made a push to improve health care in the late 1970s, the infrastructure tends to favor curative or hospital care over preventative or primary health care, and southern urban areas like the capital are much better served than rural areas. These biases are reflected in budgets, staffing, and the location of health facilities. These problems mean that the rural poor will tend to have the worst access to health care, and therefore women are underserved by Togo's health care system. The costs of transportation to and from a health center, when combined with the fee charged for services and the costs of prescribed medications mean that many families turn to traditional healers or local remedies for their health care needs. The cost of prescription medicine shot up after the devaluation of the African Financial Community (CFA) franc in 1994, prompting an increase in the informal trade of unpackaged pills in the local markets. Often entrepreneurs in this trade, generally women, have little reliable information about the indications or dosage for the medicines they sell.[7]

Limited access to professional health care affects women in pregnancy and childbirth, as well as the health of their children. Trained health personnel attend about half of the births in Togo, and only forty percent of pregnant women receive tetanus shots. Maternal mortality from 1990–1998 was 480 per 100,000 live births. Infant mortality has declined from 158 per 1,000 live births in 1960, to 80 per 1,000 live births in 1998.

Diseases and Disorders

There are many endemic diseases that affect the Togolese population, including malaria, which was considered the deadliest in 2002. The morbidity rate of this disease has remained consistent over time; from 1988 to 1997 about 34 percent of sufferers died each year.[8] Forty percent or fewer of one-year-olds received immunizations for polio, measles, and diphtheria during 1990–1998, whereas closer to 75 percent were vaccinated against tuberculosis. Between 20 and 25 percent of Togolese children from infants to five-year-olds are underweight, though most children are breastfed for nearly two years, providing an important source of nourishment.[9] However, children are particularly prone to diarrheal diseases and respiratory infections that also claim many lives in Togo each year.

AIDS

The incidence of tuberculosis is on the rise in Togo, but this is likely a result of the AIDS pandemic, which is the highest profile disease in Togo as in much of Africa. The figures for HIV/AIDS in Togo are only estimates, but close to 6 percent of the population may have been infected in 1999. Some 130,000 may be living with AIDS, including 66,000 women, and annually about 14,000 people die of the disease.[10] The AIDS patients put a considerable burden of care on an overtaxed health care system, and the number of children orphaned by the disease is on the rise. In Togo, as in other African countries, the family networks that formerly took responsibility for indigent relations are strained by the number of AIDS orphans, and the social stigma associated with HIV-positive relations can also prevent families from providing care for sufferers. For these reasons, the AIDS epidemic has had an impact beyond the mortality figures, and the situation is likely to get worse in the coming years.

Female Genital Cutting

Though the practice of female genital cutting is officially outlawed, it is still practiced by some ethnic groups in Togo. An estimated one in eight girls have some version of the procedure performed on them in childhood. This is somewhat lower than the rate in neighboring countries, but despite this, many Americans became aware of the problem of excision in Africa thanks to a Togolese woman who fled to the United States to avoid the procedure in 1994. Her highly publicized case became a landmark of United States immigration law with respect to genital cutting. Fauziya Kasinga, then age seventeen, had been protected by her father from the procedure, but after his death his relatives took control of the family and tried to force Kasinga to marry and undergo excision. Her mother and sisters helped her escape to the United States, where she asked for asylum. Instead, she spent fifteen months in prison before her story was told in the *New York Times*. The description of her poor treatment by the Immigration and Naturalization Service and prison officials provoked such outrage that she was released. Kasinga was ultimately awarded asylum and is the first such case in U.S. history. She and her lawyer collaborated on a book describing her experiences in Togo and in the United States.

Togo's National Assembly passed legislation outlawing female genital cutting in October 1998. The practice, however, remains largely in the realm of family or local tradition, and outside the scope of formal law enforcement. Some women's groups have undertaken awareness and education campaigns to highlight the dangers of the practice and to encourage opinion leaders, particularly in the central region of Togo, to change local customs.[11]

POLITICS AND LAW

Political Participation

Women are not yet well represented at the highest levels of government in Togo. At most times during the last decade women held one or two cabinet positions, often those related to health and family protection. In the eighty-one-member National Assembly elected in 2002, women hold only 6 seats (7.4 percent). As of 2000, only one of nine municipal mayors and one of forty-five municipal councilors were women. It is possible for women to form their own trade unions in Togo but activity in this area has been limited to organizations of domestic servants lobbying for a minimum wage.

Prior to Togo's political liberalization in the early 1990s, women's participation in government was channeled through the women's branch of the one legal party, the Togo's People's Assembly. When opposition groups made their push for democracy in 1991, the number of women's organizations exploded. With new freedoms of the press and association, women had new avenues to express their concerns. Groups of professional women, such as lawyers and merchants, became prominent, as well as groups raising awareness about women's rights. Beyond organizations oriented to women's concerns, the changes that came in the early 1990s improved the opportunities for individual political participation in general, and many women were able to take advantage of these opportunities, no matter what their agenda. Though President Eyadéma was able to reassert his power and remains president today, a new constitution was passed in 1992 that provided for greater participation of all groups. Many Togolese agree that though the political situation remains difficult, ordinary people have greater freedoms today than they did prior to the early 1990s.[12]

Women's Rights

Despite the low numbers of women in government, there have been several important pieces of legislation passed with reference to women's rights. The government undertook a family planning and population policy in 1975, though Togo's government in 2002 claims it is satisfied with the current rate of population growth. Another important document is the 1980 Family Code, which details laws related to women, children, and inheritance. In some ways, the code protects the rights of women, including their right to choose their husbands freely and to oppose a second polygamous marriage by their husbands. But in other areas it falls short of international conventions on women's rights like the Convention on the Elimination of All Forms of Discrimination Against Women, which Togo has ratified. The Family Code stipulates that the husband is the head of the household (Article 101), which poses a problem for Togolese households headed by women. This article also has an important effect on children, who inherit the nationality of the head of the household. In married households, a husband may forbid his wife to seek employment outside the home (Article 109).

Discrimination on the basis of gender is outlawed by Togo's 1992 constitution, but not all women are aware of their rights or feel that national government can offer them redress. In a small survey of about fifty women, 94 percent knew of national laws protecting women's rights, but felt that customary laws were predominant in the lives of most women. A vast majority cited ignorance of the laws, reluctance on the part of men and traditional authorities to change, and lack of specificity in the laws as reasons that women's rights were not more widely protected.[13]

Women's Movements

The history of activism by women in Togo includes several notable movements, including the "revolt" of the women merchants of Lomé in 1933 against new taxes imposed by the French colonial government. As one market woman recalled, "The house of Savi de Tové [a local leader] was sacked. The fetish women came from Bè to join the movement and bared their bottoms in broad daylight in his compound, to show their contempt; his wells were filled with garbage. That's how we punished Savi de Tové for his complicity with the [French] government."[14]

During that uprising, and again in the political upheaval of the early 1990s, Togolese women were moved to demonstrate for the release of prominent activists from prison. The mobilization of women at such times appears to have been designed to signal the extremity of the situation, as well as to deter security forces who might otherwise be prone to harsh repression. When police beat participants at a women's demonstration in March 1991 many local observers felt that Eyadéma's regime had discredited itself by stooping so low. Though women's activism channeled through associations is much more common, women in Togo do have a history of mobilizing to fight for their rights.

RELIGION AND SPIRITUALITY

Togo is a land of religious pluralism, where almost 30 percent of the population are Christian, and about 12 percent are Muslim. The remainder participates in traditional or indigenous belief systems, one of the best know is vodoun (or voodoo), practiced in the southern region of Togo, and also in neighboring Benin.

Women play an important role as vodoun priestesses (*mambo*), whose practices include animal sacrifice and spirit possession. Another religious role for women in Togo is that of intermediaries for the Mami Wata, which is a powerful and beautiful water spirit often depicted carrying serpents. Mami Wata followers are generally clad in long white garments and may assist people in contacting or appeasing the spirit.

VIOLENCE

Domestic Violence

Though many forms of violence against women are outlawed by Togo's penal code, some Togolese women continue to be victims of domestic abuse. Civil law prohibits a husband from abandoning his family, taking another wife against his current wife's will, or forcing female children to marry against their will: there is no specific law against adultery or incest.[15] There are no reliable statistics on the incidence of domestic violence, but a number of women's organizations do provide counseling and legal support for women who face an abusive relationship.

Rape/Sexual Assault

By law a man may not threaten, rape, or injure a woman. There are currently no explicit laws governing sexual harassment, adultery, pedophilia, and incest.[16] There are no reliable statistics on the incidence of rape, but a number of women's organizations do provide counseling and legal support for women.

Trafficking in Women and Children

In Togo, as in many West African countries, trafficking in women and children is often disguised as some form of employee training or apprenticeship. With the expense of formal education and a relatively high level of unemployment for graduates, many families view learning a trade or leaving home for wage labor as viable options for at least some of their children. Young girls may be put to work as domestic servants for a family which may purport to undertake girls' "education." It is more likely, however, that girls' parents will receive occasional payments, while girls are offered room and board but no schooling.[17]

Young women may also be coerced into prostitution with the promise of employment. Some groups of children have been intercepted as they were transported across national borders in West Africa, including Togo, apparently destined for work as plantation hands. International condemnation of such practices has prompted the authorities to crack down on such trafficking, but the demand for labor combined with the high number of children born to poor families suggests that the practice will persist while economic circumstances in Togo remain depressed.

OUTLOOK FOR THE TWENTY-FIRST CENTURY

Women in Togo face poverty and discrimination that undermine their quality of life and that of their children. However, larger issues like the political and economic difficulties of recent years mean that all Togolese, male and female, have concerns that must be addressed by government and aid organizations locally, nationally, and internationally. Establishing an inclusive political system and a secure base for economic activity are the first steps in improving the lives of women. The structural and organizational foundation of an equitable society has been laid, though some institutionalized biases against women, such as articles in the Family Act that favor men, need to be corrected. In many cases, however, the changes that will most benefit women will not take place in a legal setting, but in cultural or family practices. Togo is fortunate to have active women's organizations which have identified important concerns and are working to change attitudes and behaviors to the benefit of women. But as long as Togo is condemned internationally as undemocratic, international financial support will have trouble finding these groups: it is hoped that the twice-delayed Fall 2002 elections are the first step toward solving this problem. A weak domestic economy also means that local funds will be unavailable, and the Togolese people will be distracted from issues of gender equality by their concerns for basic survival. Without fundamental changes in the Togo's political and economic condition, the situation of women will remain inferior to that of men well into the twenty-first century.

NOTES

1. *CIA World Factbook: Togo*, www.cia.gov/cia/publications/factbook/geos/to.html.

2. Ibid.

3. "Bilan commun de pays," *System des Nations Unies au Togo*, 25 July 2000, www.pnud.tg.

4. United Nations Development Programme, www.undp.org/.

5. Ibid.

6. John Asamoah, "Togo: Quand les commercantes font la sourde oreille," *Jeune Afrique Economie* no. 215 (April 1996).

7. Dominique Seshie, "Togo: Pharmacies par terre et repression," *Jeune Afrique Economie* no. 229 (November 1996).

8. "Bilan commun de pays," 34.

9. Population Reference Bureau, *Togo: Demographic Highlights 2001*, www.prb.org.

10. Ibid.

11. "Genital and Sexual Mutilation of Females: CIAF-Togo Report on Consciousness Raising," *Women's International Network (WIN) News* 25, no. 3 (July 1999).

12. Based on interviews conducted by the author in Togo, 1998–1999. Jennifer C. Seely, "Transitions to Democracy in Comparative Perspective: The National Conferences in Benin and Togo" (Ph.D. diss., Washington University, 2001).

13. *Comprendre un peu plus les droits de la femme au Togo (Understand better the rights of women in Togo)*, CUSO-Togo, Lomé, 1998.

14. Silivi d'Almeida-Ékué, *La Révolte des Loméennes, 24–25 Janvier 1933* (Lomé: Les Nouvelles Éditions Africaines du Togo, 1992), 84.

15. *Guide pour la prise en charge des femmes victimes de violence (Guide for taking care of women who are victims of violence)*, WiLDF/FeDDAF, Lomé, n.d.

16. Ibid.

17. Dominique Seshie, "Togo: Comment en finir avec le travail des enfants," *Jeune Afrique Economie* no. 235 (February 1997).

RESOURCE GUIDE

Suggested Reading

Curkeet, Abigail Anne. *Togo: Portrait of a West African Francophone Republic in the 1980's*. Jefferson, NC: McFarland, 1993.

Kassindja, Fauziya. *Do They Hear You When You Cry?* New York: Delacorte Press, 1998. Moving account of a young woman who seeks asylum in the United States after fleeing the prospect of female circumcision in Togo. Also provides an excellent account of family life in Togo and of the vulnerability of women within a system of kin relations.

Packer, George, and Philip Gourevitch. *The Village of Waiting.* New York: Farrar, Straus & Giroux, 2001. Written by a Peace Corps volunteer serving in Togo, this book provides a view of village life from the perspective of an American schoolteacher.

Rosenthal, Judy. *Possession, Ecstasy, and Law in Ewe Voodoo.* Charlottesville: University Press of Virginia, 1998.

Videos/Films

God Gave Her a Mercedes Benz. 1992. Filmmakers Library (French with English subtitles). This documentary by Katia Forbert Petersen presents the story of one Nana Benz who sells cloth in Lomé's central market.

Women with Eyes Open (Femmes aux Yeux Ouverts). 1994. California Newsreel. Filmmaker Anne-Laure Folly is from Togo, and her film portrays the lives of West African women who are organizing and fighting for their rights.

Web Sites

Friends of Togo Fufu Bar, www.concentric.net/~jmuehl/togo.shtml.

Mami Wata Home Page, www.mamiwata.com.

Republic of Togo, www.republicoftogo.com/english/index.htm.

Republic of Togo Official Page, www.afrika.com/togo.

Organizations

Comité Nationale de la Santé des Femmes
B.P. 123
Sokodé, Togo

Affiliated with the Inter-African Committee (CIA) on traditional practices affecting the health of women and children in Africa. National Committee of Women's Health.

Commission des Droits de l'Homme et de la Condition de la Femme, Soroptimist International Club de Lomé
Adjoa S. Aquereburu, Coordinator
B.P. 423
Lomé, Togo

Organization of professional women devoted to maintaining a high level of morale among professional and businesswomen, as well as improving the Women's Statute and increasing access to education for all women, including handicapped women.

Groupe de Reflextion et d'Action Femme, Démocratie et Développement (GF2D)
Télé Amendah, Coordiantor
Foyer Pie XII—B.P. 14455
Lomé, Togo

Women providing services to women including legal advice and assistance and training in law and communications.

Union Nationale des Femmes Togolaises (UNFT)
Madame Aithnard, President
National Union of Togolese Women
Immeuble RPT
Lomé, Togo

Women's arm of the ruling party, designed to reinforce women's rights and promote the Women's Statute.

Women in Law and Development in Africa (WiLDAF)/Femmes, Droit et Developpment en Afrique (FeDDAF)
B.P. 7755
Lomé, Togo
Email: wildaf@cafe.tg

A pan-African nongovernmental organization designed to promote respect for women's rights in Africa, and to facilitate women's use of the law for purposes of development.

SELECTED BIBLIOGRAPHY

Bendokat, Regina, and Maurizia Tovo. *A Social Protection Strategy for Togo*. World Bank Social Protection Discussion Paper no. 9920. July 1999.

Population Reference Bureau. *Togo: Demographic Highlights 2001*. www.prb.org.

System des Nations Unies au Togo. *Bilan Commun de Pays*. July 2000. www.pnud.tg.

U.S. Department of State. *Togo Country Reports on Human Rights Practices 2001*. www.state.gov/g/drl/rls/hrrpt/2001.

World Bank. *Togo: Overcoming the Crisis, Overcoming Poverty*. World Bank Report no. 15526-TO. 25 June 1996.

21

UGANDA

Rebecca Mukyala

PROFILE OF UGANDA

Uganda is a landlocked country located in the East African Great Lakes region. It is bordered by the Democratic Republic of Congo to the west and Rwanda and Tanzania to the south. Kenya, the country's doorway to the coast and ocean-based trade, lies to the east, while the Sudan lies to the north. The country covers a surface area of 241,038 square kilometers and is endowed with extensive water bodies that include Lakes Albert and Edward on the western border with the Democratic Republic of Congo. To the south lies the biggest lake in the region, Lake Victoria, which is shared by the three East African countries of Uganda, Kenya and Tanzania. In the middle of Uganda lies Lake Kyoga. The Nile River is the most significant because of its economic potential. It traverses the country from the south in Lake Victoria through the Lakes Kyoga and Albert to Nimule in the Sudan, Egypt and finally to the Mediterranean Sea in northern Africa. These waters provide Uganda with hydroelectricity, for both domestic use and for export. And it is also a basis for the fishing and tourist industry.

The current total population of Uganda stands at an estimated

figure of about 25 million people, who are unevenly distributed throughout the country. Some districts, especially in the southern, western, central, and eastern regions, are generally more densely settled than the northern districts. This apparently is because the former regions enjoy a relatively well-developed economic base in addition to the relative peace for the last seventeen years under the National Resistance Movement regime. The current level of urbanization is very low. Only 14.2 percent of the population lives in the growing urban areas.[1] The infrastructure in most of these centers is poor and generally lacks amenable facilities.

There are a multiplicity of ethnic groups—around fifty-six in Uganda. The political salience of particular groups has been notable. Historically, political organization patterns differed remarkably with some ethnic communities having fully developed political organizational structures such as king and chiefdoms while others were organized groups of extended families, relating only through clan heads and leaders. The former category included the Buganda, Ankole, Toro and Bunyoro kingdoms, and the Busoga chiefdom.

The colonial administration modeled the present nation on the British prototype with variations following the Buganda political practice that allowed for indirect rule as a governance strategy. This put Buganda at the center of national politics, a position reinforced by its central geographic position and that has intermittently influenced the country's politics. The Ganda people make up 19 percent of the country's population, Ankole/Hima make up another 10 percent, Kiga 9 percent, and Soga 9 percent.

When the National Resistance Movement government took power in Uganda in 1986, the country's economic and social infrastructure had been laid to waste due to lack of maintenance and destructive civil wars. Most skilled personnel had fled the country. The agricultural sector, the mainstay of the economy, had declined precipitously, while industrial production was cut in half. The country had plunged into severe macro-economic imbalance. The new regime made an ardent pledge to promote equity through enabling hitherto disenfranchised groups to participate in politics. Hence, women, youth, workers, and persons with disabilities were given quotas in both legislative and administrative bodies at the national level and in local governing authorities up to the village local council. This encouraged those groups to participate in decision-making. Increasingly more women began to vie for elective positions.

Women constitute slightly above 51 percent of the nation's population. In relative terms, the country has had a high population growth rate of 3.4 percent per year. As of 2001, the total fertility rate was around 6.9 percent.[2] Consequently, the health status of the people is generally poor and the basic welfare indicators are discouraging. For example, the under-five mortality rate was 185 per 1,000 live births in 1970 and 64 per 1,000 live births in 2000–2001.[3] The infant mortality rate was 110 per 1000 in

1970, while it was 88 per 1000 in 2000–2001. Life expectancy at birth was 46.4 years and 42 years for the same periods respectively.

OVERVIEW OF WOMEN'S ISSUES

Despite Uganda's impressive political pronouncements on gender issues, the majority of the women in Uganda are yet to qualitatively benefit from the government's celebrated empowerment policies. An average Ugandan woman is still overburdened by work, illiteracy and the need for better medical treatment. In the rural areas, where the majority of the women reside, they are yet to make inroads into the oppressive predominantly male-controlled political system. Only a few women have made it to key positions in the local councils, especially at the sub-county and district levels.

Since 43 percent of women are illiterate, they are forced into limited social economic development opportunities, especially in rural areas. They labor primarily within the subsistence economy, while men control much of the cash economy. Hence women have limited opportunities to earn cash compared with men. Traditionally, men controlled women's access to productive assets, especially land. Moreover, incomes from the sale of crops and livestock are managed and controlled by men, as the presumed heads of households.

Women in the local government have the potential to make a big difference because the local governments are presently handling a lot of development funds and are planning and executing development projects. They are therefore important grounds from where gender equity could be promoted. Men continue to dominate these arenas with women settling for representative seats as secretaries for women and often appointed as vice chairpersons, or as members on the various sectoral committees.

EDUCATION

The current education system has evolved from the informal traditional indigenous education systems. Around the late 1880s, formal education was introduced: most schools were managed and owned by voluntary agencies, including the Christian missionary societies and Muslim communities, whose training focused on religious instruction for the faithful.

Opportunities

Education today is associated with increasing choices and opportunities for society, in terms of its potential to improve the quality of family life, health, nutrition, and to help lower maternal and child mortality rates and decrease birth rates. Education also improves a person's sense of security

Primary school class, Kampala, Uganda. Photo © TRIP/P. Joynson-Hicks.

by empowering individuals by providing knowledge of alternatives and hence an avenue in the reduction of personal vulnerability. It is therefore regarded as the single most important investment for developing countries.

The prospects of reversing this state of affairs are bleak. Even with the different opportunities in place through the Universal Primary Education Program, the overall primary school enrollment is biased against girls. Seventy-one percent of boys of schoolgoing age, as compared to 63 percent of girls, are enrolled in school. About 40 percent of the girls that are enrolled in school will drop out due to lack of adequate sanitary facilities and early pregnancy and sexual harassment by the teachers and peers of the opposite sex.[4]

To address gender imbalances in education, several innovative programs have been adopted that address the needs of girls and women, including:

Functional Adult Literacy for the adults;

Complementary Primary Education for the children who have faced setbacks and have had to drop out for periods of time in the educational cycle;

Alternative Basic Education for Karamoja, specifically instituted for the Karamoja region to address the needs of the pastoralists;

Child-centered Alternative for Nonformal Community-based Education for fishing communities and similar communities whose workday is not compatible with the formal routine of schools;

Basic Education in Urban Poverty Areas for the urban poor communities; and

Educational Assessment and Resources Services for the less privileged and especially persons with disabilities.

Regardless of all these privileged special groups, Universal Primary Education Program, instituted in 1997, is aimed in part at increasing educational opportunities for girls. At the tertiary level Makerere University, the largest university in Uganda, has instituted affirmative action for entering women to increase chances for female students to access higher education.

Finally, in some districts (e.g., Luwero), scholarship programs target exceptionally bright children who might fail to proceed to senior secondary school for lack of school fees.

Literacy

Although women manage development processes, their educational status is unfortunately lower than that of the men. Women's literacy rates are very low. Female adult literacy rate is around 57 percent, whereas the male adult literacy rate stands around 78 percent.

EMPLOYMENT AND ECONOMICS

Farming

The country's economic potential and its economic comparative advantage lies in agro-based ventures. Overall, the population in Uganda is agrarian. Agriculture contributes to 43 percent of the gross domestic product (GDP) and 90 percent of the country's exports (1999). It is a source of livelihood for 85 percent of population who live in rural areas as peasant farmers. However, there is a high potential for minerals, mainly copper, limestone, volcanic ash, iron ore, cobalt, and of recent, petroleum. Investors have expressed interest in this sector.

Although the economy has registered encouraging leaps in growth over the last decade, poverty at the household level remains glaring. Women remain the majority of the agricultural workforce (71 percent). One of the key constraints for women in the economy, especially in the agricultural sector, is their lack of household decision-making authority concerning assets such as agricultural land and produce. Even when women are cultivating on their own, it is the husband who generally decides on the use of the proceeds from her fields. As women are frequently the ones charged with overseeing the family's well being, agricultural, livestock, and fisheries development will have less of an impact until women are able to gain more power in household decisionmaking.

Paid Employment

The employment status of a woman depends on where she lives, whether she is married, and how many children she has. One is more likely to find divorced, separated and/or widowed women employed than married women. There also are more employed women in rural areas than in urban areas. This can be explained by women's different skills. While in the rural areas one is able to find a variety of job opportunities without formal skills, this is less likely in urban areas.

Informal Economic Activities

Most women (63 percent) are self-employed. Women constitute the majority of the workers in the informal sector, selling in markets and on the streets as food vendors. About 28 percent work for a relative and 9 percent work for a nonrelative. Most of these women work in the informal economy that is untaxed, unlicensed, and unregulated.

Entrepreneurship

A growing number have ventured into bigger business as exporters and importers of merchandise especially from Dubai, but also Kenya, Thailand, and other countries. These women traders have been subjected to rough times, being maligned by their business rivals as women who go for prostitution instead of trading. This has caused them a lot of stress and even affected their familial relations. Today there are also women who have ventured into big business and into the manufacturing industries, making shoes and other products.

Pay

A substantial number of women (35 percent) work for both cash and in-kind payments. Only 27 percent work for cash only; 29 percent are not paid, and 9 percent get paid in kind only (2000). The government has given women the opportunity to develop substantial economic resources of their own and to attain high renown as political leaders.

Support for Mothers/Caretakers

Maternal Leave

Women working in the formal sector—both public and private—are entitled to forty-five days maternity leave after delivery. This luxury of maternal leave is out of reach of their counterparts in the agricultural and informal sectors, as well as for domestic workers.

Child Care

Vital statistics about child care and support are not easily obtained. It is still notable, however, that the welfare of children is tied to the welfare of women and where the well being of women is compromised, that of the children is generally also violated. Child care continues to be the most basic domestic responsibility of women. A limited number of organizations are involved in caring for disadvantaged children, like the Young Women Christian Association. There are also some nursery schools in the growing urban centers, but affordability and access make them out of reach for most parents.

For women working in the public sector, there are hardly any daycare facilities at their places of work or in their neighborhoods. For those in the informal sector, the situation is even worse. Children are frequently found in markets alongside their mothers' merchandise. And in markets where limited space restricts movement, children are sometimes tethered on ropes or strings by their mothers to prevent them from wandering off while the mother is busy attending to customers. In other restricted Kampala City Council markets children are hidden in merchandise boxes.

Inheritance, Property, and Land Rights

Inheritance, property, and land rights are still cast in the traditional cultural realm, which is biased against women. Often themselves regarded as part of men's property, most women do not inherit or have property rights. Land is the most important resource in Uganda because people depend on it for cultivation, hence their livelihood, yet women own only 7 percent of land. The majority of the women in rural areas enjoy only user rights on the land they cultivate. Women are generally dependent on men to access that land.

In patrilineal societies, women generally do not inherit land. Fathers will not bequeath land to their daughters because girls will marry outside the clan, taking the land with them to another clan. Husbands often do not bequeath land to their wives for the same reason.

Although various pieces of legislation have the potential to help women obtain rights to property, traditional cultural values still dictate practice. Control of land and also positions of political authority are exclusive prerogatives of men in which women are conceived as inferior. Key legislative changes regarding women's access to land through common property arrangements were denied and the Domestic Relations Bill that would improve women's property rights has been stalled.

Social/Government Programs

Gender Budgets

Uganda, Tanzania, and South Africa have been leaders in developing African gender budgets and analyzing national budgets for gender impact. The concept of a gender budget introduces the idea of harmonizing development plans and policies in order to engender a responsive address to the needs of the intended beneficiaries of the development policies. In gender budgets, development resources are sensitively allocated so that the differential impacts of budgets on communities and people (rich women/ men, girls/boys, persons with disability, the poor, and other marginalized groups) are equitable. This is possible because gender budgets expose the gendered nature of the economy and economic decisionmaking and work to transform the plans and budgetary processes so that the delivery of public goods and services is equitable. Various women's organizations like the Forum for Women in Democracy (FOWODE) have been studying the government's budget in order to make recommendations toward tailoring it to better serve the interests of women and other economically marginalized groups.

FAMILY AND SEXUALITY

Most families are extended in nature, encompassing relatives such as cousins, nephews, uncles, aunts and grandparents. Although in some cases the family institution is being transformed into a more nuclear unit, the visible activity of the extended family continues to influence the organization of all the social, economic and political realms of society in Uganda, and this may remain so for the next couple of decades.

The extended family unit still serves as a shock absorber in periods of political turmoil and civil strife that have negatively impacted the economy. The extended family remains the most important productive and reproductive unit. It is as well the primary survival structure of last resort, ensuring the survival of orphans, widows and people in dire need of support, especially in periods of civil unrest and unprecedented death rates due to the HIV/AIDS epidemic. In recent years, however, the extended family has come under strain due to increasing demands being placed on relatives due to poverty and the HIV/AIDS crisis.

Gender Roles and Division of Labor

At the household level, the ability of women to control their life is highly curtailed. Many women, for example, cannot make decisions about their own health care. Only 44 percent are able to decide when to seek health care while 38 percent will wait for their husbands to give them approval. They cannot decide on the purchase of large properties, especially assets like land. Only 11 percent will determine alone when to make large household purchases and 53 percent of the men decide on the regular household purchases. Recent studies reveal that 83 percent of women decide on the meals they eat.[5] It is men who frequently decide when women can visit their families and friends and if women can attend associational meetings, thereby regulating women's social life.

Even unmarried women are curtailed in these respects. Only 46 percent will decide on their own when to see a health care provider and 42 percent have someone, such as a male relative, who decides for them.[6] Overall, only one in every four women has some say on their welfare. As a rule, older women have more say than the young females, especially those between fifteen and nineteen years of age.

Marriage

In marriage, a Ugandan woman can elect to marry according to any of the four sets of rules: civil, Christian, traditional/customary, and Islamic/shari'a law. The most restrictive regime for women's rights are the customary and shari'a laws that regulate Muslim marriages.

Reproduction

Family planning is not widespread. The situation is made worse by a culture that prizes large numbers of children of both sexes. A mother who begets only boys, for example, will try until she has an equal number of both sexes. Inheritance through male lineage and the practice of polygamy tends to encourage competitive reproduction among women so that they obtain equal access to the "husband's estate."

Contraception and Abortion

About 70 percent of Ugandan women surveyed have favorable attitudes regarding family planning, however, only 23 percent of women in their childbearing years are currently using contraceptives.[7] This is because the incentive to use contraceptives is low, as is awareness about what is available, and access to reproductive technologies is difficult.

The rules on sexuality are enshrined in the various Ugandan cultures through traditional and patriarchal norms, values and practices. The different communities still wield the power to protect these values. Thus men generally make decisions about when and with whom to have sex. Two-thirds of married women will only refuse sex when they suspect that their husband has a sexually transmitted infection; has had sexual intercourse with other women; and when the woman has just delivered, is not in the mood or is tired.[8] A mere 4 percent said one could refuse without reason. Ninety percent of the respondents said that sexually transmitted infections and recent delivery were the most important reasons for refusing sex.

HEALTH

Health Care Access

The country's health infrastructure is still poor. The system comprises referral hospitals, subdistrict hospitals, health centers, dispensary/maternity units, and clinics. Overall, the system is structured into three tiers; a referral tier, district tier, and the subdistrict health centers. The Ministry of Health manages the referral tier, while the Directorate of District Health Services runs the lower tiers.

The day-to-day management of the health system falls under government and nongovernment organizations (NGOs), mainly religious/mission based bodies, which operate on private non-profit basis. The government controls around 40 percent of the system, providing up to 60 percent of clinical facilities. The remaining 60 percent are operated by the NGO sector, delivering 40 percent of clinical services. The NGOs are known for greater staff productivity and capacity utilization.

The private sector has also begun to enter the health field, especially in the capital city of Kampala, where approximately four privately run hospitals have been started. There are, however, a substantial number of privately managed clinics and drug shops scattered throughout the country.

There is a generalized lack of highly qualified personnel in most health units, with the overwhelming majority of the workforce (60 percent) made up of either nurses' aides, and/or other apprentice health workers. The delivery of health services of the basic primary/preventive health care to the communities primarily relies on the support of functionaries constituted by the community health workers and traditional birth attendants who have been trained as a move to augment better service delivery.

Diseases and Disorders

Three-quarters of the health system is curative. Preventive and public health measures are relatively limited due to insufficient budgetary provisions, even though preventive care would greatly reduce the high mortality rates, mostly due to communicable diseases. About 70–80 percent of the people suffer from preventable diseases like HIV/AIDS, tuberculosis, malaria, pneumonia, and diarrhea. The most common illnesses listed in order of prevalence include malaria, respiratory tract infection/pneumonia, tuberculosis, diarrhea, anemia, HIV/AIDS, meningitis, malnutrition, tetanus and trauma.

Maternal health indicators are disheartening. Maternal mortality stands at 505 deaths per 100,000 women. Nine out of ten (91 percent) expectant mothers receive antenatal care; only 9 percent are able to have the attention of a doctor.[9] It is common to find that an expectant mother is receiving antenatal care from both the modern and traditional caretakers simultaneously. Most deliveries (62 percent) take place outside of a health facility and only 10 percent of women receive postnatal care.

AIDS

HIV, the virus that causes AIDS is a nascent health, reproductive and security problem, emerging as the fourth leading cause of mortality in the country. However, there is still social stigma attached to HIV/AIDS, which renders voluntary reporting difficult.

POLITICS AND LAW

Political Participation

The policy and regulatory environment in Uganda has improved considerably in favor of women. The Ministry of Gender, Labor, and Social Development notes that out of 17,000 persons in strategic decisionmaking positions in Uganda, 39 percent are women. This compares positively with the 1988 figures when women represented a dismal 6 percent of legislators, managers and other decisionmakers combined. The presence of women in the decisionmaking arenas has enabled their voices to be heard in policy circles. Women also made important contributions to the 1995 constitution-making process, both in influencing and drafting the new constitution.

Until the mid-1980s women's involvement in "politics" was minimal other than as voters. For example, in 1980 there was only one woman member of parliament. After 1986, the government adopted an affirmative action policy that ensured that women were represented in every elected body from the lowest political organization in the villages to the highest legislative body, the parliament. This arrangement has been enshrined in the 1995 constitution and was further strengthened by the enactment of the Local Government Act of 1997, which provides for the continued and wider devolution of administrative and managerial powers to village communities. Women hold one third of the seats in local councils.

Women can stand for parliamentary seats in each of the 53 districts on a women-only ticket as well as on the open constituent ticket. Although many look at this arrangement as a way to enable women to get the experience to stand for the open seats in parliament, others have seen the women's seats as a way to prevent women from directly vying for power in a man's world. At the local levels, women who defy the social expectations to dare on the men's seats have been ridiculed.[10] Women now hold 25 percent of all seats in parliament and 26 percent of all cabinet positions. They hold 44 percent of all civil service posts in the Public Service Commission, 12 percent of the nonpolitical decisionmaking positions at the national levels, and 14 percent in the central government decisionmaking positions. Altogether, women constitute 57 percent of political and civil service decisionmakers at the district level. In relative terms women are more represented in local governments with 42 percent of the political leadership especially at the subcounty level.[11]

The judicial sector has the highest levels of female representation in the nonpolitical service in which women hold 25 percent of all positions in the Court of Appeals, 26 percent in the High Court, and represent 30 percent of chief magistrates.

Enormous constraints remain for women in leadership. Patriarchal values dictate that the public realm is for men only. Many husbands will not permit their wives to run for office or to participate in political meetings, fearing it will detract from their work in the home and their roles as mothers and wives. Additionally, socialization has inhibited women from vying for political positions, especially involving competition with men. And this is aggravated by the lack of professional and educational qualifications among women.

Women's Rights and Women's Movements

The basis of the legal framework for women's emancipation is the Convention on the Elimination of All Forms of Discrimination against Women (CEDAW), to which Uganda is a signatory. Article 10 of the convention guarantees equal rights between women and men in all realms of social life. Equal rights have been advanced through the government's Gender Policy and have been reiterated in all other important policies and legal instruments such as the Republic of Uganda's 1995 constitution, the 1997 Local Government Act, and in all sectoral policies and programs.

While the government has made positive efforts to promote women's leadership, women themselves have also been active in pressing for leadership roles and to improve the status of women. Women have come together to address virtually every area of concern through internationally affiliated organizations like the Forum for African Women Educators (Uganda), Uganda Women Lawyers and locally initiated national organizations like Uganda Women Efforts to Save Orphans, the National Community of Women Living with AIDS, Action for Development, Forum for Women in Democracy and the National Association of Women Organizations in Uganda. The Kitgum Concerned Women Association is an outgrowth of Concerned Parents' Association of Kitgum dealing with reception, psychological support, and reintegration of children into their families after being abducted by the northern warlord Joseph Kony and his Lord's Resistance Army. Women also belong to professional associations of lawyers, doctors, engineers, businesswomen and other organizations aimed at improving the status of women in these fields. In addition to these organizations there are community-based women's organizations involving the average Ugandan woman that are engaged in collective farming, savings, income-generating projects, marketing of produce and goods, literacy and other educational activities, as well as cultural and sports activities.

The women's movement is still in its nascent stages in Uganda. Nevertheless, women have made their mark on the political and social economic scene of the country and women today are visible in public office, in the military, and in virtually every sector, especially the private sector. Women are excelling in educational and professional achievements.[12] Citizens are aware of the need for gender equality. Many are moving away from focusing on modeling good housewives to agitating for the provision of social welfare and social equity.

Aware of the importance of the press to their future, women have learned to maintain cordial relationships with the press. This has paid off, as evident in the mass media, where progressively women's images have shifted from negative to positive press coverage. The views of women leaders on national and other issues are now presented more favorably in the most popular dailies. There is a "Women Vision" pullout in every Wednesday *New Vision Daily*, which has unearthed violence against women and is changing societal attitudes from negative to sympathy and respect. It also draws attention of high authority to the oppression of women in the peripheral social niches. For example, the rape and forced marriage of a virgin was recently exposed and a presidential directive was issued to bring the perpetrators to book.[13]

Men have more access to mass media than women, especially the radio. Recent statistics report that three out of every four people in the population—more men than women—listen to radio only once a week.[14] About 24 percent of men, compared to 15 percent of women read a newspaper. Women have learned to promote their cause by establishing magazines (*Women Arise* by ACFODE), founding a radio station (Radio Mama), and founding an association for journalists and writers (the Uganda Association of Media women/UMWA and FEMRITE). All are aimed at championing the women's cause, promoting their political actions in society, and selling their views to society.

RELIGION AND SPIRITUALITY

About 45 percent of Ugandans are Catholic, 39 percent are members of the Anglican Church of Uganda (Episcopalian), and 11 percent are Muslim.

Women's Roles

Historically, women in Uganda played important roles as priestesses, spirit mediums, and religious specialists. With the coming of Christianity and Islam, women lost many of these leadership roles even though women are very active in the laity and in church-related women's organizations like the Protestant Mother's Union and the Uganda Muslim Women's Association.

While the Church of Uganda has fifty women clergy, they do not hold high-ranking positions and are generally relegated to the role of assistant parish priest or pastor. Women cannot be ordained as priests in the Catholic Church. Various orders of sisters, like the Bannabikira Sisters, have been pioneers in the area of girls' education and have sought to increase opportunities for girls and encourage them to use their educational opportunities to advance themselves. Other sisters serve in hospitals and dispensaries as administrators, nurses, midwives, and as laboratory technicians. While the church has generally failed to draw on the leadership skills even of sisters who have obtained their Ph.D.s, some nuns have served leadership roles in other capacities. For example, Sr. Margaret Magoba, a former headmistress of Sacred Heart High School in Rukungiri District, was appointed by Uganda's president to head the Electoral Commission in Kampala District.

Women in both Protestant and Catholic churches are today actively pressing to expand their leadership roles.[15] Therese Tinkasimire, a Catholic sister and head of the Department of Religious Studies at Makerere, has called on African Catholic Bishops to act on their belief that men and women are equal before God. Tinkasimire wrote:

> At the Parish level, the priest or pastor and his curate and all the immediate subordinates are men. The Parish council, where all the decisions are made, is comprised of ninety percent men. Ironically, the implementors of these decisions are women. Going up the ladder to the Diocesan level, the situation becomes even worse. There are no women representatives on the Diocesan Council. In some Dioceses, the Bishop dictates to women what they are supposed to do. . . . Catholic women would like to be admitted into the inner circles of church ministry. . . . As it is now, the gifts and talents of women are not being fully utilised by the church.[16]

VIOLENCE

Domestic violence, rape and other forms of violence against women and girls have been key issues taken up by almost all major women's rights organizations in Uganda, which have addressed the issues by providing counseling services, carrying out advocacy and seeking legislative changes, and by providing legal aid.

Domestic Violence

Domestic violence is rampant in Uganda as it is elsewhere in the world. A 1997 survey of women in the Lira and Masaka districts found that among women aged twenty to forty-four, over 41 percent faced domestic violence in their current relationships.[17] Wife abuse is related to women's lack of power within the household and the husband's dominance. Women who challenge male authority in the home increase their risk of being beaten or threatened with physical violence. Even though Uganda is a leader in enacting laws that criminalize domestic and sexually related violence, women do not always have the resources to seek shelter from their abusers or to take them to court nor do women always want to bring their cases to court. Beating is seen as a man's prerogative, which makes law enforcement reluctant to intervene. Similarly, delays in bringing capital offense cases to trial in situations where a husband killed his wife remain common.

Rape/Sexual Assault

Police and court records indicate that cases of defilement (statutory rape of girls under the age of consent) are increasing at alarming rates. The Commissioner General of Prisons indicated that 4,000—or 38 percent—of capital cases during 2001 were defilement cases.[18] Many of these men prey on girls with the belief that girls under the age of consent are free of the HIV virus. Although defilement carries a maximum sentence of death, this punishment has never been set for a convicted rapist.

War and Military Repression

A significant number of women and girls have also been victims of abduction and rape by rebels of the Lord's Resistance Army (LRA) in the northern part of the country, where the LRA has been fighting government forces. Some have been taken as sex slaves, forced into marriages, and infected with sexually transmitted diseases as a result of rape.

OUTLOOK FOR THE TWENTY-FIRST CENTURY

The general outlook regarding the status of women in Uganda borders on hope and skepticism. Although the government has to a large extent demonstrated its willingness to promote gender equity, the seemingly immutable cultural traditions that call on women to remain in the domestic sphere continue to frustrate these efforts. The fact that large numbers of women remain uneducated further limits their chances to take advantage of the woman-friendly political environment.

Much will depend on the more general political environment in Uganda and whether peace and stability can be maintained within a framework of political liberalization. The challenges of the upcoming period call for unrelenting and undivided focus by the government in promoting genuine participation of women in critical policymaking bodies. There is also need to deepen structural reforms, particularly in the financial and state managed business sectors, and to build up an effective public service delivery system especially at the local governing levels.

Policymakers and implementers will have to promote genuine participation of women. Women are coming to recognize that their advantage is in numbers. If women compromise 51 percent of the adult population, they have an edge over the men in this regard. If women take a greater interest in public office, they may feature even more prominently in politics. Many grassroots women believe that women need to be in the executive to have an impact.

Women remain constrained by customary practices, religious beliefs, illiteracy and a lack of political awareness. However, the trends suggest that the stage has been set for women's advancement as more women are accessing education, improving their economic circumstances and seeking political office.

NOTES

1. United Nations Development Programme (UNDP), *Human Development Report 2002*, http://hdr.undp.org.

2. Uganda Demographic and Health Survey (UDHS) 2000–2001, www.ubos.org/newudhs.html.

3. UNDP, *Human Development Report 2002*; UDHS 2000–2001.

4. *Women and Men in Uganda: Facts and Figures 1999*, www.Uganda.co.ug/misr.

5. Food and Agriculture Organization of the United Nations, (FAO), "IFAD's Gender Strengthening Programme for East and Southern Africa," *Uganda Field Diagnostic Study (Draft)* (Rome, 2000).

6. Ibid.

7. UDHS 2000–2001.

8. Ibid.

9. Ibid.

10. *Women and Men in Uganda: Facts and Figures 1999*.

11. *Women and Men in Uganda: Facts and Figures 2000*, www.uganda.co.ug/misr.

12. Aili Mari Tripp, *Women and Politics in Uganda* (Madison: University of Wisconsin Press, 2000).

13. *New Vision Daily*, www.newvision.co.ug. *The Monitor*, www.monitor.co.ug.

14. UDHS 2000–2001.

15. Sister Therese Tinkasimiire, "Women's Contributions to Religious Institutions in Uganda (1962–2001)," in *The Women's Movement in Uganda: History, Challenges, and Prospects*, eds. Aili Mari Tripp and Joy Kwesiga (Kampala: Fountain, 2002).

16. Therese Tinkasimire, "Women in Decision-Making Within the Catholic Church in Uganda," *Arise* 18 (July–September 1996): 12–13.

17. Center for Health and Gender Equity, "Ending Violence Against Women" Series L, no. 11, *Issues in World Health* 27, no. 4 (December 1999), www.jhuccp.org/pr/11/violence.pdf.

18. UN OCHA Integrated Regional Information Network, "East Africa: Special Report on Violence Against Women," IRIN News Service, Nairobi, 8 March 2002.

RESOURCE GUIDE

Suggested Reading

Behrend, Heike. *Alice Lakwena and the Holy Spirits: War in Northern Uganda, 1986–97.* Oxford: James Currey, 1999.

Hanson, Holly. "Queen Mothers and Good Government in Buganda: The Loss of Women's Political Power in Nineteenth Century East Africa." In *Women in African Colonial Histories*, edited by Jean Allman, Susan Geiger, and Nakanyike Musisi, 219–36. Bloomington: Indiana University Press, 2002.

Snyder, Margaret. *Women in Africa Economies: From Burning Sun to Boardroom*. Kampala: Fountain, 2000.

Tamale, Sylvia. *When Hens Begin to Crow: Gender and Parliamentary Politics in Uganda*. Boulder: Westview Press, 1999.

Tripp, Aili Mari. *Women and Politics in Uganda*. Madison: University of Wisconsin Press, 2000.

Videos/Films

The Cutting Edge: Uganda. 1996. 10 min. A short film that profiles the success of the REACH project in Uganda. REACH offers young women an alternative to the genital cutting initiation into womanhood.

I Have a Problem, Madam. 1995. 59 min. Maarten Schmidt and Thomas Doebele. Ugandan women are helped with their legal problems by female lawyers involved in FIDA-Uganda.

Mama Wahunzi. Lawan Jirasuradej. 2001. 57 min. Thailand United States. Subtitled. Available from www.wmm.com/index.htm *Mama Wahunzi* (literally "women blacksmiths" in Swahili) is a documentary video about three Ugandan and Kenyan women who are handicapped. They meet at a metal workshop sponsored by the American organization Whirlwind Wheelchairs International. They learn wheelchair-building skills and eventually become entrepreneurs. The film shows how they combat stereotypes of disability, gender and poverty.

Web Sites

Bibliography of Research on Uganda Women 1986–2001, www.wougnet.org/documents.html.

Department of Women and Gender Studies, Makerere University, www.makerere.ac.ug/womenstudies/index.htm.

Essay on women's art in Uganda, www.theartroom-sf.com/trippessay.htm.

United Nations Women Watch profile of Uganda, www.un.org/womenwatch/world/africa/uganda.htm.

Women of Uganda Network, www.wougnet.org/.
Links to women's organizations in Uganda, reference material, and other information pertaining to women in Uganda.

Organizations

Action for Development (ACFODE)
P.O. Box 16729
Kampala, Uganda
Email: acfode@starcom.co.ug

Action for Development is a nonprofit devoted to improving the "professional, personal, legal, economic, and educational status of women."

Association of Uganda Women Lawyers—FIDA(U)
P.O. Box 2157
Kampala, Uganda
Phone: 256-41-530848
Fax: 256-41-530848
Email: fidauganda@africaonline.co.ug

Legal aid for women, children and other marginalized groups.

Disabled Women in Development (DIWODE—Uganda)
P.O. Box 2154
Kampala, Uganda
Phone: 256-77-385601
Email: diwode98@hotmail.com
Web site: www.users.anytimenow.com/diwode_web

DIWODE educates the public about disability and helps disabled women economically.

Forum for Women in Democracy (FOWODE)
P.O. Box 7176
Kampala, Uganda
Phone: 256-41-540241/2
Fax: 256-41-540243
Email: fowode@utlonline.co.ug
Web site: www.nic.ug/fowode

FOWODE works toward gender equality through advocacy, training research, and publishing.

National Association of Women Organisations in Uganda (NAWOU)
P.O Box 1663
Kampala, Uganda
Phone: 256-41-258463/257730
Fax: 256-41-345293
Email: nawou@uol.co.ug
Web site: www.nawou.interconnection.org

NAWOU promotes a network of women organizations.

Uganda Media Women's Association (UMWA)
P.O. Box 7263
Kampala, Uganda

Phone: 256-41-543996/256-77-469363
Fax: 256-41-543996
Email: umwa@swiftuganda.com
Web site: www.interconnection.org/umwa

UMWA is a media forum to promote women's rights and those of other marginalized people.

Uganda Women Entrepreneurs Association (UWEAL)
P.O. Box 10002
Kampala, Uganda
Phone: 256-41-343952
Fax: 256-41-257177

Uganda Women's Network (UWONET)
P.O. Box 27991
Kampala, Uganda
Phone: 256-41-543968
Fax: 256-41-543968
Email: uwonet@starcom.co.ug

SELECTED BIBLIOGRAPHY

Musisi, Nakanyike. "The Politics of Perception or Perception as Politics? Colonial and Missionary Representations of Baganda Women, 1900–1945." In *Women in African Colonial Histories*, edited by Jean Allman, Susan Geiger, and Nakanyike Musisi, 95–115. Bloomington: Indiana University Press, 2002.

———. "Women, 'Elite Polygyny,' and Buganda State Formation." *Signs* 16, no. 4 (1991): 757–86.

Sorensen, Penilla. "Commercialization of Food Crops in Busoga, Uganda, and the Renegotiation of Gender." *Gender and Society* 10, no. 5 (October 1996): 608–28.

Tinkasimire, Therese. "Women in Decision-Making Within the Catholic Church in Uganda." *Arise* 18 (July–September, 1996): 12–13.

Tripp, Aili Mari. "The Politics of Autonomy and Cooptation in Africa: The Case of the Ugandan Women's Movement." *Journal of Modern African Studies* 39, no. 1 (March 2001): 101–28.

———. "Women's Mobilization in Uganda (1945–1962): Non-Racial Ideologies within Colonial-African-Asian Encounters." *International Journal of African Historical Studies* 35, no. 1 (2002): 1–22.

Uganda Bureau of Statistics (UBOS). *Uganda Demographic and Health Survey, 2000–2001*. www.ubos.org/newudhs.html.

Wallman, Sandra, in association with Grace Bantebya-Kyomuhendo et al. *Kampala Women Getting By: Wellbeing in the Time of AIDS.* London: James Currey, 1996.

22

ZIMBABWE

Mary J. Osirim

PROFILE OF ZIMBABWE

Zimbabwe (formerly known as Rhodesia or Southern Rhodesia) is a land-locked nation in southern Africa with a population of approximately 12.5 million people. Under the auspices of the British South Africa Company, Cecil Rhodes, in an effort to discover gold in southern Africa, led over 500 men from South Africa into what was then known as "Zambesia" and established a new British colony in 1890.[1] At the time, there were two major black African ethnic groups resident in the area—the Shona- and Ndebele-speaking peoples. Despite attacks by the Shona and Ndebele populations in the late 1890s, the British established a race-based system of stratification, designated the most arable land for white settlers and banished black Africans to the least desirable land. The Land Apportionment Act of 1930 codified these policies and gave the majority of the land to the white minority thereby effectively restricting blacks to the rural reserves and limiting their access to the cities.

British rule became particularly harsh under Ian Smith, who in 1965 issued a Unilateral Declaration of Independence from Britain. The situation became quite intolerable for blacks who took

up arms in 1969 in a bitter liberation struggle in which women and men fought against the Smith regime. The Lancaster House Agreement in 1979 ended the war with the Zimbabwe African National Union under the leadership of Robert Mugabe and the Zimbabwe African People's Union under the leadership of Joshua Nkomo representing the majority of black Africans in the negotiations. After ninety years of colonial rule, Zimbabwe emerged as an independent nation in April 1980 with Mugabe as head of state.

Today, Zimbabwe is a multiracial society with a black majority government but where whites still control much of the formal sector of the economy. Although the Mugabe regime appeared to be aspiring to establish a socialist economy in the first postindependence decade, by 1990 it had clearly adopted a market-oriented approach. Throughout the postindependence period, Zimbabwe remained dependent on agricultural exports for much of its foreign exchange, with tobacco as the number one export constituting 29 percent of foreign exchange earnings.[2] Other agricultural exports include corn, cotton, wheat, coffee, sugarcane, peanuts, sheep, goats, and pigs. While blacks constitute 98 percent of the population of the country and whites are 0.8 percent, whites by and large control the large-scale commercial farming sector. Approximately 4,500 white commercial farmers own farms whose average size is 2,000 hectares, compared to the 1 million black commercial farm families who are still farming the least arable land in plots of about three hectares per family.[3] There is also a small-scale commercial farming sector owned mainly by blacks of about 8,500 farms averaging 125 hectares each. Most blacks remain as poor subsistence farmers.

Until recent years, Zimbabwe was the second-largest industrial economy in sub-Saharan Africa after South Africa, with a diversified economic base and self-sufficient in food production.[4] Mining has also been an important contributor to export earnings, particularly gold and ferroalloys. Zimbabwe manufactures food, clothing, fertilizers, metal products, and electrical machinery and engages in vehicle assembly.[5] Whites have largely controlled the mining and manufacturing sectors. Since the late 1990s, however, Zimbabwe has been enmeshed in a major economic crisis, which has escalated into a political crisis in the new millennium. Since 2000, land appropriations by black former combatants are illustrative of the long history of racial and class exploitation and contemporary political struggles.

The Shona- and Ndebele-speaking populations are still the largest ethnic groups in the country and constitute about 80 percent and 16 percent of the total population respectively. Smaller black ethnic groups including the Tonga and other migrants from the region constitute another 2 percent, with mixed race and Asian populations comprising about 1 percent of the population and whites are 0.8 percent.[6] Zimbabwe recognizes three national languages: Shona, Ndebele, and English. The vast majority of the population (about 75 percent) is either Christian or a mixture of Christian and indigenous faiths, about 24 percent belong to indigenous faiths, with

Muslims and others constituting about 1 percent of the population.[7] The majority of Zimbabweans live in the rural areas (about 65 percent) compared to 35 percent of the population that lives in cities.[8]

There are 101 women for every 100 males in Zimbabwe with a life expectancy of 42.5 years for women and 43.2 for men, with an overall life expectancy of 42.9 years in 2000.[9] With the end of colonialism, expanded educational opportunities and greater access to contraceptives for women resulted in substantial drops in the fertility rate in Zimbabwe. It has declined in the past few decades to 3.2 children per woman today of childbearing age, compared to 4.8 children in the mid-1990s and 7.5 children in 1960. Births to teenage mothers are about 9 percent of all births in the country.[10] The infant mortality rate was estimated at 62.6 deaths per 1,000 live births in 2001.[11] The maternal mortality rate is 570 deaths per 100,000 live births.[12]

OVERVIEW OF WOMEN'S ISSUES

At the time of independence in 1980, Zimbabwe held much promise for the future of women in that nation. Since women had fought alongside men in the liberation war, the new regime under Mugabe proclaimed that it intended to promote equality between women and men. Unfortunately, economic crisis in the 1990s coupled with more recent political crisis has resulted in a decline in the status of Zimbabwean women. Despite the many challenges of the past decade, particularly those that have disproportionately affected poor and low-income women, Zimbabwean women remain active agents of change who are committed to the development of their communities and their society.

EDUCATION

Opportunities

Black women entered the postindependence period at a major disadvantage with respect to educational and occupational attainment. The movement of blacks was significantly restricted under colonial rule to preserve the best positions in the society for whites. Black women were the most disadvantaged in this system and were mainly restricted to the rural reserves where they were expected to eke out a living from particularly poor farmland. Although some black men did receive formal education and skills training to enable them to assume positions as low-level civil servants in the colonial regime, most black women received very little formal education, if any, and those who did were lucky to receive about four years of schooling. Besides a rudimentary level of education in reading and mathematics, black women were mainly trained in domestic skills often including sewing and knitting. A black woman was more likely to receive such education if she lived on or very near a mission.[13]

When the Mugabe government came to power in 1980, it was determined to begin to right the wrongs of the colonial period and significantly expanded educational opportunities for black Zimbabweans in the first few years after independence. The government instituted free primary education for all. Expenditures on education increased substantially from 1980–1982 and continued to increase until 1986 although by small amounts. By 1986, girls constituted 48.8 percent of primary school enrollments.[14] Secondary education was heavily subsidized in this period and enrollments in the first form of secondary school multiplied nearly eight times from 1980 to 1986. Young women were 50 percent of primary school enrollment, which places Zimbabwe among the highest ranked countries in the world in this area. Unfortunately, young women were 44 percent of secondary school enrollment and only 27 percent of university and other tertiary-level enrollments.[15] Total enrollments in all educational levels more than doubled from 1980 to 1986.[16]

The state's spending on education, however, did not continue unabated into the 1990s. In fact, the economic crisis that hit Zimbabwe in 1989–1990 resulted in the adoption of an Economic Structural Adjustment Program (ESAP) in 1991. In the first year of its adjustment program, the state reduced its spending on many social services including education, which declined from 18.4 percent of the federal budget in 1990–1991 to 16.3 percent of the budget in 1991–1992.[17]

Since the adoption of the ESAP in 1991, the state has reinstituted the payment of school fees for primary education and thus reneged on its earlier policy of universal free primary education. The payment of school fees is particularly problematic in the case of young girls from poor and low-income families in countries undergoing major economic crisis. In Zimbabwe, as well as in many other southern nations, the adoption of the ESAP has meant that many young girls have been removed from elementary and secondary schools. With increased unemployment and rising costs for basic necessities, poor and low-income families who have difficulties paying school fees often try to keep their sons in school as insurance for their old age. In such cases, daughters are often removed or not allowed to start school.

Parents' decisions in these cases are also related to the broader processes of gender-role socialization. In both Shona and Ndebele families, young girls are primarily raised to become wives and mothers as adults and from an early age they are trained to assume such responsibilities in their families of origin. Therefore, responsibilities for cooking, housekeeping and child care are part of the early socialization of young girls. It is also increasingly expected that women will engage in income-generating activities outside of the home in agriculture, the informal sector, or in the formal labor market. Upon the payment of brideprice in marriage, Shona and Ndebele women leave their natal homes and join the families of their spouses. Thus families, particularly the poor fathers of young girls, regard investments in their daughters' education as a waste of resources, especially under difficult economic conditions. The education of young women in Zimbabwe has often been seen as expendable in such circumstances.

The continuation of the British colonial education system in Zimbabwe has also been a deterrent to the education of young women. In addition to the increasing costs of education, many young women are unable to receive their secondary school certificate because they are unable to pass the sufficient number of O-level examinations that are generally taken when students have completed the fourth form in secondary school. Students who do not receive their O-level certificates are not able to attain positions in the formal sector of the economy. Needless to say, such students are also unable to attend upper-level secondary schools and gain admission to universities in Zimbabwe. Most of these students do not have the requisite funds to retake the examinations, since one must first reenroll in school before registering to take the tests. Many young women find it difficult to pass their O-level exams in various subjects because of the many domestic responsibilities they shoulder both before and after school that limits the amount of time available for studying.

Finally, early pregnancies also prohibit many young women from completing their secondary schooling. The majority of high schools in Zimbabwe force young women to leave school once they become pregnant. Many young women face some or all of these structural barriers that limit their levels of educational attainment and restrict their access to formal sector positions.

Literacy

Today a gap still persists in the literacy rate between women and men and substantial barriers remain that preclude women from gaining parity with men in higher education. By the beginning of the new millennium, the literacy rate for women was 84.7 percent compared to 92.8 percent for men.[18]

EMPLOYMENT AND ECONOMICS

Farming

The two major areas of employment for women are agriculture and informal sector activities, with many women still concentrated in subsistence agriculture.

Paid Employment

Currently, women in Zimbabwe aged fifteen to sixty-four have an official labor force participation rate of 41 percent. Women compose 34 percent of the labor market.[19] Much of the work that women do, however, is not accounted for in official labor force statistics, especially those in subsistence agriculture and some informal sector positions. Thus the female economic activity rate of 65.3 percent for women aged fifteen to sixty-four, as estimated by the UN Development Programme, provides a more complete picture of women's significant contributions to the economy in both the formal and informal sectors.[20]

Women particularly lag behind men in administrative and managerial positions, where there are just 18 women in such positions for every 100 men. In the professional and technical fields, women occupy 67 positions for every 100 positions held by men. As in most other nations around the world, professional women are concentrated in the gender-typed fields of teaching and nursing. Unlike the case in the North, women hold only 37 of clerical positions for every 100 positions in these areas held by men. They also hold 42 service positions for every 100 jobs in this field held by men.[21]

Informal Economic Activities

Many positions in the informal sector are also segregated by gender. Despite the state's efforts in the early 1980s to provide training for women in nontraditional fields, most women's firms are still concentrated in the service-oriented, low-wage end of this sector. Men's enterprises are more likely to involve manufacturing and the sale and service of high technology goods. Women's activities in the informal sector are most often viewed as an extension of their domestic responsibilities and often remain invisible. They remain concentrated in the trade of food and household goods, domestic service, food processing and/or preparation, beer brewing, prostitution, hairdressing, knitting, crocheting, handicrafts, and pottery making.

With the beginning of the economic crisis and the adoption the ESAP in the early 1990s, women faced increasing pressure to engage in income-generating activities. Since the state was mandated to cut its expenditures with the establishment of the ESAP, over 30,000 civil servants lost their jobs. This mainly male population was encouraged to start small enterprises as a means to earn a living. At the same time, many men were encouraging their wives to assume more financial responsibilities and to seek employment outside of the home. Thus, the informal sector grew as a result of the economic crisis. Many women in this sector faced increased competition from other women as well as men. As a result, they earned less, were expected to extend credit to many customers, and experienced declining profits.

Entrepreneurship

Urban women entrepreneurs often provide education and training for poorer rural relatives. Many young women are brought to the cities and trained in hairdressing or sewing, for example, within the shops of their older female relatives.

Men began to enter some of the fields historically dominated by women, such as food vending. Men continue to enjoy an advantage over women in small and microenterprises precisely since the former generally have greater social capital which provides them with more access to loans, technology and training. In addition, women are still hampered by gender-role socialization and gender discrimination. Many market women, however, have been able to sustain their economic activities through their participation in rotating credit schemes or "rounds" as they are called in Zimbabwe. These informal associations provide women who cannot receive bank loans with needed lump-sum payments to keep many businesses afloat given declining sales and the increasing cost of inputs.

Pay

The earnings of women and men are generally quite separate in Shona and Ndebele households. Women often try to keep the exact amount of their earnings secret, especially when they are entrepreneurs since under customary law in these groups, a husband as head of the household is entitled to a wife's income. This issue is particularly salient during periods of economic crisis since knowledge of a wife's earnings might reduce a husband's contributions even further. This is a problematic situation for wives and mothers, not because they do not want to contribute to the support of their children (since they most often believe that they have a responsibility to assist in the support of their children and view this as a focal part of their identities), but because "extra" resources for men are most often used for alcohol consumption and/or "outside" wives/women and not for support of their families.

Support for Mothers/Caretakers

Women continue to meet obligations to their extended families. Poor and low income women are very likely to give regular payments of money to their parents and often to their in-laws.

Child Care

The Ministry of Cooperative and Community Development and Women's Affairs in 1981 stated one of its primary goals was to provide access to adequate daycare and community centers. However, in light of the economic crisis of the late 1980s, many social services were curtailed.

Inheritance, Property, and Land Rights

Many women believed that the Legal Age of Majority Act, passed in 1982, was designed to give them legal status as majority citizens with full legal rights. Under this legislation, women would be able to engage in contracts and own property in their names, rights that black women were denied under colonialism. Many women believed that the Act removed the legal basis for discrimination against them and established their equality with men.

In 1999, a major Supreme Court decision involving inheritance rights, however, raised serious doubts about the status of this act, as well as the constitution. The Magaya case involved a fifty-eight-year-old seamstress who sued her stepbrother for ownership of their deceased father's land after the stepbrother evicted her from the home. "Under the Zimbabwean constitution and international human rights treaties, Magaya had a right to the land."[22] The Supreme Court ruled in a 5–0 decision that women should not be able to inherit land because of "the consideration in the African society, which amongst other factors, was to the effect that women were not able to look after their original family of birth because of their commitment to the new family through marriage."[23] Such a ruling appeared to ignore the statutory law and gave precedence to customary law. It represents another example of the deterioration of the state's commitment to women in recent years.

Under customary law, a widow was generally entitled to a year's support before the distribution of her husband's property, usually to his male relatives. The widow could then choose to be inherited by one of her husband's male relatives (most often a brother), live independently in the village, or return to her family of origin. The children of her marriage would stay with her deceased husband's family, with the exception of young children who might remain with their mother until they are about seven years of age. Gaining inheritance from the estate of a deceased spouse remains a struggle for both Shona and Ndebele women in Zimbabwe.

Social/Government Programs

With the advent of the ESAP, which was created in response to the economic crisis of the late 1980s, the state substantially reduced its support for social services. This has disproportionately affected women and children. Substantial subsidies have been removed from education, health care, transportation and housing and user fees have been reinstituted for education and health care, even for the poorest citizens. The state's overall commitment to improving the status of women was further eroded by the downgrading of the Ministry of Cooperative and Community Development and Women's Affairs to a unit within the major party in power, ZANU-PF, and later to a desk in the president's office.

In the postindependence period, Zimbabwean women have made important strides in the labor market, although recent problems in the polity and the economy have seriously jeopardized their earlier gains. The state's efforts to improve the status of women in the economy began with their establishment of the Ministry of Cooperative and Community Development and Women's Affairs in 1981. This agency was given the responsibility of working to eliminate all forms of discrimination against women. Some of its major goals were:

1. To assist women in attaining economic independence.

2. To ensure the availability and access to adequate social services for women, including access to health care, daycare, and community centers.

3. To ensure the development of technology that would lead to reductions in women's domestic responsibilities and enhance their productivity.[24]

This agency also attempted to mainstream women's issues throughout various ministries in the government, particularly to provide greater opportunities for women in the formal labor market. In addition, the government also promoted the training of women and young girls in male-dominated fields, such as carpentry and welding. Thus, the City Councils of Harare and Bulawayo, the two major cities in the nation, established training facilities in nontraditional fields for women.

During the early postindependence years, the Ministry of Cooperative and Community Development and Women's Affairs along with the state also recognized the pivotal roles that women played in the informal economy. Women own over 64 percent of all urban informal-sector establishments.[25] To improve their earnings and further secure their business endeavors, the state encouraged the extension of credit to women for small and microenterprises through the Ministry of Trade and Commerce, ZIMBANK, and the Small Enterprises Development Corporation.[26] Such efforts were an important first step in providing business loans for women who had historically been severely restricted in their access to credit.

FAMILY AND SEXUALITY

Gender Roles and Division of Labor

Women also continue to shoulder the major responsibilities for housework and child care. Both Shona and Ndebele women are traditionally assigned the duties of cleaning the house and clothing, providing and preparing food, and caring for children. Men in these groups are responsible

Rural Zimbabwe woman with baby. Sister Constantia Treppe/ Art Directors & TRIP.

for the financial support of the family, which includes paying for the family residence, the utilities, school fees, and food. Under conditions of economic crisis and the ESAP many men have either reduced the amount of money that they provide for the food allowance and expect their wives either to make up the difference or to pay for the entire food bill. Women are also expected to buy clothing for themselves and their children, as well as pay school fees.[27]

Women's responsibilities in providing for their children have also escalated in Zimbabwe with the growth in female-headed households. Women head approximately 25–40 percent of all households in southern Africa.[28] Both the legacy of forced labor migration under colonialism and continued labor migration today contribute to this phenomenon. In addition, escalating poverty, unemployment, HIV/ AIDS and domestic violence all contribute to the increase in the number of female-headed households. Like the situation throughout the world, such households are disproportionately poor.

Marriage

Zimbabwe has a dual legal system where both statutory and customary law are recognized. Under Shona and Ndebele customary law, prospective spouses are expected to pay a bridewealth (*lobola*) to the prospective wife's family. The state also expects these marriages to be registered. Once the brideprice has been paid, the wife becomes part of the husband's family and any children resulting from that union belong to the husband's family. Marriages under customary law can be polygamous. There are also unregistered customary marriages (*mapoto*) that entail no family arrangements or *lobola*. These marital forms coexist with marriages under statutory law, which are most often performed within churches or courts of law.

Reproduction

Sex Education

Historically, members of the extended family were responsible for providing sex education to Zimbabwean youth. For young girls, such education occurred most often in discussions with their aunts; for young boys, in conversations with their uncles. Given the HIV/AIDS pandemic ravaging the country today, official sex education classes are provided in schools with an emphasis on combating the AIDS virus. Since 1993, the government, working in tandem with UNICEF, has implemented an AIDS Program for Schools in Zimbabwe that is modeled on an earlier initiative undertaken in Uganda in 1987.[29] Despite these efforts in the early 1990s, the state did not develop an official AIDS policy until 1999. In that same year, the government enacted an AIDS levy to increase the funding allocated in the budget of the Ministry of Health and Child Welfare to fight the disease.[30]

In addition to the formal classes on sex education, many local nongovernmental organizations (NGOs) are providing sex education aimed at Zimbabwean youth and women. Many of these efforts are focused on peer education programs, such as the Matabeleland AIDS Council. Peer educators engage in informal discussions in the schools and in the community with Zimbabwean youth about AIDS and other sexually transmitted diseases.[31]

Such efforts are especially important for young women, who have much higher HIV/AIDS infection rates than their male counterparts.[32] Several factors account for the higher rate of infection among young women, including the persistence of gender-based inequality that disproportionately subjects women to poverty and thus leads some women to exchange sex for money and/or food. In addition, young women are subject to rape by older men who believe that the former are either free of the virus and/or that sexual relations with young girls will cure infected men of the disease. Other local efforts to fight AIDS can be noted in the work of the Zimbabwe National Traditional Healers Association, a group of spirit mediums, herbalists, and faith healers. They are involved in a project that aims to reduce the rate of HIV/AIDS transmission, promote greater awareness about the disease, and provide care for those suffering from AIDS.[33]

International NGOs and multilateral agencies have also played a major role in promoting information about AIDS in Zimbabwe.[34] Unfortunately, the country's current economic and political crises have led to some reductions in support for AIDS education from the international community.

Contraception and Abortion

From 1995 to 2000, it was estimated that approximately 54 percent of adults used contraceptives.[35] Birth control pills, intrauterine devices, condoms, and injections are available in Zimbabwe, although these are generally less accessible to the poor in rural areas. In general, contraceptive adoption has been lowest in rural areas, where only 48 percent of women were estimated to be using some form of birth control in 1995.[36] Abortion is only permitted in Zimbabwe if the pregnancy was caused by rape or incest.[37]

Teen Pregnancy

Roughly 9 percent of all births in the country are to teenage mothers.[38]

HEALTH

Health Care Access

The Zimbabwean state increased spending on health care in the first decade after independence. Primary health care was free at rural clinics and low cost for the urban poor. With the introduction of the ESAP in 1990, however, the state reimposed user fees and this had an especially devastating impact on low-income women and children.

Diseases and Disorders

One example of the dangers of economic cutbacks was the reduction in the number of women and children seeking health services. In 1991, UNICEF ranked Zimbabwe second in sub-Saharan Africa for the immunization of children against measles. By 1993 measles became a killer disease in that country because of the decline in the number of children obtaining immunizations from health centers.[39] In 1995 the minister of health announced the return of free health care to the rural population.

AIDS

Zimbabwe is experiencing one of the most major public health crises in the world. Over 33 percent of its population are living with HIV/AIDS, the second highest infection rate of any nation.[40] In Zimbabwe, HIV/AIDS is transmitted primarily through heterosexual relations. The high rates of male labor migration in the southern Africa region have made this area of the world especially vulnerable to high rates of HIV/AIDS. During the early 1990s the state television station provided several public service announcements about the disease and condoms were quite readily available in urban shops. In 1995 it was estimated that 97 out of every 100 women had received information about HIV/AIDS, most of it from the health authority and the mass media.[41] Nongovernmental organizations such as the Musasa Project have also engaged in efforts to reduce the spread of AIDS. In 1996 they began a "Gender Violence and HIV/AIDS Program," which consisted of a study to explore the relationships between sexually transmitted diseases and domestic abuse. The organization also developed a pilot program to work with urban women around these issues.[42] Given the current economic crisis in the country, the state is especially limited in its abilities to provide the necessary education and health care to sustain the population under such trying conditions.

POLITICS AND LAW

Zimbabwe is officially a parliamentary democracy with three branches of government—the executive, a 150-member House of Assembly at the legislative level, and a Supreme Court at the judicial level. There are several political parties in Zimbabwe, although for many years, Mugabe's party, the Zimbabwe African National Union–Patriotic Front, dominated the political scene. Today, the Movement for Democratic Change has emerged as a formidable challenger.

Suffrage and Political Participation

White women in Zimbabwe were granted the right of restricted suffrage in 1919 and were not given full suffrage until 1957. It was not until 1980 that all blacks achieved the right to vote. All citizens of Zimbabwe over eighteen years of age have the right to vote.[43]

In the early postindependence period, some women were appointed to the cabinet heading such ministries as: education, natural resources, tourism, cooperative and community development, and women's affairs. Women's representation in parliament has remained at about 10 percent over the past twenty years.[44]

Women's Rights and Women's Movements

Since the 1990s, women have played an important role in the development of civil society through their work in nongovernmental organizations. Some of these groups are national-level organizations, while others work at the grassroots level designed to meet the needs of poor and low-income women. There is a wide range of organizations at each of these levels. At the national level, there are service organizations, professional associations, development research centers, human rights/women's rights groups, women-in-development organizations, and associations affiliated with political parties. Such organizations have assisted women with access to credit for their enterprises, legal assistance in cases of divorce, child custody and inheritance claims, employment, health care, and continuing education, among other areas. Included among these organizations are the Zimbabwe Women's Resource Center and Network (the premier documentation center on women's lives in Zimbabwe and an umbrella organizations for many NGOs), the Zimbabwe Women's Finance Trust, the Zimbabwe Women's Bureau, Women and Law in Southern Africa, the Women's Action Group, and the Musasa Project. At the local level, rotating credit schemes (known as "rounds"), burial societies, and ethnic/village associations have proved to be very important in the empowerment of low-income women.

RELIGION AND SPIRITUALITY

Since the beginning of colonialism, Christianity has been growing in Zimbabwe. Beginning in the early twentieth century, the mission churches provided some very important services for women and men in the country including: formal education—for women this generally meant about four years of elementary education if they were living on or near a mission; health services—churches established hospitals and clinics and provided treatment for their members; and extension services—that primarily benefited church members who were farmers. In the cities, the mission churches were also notable organizations in establishing social networks for populations from specific rural areas.[45]

Women's Roles and Religious Practices

In both rural and urban areas, women established Christian church organizations associated with the missions that increased social ties among black and white women. These groups enabled women to share domestic skills, engage in Bible study and participate in a unique form of Christian fellowship.[46]

On the other hand, many of the mission churches were sources of racial hostility and they often ignored the existence of indigenous faiths that were prominent in the country, which included beliefs in the powers of witchcraft, ancestral spirits and spirit mediums. Some black Zimbabweans, therefore, established independent Christian churches during colonialism that continued into the postindependence period. One of the early independent black churches was the African Apostolic Church, which practices faith healing. Such spirit-type churches engage in exorcisms to drive troubling spirits and witches out of their members.

Within Zimbabwean traditional faiths, women have occupied notable roles as spirits and spirit mediums. In Shona indigenous religion, women could have domain over a chiefdom as a lion spirit who controls an area or population through the senior man of her lineage.[47] Lion spirits are associated with power and fearlessness and they are the protectors of their people. They possess healing powers. Women also occupy roles as spirit mediums and in these more public roles they amaze the local populations with their ritual dress and appearance. These mediums may be approached to deal with matters of inheritance and succession to positions of power within chiefdoms.[48] Politically, the spirit mediums occupied significant roles as agents of resistance against the colonial regime.[49] In traditional religions, women also occupy positions as witches. Among the Shona, witchcraft is generally regarded as responsible for the major problems in society including death, disease and family conflicts.

Today, traditional religions coexist with established Christian churches in Zimbabwe. Roman Catholics, Anglicans, and Methodists are among the largest Christian denominations in the country. Women are regarded as the "backbone" of the established and independent churches, since they most often constitute the majority of the congregations.[50] As in many other parts of sub-Saharan Africa, significant growth can be noted among the evangelical churches in the 1990s, whose congregations have grown by an estimated two million persons in the past decade.

VIOLENCE

The economic and political crises, from 2000 and continuing through 2002, caused in part by Mugabe's failed fiscal policies, the nation's participation in the war in the Democratic Republic of the Congo, the seizure of white-owned farms, violence against the opposition, drought, and rigged elections, has had a very devastating impact on women as well as men. Several black women who worked on white commercial farms have suffered physical violence at the hands of those involved in the seizures. In fact, the current unemployment rate of 50 percent and the general economic crisis have led to increased physical and economic violence against women.

Domestic Violence and Rape

Zimbabwe's national report to the Fourth World Conference on Women in Beijing in 1994 stated that "domestic violence is the most prevalent form of violence against women, and that this works against a picture that a home is a safe place."[51] In 1997, the Zimbabwean police reported that "more than 20 women are physically assaulted by their spouses daily."[52] In fact, nearly half of all murders of women in Zimbabwe are committed by their husbands, their lovers, or former husbands.

The number of reported rapes has also increased since the early 1990s.

Domestic violence and rape are acts of male power and control. They clearly reinforce patriarchy in Zimbabwean society. While this type of male control certainly is part of the explanation for the increase in domestic violence and rape in Zimbabwe, the economic crisis, the adoption of ESAP, globalization, and the resulting decline in socioeconomic status for many men in that nation are also major explanatory variables for the rise in abuse against women. Shona and Ndebele men were traditionally viewed as the heads of their households responsible for the financial upkeep of their families. The massive layoff of men in the formal sector coupled with women's increasing labor force participation and greater roles in civil society have prompted some men to feel that their dominant roles in society are being threatened.

There are currently no specific laws against domestic violence and marital rape in Zimbabwe. Under statutory law, rape consists of sexual intercourse with a woman without her consent. Under Shona customary law, the consent of the young woman is not the central issue; the focus instead is on the consent of the family to the relationship. It has been noted that "according to the theory of Shona law all sexual relations, unless sanctioned by a valid marriage, are unlawful and actionable."[53] Thus, it is clear that sex within a relationship not approved by the family is not only immoral, but also an affront to the control of the family. On the other hand under customary law, rape cannot exist within marriage. Differences between statutory and customary law regarding the meaning of rape are likely to pose serious problems for women who experience this abuse.

The women's movement in Zimbabwe has been especially important in drawing attention to rape and domestic violence and in broadening the perspective of many in that nation and internationally on the definition of abuse. The Musasa Project is a model organization in its efforts to reduce violence against women and children in Zimbabwe. Established in 1988, the organization is committed to educating the public and especially policymakers about domestic violence, with its psychological and economic abuse components. Musasa provides one-on-one counseling sessions for women and children, as well as for the perpetrators of the abuse. The organization runs the only shelter for women and children in Harare. It has also been successful in establishing partnerships with the police, lawyers' associations, and the Ministries of Health and Justice.

OUTLOOK FOR THE TWENTY-FIRST CENTURY

Since 2000, women in Zimbabwe have experienced a significant decline in their socio-economic status and in their general health and welfare. These problems are rooted in the economic crisis of the 1990s, the more recent political crisis, Zimbabwe's position in the global economy, as well as the legacy of colonialism. The active participation of many Zimbabwean women in civil society today, particularly through national-level organizations and grassroots associations, however, signals promise for the future. Despite the many formidable challenges from the state, these women are rebuilding society from the bottom up and challenging institutions and practices which hinder their development.

NOTES

1. Christine Sylvester, *Zimbabwe: The Terrain of Contradictory Development* (Boulder: Westview Press, 1991).

2. For this and other basic facts on Zimbabwe's economy and society, refer to the government factbook on the web: www.odci.gov/cia/publications/factbook/geos/zi.html. A more comprehensive source of development indicators can be found on the web site for the United Nations Development Programme at http://hdr.undp.org.

3. Sam Moyo, John Makumbe, and Brian Raftopoulos. *NGO's, the State, and Politics in Zimbabwe* (Harare: Sapes Books, 2000); N. P. Moyo, ed., *The Informal Sector in Zimbabwe: Its Potential for Employment Generation* (Harare: Ministry of Labor, Manpower Planning, and Social Welfare, 1984).

4. Colin Stoneman and Lionel Cliffe, *Zimbabwe: Politics, Economics, and Society*, (London: Pinter, 1989).

5. Moyo, Makumbe, and Raftopoulos, *NGO's, the State, and Politics in Zimbabwe.*

6. www.odci.gov; Morgan Robin, ed., *Sisterhood Is Global* (New York: Free Press, 1996); Sylvia Chant and Cathy McIlwaine, *Three Generations, Two Genders, One World: Women and Men in a Changing Century* (London: Zed Books, 1998).

7. Morgan, *Sisterhood Is Global.*

8. http://hdr.undp.org.

9. http://hdr.undp.org/reports/global/2002/.

10. Naomi Neft and Ann Levine, *Where Women Stand: An International Report on the Status of Women in 140 Countries* (New York: Random House, 1997). Sylvia Chant and Cathy McIlwaine, *Three Generations, Two Genders, One World: Women and Men in a Changing Century* (London: Zed Books, 1998).

11. *U.S. Government Factbook, Zimbabwe*, www.odci.gov.

12. Neft and Levine, *Where Women Stand.*

13. Carol Summers, "Native Land Policy, Education, and Development: Social Ideologies and Social Control in Southern Rhodesia, 1890–1934" (Ph.D. diss. 1991), Gay Seidman, "Women in Zimbabwe: Post-Independence Struggles," *Feminist Studies* 10, no. 3 (1987).

14. Mary J. Osirim, "Women, Work, and Public Policy: Structural Adjustment and the Informal Sector in Zimbabwe," in *Population Growth and Environmental Degradation in Southern Africa*, ed. Ezekiel Kalipeni (Boulder: Lynne Rienner, 1994); Stoneman and Cliffe, *Zimbabwe.*

15. Neft and Levine, *Where Women Stand.*

16. Stoneman and Cliffe, *Zimbabwe.*

17. Mary J. Osirim, "Trading in the Midst of Uncertainty: Market Women, Adjustment, and the Prospects for Development in Zimbabwe," *African Rural and Urban Studies* 2, no. 1 (1995); Austin Chakaodz, *Structural Adjustment in Zambia and Zimbabwe: Reconstructive or Deconstructive* (Harare: Third World Publishing House, 1993).

18. UNDP, http://hdr.undp.org.

19. Neft and Levine, *Where Women Stand.*

20. UNDP, http://hdr.undp.org.

21. Neft and Levine, *Where Women Stand*.

22. Sisterhood Is Global Institute, www.sigi.org/alert/zimb0699.htm.

23. Ibid.

24. Osirim, "Women, Work, and Public Policy." Ministry of Cooperative and Community Development and Women's Affairs, *Policy Statement* (Harare: Ministry of Cooperative and Community Development and Women's Affairs, 1981).

25. Saito Katrine, *The Role of Women in the Informal Sector in Zimbabwe* (Washington, DC: World Bank, 1990).

26. Osirim, "Women, Work, and Public Policy."

27. During four fieldwork visits to Zimbabwe from 1991 to 1999, I conducted in-depth interviews among 158 women microentrepreneurs. Most of these women reported that they had to meet the increasing costs for food, education and clothing from their earnings and in many cases, women were paying all of the fees in these areas.

28. Mary J. Osirim, "Beyond Simple Survival: Women Microentrepreneurs in Harare and Bulawayo, Zimbabwe," in *Courtyards, Markets, and City Streets: Urban Women in Africa*, ed. Kathleen Sheldon (Boulder: Westview Press, 1996); Pat Made and M. Whande, "Women in Southern Africa: A Note on the Zimbabwe Success Story," *Issues: A Journal of Opinion* 17, no. 2 (1989).

29. United Nations Children's Fund (UNICEF), "UN AIDS Best Practices in School AIDS Education: The Zimbabwe Case Study" (1997), www.unicef.org/programmes/lifeskills/sitemap.html.

30. Lisa Garbus and Gertrude Khumalo, HIV/Insite (2002), Center for HIV Information, A Collaborative Project of the AIDS Policy Research Center, Zimbabwe and the University of California, San Francisco, http://hivinsite.ucsf.edu/pdf.

31. Jessica De Ruijter, "Zimbabwe: Prevention HIV/AIDS Through Peer Education," *The Watchdog: The Youth Coalition's Quarterly Newsletter* (2001), www.youthcoalition.org/watchdog.engine.php/v4n3/126.

32. Simon Gregson, Heather Waddell and Stephen Chandiwana, "School Education and HIV Control in Sub-Saharan Africa: From Discord to Harmony," *Journal of International Development* vol. 13 (2001): 467–85.

33. Garbus and Khumalo, HIV/Insite.

34. Ibid.

35. UNDP, http://hdr.undp.org.

36. Ciru Getecha and Chipika Jesimen, *Zimbabwe Women's Voices* (Harare: Zimbabwe Women's Resource Center and Network, 1995).

37. Neft and Levine, *Where Women Stand*; Morgan, *Sisterhood Is Global*.

38. Neft and Levine, *Where Women Stand*.

39. Osirim, "Trading in the Midst of Uncertainty," Chakaodza, *Structural Adjustment in Zambia and Zimbabwe*; Kamidza Richard, "Structural Adjustment Without a Human Face," *Southern Africa: Political and Economic Monthly* 7, no. 6 (1994); United Nations International Children's Education Fund, *The Progress of Nations* (New York: UNICEF, 1993).

40. UNDP, http://hdr.undp.org.

41. Getecha and Jesimen, *Zimbabwe Women's Voices*.

42. Mary J. Osirim, "Making Good on Commitments to Grassroots Women: NGO's and Empowerment for Women in Contemporary Zimbabwe," *Women's Studies International Forum* 24, no. 2 (2001).

43. *Worldwide Guide to Women in Leadership*, www.guide2womenleaders.com/Zimbabwe_parl.htm.

44. http://hdr.undp.org; Morgan, *Sisterhood Is Global*.

45. Michael Bourdillon, *The Shona Peoples* (Harare: Mambo Press, 1987).

46. Terri Barnes and Everjoyce Win, *To Live a Better Life* (Harare: Baobab Books, 1992).

47. Bourdillon, *The Shona Peoples*.

48. Ibid.

49. Norman Etherington, "Recent Trends in the Historiography of Christianity," *Journal of Southern African Studies* 22, no. 2 (1996).

50. Barnes and Win, *To Live a Better Life*.

51. Ministry of National Affairs, Employment Creation, and Co-operatives, *The National Reports to the Fourth World Conference on Women* (Harare: Ministry of National Affairs, Employment Creation, and Co-operatives, 1994).

52. Tichagwa, *Beyond Inequalities*.

53. Alice Armstrong, *Culture and Choice: Lessons from Survivors of Gender Violence in Zimbabwe* (Harare: Violence Against Women Research Project, 1998).

RESOURCE GUIDE

Suggested Reading

Armstrong, Alice. *Culture and Choice: Lessons from Survivors of Gender Violence in Zimbabwe*. Harare: Violence Against Women in Zimbabwe Research Report, 1998.

Berger, Iris, and E. F. White. *Women in Sub-Saharan Africa: Restoring Women to History*. Bloomington: Indiana University Press, 1999.

Daniels, Lisa. "What Drives the Small-Scale Enterprise Sector in Zimbabwe: Surplus Labor or Market Demand?" In *African Entrepreneurship: Theory and Reality*, edited by Anita Spring and Barbara E. McDade. Gainesville: University Press of Florida, 1998.

Dashwood, Hevina. *Zimbabwe: The Political Economy of Transformation*. Toronto: University of Toronto Press, 2000.

Horn, Nancy. *Cultivating Customers: Market Women in Harare, Zimbabwe*. Boulder: Lynne Rienner, 1994.

Jenkins, Carolyn, and John Knight, *The Economic Decline of Zimbabwe. Neither Growth Nor Equity*. New York: Palgrave, 2002.

Osirim, Mary J. "Making Good on Commitments to Grassroots Women: NGO's and Empowerment for Women in Contemporary Zimbabwe." *Women's Studies International Forum* 24, no. 2 (2001).

Parpart, Jane. *Gender, Patriarchy, and Development in Africa: The Zimbabwean Case*, Women and Development Working Paper no. 254. East Lansing: Michigan State University, 1995.

Schmidt, Elizabeth. *Peasants, Traders, and Wives: Shona Women in the History of Zimbabwe, 1870–1939*. Portsmouth, NH: Heinemann, 1992.

Sylvester, Christine. *Zimbabwe: The Terrain of Contradictory Development*. Boulder: Westview Press, 1991.

Videos/Films

Everyone's Child. 1996. Screenplay by Dangarembga et al. Media for Development Trust.

Neria. 1992. Based on a story by Tsitsi Dangarembga. Media for Development Trust.

Web Sites

Sisterhood Is Global Institute, www.sigi.org/alert/zimbo699.htm.
Founded in 1984 and established in conjunction with the publication of the first edition of the book *Sisterhood Is Global* in that same year. The institute "seeks to deepen the understanding of women's rights at the local, national, regional and global levels and to strengthen the capacity of women to exercise these rights."

United Nations Development Programme, http://hdr.undp.org.

U.S. Government World Factbook, Zimbabwe, www.odci.gov/cia/publications/factbook/geos/zi.html.

Organizations

Musasa Project
64 Selous Avenue
P.O. Box A712, Avondale
Harare, Zimbabwe
Phone: 263-4-734381

Women in Law and Development in Africa (WILDAF)
P.O. Box 4622
Harare, Zimbabwe
Phone: 263-4-752105/751189
Fax: 263-4-781886
Email: wildaf@mango.zw

Zimbabwe Women's Bureau
43 Hillside Road
P.O. Box CR 120, Cranborne
Harare, Zimbabwe
Phone: 263-4-747905
Fax:263-4-747809

Zimbabwe Women's Finance Trust Ltd.
10 Masooha Ndlovu Way
Parktown Prospect
Hatfield, Harare, Zimbabwe
Phone: 263-4-670201
Fax: 263-4-723198

Zimbabwe Women's Resource Centre & Network (ZWRCN)
288 Herbert Chitepo Avenue (corner of 7th Street)
P.O. Box 2192
Harare, Zimbabwe
Phone: 263-4-737435
Fax: 263-4-720331
Email: zwrcn@zwrcn.org.zw

SELECTED BIBLIOGRAPHY

Armstrong, Alice. *Culture and Choice: Lessons from Survivors of Gender Violence in Zimbabwe*. Harare: Violence Against Women Research Project, 1998.

Barnes, Terri, and Everjoyce Win. *To Live a Better Life*. Harare: Baobab Books, 1992.

Bourdillon, Michael. *The Shona Peoples*. Harare: Mambo Press, 1987.

Chakaodza, Austin. *Structural Adjustment in Zambia and Zimbabwe: Reconstructive or Deconstructive*. Harare: Third World Publishing House, 1993.

Chant, Sylvia, and Cathy McIlwaine. *Three Generations, Two Genders, One World: Women and Men in a Changing Century*. London: Zed Books, 1998.

Downing, Jeane. "The Growth and Dynamics of Women Entrepreneurs in Southern Africa." Paper presented at the annual meeting of the African Studies Association, St. Louis, Missouri, 1991.

Etherington, Norman. "Recent Trends in the Historiography of Christianity." *Journal of Southern African Studies* 22, no. 2 (1996).

Getecha, Ciru, and Chipika Jesimen. *Zimbabwe Women's Voices*. Harare: Zimbabwe Women's Resource Center and Network, 1995.

Holleman, John. *Shona Customary Law*. London: Oxford University Press, 1952.

Kamidza, Richard. "Structural Adjustment Without a Human Face." *Southern Africa: Political and Economic Monthly* 7, no. 6 (1994).

Made, Pat, and M. Whande. "Women in Southern Africa: A Note on the Zimbabwe Success Story." *Issues: A Journal of Opinion* 17, no. 2 (1989).

Ministry of Cooperative and Community Development and Women's Affairs. *Policy Statement*. Harare: Ministry of Cooperative and Community Development And Women's Affairs, 1981.

Ministry of National Affairs, Employment Creation, and Co-operatives. *The National Reports to the Fourth World Conference on Women*. Harare: Ministry of National Affairs, Employment Creation, and Co-operatives, 1994.

Moghadam, Valentine. "Women's NGO's in the Middle East and North Africa: Constraints, Opportunities, and Priorities." In *Organizing Women: Formal and Informal Women's Groups in the Middle East*, edited by D. Chatty et al. New York: Oxford University Press, 1997.

Morgan, Robin, ed. *Sisterhood Is Global*. New York: Free Press, 1996.

Moyo, N. P., ed. *The Informal Sector in Zimbabwe: Its Potential for Employment Generation*. Harare: Ministry of Labor, Manpower Planning, and Social Welfare, 1984.

Moyo, Sam, John Makumbe, and Brian Raftopoulos. *NGO's, the State, and Politics in Zimbabwe*. Harare: Sapes Books, 2000.

Muchena, Olivia. *Women's Employment Patterns, Discrimination, and Promotion of Equality in Africa: The Case of Zimbabwe*. Addis Ababa: International Labour Organisation, 1986.

Musasa Project Trust. *Musasa News*, June–October 1998.

Neft, Naomi, and Ann Levine. *Where Women Stand: An International Report on the Status of Women in 140 Countries*. New York: Random House, 1997.

Osirim, Mary J. "Beyond Simple Survival: Women Microentrepreneurs in Harare and Bulawayo, Zimbabwe." In *Courtyards, Markets, and City Streets: Urban Women in Africa*, edited by Kathleen Sheldon. Boulder: Westview Press, 1996.

———. "Making Good on Commitments to Grassroots Women: NGO's and Empowerment for Women in Contemporary Zimbabwe." *Women's Studies International Forum* 24, no. 2 (2001).

———. "Trading in the Midst of Uncertainty: Market Women, Adjustment, and the Prospects for Development in Zimbabwe." *African Rural and Urban Studies* 2, no. 1 (1995).

———. "Vehicles for Change and Empowerment: Urban Women's Organizations in Nigeria and Zimbabwe." *Scandinavian Journal of Development Alternatives and Area Studies* 17, nos. 2–3 (1998).

———. "Women, Work, and Public Policy: Structural Adjustment and the Informal Sector in Zimbabwe." In *Population Growth and Environmental Degradation in Southern Africa*, edited by Ezekiel Kalipeni. Boulder: Lynne Rienner, 1994.

Parpart, Jane. *Gender, Patriarchy, and Development in Africa: The Zimbabwean Case* Women and Development Working Papers no. 254. East Lansing: Michigan State University, 1995.

Saito, Katrine. *The Role of Women in the Informal Sector in Zimbabwe*. Washington, DC: World Bank, 1990.

Seidman, Gay. "Women in Zimbabwe: Post-Independence Struggles." *Feminist Studies* 10, no. 3 (1984).

Stoneman, Colin, and Lionel Cliffe. *Zimbabwe: Politics, Economics, and Society*. London: Pinter, 1989.

Summers, Carol. "Native Land Policy, Education, and Development: Social Ideologies and Social Control in Southern Rhodesia, 1890–1934." Unpublished Ph.D. diss., Department of History, Johns Hopkins University, 1991.

Sylvester, Christine. *Zimbabwe: The Terrain of Contradictory Development*. Boulder: Westview Press, 1991.

Tichagwa, W. *Beyond Inequalities: Women in Zimbabwe*. Harare: Southern African Research and Documentation Center, 1998.

UNICEF. *The Progress of Nations*. New York: United Nations Children's Fund, 1993.

APPENDICES

Basic Education and Literacy

Country	Combined 1st/2nd level gross enroll- ment ratio (per 100), 1992, 1997		Girl's share of 2nd-level enrollment, 1992–1997 (%)	Illiterate, 1985–1997 (%)			
				Ages 15–24		Ages 25+	
	Female	Male		Female	Male	Women	Men
Algeria	82	90	48	38	14	80	50
Benin	35	63	—	73	45	88	67
Botswana	93	90	52	8	14	40	47
Burkina Faso	—	—	35	80	57	—	—
Burundi	—	—	39	52	40	82	57
Cameroon	53	63	—	29	15	68	43
Cape Verde	80	85	49	14	10	63	35
Central African Republic	26	43	29	65	37	87	60
Chad	23	47	20	—	—	—	—
Congo	78	92	43	5	3	—	—
Comoros	—	—	—	40	28	—	—
Côte d'Ivoire	38	58	32	62	40	85	64
Dem. Rep. of the Congo	41	62	31	—	—	—	—
Djibouti	22	31	41	62	38	87	63
Egypt	81	93	45	46	29	79	50
Equatorial Guinea	—	—	35	6	2	—	—
Eritrea	33	41	42	—	—	—	—
Ethiopia	20	33	43	52	48	—	—
Gabon	—	—	47	—	—	—	—
Gambia	46	62	38	55	39	—	—
Ghana	50	64	—	15	8	—	—
Guinea	20	41	26	—	—	—	—
Guinea-Bissau	—	—	—	71	22	—	—
Kenya	66	68	—	14	8	54	26
Lesotho	84	72	59	2	19	—	—
Liberia	—		—	51	18	—	—
Libya	—	—	—	9	<1	—	—
Madagascar	51	51	49	—	—	—	—
Malawi	94	106	18	51	30	75	37
Mali	20	33	34	81	62	91	76
Mauritania	42	54	34	62	43	83	59
Mauritius	84	82	50	8	9	31	17
Morocco	54	71	42	54	29	80	53
Mozambique	27	38	39	58	27	—	—
Namibia	108	103	54	10	14	35	27
Niger	14	23	35	90	75	97	87
Nigeria	61	77	46	21	13	—	—
Reunion	—		50	—	—	—	—

Basic Education and Literacy (*continued*)

Country	Combined 1st/2nd-level gross enrollment ratio (per 100), 1992, 1997		Girl's share of 2nd-level enrollment, 1992–1997 (%)	Illiterate, 1985–1997 (%)			
				Ages 15–24		Ages 25+	
	Female	Male		Female	Male	Women	Men
Rwanda	52	55	44	23	17	—	—
Sao Tome and Principe	—	—	—	8	4	54	21
Senegal	37	48	37	72	51	88	70
Seychelles	—	—	49	2	3	21	23
South Africa	118	115	54	10	9	—	—
Sudan	40	47	47	41[a]	22[a]	74[a]	43[a]
Swaziland	92	96	51	16	17	46	37
Tanzania	41	42	46	17	7	—	—
Togo	59	92	27	—	—	—	—
Tunisia	86	91	48	28	7	68	42
Uganda	44	54	38	37	23	67	37
Zambia	63	72	—	28	20	53	25
Zimbabwe	84	89	46	4	6	33[b]	17[b]

a—Data refer to northern states only and do not include homeless and/or nomad populations.
b—Data refer to ages 25–64 years.

Source: Adapted from United Nations Department of Economic and Social Affairs, *The World's Women 2000: Trends and Statistics* (New York: United Nations, 2002). The United Nations is the author of the original material. Used with permission.

Convention on the Elimination of All Forms of Discrimination Against Women (CEDAW)

Country	Year ratified	Convention Access	Plan provided to the U.N. Secretariat for implementation of Beijing Platform for Action, 2000
Algeria	1996	Yes	Yes
Angola	1986	Yes	Yes
Benin	1992		—
Botswana	1996	Yes	Yes
Burkina Faso	1987	Yes	Yes
Burundi	1992		Yes
Cameroon	1994	Yes	—
Cape Verde	1980	Yes	Yes
Central African Republic	1991	Yes	—
Chad	1995	Yes	—
Comoros	1994	Yes	—
Congo	1982		Yes
Côte d'Ivoire	1995	Yes	—
Dem. Rep. of the Congo	1986	—	
Djibouti	1998	Yes	—
Egypt	1981		Yes
Equatorial Guinea	1984	Yes	—
Eritrea	1995	Yes	Yes
Ethiopia	1981		Yes
Gabon	1983		—
Gambia	1993		—
Ghana	1986		Yes
Guinea	1982		Yes
Guinea-Bissau	1985	—	
Kenya	1984	Yes	Yes
Lesotho	1995	Yes	—
Liberia	1984	Yes	—
Libya	1989	Yes	—
Madagascar	1989	—	
Malawi	1987	Yes	Yes
Mali	1985		Yes
Mauritius	1984	Yes	—
Morocco	1993	Yes	Yes
Mozambique	1997	Yes	Yes
Namibia	1992	Yes	Yes
Niger	1999	Yes	Yes
Nigeria	1985		Yes
Rwanda	1981		—
Senegal	1985		Yes
Seychelles	1992	Yes	—

Convention on the Elimination of All Forms of Discrimination Against Women (CEDAW) (*continued*)

Country	Year ratified	Convention Access	Plan provided to the U.N. Secretariat for implementation of Beijing Platform for Action, 2000
Sierra Leone	1988	—	
South Africa	1995	Yes	—
Sudan	—		Yes
Swaziland	—		Yes
Tanzania	1985	Yes	
Togo	1983	Yes	—
Tunisia	1985		Yes
Uganda	1985		Yes
Zambia	1985		Yes
Zimbabwe	1991	Yes	Yes

Source: Adapted from United Nations Department of Economic and Social Affairs, *The World's Women 2000: Trends and Statistics* (New York: United Nations, 2002). The United Nations is the author of the original material. Used with permission.

Economic Activity Indicators

Country	Adult (age 16+) economic activity rate (%)				Women in the labor force 1995–2000 (%)
	1990		1995–2000		
	Women	Men	Women	Men	
Algeria	19	76	24	76	24
Angola	74	90	73	90	46
Benin	76	85	75	84	49
Botswana	66	84	46	60	47
Burkina Faso	78	91	77	90	47
Burundi	83	93	83	93	50
Cameroon	47	87	48	86	37
Cape Verde	43	88	45	88	39
Central African Rep.	70	89	69	87	47
Chad	66	89	67	88	44
Comoros	63	86	63	86	42
Congo	58	84	58	83	43
Côte d'Ivoire	43	89	44	88	32
Dem. Rep. of the Congo	62	85	62	85	43
Egypt	27[a]	73[a]	20[a]	72[a]	21[a]
Equatorial Guinea	45	90	46	89	36
Eritrea	76	87	75	87	47
Ethiopia	58	86	72	90	46
Gabon	63	84	63	84	44
Gambia	69	91	70	90	44
Ghana	82	82	81	83	51
Guinea	79	88	78	87	47
Guinea-Bissau	57	92	57	91	40
Kenya	75	90	74	89	46
Lesotho	46	86	47	85	37
Liberia	54	85	54	84	39
Libya	21	81	23	78	21
Madagascar	70	90	69	89	44
Malawi	80	88	79	87	49
Mali	73	90	72	90	46
Mauritania	65	87	64	87	44
Mauritius	35	81	39	80	33
Morocco	39	80	30	79	28
Mozambique	84	92	83	91	49
Namibia	54	82	54	81	41
Niger	70	94	70	93	44
Nigeria	47	88	48	87	36
Reunion	45	67	47	68	43
Rwanda	84	94	85[b]	87[b]	56[b]
Senegal	61	86	61	86	42
Sierra Leone	42	85	44	84	36
Somalia	64	88	64	87	43

Economic Activity Indicators (*continued*)

| Country | Adult (age 15+) economic activity rate (%) | | | | Women in the labor force 1995–2000 (%) |
| | 1990 | | 1995–2000 | | |
	Women	Men	Women	Men	
South Africa	46	80	46	79	37
Sudan	31	87	33	86	28
Swaziland	40	80	41	80	37
Tanzania	83	89	83	89	49
Togo	53	88	53	87	39
Tunisia	33	80	24	73	24
Uganda	81	92	81	91	48
Zambia	66	87	66	86	45
Zimbabwe	67	86	67	86	45

a—Data estimated to correspond to standard age groups
b—Urban areas

Source: Adapted from United Nations Department of Economic and Social Affairs, *The World's Women 2000: Trends and Statistics* (New York: United Nations, 2002). The United Nations is the author of the original material. Used with permission.

Higher Education

Country	3rd-level students per 1,000 population, 1992–1997		Women's share of 3rd-level enrollment, 1992–1997 (%)
	Women	Men	
Algeria	10	14.7	—
Angola	—	—	—
Benin	0.9	4.2	19
Botswana	5.5	6.4	47
Burkina Faso	0.4	1.3	23
Burundi	0.4	1.1	27
Central African Republic	0.3	2.1	15
Chad	0.1	1	13
Congo	—	—	—
Côte d'Ivoire	2.1	6	25
Dem. Rep. of the Congo	—	—	—
Djibouti	0.2	0.3	44
Egypt	14.7	23.2	—
Equatorial Guinea	—	—	—
Eritrea	0.2	1.7	13
Ethiopia	0.2	1	19
Gabon	—	—	—
Gambia	1.1	1.9	36
Guinea	0.2	1.9	11
Lesotho	2.4	2.1	54
Libya	—	—	46
Madagascar	1.6	1.9	45
Malawi	0.3	0.8	30
Mauritania	1.3	6.2	18
Mauritius	5.8	6.1	51
Morocco	9.3	13.3	41
Mozambique	0.2	0.6	25
Namibia	8.9	5.8	61
Niger	—	—	—
Nigeria	—	—	—
Reunion	—	—	—
Rwanda	—	—	—
Seychelles	—	—	—
South Africa	14.6	15.9	48
Sudan	—	—	—
Swaziland	5.4	7.5	44
Tanzania	0.1	0.7	16
Togo	1.1	5.3	17
Tunisia	12	14.6	45
Uganda	1	2.2	33
Zambia	—	—	30
Zimbabwe	3.7	9.1	37

Source: Adapted from United Nations Department of Economic and Social Affairs. *The World's Women 2000: Trends and Statistics* (New York: United Nations, 2002). The United Nations is the author of the original material. Used with permission.

HIV/AIDS, Maternity Care, and Maternal Mortality Indicators

Country	Estimated number of adults and children with HIV/AIDS, 1997 (in thousands)	Women with HIV/AIDS, 1997 estimate (%)	Pregnant women who received prenatal care,[a] 1996 (%)	Deliveries with skilled attendant, 1996 (%)	Maternal mortality ratio (per 100,000 live births), 1980–1998
Algeria	—	—	58	77	220
Angola	110	52	25	17	—
Benin	54	50	60	38	500
Botswana	190	49	92	77	330
Burkina Faso	370	49	59	43	—
Burundi	260	50	88	24	—
Cameroon	320	48	73	58	430
Cape Verde	—	—	99	99	55
Central African Republic	180	50	67	46	1,100
Chad	87	51	30	15	830
Comoros	—	—	69	24	500
Congo	100	49	55	50	—
Côte d'Ivoire	700	49	83	45	600
Dem. Rep. of the Congo	950	50	66	—	—
Djibouti	33	50	76	79	—
Egypt	—	10	53	46	170
Equatorial Guinea	2	48	37	5	—
Eritrea	—	—	19	6	1,000
Ethiopia	2		48	20	8
Gabon	23	50	86	80	600
Gambia	13	48	91	44	—
Ghana	210	50	86	44	210
Guinea	74	50	59	31	670
Guinea-Bissau	12	52	50	—	910
Kenya	1,600	49	95	45	590
Lesotho	85	50	91	50	—
Liberia	44	50	83	58	—
Libya	—	—	100	76	75
Madagascar	9	50	78	57	490
Malawi	710	49	90	55	620
Mali	89	50	25	24	580
Mauritania	6	49	49	40	550
Mauritius	—	—	99	97	50
Morocco	—	—	45	40	230
Mozambique	1,200	48	54	30	1,100
Namibia	150	50	88	68	230
Niger	65	51	30	15	590

Nigeria	2		50	60	31
Reunion	—	—	95	97	—
Rwanda	370	49	94	26	—
Sao Tome and Principe	—		—	—	—
Senegal	75	50	74	47	560
Sierra Leone	68	50	30	25	—
Somalia	—	—	40	2	—
South Africa	2,900	50	89	82	—
Sudan	—	—	54	86	550
Swaziland	84	51	70	56	230
Tanzania	11,400	49	92	44	530
Togo	170	51	43	32	480
Tunisia	—	—	71	90	70
Uganda	930	49	87	38	510
Zambia	770	51	92	51	650
Zimbabwe	1,500	51	93	69	400

a—Attended at least once during pregnancy by skilled health personnel for pregnancy-related issue.

Source: Adapted from United Nations Department of Economic and Social Affairs, *The World's Women 2000: Trends and Statistics* (New York: United Nations, 2002). The United Nations is the author of the original material. Used with permission.

Household and Childbearing Indicators

Country	Average number of household members, 1991–1994	Women-headed households, 1991–1997 (%)	Contraceptive use, married women, 1991–2000 (%)	Total fertility rate (births per woman)		Births per 1,000 women aged 15–19, 2000–2005
				1990–1995	2000–2005	
Algeria	7.0[a]	11[a]	52[bc]	4.1	2.8	20
Angola	—	—	—	7.2	7.2	229
Benin	5.9	18	16	6.5	5.7	113
Botswana	4.8[a]	47	33[a]	4.9	3.9	63
Burkina Faso	6.2[a]	7	12	7.1	6.8	151
Burundi	4.6[a]	25[a]	9[a]	6.8	6.8	60
Cameroon	5.2[a]	18	19	5.7	4.7	127
Cape Verde	5.0[a]	38[a]	53	3.9	3.2	72
Central African Republic	4.7[a]	21	15	5.6	4.9	141
Chad	—	—	—	6.3	6.3	146
Comoros	6.2	25	21	5.8	5	77
Congo	—	22	4	6.7	6.7	195
Côte d'Ivoire	6.0[a]	15	15	5.7	4.6	121
Dem. Rep. of the Congo	—	—	8	6.7	6.7	230
Djibouti	6.6	18	—	6.3	5.8	65
Egypt	4.9[a]	13	56	3.8	2.9	34
Equatorial Guinea	—	—	—	5.9	5.9	192
Eritrea	31	5	6.1	5.3	112	
Ethiopia	—	—	8	6.8	6.8	78
Gabon	—	—	—	5.2	5.4	161
Gambia	—	—	12[a]	5.6	4.8	139
Ghana	4.8[a]	37	22	5.3	4.2	78
Guinea	7.2	7	6	6.4	5.8	168
Guinea-Bissau	7.9	—	—	6	6	195
Kenya	5.2[a]	33	39	5.4	4.2	90
Lesotho	5.1[a]	—	23[d]	5	4.5	67
Liberia	5.0[a]	19[a]	6[a]	6.8	6.8	230
Libya	—	—	40	4.1	3.3	35
Madagascar	4.5	22	19	6.2	5.7	136
Malawi	4.3[a]	26	31	7.2	6.3	152
Mali	5.6[a]	8	7	7	7	195
Mauritania	—	—	3[a]	6.1	6	147
Mauritius	4.4[a]	18[a]	75	2.3	1.9	34
Morocco	6.0[a]	15	50	3.9	3	28
Mozambique	—	27	6	6.4	5.9	129
Namibia	5.2	39	29	5.8	4.9	81
Niger	6.4[a]	10[a]	8	8	8	233
Nigeria	5.4[a]	14[a]	15	6.4	5.4	104

Reunion	3.8[a]	—	67[a]	2.4	2.1	20
Rwanda	4.7	25	21	6.7	5.8	60
Sao Tome and Principe	4.3	33	—	—	—	—
Senegal	8.8	18	13	6.1	5.1	100
Seychelles	4.5[a]	—	—	—	—	—
Sierra Leone	5.7[a]	11[a]	4[a]	6.5	6.5	212
Somalia	—	—	1[a]	7.3	7.3	213
South Africa	5.8[e]	—	62	3.3	2.9	73
Sudan	6.3[a]	13[a]	8[g]	5.3	4.5	57
Swaziland	—	40[a]	20[af]	5.3	4.4	81
Tanzania	5.2[a]	22	25	5.9	5	92
Togo	5.1[a]	26[a]	14	6.2	5.4	93
Tunisia	5.4[a]	11[a]	60	3.1	2.1	17
Uganda	5.4[a]	29	15	7.1	7.1	211
Western Sahara	—	—	—	4.8	3.8	83
Zambia	5.6	17[a]	24	6.3	5.7	146
Zimbabwe	5.2[a]	33	54	5.5	4.5	105

a—Data refer to a year between 1985 and 1990.
b—Excluding sterilization.
c—For all ever-married women of reproductive age.
d—For all women of reproductive age.
e—Excluding Bophuthatswana, Ciskei, Transkei, and Venda.
f—Including single women of reproductive age who have borne a child.
g—North Sudan only.

Source: Adapted from United Nations Department of Economic and Social Affairs, *The World's Women 2000: Trends and Statistics* (New York: United Nations, 2002). The United Nations is the author of the original material. Used with permission.

Life Expectancy and Infant Mortality

Country	Life expectancy at birth, 2000–2005		Life expectancy at age 60, 2000–2005		Infant mortality rate (per 1,000 live births), 2000–2005	
	Female	Male	Women	Men	Female	Male
Algeria	72	69	20	17	40	45
Angola	47	45	15	14	109	127
Benin	56	52	17	16	74	87
Botswana	36	37	18	15	63	72
Burkina Faso	49	47	16	15	81	92
Burundi	41	40	16	14	103	120
Cameroon	51	49	17	16	74	84
Cape Verde	73	67	21	17	47	53
Central African Republic	46	43	17	15	82	105
Chad	47	45	15	14	108	124
Comoros	62	59	17	15	62	72
Congo	54	50	18	15	58	74
Côte d'Ivoire	48	48	17	15	75	87
Dem. Rep. of the Congo	53	51	17	16	71	83
Djibouti	42	39	16	14	109	125
Egypt	70	67	17	15	38	43
Equatorial Guinea	54	50	16	15	91	106
Eritrea	54	51	16	15	78	87
Ethiopia	44	43	16	15	99	113
Gabon	54	52	17	16	74	86
Gambia	49	46	16	14	106	124
Ghana	58	56	18	16	57	67
Guinea	49	48	15	15	111	118
Guinea-Bissau	47	44	15	14	111	131
Kenya	50	49	18	16	53	64
Lesotho	40	41	17	15	108	114
Liberia	57	55	16	15	73	85
Libya	73	69	20	16	25	26
Madagascar	55	53	16	15	86	96
Maiawi	39	40	17	15	128	132
Mali	53	51	23	21	116	125
Mauritania	54	51	16	15	89	104
Mauritius	76	68	20	16	14	18
Morocco	71	67	18	17	38	46
Mozambique	39	37	15	14	117	138
Namibia	44	44	18	16	61	69
Niger	46	46	15	14	123	129
Nigeria	52	52	17	16	76	81
Reunion	79	71	23	17	8	9
Rwanda	42	40	16	14	112	126
Senegal	56	53	14	13	53	60

Sierra Leone	42	39	14	13	135	157
Somalia	51	47	16	15	104	121
South Africa	48	46	18	13	55	64
Sudan	58	56	17	16	73	83
Swaziland	38	38	17	15	84	99
Tanzania	52	50	16	15	69	76
Togo	53	51	17	16	68	81
Tunisia	72	70	19	17	24	27
Uganda	47	45	16	14	87	101
Western Sahara	66	62	17	15	48	59
Zambia	42	43	16	15	76	83
Zimbabwe	42	43	18	16	51	59

Source: Adapted from United Nations Department of Economic and Social Affairs. *The World's Women 2000: Trends and Statistics* (New York. United Nations, 2002). The United Nations is the author of the original material. Used with permission.

Maternity Leave Benefits, As of 1998

Country	Length of leave (weeks)	Wages paid in covered period (%)	Provider of coverage
Algeria	14	100	Social Security
Angola	13	100	Employer
Benin	14	100	Social Security
Botswana	12	25	Employer
Burkina Faso	14	100	S.S./Employer
Burundi	12	50	Employer
Cameroon	14	100	Social Security
Central African Rep.	14	50	Social Security
Chad	14	50	Social Security
Comoros	14	100	Employer
Congo	15	100	50% Employer/50% S.S
Côte d'Ivoire	14	100	Social Security
Dem. Rep. of the Congo	14	67	Employer
Djibouti	14	50 (100 for public employees)	Employer/S.S.
Egypt	7	100	S.S./Employer
Equatorial Guinea	12	75	Social Security
Eritrea	9	—	—
Ethiopia	13	100	Employer
Gabon	14	100	Social Security
Gambia	12	100	Employer
Ghana	12	50	Employer
Guinea	14	100	50% Employer/50% S.S.
Guinea-Bissau	9	100	Employer/S.S.
Kenya	8	100	Employer
Lesotho	12	0	—
Libya	7	50	Employer
Madagascar	14	100a	50% Employer/50% S.S.
Mali	14	100	Social Security
Mauritania	14	100	Social Security
Mauritius	12	100	Employer
Morocco	12	100	Social Security
Mozambique	9	100	Employer
Namibia	12	as prescribed	Social Security
Niger	14	50	Social Security
Nigeria	12	50	Employer
Rwanda	12	67	Employer
Sao Tome and Principe	10	100 or 60 days	Social Security
Senegal	14	100	Social Security
Seychelles	14	flat rate for 10 weeks	Social Security

Somalia	14	50	Employer
South Africa	12	45	Unemployment Insurance
Sudan	8	100	Employer
Swaziland	12	0	—
Tanzania	12	100	Employer
Togo	14	100	50% Employer/50% S.S.
Tunisia	4	67	Social Security
Uganda	8	100 for month	Employer
Zambia	12	100	Employer
Zimbabwe	13	60/75	Employer

Source: Adapted from United Nations Department of Economic and Social Affairs, *The World's Women 2000: Trends and Statistics* (New York: United Nations, 2002). The United Nations is the author of the original material. Used with permission.

Women Administrators and Managers, 1985–1997 (%)

Country		Country	
Algeria	6	Mali	20
Botswana	26	Mauritania	8
Burkina Faso	14	Namibia	21
Burundi	13	Nigeria	6
Cameroon	10	Rwanda	46
Cape Verde	23	Seychelles	29
Central African Rep.	9	Sierra Leone	8
Côte d'Ivoire	10	South Africa	19
Djibouti	2	Swaziland	15
Egypt	16	Tunisia	9
Ethiopia	8	Uganda	14
Lesotho	33	Zambia	6
Malawi	8	Zimbabwe	15

Source: Adapted from United Nations Department of Economic and Social Affairs, *The World's Women 2000: Trends and Statistics* (New York: United Nations, 2002). The United Nations is the author of the original material. Used with permission.

Women in Government

| Country | Parliamentary seats in single or lower chamber occupied by women (%) | | | Women in decision-making positions (%) | | | |
| | | | | Ministerial level | | Sub-ministerial level | |
	1987	1995	2001	1994	1998	1994	1998
Algeria	2	7	3	4	0	8	10
Angola	15	10	16	7	14	2	10
Benin	4	8	6	10	13	0	5
Botswana	5	9	17	6	14	6	20
Burkina Faso	—	4	8	7	10	14	10
Burundi	9	—	14	7	8	0	0
Cameroon	14	12	6	3	6	5	6
Cape Verde	12	8	11	13	13	9	50
Central African Republic	4	4	7	5	4	17	6
Chad	—	16	2	5	0	0	6
Comoros	0	0	—	0	7	0	0
Congo	10	2	12	6	6	0	0
Côte d'Ivoire	6	5	9	8	3	0	3
Dem. Rep. of the Congo	5	5	—	6	—	7	—
Djibouti	0	0	0	0	0	3	3
Egypt	4	2	2	4	6	0	4
Equatorial Guinea	3	8	5	4	4	0	5
Eritrea	—	21	15	7	5	13	6
Ethiopia	1	5	8	10	5	10	16
Gabon	13	6	9	7	3	12	9
Gambia	8	—	2	0	29	7	17
Ghana	—	8	9	11	9	12	9
Guinea	—	7	9	9	8	8	20
Guinea-Bissau	15	10	8	4	18	19	16
Kenya	2	3	4	0	0	4	9
Lesotho	—	5	4	6	6	21	15
Liberia	6	6	8	5	8	0	6
Libya	—			0	7	0	0
Madagascar	1	4	8	0	19	4	8
Malawi	10	6	9	9	4	9	4
Mali	4	2	12	10	21	0	0
Mauritania	—	0	4	0	4	6	6
Mauritius	7	3	6	3	—	7	—
Morocco	0	1	1	0	0	0	8
Mozambique	16	25	30	4	0	9	15
Namibia	—	18	25	10	8	2	17
Niger	—	4	1	5	10	19	8
Nigeria	—	—	3	3	6	11	4
Rwanda	13	17	26	9	5	10	20
Sao Tome and Principe	12	7	9	0	0	20	33
Senegal	11	12	17	7	7	0	15

Women in Government (*continued*)

| Country | Parliamentary seats in single or lower chamber occupied by women (%) | | | Women in decision-making positions (%) | | | |
| | | | | Ministerial level | | Sub-ministerial level | |
	1987	1995	2001	1994	1998	1994	1998
Seychelles	16	27	24	31	33	21	16
Sierra Leone	—	—	9	0	10	2	11
Somalia	4	—	—	0	0	0	0
South Africa	2	25	30	6	—	2	—
Sudan	8	8	10	0	0	0	0
Swaziland	4	3	3	0	6	6	16
Tanzania	—	11	22	13	13	4	11
Togo	5	1	5	5	9	0	0
Tunisia	6	7	12	4	3	14	10
Uganda	—	17	25	10	13	7	13
Zambia	3	7	10	5	3	9	12
Zimbabwe	11	15	10	3	12	25	6

Source: Adapted from United Nations Department of Economic and Social Affairs, *The World's Women 2000: Trends and Statistics* (New York: United Nations, 2002). The United Nations is the author of the original material. Used with permission.

INDEX

Ethiopia, 140; in Guinea, 191; in Mali, 241 n.31; in Senegal, 377; in sub-Saharan Africa, 9; in Sudan, 446

Infrastructure: in Burundi, 57, 67; in Eritrea, 110; in Somalia, 391

Inheritance, right of: in Botswana, 31; in Burundi, 63, 72; in Cameroon, 83, 87; in Eritrea, 115; in Ethiopia, 132, 134; in Guinea, 185; in Kenya, 207–8; in Mali, 230, 238, 239; in Mozambique, 251, 259; in Namibia, 274; in Niger, 305, 307; in Nigeria, 12, 318; in Senegal, 372; in Somalia, 393–94; in South Africa, 414; in sub-Saharan Africa, 1, 5, 12, 15; in Sudan, 443; in Tanzania, 461, 465; in Togo, 474; in Uganda, 491, 493; in Zimbabwe, 512, 518

Inputs access, in sub-Saharan Africa, 4, 6

Institute of Agricultural Research (Ethiopia), 132

Inter-African Committee on Traditional Practices Affecting the Health of Women and Children, and Ethiopia, 137, 138, 140, 144

Internally displace persons (IDP): of Burundi, 56–57, 58, 59, 68, 71–72, 73, 74, 75; of Eritrea, 111

International Convenant on Economic, Social, and Cultural Rights, and Kenya, 214

International Covenant on Civil and Political Rights, and Kenya, 214

International donors: and Burundi, 70; and Kenya, 208; and Mali, 226, 227, 231, 234, 240; and Rwanda, 348; and Tanzania, 462; and women's movements, 11

International Federation of Women Lawyers (FIDA), in Ghana, 167, 170, 171

International Labor Organization (ILO): and Eritrea, 113, 114; and Ethiopia, 133; and Rwanda, 346; and Sudan, 442

International Monetary Fund

(IMF): in Cameroon, 82, 88–89; in Ethiopia, 127, 135; in Ghana, 156; in Mozambique, 250, 252; in Niger, 296, 301, 307; in Nigeria, 319; in Rwanda, 347; in Senegal, 366; in sub-Saharan Africa, 6; in Sudan, 446, 452

International Muslim Women's Union, 449

International Planned Parenthood Association, and Eritrea, 116

International Planned Parenthood Foundation, and Cameroon, 91

Intestinal parasites, in Niger, 303

Iodine deficiency, in Guinea, 190

Islam and Muslims: in Burundi, 73; in Cameroon, 84, 99; in Eritrea, 110; in Ethiopia, 127, 145; in Ghana, 156, 165, 168; in Guinea, 179, 181, 194; in Kenya, 209, 214, 215; in Mali, 226, 238; in Mozambique, 259, 261; in Niger, 296, 301, 306; in Nigeria, 313, 315, 316–17, 320; in Rwanda, 356; in Senegal, 365, 368, 373, 376, 377, 379, 380–81, 382, 383; in Somalia, 389, 395, 397, 399; in South Africa, 426; in sub-Saharan Africa, 12; in Sudan, 439, 443, 449, 450; in Tanzania, 465, 466; in Togo, 479; in Uganda, 487, 497; in Zimbabwe, 507

Islamic Association of Niger (AIN), 306

Islamic law: in Ghana, 163; in Guinea, 187; in Mozambique, 259; in Niger, 2, 306, 307; in Nigeria, 2, 12–13, 320, 321, 327, 331, 333; in Senegal, 372, 374; in Somalia, 393, 402 n.19; in sub-Saharan Africa, 2; in Sudan, 438, 439, 445, 450; in Uganda, 493

Islamic Women's Association, 238–39

Israel, and Ethiopia, 148

IUDs (intrauterine devices). See Contraception; Family planning

Jews and Judaism: in Ethiopia, 127, 145; in South Africa, 426

Kabuye, Rose, 354

Kairos Document, 427

Kalanga, 20

Kanigi, Sylvie, 70

Kasinga, Fauziya, 477

Kayibanda, Gregoire, 352

Kazibwe, Wandera Specioza, 10

Keita, Modibo, 237

Kenya: AIDS in, 211–12; British rule of, 202–3, 213; economics in, 204–8, 209, 216; education in, 203–4, 208, 209, 214; employment in, 205; female genital cutting in, 9, 212–13; gender roles and division of labor, 209; health in, 208, 209, 210–13, 214; land alliance/coalitions in, 5; marriage in, 209–10, 214; outlook for twenty-first century, 216–17; political leadership and decision-making in, 10; political participation in, 10; politics and law in, 213–14; profile of, 201–2; religion and spirituality in, 215; social/government programs in, 208; and Somalia, 401 n.2; and trafficking in women and children, 14, 216; violence in, 13, 208, 215–16; women's issues in, 202–3; women's movements in, 11; women's rights in, 213, 214

Kenya Anti-Corruption Authority, 208

Khat, 393, 395, 402 n.16

Kidnapping: in Ethiopia, 126, 129, 144, 146, 147; in Somalia, 13; in South Africa, 430

Kitgum Concern Women Association, 496

Konaré, Alpha Oumar, 226, 238

Kony, Lord, 496

Kountché, Seyni, 304

Kufour, John, 155, 166

Kwelagobe, Mpule, 41

Labour Act of 1992 (Namibia), 275–76

Lancaster House Agreement, 506

Land Act and Village Land Act (1999), 5, 461, 465

Land Apportionment Act of 1930 (Zimbabwe), 505

SIX-VOLUME COMPREHENSIVE INDEX

22; in Bahrain, 46, 51; in Egypt, 72–73, 85, 86–87; in Iran, 127–28; in Iraq, 155; in Israel, 172; in Jordan, 196, 202, 206; in The Occupied Territories, 317, 319–20; in Saudi Arabia, 342–43; in Syria, 363; in Tunisia, 382, 389, 390, 392, 398; in UAE, 423; in Yemen, 448. Development, policies and progress: **Sub-Saharan Africa**: in Botswana, 20, 26, 34, 35; in Burundi, 72; in Cameroon, 97; in Eritrea, 110; in Ethiopia, 127, 135, 143; in Kenya, 214; in Mali, 230; in Somalia, 393; South Africa, 414, 415; in Tanzania, 457, 465 Development, *The Botswana Human Development Report 2000*: 34

Devices, intrauterine (IUDs). *See* Contraception; Family planning

DeVries, Sonja: **No. America/ Caribbean**: in Cuba, 94

Diakhate, Diouma Dieng: **Sub-Saharan Africa**: in Senegal, 370

Diarrhea (*see also* Diseases and disorders): **Sub-Saharan Africa**: in Kenya, 211; in Togo, 476; in Uganda, 494

Diogo, Luisa: **Sub-Saharan Africa**: in Mozambique, 258

Diop, Sokhna Magat: **Sub-Saharan Africa**: in Senegal, 381

Diouf, Abdou: **Sub-Saharan Africa**: in Senegal, 365

Disabilities, women with (*see also* Children, disabled): **Asia/Oceania**: in Afghanistan, 20. **Middle East/No. Africa**: in Algeria, 29; in Jordan, 207; in Yemen, 448, 453

Disappearances (*see also* Kidnapping; Military, repression by): **Central/So. America**: in Argentina, 13, 30–31, 37 n.2, 40 n.60; in Central and South America, 9; in El Salvador, 225, 239, 241; in Guatemala, 281–82;

in Honduras, 314, 323; in Peru, 429

Discrimination, gender-based (*see also* Gender roles and division of labor; Harassment, sexual; Law, religious; Unions, labor; Women, unmarried, health care for; Working conditions): **Europe**: 3; in Armenia, 35–36; in Bulgaria, 103, 104; in Georgia, 5; in Poland, 482, 486, 496, 497, 498; in Portugal, 512, 513, 519, 523 n.2; in Russia, 550, 555; in Serbia and Montenegro, 579; in Slovakia, 591, 596; in Turkey, 677. **Middle East/No. Africa**: in Algeria, 17, 22, 26; in Bahrain, 48; in Iran, 109, 113–14; in Iraq, 162; in Israel, 171, 173, 179; in Jordan, 197, 216, 221; in Lebanon, 245; in Morocco, 286; in Syria, 376; in Tunisia, 383, 387, 402. **No. America/Caribbean**: Bahamas, 17; Canada, 54, 56–57, 58–59; Dominican Republic, 108–9; Trinidad and Tobago, 304, 309

Discrimination, of migrants: **Middle East/No. Africa**: in Iran, 137–38; Iranians, 138; in Jordan, 197

Diseases, sexually transmitted (STDs). *See* HIV/AIDS; Sexually transmitted diseases (STDs)

Diseases and disorders (*see also* specific types of): **Asia/Oceania**: in Afghanistan, 19–20; in Australia, 45–46; in Bangladesh, 70; in Cambodia, 95–96; in Central Asia, 118; in China, 140–41; in India, 171–72; in Laos, 273; in Myanmar, 326; in New Zealand, 374; in Pakistan, 392; in Papua New Guinea, 412; in Taiwan, 487; in Thailand, 513–14; in Uzbekistan, 545, 547. **Central/So. America**: in Argentina, 28–29; in Belize, 53; in Chile, 133–34; in Colombia, 165; in Ecuador, 212–13; in El Salvador, 237–38; in French Guiana, 262; in Guatemala, 273–

74; in Nicaragua, 344–45; in Panama, 371; in Suriname, 44. **Europe**: in Albania, 23, 24–25, 271; in Armenia, 39; in Austria, 50, 53–54; in Belgium, 76–77; in Bulgaria, 107–8, 271; in Croatia, 124; in Czech Republic, 141; in Denmark, 158; in Estonia, 176–77; in Finland, 199; in France, 212, 213, 214; in Germany, 246–47; in Greece, 270, 271; in Hungary, 281–82, 289–90; in Iceland, 305–6; in Ireland, 326–28; in Italy, 357–58; in Kosovo, 380; in Latvia, 392; in Lithuania, 409–10, 413; in Macedonia, 425–26; in Malta, 438; in Netherlands, 451–52; in Norway, 470; in Poland, 493; in Portugal, 518–19, 523; in Romania, 535, 536–37; in Russia, 557, 559–61; in Slovakia, 588, 593; in Spain, 610; in Sweden, 634–35; in Switzerland, 659, 660; in Turkey, 686–87, 699 n.65; in Ukraine, 713–14; in United Kingdom, 731–32. **Middle East/No. Africa**: in Algeria, 26; in Bahrain, 54; in Iraq, 158, 160; in Israel, 177; in Jordan, 214, 215; in Libya, 270; in Morocco, 282; in The Occupied Territories, 325–26; in Syria, 369; in UAE, 421; in Yemen, 452–53. **No. America/Caribbean**: Canada, 63–64; Cuba, 100–101 n.34; Dominican Republic, 119; French Caribbean, 144; Haiti, 165–67; Mexico, 214; Netherlands Antilles, 241; OECS, 266; Puerto Rico, 287–89; sexually transmitted, 64; Trinidad and Tobago, 317–19; United States, 340–43. **Sub-Saharan Africa** (*see also* Tuberculosis): in Botswana, 35, 36; in Guinea, 190; in Kenya, 211; in Mozambique, 255; in Niger, 303; in Somalia, 396; in Togo, 476; in Uganda, 494

Divorce (*see also* Alimony; Annulments, marriage; Children, custodial rights concerning;

Cuba, 80; Dominican Republic, 108, 111; Haiti, 157; Jamaica, 183; Netherlands Antilles, 234–35. **Sub-Saharan Africa**: 2, 4; in Botswana, 28–29; in Cameroon, 84, 86; in Eritrea, 113–14; in Ethiopia, 132–33; in Ghana, 159–60; in Guinea, 181; in Kenya, 205; in Mali, 229–30; in Mozambique, 248; in Namibia, 275; in Niger, 296, 299–300; in Nigeria, 316–17; in Senegal, 368, 370; in Somalia, 392; in Sudan, 441; in Togo, 473; in Uganda, 490, 491; in Zimbabwe, 508, 510, 513

Economy, national (*see also* Income, annual per capita; Gross domestic product [GDP]; Gross national product [GNP]): **Asia/Oceania**: of Afghanistan, 10, 15; of Bangladesh, 58; of Cambodia, 86; of China, 126–27, 130; of Indonesia, 190–91; of Japan, 220; of Korea, 241; of Laos, 266, 269; of Malaysia, 284; of Myanmar, 316–17, 322; of Nepal, 344, 345; of New Zealand, 368; of Pakistan, 385; of Papua New Guinea, 406–7; of Philippines, 419, 422; of Taiwan, 476; of Thailand, 503–4, 506; of Turkmenistan, 109; of Uzbekistan, 542; of Vietnam, 561–62. **Central/So. America**: of Argentina, 13–14, 16; of Belize, 49–50; of Bolivia, 62; of Brazil, 86; of Chile, 123; of Colombia, 154; of El Salvador, 223, 229; of French Guiana, 258, 259; of Guatemala, 268; of Guyana, 293–94; of Honduras, 314; of Nicaragua, 336, 338–39, 340; of Paraguay, 400, 401 n.19; of Peru, 413, 415; of Suriname, 441; of Uruguay, 456; of Venezuela, 478, 480–81. **No. America/Caribbean**: of Barbados, 33; of Cuba, 79. **Sub-Saharan Africa**: of Botswana, 19–20, 25–32, 43; of Burundi, 57, 60–64; of Cameroon, 82, 84–89; of Eritrea, 110, 113–15;

121; of Ethiopia, 127, 130–36; of Ghana, 156, 158–62; of Guinea, 180, 181, 183–86, 193–94; of Kenya, 204–8, 209, 216; of Mali, 228–31, 234, 240; of Mozambique, 245, 247–53, 263; of Namibia, 272, 274–76; of Niger, 296, 298–301; of Nigeria, 311–12, 315–20; of Rwanda, 339, 345–47; of Senegal, 365–66, 367, 369–72, 383; of Somalia, 392–94; of South Africa, 407, 408, 411–17; of Sudan, 440–44; of Tanzania, 457, 459–62, 466; of Togo, 472–74, 481; of Uganda, 486, 489–92; of Zimbabwe, 506, 507, 509–13, 514, 519, 520

Economy, oil production influences (*see also* Oil industry): **Middle East/No. Africa**: in Algeria, 15, 24; in Bahrain, 47, 48; in Iran, 106; in Iraq, 159. **Sub-Saharan Africa**: in Cameroon, 82; in Nigeria, 311–12

Economy, reform of. *See* International Monetary Fund (IMF); Reform, economic

Ecotourism (*see also* Tourism): **Central/So. America**: in Belize, 49

Eduards, Maud: **Europe**: in Sweden, 621, 640

Education: Decade of Development in Education: **Sub-Saharan Africa**: Mali, 231

Education (*see also* Literacy): **Asia/Oceania**: 3, in Afghanistan, 12–13; in Australia, 32; in Bangladesh, 60–61; in Cambodia, 87–88; in Central Asia, 112; in China, 129; in India, 157; in Indonesia, 191–92; in Japan, 221–22; in Korea, 243–45; in Malaysia, 284–85; in Micronesia, 302–3; in Myanmar, 318; in Nepal, 346–47; in New Zealand, 368; in Pakistan, 386–87; in Papua New Guinea, 408; in Philippines, 420–21; in Sri Lanka, 443; in Taiwan, 473; in Thailand, 504–5, in Uzbekistan,

537–38; in Vietnam, 563. **Central/So. America**: in Argentina, 15; in Belize, 48; in Bolivia, 61; in Brazil, 87; in Colombia, 155–56; in Costa Rica, 186; in Ecuador, 203; in El Salvador, 227; in French Guiana, 258; in Guatemala, 266; in Guyana, 294–95; in Honduras, 316; in Nicaragua, 337; in Panama, 362–63; in Paraguay, 384; in Peru, 413–14; in Suriname, 440–41; in Uruguay, 457–58; in Venezuela, 479–80. **Europe**: 1, 3, 8, 14 n.15; in Albania, 19; in Armenia, 35; in Austria, 47–48; in Belarus, 62–63; in Belgium, 72; in Bosnia and Herzegovina, 88; in Bulgaria, 102; in Croatia, 121, 122; in Czech Republic, 136; in Denmark, 153; in Estonia, 168–69; in Finland, 192–93; in France, 206–7, 603; in Georgia, 224; in Germany, 234–35, 256 n.5; in Greece, 265; in Hungary, 282–83; in Iceland, 298–99; in Ireland, 316–17, 603; in Italy, 342–43, 363, 365 n.25; in Kosovo, 375–76; in Latvia, 388, 395; in Lithuania, 403–4, 414–15; in Macedonia, 423; in Malta, 434–35; in Netherlands, 445–46; in Norway, 464–65, 466, 474; in Poland, 482–83; in Portugal, 512–13, 517; in Romania, 530–31; in Russia, 547–48; in Serbia and Montenegro, 578–79; in Slovakia, 589; in Spain, 602–3; in Sweden, 603, 622–24; in Switzerland, 655, 665; in Turkey, 3, 672, 674–76, 684, 688, 697 n.24; in Ukraine, 708; in United Kingdom, 3, 721–22, 734. **No. America/Caribbean**: Bahamas, 16–17; Barbados, 35; Canada, 51–53, 54; Cuba, 82–83; Dominican Republic, 109–10; French Caribbean, 138; Haiti, 155–56, 160–61; Jamaica, 180–82; Mexico, 207–8; Netherlands Antilles, 233–34; OECS, 254–55; Puerto Rico,

Fundamentalism, religious, harassment of women and (*see also* Segregation and separation): **Asia/Oceania** (*see also* Hamas [Movement of Islamic Resistance]; Law; Politics; Veiling): in Afghanistan, 12, 23; in Bangladesh, 72; in Pakistan, 386, 398 n.8

Fundamentalism, religious, politics and: **Middle East/No. Africa**: in Algeria, 17, 27, 30, 32; in Egypt, 100 n.29; in Iran, 126, 127, 128, 131; in Jordan, 220; in Saudi Arabia, 344, 346; in Syria, 371–72.

Fundamentalism, religious, violence and oppression via (*see also* Veiling; Violence): **Middle East/No. Africa**: in Algeria, 17, 20, 33; in Iran, 137

Fürst, Gunilla: **Europe**: in Sweden, 623

Gandhi, Indira: **Asia/Oceania**: in India, 172, 180. **Europe**: effect on Bulgaria, 110

García, Domitila: **No. America/Caribbean**: in Cuba, 90

Garment industry (*see also* Industry; Sweatshops; Textile industry): **Asia/Oceania**: in Bangladesh, 63, 76; in Cambodia, 89; in Nepal, 345; in Sri Lanka, 446

Gaskin, Molly: **No. America/Caribbean**: in Trinidad and Tobago, 312

Gays. *See* Homosexuality; Lesbianism; Same-sex

GDP. *See* Gross domestic product (GDP)

Gedle, Shewareged: **Sub-Saharan Africa**: in Ethiopia, 144

GEM. *See* Gender Empowerment Measure

Gender, decision making and: **Middle East/No. Africa**: in Egypt, 74; in Israel, 172; in Morocco, 283; in Saudi Arabia, 350; in Tunisia, 390; in UAE, 416, 424

Gender, family responsibilities

and (*see also* Family; Gender, public v. private spheres; Households, female-headed): **Middle East/No. Africa**: in Algeria, 24; in Bahrain, 51; in Egypt, 74; in Iran, 108, 118; in Lebanon, 246; in Libya, 266, 268; in Morocco, 285, 293, 294, 307; in The Occupied Territories, 323; in Syria, 365; in UAE, 424

Gender, public v. private spheres: **Middle East/No. Africa**: in Bahrain, 51, 60–61; in Egypt, 85; in Iran, 118; in Iraq, 156, 161; in Israel, 175; in Lebanon, 250; in Libya, 264; in The Occupied Territories, 321; in Tunisia, 390, 391

Gender Advocacy Project: **Sub-Saharan Africa**: in South Africa, 428, 429

Gender budgets: **Sub-Saharan Africa**: 7–8; in South Africa, 416–17, 491; in Tanzania, 8, 491; in Uganda, 8, 491–92

Gender Center: **Sub-Saharan Africa**: and Ghana, 170

Gender Development Index: **Asia/Oceania**: Cambodia in, 86; Laos in, 266; in Malaysia, 285. **Central/So. America**: Costa Rica in, 190; Guatemala in, 266

Gender Difference Index (UNDP): **Asia/Oceania**: Korea in, 242

Gender discrimination. *See* Discrimination, gender-based

Gender Empowerment Measure (GEM): **Asia/Oceania**: Malaysia in, 291; Taiwan in, 472–73. **No. America/Caribbean**: 122

Gender equality (*see also* Benefits; Inheritance and property rights; Laws; Pay; Property, right to own; Rights): **Europe**: 2–3, 5–6, 13; in Armenia, 40; in Austria, 47, 50–51; in Belgium, 72, 73, 77–78, 82; in Bosnia and Herzegovina, 88, 90, 92–94, 96, 96 n.3; in Bulgaria, 102, 105; under communism, 1, 4, 8, 18,

34, 40, 105, 168, 234, 235, 292, 403, 406, 546, 547–48, 556, 557, 561–52, 588, 592; in Croatia, 122, 125, 126; in Czech Republic, 136, 145; in Denmark, 3, 4, 152, 159, 161; in Estonia, 168, 177–78, 182–83; in Finland, 3, 6, 189–90, 191–92, 200, 202; in France, 206, 208–9, 218–19; and gender mainstreaming, 4, 82, 159, 161, 273, 318, 329, 716; in Georgia, 226, 227; in Germany, 234, 236, 238–39, 247, 248–49, 255–56; in Greece, 272, 273, 274; in Iceland, 3, 298, 309–10; in Ireland, 318, 322, 329, 331, 334–35; in Italy, 8, 351–52, 353, 355, 365 n.25; in Kosovo, 375, 381, 383; in Latvia, 389; in Lithuania, 402–3, 404, 410–11, 412, 415; in Macedonia, 422, 423, 424, 426–27; in Malta, 436, 440; in Netherlands, 445, 453, 454, 457; in Norway, 3, 467, 468, 469, 471–72, 474; in Poland, 485, 488, 495, 496; policies of European Union (EU) regarding, 1, 3–4, 82, 145, 155, 161, 182, 206, 264–65, 266, 267, 496, 540, 594, 606, 719; in Portugal, 513, 523; in Romania, 530, 531, 537–38, 540; in Russia, 547–48, 550, 553, 554–55, 564; in Slovakia, 588, 592, 596; in Soviet Union, 1; in Spain, 601, 602, 607–8, 612–13; in Sweden, 3, 9, 621–23, 624, 625–26, 631, 636, 637, 642; in Switzerland, 656, 657, 661; in Turkey, 672, 677, 679, 680, 690–91; in Ukraine, 4, 709, 714, 716; in United Kingdom, 719, 721, 723, 727, 734, 735, 738. **Middle East/No. Africa**: in Algeria, 21, 29; in Bahrain, 58; in Egypt, 85; in Iraq, 152–53, 161, 163; in Israel, 171, 178, 179; 182; in Jordan, 220–21; in Libya, 267; in Morocco, 282, 301; in Saudi Arabia, 344–45; in Syria, 362, 370, 371; in Tunisia, 391, 399; in UAE, 422. **Sub-Saharan Africa**: in Botswana, 31, 32, 36,

Bolivia, 68; in Colombia, 167; in Ecuador, 212; in Nicaragua, 344; in Panama, 371; in Paraguay, 392; in Peru, 424; in Uruguay, 462. **No. America/Caribbean**: *Gender Focused Interventions to Address the Challenges of the HIV/AIDS Epidemic* (study), 25

HIV/AIDS, incidence of: **Asia/Oceania**: 7; in Australia, 45; in Bangladesh, 71; in Cambodia, 95; in Central Asia, 118; in China, 140; in India, 171; in Indonesia, 202–3; in Japan, 230; in Korea, 255; in Laos, 273; in Malaysia, 289; in Micronesia, 307; in Myanmar, 326; in Nepal, 355; in New Zealand, 374; in Pakistan, 392; in Philippines, 427; in Sri Lanka, 452; in Taiwan, 486; in Thailand, 514; in Uzbekistan, 547; in Vietnam, 567. **Central/So. America**: in Belize, 53; in Bolivia, 68; in Brazil, 100; in Chile, 133; in Colombia, 166; in Ecuador, 212; in El Salvador, 238; in French Guiana, 262; in Guatemala, 274; in Guyana, 302; in Honduras, 322; in Panama, 371; in Paraguay, 392; in Peru, 423–24; in Suriname, 445–46; in Uruguay, 463; in Venezuela, 486

HIV/AIDS, organizations and studies: **No. America/Caribbean**: *Gender Focused Interventions to Address the Challenges of the HIV/AIDS Epidemic* (study), 25. **Sub-Saharan Africa**: Botswana Network of AIDS Service Organizations (BONASO), 36; National AIDS and STI Control Program (NASCP), 324; National AIDS Prevention Department (Cameroon), 93; National Committee for the Prevention of AIDS (CNLS) (Cameroon), 93; National Community of Women Living with AIDS, 496; National Program to Combat AIDS

(Guinea), 190; Organization for Social Service for AIDS, in Ethiopia, 139

Hoa Hao: **Asia/Oceania**: in Vietnam, 569

Holland. *See subentries for* Netherlands

Holocaust (*see also* Judaism, World War II): **Europe**: 13 n.3; Denmark, 160

Homelessness (*see also* Immigrants; Refugees): **Asia/Oceania**: in Australia, 41. **Central/So. America**: in Bolivia, 71

Homosexuality (*see also* Adoption by same-sex couples; Lesbianism; Rights, transgender; Same-sex): **Middle East/No. Africa**: in Bahrain, 60; in Egypt, 84; in Iran, 129; in Iraq, 163; in Israel, 179–80; in Libya, 273; in Morocco, 303; in The Occupied Territories, 329; in Tunisia, 399; in UAE, 420; in Yemen, 459. **No. America/Caribbean**: Bahamas, 22; Canada, 60, 61; Cuba, 93–94; Dominican Republic, 119

Honduras, British. *See subentries for* Belize

Hong Kong: **Asia/Oceania**: 132

Honor, family (*see also* Abaya; Adultery; Chastity; Fidelity; Murder, of women; Veiling; Violence, domestic; Virginity): **Middle East/No. Africa**: in Bahrain, 52; in Egypt, 75–76, 97; in Iran, 115, 123; in Iraq, 153, 165; in Jordan, 210, 224, 226–27; in Lebanon, 246, 248, 249; in Libya, 269, 275; in Morocco, 292, 293, 307; in The Occupied Territories, 324; in Syria, 363, 366, 374; in Tunisia, 390.

Honor killings (*see also* Adultery; Chastity; Fidelity; Murder, of women; Violence): **Asia/Oceania**: in Pakistan, 395

Hospitality industry (*see also* Employment, service sector; Sex tourism; Tourism): **Asia/Oceania**: in New Zealand, 370–71

Hotlines, for domestic violence (*see also* Shelters for battered women; Violence): **Middle East/No. Africa**: in Tunisia, 402. Houda-Pepin, Fatima: **No. America/Caribbean**: in Canada, 66

Household work (*see also* Work, unpaid): **Asia/Oceania**: in Australia, 36, 41–42; in India, 164; in Indonesia, 198–99; in Japan, 223, 227; in Korea, 246, 249–50, 252; in Laos, 271; in Myanmar, 319, 323; in New Zealand, 369, 370; in Pakistan, 387, 390; in Philippines, 422; in Taiwan, 473, 475, 477, 492; in Uzbekistan, 540–41. **Central/So. America**: in Argentina, 23; in Bolivia, 65–66; in Brazil, 94; in Chile, 126, 129, 136; in Costa Rica, 190; in Ecuador, 208; in El Salvador, 230; in Guatemala, 270; in Honduras, 319; in Nicaragua, 341; in Panama, 367; in Suriname, 444; in Uruguay, 460, 461; in Venezuela, 483. **Sub-Saharan Africa**: 3; in Botswana, 29, 32; in Cameroon, 86; in Eritrea, 112, 113, 114; in Ethiopia, 131, 143; in Ghana, 157, 159, 160, 162; in Guinea, 187, 188; in Mozambique, 253; in Niger, 301; in Nigeria, 320; in Rwanda, 342; in Somalia, 391, 392; in South Africa, 417, 418; in Sudan, 440; in Tanzania, 460, 462, 463; in Togo, 474, 475; in Zimbabwe, 513

Households, female-headed (*see also* Divorce; Marriage, woman): **Middle East/No. Africa**: in Algeria, 24; in Iran, 120; in Jordan, 207; in Morocco, 286; in The Occupied Territories, 319, 320, 323; in Syria, 357; in Tunisia, 391–92; in Yemen, 447. **No. America/Caribbean**: Canada, 39, French Caribbean, 141–42; Jamaica, 188, 189; Netherlands Antilles, 239; OECS, 253–54; Puerto Rico, 280, 283; Trinidad and

Netherlands Antilles, 239–40; OECS, 261, 263; United States, 338–39, 344–45. **Sub-Saharan Africa**: Cameroon, 91; Eritrea, 116; Ethiopia, 137

International Women's Day: **Europe**: 79. **Middle East/No. Africa**: in Tunisia, 399. **No. America/Caribbean**: 67

International Women's Decade (1975–1985), **Asia/Oceania**: 1; legal changes during and after, 7; and Sri Lanka, 442. **Central/So. America**: and Panama, 372; and reform, 8; and Venezuela, 494. **Middle East/No. Africa**: in Jordan, 217, 224. **No. America/Caribbean**: 15–16

International Year of the Woman (1975): **Asia/Oceania**: 1; and Papua New Guinea independence, 407; and women's rights, 8. **Central/So. America**: and Brazil, 105; and Panama, 372. **No. America/Caribbean**: 124

Internet, use of: **Asia/Oceania**: in Korea, 259; and Philippines, 427; in Taiwan, 491. **No. America/Caribbean**: in Canada, 53

Internet violence (*see also* Violence): **Asia/Oceania**: in Korea, 259

Intifada. *See* Palestinians, resistance movement of

Investment, foreign. *See* Banking; Foreign investment; International Aid

Iragary, Luce: **Europe**: in Mexico, 216

Islam and Muslims (*see also* Hamas [Movement of Islamic Resistance]; Fundamentalism, religious; Law, Islamic [*shari'a*]; Law, religious; Organizations, religious; Ramadan; Shi'ism; Sunni Muslims; Veiling): **Asia/Oceania**: 6; in Afghanistan, 21–22; in Bangladesh, 57, 65; in Central Asia, 119–20; in China, 145; in India, 158; in India, 167, 176, 177; in Indonesia, 197, 199–200, 201, 207–8; in Malaysia,

283, 288, 289, 290, 292–94; in Myanmar, 330; in Nepal, 344; outline of, 401 n.54; in Pakistan, 384, 386, 390, 391, 393–95, 398 n.8; in Philippines, 417, 420, 432, 434; in Sri Lanka, 441, 443–44, 444, 449, 457–58; in Taiwan, 491; in Thailand, 518; in Uzbekistan, 533, 535, 538, 542, 549, 550–52, 552; in Vietnam, 569. **Central/So. America**: 4; 35; in Guyana, 305; in Suriname, 447. **Europe**: in Albania, 27; in Austria, 55; in Belgium, 80; in Bosnia and Herzegovina, 88, 94; in Bulgaria, 110; in Croatia, 120, 127; in Denmark, 152; in Finland, 201; in France, 5, 206, 207, 217; in Georgia, 224; in Germany, 251, 252; in Greece, 275; in Kosovo, 283, 380; in Macedonia, 427–28; in Netherlands, 444, 456; in Russia, 546; in Switzerland, 663; in Turkey, 10, 671, 673, 675, 679, 684, 689–90, 691–92, 694, 696, 696 n.3, 697 n.26, 699 n.78; in United Kingdom, 736. **Middle East/No. Africa**: in Egypt, 90–92, 94; in Iraq, 157; in Jordan, 205; in Morocco, 307. **Sub-Saharan Africa**: 12; in Burundi, 73; in Cameroon, 84, 99; in Eritrea, 110; in Ethiopia, 127, 145; in Ghana, 156, 165, 168; in Guinea, 179, 181, 194; in Kenya, 209, 214, 215; in Mali, 226, 238; in Mozambique, 259, 261; in Niger, 296, 301, 306; in Nigeria, 313, 315, 316–17, 320; in Rwanda, 356; in Senegal, 365, 368, 373, 376, 377, 379, 380–81, 382, 383; in Somalia, 389, 395, 397, 399; in South Africa, 426; in Sudan, 439, 443, 449, 450; in Tanzania, 465, 466; in Togo, 479; in Uganda, 487, 497; in Zimbabwe, 507

Islamic law. *See* Law, Islamic; Law, religious

Israel, and Ethiopia: **Sub-Saharan Africa**: 148

IUDs (intrauterine devices). *See* Contraception; Family planning

Jäätteenmäki, Annel: **Europe**: in Finland, 189

Jacobs, Aletta: **Europe**: in Macedonia, 452–53

Jagan, Cheddi: **Central/So. America**: in Guyana, 306

Jagan, Janet: **Central/So. America**: in Guyana, 302, 303

Jagdeo, Bharrat: **Central/So. America**: in Guyana, 303, 305

Jalal, Massouda: **Asia/Oceania**: in Afghanistan, 21

James, Carol: **No. America/Caribbean**: in Trinidad and Tobago, 312

Japan, influence on: **Central/So. America**: Brazil, 86; Peru, 412, 424

Jehovah's Witnesses, religion of: **Central/So. America**: in Peru, 428

Jesuits, in Panama: **Central/So. America**: 363

Jews. *See* Judaism; Law, Jewish

Jhvania, Zurab: **Europe**: 228

Job flexibility: **No. America/Caribbean**: 3 in United States, 34–35

Job placement services: **No. America/Caribbean**: Bahamas, 20

Job/career opportunities: (*see also* Education; Employment; Work): **Asia/Oceania**: 4; in Afghanistan, 13; in Australia, 33; in Bangladesh, 61; in Cambodia, 87, 88; in China, 128, 130; in India, 159; in Japan, 224; in Micronesia, 304; in Myanmar, 319; in Pakistan, 388; in Philippines, 422; in Sri Lanka, 445. **Central/So. America**: in Argentina, 19; in Belize, 50; in Brazil, 88; in Ecuador, 205; in French Guiana, 259; in Panama, 364; in Suriname, 442; in Uruguay, 457, 458. **Europe**: in Albania, 19–20; in Armenia, 35; in Austria, 48; in Belarus, 63–

minican Republic, III; French Caribbean, 140–41; Jamaica, 182–83, 184; Mexico, 209; Netherlands Antilles, 235; OECS, 258–59; Puerto Rico, 278–80; Trinidad and Tobago, 309–10; United States, 330, 331, 332–33. **Sub-Saharan Africa**: in Botswana, 29; in Burundi, 62; in Eritrea, 114; in Ethiopia, 133; in Ghana, 160; in Guinea, 181, 184; in Kenya, 206; in Namibia, 275; in Nigeria, 317; in Senegal, 371; in South Africa, 411, 413; in Sudan, 439, 442; in Tanzania, 459–60; in Togo, 474; in Uganda, 490; in Zimbabwe, 511

Pay, formal workforce: **Middle East/No. Africa**: in Iran, 113, 114; in Iraq, 152–53; in Israel, 171, 172; in Jordan, 200, 202, 203–4; in Lebanon, 241; in Morocco, 282, 286; in Syria, 362; in Tunisia, 386; in Yemen, 438, 444

Pay, informal workforce: **Middle East/No. Africa**: in Jordan, 198, 199; in Morocco, 286, 287; in Tunisia, 386; in UAE, 416, 417

Pay, minimum wage standards of: **Asia/Oceania**: in Bangladesh, 65; in Cambodia, 89; in Indonesia, 195; in Laos, 269; in Nepal, 349; in Philippines, 423; in Thailand, 508. **Central/So. America**: in Guatemala, 269; in Guyana, 297. **Middle East/ No. Africa**: in Egypt, 71; in Israel, 173; in Jordan, 204; in Morocco, 286, 287; in the Occupied Territories, 318; in Tunisia, 386, 387

Pay, overtime: **Asia/Oceania**: in Bangladesh, 64, 65; in Cambodia, 89–90; in China, 132. **Central/So. America**: in Chile, 129; in Guyana, 298

Peacebuilding: **Sub-Saharan Africa**: 13–14; in Burundi, 58, 59, 71, 72–73; in Mozambique, 260; in Rwanda, 355; in Somalia,

397, 398–99, 403 n.30, 501; in Sudan, 451

Pedophilia (*see also* Child, sexual abuse of): **Asia/Oceania**: in Philippines, 427, 434

Pélé: **Central/So. America**: Brazil, 95

Peña, Lorena (Rebecca Palacio): **Central/So. America**: El Salvador, 243

Penal code. **Middle East/No. Africa**: *See* Code, penal

Penal Code Amendment Act of 1998 (Botswana): **Sub-Saharan Africa**: 43

Pension, benefits (*see also* Retirement): **Middle East/No. Africa**: in Iraq, 154; in Israel, 171; in Jordan, 207; in Libya, 267; in Morocco, 303; in Tunisia, 387. **No. America/Caribbean**: Canada, 54; French Caribbean, 141; Puerto Rico, 279–80

Pentecostal religion: **Central/So. America**: in Uruguay, 467

Pérez Jiménez, Marcos: **Central/ So. America**: Venezuela, 487, 492

Perón, Eva Duarte de (Evita): **Central/So. America**: Argentina, 29

Perón, Isabel (María Estela Martínez): **Central/So. America**: 7; Argentina, 25

Perón, Juan: **Central/So. America**: 7; Argentina, 20, 22, 25, 29

Personal Law for Muslims Act of 1991: **Sub-Saharan Africa**: Sudan, 441

Personal status code. *See* Code, personal status (CSP)

Philip, King of Spain: **Asia/Oceania**: Philippines and, 418

Piece work. *See* Employment, piece-work

Pilgrimage, religious (*see also* Menstruation, rituals and; *entries beginning with* Religion; *with* Rituals): **Middle East/ No. Africa**: from Egypt, 95; from Iran, 130, 132–33; from Libya, 274; from Morocco,

304, 305, 306; from Yemen, 460

Ping Lu: **Asia/Oceania**: Taiwan, 491

Ping Ying Chang: **Asia/Oceania**: Taiwan, 491

Pinochet Ugarte, Augusto: **Central/So. America**: Chile, 123, 131–32, 135

Planned Parenthood. *See* International Planned Parenthood:

Plastic surgery (*see also* Beauty, concept of): **Central/So. America**: in Brazil, 87, 101; in Venezuela, 487–88

Pol Pot: **Asia/Oceania**: Cambodia, 85, 86

Police: **Asia/Oceania**: in Bangladesh, 74; in Philippines, 433. **Central/So. America**: in Bolivia, 72; in Suriname, 448; in Uruguay, 469

Police, rape victim reports and (*see also* Rape, custodial): **Asia/ Oceania**: in Thailand, 521.

Police, women as: **Central/So. America**: in Brazil, 108–9; in Ecuador, 214; in Peru, 430; in Uruguay, 468. **Middle East/ No. Africa**: in Algeria, 20, 31; in Iraq, 152, 163; in UAE, 417, 424

Police stations handling violence against women (*see also* Police, women as): **Central/So. America**: in Nicaragua, 350; in Peru, 430.

Political leadership and decision-making: **Sub-Saharan Africa**: 1, 10, 11, 12, 15; in Botswana, 38, 41, 45 n.19; in Burundi, 58, 69; in Cameroon, 94–96; in Eritrea, 117, 119; in Ethiopia, 141–42, 143; in Guinea, 191–93; Guinea Bissau, 10; in Kenya, 214; in Namibia, 281–83; in Niger, 304–5; in Nigeria, 313–14; in Rwanda, 10, 350–52; in Somalia, 397–98; in Sudan, 448; in Uganda, 10, 499–500

Political organizations. *See* Organizations, political

Political participation by women

anism, religion of; Seventh Day Adventists, religion of): **Asia/ Oceania**: in Indonesia, 207–8; in Micronesia, 308; in Taiwan, 491; in Vietnam, 569. **Central/ So. America**: in Argentina, 35; in Chile, 130, 139; in Colombia, 154, 173; in Costa Rica, 194; in Guatemala, 265–66, 280; in Honduras, 315; in Nicaragua, 348, 349; in Panama, 362, 368; in Peru, 428; in Suriname, 447; in Uruguay, 467. **Europe**: in Austria, 55; in Bosnia and Herzegovina, 88; in Croatia, 120, 127; in France, 217; in Germany, 251, 252; in Latvia, 394; in Netherlands, 444, 455–56; in Slovakia, 595; in Switzerland, 663; in United Kingdom, 735–36. **Sub-Saharan Africa**: 12; in Botswana, 42; in Cameroon, 99; in Guinea, 194; in Kenya, 215; in Mozambique, 261; in Namibia, 286; in Rwanda, 356; in Senegal, 380; in Uganda, 497, 498

Protests. *See* Unrest

Provisional National Defense Council (PNDC): **Sub-Saharan Africa**: 155, 166, 167

PSL. *See* Law, Personal Status (PSL)

Public, women in. *See* Gender, public v. private spheres; Segregation and separation

Public Service Act (1994) (Sudan): **Sub-Saharan Africa**: 442

Purdah (*see also* Segregation and separation): **Asia/Oceania**: in Afghanistan, 23; in Bangladesh, 60, 72; in Pakistan, 387, 394, 400 n.34

Putin, Vladimir: **Europe**: Russia, 569

Qat. *See* Drugs, alcohol use and

Qigong: **Asia/Oceania**: Chile, 145

Qur'an, interpretation of (*see also* Law, Islamic): **Asia/Oceania**: 22, 293, 401 n.54. **Middle East/ No. Africa**: in Bahrain, 61; in

Egypt, 78, 86; in Iraq, 163; in Morocco, 304; in The Occupied Territories, 330; in Syria, 372; in UAE, 419, 420

Quakers: **Europe**: United Kingdom, 735

Queiroz, Carlota: **Central/So. America**: Brazil, 8

Quezon, President: **Asia/Oceania**: Philippines, 429

Quota laws (*see also* Political participation by women; Suffrage): **Asia/Oceania**: 7; in Australia, 46–47; in Bangladesh, 71; in India, 173; in Nepal, 356; in Pakistan, 393; in Sri Lanka, 454; in Taiwan, 471, 472, 488. **Central/So. America**: 8; in Argentina, 30; in Bolivia, 70; in Brazil, 103; in Central and South America, 8; in Costa Rica, 192; in Ecuador, 213; in Paraguay, 393; in Venezuela, 488. **Europe**: in Belgium, 77; in Bosnia and Herzegovina, 91; in Croatia, 125; in Denmark, 159; in France, 7, 215; in Germany, 7, 248–49; in Greece, 273; in Italy, 358; in Kosovo, 381; in Norway, 471; in Portugal, 519–20; in Spain, 7, 612; in Sweden, 623. **Middle East/No. Africa**: in Jordan, 190, 218–119. **Sub-Saharan Africa**: 11; and Botswana, 37; and Cameroon, 96, 100; in Ghana, 167; in Namibia, 282–83, 290; in Somalia, 398; in Tanzania, 464; Tunisia, 11

Race relations (*see also* Class; Discrimination, gender based; Indigenous peoples): **No. America/Caribbean**: Canada, 52, 69, 72; Cuba, 91, 94–95; Netherlands Antilles, 230–31

Racial factors (*see also* Class; Indigenous peoples): **Central/ So. America**: in Brazil, 86, 88–91, 94–95, 97, 101, 106, 109; in Ecuador, 204; in Guyana, 304; in Panama, 365; in Venezuela, 486.

Radio. *See* Media

Rahman, Sheik Mujibur: **Asia/ Oceania**: Bangladesh, 58

Rahman, Ziaur: **Asia/Oceania**: Bangladesh, 58, 71

Rahmonov, Emomal: **Asia/Oceania**: Central Asia, 108

Rama IX, King Bhumipol Adulyadej: **Asia/Oceania**: Thailand, 503

Rama V, King Chulalongkorn: **Asia/Oceania**: Thailand, 505

Ramadan (*see also* Religion and spirituality; Rituals, religious practices and): **Asia/Oceania**: India, 177; Malaysia, 293; Pakistan, 401 n.54. **Middle East/ No. Africa**: in Egypt, 95; in Iran, 132; in Iraq, 163; in Libya, 265, 274; in Morocco, 304, 305, 306

Ramos, Fidel: **Asia/Oceania**: Philippines, 419, 420, 426, 427, 432

Rana, Jung Bahadur: **Asia/Oceania**: Nepal, 344

Rape, custodial (*see also* Child, sexual abuse of): **Asia/Oceania**: in India, 179; in Sri Lanka, 459; in Uzbekistan, 552. **Central/So. America**: in Bolivia, 74

Rape, date: **Asia/Oceania**: in New Zealand, 377

Rape, deaths connected to: **Asia/ Oceania**: in Myanmar, 332

Rape, marital (*see also* Violence, domestic): **Asia/Oceania**: in India, 179; in Indonesia, 209; in Japan, 234; in Nepal, 357, 360; in Philippines, 433; in Sri Lanka, 458, 459; in Uzbekistan, 552; in Vietnam, 569. **Central/ So. America**: in Belize, 54; in Chile, 141–42; in Peru, 430, 431; in Suriname, 448. **Middle East/ No. Africa**: in Iran, 133, 134; in Jordan, 226; in Lebanon, 252, 253; in Morocco, 308; in Syria, 374; in Tunisia, 403; in Yemen, 462. **Sub-Saharan Africa**: in Cameroon, 100; in Ethiopia, 146; in Ghana, 167–

68, 170, 171; in Kenya, 216; in Namibia, 288–89; in Niger, 307; in South Africa, 428; in Tanzania, 460–61; in Zimbabwe, 520.

Rape, punishment of: **Asia/Oceania**: 7; in Australia, 50; in China, 146; in Indonesia, 209; in Laos, 277; in Malaysia, 294, 295; in Myanmar, 331; in Nepal, 359. **Central/So. America**: in Brazil, 108; in Paraguay, 398–99; in Peru, 431. **No. America/Caribbean**: Bahamas, 29. **Sub-Saharan Africa**: Combating of Rape Act in Namibia, 288; Tanzania, 465, 466

Rape, services for victims of (see also Police, rape victim reports and; Police, and stations handling violence against women; Shelters for battered women): **Asia/Oceania**: in India, 178; in Japan, 233–34; in Korea, 259; in Myanmar, 331; in Sri Lanka, 459; in Uzbekistan, 553. **Central/So. America**: in Argentina, 36; in Belize, 54; in Bolivia, 74; in Costa Rica, 194; in Paraguay, 399. **Sub-Saharan Africa**: Cameroon, 100

Rape, shame associated with (see also Honor killings; Murder, of women): **Asia/Oceania**: in Central Asia, 120–21; in India, 179; in Myanmar, 319, 331; in Uzbekistan, 552–53. **Central/So. America**: in Guyana, 306

Rape, underreporting of: **Asia/Oceania**: in Cambodia, 98; in Central Asia, 120–21; in China, 146; in India, 179; in Japan, 234; in Malaysia, 295; in Taiwan, 493; in Thailand, 521; in Uzbekistan, 552. **Central/So. America**: in Bolivia, 74; in Guyana, 306

Rape, unsympathetic treatment of: **Asia/Oceania**: in Central Asia, 121; in India, 179; in Indonesia, 210–11; in Thailand, 521; in Uzbekistan, 552

Rape Crisis South Africa: **Sub-Saharan Africa**: 428, 429

Rape/sexual assault: **Asia/Oceania** (see also Incest; Pedophilia).: in Cambodia, 98; in Central Asia, 120–21; in Indonesia, 209–11; in Japan, 234; in Laos, 277; in Malaysia, 295; in Nepal, 359; in New Zealand, 377; in Pakistan, 401 n.57; in Papua New Guinea, 415; in Philippines, 433; in Taiwan, 493; in Uzbekistan, 552–53. **Central/So. America**: in Argentina, 31, 36; in Belize, 54; in Brazil, 109; in Chile, 141–42; in Colombia, 175; in El Salvador, 247; in Guatemala, 281; in Nicaragua, 350; in Paraguay, 397, 398–99; in Peru, 431; in Suriname, 448; in Uruguay, 468–69; in Venezuela, 495–96. **Europe**: in Albania, 28; in Armenia, 41; in Austria, 56; in Belarus, 67; in Belgium, 81; in Bosnia and Herzegovina, 129, 584; in Bulgaria, 111; in Croatia, 128, 129, 584; in Czech Republic, 143–44; in Denmark, 161; in Estonia, 12, 181; in Finland, 202; in France, 218; in Germany, 253, 254; in Greece, 276; in Iceland, 309; in Ireland, 334; in Kosovo, 382; in Lithuania, 413, 414; in Macedonia, 428; in Netherlands, 456; in Norway, 474; in Poland, 500; in Portugal, 522; in Romania, 539–40; in Russia, 567; in Spain, 616–17; spousal rape, 128, 202, 253, 254, 428, 540, 567, 664, 695, 736; in Sweden, 641; in Switzerland, 664; in Turkey, 695; in United Kingdom, 738. **Middle East/No. Africa**: in Bahrain, 62; in Egypt, 97; in Iran, 134, 137; in Iraq, 165; in Israel, 176; in Jordan, 226, 228; in Lebanon, 249, 252; in Libya, 275; in Morocco, 296; in The Occupied Territories, 332; in Syria, 375; in Tunisia, 402–3; in UAE, 425; in Yemen, 462. **No. America/Caribbean**: Bahamas, 28–29;

Barbados, 44; Canada, 73; Caribbean, 9; Dominican Republic, 126; Haiti, 171; Jamaica, 195–96; Mexico, 220–21; Netherlands Antilles, 244–45; Puerto Rico, 292; and slavery, 230; Trinidad and Tobago, 323, United States, 348–49. **Sub-Saharan Africa**: 12, 13; in Botswana, 43; in Burundi, 13, 74; in Cameroon, 100; in Eritrea, 120; in Ethiopia, 126, 128–29, 132, 139, 144, 146–47; in Ghana, 164, 167, 170; in Guinea, 195; in Kenya, 204, 216; in Mali, 239; in Mozambique, 261, 262–63; in Namibia, 281, 285, 288–89; in Nigeria, 331–32; in Rwanda, 13, 342, 350, 357; in Senegal, 382; in Somalia, 391, 395, 397, 400; in South Africa, 409, 421, 428–30, 431; in Sudan, 13, 445, 451; in Tanzania, 460, 466–67; in Togo, 480; in Uganda, 499; in Zimbabwe, 516, 519–20

Rastafarianism, religion of: **No. America/Caribbean**: 194–95, 322

Rawlings, Jerry: **Sub-Saharan Africa**: Ghana, 155, 166, 167

Rawlings, Nan Konadu Agyeman: **Sub-Saharan Africa**: Ghana, 167

Reagan, Ronald: **Central/So. America**: El Salvador, 225, 239

Rebick, Judy: **No. America/Caribbean**: Canada, 67

Reconciliation of indigenous peoples: **Asia/Oceania**: Australia, 29–30

Red Cross: **Sub-Saharan Africa**: in Botswana, 38

Reebok, in Indonesia: **Asia/Oceania**: 196

Reform, economic (see also International Monetary Fund [IMF]): **Middle East/No. Africa**: in Bahrain, 62; in Iran, 107; in Jordan, 196; in Syria, 363; in Tunisia, 382. **Sub-Saharan Africa**: in Ghana, 156,

165; in Kenya, 208, 217; in Mali, 231

Reform, education: **Central/So. America**: in Chile, 124; in El Salvador, 228; in Guatemala, 267; in Paraguay, 383; in Peru, 414; in Uruguay, 460; in Venezuela, 479–80. **Middle East/No. Africa**: in Iran, 107, 110–11, 127; in Jordan, 192; in Tunisia, 384

Reform, land. *See* Land reform

Reform, legal. *See* Law, reform

Reform, political: **Middle East/No. Africa**: in Egypt, 86, 90; in Iran, 127; in Iraq, 156; in Lebanon, 250; in Tunisia, 381

Refugees: **Asia/Oceania**: from Afghanistan, 11–12, 12–13, 23–24, 24–25; in Australia, 31; in Myanmar, 333–34; in Sri Lanka, 460. **Central/So. America**: to Belize, 48; in El Salvador, 225; from El Salvador, 246; from Guatemala, 282; from Peru, 432; from Suriname, 449. **Middle East/No. Africa** (*see also* Palestinians, as refugees): from Afghanistan, 137; from Iran, 137; in Jordan, 193, 198–99, 200; in Lebanon, 240, 251; in The Occupied Territories, 314, 320–21; in Syria, 360; Reintegration of Demobilized Fighters (MITYAS). **Sub-Saharan Africa**: in Eritrea, 119

Refugees, education of: **Asia/Oceania**: from Afghanistan, 12–13, 24. **Central/So. America**: in Guatemala, 267

Religion (*see also specific religions*; Ancestor worship; Evangelism; Fundamentalism, religious; Liberation theology; Pilgrimage, religious; Religion and spirituality; Rituals, religious practices and): **Asia/Oceania**: 6; in Australia, 48–49; birthplace of, 2; in Cambodia, 97–98; in Central Asia, 114, 119–20; in China, 144–45; in India, 156, 157, 162; in India, 158; in Laos, 276; in Malaysia, 283, 292–94;

in Micronesia, 308–9; in Myanmar, 327, 329–30; in Nepal, 344; in New Zealand, 377; in Sri Lanka, 441; in Taiwan, 491; in Uzbekistan, 533, 550; in Vietnam, 569. **Central/So. America**: in Central and South America, 4; in Costa Rica, 194; in Suriname, 447; in Uruguay, 467. **No. America/Caribbean**: Bahamas, 27–28; Barbados, 43–44; Canada, 49–50, 62, 70–71; Cuba, 79, 86, 94–97; Dominican Republic, 125–26; French Caribbean, 146; fundamentalism in, 322; Haiti, 168–70; Jamaica, 194–95; Mexico, 39, 42, 217–20, 223 n.38; Netherlands Antilles, 231, 233–34, 243–44; OECS, 267; Puerto Rico, 290–91; Trinidad and Tobago, 302, 321–22; United States, 346–47

Religion, education and. *See* Education, religious

Religion, independent churches: **Sub-Saharan Africa**: 12; in Ghana, 169; in Zimbabwe, 518

Religion, indigenous (*see also specific religions*; Ancestor worship; Rituals, religious practices and): **Asia/Oceania**: in Thailand, 511, 519–20. **Central/So. America**: in Bolivia, 73; in Central and South America, 4; in Chile, 139; in Colombia, 173–74; in Ecuador, 216; in Guatemala, 279–80; in Paraguay, 396; in Peru, 428–29; in Suriname, 447

Religion, law and. *See* Law

Religion, new: **Asia/Oceania**: in Japan, 221, 233

Religion, New Age: **Central/So. America**: in Argentina, 36

Religion, patriarchy in: **Asia/Oceania**: 6; in New Zealand, 377. **Central/So. America**: in Costa Rica, 194; in Guyana, 305

Religion, politics and: **Central/So. America**: in Argentina, 34–35. **Middle East/No. Africa**: in Bahrain, 57–58; in Iran, 133;

in Jordan, 222, 224; in Saudi Arabia, 340–41, 342, 344–45, 348, 350; in Syria, 373; in Yemen, 460. *See also* Fundamentalism, religious, and politics; Organizations, women's political; Reform, political. **Sub-Saharan Africa**: 2; in Mali, 238–39; in Nigeria, 327, 333

Religion, women's roles in: **Asia/Oceania**: 6; in Afghanistan, 21; in Australia, 49; in China, 145; in India, 175–76; in Indonesia, 207–8; in Japan, 232; in Laos, 276; in Malaysia, 293; in Myanmar, 330; in Nepal, 358; in Pakistan, 394; in Papua New Guinea, 415; in Philippines, 431–32; in Sri Lanka, 456–57; in Taiwan, 491–92; in Thailand, 519; in Uzbekistan, 550–51; in Vietnam, 569. **Central/So. America**: in Argentina, 34–35; in Brazil, 107–8; in Chile, 139–40; in Costa Rica, 194; in Ecuador, 216; in El Salvador, 246; in Nicaragua, 348; in Panama, 375; in Paraguay, 396–97; in Peru, 428; in Suriname, 447; in Uruguay, 467. **Middle East/No. Africa**: in Egypt, 93, 94, 95; in Iran, 127–29; in Israel, 174; in Jordan, 212, 222, 225; in Lebanon, 246, 251; in Libya, 274; in Saudi Arabia, 340, 341–42; in Tunisia, 391; in Yemen, 460. **No. America/Caribbean**: Bahamas, 28; Barbados, 43–44; Jamaica, 194–95; Mexico, 218–20; Netherlands Antilles, 243; United States, 347

Religion and spirituality (*see also specific religions*): **Europe**: 2; in Albania, 27; in Armenia, 40–41, 42 n.13; in Austria, 55; in Belarus, 67; in Belgium, 77, 78, 79, 80; in Bosnia and Herzegovina, 88, 94; in Bulgaria, 110; in Croatia, 120, 123, 127–28; in Czech Republic, 140, 142–43; in Denmark, 152, 160; in Estonia, 180–81; in Finland, 201; in

Uganda, 486, 489, 491; in Zimbabwe, 507, 513

US Agency for International Development (USAID): **Europe**: 712. **Middle East/No. Africa**: in Egypt, 87; in Jordan, 206, 210; in The Occupied Territories, 319, 320. **Sub-Saharan Africa**: in Ghana, 165; in Senegal, 372

US National Endowment for Democracy: **Sub-Saharan Africa**: 449

USAID. *See* US Agency for International Development (USAID)

Usena, Edidiong: **Sub-Saharan Africa**: in Nigeria, 328

Uwilingiyimana, Agathe: **Sub-Saharan Africa**: in Rwanda, 353

Vaccinations. *See* Immunization; Medicine, access to

Vaginismus (*see also* Health; Virginity) **Europe**: 687, 699 n.65

Vankovska, Biljana: **Europe**: in Macedonia, 427

Vargas, Getúlio: **Central/So. America**: in Brazil, 93, 103

Vargas, Virginia: **Central/So. America**: in Peru, 426

Vasectomy. *See* Sterilization, reproductive

Vásquez, Horacio: **No. America/Caribbean**: in Dominican Republican, 127

Vatican II. *See* Second Vatican Council

Veiling (*see also* Abaya): **Asia/Oceania**: in Afghanistan, 10, 14, 16, 23; in Bangladesh, 72; in India, 176; in Indonesia, 211; in Malaysia, 293; in Pakistan, 390; in Uzbekistan, 535–36, 544, 554 n.5. **Middle East/No. Africa**: 4–7, 9; in Algeria, 17, 33, 36 n.5; in Bahrain, 52; in Egypt, 75–76; in Iran, 110, 111; in Iraq, 156, 164; in Libya, 268; in Morocco, 290; in the Occupied Territories, 330; in Saudi Arabia, 345–47; in Syria, 364, 366;

in UAE, 417, 425; in Yemen, 449.

Veiling, politics of: **Middle East/No. Africa**: in Egypt, 75–76, 89, 90; in Iran, 114, 125, 126, 128, 136, 137; in Libya, 268; in Saudi Arabia, 346–47; in Syria, 366; in Yemen, 460

Velandia, Manuel: **Central/So. America**: in Columbia, 172

Velasco, Juan: **Central/So. America**: in Peru, 418

Velázquez, Nydia: **No. America/Caribbean**: in Puerto Rico, 289

Vendors. *See entries beginning with* Employment; Entrepreneurs, women as

Verstand-Bogaert, A.E.: **Europe**: in Netherlands, 447

Verwoerd, Hendrik: **Sub-Saharan Africa**: in South Africa, 409

Viall, Jenny: **Sub-Saharan Africa**: in South Africa, 421

Vicenti, Azucena de: **Central/So. America**: 11 n.18

Vike-Freiberga, Vaira: **Europe**: in Latvia, 393

Villa El Salvador, Peru: **Central/So. America**: in Peru, 418, 432

Violence (*see also* Death, by violence; Fundamentalism, religious, violence and oppression via; Internet violence; Murder, of women; Rape; Police, rape victim reports and; Police stations handling violence against women; Torture, of women): **Asia/Oceania**: in Bangladesh, 74; in Philippines, 432–33. **Central/So. America**: in Bolivia, 73; in Colombia, 153–54, 171, 174; in El Salvador, 247. **Europe**: 2, 11–12; in Albania, 5, 28–29; in Armenia, 41; in Austria, 51, 55–57; in Belarus, 67; in Belgium, 72, 81–82; in Bosnia and Herzegovina, 5, 90, 94–96, 97 nn.9, 10, 98 n.11, 129, 584; in Bulgaria, 111; in Croatia, 5, 121, 127, 128–29, 584; in Czech Republic, 143–45; in

Denmark, 152, 156–57, 160–61; domestic, 3, 4, 5, 12, 28, 41, 51, 56, 81, 94–96, 111, 121, 127, 128, 143, 156–57, 160–61, 181, 201–2, 218, 229, 253–54, 275–76, 292, 308, 334, 360–61, 363, 367 n.77, 382, 395, 414, 428, 439, 456, 457, 474, 499–500, 501, 522, 530, 539, 566–67, 583–84, 602, 616, 639–40, 664, 686, 689, 693–95, 736–38; in Estonia, 181; in Finland, 201–2; in France, 218; in Georgia, 5, 229; in Germany, 12, 253–55, 258 n.54; in Greece, 275–76; in Hungary, 292; in Iceland, 308–9; in Ireland, 333–34; in Italy, 342, 358, 360–61, 363; in Kosovo, 5, 13 n.3, 382–83; in Latvia, 394–95; in Lithuania, 402, 413–14; in Macedonia, 5, 110, 383, 428; in Malta, 439; in Montenegro, 12; in Netherlands, 456, 457; in Norway, 474; in Poland, 497, 499–501; in Portugal, 522–23; in Romania, 10, 12, 530, 539–40; in Russia, 5, 546, 566–69; in Serbia, 12; in Serbia and Montenegro, 5, 383, 583–84; in Slovakia, 588, 594, 595–96; in Spain, 602, 613–14, 615–17; in Sweden, 637, 639–42, 643; in Switzerland, 664–65; in Turkey, 686, 689, 692–95; in Ukraine, 708, 715–16; in United Kingdom, 734, 736–38. **Middle East/No. Africa** (*see also* Repression): in Algeria, 21; in Iran, 134. **No. America/Caribbean**: Bahamas, 28–30; Canada, 71–72; Caribbean, 9; Cuba, 97–99; deaths from, 24, 71–72, 267; Dominican Republic, 126–28; elder abuse, 20; French Caribbean, 146; Haiti, 170–72; Jamaica, 195–97; Mexico, 220; Netherlands Antilles, 244–46; OECS, 267; Puerto Rico, 291–92; sexual, 42–43, 68, 180, 317; Trinidad and Tobago, 323; United States, 347–48. **Sub-Saharan Africa** (*see also* Civil conflict): 13–14; in